THE NEW
COMPLETE
HOYLE

REVISED

BY

ALBERT H. MOREHEAD
RICHARD L. FREY
GEOFFREY MOTT-SMITH

REVISED BY

RICHARD L. FREY
TOM SMITH
PHILLIP ALDER
MATT KLAM

THE NEW COMPLETE HOYLE

REVISED

THE AUTHORITATIVE GUIDE TO THE OFFICIAL RULES OF ALL POPULAR GAMES OF SKILL AND CHANCE

Doubleday

New York   London   Toronto   Sydney   Auckland

PUBLISHED BY DOUBLEDAY
division of Bantam Doubleday Dell Publishing Group, Inc.
1540 Broadway, New York, New York 10036

Library of Congress Cataloging-in-Publication Data

The new complete Hoyle, revised: The authoritative guide to the official rules of
all popular games of skill and chance by Albert H. Morehead, Richard L. Frey,
Geoffrey Mott-Smith.—Rev. / revised by Richard L. Frey . . . [et al.]
       p.   cm.
Rev. ed. of: Hoyle's rules of games. 1983.
1. Cards.   2. Hoyle, Edmond, 1672–1769.   3. Board games.
I. Morehead, Albert H. (Albert Hodges). II. Frey, Richard L.
III. Mott-Smith, Geoffrey. IV. Hoyle's rules of games.
GV1243.H88   1991
794—dc20   90-32576
                                                              CIP

ISBN 0–385-24962-4

Designed by Diane Stevenson, SNAP-HAUS GRAPHICS

Illustrations by Jackie Aher

FOREWORD

Who Is Hoyle?

THE only truly immortal human being on record is an Englishman named Edmond Hoyle, who was born in 1672 and buried in 1769 but who has never really died.

Hoyle wrote "short treatises" on five different games. They were bound together in one volume in 1746. This was the first edition of "Hoyle's Games." Within the year plagiarists were putting Hoyle's name on other books that gave rules and advice for playing games. By the end of the nineteenth century dozens of such books had appeared, different books by different writers but all bearing the name of this same Edmond Hoyle. Into the twentieth century it has continued. Every few years, as sure as fate, one may see another book "by Hoyle" appear on the market.

Furthermore, there are countless millions who own one of the innumerable Hoyle books and in whose minds Hoyle is a living man, "the man who wrote the book," who probably lives in New York or Los Angeles or Miami or wherever authors live; to whom a letter may be addressed if a ticklish problem arises, and who might even be gotten on the other end of a long-distance telephone call if the problem were sufficiently urgent.

No less does this concept of a living Hoyle persist among authors and publishers. In a recent book on Poker, the author castigated "Hoyle's laws"; his publisher, no doubt fearful that Mr. Hoyle would sue, softened the tone of the attack. (Hoyle himself died at least fifty years before Poker was invented.) The managing editor of a Reno newspaper, asked what rules were being followed in the Nevada gambling houses, replied, "Hoyle was out here and put the rules in his book." Not even the "experts" who write books and articles about rules are immune; constantly, in citing some law or other, they begin with "Hoyle says." Yet they might be quoting from any of hundreds of "Hoyle" books, of which at least ten different ones are still on sale. And Edmond Hoyle himself never wrote or saw a word of any of these books.

Among writers on games who know all about the Hoyle history, the prestige of the immortal old man is immense. Surely no one in history ever made a greater name for himself in the realm of games than Ely Culbertson. Nevertheless, Culbertson's book of games was called "Culbertson's Hoyle." The worthiest successor to Edmond Hoyle, over a period that stretched from 1880 into the 1920s, was the old Scotsman R. F. Foster, but after a brief, futile effort to sell his "Encyclopedia of Games" he gave up and thereafter his book carried the simple and eloquent title "Hoyle." If Edmond Hoyle has any peer in immortality, it's no gamester. It's Noah Webster.

BILL ROOT

PREFACE TO THE NEW REVISED EDITION

For millions of people the world over, the best and cheapest form of entertainment is still provided by two decks of playing cards. Whether the game is All Fives or Zioncheck, they play according to Hoyle.

There is hardly a household that does not have a "Hoyle" on its bookshelves. Players have found that most games are more enjoyable if they are played according to the rules. This eliminates arguments and assures that everyone is treated fairly. But to be effective, a rules book must be current.

It is rather ironic that the master guru of games should be an Englishman, Edmond Hoyle, who died more than two hundred years ago—before most of the games in a modern "Hoyle" were devised. If Mr. Hoyle is looking down on us from above, he must be particularly happy with the three personalities who combined to pay homage to his name in this version: the late Geoffrey Mott-Smith, bridge champion and games authority, was largely responsible for the mathematical work; the late Albert H. Morehead, lexicographer and bridge editor for the *New York Times* and Encyclopaedia Britannica. And the late Richard L. Frey, prolific and facile writer on bridge and other games, who died shortly after completing this latest update. Together, they, with the assistance of Phillip Alder, Tom Smith, and Matt Klam, combined expertise in every facet of this book.

Here you will find up-to-date laws of Contract and Duplicate Contract Bridge; rules of all popular card and board games, as well as the playing strategy for many, such as Poker, Blackjack, Backgammon, and Chess. Also included is a new section on casino gambling games, plus new variations of old favorites. This is more than an important reference book; it is also fascinating to read.

About This Book

THE games described or mentioned in this book are listed alphabetically in the following Contents pages. In the text they are arranged, not alphabetically, but according to the type of equipment used and the "family" to which each game belongs.

Attention is called to several added features:

• The historical notes on the origins of games, in connection with every family and every principal variant.

• Indication of the character of many games now obsolete, but frequently mentioned in literature.

• The appendix, containing useful collateral information. The general arrangement of the book is as follows:

Contents

CONTENTS

CONTENTS

CONTENTS

CONTENTS

CONTENTS

CONTENTS

CONTENTS

CONTENTS

CONTENTS

CONTENTS

CONTENTS

CONTENTS

CONTENTS

CONTENTS

THE NEW
COMPLETE
HOYLE

REVISED

POKER

POKER

Referred to by some as the national card game of the United States, Poker is also an international game, popular almost anywhere cards are played. It has many forms, and is played differently in different lands and communities, but the basic principle is everywhere the same: to build "structures" consisting of two or more cards of a kind . . . sequences of cards . . . hands composed all of the same suit.

Poker in its present form is relatively new as games go. Its ultimate ancestor was perhaps the Persian game Às Nàs, perhaps an earlier Oriental game. A similar game of structures appeared in England in the eighteenth century as Brag; in France as Commerce. The German equivalent was Pochen (to bluff), which the French called Poque and the Americans corrupted to Poker. This name became so thoroughly identified with the game that at first any game of structures was called a Poker game: The Spanish Conquian became not merely Rum, but "Poker Rum" ("rum," that is, "queer," Poker).

At first Poker was a rough, tough, ask-no-quarter-give-no-quarter gamblers' game played by men in shirtsleeves. In the twentieth century, however, it has become a social game of both sexes, played in the parlor for nominal stakes and sometimes for none at all. Originally it was a slow, serious game; more lately it has been "pepped up" by the introduction of new variants and by promiscuous use of "wild cards." Nearly all Poker games today are of this "pepped-up" variety.

The laws and customs of Poker have kept up with the changing times. When R. F. Foster drafted a code of Poker laws in the 1890s, his object was to prevent cheating, which was then prevalent. The code of ethics was amoral; there was no ban on lying or trickery in almost any form. In almost no case did a violation call for a penalty.

Such laws and ethics are not compatible with the drawing-room atmosphere of present-day Poker, but it has proved difficult for would-be lawmakers to break through the old traditions or to standardize laws which are traditionally subject to an unlimited number of "house rules" established by any club or host who has his own ideas of propriety. Yet it was just such a task that was eventually accomplished in the standardization of the Bridge laws. In many cases the old Poker customs are inequitable or unjust, and sensible players will continue to improvise improvements on the laws until they are given a code they can adopt without outrage to their sense of equity and justice.

A start in that direction was made in a code of laws written by Oswald Jacoby in 1940. A code of Poker laws was published by the United States Playing Card Company in 1941; and during World War II, when much Poker was played in the armed services, Lieutenant George S. Coffin made a complete revision of that code. A description of Poker procedure in both casual and professional games was published in *The Modern Hoyle* (1944) by Albert Morehead. In 1988, Bob Ciaffone, in conjunction with the Las Vegas Hilton Poker room, compiled an updated set of rules which is referred to as standard for card clubs. Los Angeles Poker clubs publish rules which are strictly followed in the games they host. All these and other sources are reflected in the Poker laws that follow.

STANDARD POKER LAWS

Applying to All Forms of the Game

PLAYERS

Any number of players from two to fourteen may play in a single Poker game, depending on what form of the game is selected.

The original players in any game may by agreement limit the eventual number of players. Additional players who wish to enter a full game may replace players who leave, in the order in which application to enter the game was made. A full game may agree to allow one or more "rovers." A "rover" sits in an active player's seat for a full round while the active player takes a break. After the round is completed, the "rover" roves to a different seat, replacing a different active player for one full round.

CARDS

The pack of 52 is used, with the cards in each suit ranking: **A** (high), **K**, **Q**, **J**, **10**, **9**, **8**, **7**, **6**, **5**, **4**, **3**, **2**. There is no rank of suits.

Wild Cards. Any card or cards may be designated, by unanimous agreement, as *wild*. The holder of a wild card may designate any other card for which the wild card stands; thus, when deuces are wild, the holder of ♣**2** ♡**Q 9 7 4** may designate the ♣**2** as ♡**A**; but he may not cause a wild card to represent any card which he actually holds in his hand. In the foregoing example, he could not make ♣**2** represent ♡**Q**, for he already has that card.

The Joker. It is quite usual to play with a 53-card pack, including the joker, the joker being wild.

The Bug. The joker in a 53-card pack is often designated as the *bug*. The bug is a wild card with limitations: It may be counted as an ace, and it may be counted as a card of any suit and rank necessary to make a *flush*, or *straight* (which terms are defined in the next section).

OBJECTS OF THE GAME

Each player endeavors to hold a better *poker hand* than any other player in the game. Except in a very few variants of Poker, a poker hand consists of exactly five cards, though the five cards may be selected by the player from a greater number of cards available to him.

Rank of Poker Hands. The following list states the combinations which make up valuable poker hands, and their rank. The combinations and rankings given are standard for virtually all Poker games.

Straight flush ranks highest. It consists of five cards in suit and sequence, with the ace ranking either high or low: ◇**A K Q J 10** (the highest possible hand, also called a *royal flush*), or ◇**5 4 3 2 A**, or any sequence in between, as ♠**10 9 8 7 6** or ♣**8 7 6 5 4**, is a straight flush.

Four of a kind is next highest. It consists of the four cards of any one rank together with any fifth card; for example, ♡**7** ◇**7** ♣**7** ♠**7** ◇**Q** constitute four sevens.

A *full house* ranks next; it consists of any three of one kind and any pair of another kind, as ♠**6** ♡**6** ◇**6** ♣**A** ♠**A**. It is referred to by the three of a kind it contains; the example shown would be "sixes full."

A *flush*, ranking next, consists of any five cards of the same suit, but not in sequence, as ◇**J** ◇**9** ◇**8** ◇**6** ◇**3**, referred to as a "jack-high flush."

A *straight* consists of any five cards of two or more suits in sequence of rank, with the ace ranking either high in the sequence **A–K–Q–J–10** or low in the sequence **5–4–3–2–A**. It ranks next under a flush.

Three of a kind are any three cards of the same rank plus two other cards which do not constitute a pair and do not include the fourth card of the same rank; ♠**9** ◇**9** ♡**9** ♣**K** ◇**3** would be referred to as "three nines."

Two pairs, which rank next under three of a kind, constitute two cards of one rank, two cards of another rank, and any fifth card which is of neither of those ranks; it is referred to by the higher of the two pairs. Thus, ♠**Q** ♣**Q** ♠**8** ♣**8** ♠**4** would be "queens up."

Any two cards of the same rank, together with three other cards which do not combine with the other two to form any of the higher-ranking hands listed above, are a *pair*; ♠**K** ♣**K** ♡**7** ♡**6** ♡**4** are a pair of kings.

No pair—the lowest-ranking hand—losing to any hand containing a pair or any better combination, consists of any five cards not meeting the specifications above.

Object of Betting. The players in the game bet with one another as to which has the best poker hand. Each deal is a separate game, in that its result does not affect any preceding or subsequent deal. All the bets are placed together and form a *pot*. A player who does not wish to bet that he has the best hand may *drop*, thus relinquishing any chance to win the pot.

The ultimate object in Poker is therefore to win the pot, whether by actually holding the best hand or by inducing other players to drop and leave the pot to be taken, uncontested, by a single player still willing to bet.

SEQUENCE OF PLAY

Rotation. The turn to deal, the cards as they are dealt, and the turn to bet all pass from player to player to the left. Once a player has dropped, the turn skips him and takes up with the next player to his left who has not dropped.

Chips. The unit of exchange is almost invariably the poker chip, which may represent money or may merely be a token whereby victory and the extent of victory are measured.

In most forms of Poker, the pot is formed before the deal and begins by the contribution of an *ante* from each player. Such an ante is usually a chip of low value, and every player makes the same ante.

Procedure. First the cards are shuffled and dealt by the proper dealer; then there may be one or more *betting intervals* in which the players may bet on their hands (or, if unwilling to bet, may drop); and, at the end of the last betting interval, there is a *showdown* at which each player who has not previously dropped exhibits his cards face up. Whichever of these players has the highest-ranking poker hand wins the pot and gathers it in, after which the same sequence of play is repeated for the next pot.

PRELIMINARIES

The Banker. One of the players is selected as the banker. All available poker chips are given to him, for issuance to the other players. Each other player purchases chips from the banker, and may redeem such chips as he has at any time by returning them to the banker for their value. This is called *cashing in.*

Betting Limits. The players in the game must agree unanimously upon the values of chips and the limits of betting. There should be a minimum limit for each bet, and a maximum limit.

There are several methods of establishing the maximum limits. These are described on pages 10–11.

VALUES OF CHIPS

The players in the game determine the value of different-colored chips. In many games, white chips are assigned the lowest value. Red chips represent five white chips; blue chips represent ten or twenty white chips; black or yellow chips represent one hundred white chips.

While the original stakes and limits must be established by unanimous agreement, each player who enters the game thereafter is bound by the agreement previously reached unless there is again unanimous agreement to change.

Time Limit. Before beginning play, the original members of the table should establish an hour at which the game will end. They and all players who enter the game later are bound by this agreement. However, any player is free to leave the game at any earlier time.

The Kitty. By unanimous agreement the players may establish special pool, to defray the cost of playing space, equipment, refreshments, or any other expense incidental to the game.

Penalties for infractions of rules, when payable in chips, are paid to this "kitty"; and, if such payments are insufficient, one white chip may be *cut* from each pot and placed in the kitty. A maximum limit should be put on the kitty, and no other payments made to it after this maximum is reached.

No player owns a proportionate share of the kitty unless, at the time the game breaks up, there is a surplus in it after allowance for all expenses. Any such surplus is divided among players who are still present and who are in the game at the time the kitty reaches its maximum amount and payments to it are suspended.

Seating. In most games, players choose seats on a first come, first served basis. The players may decide to choose seats by picking cards and sitting according to the rank of the cards. When a new player arrives, any active player may change seats with an empty spot before the new player picks his seat.

Players who wish to exchange seats may do so unless some other player objects.

THE SHUFFLE, CUT AND DEAL

Any player may shuffle the pack of cards, have them cut by the player at his right, and deal them one at a time, face up, in rotation beginning with the player at his left, until a jack falls to any player; that player becomes the first dealer.

The Shuffle. Any player may shuffle, the dealer last. The cards must be shuffled at least three times.

The Cut. The player at dealer's right must cut the pack, leaving at least five cards in each packet. (Traditionally, the player at dealer's right could refuse to cut, whereupon the cards had to be dealt uncut. The obligatory cut, however, is in accordance with the custom of most other card games.)

Dealing. In all Poker games, the cards are dealt one at a time in rotation to each player in the game, including the dealer, eldest hand being the first to receive cards. The number of cards dealt to each player, and which, if any, are dealt face up, depend upon the form of Poker being played. These rules are given under each variant of Poker described hereafter.

BETTING

In any form of Poker there are one or more *betting intervals*.

In each betting interval, one player in the game has the privilege or duty of making the first bet. Each player in rotation after him may either

(a) *drop*, by discarding his hand; in this case, he no longer participates in the pot, and cannot win the pot regardless of what may later occur;

(b) *call*, which means that he places in the pot enough chips to make his contribution to the pot *during that betting interval* as great as the contribution of any other player, but no greater;

(c) *raise*, which means that he places in the pot enough chips to call, plus one or more additional chips.

To illustrate this: There are seven players in the game, designated as A, B, C, D, E, F and G. A is the first bettor. A bets one chip. B calls by putting in one chip. C drops, discarding his hand. D raises, putting in three chips—one chip to call and two to raise. E calls, putting in three chips. F raises, putting in six chips—three to call and three to raise. G drops.

It is now the turn of A again. A calls, putting in five chips; this makes his total contribution to the pot six chips during this betting interval. B drops; he relinquishes his chance to win the pot, and the chip he previously put in the pot remains there. D calls, putting in three chips to bring his total contribution up to six. E raises five chips by putting in eight chips. F raises by putting in ten chips. A drops, thus losing the six chips he had already put in. D calls by putting in ten chips. E calls by putting in five chips, and now the betting interval is ended. D, E and F are still in the pot, and each during this betting interval has put sixteen chips into the pot.

A betting interval ends when every active player has had at least one turn to bet and when the bets have been *equalized*—that is, when every player has either contributed the same amount as every other player has contributed during the betting interval, or has dropped.

Method of Betting. A player may drop or bet only in turn. When his turn comes, a player should announce whether he is dropping, betting, calling or raising; and if he is betting or raising he should announce the amount of the bet or raise.

Before putting any chips in the pot, a player should stack them just outside the pot and permit the other players to see them, so they may be sure that he is putting in the correct number of chips.

However, regardless of announcement, a player is deemed to drop if he discards his cards, mixes them with other discards, or throws or pushes them away from him on the table.

A player is deemed to have bet the number of chips put into the pot if he is the first player to put any chips in the pot during the betting interval and if he fails to announce the amount of his bet.

A player is deemed to call if he puts a number of chips into the pot without announcing it, always provided he puts in at least as many as are required to call.

But a player must announce a raise or his bet may be construed as a call only.

Checking. In many forms of Poker, a player in turn is permitted to make "a bet of nothing" by saying "Check," provided no previous player has made a bet during that betting interval. The effect of the check is that the player merely wishes to stay in the pot by making a bet so insignificant that it is not worth the trouble of putting that amount into the pot. If the first bettor checks, each active player thereafter may check until any player chooses to bet, after which a player may stay in the pot only by at least calling the previous bet.

Raising after checking is legal; however, by unanimous agreement, players may decide not to allow it.

BETTING LIMITS

In almost any Poker game it is desirable to limit the amount the first bettor may bet, or the amount by which any player thereafter may raise the last previous bet.

In most games, the limit is equivalent to the value of the highest-valued chip issued.

It is also desirable to limit the number of raises any one player may give in any one betting interval; the recommended limit is three raises per player.

There are several other methods of establishing betting limits, described below.

Variable Limit. In Draw Poker, the limit may be made greater after the draw than before, as five chips before the draw and ten chips after the draw. In Stud Poker, the limit may be higher after the last card has been dealt than in any previous betting interval. These forms of the game are described later.

Pot Limit. A player who wishes to raise may call the preceding bet and then may raise by as many chips as there are in the pot at the time.

Bet the Raise. The most by which a player may raise is the greatest number of chips any player has previously put into that pot at any one time: If the first bet is one chip, the limit for a raise is one chip; if a player raises by putting in two chips, the limit from then on is two chips; and so forth. To know the limit the player must only remember the largest contribution made to the pot by any player in a single turn.

Table Stakes. Each player begins the game by buying one hundred chips from the banker. These and any other chips bought from the banker are called a *take-out*. By agreement the players may vary the size of the take-out, making it fifty, or two hundred, or any other number; but whatever the unit established for the take-out, all purchases of chips from the banker must be in that unit.

The limit for each player in any one pot is the number of chips he has at the time. He may not remove or cash in any chips until he leaves the game. A player may add to his stack of chips by additional purchases from the banker, except that he may not make any purchase between the time the deal is begun and the showdown.

A player may purchase less than the take-out unit only upon his statement that he is unable to purchase the entire take-out unit, and if he loses these chips he must leave the game.

If a player has too few chips to call a bet, he may call for whatever chips he has, and continue play without further contribution to the pot, competing in the showdown. When this occurs, no other player puts into the pot more than the lowest amount for which any player has called. Additional bets are not withdrawn by the other players, however; they become *side money* and are placed in other pots kept separate from the main pot.

When a player has insufficient chips to call a bet made into a side pot, he may call for what he has, whereupon the excess of any bet against him becomes a second side pot. Theoretically, three or even more side pots could be created, though more than one side pot is extremely rare.

At the showdown, every player who has not dropped competes for the main pot; but to determine the winner of a side pot, only the hands of the players who contributed the full amount to that side pot are compared.

If a player refuses to call a bet made into a side pot, though able to do so, he must drop out of the competition not only for the side pot but for all other pots.

Short Showdown. In any Poker game, regardless of the limit, it is traditional that a player who is physically unable to call a bet may have a showdown by putting into the pot whatever chips he has left. If he loses, he must withdraw from the game. If other players in the pot wish to make further bets, side money is created as described under Table Stakes.

THE SHOWDOWN

When the bets have been equalized in the last betting interval, every player who has not previously dropped must expose all his cards face up on the table. The highest-ranking poker hand wins the pot.

It is not necessary for a player to announce the value of his poker hand as he puts it down, nor is he bound by any such announcement if he makes it. "The cards speak for themselves." The player with the winning hand takes in the pot. If a player begins to take in the pot even though he does not have the winning hand, a player with a better hand must protect himself by promptly objecting; if he does not object before the pot has been gathered in, he may no longer claim it and it belongs to the player who took it.

If any wild cards are being used, the player holding them must indicate their rank or suit when he shows them. Thereafter, the cards speak for themselves. If he fails to designate a wild card as such, it is taken at its face value.

If at any stage of the game every player but one has dropped, the latter takes the pot without showing any of his cards.

Five of a Kind. When there are one or more wild cards, the highest-ranking poker hand is five cards of the same rank or so designated. Such a hand ranks higher than a straight flush.

Breaking Ties. When two players have hands of the same type, the higher-ranking hand is determined as follows:

If each has a straight or straight flush, the one including the highest card wins (**6, 5, 4, 3, 2** beats **5, 4, 3, 2, A**).

If each has three of a kind, four of a kind, or (with wild cards) five of a kind, the one composed of the higher-ranking cards wins. When there are many wild cards, two players may have three or four of a kind in the same rank. The tie is then broken by the unmatched cards, as described in the two next paragraphs.

If each has two pairs, the one with the highest pair wins; **A, A, 3, 3, 4** beats **K, K, Q, Q, 5**. If each has the same higher pair, the hand with the higher of the two lower pairs wins; **A, A, 6, 6, 5** beats **A, A, 5, 5, 9**. If each has the same two pairs, the one with the higher fifth card wins; **A, A, 6, 6, 7** beats **A, A, 6, 6, 5**.

If each has one pair, the higher pair wins; **K, K, 5, 3, 2** beats **J, J, A, K, Q**. If the two pairs are the same, the winner is determined by comparison of the other three cards in the two hands, depending first on the highest card (**J, J, A, 3, 2** beats **J, J, K, Q, 10**); then on the next higher card (**J, J, A, 4, 3** beats **J, J, A, 3, 2**); and finally on the third card (**J, J, A, K, 7** beats **J, J, A, K, 6**).

If each has a flush, or if each has a hand of lower rank than one pair, the hand containing the highest card wins; **A, 7, 5, 3, 2** beats **K, Q, J, 7, 4**. The highest cards in the two hands being identical, the winner is determined by the rank of the next-highest card, and so on down to the lowest card in the two hands, if necessary.

When two players have hands which are in all respects identical, except for the suits of the cards, and when they are jointly highest in the showdown, they divide the pot as evenly as possible and determine ownership of an odd chip or chips by lot. In determining the rank of poker hands, the suits are meaningless.

IRREGULARITIES

The laws of Poker are not designed to prevent cheating, for which there is no remedy except to refuse to play with the guilty party. The purpose of the laws and penalties for infractions of laws is to protect innocent players from loss because of irregularities committed by other players in moments of carelessness or overanxiety to win. Poker clubs in Los Angeles and Las Vegas have clearly written rules and penalties that are adhered to with good grace, as they are in bridge. Adoption of standard laws should reduce arguments, prevent ill-feeling, and thereby make the game more pleasant.

The irregularities and penalties listed in the section below apply in any form of Poker. Irregularities which can occur only in a specific form— as in Draw Poker, or in Stud Poker—are separately listed where those games are described.

In some cases, irregularities call for the payment of a penalty in chips. This payment should be made to the kitty if there is one, or if its maximum has not already been reached; otherwise the payment should be made to the current pot and goes to the winner of that pot.

The Dealer's Responsibility. In the case of any irregularity, the dealer is responsible for stating the fact and the penalty. He may not state a penalty or means of rectification contrary to these laws. In case of a dispute by a player concerned, all inactive players will constitute a committee whose majority decision can override the decision of the dealer; if there is only one such player, or if there is no clear majority, all the players at the table shall decide the issue by majority vote.

Calling for New Cards. Before any deal, any player may call for a change to a different pack of cards, and the substitution demanded must be made if a perfect pack is available for the purpose and if the pack previously in use, if perfect, has been dealt at least once by each player in the game.

Incorrect Pack. The first player to deal with any pack is responsible for checking it and must pay a penalty of five chips if he begins to deal without checking the pack and it proves to be incorrect.

If a pack is proved to be incorrect before the pot has been taken in, that deal is void and each player withdraws from the pot as many chips as he has put in it, but results of previous deals are not affected.

New Shuffle and Cut. At any time before the dealer has dealt any player his second card, a player who has not intentionally seen the face of any card may demand a new shuffle and cut and a new deal by the same dealer, if: The shuffle and cut were omitted or not as provided by law; or the wrong player is dealing; or a card was exposed in cutting.

A new shuffle and cut may be demanded at any time before a bet is made, if two or more cards are found faced in the pack.

If the deal is not completed and the cards still to be dealt become so mixed with other cards that they cannot be identified, all dead cards (undealt cards plus discards) must be shuffled and cut before the deal is resumed and the player responsible for mixing the cards must pay a penalty of five chips.

The dealer may never deal the bottom card of the pack. If he reaches this card and the deal is not completed, all dead cards must be shuffled and cut, and the deal resumed.

Misdeal. In the event of a misdeal, the next dealer in turn deals, after a new shuffle and cut; any ante placed in the pot remains there, but the regular ante is made for the next pot also. It is a misdeal if: Attention is called in time to an irregularity in the shuffle or cut or to a deal out of turn; or if the pack is discovered to be imperfect at any time before the pack has been taken in; or if at the end of the deal more than two players prove to have irregular hands; or if a misdeal is called as provided on page 18.

Incorrect Number of Cards. If in dealing the dealer gives a card to the wrong player, he may rectify the deal before proceeding, transferring such cards as are necessary.

Incorrect Number of Hands. If dealer omits a player, he must give his own hand to the omitted player nearest his left. If dealer deals too many hands, he must assign one hand to each player and the excess hand or hands become dead.

Irregularity in Betting. In correction of an irregularity in betting, no chips once placed in the pot may ever be removed.

If a player bets, calls or raises out of turn, the turn reverts to the proper player. When the offender's turn comes, he is deemed to have bet the number of chips he put in, if no player previously bet during that betting interval; or to have called the last preceding bet if the number of chips he put in is at least sufficient to call. If he put in too few chips to call, he may add enough chips to call. He may not raise, and if he put in more chips than he needed to call, those chips are forfeited to the pot. If he put in insufficient chips to call, and does not wish to add enough to call, he must drop and forfeit whatever chips he put in.

If a player drops out of turn, and there is more than one player ahead of him who has not acted, when his turn comes he must put in enough chips to call any bet made in the meantime, but his hand is dead and cannot win the pot.

If a player announces a bet, in or out of turn, and does not accompany the announcement with a contribution of chips to the pot, the announcement is void. But if a player announces a call or raise, and puts into the pot too few chips to match his announcement, he must on demand put in as many additional chips as were called for by his announcement. If he puts into the pot more chips than he announced, the additional chips are forfeited to the pot unless the improper announcement was a slip of the tongue which is corrected before any other player calls attention to it.

Looking at Dead Cards. A player may not look at cards of the pack remaining after the deal is completed, or at the discards of other players, and if he does so look he must pay a penalty of three chips; except that a player may demand examination of these cards on a claim that the pack is incorrect.

Exposure of Cards. A player should not expose any cards in his hand not required to be exposed by the rules of the game. If he does so accidentally, there is no penalty. If he does so intentionally, or if he does so repeatedly by carelessness, he must pay a penalty of two chips.

Showdown. A player who has made or called the final bet and who does not show his entire hand face up in the showdown pays a penalty of ten chips. (Unless there are at least two such players after the final betting interval, there is no showdown and no exposure is required.)

DRAW POKER

In the original Poker game, each player received five cards face down, did not show any of them until the showdown, and never had a chance to improve beyond the five cards originally dealt to him. This was "Straight Poker."

Draw Poker was the first of a long line of innovations designed to speed up the game and create more betting action. Each player was given hope beyond his original five cards, for he could discard any number of them and receive new cards to replace them.

Continued attempts to liven up the game by encouraging betting led to eventual adoption of a rule that in certain circumstances (as after a passed out deal, or after some player held a big hand) the next pot should be a "jack," meaning that the stakes would be jacked up by raising the limit and increasing the amount of the ante. This created bigger pots, and so that no very weak hand could win such a pot by default, the rule was added that the betting could not even be begun on a hand weaker than a pair of jacks. The resultant game, Jackpots, eventually came to be played in the United States almost to the exclusion of other forms of Draw Poker. In countries other than the United States, an earlier form of Draw Poker known as Blind and Straddle continues to be more popular.

Jackpots

THE ANTE

Before each deal, each player in the game antes one white chip. (By unanimous agreement, each dealer may ante for all players. This comes to the same thing in the long run and saves a great deal of trouble.)

PLAYERS

Seven make the best game, eight make a full table. When eight play, dealer may sit out each round (when dealer takes cards, it is sometimes necessary to shuffle the discards before completing the draw; but many players would rather do this than force the dealer to be idle for a full deal).

If fewer than five are in the game, the pack may be *stripped* (see page 27).

DEALING

Each player receives five cards, all face down, dealt as described on page 8.

OPENING THE POT

The first betting interval commences when the deal is completed. Eldest hand has the first turn. He may either:

(a) *Open* the pot by making a bet, if he has a pair of jacks or any higher-ranking poker hand; or

(b) *Check*, meaning that he does not make a bet at the time but reserves the right to call or raise a bet later. (Instead of "Check" many players say "Pass" to signify inability or disinclination to open the pot on the first round. When this is permitted, the game is "pass and back in." In all other forms of Poker, the rule is "pass and out," that is, to pass is to drop out without the right to reënter later.) A player may check whether or not he has as good a hand as a pair of jacks.

If eldest hand checks, the next player in rotation may either open or check; and so on. Once any player makes a bet, the pot is open and each player in turn thereafter must either drop, call or raise.

Deal Passed Out. If every player including the dealer checks on the first round, the deal is passed out. Each player antes another chip. The next player in turn deals. (If dealer is anteing for all players, only the next dealer in turn antes.)

THE DRAW

When the bets in the first betting interval have been equalized, dealer picks up the undealt portion of the pack. Each player who is still in the pot, in rotation beginning nearest the dealer's left, may discard one or more cards, face down, at the same time announcing the number of cards he has discarded. The dealer then takes an equivalent number of cards from the top of the pack and gives them to that player, to restore his hand to five cards.

Each player in his turn receives the full number of cards demanded before the next player discards and draws.

Dealer draws last, and must announce the number of cards he discards.

Standing Pat. A player who does not wish to draw to his original five cards must so signify by announcing the fact or by knocking on the table when his turn to draw comes. Such a player *stands pat*.

Limiting the Draws. When there are six or more in the game, no player should be permitted to discard and draw more than three cards.

Splitting Openers. The player who opens the pot is permitted to discard one or more of the cards essential to the combination which permitted him to open, and must announce that fact. He is permitted to place his discard face down near the pot, so that it can be referred to later as evidence that he held proper openers. These discards may not be shuffled if additional cards are needed.

Disposition of Discards. The player next in turn to deal should gather in all cards as they are discarded, keeping them face down and not looking at the faces of any of them.

Shuffling the Discards. If dealer has given the next-to-last card of the pack, and if the demands of the players in the draw are still not satisfied, he must shuffle together the bottom card and all cards previously discarded, have them cut by the player who will next receive a card in the draw, and proceed with the draw with the new pack so created. The discard of the opener and the discard of the player next to receive cards are not included if they have been kept separate and can be identified.

Reviewing the Draws. At any time during the draw, until the first legal bet has been made thereafter, any player may demand that each other player state the number of cards he drew, and the other players must so state, truthfully.

FINAL BETTING AND SHOWDOWN

When the draw is completed, the player who opened the pot must either check or bet. If this player has dropped, the next player in the pot to his left has the first turn. Each other player in turn may then check, or, if any bet has been made, may either call, raise or drop until the bets are equalized.

When all players have checked, or when all bets are equalized, every player who has not previously dropped shows his full hand in the showdown and the highest-ranking poker hand wins the pot.

PROVING OPENERS

Before his hand is discarded for any reason, the opener must prove that he held sufficient strength to justify opening the pot.

If the opener's hand is in the showdown, he must show his entire hand and may add his discards, if necessary, to indicate what original cards represented his openers.

If the opening bet is not called, or if the opener drops after opening, or if the opener makes the only bet after the draw and is not called, he must show face up enough cards (combined with his discards) to prove that he held openers, and he must show his other cards face down to prove that he held no more than five cards.

Inability to prove openers is subject to penalty—see "False Openers" below.

IRREGULARITIES IN DRAW POKER

The following sections apply only to Draw Poker. Remedies and penalties for irregularities which may occur not only in Draw Poker but also in other forms of Poker are covered in the general laws on page 12.

17

Card Exposed in the Deal. If one card is exposed in dealing, the player to whom it is dealt must keep it and there is no misdeal. If more than one card is exposed in dealing, a misdeal may be called by any player receiving such an exposed card, provided that player has not intentionally seen the face of any other card dealt to him. See the rules governing the misdeal, on page 13.

If a player other than the dealer causes the exposure of a card by touching or reaching for any card dealt, before the deal is completed, he must pay a penalty of two chips. If the card caused to be exposed is his own, he may not call a misdeal.

Foul Hand. If a player's hand is foul, he cannot win the pot. He is deemed to drop whenever the irregularity is discovered, and any chips he has placed in the pot are forfeited. If he has made the final bet and has not been called, the chips in the pot remain there for the next deal.

Incorrect Hand. If one player is dealt too many cards and announces the fact before he has looked at the face of any of them, the dealer must draw the excess from his hand and restore it to the top of the pack. If a player is dealt too many cards and has seen the face of any of them, his hand is foul.

If a player has too few cards and has not seen the face of any of them, the dealer shall deal him enough cards from the top of the pack to give him the proper number. Such dealing follows the restoration to the top of the pack of any cards taken from the hands of players with too many cards. If more than one player has too many cards and is entitled to have his hand corrected, the dealer must restore the pack by placing one card at a time from the hands of such players in counter-clockwise rotation; if more than one player has too few cards, the dealer then deals additional cards to those hands one at a time in regular rotation.

If a player has too few cards and has seen the face of any of them, he may play on but may never have his hand filled out to the full five cards (if he discards two cards, he may not draw more than two cards, and so on). A hand with fewer than five cards may never constitute a straight, flush or straight flush.

Card Exposed in the Draw. If the first card drawn by a player is exposed in the draw, the player must accept that card. If any other card demanded by that player is exposed in the draw, such card must be placed among the discards. After all other players have drawn, such exposed card is replaced by the dealer.

A player entitled to receive such replacements after the completion of the regular draw may demand that the remainder of the pack be shuffled by the dealer and cut by himself before his draw is completed; except that if he has intentionally seen the face of any other card dealt to him in the draw, he forfeits this right.

Incorrect Number of Cards Drawn. If a player does not receive the exact number of cards he asked for, he may cause the dealer to make correction provided he has not looked at the face of any of the cards drawn.

If the next player in turn has received one or more cards in the draw, a player who has received the wrong number may play on with a short hand if this causes him to have too few cards, and may leave the excess on the table, unseen, if the draw would have given him too many cards.

If a player receives too many cards in the draw and looks at all of them, his hand is foul.

If a player permits another player to his left to draw out of turn, the former may not receive cards in the draw; but he may stand pat and play on if he has not already discarded, and he may play on with a short hand if he has already discarded.

Error in Review on Draws. If dealer fails to state the number of cards drawn, or if any other player on proper demand gives an incorrect reply as to the number of cards he drew, the offender must pay a penalty of five chips.

However, a player who is asked to review his draw after the first bet has been placed in the final betting interval is not bound to reply or, if he does reply, to make a truthful reply.

FALSE OPENERS

If the opener cannot prove on demand that he held openers, his hand is foul. If all other players have dropped, each other player may withdraw from the pot any chips, except his ante, that he has contributed. The antes and any chips contributed by the opener remain for the next deal.

If, at any time before the bets in the first betting interval are equalized, the opener announces voluntarily that he does not have openers, all bets except antes and except the opener's chips are withdrawn from the pot. The players in turn to the opener's left may open. If no one opens, the remaining chips go over to the next deal. If anyone opens, the false opener may play, but chips he previously put in the pot are forfeited.

The opener is deemed to lack openers if his hand contains more than five cards.

Progressive Jackpots

This is the same game as Jackpots, except that when a hand is passed out and everyone antes again, at least a pair of queens is required for openers in the next deal; if this is passed out, at least a pair of kings is required in the next deal; if this is passed out, at least a pair of aces in the next deal. The sequence is seldom carried beyond a pair of aces.

Straight Draw Poker

This game is sometimes referred to as "Pass-out" and sometimes as "Bet or Drop." It differs from Jackpots as follows:

No minimum holding is required to make the opening bet before the draw.

In each turn, a player must either bet—at least one white chip, usually called a "white check"—or drop. Once he has dropped he may no longer compete for the pot. If any bet has been made before him, he must at least call to stay in.

Blind Opening

This form of Draw Poker, in the United States also called "Blind Tiger" (and in former times called "Blind and Straddle"), has become the standard form of Poker in most countries. Except in big-city clubs, it is little played in the United States.

Betting. Before the deal, the dealer puts one chip in the pot. This is the *ante*. The player at his left (formerly called the *age*) must put in one chip to open the pot; this bet is the *blind*. The next player to the left must put in two chips, constituting a *blind raise* of one chip; this bet is sometimes called the *straddle*. All these bets are made before any cards are dealt.

When the cards have been dealt and the players have looked at their hands, the turn begins at the left of the last blind bettor. Each player in turn may stay in by calling or raising the highest previous bet; in some games the first voluntary bet must be a raise, so the first voluntary bettor would have to put in three chips, or in some games four chips (called a *double*). The limit before the draw is usually two chips. In some games the ante and blind are two chips each, the blind raise four chips, and the first voluntary bet six or eight chips; if it is six chips, the limit before the draw is two chips, and if it is eight the limit is four. The blind bettors (including the dealer) count their blind bets toward what they later need to call.

Once a voluntary bet is made, betting proceeds as in any other form of Draw Poker. After the draw, there is a final betting interval in which the limit is usually four or five chips. In this betting interval there is usually a one-chip minimum bet, but in some games players are permitted to "check free" (stay in without betting) until a bet is made.

When no player before the age makes a voluntary bet in the first betting interval, the age may either call the blind bet, or raise, or propose to the blind raiser that they divide the dealer's ante. If the blind raiser refuses the proposal, the age may raise, call, or drop.

STUD POKER

Seven-card Stud

Any procedure not specifically described below is governed by the standard laws beginning on page 5.

PLAYERS

Seven, eight, or nine make the best game. Stud Poker is a better game for two, three, or four players than is Draw Poker, for there is more action in betting.

DEALING

After the preliminaries as described in the standard laws, the dealer gives one card to each player in rotation face down; then a second card to each player face down; then a third card to each player face up.

A player's face-down cards are his "hole cards" and are not shown until the showdown.

After these cards have been dealt, the pack is temporarily laid aside and the deal is interrupted for a betting interval. When the bets have been equalized, the dealer gives another face-up card, in rotation, to each player who has not dropped. The deal is again interrupted for a betting interval. After this betting interval, a third face-up card is given to each player who has not dropped, and after another betting interval each player receives a fourth face-up card. There is another betting interval after which each player receives a final card face down, completing his hand of seven cards. Now there is a final betting interval, after which each player who is in the showdown turns up his hole cards. Each hand is examined to determine the highest Five-card Poker hand that can be constructed from each player's seven cards. The player with the highest five-card hand takes the pot.

BETTING

There is no ante in Stud Poker, except by agreement.

In the first betting interval, the player with the highest card showing must make a bet; if two or more players tie for highest-showing card, the player nearest the dealer's left (that is, the player who received his card first) bets first.

In any subsequent betting interval, the highest Poker combination which is showing designates the player with the first right to bet. Thus, a player whose first two cards are **A**, **6** will bet first as against a player whose first two cards are **K**, **Q** or **A**, **5**, or as against a player whose first two cards are also **A**, **6** but who sits at the left. A player whose first three cards are **2**, **2**, **3** will bet ahead of a player whose first three cards are **A**, **K**, **Q**.

After the first betting interval, it is not obligatory to bet. The first bettor may check, and any player thereafter may check if there has been no previous bet.

The betting is governed by the standard laws.

DEALER'S OBLIGATIONS

The dealer is expected to designate the player who must bet first in each betting interval, as by pointing to the proper player and saying "First queen bets," and if dealer is in error any player may demand a correction until at least two players in rotation have checked or bet.

The dealer is also expected to call attention to combinations of three showing cards which make it possible that the holder will eventually have a straight or a flush; thus, if all three of a player's showing cards are hearts, the dealer should announce "Possible flush." If a player's first three cards are **9**, **8**, **6**, the dealer should announce "Possible straight."

BETTING LIMIT

It is customary in Stud Poker to have one limit—such as a red chip—for bets and raises during the first three betting intervals, and a higher limit—such as one blue chip—for the final betting interval, and also for any earlier betting interval in which any player has an "open pair."

In some circles the limit is graduated round by round—one chip in the first betting interval, two in the second, three in the third, and four in the fourth or in any betting interval when there is a pair showing.

IRREGULARITIES

Only irregularities peculiar to Stud Poker are dealt with here. Other irregularities and the remedies and penalties for them will be found on page 12.

Misdeal. No misdeal may be called after all hole cards and at least one face-up card have been dealt.

When there is a misdeal, the same dealer deals again.

Dropping. A player who drops must turn his face-up cards down, and should not expose his hole card. (He is said to *fold*.) A player who drops but does not turn his cards face down must pay a penalty of two chips.

Card Improperly Exposed. If dealer deals any player's first card face up, he must deal that player's second card face down to serve as his hole card.

If dealer deals both of a player's first two cards face up, that player may stay in and dealer must deal his third card face down. There is no penalty on the dealer if he improperly deals any one of the first three cards face up to a player; but if, having dealt the first three cards face up to a player, dealer also gives that player his fourth card face up, such player may withdraw from the pot all the chips he has placed in it and drop out; or that player may stay in and dealer must give him his fifth card face down.

If dealer has given a player all five of his cards face up, that player may either stay in or may drop out and withdraw from the pot all the chips he has placed therein, and dealer must pay a penalty of twenty chips.

Card Faced in Pack or Prematurely Dealt. Any card dealt by the dealer before the close of a betting interval, or found faced in the pack, is dead and must be discarded. The deal is continued, each player receiving the card he would have received in regular rotation if no such card had been prematurely exposed or found faced; and when all cards in regular rotation have been dealt, players who failed to receive cards on that round shall be served in rotation from the top of the pack.

A player who would have received an exposed card may demand a shuffle and cut of the remaining cards before a replacement card has been dealt to him.

Impossible Call. If a player calls a bet in the last betting interval, though it is impossible for him to have a hand which would beat the four cards of the hand showing against him, and if attention is called to this before the pot is gathered in, the player who so called may withdraw the number of chips with which he called the bet, unless at the time he called there was a player to his left who had not dropped.

FIVE-CARD STUD

This is the original Stud game from which Seven-card Stud and all other Stud variations came. Five-card Stud is rarely played today because it is slow and less interesting than Seven-card Stud and variations.

Each player receives a face-down card and a face-up card before the first betting interval. There are three more rounds of cards dealt face up, one at a time, with a betting interval after each. After the final betting interval, each player turns up his hole card, and the player with the highest poker hand takes the pot.

Hold 'Em

Any procedure not specifically described below is governed by standard laws beginning on page 5.

PLAYERS

Eight, nine, or ten make the best game; however, any number from two to twenty-three can theoretically play. Normally, the game is not played with more than eleven players because dealing becomes clumsy.

DEALING

After the preliminaries as described in the standard laws, the dealer gives two face-down cards to each player.

A player's face-down cards are his "hole cards," and are not shown until the showdown.

After the hole cards are dealt, the pack is temporarily put aside and the deal is interrupted for a betting interval. When the bets have been equalized, the dealer turns up three cards in the middle of the table. This is called the "flop." The deal is again interrupted for a betting interval. When the bets have been equalized, the dealer turns up a fourth card, after which there is a betting interval. Now the dealer turns up a fifth and final card, after which there is a final betting interval. Each player now turns up his two hole cards and the player who can construct the best Five-card Poker hand using any combination of his two hole cards and the five cards on the flop wins the pot.

BETTING

There is no ante in Hold 'Em Poker, except by agreement. The player to the dealer's left must make the first bet regardless of his cards. This is called the "blind." By agreement, there can be two or more blinds.

In the first betting interval, the players after the blind must act in turn, either dropping, calling the blind bet, or raising.

In each of the three remaining betting intervals, the player to the dealer's left always acts first. However, there are no forced bets except for the first betting interval.

The betting is governed by the standard laws.

BETTING LIMIT

It is customary in Hold 'Em Poker to have one limit for the first two betting intervals and a higher limit for the last two betting intervals. Some circles have graduated limits for each betting interval.

IRREGULARITIES

Only irregularities peculiar to Hold 'Em Poker are dealt with here. Other irregularities and the remedies and penalties for them will be found in the standard laws.

Card Improperly Exposed. If the dealer accidentally exposes one of the player's hole cards while dealing, that card is considered dead. The deal is continued, each player receiving the card he would have received in regular rotation if no card had been prematurely exposed; and when all cards in regular rotation have been dealt, players who failed to receive cards shall be served in rotation from the top of the pack.

Card Found Face Up in the Pack. Any card found face up in the pack is considered dead and placed with the discards. If this occurs during the dealing of hole cards, follow the same procedure as if the card had been exposed. If a card is found face up while dealing the flop, fourth, or fifth cards, the next card in the deck is substituted for the dead card.

Flop, Fourth, or Fifth Card Dealt Too Early. If the dealer begins dealing any part of the flop before the prior betting interval has been completed, the exposed cards are reshuffled into the pack. The interrupted betting interval is completed, and then the flop, fourth, or fifth cards are redealt.

Hold 'Em Variations

Hold 'Em can be made more interesting by various modifications. The most popular forms change the number of hole cards each player receives to three, four, or five cards. Most variations change the requirement from using any combination of hole cards to using exactly two hole cards and three cards from the flop.

VARIATIONS OF POKER

Optional Laws

SPECIAL HANDS

Depending upon the locality in which the game is played, and the personal preferences of the players, certain special combinations of cards may be given values along with the standard poker hands enumerated on page 6. Some of these hands are:

Big Tiger, or Big Cat. King high, eight low, no pair. Ranks above a straight, below a flush.

Little Tiger, or Little Cat. Eight high, three low, no pair. Ranks above a straight, below a Big Tiger.

Big Dog. Ace high, nine low, no pair. Ranks above a straight, below a Little Tiger.

Little Dog. Seven high, deuce low, no pair. Ranks above a straight, below a Big Dog.

Skeet, or Pelter. Nine, five, deuce, with one card between the nine and five in rank and one card between the five and deuce in rank, no pair. Ranks above a straight, below a flush. The skeet is seldom played when Tigers and Dogs are also played. When all five cards of a skeet are of the same suit, the hand is a Skeet Flush and ranks above a straight flush.

As between Tigers (Cats), Dogs and Skeets, ties are broken as in the case of any other poker hand containing no pair—by the highest card, then the next highest, and so on.

Skip Straight. This is also called a Dutch Straight, or Kilter. It consists of a progression of cards each separated by one step in rank from the adjacent one—for example, **Q, 10, 8, 6, 4** or **K, J, 9, 7, 5**. It ranks above three of a kind but below a straight. As between two skip straights, the one containing the highest-ranking card wins.

Round-the-Corner Straight. A sequence of cards, treating the thirteen cards as an unending sequence, so that **3, 2, A, K, Q** is a "straight." Beats three of a kind, loses to a skip straight or straight. As between two round-the-corner straights, the one with the higher card at the top of the sequence wins: **5, 4, 3, 2, A** beats **4, 3, 2, A, K**.

Blaze. Any five face cards. Beats two pairs, loses to three of a kind; however, a blaze including three of a kind need not be called a blaze. As between two blazes, each composed of two pairs, ties are broken as between any two hands composed of two pairs.

Four Flush. This is played principally in Stud Poker, whereas the other special hands are played principally in Draw Poker; however, in many Jackpot games, a player is permitted to open on a four flush even though that hand is given no special value in the showdown. In Stud Poker, a four flush (when played) beats a pair but loses to two pairs. A four flush is any hand containing four cards of one suit. As between two four-flush hands, the one containing a pair beats one containing no pair; if neither contains a pair, ties are broken as between any two hands containing no pair.

POPULAR WILD CARDS

The following are most frequent choices of cards to be designated as wild:
Deuces;
One-eyed cards, or "cards with profiles" (♠J, ♡J and ◇K);
Low hole card in each hand (in Seven-card Stud);
Any card selected in the hand and all other cards of the same rank in the same hand;
Any card selected by the player, but only the one card.

DOUBLE-ACE FLUSHES

When it is not required (in accordance with the rules given on page 11) that a player designate a wild card as some card other than the ones he already holds, a flush may be headed by two or even three aces; thus, if deuces are wild, the holding ◇A ♣2 ◇7 ◇5 ◇4 would beat ♠A ♠K ♠9 ♠8 ♠5, because the holder of the former hand could cause the ♣2 to serve as an additional ◇A.

In games in which the low hand wins, and in which ace ranks as the low card, some permit a hand to be designated as "Double Ace Low," and yet be deemed not to contain a pair.

STRIPPED DECK

When there are fewer than five players in the game, all the deuces, threes and fours may be removed from the pack, making a pack of 40 cards. The purpose of this is to increase the number of high pairs which may be dealt. When the five is the lowest card remaining in the pack, the combination **8, 7, 6, 5, A** is a straight. When the pack has so been stripped, a full house is more likely to occur than a flush, wherefore (under the theory by which poker hands are ranked) a flush should beat a full house in the showdown; however, this ranking of the hands is only by unanimous agreement of the players.

ROYALTIES

Royalties, or *premiums*, or *bonuses*, (in England, *penalties*), are sometimes paid by unanimous agreement of the players, made before the game begins. In such cases, any player holding four of a kind receives one red chip from each other player, and any player holding a straight flush receives one blue chip from each other player. Such payments are made regardless of the result of the pot: If a player holds four of a kind and loses the pot to a straight flush, the former nevertheless receives his royalty of one red chip per player.

Poker Variations

There is an indeterminate number of games based on Poker, and many of these games have several different names. Most of them were originally devised, or are devised from time to time, to break the monotony of a regular Poker game (or, at least, what seems to the average player to be monotony.) The variations which have proved most popular over a period of time are described in the following pages.

In most of these games, the standard poker hands as listed on page 6 have value in the showdown and determine the winner. When any of the standard poker hands are not counted, or when any of the optional hands (page 26) are counted, that fact is noted in the description of the variation. In some cases, each hand in the showdown consists of fewer than five cards; though a player be dealt as many as ten cards, he must select his best five for the showdown.

Low Poker, or Lowball

Straight Draw Poker is played, as described on page 15. There is no minimum requirement for betting, and in each turn a player must either bet (or at least call the previous bet) or drop. Straights and flushes do not count.

In the showdown, the lowest hand wins the pot, with the ace the lowest card in the pack. Since straights do not count, the lowest possible hand is **5**, **4**, **3**, **2**, **A**, which is called a *bicycle*. Aces are low in every case; a pair of aces ranks lower than a pair of deuces.

Low Poker is frequently played in connection with a Jackpots game. If a deal is passed out at Jackpots, the cards are not gathered up and reshuffled; instead, the betting takes up with eldest hand and the game becomes Lowball.

Variant. Occasionally, but rarely, Lowball is played with no difference from the standard rank of the hands, so that the lowest possible hand is **7**, **5**, **4**, **3**, **2** of two or more suits; straights and flushes count, and the ace ranks high. In the showdown the cards speak for themselves, and the combination **5**, **4**, **3**, **2**, **A** is a straight; the holder is not permitted to call the ace the high card in his hand, and thus have a lower ranking hand than, for example, a pair in some other hand.

High-Low Poker

Any standard form of Poker may be played, but in the showdown the highest-ranking poker hand and the lowest-ranking poker hand divide the pot equally. The lowest-ranking hand is either **7**, **5**, **4**, **3**, **2**, or **6**, **4**, **3**, **2**, **A** or **5**, **4**, **3**, **2**, **A** depending on agreement. If the best low hand is **7**, **5** or **6**, **4**, then the hand must contain two or more suits. If there is a chip left over after the pot has been divided as evenly as possible, that chip goes to the high hand. If two or more players tie either way, they divide the pot.

High-Low Stud

Regular five-card Stud Poker is played, but in the showdown the high and low hands divide the pot. Before taking his last card, any player has the option of turning up his hole card and taking his last card face down. If the dealer improperly exposes such a card, the player may not take it; and after all other players still in the pot have been served, the player receives the next card from the top of the pack. The penalty on the dealer is that, if he is still in the pot, his hand becomes foul.

High-Low Seven-card Stud

Seven-card Stud is played as described on page 21, but in the showdown each player may select any five of his cards to represent his high hand, and any five of his cards to represent his low hand. High and low split the pot, but the same player may win both ways.

Declarations. In many games, each player is required to declare, after the bets have been equalized in the last betting interval but before any face-down cards are exposed for the showdown, whether he is going for high, for low, or for both. He is bound by his announcement, and if he declares for high, he may not compete for low; if he declares for low, he may not compete for high; and if he declares for both, he must at least tie for winning hand both ways or he cannot win either way, and even if there is only one other player in the showdown, that player takes the entire pot.

Others play that each player in the showdown must decide in advance whether he will go for high, for low, or for both, but need not make his decision public. Without permitting other players to see him, he must take into his hand a white chip if he is going for low; a red chip if he is going for high; a blue chip if he is going for both.

Eight or Better High-Low Poker

As in High-Low Poker, any standard form of Poker may be played as Eight-Or-Better. At the showdown, the highest hand splits with the lowest hand only if the lowest hand is an eight low or better. If no player has an eight low or better, the high hand takes the whole pot. This game is not played with declarations.

Dealer's Choice

In the usual informal Poker game, the dealer may choose which form or variation of Poker will be played. Sometimes he is not limited to forms of Poker, but may select such games as Fan Tan, Red Dog, or any other game suitable to the number of players at the table. Sometimes each dealer in turn plays a series of games, and this is known as "Garbage."

There is one special rule applicable to Dealer's Choice: When the game selected is Jackpots, or any other game in which the hand can be passed out, when a hand is passed out everyone antes again but the same dealer redeals. Otherwise the next dealer in turn would lose his right to select a game.

Spit in the Ocean

Each player gets four cards, dealt one at a time face down. The dealer then places one card face up in the center of the table. This card is wild, and every other card of the same rank is wild. The card thus shown in the center of the table is considered to be the fifth card of every player in the game.

In most games of Spit in the Ocean, every player antes before the deal. There are several methods of betting:

Variant 1. There is only one betting interval, which occurs after the deal is completed. When the bets are equalized, there is a showdown.

Variant 2. As in Stud Poker (except that the cards are dealt face down) there is a betting interval after each round of one card is dealt to each player who has not dropped, and a final betting interval after the card is faced in the center.

Variant 3. After the face-up card is dealt, there is a betting interval; then each player who has not dropped may discard one or more of his face-down cards and draw enough cards, also face down, to restore his hand to four cards. The rules of Draw Poker apply. There is then a final betting interval before the showdown.

Spit in the Ocean Variation

Each player receives four cards face down as in Spit in the Ocean, then three cards are dealt face down to the center of the table. One of these cards is turned face up, and there is a betting interval; then another card is turned face up and there is a betting interval; finally the third card is turned face up and there is a betting interval. Each player may select one of the center cards, but only one, to represent the fifth card in his hand. So far as he is concerned, the card selected and all other cards of the same rank are wild.

Mexican Stud, or Flip

Stud Poker is played, except as follows: Each player receives his first two cards face down, and may turn up one of them, after which there is a betting interval; each round thereafter is dealt face down, but after the deal each player must turn one of his face-down cards up. Thus there is only one hole card in each hand at any one time.

Each player should select the card to turn up before any other player has turned up his card, so that all cards are turned up simultaneously; but if any player turns his card up before the other players have selected theirs, any other player may change his selection before turning up his card.

Cincinnati

Among the many names for this game are Lame Brains, Rickey de Laet and, in one variant, Criss-Cross.

Five cards are dealt face down to each player, one at a time, and five more face-down cards are dealt to the center of the table. One of the cards in the center is turned face up, and there is a betting interval; then another, and so on, with a betting interval after each card, until all five are exposed. In the showdown, each player selects five cards from among the ten cards of his hand and the exposed cards on the table. No card is wild unless the dealer so designates before dealing.

Criss-Cross. The center cards are laid out in the form of a cross, and the center card is turned up last. Each player must select one or the other bar of the cross, giving him only eight cards to select from. Otherwise the game is the same as Cincinnati. The dealer may, if he wishes, designate the center card and all other cards of the same rank to be wild cards. This designation must be made before the deal begins.

The Wild Widow

Each player receives four cards face down, then a card is faced in the center. This does not become a part of any player's hand, but other cards of the same rank are wild. There is a betting interval, then each player who has not dropped receives another card face down and there is another betting interval, followed by a showdown.

Shotgun

Draw Poker is played, except that after each player has received three cards the deal is interrupted for a betting interval; then each player who has not dropped receives another face-down card, and there is another betting interval; then each player who has not dropped receives a fifth face-down card and there is another betting interval. There is then a draw, followed by a final betting interval and showdown.

Double-barreled Shotgun

Shotgun, as described in the preceding paragraph, is played as a high-low game; and there are four additional betting intervals, because after the draw each player turns up one card of his hand at a time, with a betting interval following each. High and low hands split the pot.

Two Pots to Win

Any form of Poker may be played, but the pot accumulates until any player has won the pot a second time, whereupon he takes the pot.

Two-card Poker, or Hurricane

Each player receives only two cards, dealt one at a time, face down. There is a betting interval, and the high hand in the showdown wins the pot. Usually all players ante before the deal. Straights and flushes do not count in the showdown; a pair of aces is the highest possible hand.

High-Low Two-card Poker. This is usually played with deuces wild, and with the ace counting either high or low; the high and low hands split the pot, so that a holding of **A, 2** is an unbeatable hand both ways, being a pair of aces for high and deuce-ace (double ace) for low. Often declarations are required before the showdown, as explained on page 29.

Three-card Poker, or Three-card Monte

One card is dealt face down to each player, with a betting interval; then one card face up to each player, with a betting interval; then another card face up to each player, which ends the deal. There is a final betting interval and a showdown. The highest possible hand is a straight flush (three cards in sequence in the same suit); then three of a kind, then a flush (all three cards of the same suit), then a straight (any three cards in sequence), then a pair, and then high card.

English Stud

Each player is dealt two cards face down and one card face up, after which there is a betting interval; another face-up card is dealt to each, followed by a betting interval; and then another card face up, followed by a betting interval. Each player may then discard one card and receive a replacement for it, dealt up or down in accordance with whether the card discarded was up or down, and there is a betting interval. Each player may then make a second discard and get a replacement, followed by a betting interval; then a third and last discard and replacement, followed by a final betting interval and showdown. After each discard and draw, each player must always have two cards face down and three cards face up.

If the dealer replaces a card face up when it should have been replaced face down, the replacement card is dead; after other hands have been given their cards, the dead card is replaced with the third card from the bottom of the pack. If the dealer makes this mistake more than once, his own hand is foul.

Baseball

Either five-card or seven-card Stud Poker is played, with the following special rules:

All nines are wild.

Any three in the hole is wild.

If a player is dealt a three face-up, he must either "buy the pot," which means that he puts into the pot as many chips as are already there, in which case his exposed three and all other threes are wild; or he must drop out of the pot. If he does buy the pot, no other player need match that amount to stay in.

A player who is dealt a four face-up is immediately dealt another face-up card in addition to the four.

However many cards a player may have at the end, he must select five of them to be his hand in the showdown.

Butcher Boy

The cards are dealt in rotation face up. When a duplicate of any card previously dealt appears, it is transferred to the player who received the card of that rank previously. There is a betting interval, with this player betting first.

When bets are equalized, the deal resumes, the next card being dealt to the player who would have gotten the last card (or, if he has dropped, to the active player nearest his left).

This process continues until any player has four of a kind, at which point the game ends and that player takes the pot.

As many play, at this point the pot is divided between the high and low hands, the player with four of a kind being high even though another player has a straight flush in five cards. As among the other hands, each must select five cards if he has more than five. In a hand of fewer than five cards, a missing card ranks as the lowest card in the pack, so that **7, 5, 4, 3** is lower than **7, 5, 4, 3, 2**.

Knock Poker

This game is not played in Dealer's Choice games, but is an excellent game for two, three, or four players and may be played by five or more. It is a combination of Poker and Rummy.

Each player is dealt five cards, as in Draw Poker; the remainder of the deck is placed face down in the center, and the top card is turned up to form a discard pile, as in Rummy.

Each player in turn must draw either the top of the discard pile or the top card of the stock, and then must discard one card face up on the discard pile. This process continues until, after drawing and before discarding, a player knocks. When he knocks, every other player gets a turn to draw and discard until it comes around to the knocker again, at which time there is a showdown; having knocked, a player may no longer draw.

Settlement. Each player antes one chip before the deal, and this pot goes to the highest hand in the showdown. After a knock, each player after drawing but before discarding may either drop and pay the knocker one chip, or may stay in. If the player stays in and the knocker is high, he pays the knocker two chips; but if the knocker is not high the knocker pays him two chips.

Bonuses. Many play that bonuses are paid (by every other player in the game, whether or not he has dropped) for knocking and winning without drawing a card (two chips per player); for winning with a royal flush (four chips per player); for winning with any other straight flush (two chips per player); for winning with four of a kind (one chip per player).

Irregularities. On the first round, a hand with six cards discards without drawing; a hand with four cards draws without discarding. An irregular hand discovered at any later time is foul.

If a player draws more than one card from the stock in one turn, his hand is foul; the cards he drew in that turn are placed on the discard pile face up, and the next player has his choice of them.

Variants. Some play that the showdown follows immediately upon a knock, no player having a chance to draw again after the knock, the high hand winning the antes. There is no penalty on the knocker if his is not the high hand. In other circles, it is also played that each time a player draws another card, he must put a chip into the pot.

Cold Hands

Each player puts up an agreed amount, after which the cards are dealt, face up, one at a time until each player has five. The highest poker hand showing takes the pot. Some play that one may discard from a cold hand and draw, as in Draw Poker.

Freezeout

Any form of Poker may be played; usually, the game is either Straight Draw Poker or Stud Poker. Each player takes an original stake; it is not necessary for all players to start with the same amount. No player may add to his original stake nor drag down any part of it or of his winnings after play begins. When a player loses all he has, he drops out and play continues among the remaining players until one player has all the starting stakes.

Red and Black

The rules follow Draw Poker except in the rank of the cards. Instead of determining the winner by poker hands, each player in the showdown counts the point value of his hand. All red cards count plus, and all black cards count minus; each ace counts 1 point, each face card 10 points, and each other card its index value. The hand with the highest plus total in the showdown wins the pot; or the game is played high-low, with the greatest plus hand dividing the pot with the greatest minus (or, if there is no minus hand, with the lowest plus).

Up and Down the River, or
Put and Take

Dealer gives each player five cards, face up, one at a time. He then turns up five cards to the center, one at a time, as "put" cards. As each card is turned, each player having a card of the same rank in his hand must put in the pot as many chips as the rank of the cards, counting a king as 13, queen 12, jack 11, ace 1 and other cards their index numbers. If a player has two or more cards in his hand of the rank turned, he must put up individually for each. When the five "put" cards have been turned, the dealer turns up five "take" cards and this time each player takes from the pot the number of chips equivalent to the rank of the card for each card of similar rank in his hand.

Some play that the first card of each series turned by dealer calls for 1 chip, the second card 2 chips, the third 4, the fourth 8, and the fifth 16. When this variation is played, the rank of the card does not affect the number of chips put in the pot.

This is played as a banking game, the dealer taking any excess remaining in the pot and supplying any deficiency; but there is no advantage to the dealer.

POKER STRATEGY

Poker is widely known as a game of mathematics and psychology. As to which of these elements is the more important, there apparently is a great deal of disagreement. Of the many writers on Poker, some have swayed toward one side, others toward the other.

Nevertheless, it would seem that anyone who places psychology first is overlooking a vital consideration: Poker is a game of betting, and a player who consistently places bets at unfavorable odds is almost sure to lose.

Suppose there are three chips in the pot, and it will cost you one chip to play. But you know that the odds are five-to-one against your winning the pot on the cards you hold. That is to say, if you play the same sort of hand six times, you will win only one pot. If you go into six such pots, you will pay out five chips for the times you lose and get back only three chips for the time you win, a net loss of two chips.

The player must also consider future rounds of betting before acting on the current betting round. In the preceding example, if three chips will be won on the next betting rounds when the hand is won, then the call becomes profitable. However, if calling a one-chip bet leads to being "sucked in" to calling additional losing bets on later rounds, then the error becomes compounded.

To some extent, therefore, a Poker player's first job is to learn the odds against his winning the pot on the various hands he might hold. He must make sure that the pot is offering him adequate odds every time he bets.

POKER PROVERBS

There are many time-honored proverbs that have been handed down by generations of Poker players. Not all of these may be relied upon in all forms of Poker; not all of them are 100% true in any form of Poker; but by and large they are a better crop than any other game has produced. Here are some of them:

Don't throw good money after bad. Money once put into the pot belongs to the pot. It no longer belongs to the player who put it there. In deciding whether to bet, or to call a bet, a player should pay no attention to whatever chips he has previously put into the pot; if he does, and consequently makes an unsound bet, he is throwing good money after bad.

Don't bet into a one-card draw. This applies only at Draw Poker, and means that if an opponent drew only one card it is not wise to bet against him; it is better to wait and see what he will do. The theory here is that he may have been drawing to a flush or straight possibility, so his hand will be worthless if he failed to fill and will probably be the winning hand if he did fill. Thus a bet becomes pointless. He will not call it if his hand is worthless, and he will raise and win if his hand is good. Nevertheless, this proverb is more a warning than a rule. The circumstances may make it clear that the opponent was not drawing to a flush or straight, but rather to two pairs. If there is no chance that he will bet on his two pairs, it is winning play in the long run to bet against him and make him call.

Don't play if you can't beat the board. This applies to Stud Poker, the "board" being the exposed cards of the other players, and ability to beat the board being the holding of a combination higher than any of those exposed cards. This is generally a good rule; it is a 100% rule if any player has a pair showing and you have no pair.

Don't bet into a possible cinch hand. This is another Stud Poker rule. A "possible cinch hand" is an opponent's holding which, combined with the proper hole card, may give him a combination you cannot possibly beat. If you bet into such a hand, he may raise back without fear that you can beat him. This is another good rule which nevertheless has its exceptions. The exceptions are based on the circumstances of the previous betting, which may indicate that his having a dangerous hole card is extremely unlikely.

Raise immediately if you hold two pairs before the draw. This is a Draw Poker rule, and as usually quoted it is far too broad to be reliable. Whether or not you raise on two pairs depends largely on your position at the table; the matter will be dealt with in greater detail later.

THE POKER HANDS

In general, the various tables of Poker probabilities given below are of little value while a game is in progress, but do furnish some background to the study of the game: For one thing, they show the relative probability of the various hands, and emphasize the infrequency with which the best of these combinations occur; and they give some picture of how the incidence of good hands increases when the pack is stripped, or when wild cards are counted.

The 52-card pack provides 2,598,960 possible different combinations of five cards, which is to say, that many different Poker hands.

Possible Poker Hands in a 52-card Pack

Straight Flush (including 4 Royal flushes)	40
Four of a Kind	624
Full House	3,744
Flush	5,108
Straight	10,200
Three of a Kind	54,912
Two Pairs	123,552
One Pair (84,480 of each, aces to deuces)	1,098,240
No Pair:	

Ace High	502,860	
King High	335,580	
Queen High	213,180	
Jack High	127,500	
Ten High	70,380	
Nine High	34,680	
Eight High	14,280	
Seven High	4,080	
		1,302,540
Total		2,598,960

Possible Poker Hands in a 40-card Pack

(STRIPPED OF 2S, 3S, AND 4S)

Straight Flush	28
Four of a Kind	360
Flush	980
Full House	2,160
Straight	7,140
Three of a Kind	23,040
Two Pairs	51,840
One Pair	322,560
Less than One Pair	249,900
Total	658,008

Possible Poker Hands in a 32-card Pack

(STRIPPED TO THE SEVENS)

Straight Flush	20
Flush	204
Four of a Kind	224
Full House	1,344
Straight	5,100
Three of a Kind	10,752
Two Pairs	24,192
No Pair	52,020
One Pair	107,520
Total	201,376

Possible Poker Hands in a 53-card Pack

(WITH THE JOKER INCLUDED AS A WILD CARD)

Five of a Kind	13
Straight Flush	204
Four of a Kind	3,120
Full House	6,552
Flush	7,804
Straight	20,532
Three of a Kind	137,280
Two Pairs	123,552
One Pair	1,268,088
Less than one pair	1,302,540
Total	2,869,685

Possible Poker Hands with Deuces Wild

	Number of Deuces					
	None	*One*	*Two*	*Three*	*Four*	*Total*
Five of a Kind		48	288	288	48	672
Royal Flush	4	80	240	160	..	484
Straight Flush	32	576	2,232	1,232	..	4,072
Four of a Kind	528	8,448	19,008	2,832	..	30,816
Full House	3,168	9,504	...	...	..	12,672
Flush	3,132	7,264	2,808	...	..	13,204
Straight	9,180	37,232	19,824	...	..	66,236
Three of a Kind	42,240	253,440	59,376	...	..	355,056
Two Pairs	95,040	...	...	...	..	95,040
One Pair	760,320	461,728	...	...	..	1,222,048
No Pair	798,660	...	...	...	..	798,660
Total	1,712,304	778,320	103,776	4,512	48	2,598,960

It should be noted that as cards are stripped from the pack, or as wild cards are introduced, the number of "good" hands is increased. Theoretically, this makes no difference whatsoever; the value of any poker hand is purely relative. The average player, however, accustomed to Jackpots, does not like to open a pot on less than jacks and does not think he has a good hand unless he has considerably more than that. Thus the introduction of wild cards, or the stripping of the pack, so that three or four players taking part in a game may still have some action. If four play Jackpots with a full pack, nothing wild, they will probably pass out half the deals; if they play with a pack stripped to forty cards, nothing wild, almost three out of four hands will probably be opened.

Of far more importance to the practical player are the calculations which indicate when to open a pot; when to stay in; when to raise.

OPENING THE POT

It may be flatly stated that a player should not make the opening bet unless he probably has the highest hand at the table. In Draw Poker, a player will not have assurance of the highest hand; he "probably" has the highest hand when mathematically it is more likely (be it ever so slightly) that he has the highest hand than that any other player can beat him.

If the game is Straight Draw Poker, there is no legal minimum for making the opening bet and the matter is merely one of counting the players yet to speak—that is, the players who have not yet passed out. In a seven-hand game, the first bettor ("under the guns") will always have six such men behind him; the second bettor will have five if the first has passed, and so on. The minimum strength which justifies a bet is as follows:

PLAYERS YET TO SPEAK	STRENGTH REQUIRED
7	Pair of Aces
6	Pair of Kings
5	Pair of Kings
4	Pair of Queens
3	Pair of tens
2	Pair of eights
1	Ace-King high

Most Draw Poker games, however, are Jackpots; and a player with only three, two or one opponent yet to be heard from nevertheless cannot open without jacks. In the first position, the strength required is the same as though there were no minimum openers. In the last three positions, a player should open if he has at least a pair of jacks. It will be noted that the table above provides for an eight-hand game, since otherwise there could not be seven players after the first bettor. The usual game is no more than seven-handed, and in such a game a pair of kings justifies an opening in any position.

Except in rare cases, in which one purposely defies mathematical considerations for psychological reasons, it is wisest to open the pot whenever holding the required strength.

WHEN TO STAY IN

The principle which must be learned by most Poker players, even experienced ones, is this: Unless you have reason to think your hand is the best at the time that you put your chips in the pot, do not stay in after someone else has bet. There are cases, when a number of players are already in the pot and when it has not been raised, when a player may stay in because he thinks he has the high pair (that is, he has a pair of aces) even though it is likely that some other player has two pairs. In general, however, the best hand going in is the best hand coming out and one should not go in unless he expects to be the best hand coming out.

The following table assumes that every player in the game has a pair, and shows the expectancy of winning the pot that each player enjoys before he draws:

Wins in a Hundred Pots

NUMBER IN POT	NEEDED FOR EVEN BREAK	HIGH PAIR	2ND PAIR	3RD PAIR	4TH PAIR	5TH PAIR	6TH PAIR	7TH PAIR
2	50	76½	23½					
3	33⅓	58½	21	20½				
4	25	47	19½	19	14½			
5	20	38⅓	18½	17½	13⅔	12		
6	16⅔	31¾	17	16¼	13	11½	10½	
7	14²⁄₇	27	16	15	12½	11	10	8½

The way to read the table is this: If only two players are in the pot, the one with the higher pair stands to take out 76½ chips for every 50 he puts in, a clear profit of 26½ chips on his investment of those 50. With six in the pot, a player may go in with the second-best pair and break about even, showing an inconsiderable profit; if there are fewer than six in the pot, the player with the second-best pair stands to lose in the long run.

It should be particularly noted that only the relative rank of the pairs is important; it does not greatly matter what pairs they are. If your opponent has a pair of aces, you have no appreciably better chance against him with a pair of kings than with a pair of deuces.

Therefore, in a conservative game it may be assumed that every additional player who stays in believes he has a better hand than any of the players before him. On this is based the following table of the minimum strength required to stay in when the pot has already been opened and others are in it:

PLAYERS ALREADY IN POT	REQUIRED TO STAY IN
1	Kings
2	Two low pairs
3	Queens up
4	Kings up
5	Aces up
6	Three of a kind

In fact, some of the two-pair hands listed would be too weak if it could not be assumed, when four or five players have already stayed, that one of the foregoing players may be in on a one-card draw to a straight or flush, draws which are justified only when several other players are already in the pot.

Odds Offered by the Pot. As previously noted, the decision to stay in or to drop is based always on the chance of winning the pot, the number of chips required to play, and the size of the pot. There are other factors to consider—for example, the danger that the pot will be raised—but usually it is proper to play when the chance of winning is greater than the odds offered.

For this reason, every chart or table given here must be modified by an actual count of the pot at the time the decision is made. This must be an "eye" count; Poker etiquette does not usually permit one to delay the game by stopping for an actual count of the chips. Usually the count is more or less automatic, once one has fixed in mind the amount of the ante and the size of the customary opening bet. If the ante is large and the bets small, it is advisable to play on a considerably weaker holding than those listed. *For example:* In a Jackpots game with an ante of ten chips and an average opening of two chips, the pot has been opened and one other player has stayed in. A third player finds himself with a low pair; the odds are four-to-one against his winning the pot. But there are fourteen chips in the pot and he must put up only two; he is being offered seven-to-one odds. If he is last man, he should stay; the odds are proper, and the pot cannot be raised. If there are three or four players ahead of him still to speak, he should drop; if one or two other players come in it will decrease his chance of winning, and if the pot is raised it will greatly decrease the odds he is being offered.

Flushes and Straights. At the start of a Draw Poker hand, you can see only five cards. There are forty-seven cards you do not know. If you hold four cards of a suit, nine of the unknown forty-seven cards are of the same suit as your four, and if you draw one of them you will have a flush. Therefore if you stay and draw one card, you have nine chances in forty-seven to fill your flush. The odds are 38-to-9, or somewhat more than 4-to-1 against you.

If you have a bobtail straight, such as **8, 7, 6, 5**, the odds are 39-to-8, or almost 5-to-1 against filling it, for there are only eight cards which will help you (in this case, the four nines and the four fours). If you have a straight possibility which only one card will fill—such as **A, K, Q, J**, or **9, 8, 6, 5**—the odds are 43-to-4, or almost 11-to-1 against you.

It would seem that you should draw to a flush only when the pot gives you at least 4-to-1 odds; to a bobtail straight only when the pot gives you 5-to-1 odds; to an inside, or one-end straight practically never, since you can so rarely expect to be offered as much as 11-to-1 by the pot.

Actually, it is wise to stay on a flush when the pot offers slightly under 4-to-1—for example, when there are already seven chips in the pot and it costs two to stay in. When you do fill, you will probably win the pot, and very often you can make a sizable bet or raise which one or two other players will call. This compensates for the times you do not fill, and makes some allowance for the disastrous occasions when you will fill your flush and be beaten by a better hand. On the balance, you will win somewhat more than you will lose.

Likewise, though the odds are 5-to-1 against filling a bobtail straight, you have a slight advantage when you stay against 4-to-1 odds—that is, when there are already eight chips in the pot and it costs two to go in.

It is seldom wise to play on these hands if the pot has been raised, however, except in exceptional games where the pot is enormous and the limit low. Every raise and re-raise not only reduces the odds offered by the pot, but also warns of the danger that another player will have a better hand than yours even if you fill.

Conforming to the Custom. In most Poker games the play is not nearly so conservative as it has been described here. When playing in such games, you should be considerably more liberal about staying in and raising. There are several reasons for this: First, since the other players are playing liberally, you will be offered better odds by the pot on weaker hands outstanding against you; second, the pot will be larger and the winnings on your good hands greater, permitting you to speculate more on your doubtful hands; third, you will avoid the stigma of being a poor sport. A good criterion in such games is to be just a bit more conservative than the average of the game—not so much so that it is readily noticeable, but enough so to maintain your advantage. Thus, if mathematics would demand that in a certain position you have two pairs to stay, but the custom of the game is to stay on any low pair, you might adopt the style of staying when you have at least queens, or kings.

DRAWING CARDS

The first bit of advice in connection with drawing is very obvious, yet so widely violated that it deserves mention: Do not discard or otherwise indicate how many cards you intend to draw, until every player before you has drawn. The information you give in advance may help those before you to decide how many to draw. Throwing in your discards prematurely may, in some cases, cause them to be shuffled up with the other discards, and when your turn comes you may get back one or more of the cards you threw away and do not want.

The second thought is this: Before deciding how many to draw, have clearly in mind your object in drawing: Is it to improve your hand, or is it to deceive the other players?

If it is almost a foregone conclusion that your hand will win without improvement, you should draw (or fail to draw) in accordance with the impression you want to give of your hand, so that you will be called when you bet after the draw. For example, you hold three tens. The pot was opened ahead of you, you raised, everyone else dropped out and the opener stayed in without raising. He draws three cards; you should draw only one. The odds are almost 8-to-1 that he will not get three of a kind, while if he opened on a pair of aces or kings and happens to get two pairs, he is likely to bet or call.

If your object is to improve your hand, you may be governed by the following tables showing the chances of improving a pair, or three of a kind (the chance of improving a straight or flush possibility has already been given):

Drawing Three Cards to a Pair

TOTAL NUMBER OF CASES: 16,215

RESULT	FAVORABLE CASES	ODDS AGAINST
Two pair	2,592	5.25 to 1
Triplets	1,854	7.74 to 1
Full House	165	97.3 to 1
Four of a Kind	45	359 to 1
Any improvement	4,656	2.48 to 1

Drawing to a Pair and Ace Kicker

TOTAL NUMBER OF CASES: 1,081

RESULT	FAVORABLE CASES	ODDS AGAINST
Aces up	126	7.58 to 1
Another pair	20	17 to 1
Total two pair	186	4.81 to 1
Triplets	84	12 to 1
Full House	9	119 to 1
Four of a Kind	1	1080 to 1
Any improvement	280	2.86 to 1

Drawing Two Cards to Triplets

TOTAL NUMBER OF CASES: 1,081

RESULT	FAVORABLE CASES	ODDS AGAINST
Full House	66	15½ to 1
Four of a Kind	46	22½ to 1
Any improvement	112	8⅔ to 1

Drawing One Card to Triplets

TOTAL NUMBER OF CASES: 47

RESULT	FAVORABLE CASES	ODDS AGAINST
Full House	3	14⅔ to 1
Four of a Kind	1	46 to 1
Any improvement	4	10¾ to 1

Odd Draws

DRAW	ODDS AGAINST	RESULTS
Four to an Ace	11 to 1	Two pairs or better
Three to A–K of same suit	12 to 1	Two pairs or better
Two to straight flush (e.g. ◇ J 10 9)	11 to 1	Straight or better
except: K, Q, J or 4, 3, 2	13½ to 1	Straight or better
A, K, Q or 3, 2, A	20 to 1	Straight or better
Two to a flush	23 to 1	Flush
Two to open-end straight	22 to 1	Straight

There are other odd draws, rarely seen but worth recognizing when need for them arises. For example, a player who has two low pairs is reasonably sure that to win the pot he must beat another hand which contains two higher pairs. The odds against his winning, if he makes the normal draw of one card, are 11-to-1 (approximately). If he throws away one of the pairs and draws three cards to the other, the odds are only about 8-to-1 against him. If his odd card happens to be an ace, he can hold it as a kicker and make even a further reduction (though a slight one) in the odds against him. Nevertheless, it is seldom wise to split two pairs, because it is so seldom possible to be sure that the opponent has two higher pairs and not some other hand; and one may at least know that if he draws one card to his two pairs and gets a full house, he is almost sure to win the pot.

RAISING

Either of two reasons may prompt a raise. The first is a simple one: The player feels that he has the winning hand and wants to make the other players put as many chips as possible into the pot. The other possible reason is to drive the other players out because if they stay in one of them may improve and win the pot.

Take, for example, the classic case, the hand with two pairs in Draw Poker. This hand has a 3-to-1 chance to win against one opponent; a 53-to-47 chance against two opponents; but the odds are approximately 3-to-2 against it when there are three opponents, and 7-to-3 against it when there are four opponents. Suppose you hold such a hand and the player at your right opens. The ante is ten chips, and it costs two to play. If you raise and thereby drive out all the other players, your average winning on the hand will be approximately ten chips. If you fail to raise and in consequence other players come in, you will still show a profit on the hand but it will average only seven chips. In such a case it pays to raise.

Likewise, in Stud Poker you figure to win when you have a low pair back to back, but you are likely to win less if several opponents stay against you than if you drive all but one or two of them out by an immediate raise. Therefore, standard practice is to raise on the first round.

When you are sure you have the best hand, and you are likely to have the best hand even if several other players stay in and draw cards, it is not wise to raise too quickly. Raising here is largely a matter of position; if you are the last man to speak, and three or four other players have already come in, you raise because you will not scare out any other players after you. If you are next to the opener (or to the first bettor in Stud) you simply chip along and hope as many other players as possible will come in. You can raise later.

In most cases when you raise on what you believe to be the winning hand, the time of your raise and the amount of your raise will depend on your knowledge of the habits of the players against you. Against one player you may make a small bet because he will make a "cheap" call but might not call for a larger amount; against another player you may make a large bet because he will think you are bluffing, whereas a smaller bet he would think to be genuine.

BLUFFING

The most dangerous of all the Poker proverbs is this: "You should occasionally bluff even when you think you will lose, just for advertising purposes. Then you are more likely to be called when you have good hands."

One point that cannot be overemphasized is that the object of every bet is to win the pot. You should bluff when you think you have a better-than-even chance of winning by it. You need not worry about the "advertising." Bluffing is a losing game at best, and the advertising will take care of itself in the cases when you do not get away with your bluff.

Successful bluffing is a matter of grasping at unexpected opportunities. A player may occasionally set the stage for a successful bluff, but it is rarely worthwhile to do so. It must also be borne in mind that it is easier to bluff good players than poor players. Good opponents will observe when one's play has been typical of the play of a good hand, and may drop out. Poor opponents will probably call. In fact, poor opponents call almost everything and it is neither wise nor necessary to bluff against them.

PSYCHOLOGY

"Psychology" is "the study of the mind." That is precisely what is meant by psychology in Poker. One studies the habits and the voluntary or involuntary customs of the other players. From this he learns to judge their manners and mannerisms when they have strong hands, and when they have weak hands; the bets they make when they want to be called and the bets they make when they do not want to be called; and all the other set patterns into which the play of most Poker players will inevitably fall. These patterns are not stereotyped, and no set rules may be laid down about them.

The corollary is that the winning player must be careful not to let the other players get too much evidence as to his own style of play. He should not show his hand when he has bluffed successfully, however strong his inclination to gloat. He should not show his hole cards in Stud Poker unless he has to.

SPECIAL CONSIDERATIONS

In many forms of Poker, or in standard forms played with different stakes and limits, there are special considerations.

The Bug. A straight is good enough to win in almost every case, and drawing to a three-card sequence plus the Bug (the joker), such as **Bug–10–9–8**, is twice as good as the draw to a usual bobtail straight. Such a hand is therefore worth a play in many cases where a bobtail straight such as **J–10–9–8** would be dropped, and is even worth a raise when three other players are already in the pot. This is not true of draws to a flush.

High-Low Poker. There is no exact concordance between the winning chances of good high hands and good low hands; a full house has a better chance to win high than a seven-high hand to win low. When many players are raising and re-raising, a good low hand should be viewed with caution and the holder should be content to call; a good high hand should be played as strongly as in a Jackpots or regular Draw Poker game.

High-Low Seven-card Stud. At the start, you should play for low, not for high. The holding **7–5–4** is far better than an original holding of a pair of kings. A possibility for low can turn into a hand which is good both high and low; an original holding of high cards can almost never turn into a good low hand.

Deuces Wild. The average winning hand in a five- or six-hand game is three aces, including at least one deuce. A "natural" combination is not so good as a combination including one or more deuces, because the chance that other players will hold deuces is increased. When the pot has been opened, it is seldom wise to stay in without a deuce in the hand, unless holding three of a kind or better.

Table Stakes Games. When a player is down to his last five or ten chips, and the pot is large, the odds he is offered by the pot (assuming he has a choice between dropping and staying in) are enormous. Furthermore, his losses are limited; he cannot lose any more even though he draws a good hand and is unfortunate enough to have someone else draw a better hand.

Two Pots to Win. When it is necessary to win the pot twice in order to collect it, a player who has won a pot has an enormous advantage. A player who has not won a pot, when several other players have, should be even more conservative than usual; a player who has won a pot should play on almost anything.

RUMMY

RUMMY—THE BASIC GAME AND ITS VARIATIONS

Although it is the newest family of games, Rummy and its variants have enlisted a huge following in the United States, comparable to that of the perennial leaders, Contract Bridge and Poker.

Rummy derives from Conquian, also called Coon-Can. Little is known of the origin of Conquian. The name is Spanish (*con quien*, with whom) and the game is widely played in Mexico, whence it spread to Texas and other Southern states. But "games of structure" are very old indeed; the great majority of the games devised during the cradle period in Europe (17th century) involved some preliminary melding, regardless of whether the subsequent play if any was for tricks, points, or stops. Conquian may trace its lineage to this time.

There is nothing in modern Conquian to suggest why it was called "with whom?" The name is more suitable to a game of temporary partnerships, such as Call-Ace Euchre. Perhaps the original Conquian was such a game and the name was misapplied to an entirely different pastime. In the United States, Coon-Can acquired a new name, Rum. It has been suggested that the title was in imitation of the "Whiskey" in Whiskey Poker, which is no longer played; the theory is not far-fetched, since later the game of Gin was deliberately so named "to keep the liquor in the family." Rum became generally Rummy, and Gin was softened to Gin Rummy, by the same bowdlerism that changed Vive l'Amour to Pig and Oh Hell to Blackout.

The basic game of the family, Rum, has largely given way to more elaborate variants. For two players, Gin and Knock Rummy are preferred; for three, Five Hundred Rum; for four, Partnership and Persian Rummy; for five or more, Double Rum and Liverpool Rum.

PLAYERS

From two to six may play.

CARDS

The pack of 52. The cards in each suit rank: **K** (high), **Q**, **J**, **10**, **9**, **8**, **7**, **6**, **5**, **4**, **3**, **2**, **A**.

PRELIMINARIES

Cards are drawn for deal; lowest card has choice of seats and deals first. Other players may take seats at random. Dealer has the right to shuffle last, and the pack is cut by the player at his right. The cut must leave at least four cards in each packet.

DEALING

Cards are dealt one at a time, to the left, beginning with eldest hand. Each hand comprises: with two players, ten cards; with three or four, seven cards; with five or six, six cards.

The rest of the pack is placed face down to form the *stock*. The top card is turned up and set beside the stock to commence the *discard pile*.

In two-hand, the winner of each hand deals next. With more players, the deal rotates in turn to the left.

OBJECT OF PLAY

In all games of this family, the immediate object of play is to form the hand into *sets*. A set may be of either of two types: a *group* of three or four cards of the same rank, or a *sequence* of three or more cards of the same suit. In straight Rummy, ◇**A 2 3** is a sequence, but ◇**A K Q** is not.

THE PLAY

Each player in turn must *draw* one card, either the top card of the discard pile or the top of the stock. He may then *meld* (place on the table) any *set* he holds. If he has more than one set, he may meld all in the same turn. He need not meld when able, but may keep the set in his hand. To complete his turn, the player must *discard* one card, face up on the discard pile.

Any player in turn may *lay off* (add one or more matching cards) on any melded set, his own or another player's. He may meld and lay off in the same turn.

The first player to get rid of all his cards, by melding, wins the deal, and play ends. When the draw enables him to meld all his remaining cards, he need not discard. But he may *go out* by the help of the discard, after melding all but one card.

If no player has gone out by the time the stock is exhausted, the discard pile is shuffled and placed face down to form a new stock, and play continues until some player is able to go out.

SCORING

Each other player pays to the winner the count of all cards left in his hand, reckoning each face card as 10, each ace as 1, and each other card its index value. If the game is played for a stake, settlement is made after each deal. In social play, game may be set at 100 or more, and the first to amass that total is declared the winner.

IRREGULARITIES

Play out of Turn. If a player is not stopped before he has completed his turn by discarding, it stands as a play in turn and intervening players lose their turns. If the player out of turn has taken the top card of the stock, it is too late for rectification after he has added that card to his hand.

Illegal Draw. If, by playing out of turn or by drawing more than one card from the top of the stock, a player sees a card to which he is not entitled, that card is placed face up on top of the stock. The next player in turn may either take the card or may have it put in the center of the stock, face down, and proceed to play as if no irregularity had occurred.

Incorrect Hand. A player with too many cards discards without drawing; a player with too few cards draws without discarding, until his hand is restored to the correct number. If, after a player goes out, another player has too many cards he simply pays the value of all cards in his hand; if he has too few cards, he is charged 10 points for each missing card.

Cards Laid Down Illegally. If a player lays down cards which are not in fact a matched set, they must be restored to his hand if discovered at any time before the cards have been mixed. An opponent's card laid off on such a set remains on the table, but no card may then be added unless three or more cards, which themselves form a matched set, have been laid off on it. If a player announces that he is out when he is not able to get rid of all his cards, he must lay down and lay off all he can. In either case play proceeds as if no irregularity had occurred.

STRATEGY

Keen observation of the discards helps both toward improving one's own hand, and blocking the opponent's. A knowledge of what cards are dead (buried in the discard pile) often shows that a combination of cards is not worth holding because it cannot be improved. Noticing what an opponent picks up will give a clue to what he has in his hand. Attention to what cards have *not* been discarded may be an even better guide to an opponent's hand.

Building Sets. The more chances there are to improve a combination of cards, the better it is. The combination ♣Q ◇Q J has four chances—♠Q, ♣Q, ◇K, ◇10—and so is better than ♣K Q ◇Q, which only three cards can improve. It must be remembered that a dead card must not be counted as a chance; if an eight has been discarded previously, ♠8 ♣8 7 is no better than ◇6 ♡6 4, assuming that both black sixes and ♡5 are still available.

As between combinations offering the same number of chances, the lower is usually better to hold. With this hand:

$$\text{7–7–7–7} \qquad \heartsuit \, \textbf{Q J} \qquad \diamondsuit \, \textbf{4 3}$$

if $\heartsuit$**K 10** and $\diamondsuit$**5 2** are yet to be seen, one of the hearts should be discarded rather than one of the diamonds. If an opponent goes out there will be less to pay for the diamonds.

It is somewhat better to play for sequences than to hold pairs. Having turned a pair into three of a kind, one can draw only one card—the fourth of that kind—to improve the set and after that no improvement will be possible. Having made a sequence, one can improve it with either of two cards—the card matching either end—and then continue to improve it.

Discarding. In general, the highest unmatched cards in the hand should be discarded first; kings first of all, since they will fit into sequences only at one end. However, with choice of discards those closest together in rank should usually be retained. Holding:

$$\heartsuit \, \textbf{K Q} \qquad \spadesuit \, \textbf{Q} \qquad \spadesuit \, \textbf{3 2} \qquad \diamondsuit \, \textbf{10} \qquad \heartsuit \, \textbf{9} \qquad \clubsuit \, \textbf{J}$$

it is better to throw $\clubsuit$**J** than $\diamondsuit$**10**. The latter, held with $\heartsuit$**9**, will become a four-chance combination if either $\heartsuit$**10** or $\diamondsuit$**9** is drawn. The $\clubsuit$**J** may also serve as "bait" to convince an opponent that he may safely discard $\clubsuit$**Q** or $\heartsuit$**J**.

Discarding should be directed toward reducing the count of the cards in the hand, especially when the hand is a poor one and offers little hope of going out. With a good hand, it is better to hold $\heartsuit$**Q J** than $\clubsuit$**5 3**, but if the hand is poor the hearts, which will cost 20 points if left in the hand, should be discarded and the club combination, which can cost no more than 8 points, should be retained.

A "good" hand is one which contains a set after the second draw at latest, and which can go out by addition of at most two cards to the hand; for example:

$$\text{Q–Q–Q} \qquad \clubsuit \, \textbf{10 8} \qquad \diamondsuit \, \textbf{8} \qquad \spadesuit \, \textbf{3 A}$$

From this hand $\clubsuit$**10** is discarded, since there is almost as much chance of drawing $\spadesuit$**2** as of drawing $\clubsuit$**9** (mathematically there is the same chance for either card, but the opponent is more likely to discard $\clubsuit$**9** than $\spadesuit$**2**).

Blocking. There must be constant effort to block the opponent by refusing to discard cards he can use. The ideal discards are "dead" cards—in this sense, cards which are unlikely to make sets because their mates have been discarded previously. (For example, $\heartsuit$**8** is dead if $\heartsuit$**9**, $\heartsuit$**7** and two other eights have been discarded or are out of play for any other reason.) In two-hand play, the opponent may be able to use any live card. In three- or four-hand play, no one but the left-hand opponent can take the discard, and there is less danger in discarding live cards.

For example, with only ten or twelve cards left in the stock, a player draws a king. He has no king in his hand, and no king has been discarded. There is so slender a chance that all the other kings remain in the stock that it may be disregarded; and since any player with a lone king would have discarded it, it is obvious that someone is holding two or three kings.

There is constant opportunity for card-reading in the cards picked up by opponents from the discard pile. When the opponent picks up ♣8 and later discards ♢8, he is placed with a sequence in clubs. In games in which laying off is permitted, this permits certain unmatched cards to be retained with safety. At all times it warns against dangerous discards.

Picking Up. It seldom pays to pick up the last discard unless it forms a set. For example, to pick up a discarded ♡8 when holding ♡7 and ♣8, in order to have a four-chance combination, is generally losing tactics. The opponent will be warned not to discard anything that might match ♡8, and the chance of completing a set from that combination will immediately be reduced because the matching card can be drawn only from the stock.

Going Down. Some player is usually able to go out before the stock is exhausted. To hold up a set for fear some other player, by laying off on it, will be enabled to go out sooner, is dangerous if the set is composed of high cards. With three aces, or **A–2–3**, it is a different matter; they may be held because the cost will not be great in any event. In general, it is best to wait no longer than the point at which half the stock is gone; then such high sets as one has should be melded.

A similar principle governs waiting to "go rummy," in games in which that pays double.

Rummy Variations

Among the variations from the foregoing rules, found in various localities, are the following:

Sequences. The ace ranks either below the two or above the ace, so that ♢**A 2 3** and ♢**A K Q** are both correct sequences. Or, as some play, the sequence in the suit is circular, so that ♢ **K A 2** may be melded " 'round the corner."

Laying Off. Cards may be laid off on adverse melds, during play. Or, another variation, cards may be added only to one's own melds, during play, but when one player goes out all others may lay off on his melds.

Final Discard. The player who goes out must complete his turn with a final discard. Consequently, when reduced to two cards or one the player cannot make a new meld but must depend upon laying off on previous melds. This rule is usually combined with allowing the player to lay off on adverse melds.

Rummy. The winner collects double if he melds his whole hand at one time, having made no previous meld. This is called *going rummy*. Some play that no melding at all is permissible; the first to form his entire hand into sets shows it and wins.

"Rummy." If a player discards a card that he could have laid off on an existing meld, any other player may call "Rummy!" pick up and meld the card, and then make a discard.

Block. If none has gone out by the time the stock is exhausted, play ends, and the hand with the lowest count wins. Each other hand pays the winner the difference of the counts. If two or more tie for low count, they divide the winnings.

Borrowing. A player may borrow a card from any of his previous melds to complete a new meld, provided that he leaves a correct meld of at least three cards. Thus he may borrow one card from a group of four, or cards from either or both ends of a sequence if three remain.

Coon-can, Double Rum, or Two-pack Rum

Two full packs plus two jokers, 106 cards in all, are shuffled together. Each hand receives ten cards. A group comprises three or more cards of the same rank, regardless of suits. The joker is a *wild* card—it may be used to complete any group or sequence. If a joker is melded as the end card of a sequence, it may be moved to accommodate the natural card. *Example:* A player melds ♠**5**, ♠**6**, and joker ranking as ♠**7**. The player may later add the ♠**8**, or he may add ♠**7**, whereupon the joker ranks as ♠**8**. Some play that an opponent holding the natural card replaced by the joker may exchange it for the joker, thus gaining possession of the latter. In scoring, jokers count 15 each, aces 11, face cards 10, other cards their index value.

Kaluki

In this double-deck rum game, aces rank high or low, and each player is dealt 15 cards. Aces count 15 points, honor cards 10, other cards their face value. Jokers are wild and when melded count the same as the card it represents. A joker in hand counts 25. The first meld must total 51 or more. A player may not draw the discard or lay off until he has melded, except he may take the discard if he correctly melds at that turn. A melded joker may be traded by any player in exchange for the natural card it represents. The player who goes out scores all the points remaining in the other hands.

Boat House Rum

The number of cards dealt to each hand is 9 minus the number of players. A player may draw the top of the stock or the top of the discard pile, but if he elects the latter, he must take one additional card, either the top of the stock or next discard. No melds are shown until one player is able to *go rum* by laying down a hand completely formed in sets. The winner collects the count of *unmatched cards* in every other hand. The last card of the stock may not be drawn; if no player goes rum, each player puts up chips to the amount of his unmatched cards and the pool goes to the next winner.

Conquian

The original Conquian changed somewhat as its name became Coon-can, and finally was almost indistinguishable from Double Rum, described on the preceding page.

PLAYERS

Two

CARDS

The pack of 40, made by discarding all face cards from the pack of 52. The cards in each suit rank: **10** (high), **9**, **8**, **7**, **6**, **5**, **4**, **3**, **2**, **A**. (The regular Spanish pack is made by discarding the eights, nines and tens from the pack of 52; the jack is then in sequence with the seven. But stripping out the face cards instead avoids confusion.)

PRELIMINARIES—as in Rummy

DEALING

Each hand receives ten cards, dealt in rounds of two at a time. The rest of the pack is placed face down to form the stock.

THE PLAY

Non-dealer commences by turning the top card of the stock face up. If he wishes, he may take this card into his hand. If he does not want it, he *passes*, and dealer has the right to take the *turn-up*. If dealer also does not want it, he casts it aside face down and turns up the next card. And so following—the player who turns up from the stock has first claim to the card; if he refuses it, opponent may take it; if both refuse, it is discarded face down and the second to refuse turns up a new card.

Any time that a card is taken into the hand, the player discards one card face up on the stock. Opponent then has a right to take this card, or cast it out of play and turn up from the stock. Once cast out, face down, a card remains out of play.

A card may be taken into the hand on speculation; it need not be melded immediately.

Object of Play is to form sets, as in Rum. A set may be melded immediately it is formed, or held in the hand so long as the owner wishes. Melding must be done in the player's turn, before he refuses the turn-up or before he discards.

A player may lay off additional cards on his own melds, and may also borrow from his own melds to make new ones provided that he leaves a correct meld in so doing. *Example:* From **♣8 7 6 5** he may borrow **♣8** or **♣5**, but not **♣7** or **♣6**.

Forcing. A player may compel opponent to take the turn-up or discard, if it can be added to one of opponent's melds. The object in so forcing is to compel a discard from opponent, possibly breaking a pair or part-sequence.

GOING OUT

To *go out*, a player must meld eleven cards: consequently, his last play must be a draw, which is melded, not followed by a discard.

SCORING

Each deal is a separate game. When one player goes out, he wins, and the other pays him one chip. If neither goes out by the time the stock is exhausted, each player antes a chip and the pool goes to the winner of the next game.

IRREGULARITIES

If a player turns up and sees more than one card of the stock, his opponent has first right to any such card illegally seen, regardless of the normal procedure of the game. Any other irregularity must be corrected on demand of the non-offender before his next play. If not corrected by this time, it stands as regular and play proceeds.

STRATEGY—See also Rummy, "Strategy"

The skillful player is deadliest in his use of the privilege of "forcing." A player with two cards left in his hand should usually be forced. For example, a player has melded **A–A–A–A**, **♡3 4 5 6**. He holds **9–9**. His opponent, however, discards **♡7**, forcing him to add the **♡7** to the sequence on the table and discard a nine. Previously, drawing any nine would have given him eleven cards down; now, to get eleven cards down he must draw **♡2** and ♡**8**, or ♡**8** and ♡**9** in that order—and one of those cards may be dead.

It must also be remembered that holding a card that prevents the opponent from going out will usually prevent one from going out himself. The exception is when one player holds, for example, ◇**5 6** and the other player has ◇**8 9**, or two sevens, whereupon ◇**7** will put either out. This is seldom the case, and it is usually necessary to throw the dangerous card early and risk losing, or hold it and try to block the game.

Knock Rummy

The drawback of some variants, e.g., Persian Rummy, is that each deal takes a long time to play. Knock Rummy is at the other extreme: it is a fast-moving "murder and sudden death" proposition. Eldest hand may knock on sight of his hand, and more than ten turns per deal is rare. Knock rummy has also been called Poker Rum.

PLAYERS

From two to five.

CARDS

The pack of 52, the cards ranking as in Rummy.

DEALING

When two play, each receives ten cards; three or more, seven cards; dealt as in Rummy.

THE PLAY

Drawing, discarding, and rules as to sets are as in Rummy, but there is no melding. All sets are kept in the hand until a player is ready to knock, that is, lay down his whole hand and thereby end the play. A player may knock in his turn, after drawing, regardless of how far the play has progressed or even whether it has begun, and he duly discards one card.

SCORING

When any player knocks, each player counts the *deadwood* in his hand— the cards not matched with others in sets. Face cards count 10 each, all other cards their index value. The hand with the lowest total in deadwood collects from each other hand according to the difference of the counts. If the knocker is lowest, there is no further payment. But if another hand is lower than the knocker, this player wins from all and collects an extra penalty of 10 from the knocker. (Some play that the knocker in this case pays double.) If a player ties the knocker for low count, this player collects the winnings, while the knocker neither pays nor collects. If two or more players other than the knocker tie for low score, they divide the winnings.

If a player *goes rum* by knocking with a hand completely formed in sets, he collects an extra 25 from each player besides the count of his hand. A *rum hand* cannot be tied; if another besides the knocker has a complete hand, he pays the knocker 25.

STRATEGY—*See also Rummy, "Strategy"*

In two-hand play, many players knock on first turn if they are slightly below "average" (which is 65). That is, they knock with a deadwood count of 60 or less in their original ten cards. On the second turn, a count of 40 or under is a good knock. Thereafter, the minimum should be decreased by about 10 points per turn.

In three-hand play (when average for the seven cards is 45) it is wise to knock on the first turn with 35; in four- or five-hand play, with 30. After every one has had one turn, 20 is the lowest safe count for a knock. After two turns around, it is unwise to knock with less than 15, and thereafter the count should be under 10.

Unmatched face cards and tens should, of course, be discarded first, and very low cards should be held even when they do not promise to match other cards in the hand in forming sets. The principle is to avoid heavy losses on poor hands so as to make the most of the winnings on good hands.

GIN RUMMY

This variant is essentially Knock Rummy with a limitation on knocking designed to give more defense to a player who is dealt a poor hand. Its invention is credited to E. T. Baker, a member of the Knickerbocker Whist Club of New York, in 1909. He called it Gin for the alcoholic drink, by analogy with the name of the parent game, which was then called Rum. It was played as a minor game in New York clubs for several decades until in 1941 it became a fad in Hollywood and received nationwide publicity.

PLAYERS

Two. But see also the methods by which three or more may play (page 68).

CARDS

The pack of 52. In practice, two packs are used alternately. The cards in each suit rank: **K** (high), **Q**, **J**, **10**, **9**, **8**, **7**, **6**, **5**, **4**, **3**, **2**, **A**.

PRELIMINARIES

Cards are drawn; higher card has choice of seat and deal. None of the four end cards of the spread pack may be drawn. If cards of the same rank are drawn, the higher is fixed by the suits, which rank: spades (high), hearts, diamonds, clubs. The player winning the right may either deal first himself or require opponent to do so. Thereafter, the winner of each hand deals the next.

Dealer has the right to shuffle last. Non-dealer cuts the pack.

DEALING

Each hand receives ten cards, dealt one at a time beginning with non-dealer. The rest of the pack is placed face down to form the *stock*. The top card of the stock is turned up and placed beside the stock, to form the first *upcard*.

THE PLAY

Non-dealer may take the first upcard or refuse it; if he refuses, dealer has the same option. If dealer also refuses, non-dealer draws the top card of the stock. Thereafter, each in turn draws a card, either the upcard or top of the stock, and then discards one (the new upcard) card face up on the previous discards.

The object of play is to form the hand into *matched sets:* three or four cards of the same rank, or sequences, three or more cards in sequence in the same suit. Cards that do not form part of a set are called unmatched cards.

After drawing, a player may *knock* if his unmatched cards (less one discard) count 10 or less. In this reckoning, each face card counts 10, each ace 1, each other card its index value. On knocking, the player lays down ten cards, arranged in sets and with the unmatched cards segregated, then discards the eleventh card. If all ten of his cards are matched, his count is 0 and he is said to *go gin.*

If neither player has knocked by the time the fiftieth card has been drawn (and a following discard made), the cards are abandoned and there is no score for the deal.

LAYING OFF

Opponent of the knocker may *lay off* any of his unmatched cards that fit upon the knocker's matched sets, thereby reducing his own count of unmatched cards.

SCORING

If the knocker has the lower count in unmatched cards, he wins the difference of the counts. Should the opponent have an equal or lesser count, he is said to *undercut* the knocker. The opponent then scores the difference (if any) in the counts, plus a bonus of 25 points (in some games, 10 or 20 points). The knocker cannot be undercut if he has gone gin. A player who goes gin scores the opponent's count of unmatched cards, if any, plus a bonus of 25 (in some games, 20).

Game. The first player to accumulate 100 (or 200) points wins the game. A 100-point *game bonus* is added to his score. Each player then adds to his score 25 points (in some games, 20) for each hand he has won; this is called a *box,* or *line, bonus.* The winner wins the difference in total scores. If the loser did not score a point, this difference is doubled; such a game is called a *shutout,* or *schneider,* and the loser is said to be *skunked.*

IRREGULARITIES

New Deal. A deal out of turn may be stopped at any time before the upcard is dealt; thereafter it stands as a correct deal.

There must be a new deal by the same dealer if it is found, before the completion of the deal, that the pack is imperfect or that a card is faced in the pack; or if a card is exposed in dealing, or if a player has looked at the face of a card.

Irregular Hands. If either player's hand is discovered to have an incorrect number of cards before that player has made his first draw, there must be a new deal.

After the first draw, if it is discovered that both players have incorrect hands, there must be a new deal. If one player's hand is incorrect and the other player's hand is correct, the player with the correct hand may decide either to have a new deal or to continue play. If play continues, the player with the incorrect hand must correct his hand by drawing without discarding, or by discarding without drawing, and may not knock until his next turn to play.

After a knock, a player with too few cards is charged 10 points for each card missing, and may not claim the undercut bonus; if the knocker's opponent has more than ten cards, the hand may not be corrected, the offender may not claim an undercut bonus, and can lose or tie but may not win the hand.

If the player who knocks has an incorrect number of cards, the penalty for an illegal knock applies.

Imperfect Pack. When two packs are being used, a card from the other pack found in the stock is eliminated and play continues. If it is discovered, after the knock, that the pack is incomplete, the deal stands. Discovery that the pack is imperfect in any way has no bearing on any score that has been entered on the score sheet. (See also *New Deal,* above.)

Premature Play. If non-dealer draws from the stock before dealer has refused the upcard, the draw stands without penalty as his first play. If a player draws from the stock before his opponent has discarded, the draw stands as his proper play.

Illegally Seeing a Card. If a player drawing in turn sees any card to which he is not entitled, every such card must be placed face up next to the discard pile. The offender may not knock until his next turn to play, unless he is gin. The non-offender has the sole right to take any of the exposed cards until first thereafter he draws from the stock; then the offender has the same right until first thereafter he draws from the stock; when each player has drawn from the stock, the exposed cards are placed in the discard pile.

If a player drawing out of turn sees a card to which he is not entitled, the rule given in the preceding paragraph applies, except that the offender may never take such cards, but may draw only his opponent's discard or the top card of the stock in each turn.

Exposed Card. A card found exposed in the stock, or in the other pack or away from the table, is shuffled into the stock and play continues. Accidental exposure of a card in a player's hand is not subject to penalty.

Illegal Knock. If a player knocks with a count higher than 10, but his opponent has not exposed any cards before the error is discovered, the offender must leave his hand face up on the table until his opponent has completed his next play. However, if the knocker's hand is illegal only with respect to the count of his unmatched cards, his opponent may accept the illegal knock as legal.

If the knocker has more than 10 points, and the error is discovered after the opponent has exposed any of his own cards but before he has laid off any cards, the opponent may choose which of the following penalties to apply: To make the knocker play the rest of the hand with all his cards exposed; or to permit the offender to pick up his hand, in which event the offender may not score for any undercut or gin bonus in that hand.

If the knocker has an incorrect number of cards, his opponent may demand a new deal; or may require the offender to play with his hand exposed and to correct his hand on his next play or plays, either by drawing without discarding or by discarding without drawing.

If a player, after knocking, inadvertently discards a card which makes his knock illegal, he may replace that discard with a discard which makes his knock legal.

Looking Back at Discards. Players may agree in advance that looking back at discards will be permitted. In the absence of such agreement, a player who looks back at a covered discard loses his right to his next draw.

STRATEGY—See also Rummy, "Strategy"

In Gin Rummy, sets and cards that can be laid off do not count against the loser. This is the principal difference between Gin and other Rummy games, and affects the strategy of Gin in several respects.

Most important is the effort to keep two or three very low cards—aces, twos and threes—at all times, even when they are not matched and offer no prospect of forming sets. If the opponent wins, having the low cards reduces the loss. Most Gin hands are won on holdings of six or seven matched cards (two sets) plus other cards counting to 10 or less.

The initial effort to get some low cards into the hand means that the early discards are usually face cards and tens, even more than in other Rummy games. For the first two or three turns it will often pay to hold high pairs and two-card sequences, hoping the opponent's discards will fill them. After the fourth turn it is unsafe to hold them.

In the first four or five turns one should knock as soon as he can get his count down to 10. Very occasionally he may be wary of knocking with 9 or 10 on the fifth turn, for example if his opponent has picked up one or two discards, or has discarded a low card, especially an ace or deuce. But generally one should knock whenever he can do so in an early turn.

In later play—after the eighth turn—a count of about 5 justifies a knock. If a player has picked up more than one card from the discard pile to form sequences, or three of a kind, he should beware of knocking at all this late in the game. His opponent has been warned and may be holding one or more cards that can be laid off, permitting an undercut.

Waiting for gin, although able to knock, is seldom justified unless the opponent can be assumed to have a weak hand. Otherwise the opponent may go gin and the loss often represents a difference of 50 or more points.

Hollywood Gin

Hollywood Gin is played the same as standard Gin Rummy, but differs in how its score is kept. Each hand is scored as though three games were being played simultaneously. The scoresheet contains three double-columns for Games 1, 2, and 3. The first score made by a player is entered in Game 1; his second score is entered in Game 1 and again in Game 2; his third score and subsequent scores are entered under all three games. When any one game terminates, Game 4 may be opened up, and so on continuously, or the two remaining games may be finished without further extension, which is used in this form of scoring. If a player is shut out in Game 1, his first score is entered in Game 2 alone, and his second in Games 2 and 3. Game and box bonuses are awarded to each column independently of the other games in progress.

Round-the-Corner Gin

This form of Gin Rummy may be played in any variant of that game, with the following differences in procedure:

Ace may rank high or low in a sequence and sequences may go around the corner (**A-2-3**, **A-K-Q**, **K-A-2**, etc.). As an unmatched card, an ace counts 15 points.

If the knocker goes gin but his opponent can reduce his own count to zero, neither player scores on that hand.

Game ends when one player reaches 125 points. In any partnership game, it takes 25 points more to end the game than when regular Gin Rummy is played.

Players may at all times inspect the previous discards.

Oklahoma Gin

In Oklahoma Gin the rank of the upcard fixes the maximum number of points with which a player may knock in that deal. Thus, if the upcard is a five, the knocker must have 5 points or less. Any face card counts 10. Most play that an ace calls for a Gin hand, not merely a count of 1. A usual added rule is that when the upcard is a spade all scores accruing from that deal are doubled.

A version of Oklahoma that is widely played in clubs is to use a second deck to determine the knock card. Each deal the next card is faced, but these cards have no other effect on the play. With the first deck, 11 cards are dealt to the non-dealer and 10 to the dealer. After non-dealer has discarded, play continues as in Gin. In the scoring, an undercut is worth 20 game points plus one additional box, which is indicated by circling the numeral 1 opposite that score. A player who goes gin receives two additional boxes and 25 game points. If a player *gins off* (lays off all of his unmatched cards on the knocker's sets), the bonus is three boxes in addition to 25 or 30 game points. Hollywood scoring is used and games are 150 points. For winning a game, the premium is 150 points; each box for line score and bonus awards counts 25 points. The loser deals the next hand.

Gin Rummy for 3, 4, 5, and More

Three-hand Play. In the most popular method, only two play at a time. Each player cuts; lowest stays out the first hand, next-lowest deals. After the end of each hand the loser goes out and the idle player takes his place. Each player has his own scoring column for the hands he wins. The game ends when any player reaches 100, and after game and box bonuses have been added, each player settles separately with each other player (a player who is shut out pays the extra points only to the winner). An idle player may not advise either other player.

A second method is to play *chouette* (see page 587). One player is in the box. He plays a regular two-hand game against one of his opponents (the captain), but if he loses he pays both opponents and if he wins he collects from both. The opponents may consult but the captain has the final decision. When the captain loses a hand, the other opponent becomes captain. When a game ends, the captain becomes the man in the box.

A third method is for all three to play. Each receives ten cards. If the player at dealer's left refuses the first upcard, either other player, in turn, may take it. A player in turn may take either opponent's previous discard (unless one has already been taken). When a player knocks, the other players may lay off only on the knocker's original matched sets (if the knocker has ♡**9 8 7** and one opponent lays off ♡**6**, the other may not add ♡**5**). An individual score is kept for each player. Game is 200, and each player settles separately with each other player. There is no undercut bonus; if the knocker is undercut, 20 points are deducted from his score, but an undercutter scores only if his score is lower than the knocker's.

Partnership Play. Four or more players, in even numbers, may play in partnerships. Each member of a side plays a two-hand game against a member of the opposing side. When all hands are finished, the scores are combined and only one side scores; for example, if one member of side A wins by 12 points and the other member loses by 10 points, side A wins the hand by 2 points. When a player knocks, play in other games may be suspended until the result is known. At the end of each game, each player changes opponents. Game is 125 when there are four players, 150 when there are six or eight players, 175 when there are ten players, 200 when there are twelve players, etc. Drawn hands are not replayed. A player whose hand is ended may advise a teammate, if he has not seen any opposing hand.

500 RUM

This is also called Pinochle Rummy, and its family includes the popular games of Canasta, Samba, Persian Rummy, Michigan Rum, and Oklahoma.

PLAYERS

From two to eight may play. Best for three, four, or five.

CARDS

The pack of 52. With five or more players, it is advisable to use two full packs shuffled together. The cards in each suit rank: **K** (high), **Q**, **J**, **10**, **9**, **8**, **7**, **6**, **5**, **4**, **3**, **2**, **A**. The counting value of cards is as follows: **K**, **Q**, **J**, each 10; cards from **10** to **2**, index value; **ace**, 15 if left in hand or melded in a group of aces, but 1 if melded in a sequence **A–2–3**.

PRELIMINARIES

Cards are drawn; lowest has choice of seats and deals first. Other players may take places at random. Dealer has the right to shuffle last, and the pack is cut by the player at his right. The cut must leave at least four cards in each packet.

DEALING

Cards are dealt one at a time to the left, beginning with eldest hand. When two play, each receives thirteen cards. With any greater number of players, each receives seven cards. The rest of the pack is placed face down to form the *stock*. The top card is turned up and set beside it to start the *discard pile*.

OBJECT OF PLAY

To form sequences and three or more of a kind, as in Rummy.

THE PLAY

Each hand in turn draws either the top card of the stock or a card from the discard pile. *All* cards in the discard pile are available, and it is therefore spread so that all indexes are visible. But there are two restrictions upon drawing from the discard: (a) a discard may be drawn only if it is immediately melded; (b) any and all cards *above* the card drawn and melded must be taken also. (Such additional cards should be left on the table until the player's next turn, so that all others have fair opportunity to inspect and memorize them.)

After drawing from stock or discard, the player may meld as many cards as he can and wishes, and he ends his turn by discarding one card face up on the discard pile.

A player may add cards to any meld on the table—the fourth card of a group of three, or additional cards to a sequence. All such added cards are retained by the owner in front of himself, not placed with the original meld when the meld belongs to another player. Consequently, when a card fits with either of two melds (a group and a sequence), the owner must specify to which he chooses to attach it. A sequence increased by one player may be further increased by another, to the limits of the suit. *Example:* A player melds ♣Q J 10. Another adds ♣9. Any player holding ♣8 may then add it, and so on.

Play of a deal ends when one player gets rid of all cards in his hand by melding, or when the stock is exhausted. The entire stock may be drawn, and after the last discard play may continue so long as each hand in turn can draw from the discard and meld; but as soon as any hand passes, the play ends.

SCORING

At the end of play, each player adds the value of all cards he has melded, and from the total subtracts the count of cards left in his hand. *All* cards left in the hand are counted, regardless of whether they include possible melds. If the count of cards left exceeds the count of melds, the player scores minus for the deal.

A running total score is kept for each player, and when one reaches plus 500 or more, the game ends. Each player settles with each other according to the difference of their final totals. (There is no bonus for winning a game.)

IRREGULARITIES—See Rummy, "Irregularities"

STRATEGY

It is necessary to play to the score, especially as one or more players near the 500 mark. A player who is behind must play to go out, even though he must thereby relinquish chances for high-scoring melds; for if he can go out early he can cause all the others to end with minus scores for the deal and thus pull them down toward his level. When one is ahead, or when the score is not an important factor, he can usually progress toward 500 faster by picking up discards liberally and playing to meld as much as possible. Only the higher-scoring melds—those counting no less than 15—are worth taking chances for.

Until there is danger of someone's going out, an "open" set (on which another player may lay off) is held up, but dead sets like four of a kind are melded as soon as made.

500 Rum Variations

Partnerships. Four-hand 500 Rum may be played in two partnerships. Partners sit alternately. All rules are as in 500 Rum. Partners cooperate in play by discarding to help each other, and pool their scores each deal.

Persian Rummy

Persian Rummy is an elaboration of partnership 500 Rum. The pack is increased to 56 cards by the addition of four jokers. Jokers count 20 each, and may be melded only in *groups* of jokers. If all four cards of a rank are melded at once, the meld counts double. *Example:* A meld of four aces counts 120, but if three are melded first and the fourth added later, the total is only 60. An ace counts 15 at all times and ranks above the king. Thus ♡**A K Q** is a sequence, but ♡**A 2 3** is not. When any player gets rid of all his cards by melding, play ends and his side scores a bonus of 25. When the stock is exhausted each player must draw from the discard pile if by so doing he is able to play.

A game comprises two deals. The side with the higher final total score wins the difference of the totals plus a game bonus of 50.

Michigan Rum

This is an older game than 500 Rum, which is now more popular. Michigan Rum should not be confused with "Michigan."

There is no difference between Michigan Rum and 500 Rum except in the scoring. Each player scores the value of his melds as he puts them down. When a player goes out, he also scores the total of all the cards remaining in the other players' hands. The first player to reach 500 wins, and if two or more reach 500 on the same deal the higher score wins; all deals are played out.

If a player claims to go out when he cannot, he pays each opponent 20 and play proceeds. The player who made the incorrect claim is then eligible to go out legitimately.

Oklahoma

Two, three, or four may play, each for himself. A double pack (104 cards) is used, with or without a joker, which if used is wild. In any case, all deuces are wild.

Preliminaries. The players draw, and low deals first (the joker, if used, is low). Thereafter the winner of the previous hand deals. Each player receives thirteen cards, dealt one at a time. The next card is turned up and placed beside the stock. Eldest hand, and then each player in turn after him, may become the first player by taking this card; if all refuse, eldest hand draws the top of the stock and play proceeds as in Rummy.

The Play. When a deuce (or the joker) is melded, the player must name the card it represents. There is no trading for deuces, but the player who laid down the joker may reclaim it by substituting the card it represents. No other player may do this.

Ace ranks either high or low in sequences.

A player may lay off only on his own groups and sequences, and may not add to any group that already contains four of a kind.

To take the top card of the discard pile, a player must take the entire discard pile and must immediately use the top card in a meld, or lay it off on one of his previous melds. (He may also take it to trade for the joker if he previously used the joker to represent it.)

The hand ends when a player in turn melds his last card but one and discards his last card. *A player may not discard* ♠Q *if there is any other card he can discard, or unless it puts him out.*

Scoring. Each player is credited with the point value of each card he has melded, and is charged with the point value of each card left in his hand, as follows:

CARD	IF MELDED	IF LEFT IN HAND
Each ace	+20	−20
Each K, J, 10, 9, or 8	+10	−10
Each 7, 6, 5, 4 or 3	+5	−5
♡Q, ◇Q or ♣Q	+10	−10
♠Q	+50	−100
Joker	+100	−200
Each deuce	Value of card represented	−20

(A deuce representing ♠Q counts only +10)

The player who goes out receives a bonus of 100 points.

A player's net score for the deal is added to (or subtracted from) his score. The game ends when, at the end of any hand, a player has 1,000 points. If two or more players reach 1,000 on the same hand, the highest score wins the game. The winner receives a bonus of 200. Each player's score is then figured to the nearest 100 (50 or more counting as 100) and each settles separately with each other.

Blocked Game. If a player who draws the last card of the stock discards without going out, the hand ends and is scored, no one receiving the bonus of 100 for going out.

Going Out All at Once. If a player who has not previously melded goes out in one turn, 250 is added to his score but does not count toward reaching the game of 1,000. This bonus is not given to a player who goes out on his first turn.

Irregularities. If a player illegally exposes any but the top card of the discard pile, or looks at the top card of the stock, he is penalized 25 points.

CANASTA

Canasta is a form of 500 Rum, but it has also become the progenitor of a whole subfamily of games. It originated in Uruguay, soon after World War II. By 1949 it was a fad in the principal card clubs of Argentina, and from late 1949 through most of the 1950s it was the biggest game fad the United States had seen since Mah-Jongg in the early 1920s. It is significant that Canasta and Mah-Jongg are essentially much alike and that each had its boom period a few years after a World War. The word *canasta* is Spanish, meaning basket, and may first have been applied to the tray placed in the center of the table to hold the stock and discards. From Canasta arose the variants Samba, Chilean Canasta or Chile, Bolivia, and others. For a period of some months in 1950 and 1951 Canasta passed Contract Bridge as the favorite game in the United States, and after its fad had ended it remained among the card games most often played, along with other forms of Rummy, Solitaire, Contract Bridge, Poker, and Pinochle.

PLAYERS

Canasta may be played by two, three, four, five, or six players. It is best for four. (As a two-hand game, Samba is better; see page 79.)

With two or three players, each plays for himself. With four or more players, there are two partnerships. With four, partners sit opposite each other at the table. With five, two partners are opposed by three, but only two of the three play at a time, rotating so that a different one of the three is idle each deal. With six players, three on each side, partners sit alternately around the table; or three-pack Canasta, described on a later page, may be played.

CARDS

The game is played with two regular decks of 52 cards, plus four jokers, all 108 cards being shuffled together. The jokers and deuces (twospots) are wild. A wild card may be designated to be of any rank, at the pleasure of the owner.

PRELIMINARIES

Partnerships may be determined by drawing cards from the deck, spread face down on the table. The two or three highest cards drawn show the partners playing against the other two or three. Highest card has choice of seats. For purposes of the draw only, the suits rank: spades (high), hearts, diamonds, clubs; and the cards of each suit rank: ace (high), king, queen, jack, etc. to deuce (low). Jokers are void, in drawing.

The player drawing the highest card plays first; therefore, the player at his right deals first. Thereafter the deal rotates to the left, clockwise. The player at the right of the dealer cuts the deck, after any player who wishes to shuffle has done so. In the cut each packet must comprise at least four cards.

DEALING

The dealer gives eleven cards to each player one at a time clockwise, beginning with the opponent at his left and ending with himself. (When there are three players, each receives thirteen cards; with two players, each receives fifteen.) The undealt remainder of the deck is placed face down in the center of the table to form the *stock*. The top card of the stock is turned face up beside it; this is the *upcard*. All subsequent discards are laid face up in one pile, on the upcard, if the first player does not take it. Only the top discard may be seen.

RED TREYS

If the upcard is a red trey or a wild card it must immediately be covered by another card from the top of the stock, and the discard pile is then *frozen* (see below). The red treys (three-spots) are bonus cards, counting for or against the side to which they fall but never forming a part of the eleven-card hand. At his first turn to play, each player must withdraw from his hand each red trey dealt to him, put it face up on the table, then draw a card from the top of the stock to restore his hand to eleven cards. On drawing a red trey from the stock, a player must immediately face the trey on the table and draw a replacement from the stock to keep in his hand. A red trey taken in the discard pile is similarly faced, but is not replaced from the stock.

THE PLAY

The opponent at left of the dealer plays first; thereafter the turn passes to the left, clockwise. Each turn comprises a draw, a meld (optional), and a discard.

The player in turn is always entitled to draw the top card of the stock; subject to restrictions given in the following sections, he may instead take the top card of the discard pile, if he can use it in a meld. Having so taken the last discard, he must take the entire pile and add it to his hand or his melds.

A discard must always be made from the hand, never from a meld. The act of discarding ends a player's turn.

Melds. The principal object of play is to form *melds*, combinations of three or more cards of the same rank, with or without the help of wild cards. (Sequences are not valid melds in Canasta.) A meld is valid if it contains at least two *natural* (not wild) cards of the same rank, and not more than three wild cards. But black treys may not be melded unless the player *goes out* in the same turn. Jokers and deuces may never be melded separately from natural cards. A meld must be laid face up on the table, in some proper turn of the owner. All the melds of both partners are placed before one of them.

A player may add one or more cards of the same rank or wild cards to a meld previously faced by himself or his partner. Wild cards in any number may be added to a completed canasta, but no other meld may contain more than three wild cards.

Canastas. A meld comprising seven or more cards is a *canasta*. A canasta may be built up by an initial meld of three or more cards and addition of other cards later. Seven natural cards form a *natural canasta*, valued at 500. A canasta formed with help of one to three wild cards is *mixed* and is valued at 300. Additional cards added to a canasta do not increase the bonus, but merely add the point values of the cards. A wild card added to a natural canasta reduces it to a mixed canasta.

Minimum Count. Every card melded has a point value, as follows:

Each joker	50
Each deuce	20
Each ace	20
Each king, queen, jack, **10, 9, 8**	10
Each **7, 6, 5, 4**, and black **3**	5

The first meld made by a side is its *initial meld*. The initial meld must have a *minimum count* that depends upon the accumulated total score of that side at the beginning of the current deal, as follows:

TOTAL SCORE	MINIMUM COUNT
Minus	0
0 to 1495	50
1500 to 2995	90
3000 or more	120

A player may make two or more different melds in the same turn to achieve the minimum count. Not even a canasta may be melded initially unless the count of its cards satisfies the minimum.

After a side has made its initial meld, either partner may make any valid meld without reference to any minimum count.

Taking the Discard Pile. The discard pile is *frozen*, as concerns a side, until that side has made its initial meld. Even for the side that has melded, the discard pile is *frozen* at any time that it contains a red trey (turned as upcard) or a wild card (upcard or a later discard).

At a time when the discard pile is frozen (for both sides or his side alone), a player may draw the top card only to make a meld with two natural cards of the same rank from his hand. At a time when the discard pile is not frozen, a player may draw the top card to make a meld with two cards from his hand, either two natural cards or one natural and one wild card, or to add to a meld of his side.

In taking the discard, a player must proceed as follows (to show his legal right to it): face two cards from his hand that form a valid meld with the discard; lift off the top discard and place it with them; in the case of an initial meld, make such additional melds from his hand as are necessary to meet the minimum requirement. Next the player must take the rest of the discard pile into his hand, and he may then make all additional melds he chooses, with the aid of these cards; but these melds do not help to fulfill the minimum count.

The discard pile may not be taken when it is topped by a wild card or a black trey.

Forcing. After the last card of the stock is drawn, play continues so long as each player in turn legally takes and melds the card discarded by his right-hand opponent. It is compulsory (when the stock is exhausted) to take the discard if it is legally possible to add it to a meld. (Making a discard that the next player must take, at this time, is called *forcing*.) The play ends when the player in turn does not take the discard, either because he cannot legally or because he does not choose to.

Going Out. A player *goes out* when he (legally) gets rid of the last card of his hand, either by discard or by meld. A player may go out only if his side has melded at least one canasta. Failing this requirement, he must keep at least one card in his hand. A player need not make a discard after going out; he may meld all of his remaining cards.

Asking Permission. If able to go out before drawing, or after drawing from the stock, a player may ask his partner "May I go out?" The partner must answer "Yes" or "No" and the player is bound by the reply. Permission to go out may not be asked by a player when he has melded any card in that turn. (A player may go out without asking permission.)

When any player goes out, play ends and the deal is scored.

SCORING

The side that goes out determines its net score for the deal as follows:

(a) Total the point values of the cards in its melds.
(b) Total all bonuses under this schedule:

For going out	100
For each red trey	100
(All four red treys count 800.)	

For each natural canasta 500
For each mixed canasta 300
For concealed hand 100
(c) Total the point values of all cards left in the hand of the player whose partner went out.
(d) Subtract item (c) from the sum of items (a) and (b).

The opponents of the side that went out determine their net score for the deal in the same way, but with these differences: If this side has made no meld, the value of its red treys is deducted instead of added; point values of cards left in both hands are deducted.

If the last card of the stock is a red trey, play ends; the player drawing it may not discard and has no further opportunity to meld. Play also ends when the stock is exhausted and any player in turn fails to take the top discard. In either case the net scores are determined according to the preceding paragraph.

Scoring a Game. A game is won by the first side to reach a total of 5,000 points or more. If both sides reach 5,000 in the same deal (the final deal is played out, even though it is known that one side will reach 5,000 after play ends), the side with the higher total wins. There is no bonus for winning a game. Settlement is made on the difference of the final scores, which are the totals of the net deal scores.

The score should be recorded on paper, with one column for each side, and the record should show each net deal score together with the cumulative total of such scores for each side. (Minimum count for the initial meld is fixed by this cumulative total.)

Concealed Hand. A player goes out with a *concealed hand* if he melds all his cards in one turn, having previously melded not a single card. (In going out concealed he may not add a card to a meld of his partner's.) The player going out with a concealed hand must himself meld a complete canasta, but need not have any specific minimum count for an initial meld.

Two-hand Canasta

In two-hand Canasta, each player is dealt 15 cards. When a player draws from the stock he draws two cards, but he discards only one card in each turn. To go out, a player needs two canastas instead of one. Otherwise the rules are as in the four-hand game.

Samba

Samba follows the rules of Canasta except for the following:
Cards. Three decks of 52 cards each, plus six jokers, making 162 cards in all.

Deal. Each player receives 15 cards, regardless of the number of players.

Draw. A draw from the stock (instead of taking the discard pile) is two cards, but only one card is discarded to end the turn.

Sequence Meld or Samba. Three or more cards of the same suit and in sequence (ace high, fourspot low) are a valid meld. Such a meld may be increased by sequential cards up to a total of seven, when it becomes a *samba* and is turned face down. No card may be added to a samba, and it may never contain a wild card. A samba ranks as a canasta for purpose of going out. The bonus for a samba is 1,500.

Melding Wild Cards. Wild cards may be used only in melds of cards of the same rank, and no meld may ever contain more than two wild cards.

Adding to a Canasta. The discard pile may not be taken to add its top card to a completed canasta. Only natural (not wild) cards from the hand may be added to a canasta.

Duplicate Melds. A side may meld two or more sets of the same rank. Either partner in his turn may combine melds of like rank (to build toward a canasta).

Taking the Pack. The discard pile may be taken only (a) by melding its top card with a natural pair from the hand, or (b) when it is not frozen, by adding its top card to a meld on the table. (But note that a sequence meld may not be initiated by the top of the discard pile, plus cards from the hand; it must come wholly from the hand.)

Initial Meld. Requirements for the initial meld are:

Minus	15
0 to 1495	50
1500 to 2995	90
3000 to 6995	120
7000 or more	150

Game. Game is 10,000 points.

Going Out. A side must have at least two canastas to go out and also to count its red threes plus. (A samba is a canasta.) The bonus for going out is 200. No bonus for "concealed hand."

Red Threes. If all six red threes are drawn by one side they count 1,000.

Uruguay

Uruguay follows the rules of Canasta except for the following:

Wild Cards. Three or more wild cards, up to seven, are a valid meld. A canasta of wild cards counts 2,000.

Chile, or Chilean Canasta

Either the three-deck (162-card) Samba pack or a four-deck (208-card) pack with eight jokers is used. Sequence melds as in Samba and wild-card melds as in Uruguay are permitted.

Bolivia

Bolivia follows the rules of Samba except for the following:

Wild Cards. From three to seven wild cards form a valid meld. A canasta of seven wild cards is a *bolivia*, counting 2,500.

Samba. The samba (seven cards in suit and sequence) is called an *escalera*. It counts 1,500.

Game. Game is 15,000. The initial meld requirement stays at 150 from 7,000 up.

Going Out. A side must have two canastas, including an escalera, to go out.

Red Treys. Red treys count plus for the side if it has completed two canastas of any description; otherwise they count minus.

Black Treys. A black trey left in the hand when any other player goes out counts 100 minus. A black trey melded in going out counts only 5.

Brazilian Canasta

Brazilian Canasta is not much different from Bolivia. Game is 10,000 and the special initial meld requirements are: Score 5,000–7,000, 150; 7,000–8,000, any canasta; 8,000–9,000, 200; 9,000–10,000, a natural canasta. Any canasta of wild cards counts 2,000. Five red threes count 1,000 and all six count 1,200. Black threes may never be melded. If a side has a melded sequence of less than five cards when play ends, 1,000 points are deducted from its score.

Italian Canasta

Italian Canasta follows the rules of Samba except as noted:

Discard Pile. After the deal and before a card is turned each player replaces his red treys. Then the top card is turned. A number of cards equal to its rank (counting jack 11, queen 12, king 13, ace or joker 20) are counted off the stock to begin the discard pile. They are turned face down, and the upcard is placed face up on them.

The discard pile may be taken only by a natural pair from the hand (it is "always frozen").

Wild Cards. Deuces may be melded as an independent rank, with or without the aid of jokers as wild cards. A side that has melded deuces may not meld wild cards elsewhere until the canasta of deuces is completed.

Initial Meld. The initial meld must meet the required count without aid of any wild card. The requirements are:

TOTAL SCORE	MINIMUM COUNT
0 to 1,495	50
1,500 to 2,995	90
3,000 to 4,995	120
5,000 to 7,495	160
7,500 to 9,995	180
10,000 or more	200

Going Out. A wild-card canasta does not count as one of the two canastas required to go out. The bonus for going out is 300.

Red Treys. When a side has no more than three red treys, they count 100 each; four or more, 200 each.

Scoring. Seven deuces count 3,000; a mixed canasta of deuces, 2,000; but these bonuses go only to the side that goes out; opponents having deuce melds score only the point value of the cards. Extra bonuses: for five pure canastas, 2,000; for five canastas including a mixed, 1,000; for ten canastas of any kind, 2,000.

Game. Game is 12,000.

Cuban Canasta

Several variants of Canasta are called "Cuban." It resembles regular Canasta rather than the Samba variants. The pack (108 cards), the draw (one card at a time) and the values of cards are as in Canasta. The differences are:

Game. Game is 7,500. From 5,000 to 7,500, the initial-meld requirement is 150.

Discard Pile. The pack is always frozen. No canasta may contain more than seven cards, so the pack may not be taken to add to a five-card meld.

Canastas. In addition to natural and mixed canastas, wild cards may be melded. A canasta of seven deuces counts 4,000; four jokers and three deuces, 3,000; any other wild-card canasta, 2,000. Sequences may not be melded. A side needs two canastas to go out.

Threes. One red three counts 100, two count 300, three count 500, all four count 1,000. They count plus if the side has a canasta, otherwise minus. Black threes may not be melded. When a black three is taken in the pack it is removed from play, and if a side gets all four black threes in this way it scores 100.

OTHER GOOD RUMMY GAMES

Continental Rum

The common characteristic of many variants included under the general name Continental Rum is the elimination of the *group* as a valid set. The only kind of set recognized is the *sequence*. The object of this limitation is to speed up the play when a relatively large number of players participate. Although any smaller number may play Continental, the usual game is from six to twelve players. Other departures from the rules of Rummy (page 53) are as follows.

CARDS

The joker is added to every pack, and at least two packs of 53 cards are used, shuffled together. With six to eight players use three packs, totaling 159 cards; with nine to twelve players, use four packs, 212 cards. The ace ranks either high or low, above the king or below the two, but sequences do not go "around the corner." A sequence may have at most 14 cards, including two aces.

DEALING

Each player receives fifteen cards. The winner of one hand deals the next.

THE PLAY

Drawing and discarding is as in Rummy, but there is no melding. Play ends when one player is able to lay down a complete hand, containing no unmatched cards. A joker is *wild;* it may be designated to be any card the owner wishes in order to fill a sequence.

Rum Hand. The hand laid down must comprise at least four sequences, each of at least three cards and not more than five. The effect of this rule is to limit the hand to three possible patterns:

$$3-3-3-3-3$$
$$4-4-4-3$$
$$5-4-3-3$$

However, two or more of the sequences may be in the same suit; thus, a sequence of nine cards can be broken in a four and a five, or into three sequences of three, to comply with the rule.

SCORING

The winner of a hand collects 1 chip from each other player, plus two chips for each joker in the winner's hand.

VARIATIONS

Deuces and other cards may be designated as wild, besides the jokers. Payment for wild cards other than jokers is one chip each. In some localities, extra bonuses are paid the winner, for example: For having drawn no card, 10; for having drawn only one card, 7; for rum hand without a wild card (played only when deuces are wild), 10; for all fifteen cards of one suit, 10. The dealer receives 1 chip per player if he lifts from the full pack the exact number of cards he needs to deal each player 15 cards.

Contract Rummy

Variants of Contract Rummy are played under many different names, as Liverpool Rum, Joker Rummy, Progressive Rum, King Rummy. The first was probably the game developed by Ruth Armson, called Zioncheck. The basic idea of all is that a game comprises a fixed number of deals, and that in each deal the *rum hand* must be of prefixed character. This prescription is called the *basic contract* for the deal. It is impossible to cover all local variants, but the following is typical. Only the variations from the laws of Rummy (page 53) are given.

CARDS

With three or four players, use two packs of 52 shuffled together, plus one joker, 105 cards. With five to eight players, use three packs of 52 plus two jokers, 158 cards. The ace ranks either high or low, above the king or below the two; an ace may be *laid off* on one end of a sequence even though it includes an ace on the other end; but sequences do not go "around the corner." All aces and wild cards count 15 each.

DEALING

A game comprises seven deals. The deal rotates to the left. In each of the first four deals, each player receives ten cards; in each of the last three deals, each player receives twelve cards.

THE PLAY

Drawing and discarding is as in Rummy, with this additional feature: If the player in turn refuses the discard, any other may claim it. If two or more claim it, it goes to the hand nearest the left of the in-turn player. On receiving the discard, the claimant must also draw the top card of the stock, and he makes no discard at that time. Play then reverts to the in-turn player, who draws the top of the stock (he may not draw the next card of the discard pile, having refused the first).

The first meld by a player must be the basic contract, as defined below. Thereafter he may *lay off* cards on any melds on the table, but he may not meld any additional sets. Play ends when one player gets rid of all his cards by melding and laying off.

BASIC CONTRACT

Each set of the basic contract must comprise exactly three cards (except in the 7th deal). Having a set of four or more, the player may meld only three; the additional cards may be laid off at a later turn. The basic contracts are:

> *1st deal:* Two groups.
> *2nd deal:* One group and one sequence.
> *3rd deal:* Two sequences.
> *4th deal:* Three groups.
> *5th deal:* Two groups and one sequence.
> *6th deal:* One group and two sequences.
> *7th deal:* Three sequences, but with no unmatched
> cards; a complete hand. The first meld
> of this deal terminates the play.

Any three cards of the same rank form a valid *group* regardless of suits. When the basic contract calls for two or more sequences, they must be in different suits, or, if in the same suit, must be disconnected. *Example:* In the 3rd deal, a valid meld is ♡**A K Q, 10, 9, 8**; but illegal would be ♡**A K Q J 10 9**. It is permissible, however, to lay off connecting cards later.

WILD CARDS

Jokers are *wild*, together with any others designated by agreement. A wild card may be used to complete any set. A wild card in a sequence may be moved to either end by a player who wishes to lay off the natural card on the meld (but no sequence may be built beyond fourteen cards). When a joker is melded in a sequence, it may be claimed in exchange for the natural card by the holder thereof, provided that he has previously melded his basic contract. If two or more players are able to claim a joker, it goes to the player whose turn to play comes first.

SCORING

When play of a deal ends, each player is charged with the count of all cards remaining in his hand, as in Rummy. Winner of the game is the player having the lowest total after the 7th deal.

Panguingue

Panguingue is essentially Conquian for a large number of players. It has achieved notable popularity in the Southwest United States and on the Pacific coast; in this region there are many public gaming clubs devoted to "Pan."

PLAYERS

Any number up to about fifteen may play. The usual game is six or seven.

CARDS

Eight packs of 40 cards each, shuffled together, totaling 320 cards. The 40-card pack is made by stripping out the eights, nines and tens from the pack of 52. While the general practice is to use eight such packs, as few as five are used in some localities.

The cards in each suit rank: **K** (high), **Q**, **J**, **7**, **6**, **5**, **4**, **3**, **2**, **A**. Note that the jack and seven are in sequence. (In home play, strip the pack of face cards instead of eights, nines, and tens; the cards then rank in natural order.)

PRELIMINARIES

Cards are drawn; lowest card is eldest hand for the first deal and second-lowest is the first dealer. The rotation in Panguingue is to the *right*,* not to the left as in most games. Eldest hand chooses his seat, and dealer sits on his *left*. Other players may take seats at random.

The cards are shuffled by the player at dealer's left. At the beginning, and occasionally thereafter, all eight packs are shuffled together, in batches of manageable size. At other times, the cards that were in play during the previous hand are shuffled with a batch from the stock and then placed at the bottom thereof, so that new cards come into play from the top of the stock.

DEALING

Each player receives ten cards, dealt to the *right* in rounds of five at a time, beginning with eldest hand. The rest of the pack is placed face down to form the *stock*. In practice, the stock is cut in two; the upper part or *head* is placed in the center of the table, while the *foot* is set aside, to be brought into play only if the head is exhausted.

Rotation to the right was formerly as frequent as rotation to the left. But the latter has come to be accepted in most games and most countries. There is really no reason for preserving the archaic alternative, nor the archaic "Spanish" pack, but both are a fixture in the Panguingue clubs.

The top card of the stock is turned face up and placed beside it, to commence the *discard pile*.

The deal does not rotate: the winner of one hand becomes eldest hand in the next, and the player at his left deals.

DROPPING

After looking at his hand, each player in turn beginning with eldest hand declares whether he will stay in the deal or drop out. If he drops, he pays a forfeit of two chips. All such chips are stacked on the foot of the stock, for which reason a player who drops is said to *go on top*. These chips go to the winner of the deal. The hands discarded by players who drop are placed crosswise under the foot of the stock; they do not belong to the stock and may not be drawn if both head and foot of the stock are exhausted.

THE PLAY

Each player in turn draws one card. He may either turn up the top of the stock, and use it in a meld or discard it; or he may take the top of the discard pile, but he may take the latter only if he can meld it at once. After drawing, the player may *meld* or *lay off* as many cards as he wishes. Having done so, he discards one card from his hand. His discard goes face up on the discard pile, and his turn ends when he discards. (In many public gaming clubs, the house rule is that *no* discards may be drawn: the top of the stock must be drawn at every turn.)

MELDS

The object of play is to meld eleven cards, and the first player to do so wins the deal. As in Rummy, the valid sets that may be melded are *groups* and *sequences*. ("Pan" players have their own colloquialisms. A meld is usually called a spread; a sequence is a *stringer* or a *rope*.)

Sequence comprises any three cards of the same suit, in sequence, as ♣**J 7 6**.

Group comprises three cards of the same rank. If the rank is ace or king (which cards are called *non-comoquers*), any three cards are valid regardless of suits. *Example:* ♣**K** ♣**K** ◇**K** is a valid meld. All other ranks are governed by the rule that the three cards must be (a) of different suits, or (b) all of the same suit. *Example:* ♣**8** ♡**8** ♠**8** and ◇**Q** ◇**Q** ◇**Q** are valid melds, but not ♣**5** ♣**5** ♡**5**.

CONDITIONS

On melding one of several types of sets, a player immediately collects chips from every other player. These privileged melds are called *conditions*.

All threes, fives, and sevens are called *valle cards* (cards of value). All other ranks are *non-valle* cards. The distinction enters into the list of conditions, which is as follows:

1. Any *group* of valle cards, of different suits. (1 chip.)
2. Any *group* of valle cards, in the same suit. (4 chips in spades, 2 chips in any other suit.)
3. Any *group* of non-valle cards, in the same suit. (2 chips in spades, 1 chip in any other suit.)
4. Any *sequence* A, 2, 3. (2 chips in spades, 1 chip in any other suit.)
5. Any *sequence* K, Q, J. (2 chips in spades, 1 chip in any other suit.)

LAYING OFF

Having melded any set, a player may later *lay off* on it any additional cards that are in keeping with it. (Note that a player may lay off only on his own melds.) A *group* in different suits may be increased by cards of the same rank in *any* suit; a *group* in the same suit may be increased by cards of the same rank and suit; a sequence may be increased by additional cards in sequence of the same suit.

For each card laid off on a *condition*, the player collects again the value of the condition, except in the case of type 2 above (a group of three valle cards in the same suit), where an added card collects only 2 in spades, 1 in any other suit.

When three or more cards have been laid off on a meld, it may be split into separate melds provided that each part is valid in itself. *Example:* If a player melds ♣Q J 7, and later adds ♣K 6 5, he may break it into ♣K Q J and ♣7 6 5.

If splitting a meld forms a condition that did not previously exist, the owner duly collects for it. In the above example, the player would collect for ♣K Q J, which is a condition of type 5.

BORROWING

A player may *borrow* one or more cards from (his own) increased meld, to fill a new meld, provided that he leaves a valid meld. *Example:* If a player melds ♣K Q J, later lays off ♣7, he may then borrow ♣K to fill a new meld with two other kings. He could borrow ♣7 instead of ♣K, but could not borrow ♣Q or J as he would thereby break the sequence.

FORCING

If the top of the discard pile can be laid off on the melds of the in-turn player, he can be forced to draw it and meld it upon demand of any other player. The object of such demand is to compel the player to discard, possibly to his disadvantage.

GOING OUT

The first player to meld eleven cards wins the deal. Since the hand contains only ten cards, a player with ten cards melded continues to draw and discard, though with no card in his hand, until he draws a card he can lay off. In this situation the player at his left is not permitted to discard a card that the first could lay off, unless he has no safe card to discard. If this rule is violated, and the first player goes out thereby, the offender must pay the losses of all players for that deal.

SETTLEMENT

The winner collects, from every player who did not drop, 1 chip for winning plus the total value of all conditions melded by the winner. (Thus he collects for his conditions twice over.) Some clubs have the rule that a player who has made no meld at all must pay the winner 2 chips.

IRREGULARITIES

Wrong number of cards. If a player finds that he has more or less than ten cards, before he has made his first draw, he may discard all his cards and demand a new hand from the top of the stock. If, after his first draw, a player's hand is found incorrect, he must discard his hand and retire from that deal, must return all collections he has made for conditions, but must continue to make due payments to others for conditions and winning.

Foul meld. If a player lays down any spread not conforming to the rules, he must make it valid on demand. If he cannot do so, he must return any collections made in consequence of the improper spread and legally proceed with his turn. If he has already discarded, he must return all collections he has made on that hand, discard his hand, and retire from the play until the next deal, but must continue to make due payments to others for conditions and winning. However, if he has made the meld valid before attention is called to it, there is no penalty.

THE
WHIST
FAMILY

A Brief Introduction to Whist

Five hundred years ago, or even more, the English people began to play a game of cards which they called Triumph. Except for its name, it was not related in any way to the game of Triomphe which was already being played by the Latin peoples of Europe. In the English game of Triumph, there were four players, divided into two partnerships. The entire pack of cards was dealt out evenly among the four players. The object of each side was to win more tricks than the opposing side. There was always one triumph, or trump, suit which overrode the other suits.

References to this original game of Triumph and to the early variants of it (under such names as Ruff and Honours, or Slamm, or Whisk) appear in English literature throughout the last four hundred and fifty years and more. A sermon preached in 1529; Shakespeare's *Anthony and Cleopatra;* a poem by John Taylor published in 1621; *The Compleat Gamester*, earliest English book of games, written by Charles Cotton (whose principal fame lies in his collaboration with Izaak Walton in writing *The Compleat Angler*)—all mention or allude to this earliest of English games, which finally became internationally famous under the name of Whist, so that all games in this group have come to be called games of the Whist family. It is to this family that the twentieth-century developments of Bridge, Auction Bridge, and Contract Bridge belong.

There is no agreement on the origin of the name Whist. The word itself is a demand for silence, and some attribute the name to the atmosphere of silence which must be maintained when the game is played. Others see in Whist merely a corruption of the word whisk, which they attribute to the custom of whisking up a won trick with one of its four cards. Whatever the source of its name, the game of Whist had become so well known in England by the seventeenth century that writers on the game did not bother to tell how it was played—they assumed that every Englishman would know.

Prior to the year 1700, Whist was not a fashionable game. It was played mostly by the servants "below stairs" in the big British mansions, while the masters above played games which were more of a gambling nature, such as Quadrille, Pharaoh and Hazzard. But the early part of the eighteenth century saw a noteworthy rise in rational thinking throughout England, and even the gambling element among educated men turned from the previous games to the more scientific game of Whist. In London coffee houses, where such men assembled to talk and play, groups of gentlemen took up Whist as a subject of serious study. One of these men was Edmond Hoyle.

Hoyle may not have been a good card player himself—some of his contemporaries called him a third-rater—but he was a careful observer and writer and fully deserving of the fame which has attended his name ever since 1743, when his first book was published. The book was called *A Short Treatise on Whist*, and was one of the greatest book publishing successes in history. Whist became all the rage in fashionable British circles, and spread to all European countries. It remained the leading intellectual card game of the English-speaking world until it was supplanted by its own offspring, Bridge. Whist clubs sprang up in all parts of the world; and, in the last part of the nineteenth century, hundreds of serious players assembled periodically to compete in Whist tournaments, at which Duplicate Whist was usually played.

In 1889 a pamphlet on a game called "Biritch, or Russian Whist" was published in London. The game created little stir at the time, but soon showed up in Greece, in Egypt, and on the French Riviera. In 1894 it reached London again. Now the game was called Bridge, and introduced new features—the hand of one player, called the dummy, was exposed during the play of the cards; selection of the trump suit was the dealer's privilege and no longer a matter of chance; a new schedule of scoring was used; and doubling was permitted. Bridge was an unprecedentedly rapid success; while Whist remained the serious tournament game, before 1900 Bridge had supplanted it as the standard club game and as the party game in fashionable circles. In one form or another, Bridge has been the big game of the Whist family ever since. When Auction Bridge (which gave every player a chance to bid for the right to name the trump suit) showed up in 1904, it succeeded plain Bridge almost as rapidly as Bridge had supplanted Whist; and after Auction Bridge had reigned for some twenty years, with numerous minor changes in procedure but no essential difference from the original game, Contract Bridge arrived to assume the leading position with equal rapidity. It is Contract Bridge that is most popular today, but except for a different method of scoring it is the same game as the Auction Bridge which it replaced.

Contract Bridge dates from 1915 or before. However, in the years before 1920 it was played only in a few experimental games. In 1918, Parisians began to play a game called Plafond, which was a forerunner of Contract Bridge. The modern game dates from the winter of 1925, when Harold S. Vanderbilt of New York and some friends played some experimental games in which they developed the factor of vulnerability, large bonuses for bidding and making slam contracts, and in general the modern scoring table. By 1929, Contract Bridge had become the principal game in the clubs of New York and London and in other principal men's clubs, but Auction Bridge was still played by less serious players. The rapidity with which Contract Bridge spread after that was due largely to the showmanship of Ely Culbertson, who developed a system of bidding at Contract Bridge, wrote books on the game, played international matches and used other means to publicize it, and eventually brought Contract Bridge sharply before the public eye by playing a famous match in which his partner was his wife and their opponents were Sidney S. Lenz and Oswald Jacoby (later, Commander Winfield S. Liggett, Jr.). This match made the front pages of practically all American newspapers, day after day, and since the Culbertsons won the match by a comfortable margin of nearly 9,000 points, they acquired prestige which made Culbertson the principal name of Contract Bridge of his time. When war became imminent in Europe in 1938, Culbertson lost interest in bridge and devoted the remainder of his life to political science causes, most notably the formation of the United Nations and a campaign to give it adequate police powers. In pursuit of these activities, Culbertson lost his position as the leading bridge authority to Charles H. Goren, whose influence in the game has been even more remarkable.

In 1944, Goren, already a widely syndicated columnist and successful author, earned the top spot on the master point winners list, a position he held uninterruptedly for eighteen years, but it was the publication of his book *Point Count Bidding in Contract Bridge* in 1949 that wrought a revolution. His carefully constructed method of evaluation based on point count for high cards and distribution was so accurate and easy to learn that it swept away all other methods and attracted millions of new players to the game, giving bridge a boost not seen since the early days of Culbertson. Goren's efforts as a writer, teacher, lecturer, and TV personality as host of a successful series of "Championship Bridge" shows in the early 1960s earned him the sobriquet "Mr. Bridge," and his importance as a world figure was recognized when *Time* magazine featured him on its cover. Before his retirement in 1966 Goren had won virtually every major bridge title in the United States, and his partnership with Helen Sobel was one of the most successful and enduring in bridge history. The impact Goren has had on bridge cannot be overstated. To this day all bidding systems throughout the world are based on point-count evaluation, and the particular ideas he espoused, known as Standard America, are still widely taught and played.

CONTRACT BRIDGE

PLAYERS

Four play at a time; but five or six may participate in the same game by "cutting in"—that is, one or two players sit out each rubber while the other four play.* The positions of the four players at the table correspond to the compass points, North, South, East, and West, and there are always two partnerships, North and South being partners against East and West. Partners share equally in every result, and only one score is kept for each side.

CARDS

The 52-card pack. One pack would be sufficient for a game, but whenever they are available two packs (of contrasting back design, or, preferably, color) are used. While one pack is being dealt, the dealer's partner shuffles the other pack. Having shuffled it, he sets it down at his right.

Rank of Cards. The cards in each suit rank downward in order **A**, **K**, **Q**, **J**, **10**, **9**, **8**, **7**, **6**, **5**, **4**, **3**, **2**.

PRELIMINARIES

Before each rubber, one pack is spread face down on the table. Each player draws a card, but not one of the four cards at either end. If more than four wish to play, those drawing the lowest cards do not play in the first rubber; at the end of the first rubber, they will replace the player or players who drew the next-lowest cards. Of the four active players, the one who drew the highest card becomes the first dealer and has choice of cards and seats; the player who drew the next-highest card becomes his partner and sits opposite him; the other two players take the other two seats. Alternatively, after the cut for outs, the players recut to determine the two partnerships and who deals.

If two players draw cards of the same rank, precedence as between them is decided by the rank of the suits: spades (high), hearts, diamonds, clubs.

The Shuffle and Cut. The player at dealer's left shuffles the pack he has selected. Having shuffled, he places it at the dealer's left. The dealer transfers it to his right. The player at dealer's right must cut the pack by lifting off a packet (not fewer than five nor more than forty-seven cards) and setting

* _The winning of the first two out of three games by one side constitutes a rubber._

it down toward the dealer. The dealer completes the cut by putting the other packet on top of this one. Through all this process, the pack is kept face down.

ROTATION

The rotation is always clockwise; that is, in dealing, if South is the dealer, he will give the first card to West, the next card to North, the next to East and so on. Likewise, since South is the dealer, West will be the next dealer, then North; in bidding, when South has bid, it is West's next turn, then North's, then East's, then South's again; and in play, if North plays the first card East will play the next, then South, followed by West.

DEALING

The dealer distributes the cards one at a time face down, in rotation, beginning with the player on his left, until all have been dealt and each player has received thirteen cards. No player should touch or intentionally look at the face of any card dealt to him until the deal is completed.

THE AUCTION

When the deal is completed, each player picks up and looks at his hand, fanning it out so that he may see what he holds but no other player can. The auction period then begins, in which each player in rotation, beginning with the dealer, may continue to *call* until the auction closes. A *call* may be a pass, a bid, a double or a redouble.

Pass. A player who does not wish to make any other call says "Pass."

Bid. A bid is an offer to win a stated number of *odd tricks* (tricks in excess of six, the first six tricks being called "the book") with a named suit as trump, or with notrump. The lowest possible bid is a bid of one and, since there are thirteen tricks in all, the highest possible bid is seven. The form of a bid is: "One diamond," "One notrump," "Four spades," etc.

A bid must be *sufficient* to *overcall* the preceding bid if any. To be sufficient it must name a greater number of odd tricks, or the same number of odd tricks in a higher-ranking denomination (suit or notrump), the rank being: Notrump (high), spades, hearts, diamonds, clubs. Thus, one spade will overcall one heart; two or more clubs will overcall one spade. An insufficient bid is subject to penalty.

Double. A player in turn may double the last preceding bid if it was made by an opponent and has not previously been doubled. The effect of a double is to increase the scoring values of tricks. The literal meaning of a double is that the doubler does not believe his opponents can win as many tricks as their bid calls for. A double does not affect the sufficiency of bids; if a three-spade bid has been doubled, any player in turn may still overcall it with a bid of three notrump, or four clubs, or anything higher.

Redouble. A player in turn may redouble the last preceding bid if it was made by himself or his partner and has been doubled by an opponent. The redouble further increases the scoring values of tricks, but, like the double, does not affect the sufficiency of bids.

A double or redouble applies only to the last preceding bid. If a four-club bid is doubled, and there is a subsequent bid of four hearts, the four-heart bid counts at its usual, single, value unless it also is doubled.

Opening the Auction. The auction is said to be opened when any player makes a bid. If all four players pass originally, the deal is *passed out,* the cards are thrown in and the next dealer in turn deals. Once the auction has been opened, it must continue until it closes and the cards must be played.

Closing the Auction. When a bid, double, or redouble is followed by three consecutive passes, the auction is closed. Every card of the suit named in the final bid becomes a trump; or, if the final bid was in notrump, the cards will be played without a trump suit. Of the side which made the final bid, the member who first named the suit (or notrump) specified in that bid becomes the *declarer.* The number of odd tricks named in the final bid becomes his *contract,* and to fulfill his contract he must win that number of odd tricks. The play period commences.

THE PLAY

The player at declarer's left selects any card from his hand and places it face up in the center of the table; that is the *opening lead.* Declarer's partner then places his hand face up on the table in front of him, grouped in suits with the trumps, if any, to his right; the exposed hand of the declarer's partner is known as the *dummy.* With certain exceptions (see page 139) declarer's partner, or dummy, will take no further part in the play of the cards; declarer will select the plays from the dummy hand as well as from his own, but each in proper turn.

The object of play is to win tricks. A *trick* consists of four cards, one from the hand of each player in rotation, the first card played to a trick generally being called the *lead.* A player is required to follow suit to the card led if he can; if he cannot follow suit, he may play any card. A trick containing any trump is won by the highest trump it contains; a trick not containing a trump is won by the highest card of the suit led. The hand which wins a trick leads to the next.

When a trick is complete (contains four cards) a member of the side which won it takes in the cards, squares them up, turns them face down and places them in front of him. It is customary for one player to take in all the tricks won by his side. The tricks should be kept separated from one another so that any previous trick can be referred to if necessary. A player may turn and look back at the last trick until he or his partner has led or played to the next; after that, he may not look at any previous trick.

Play continues in this way until thirteen tricks have been played.

SCORING

Any player may keep score; one player for each side should keep score; and at least one player at the table must keep score.

The Contract Bridge score sheet is ruled with a vertical line headed "we" and "they" and the scorekeeper enters all scores made by his side on the "we" side and all scores made by his opponents on the other side. Midway on the score sheet there is a horizontal line; scores designated as *trick score* go *below the line;* all other scores (usually called the *honor score*) go *above the line.*

Trick Score. If declarer fulfills his contract by winning as many or more odd tricks than his contract calls for, he scores below the line for every odd trick named in the contract:

Score for Each ODD TRICK BID AND MADE If Trumps Were	If the contract was undoubled	If the contract was doubled	If the contract was redoubled
♠	30	60	120
♡	30	60	120
♢	20	40	80
♣	20	40	80
NT, first odd trick	40	80	160
NT, each additional odd trick	30	60	120

No trick not included in the contract may be scored below the line, regardless of the circumstances. If declarer wins more tricks than his contract calls for, their value is scored above the line (*see overtricks,* below).

Game. When a side has scored 100 or more points below the line, it has won a *game.* The scorekeeper draws a horizontal line across the entire score sheet, below the score which ended the game, to signify that a new game is beginning. A game may be made in more than one hand: A side may score 60, then its opponents may score 40, then the first side may score 40, giving it 100 points and ending the game. The opponents' trick score of 40 does not carry over to the next game, however. Each side begins the next game at zero.

Vulnerability. A side that has won a game is said to be vulnerable. A side which is vulnerable receives increased bonuses in some cases, and is subject to increased penalties when it does not fulfill its contract.

Overtricks. Any trick won by declarer in excess of his contract is called an overtrick, and is scored above the line to the credit of his side, as follows:

Score for Each ODD TRICK MADE BUT NOT BID If Trumps Were	Un- doubled	If the contract was			
		Doubled		Redoubled	
		Vulner- able	Not Vulner- able	Vulner- able	Not Vulner- able
♠ or ♡	30	200	100	400	200
♢ or ♣	20	200	100	400	200
NT	30	200	100	400	200

Doubled Contract. If declarer makes any doubled or redoubled contract, with or without overtricks, he adds 50 points to his score above the line.

Honors. When there is a trump suit, the ace, king, queen, jack, and ten of trumps are honors. If a player holds four trump honors in his hand, his side scores 100 above the line; if he holds all five trump honors, his side scores 150 above the line; if he holds all four aces at a notrump contract, his side scores 150 above the line. The player holding the honors may be declarer, dummy, or either *defender* (opponent of declarer).

Slams. If declarer fulfills a contract of six odd tricks (called a *little slam*, or *small slam*), his side scores 500 above the line if they are not vulnerable, and 750 if they are vulnerable. If declarer fulfills a contract of seven odd tricks (*grand slam*), his side scores 1000 points above the line if not vulnerable, and 1500 if vulnerable.

Undertrick Penalties. If declarer fails to fulfill his contract—that is, if he *goes down* or is *set* one or more tricks—his opponents score above the line, as follows:

IF DECLARER "Goes Down"	Regardless of the contract					
	Undoubled		Doubled		Redoubled	
	Not Vulner- able	Vulner- able	Not Vulner- able	Vulner- able	Not Vulner- able	Vulner- able
1 trick	50	100	100	200	200	400
2 tricks	100	200	300	500	600	1000
3 tricks	150	300	500	800	1000	1600
4 tricks	200	400	700	1100	1400	2200
5 tricks	250	500	900	1400	1800	2800
6 tricks	300	600	1100	1700	2200	3400
7 tricks	350	700	1300	2000	2600	4000
8 tricks	400	800	1500	2300	3000	4600
9 tricks	450	900	1700	2600	3400	5200
10 tricks	500	1000	1900	2900	3800	5800
11 tricks	550	1100	2100	3200	4200	6400
12 tricks	600	1200	2300	3500	4600	7000
13 tricks	650	1300	2500	3800	5000	7600

Rubber. A rubber ends when either side has won two games. The side which has won two games wins the rubber and adds to its score 500 points if its opponents have won a game; and 700 points if its opponents have not won a game.

All points scored by both sides, both above the line and below the line, are then added up. The side which has scored the greatest number of points wins the difference between its score and its opponents' score.

WE	THEY
(g) 500	150 (f)
(g) 750	500 (d)
(a) 50	60 (c)
(b) 120	
(e) 90	60 (c)
	70 (f)
(g) 180	
1690	840
840	
(h) 850	

Explanation of Scoring

(a) They bid three notrump and won only eight tricks, thus failing to make their contract. This one undertrick gives We a score of 50 points above the line.

(b) We bid four hearts and made their contract by winning ten tricks. The resulting 120 points is scored beneath the line. We has won the first game and is now vulnerable.

(c) They bid two spades and won ten tricks. For making their contract They received 60 points below the line, and an additional 60 points above the line for the two overtricks.

(d) We bid two diamonds, They doubled. We won only six tricks, thereby failing to make their contract by two tricks. Since We was vulnerable (by virtue of having won an earlier game), They picked up 500 "undertrick" points which are scored above the line.

(e) We bid three spades and won nine tricks, thereby making their contract. We's 90-point score is noted below the line.

(f) They bid one notrump and won eight tricks, one over their contract. They were entitled to score only 40 points below the line but since those points, combined with those from hand (c), gave them a game (100 points), it does not matter whether the overtrick is scored above or below the line. In addition, They's dummy held all four aces, giving them an additional 150 points above the line.

(g) We bid six hearts and won twelve tricks (a little slam), scoring 180 points below the line, plus 750 above the line bonus points for making the slam and an additional 500 points for winning the rubber (two games).

(h) We's total score is 1690 points, while They scored only 840. We therefore won a 9-point rubber (see Back Score following).

Back Score. It is customary to keep a record of the result of each player on each rubber that he plays. This record is kept in even hundred points. If the margin of victory includes a remainder of 50 points or more, it counts as a full 100. Any smaller remainder does not count. Thus, a rubber won by 350 points is "a four-point rubber;" a rubber won by 340 points is "a three-point rubber."

PLAYER	+	−	+	−	+	−	+	−	+	−	+	−	+	−
John	9		15		27									
Mary	9			3		15								
Jim		9		3		3								
Sue		9		9		21								
Fred				6		18								

Back Score

The first rubber was won by John and Mary, as partners against Jim and Sue. Their score was 940 points, which gave them 9 rubber points in the + column of the back score, while Jim and Sue's score shows a negative 9. In the second rubber John and Jim, playing against Mary and Fred, won by 550 points, giving them 6 rubber points in the back score. The rubber points are recorded cumulatively; thus Mary, a 9-point winner in the first rubber, had 6 points deducted from her total when she and Fred lost the second rubber. John's two rubber victories gives him a 15-point total at this point. In the third rubber John and Mary won by 1180 points from Sue and Fred. That 12-point victory gave John a cumulative back score of 27 points, while Sue shows a minus 21 point total for her two rubber loses (9 and 12 points).

BEGINNING A NEW RUBBER

When a rubber is finished, its result is entered on the back score; if there is a fifth or sixth player entitled to play in the table, such a player comes in, replacing the player next in order of precedence; the four active players cut again for seats, choice of cards and partnerships; and a new rubber is begun with a new score sheet.

Match Games. These are also called *set matches* or *set games*. By agreement, the two partnerships remain unchanged throughout the game. No back score is kept; the result of each rubber is counted in exact points and not in even hundreds; and the net difference for the entire match is recorded to the credit of the leading side, above the line, on the score sheet used for the next rubber.

After any rubber, any player may call for the pack to be spread and cards drawn for choice of cards and seats, but not for change of partnerships.

Double Rubbers. By agreement, two consecutive rubbers may be played without change of partnerships, cards or seats. Often both rubbers are scored on the same score sheet, a double line being drawn under the game that ends the first rubber.

Pivot Bridge. Four or five players often agree to play a schedule whereby each will play an equal number of times as the partner of each other. See Pivot Bridge, page 220.

Contract Bridge Strategy

VALUING THE HAND

The key to accurate bidding is proper evaluation. When a player picks up a hand his first duty is to make some rough estimate of its strength by following certain rules. For initial evaluation, he counts both *high-card points* (HCP) and *distributional points* (DP) as follows:

> High-card Points
> Ace = 4
> King = 3
> Queen = 2
> Jack = 1
> Distributional Points
> Void = 3
> Singleton = 2
> Doubleton = 1

For notrump bidding, only high-card points are counted. For suit bidding, both players base their decisions on a combination of high-card points and distributional points. As a general guideline, the two partners together must hold 20 points to make any contract, 26 points to make a game in notrump or a major suit, 28 points to make a five-level contract, 33 points to make a small slam and 37 points to make a grand slam.

Adjustments. The basic point-count structure contains several flaws. Aces and kings are slightly undervalued, while queens and jacks overvalued. No weight is given tens and nines, but these *intermediate* cards often have a crucial effect on the play. Further, honor combinations are more valuable than scattered honors, as are honors in long suits rather than short suits. *Prime* cards (aces and kings) usually retain their full value regardless of the contract, but secondary honors (queens and jacks) may be worthless, except at notrump, or in support of a suit partner has bid. When a hand contains one or more of these plus factors—prime or intermediate cards, well placed honors—it is a stronger hand than one that lacks these features. Among other adjustments a player should make are:

> Add one point when holding all four aces
> Deduct one point for an aceless hand
> Add one point for the sixth, and
> each additional card in a long suit
> Deduct one point for a 4–3–3–3 distribution

Insufficiently Guarded Honors. When an honor, or honor combination, is not supported by lower cards, such as a singleton king, queen, or jack, or a doubleton king-queen, or queen-jack, a player may not count both high-card points and distributional points for this holding. Except for a singleton ace, take the high-card value or the distributional value, whichever is higher.

Definitions

A opening bid is the first bid made. Thereafter, a bid is termed an *overcall* (of an opponent's bid), a *response* (to partner's bid), or a *rebid* (by a player who has previously bid).

Opening Suit Bids

Most hands, if opened at all, should be opened with a bid of one. The requirements are generally the same whether a player is vulnerable or not vulnerable, or whether he is first, second, third, or fourth hand.

For opening suit bids, count both high-card points and distributional points: 14 or more points make an opening bid obligatory; 13 points usually justify an opening bid, but a hand distributed 4–3–3–3 or lacking two *honor tricks* (see below) may be passed. Open a 12-point hand only with a long, strong trump suit (five cards headed by **A-Q** is the minimum).

Honor Tricks. A hand should not be opened unless it contains at least two *honor tricks*, or *quick tricks*. All players agree on the following count of honor tricks:

A-K	2 honor tricks
A-Q	1½ honor tricks
K-Q	1 honor trick
K-x	½ honor trick

Choice of Suits. Although not universal, especially in England, most players have adopted a five-card major system (hearts and spades).

If opener does not have a five-card major, he bids his longest minor (clubs or diamonds). With minors of equal length, open one diamond with four cards in each minor and one club with two three-card minors. The choice of which minor to bid may be reversed if one is considerably stronger than the other.

Bid the longest suit first. With two five- or six-card suits, bid the higher-ranking. *Exception:* Open one club for a hand with five cards in clubs and spades.

Opening Suit Bids at the Two-level. In both the Culbertson and Goren original systems, all two-bids described a powerful hand that could virtually make game on its own. That idea has been abandoned in favor of the concept of *weak two-bids.* Opening bids of two diamonds, two hearts or two spades show a hand with a good suit, usually six cards long, but less than opening-bid values. The suit should not be weaker than **Q-J-9** and the hand should not contain more than 1½ honor tricks.

An opening bid of two clubs is artificial (not meant to reflect the hand's true club holdings) and is forcing (partner must keep the bidding open). Responder may not pass a two-club bid, nor may he pass opener's rebid unless it is two notrump. Without the values to make a *positive* response (either a five-card or longer suit headed by three honors, or two of the top three honors, or a balanced hand with 1½ honor tricks) responder bids two diamonds. This bid is also artificial and does not promise a diamond suit. The opening bidder then proceeds to show his genuine suit, or to bid notrump, and the auction continues normally thereafter until game contract has been reached.

Opening Suit Bids at the Three- Four- or Five-level. These are *preemptive* (an unusually high bid) bids designed to *shut out* the opponents (discourage them from bidding). The bidder must have a very strong suit and the hand should generally conform to the *Rule of Two and Three,* which states that without support from partner, the bidder should be within two tricks of his contract if vulnerable; within three tricks of his contract if not vulnerable. Preemptive bids show weakness and should not be made on a hand containing more than 1½ honor tricks. This restriction may be relaxed opposite a partner who has passed since chances for slam are slight and there are tactical advantages to bidding what you think you can make immediately. As a general rule, three-level preempts are made on a seven-card suit, while four-level preempts suggest an eight-card suit.

Opening Notrump Bids

Bid one notrump with 16–18 high-card points. The distribution of the hand should be 4–3–3–3, 4–4–3–2, or 5–3–3–2. However, one notrump may also be a practical way to describe certain awkward hands that are distributed 5–4–2–2 or 6–3–2–2. The high cards in a notrump hand should be distributed among at least three suits. Although it is permissible to open one notrump with a five-card major or a low doubleton (King-Queen), bid the major when the hand contains both features.

An opening bid of two notrump requires 21–22 high-card points with no suit weaker than **Q x**, preferably **Q 10 x**.

In standard methods, an opening bid of three notrump shows 25–27 high-card points with no suit worse than **K x** or **Q J x**.

Responses to Opening Notrump Bids. When responder has a balanced hand simple arithmetic dictates his course of action. Over one notrump he adds his high-card points to those promised by opener and bids as follows:

Fewer than 8 points	Pass
8 to 9 points	Two notrump
10 to 14 points	Three notrump
15 to 16 points	Four notrump
17 to 18 points	Six notrump
21 points or more	Seven notrump

With 19 to 20 points, responder knows that there are enough high cards available for a small slam, or a grand slam if opener has a maximum. To show this type of hand, responder jumps to five notrump. Opener may not pass this bid. He either signs off in six notrump with a minimum holding of points for his initial action, or bids seven notrump with maximum points.

Similar considerations apply in responding to other notrump opening bids. If there are enough points for game opposite the minimum holdings the opener might have, responder raises. Responder jumps to four notrump to invite a small slam and to five notrump to invite a grand slam. Opener may accept these invitations only if he has a maximum hand.

A response in a suit to a notrump opening bid indicates a hand that will probably play better at a trump contract. Over one notrump, responses of two diamonds, two hearts, and two spades are *sign-offs*. Opener at this point may not bid again, unless he has maximum points and good support for the responder's major, in which case he may raise to the three-level. A two-club response to a one notrump opening bid is the Stayman Convention. This is an artificial bid (does not show clubs) and asks opener to show a four-card major if he has one. Without a four-card major, opener rebids two diamonds. With a hand holding both major suits, the modern tendency is to bid hearts first. After using Stayman, any further action by responder at the two-level is non-forcing; at the three-level it is forcing to game. An immediate jump response in a suit is also game-forcing.

Responses to Opening Suit Bids

Like the opening bidder, responder counts both high-card points and distributional points to determine whether his hand falls into the minimum range (6–9 points), intermediate range (10–12 points) or game-going range (13 or more points). He may not, however, include distributional values for a short suit that partner bids, or subsequently bids. With fewer than six points, responder should pass at his first turn, unless he has a very long suit that he can bid and rebid.

The first obligation of responder is to explore for major-suit fit. With a combined eight cards in a major, a suit contract is generally preferred to notrump. The principles of responding at the one-level are to bid your longest suit first, the highest-ranking with two five-card suits, and to bid *up the line* with two or more four-card suits by showing the cheapest suit first. A four-card suit of any quality may be shown, but with a 4-3-3-3 distribution, a minimum, and a poor suit, a response of one notrump should be made instead. A response at the two-level in a suit lower-ranking than partner's promises 10 or more points, although responder may violate this rule with a long, strong suit he can rebid. Any suit response is forcing; the opener must keep the bidding open to allow responder a further opportunity to describe his strength.

Raises. No raise in the bidding level should be given to partner's suit without adequate trump support. Opposite a one-bid in a major, three cards are adequate support. Four- or five-card support is required to raise a minor. Raise partner's one-bid to two with 6–10 points. With four or more trumps and 13–16 points, raise to three (forcing to game). A raise to four of a major is a preemptive bid, showing five-card support, a singleton or a void in a side suit and 5–9 points. The hand may not contain two aces. High preemptive jump raises in a minor are usually avoided because if opener has a very good hand, it may carry the pair beyond their only makable game contract of three notrump.

Notrump Responses. Count high-card points only. Respond one notrump with 6–10 points; two notrump with 13–15 points (forcing to game); three notrump with 16–18 points and 4-3-3-3 distribution. A one notrump response does not promise a balanced hand. It simply denies the strength or distribution to make a suit response.

Forcing Responses. With a hand of at least 15 points that contains a *self-sufficient* suit (a suit that will play for no more than one loser opposite a singleton in partner's hand), or excellent support for partner's suit, *jump-shift* by bidding one level higher than necessary in a new suit, such as two spades over partner's one diamond, or three clubs over partner's one heart. These responses are forcing to game and suggest a possible slam.

Responses to Weak Two-bids and Preemptive Bids. An opening weak bid at the two-level or higher announces the ability by the bidder to win a certain number of tricks with his suit as trumps. Responder can determine the number of tricks he must produce for his side to make a game by applying the Rule of Two and Three (see page 105). Tricks are not synonymous with points.

Opposite a preemptive bid, only aces and kings are to be counted as tricks; queens and jacks carry little weight. If responder chooses to bid at all, he adds the number of winners he holds to the tricks his partner expects to make and if the total is enough for game, responder bids it. Since the preempter should have a near self-sufficient suit for his bid, good trump support is not required for a raise, but with less than two-card support, responder should have one extra trick to protect against a possible additional trump loser. When partner preempts, counting tricks that are likely to be made in the play is a very easy exercise. For example, North opens three diamonds and South holds:

$$ ♠ \ J \ 10 \ 4 \ 3 \ ♡ \ A \ 6 \ 5 \ ◇ \ A \ 8 \ ♣ \ A \ 9 \ 5 \ 2 $$

Since North should have seven diamonds including the **K-Q** for his bid, South is reasonably sure of seven diamond tricks and two aces, so he should bid three notrump. The hand may not have the necessary points for game, but North's long suit compensates for this deficiency. Raises of preemptive openings should also be given when responder is not vulnerable and has a wealth of trumps, regardless of the strength of the hand. When one side has a big trump fit, it is axiomatic that the other will also have one, and raising with even a very weak hand will make it more difficult for the opponents to get together.

Rebids

Revaluation. In bidding for a suit contract a hand constantly fluctuates in value as the auction progresses. Failure to find an eight-card fit somewhere means that the hand will probably be played in notrump where only high-card points are counted. When a satisfactory fit has been located, however, distributional values increase as follows:

> Count 5 points for a void
> Count 3 points for a singleton
> Add 1 point for a high honor in partner's suit
> Add 1 point for each additional trump above eight

Opener's Rebids. If partner gives a single raise, which may show a hand of up to 10 points, pass with a minimum opening bid (15 points or fewer). A

16–18 point hand is worth a try for game, and game should be bid on any stronger hands. If partner responds one notrump, game is unlikely unless opener has 18 points or more. If opener has unbalanced distribution and a minimum, he rebids a six-card suit or lower-ranking suit at the two-level.

A suit response is forcing, so opener must bid. With a minimum his choices are to rebid a six-card suit or a very strong five-card suit, introduce a new suit at the one-level or a lower-ranking suit at the two level, raise partner's suit with adequate trump support (usually four cards, but three to a high honor is acceptable), or bid the cheapest notrump available. With a strong hand (16–18 points) opener may give partner a double raise with four-card support, bid a new suit, or jump to three in a strong, long suit of his own. Hands of 19 points or more should usually force to game. Opener may jump to two notrump with 19 points (this bid is not forcing), jump-raise partner's major to the four-level, jump to game in his own suit, or jump-shift by bidding a new suit one level higher than necessary. A jump shift is unconditionally game-forcing; responder must keep the bidding open until game is reached, no matter how sketchy his response might have been.

Responder's Rebids. Unless forced, a responder with a minimum hand is not obliged to bid again on the second round of the auction, but it is still his duty to place the contract in the best spot by taking a preference to opener's first-bid suit, bidding one notrump without support for either of opener's suits, or rebidding a six-card or longer suit. With 11–12 points or a good 10, responder can invite game by jumping to two notrump, jump-raising opener's second suit with four-card support or jumping to three in his own long, strong suit. These invitational jumps are *limit* bids and are not forcing. Other options are to bid a new suit, rebid two notrump over a two-level rebid by opener, or to raise one notrump to two. (Goren maintained that after a rebid of one notrump by opener, a new suit by responder could be passed, but most modern experts treat a new minor-suit rebid by responder as forcing.) If responder has 13 or more points he must insist on game by bidding it himself, jump-raising opener's first suit, or jump-shifting into a new suit.

Reverses. An unforced rebid of a higher-ranking suit at the two-level, or a non-jump rebid of a lower-ranking suit at the three-level by opener is a *reverse* and shows a hand of at least 17 points. In the following examples, both of South's second bids would be reverses.

South	North		South	North
1 ♣	1 ♠		1 ♠	2 ♦
2 ♥			3 ♣	

A reverse by opener is forcing for one round, but not to game. Responder may also make a reverse bid in similar fashion; his reverse is unconditionally game-forcing.

Principles of Rebidding. If the combined hands are likely to hold 26 points or more, continue to bid until game is reached. Whenever it is apparent that the combined hands do not hold as many as 26 points, pass unless a better partscore is available. To achieve the desired goals in the auction, it is desirable for each player to *limit* his hand within a fairly narrow high-card and distributional range as quickly as possible. Once one player has limited his hand, his partner will have a much better idea of where to place the contract.

Slam Bidding

Slams are fun to bid and very profitable, but points alone are not enough for slam. On many occasions it will be necessary to determine how many aces the partnership holds or to ascertain that it is not off two fast tricks in some suit.

Blackwood Four Notrump Convention. When four notrump is not a raise of an immediate preceding notrump bid, it asks for aces. Responder replies as follows:

> Five clubs shows 0 or 4 aces
> Five diamonds shows 1 ace
> Five hearts shows 2 aces
> Five spades shows 3 aces.

If the four notrump bidder continues with five notrump after the response, he is asking responder to show the number of kings he holds in exactly the same manner. A five notrump king-asking bid also guarantees possession of all four aces between the partnership because it is a try for a grand slam.

Gerber Ace-Asking Convention. Gerber is similar to Blackwood, except that it is used only after a one or two notrump opening bid or a jump response or rebid of two notrump. A jump to four clubs now asks for aces. Responder replies four diamonds with 0 or 4 aces, four hearts with 1, four spades with 2 and four notrump with 3. A continuation of five clubs by the four-club bidder asks for kings, just as in Blackwood, and carries the same proviso that the partnership has all four aces.

Cue-bids. A bid of a suit an opponent has bid is called a cue-bid. It is an artificial bid, showing a strong hand usually with "first-round control" (the ability to win a trick the first time the suit is led either by ruffing or with the ace) in the opponents' suit. Since the cue-bidder has no desire to play in the suit named, the bid is forcing. For example:

South	West	North	East
1 ♡	2 ♣	2 ♠	3 ♣
4 ♣			

South's four clubs is a cue-bid and agrees to North's spade suit as trumps. South probably has a hand like this:

♠ **K 8 6 4** ♡ **A Q J 7 5** ◇ **A J 6 2** ♣ void

In almost all cases a cue-bid suggests an eventual slam and is used to advise partner that the opponents cannot start off by winning one or more immediate tricks in their own suit. On occasion, it may be necessary to cue-bid with "second-round control" in the opponents' suit (the king or a singleton).

Cue-bids are not limited to bids of an opposing suit. When a pair has agreed on a trump suit, a bid of a new suit by either player is also a cue-bid, showing first-round control in that suit and interest in a possible slam. For example:

South	North
1 ♠	3 ♠
4 ◇	

South's four diamonds is a cue-bid, promising either the ace of diamonds or a void in the suit. In circumstances like this, certain rules must be observed. Cue-bid your cheapest first-round control first. On the above auction South has denied a first-round control in clubs because he bypassed that suit, but he may have first-round control of hearts. Once first-round controls have been shown, a player may continue by showing second-round controls. If South subsequently bids five clubs on the above auction, he is showing either the king or a singleton club, having already denied a first-round club control. When a player cue-bids he is trying for slam, so his partner should cooperate by making a cue-bid of his own if he can. Cue-bids are invaluable tools for slam exploration because most hands are not suitable for Blackwood. Each player, for example may have two low cards in a suit, a flaw that won't be revealed in the ace-asking process, but which will come to light after a cue-bidding sequence.

Defensive Bidding

Overcall of an Opponent's Bid. A simple overcall shows a good suit and at least 1½ honor tricks, but at the one-level the strength of the hand may be as low as 8–9 high-card points, or as high as 16–17. A one-level overcall may occasionally be made on a four-card suit. Simple overcalls at the two-level promise the equivalent of an opening bid and a suit of high quality. With a hand too strong for a simple overcall, make a *take-out double* (see below) first, then bid the suit.

Jump Overcalls. These are preemptive bids. The overcaller usually has a six-card suit for a jump to the two-level and a seven-card suit for a three-level jump overcall and a hand that conforms to the Rule of Two and Three (see page 105).

Notrump Overcalls. To overcall an opponent's one-bid with one notrump describes the same sort of hand as an opening one notrump bid, including a sure stopper in the opponent's suit. With a balanced hand of 19 points or more, make a take-out double (see below) and then bid the cheapest number of notrump, or jump in notrump if the hand contains a minimum of 22 high-card points.

Unusual Notrump Convention. A jump overcall in notrump at the two-level and sometimes at the four-level (but not at the three-level) describes a two-suited hand with at least five cards in two specific suits, more often 6–5 or 6–6. After an opposing opening bid in a major suit, the jump in notrump is a take-out for the minors. If the opening bid has been in a minor, two notrump is a take-out (a request to bid) for the two lowest unbid suits (hearts and the unbid minor). Most players would consider this auction to be an extension of the Unusual Notrump Convention:

West	North	East	South
1 ♠	Pass	2 ♠	2 NT

Since it's unlikely that South would want to make a natural bid in notrump opposite opponents who have both bid and found a fit, North should consider two notrump as a request for him to bid a minor.

Cue-bids. Formerly, an immediate cue-bid of the suit an opponent had opened showed a very powerful game-forcing hand with first- or second-round control in the opposing suit. In the modern game, these cue-bids are used for other purposes. Most popular is the Michaels Convention. If an opponent opens in a minor suit, a cue-bid of that suit is a take-out (a request to bid) for the majors; after a major-suit opening bid, a cue-bid of that suit is a take-out for the unbid major and a minor suit (the cue-bidder's minor is not known). Alternatively, many players prefer Upper Suit cue-bids, where the cue-bid is always a take-out for the two highest unbid suits. As with the Unusual Notrump Convention, the length of the two suits is normally 5–5 or better. The strength of the hand is less than an opening bid, or very powerful. With the latter, the cue-bidder will bid again. Conventional calls that show a two-suiter should generally be avoided on hands that qualify for a simple overcall.

In a competitive auction, cue-bids of an opposing suit by either side may be used to show a limit raise or better of partner's suit. For example:

East	South	West	North
1 ♦	1 ♠	Pass	2 ♦

North's **2 ♦** is not game-forcing, nor does it promise a control in East's suit. Instead it announces a hand of at least 10 points, including 1½ honor tricks, with three- or four-card support for partner's spade suit. If South has a minimum for his overcall and rebids **2♠**, North is free to pass. Thus, North is able to signal aspirations for game without advancing the pair to the three-level, which may be too high. A useful appendum to this application of the cue-bid is that a jump response in a new suit by North to South's overcall would be game invitational in that suit, while a cue-bid followed by a new suit by North would be game-forcing.

By opener's side, the cue-bid, previously game-forcing with first-round control of the opposing suit, may be used to distinguish between a limit and preemptive raise:

South	West	North	East
1 ♡	2 ◇	3 ◇	

If North-South have agreed that a jump to **3♡** on this sequence would be preemptive, a popular treatment among tournament players, North's cue-bid shows a limit raise—four-card heart support, or better, with 10–12 points.

Take-out Doubles. A double of an opening bid or response is for take-out, not penalties. It shows the equivalent of a light opening bid or better with support for all unbid suits, unless the doubler has an independent suit of his own and was too strong for an overcall. The partner of the doubler is under the strongest obligation to bid his longest suit, especially with a weak hand; if he passes, the opponents will surely make their contract. With 10–12 points, the partner should make an effort to get to game by jumping in his longest suit, even if the suit is only four-cards long. With a stronger hand, partner either jumps to game himself or cue-bids the opponents' suit to set up a game force. This cue-bid does not promise a control in the opponents' suit. A double is for take-out, provided partner has not bid and it is the first opportunity to double a particular denomination. As long as partner has not bid, subsequent doubles of the same denomination are still for take-out.

Any double that is not for take-out is for *business*. This business double simply states that the doubler expects to defeat the contract last bid by the opponents, thereby increasing the value of the undertrick penalties. The partner of the doubler is supposed to pass a business double, but there are many situations where it is advantageous to remove the double, either to make some more profitable bid or because the hand is too distributional for defense.

The Landy Convention. A great many conventions have been devised to cope with an opposing one notrump opening bid. Still popular with rubber-bridge players and some duplicate players is the Landy Convention, which is an overcall of two clubs in either second or fourth seat. It is an artificial take-out for the majors. Other overcalls are natural.

Modern Conventions

Stayman, Blackwood, Landy, etc., are not the only conventions that players consider essential for accurate bidding. Over the years a great many new conventions have been proposed and those that proved effective have been widely adopted. All of the conventions listed below are popular among a vast number of tournament players throughout the world and are gaining increasing acceptance among the general bridge populace. None are essential to playing the game well. A word of warning. When a pair employs a non-standard method, it is necessary that they discuss the convention thoroughly to prevent a misunderstanding. They must also advise the opponents of any special understanding they have about the meaning of bids. This is required in tournament play; it is a matter of courtesy in a social game.

Limit Raises. A standard jump raise of opener's suit from the one-level to the three-level is forcing to game. Using limit raises the double raise is only invitational. It shows four-card trump support and 10–12 points. The chief advantage of this treatment is that it distinguishes between an invitational raise based on four trumps and one with only three trumps.

Negative Doubles. In conjunction with five-card majors, where an opening bid is frequently made on a short minor and almost never in a four-card major, negative doubles are vital to locate a 4–4 major-suit fit after an opponent intervenes. When an opening bid is overcalled, a double by responder is no longer for penalties. It is for take-out for the unbid suits. North opens one club and East overcalls one spade. This would be a typical hand South would have for a negative double:

♠ 7 5 ♡ K J 8 3 ◇ K 10 9 4 2 ♣ Q 8

The double promises four-card support for the unbid major and usually four-card support for both majors if both are unbid. It does not necessarily show length in an unbid minor, but without that feature, responder should have good support for opener's suit. The range for a negative double starts at 7–8 points for a double at the one-level and moves progressively higher if an opponent bids at the two- or three-level. There is no upper limit for a negative double. A benefit of this convention is that it permits responder to more accurately describe the length of his suits, the presumption being that South would have bid two hearts on the above auction with a five-card or longer suit, unless he was too weak to make a forcing bid. Negative doubles are usually played through three spades or four diamonds, which means that a double of any overcall within that range is negative and for take-out. If responder has a hand that would qualify for a penalty double, he must pass.

Opener reacts to a negative double much as he would to a take-out double. He is obliged to bid a four-card major if he has one, jumping with a strong hand. Without a major, opener rebids normally. If an overcall is followed by two passes and opener has shortness in the overcaller's suit (two cards maximum), at least three-card support for the unbid suits and a hand suitable for defense, he is required to reopen with a double to protect his partner, who might have wanted to double for penalties. A reopening double does not show extra values. Although opener should reopen on most hands when he is short in the overcaller's suit, a double should be avoided on one- and two-suited hands, which should be bid naturally.

Responsive Double. A responsive double is a defensive tool, similar to a negative double. After an opening bid, an overall or take-out double by second hand, and a raise of opener's suit by responder, a double by fourth hand is responsive, asking partner to pick a suit, and not for penalties. For example:

West	North	East	South
1 ♡	Dbl	2 ♡	Dbl

Since North's take-out double promised four spades, there is an inference on this sequence that South does not have four spades. With that holding he would have bid two spades. Therefore, South's responsive double requests North to bid a minor. Had North overcalled one spade, instead of doubling, a responsive double by South would have the same meaning. It should be understood that the responsive doubler rarely has a good hand unless the opponents are preempting, but he should have at least 8 points to contest the auction. Responsive doubles are used only when responder raises opener's suit, and the level at which they cease being responsive is determined by the partnership.

Jacoby Transfer Bids. After an opening one notrump bid, a response of two diamonds is a transfer to hearts (responder is showing a minimum of five hearts) and a response of two hearts is a transfer to spades. Opener is obliged to bid the suit his partner has shown, although he may jump to the three-level in that suit with a maximum notrump and good trump support. There is a divergence of opinion as to other bids in the Jacoby Transfer structure. Some use two spades as minor-suit Stayman, confirming four or more cards in both minors and slam interest. Others prefer two spades to be a transfer to clubs and three clubs (or two notrump) as a transfer to diamonds.

In most cases, Jacoby Transfers enable the strong hand to become the declarer—it is desirable to have the opening lead come up to the strong hand—but equally important is that it allows responder to describe his hand more precisely. For example:

♠ K 4 ♡ K J 10 7 3 ◇ Q 6 2 ♣ 9 6 5

After an opening bid of one notrump, responder transfers to hearts by bidding two diamonds, then invites game by continuing with two notrump. Opener will now know that his partner has a balanced hand of 8–9 points with five hearts and this exactness will enable him to place the contract with great confidence.

Jacoby Transfers are also used after a two notrump opening bid and the artificial auction: South—Two clubs, North—Two diamonds; South—Two notrump, which simply shows a stronger balanced hand. In these instances, however, there is general agreement about the meaning of three spades. Responder is showing both minors and a slam-oriented hand.

Four-level transfers, known as Texas, are an extension of Jacoby. To transfer to four hearts or four spades after a one or two notrump opening bid, responder bids four diamonds or four hearts, respectively.

Splinter Bids. In general, any jump bid in an auction when a nonjump or a jump to a lower-level would be forcing is considered a Splinter Bid, showing a singleton or void in the bid suit and agreeing partner's last named suit as the trump suit. Examples:

North	South		South	North		North	South
1 ♠	4 ♣		1 ◇	1 ♠		1 ♠	2 ◇
				4 ♣		2 ♡	4 ♣

In every case, South's unusual jump to four clubs announces a singleton or void in clubs and confirms four-card support for North's last bid suit (spades in the first two auctions, hearts in the third). By their nature, Splinter Bids suggest a slam, but usually the fit must be near perfect for one to be made. A Splinter Bid on a singleton ace should be avoided.

Forcing Notrump. A one notrump response is not forcing in standard methods. With this convention, it is, but only after a one heart or one spade opening bid and only if responder is not a passed hand. Unless he can make a stronger rebid, opener rebids a six-card major, bids a lower-ranking four-card suit or bids his cheapest three-card minor, regardless of quality of that minor. The purpose of this convention is to allow responder to escape to a long suit of his own when he doesn't have sufficient strength for a two-over-one response; to find a better partscore when he doesn't have a fit for opener's major; or to make a limit raise of opener's major on three-card support.

North	South
1 ♠	1 NT
2 ♣	3 ♠

South has exactly three spades and invitational values (10–12 points). His bid is not forcing.

Jacoby Two Notrump. After a major-suit opening bid, a jump to two notrump by responder is a forcing raise of opener's major, instead of a natural bid on a balanced hand. Responder guarantees at least four trumps and a hand that may be interested in slam. Opener's rebids are conventional. A new suit at the three-level shows a singleton or void in that suit; three of the agreed major shows 16 or more points and strong slam interest; three notrump describes a sound opening bid of 14–15 points with no distributional feature; four of the agreed trump suit is a signoff with a minimum opening bid; and other four-level bids are natural with a good second five-card suit. The originator of this convention, Oswald Jacoby, suggested that a four-level jump should show precisely 6–5–1–1 distribution with six cards in the agreed major and five cards in the bid suit, but most players consider that too restrictive. Once opener has made his conventional rebid, the auction proceeds normally.

Declarer's Play

In general, the declarer must plan his play of the hand by analyzing the way he might win the most tricks. He may do this by establishing a suit (forcing out the opponents' winners in the suit so that the remaining cards will be established as tricks), ruffing losers in one hand or the other, or by *finessing* (see below). (*Ruffing* is leading a card from either declarer's hand or the dummy that will be trumped because of a void of that suit in the opposite hand.) Each hand presents its own problem, but when playing a notrump contract the declarer ordinarily counts his winners and then determines how to increase his total; when playing a suit contract, the declarer counts his losers and looks for ways to eliminate them. Some of the principles of declarer play will be discussed in the deal examples that follow.

Finesse. A finesse is an attempt to win a trick with a lower-ranking card by taking advantage of the position of higher-ranking cards held by the opponents. All of the holdings below are finesse positions. Under normal circumstances they should be played as stated. The play would be the same, of course, if declarer's and dummy's holdings were reversed.

Dummy holds	Declarer holds	Play (if second hand follows low)
x x	A Q	Lead low from dummy and play **Q**.
x x x	A Q 10	Lead low from dummy and play **10**; whether this wins or loses, enter dummy again and lead low to **Q**.
x x x	A K J	Play the **A**, then enter dummy and lead low to **J**.
x x x	A K J 10 x x	With nine cards in a suit missing **Q**, the odds are slightly in favor of playing off (*cashing*) the **A** and **K**, instead of a finesse.

117

Dummy holds	Declarer holds	Play (if second hand follows low)
x x x	A K J 10 x	Play **A**, reenter dummy then lead low to **10**. With eight cards in a suit missing **Q**, a finesse is the percentage play.
x x	A K J 10 x x	Since the odds are greater that second hand has **Q x x x** than that fourth hand has a singleton **Q**, lead low from dummy and play **10**.
x x x	A J 10	Lead low from dummy and play **10**; if this loses, reenter dummy and lead low to **J**.
x x x	A J 9	Lead low from dummy and play **9**. If this loses to **K** or **Q**, enter dummy again and lead to **J**.
Q J 10	A x x	Lead **Q** and play low from hand.
Q x x	A x x	Cash **A**, then lead low from hand and play **Q**.
J x x x	A Q 10 x x x	With ten cards in a suit missing **K**, a finesse should be attempted, so lead **J** from dummy and play low from hand.
Q J x x	A x x	Cash **A**, then lead low from hand and play **J**. If it wins, reenter hand and lead low to **Q**.
K x	x x	Lead low from hand and play **K**.
K J x	x x x	Lead low from hand and play **J**. If this loses to **Q**, lead again from hand and play **K**.
Q 10 x	K x x	Lead low from dummy and play **K**. Next lead low from hand and play **10**.
Q 9 x	J x x	Lead low from dummy to **J**. If this loses, next lead low from hand and play **9**.

Plays from the Dummy After the Opening Lead. The following are the correct plays from the dummy to an opening low-card lead by an opponent, especially at notrump contracts.

Dummy holds	Declarer holds	Play from dummy
J x	A 10 x	To assure two tricks, play **x**.
A 10 x	J x	Play **x**. If the lead has been away from **K** or **Q**, a later finesse will win two tricks in the suit.
Q x	A x x	Play **Q** in the hope the lead has been away from **K**.
Q x	A 10 x or K 10 x	Play **x** to assure two tricks.
Q x	K x x	Play **Q**.
K x x	Q x	Play **x**.
Q x or K x	J x x	Play **x**. This guarantees one trick.
K x	J x	A lead away from **A** is unlikely against a suit contract, but slightly more likely at notrump. Play **x** in a suit contract; **K** at notrump.

Dummy holds	Declarer holds	Play from dummy
J x	**A K x**	Play **J**.
A K x	**J x**	Play **x** on the chance the lead may be away from **Q**. At a suit contract winning **K** or **A** may be preferable.
10 x	**A K x** or **A Q x**	Play **10**.
10 x	**K Q x**	Play **10**.
J x	**A Q x**	Play **J**.
K Q x	**10 x**	Play **Q**.
A x	**Q x**	Play **x**.

Suit Distribution. In planning the play, declarer must consider how the cards are likely to be distributed in the defenders' hands and must be attentive to overcoming bad breaks. For an inexperienced player, a good rule of thumb is that an *odd* number of outstanding cards will break as evenly as possible, while an *even* number of cards will split unevenly. The following table gives the percentages of how the outstanding cards in a given suit will be distributed between the opponents' hands.

If the opponents hold	Those cards will divide	
2 cards in a suit	1–1	52%
	2–0	48%
3 cards	2–1	78%
	3–0	22%
4 cards	3–1	49.7%
	2–2	40.7%
	4–0	9.6%
5 cards	3–2	68%
	4–1	28%
	5–0	4%
6 cards	4–2	48.5%
	3–3	35.5%
	5–1	14.5%
	6–0	1.5%
7 cards	4–3	62%
	5–2	30.5%
	6–1	7%
	7–0	0.5%
8 cards	5–3	47.1%
	4–4	32.7%
	6–2	17.1%
	7–1	2.9%
	8–0	0.2%

Entries. Entries, cards that can win tricks, are the means by which the declarer goes from hand to dummy and back. They are valuable property and should not be wasted. When entries are scarce to one hand or the other, careful planning is needed to use them as wisely as possible. The following are some of the methods declarer has to save entries.

Dummy holds	Declarer holds	Proper play
K x x	**A Q 10** x x	Cash **A**, then lead low to dummy's **K**. If the opponent on the left "shows out"—fails to follow suit—lead low to **10**.
J 9 x	**A Q 10** x	Lead **9** from dummy and play low from hand. If **J** is led first, declarer will have to win the second trick in hand and return to dummy to pick up **K x x x** on his right.
A Q 10	**K J** x	A very flexible holding. If declarer needs entries to his hand, he can overtake **10** with his **J**, and **Q** with his **K**. If he needs entries to the board, declarer overtakes his honors with dummy's honors.
A K Q x x	x x	If declarer has no side entry to dummy and needs four tricks from this suit at a notrump contract, he plays low cards from both hands at the first trick to cater to a 4–2 split.

Defensive Play

Leads and Signals. The defenders attempt by their leads and plays to inform each other as to the nature of their holdings in the suit led. They do this by using a system of conventional leads which govern the selection of the card to lead from any specific suit holding, and by signals when they follow suit or discard. Those signals consist of the choice of the cards played.

The following table shows the proper card to lead from any given suit holding, the selection varying in some cases depending on whether the contract is in a suit or notrump. In most cases the card is selected not only for its value in giving information, but also because the lead of that particular card offers the best opportunity to win or establish tricks in the suit, or to avoid giving extra tricks to declarer.

Opening leader holds	Lead at a suit contract	Lead at a notrump contract
A K Q (alone or with others)	**K**, then **Q**	**K**, then **Q**
A K J 10 x x	**K**, then **A**	**A**, then **K**

Opening leader holds	Lead at a suit contract	Lead at a notrump contract
A Q 10 9	**A**	**Q** or **10**
A Q J x x	**A**	**Q**
A Q x x (x)	**A**	Fourth best
A J 10 x (x)	**A**	**J**
A 10 9 x (x)	**A**	Fourth best from five; 10 from four
A x x x (x)	**A**	Fourth best
A K x	**K**	**K**
A K alone	**A**, then **K**	**K**
K Q (alone or with others)	**K**	**K** or fourth best
K J 10 (alone or with others)	**J**	**J**
K 10 9 x (x)	**10**	Fourth best from five; 10 from four
Q J 10 or **Q J 9** (alone or with others)	**Q**	**Q**
Q J x or **Q J**	**Q**	**Q**
Q J x x	Fourth best	Fourth best
J 10 9 or **J 10 8** (alone or with others)	**J**	**J**
J 10 x or **J 10**	**J**	**J**
J 10 x x (x)	Fourth best	Fourth best
10 9 8 or **10 9 7** (alone or with others)	**10**	**10**
10 9 x x (x)	Fourth best	Fourth best
K J x x (x)	Fourth best	Fourth best
Any other four-card or longer holding headed by an honor not listed above	Fourth best	Fourth best
Any two cards	Highest card	Highest card
Three low cards	Highest or lowest card	Highest card
Four or five low cards	Second highest	Second highest
A J x, A x x, K J x, K x x, Q 10 x, Q x x, J x x of partner's suit	**A** or lowest card	Lowest card
Three low cards in partner's suit	Highest	Highest

The opening lead of an ace against a notrump contract asks partner to play an honor (**K**, **Q**, or **J**) in the suit led, or to give count by playing the highest card from an even holding, and the lowest from an odd holding. The lead of a king against a notrump contract requests partner to signal his attitude about whether or not the suit should be continued. Partner encourages by playing a high card and discourages by following with a low card. Although an ace is led against suit contracts from all holdings containing that card, those leads should be avoided. Aces are meant to capture other high cards, but that rarely happens when an ace is led to the first trick.

Rule of Eleven. The thirteen cards of any suit form a series of numbers of which the two is the lowest and the ace is the highest with a number of 14. Take any card in the series and subtract its number from 14 and the result is the number of higher cards in that suit; if the card is the five, for example, you subtract five from 14 and discover that there are nine higher cards.

When the leader has led his fourth-highest card, three higher cards are in his own hand; therefore, subtracting the card led from 11 will give the number of higher cards in the other three hands. This is the "Rule of Eleven," and has many applications in the play, especially at notrump contracts where fourth-best leads are common, as in the notrump holding below:

Dummy holds
♡ **K 10 3**

Opening lead is   Leader's partner holds
    ♡ **6**   ♡ **A J 7**

On the lead of ♡**6**, dummy's ♡**3** is played. Subtracting 6 from 11 leaves 5, so leader's partner knows that there are five cards higher than ♡**6** in the other three hands. He can see two in the dummy and three in his own hand; therefore the declarer can have none. On the play of ♡**3**, the leader's partner plays ♡**7** and wins the trick. When the original leader gets in again, he can lead another heart and dummy's **K** will be trapped under the partner's **A**. Had leader's partner played the **J** on the first trick, dummy could eventually have won a heart trick.

Signals in the Play. When a player unnecessarily discards or follows suit with a card which is not the lowest one available, and later plays or discards a lower card in the same suit, he has *echoed* or *high-lowed*. This series of plays acts as a signal to ask partner to continue leading that suit, or to switch to a suit where he has echoed. For example:

♠ – 9 8 5 4
♡ – 7 2
◇ – Q 8 6
♣ – A Q 9 5

N

♠ – 10 6 3
♡ – Q 8 5 3
◇ – 4 2
♣ – J 8 6 3

Lead is ◇ K   **W**   **E**

S

Spades are trumps. When East sees his partner's lead of ◇ **K**, he wants diamonds continued because he can ruff the third round. Instead of playing ◇ **2**, which would be his normal play with three or four low diamonds, he follows with ◇ **4**. West continues by leading ◇ **A** and East completes his echo by playing ◇ **2**. West leads a third round of diamonds and East ruffs with a spade to win the trick. On the other hand, if East had high diamonds and wanted the suit continued, he would make the same play of an unnecessarily high diamond to encourage partner to lead another diamond. This type of signal is known as a "come-on."

Whenever a player discards what seems to be an unusually high card, the presumption is that he is starting an echo and wants partner to lead that suit. This is an "encouraging" signal. Similarly, the discard of a low card in a suit is "discouraging." This signal advises partner to avoid leading that suit, but to shift to some other suit.

High-low signals are also used to give count. With an odd number of cards in the suit led, follow with the lowest card. With an even number, play the highest you can afford. By giving count in suits that declarer leads, the defenders help each other build a clearer picture of declarer's hand, which allows them to defend more accurately.

The Trump Echo. When a defender has a odd number of trumps, and is following suit or ruffing, he plays high-low in the trump suit. Refer to the previous example. When East ruffs the third round of diamonds, he should do so with ♠**6**. Suppose West wins a subsequent trick with ♠**A**. On this trick East will follow with ♠**3**. Having completed a trump echo, East advises partner that he still has a trump, so West can lead a fourth diamond and East will overruff dummy with ♠**10**. Trump echoes usually indicate a desire to ruff, but experienced defenders will echo in trumps even when that possibility doesn't exist to inform partner how many trumps declarer holds.

Plays from Sequences. From a sequence of cards, a player leads the highest card in the sequence. When he is following suit to his partner's lead, however, he always plays the lowest card in the sequence.

Dummy holds
◊ **8 2**

The lead is
◊ **5**

Leader's partner holds
◊ **Q J 10 3**

The leader's partner follows with ◊ **10**. If he were leading diamonds his lead would, of course, be ◊ **Q**. There is general agreement among today's players that if declarer leads this suit from dummy, second hand should play ◊ **Q** to show a sequence headed by the queen and no higher honor.

False Cards. Defensive play is governed by certain rules because the defenders cannot see each other's hand and must constantly strive to transmit information about their holdings by a series of coded signals. Occasionally a defender may judge that the information given by a conventional lead or play will not help his partner, but may help declarer judge the lie of the cards. In such a case a defender may deliberately violate the conventional rules. This is known as "false-carding," and its purpose is to deceive declarer. Since a false card also deceives partner and weakens partnership trust, there are very few instances where it is proper for a defender to indulge in this practice.

Declarer, however, should false-card at every opportunity. Since dummy cannot be deceived, an unconventional selection of plays may cause the defenders to err.

Illustrative Games

Bridge is considered the most difficult of card games and more complex than chess. To reach the correct contract the partners have to communicate with each other through a careful selection of bids, and the play and defense of a hand requires logical thought. Alexander Deschappelles, the finest whist player of his day, was able to defeat the reigning chess champion a few days after taking up the game, but he never felt that he had fully mastered whist. To illustrate how a hand of modern bridge should be bid and played, two sample games follow.

In reporting a bridge hand the order of presentation used is to show a diagram of the distribution of the cards among the four players; the diagram also states which player dealt and which side, if either, might be vulnerable. Next is a diagram that traces the flow of the bidding and reveals the opening lead. In the bidding diagram the successive bids are read across the line. Following this is a discussion of the bidding and a description of the play of the hand.

Illustrative Game No. 1

Dealer: South
East-West vulnerable

```
                    ♠ Q 6 5
                    ♡ K J 5 2
                    ◇ 8 5 2
                    ♣ K 6 3

                         N
♠ A K J 8 4 2                        ♠ 10 9 3
♡ 8                 W         E      ♡ 9 3
◇ K Q 4                              ◇ 9 7 6 3
♣ A 5 2                  S           ♣ 10 9 8 4

                    ♠ 7
                    ♡ A Q 10 7 6 4
                    ◇ A J 10
                    ♣ Q J 7
```

The bidding

South	West	North	East
1 ♡	Dbl	2 ♡	Pass
3 ♣	3 ♠	4 ♡	Pass
Pass	Pass		

Opening lead: ♠ K

NOTES ON THE BIDDING

With 14 high-card points and 3 distributional points (2 for the singleton spade and 1 for the sixth heart), South has a better than minimum opening bid. West's hand is too strong for a simple overcall, so he doubles first for take-out. After the intervening double, North bids the same as if there had been no interference, although a raise might be a shade weaker than normal. New suits by responder at the one-level are natural and forcing, but suit bids at the two level are non-forcing.

Had North passed, East would have had to bid two clubs, his best suit. North's bid relieves East of that obligation. For East to act freely in this situation he would need a long suit and about 6 points or a stronger hand. Since South's hand has been improved by partner's raise, he is interested in game. The proper way to make a game try is to bid a suit where help is needed, and South is more interested in finding partner with a high club honor than something in diamonds. A re-raise to three hearts on this auction would be competitive and discouraging; it would not be a

125

game try. West can expect to win seven or eight tricks in his own hand, so his bid of three spades is clearly justified.

North could not have a better hand on the auction. With four-card trump support and a king in a suit where partner needs help, chances of making game are excellent. Over four hearts, East and South have nothing further to contribute, and only a poor player in the West chair would gamble on a four-spade contract. He has twice told partner that he has a very strong hand, and East has been unable to act.

THE PLAY

At trick one East follows with ♠**3** to discourage a spade continuation; with two spades he would start a high-low. West, justifiably afraid that a lead of any *plain* (non-trump) suit might help declarer, *exits* (leads) safely with a trump. With trumps to spare, declarer's first duty is to draw trumps to prevent a side winner from getting ruffed away. Trumps should usually be drawn immediately unless they are needed for some other purpose. Declarer wins the trump shift, draws the outstanding trump and leads ♣**Q** to establish two clubs tricks for his side. West does best to win this trick with ♣**A** and exit with another club.

Declarer has nine sure tricks and he needs one additional diamond trick to make his contract. Under normal circumstances successive finesses of ◇**10** and ◇**J** would produce that trick, but declarer should be aware that West's strong bidding indicates that he has both of the missing diamond honors and the double finesse will fail. To extricate himself from this dilemma, declarer must eliminate all safe exit cards from the West hand. He does this by winning the second round of clubs with the jack and cashing ♣**K** before leading a diamond to the ten. When West wins this trick, he is *endplayed* (forced to make a losing return). If he returns a diamond, it will be into declarer's ◇**A J**. If West leads a spade, dummy's queen is sure to win a trick, on which declarer will discard his ◇**J**. Thus South takes six trump tricks, two clubs and two diamonds, or one diamond and a spade, and makes his game.

Illustrative Game No. 2

Dealer: East
North-South vulnerable

```
                        ♠ 5 3
                        ♡ Q 10 9
                        ◇ A 6 4
                        ♣ K Q 7 6 2

                           N
♠ K Q 10 9 7                        ♠ J 8 2
♡ K 8 4          W         E        ♡ J 7 6 3 2
◇ 10 2                              ◇ J 9
♣ J 8 4                   S         ♣ A 10 5

                        ♠ A 6 4
                        ♡ A 5
                        ◇ K Q 8 7 5 3
                        ♣ 9 3
```

The bidding:

East	South	West	North
Pass	1 ◇	1 ♠	2 ♣
Pass	2 ◇	Pass	3 ◇
Pass	3 NT	Pass	Pass
Pass			

Opening lead: ♠ **Q**

NOTES ON THE BIDDING

Again South has a better than minimum opening bid because he has a good six-card suit and three honor tricks. Many players would not overcall on the West cards, but that would be too pusillanimous, especially at this vulnerability. West has a good suit and he certainly wants partner to lead a spade and not some other suit if North becomes declarer. Although North has a near opening bid of his own, all he can do is respond in his long suit to see what develops. If South had one fewer diamond, his correct rebid would be two notrump, to show a minimum balanced hand and stoppers in the other two suits. With six diamonds, a suit rebid is preferred.

Since North has already shown approximately 11 points by responding at the two-level, his duty now is to confirm support for partner's suit by raising to three diamonds. North's raise gives South hope that he will find the ace of diamonds in partner's hand, and if so he can count on taking eight tricks in the play—six diamonds and two aces. It is not too much to expect North to contribute another trick, so game at notrump is an attractive proposition. A principle of bidding is that whenever the partnership's main suit is a minor, game in notrump should be sought if possible, because it is easier to take nine tricks in notrump than 11 in a minor.

THE PLAY

West's lead of ♠Q is a conventional lead that demands partner follow with the jack if he holds it. This lead occurs most frequently in defense of a notrump contract and is made only from a holding that includes the ten and nine. Without the nine, West's correct lead would be ♠K. Partner's encouraging or discouraging signal would then tell him whether or not to continue the suit.

When East dutifully follows with ♠J, South must not win the trick, nor the spade continuation. By *holding up* the ace until the third round, declarer seeks to exhaust the East hand of all his spades and thereby break the defenders' communications. The advantage of South's hold-up play will soon be apparent.

At trick four, declarer cashes dummy's ♢A and proceeds to run his diamond winners. In doing so he hopes that West will discard a spade. Although West is likely to have ♣A on the bidding, declarer has no choice at trick ten but to lead a club in an effort to establish his ninth trick. Now the earlier hold-up plays reap a rich reward. When East wins ♣A, he has no spade to return and no quick entry to partner's established spades. All he can do is shift to a heart, but declarer wins the ace and cashes dummy's high club for his fulfilling trick. If declarer had won either the first or second round of spades, East would have still had a spade in his hand when he won ♣A. His spade return would allow West to cash enough winners to defeat the contract.

LAWS OF CONTRACT BRIDGE

As Promulgated in the Western Hemisphere by the American Contract Bridge League

Promulgating Bodies of the 1891 Laws

The National Laws Commission
of the American Contract Bridge League

Co-Chairmen

Don Oakie	Edgar Kaplan
B. Jay Becker*	Amalya Kearse
Easley Blackwood	Robin B. MacNab
Sam Gold	George Rosenkrantz
Richard L. Goldberg	Jerome Silverman
Charles H. Goren	Ed Theus
Oswald Jacoby	Lee Hazen

Roger Stern

* Deceased

Drafting Committee for Rubber Bridge

Roger Stern   B. Jay Becker*   Edgar Kaplan
* Deceased

The Laws Committee of the World Bridge Federation
Ed Theus, Chairman

European Bridge League
Nils E. Jensen, Delegate

Card Committee of the Portland Club

Part I

The Scope of the Laws

The Laws are designed to define correct procedure and to provide an adequate remedy whenever a player accidentally, carelessly or inadvertently disturbs the proper course of the game, or gains an unintentional but nevertheless unfair advantage. An offending player should be ready to pay a prescribed penalty graciously.

The Laws are not designed to prevent dishonorable practices and there are no penalties to cover intentional violations. In the absence of penalty, moral obligations are strongest. Ostracism is the ultimate remedy for intentional offenses.

The Object of the Proprieties

The object of the Proprieties is twofold: to familiarize players with the customs and etiquette of the game, generally accepted over a long period of years; and to enlighten those who might otherwise fail to appreciate when or how they are improperly conveying information to their partners—often a far more reprehensible offense than a violation of a law.

When these principles are appreciated, arguments are avoided and the pleasure that the game offers is materially enhanced.

Part II

Preliminaries

LAW 1. THE PLAYERS—THE PACK

Contract bridge is played by all four players with a pack of 52 cards of identical back design and color, consisting of 13 cards in each of four suits. Two packs should be used, of which only one is in play at any time; and each pack should be clearly distinguishable from the other in back design or color.

LAW 2. RANK OF CARDS

The suits rank downwards in order—Spades (♠), Hearts, (♡), Diamonds (◊), Clubs (♣). The cards of each suit rank in descending order: Ace, King, Queen, Jack, 10, 9, 8, 7, 6, 5, 4, 3, 2.

LAW 3. THE DRAW

Before every rubber, each player draws a card from a pack shuffled and spread face down on the table. A card should not be exposed until all the players have drawn.

Unless it is otherwise agreed, the two players who draw the highest cards play as partners against the other two players. When cards of the same rank are drawn, the rank of suit determines which is higher.

The player with the highest card deals first and has the right to choose his seat and the pack with which he will deal. He may consult his partner, but having announced his decision must abide by it. His partner sits opposite him. The opponents then occupy the two remaining seats as they wish, and having made their selection must abide by it.

A player must draw again if he draws more than one card, or one of the four cards at either end of the pack, or a card adjoining one drawn by another player, or a card from the other pack.

Part III

The Deal

LAW 4. THE SHUFFLE

Before the first deal of a rubber, the player to the dealer's left should shuffle the pack thoroughly, without exposing the face of any card, in full view of the players and to their satisfaction. Thereafter, as each player deals, the dealer's partner shuffles the other pack for the next deal, and places the pack face down on his right.

A pack properly prepared should not be disturbed until the dealer picks it up for his deal, at which time he is entitled to the final shuffle.

No player other than the dealer and the player designated to prepare the pack may shuffle.

LAW 5. THE CUT

The pack must be cut immediately before it is dealt. The dealer presents the pack to his right-hand opponent, who lifts off a portion and places it on the table toward the dealer. Each portion must contain at least four cards. The dealer completes the cut by placing what was originally the bottom portion upon the other portion.

No player other than the dealer's right-hand opponent may cut the pack.

LAW 6. NEW CUT—NEW SHUFFLE

There must be a new cut if any player demands one before the first card is dealt. In this case, the dealer's right-hand opponent cuts again.

There must be a new shuffle, followed by a cut:

(a) If any player demands one before the dealer has picked up the pack for his deal. In this case, the player designated to prepare the pack shuffles again.

(b) If any player demands one after the dealer has picked up the pack but before the first card is dealt. In this case only the dealer shuffles.

(c) If a card is turned face up in shuffling. In this case the player who was shuffling shuffles again.

(d) If a card is turned face up in cutting. In this case only the dealer shuffles.

(e) If there is a redeal (see Law 10).

LAW 7. CHANGE OF PACK

The two packs are used alternately, unless there is a redeal.

A pack containing a card so damaged or marked so that it may be identified from its back must be replaced* if attention is drawn to the imperfection before the last card of the current deal has been dealt.

A pack originally belonging to a side must be restored on demand of any player before the last card of the current deal has been dealt.*

LAW 8. THE DEAL

The dealer distributes the cards face down, one at a time in rotation into four separate hands of thirteen cards each, the first card to the player on his left and the last card to himself. If he deals two cards simultaneously or consecutively to the same player, or fails to deal a card to a player, he may rectify the error, provided he does so immediately and to the satisfaction of the other players.

The dealer must not allow the face of any card to be seen while he is dealing. Players should not look at the face of any card until the deal is completed.**

LAW 9. ROTATION OF THE TURN TO DEAL

The turn to deal passes in rotation, unless there is a redeal. If a player deals out of turn, and attention is not drawn to the error before the last card has been dealt, the deal stands as though it had been in turn, the player who dealt the cards is the dealer, and the player who missed his turn to deal has no redress; and the rotation continues as though the deal had been in turn, unless a redeal is required under Law 10.

LAW 10. REDEAL

A redeal cancels the faulty deal; the same dealer deals again, unless he was dealing out of turn; the same pack is used, unless it has been replaced as provided in Law 7; and the cards are shuffled and cut anew as provided in Laws 4 and 5.

* See Footnote to Law 8.
** A player who violates this provision forfeits those rights to a change of pack (Law 7) or redeal (Law 10) marked with an asterisk(*).

There must be a redeal:
  (a) If, before the last card has been dealt, it is discovered that
    (i) a card has been turned face up in dealing or is face up in the pack or elsewhere;
    (ii) the cards have not been dealt correctly;*
    (iii) a player is dealing out of turn or is dealing with a pack that was not shuffled or not cut, provided any player* demands a redeal.
  (b) If, before the first call has been made, it is discovered that a player has picked up another player's hand and has seen a card in it.
  (c) If, before play has been completed, it is discovered that
    (i) the pack did not conform in every respect to the requirements of Law 1, including any case in which a missing card cannot be found after due search;
    (ii) one player has picked up too many cards, another too few;
    (iii) two or more players on opposing sides have allowed any cards from their hands to be mixed together, following a claim that a redeal is in order.

LAW 11. MISSING CARD

When a player has too few cards and a redeal is not required by Law 10 (c), the deal stands as correct, and:
  (a) If he has played more than once to a previous trick, Law 67 applies;
  (b) If a missing card is found elsewhere, not in a previous trick, that card is deemed to have belonged continuously to the deficient hand and must be restored to that hand; it may become a penalty card, as provided in Law 23 or 49, and failure to have played it may constitute a revoke.

LAW 12. SURPLUS CARD

When a player has too many cards and a redeal is not required by Law 10 (c), the deal stands as correct, and
  (a) If the offender has omitted to play to a trick, Law 67 applies.
  (b) If the offenders has picked up a surplus card from a previous trick, or from dummy's hand, or from the other pack, or elsewhere, such surplus card shall be restored to its proper place; and
    (i) If the surplus card is in the offender's hand when it is discovered, there is no penalty.
    (ii) If the surplus card had been led or played, or had been played to a previous trick, the offender must substitute for it a card of the same suit as the surplus card. The non-offending side wins that trick. When attention is drawn to the offense before the lead to the next trick, either member of the non-offending side may, without penalty, withdraw a play made subsequent to the offense, and substitute any legal play.

Part IV

General Laws Governing Irregularities

LAW 13. PROCEDURE FOLLOWING AN IRREGULARITY
(Club Law 13 on Page 151)

When an irregularity has occurred, any player—except dummy as restricted by Law 43— may draw attention to it and give or obtain information as to the law applicable to it. The

* See Footnote to Law 8.

fact that a player draws attention to an irregularity committed by his side does not affect the rights of the opponents.

After attention has been drawn to an irregularity, no player should call or play until all questions in regard to rectification and to the assessment of a penalty have been determined. Premature correction of an irregularity on the part of the offender may subject him to a further penalty (see Law 26).

LAW 14. ASSESSMENT OF A PENALTY

(Club Law 14 on Page 151)

A penalty may not be imposed until the nature of the irregularity to be penalized has been determined and the applicable penalty has been clearly stated; but a penalty once paid, or any decision agreed and acted upon by the players, stands and should not be corrected even though at some later time it may be judged incorrect, except by agreement of all four players.

LAW 15. WAIVER OR FORFEITURE OF PENALTY

The right to penalize an offense is forfeited if a member of the non-offending side
    (a) waives the penalty;
    (b) calls (Law 34) or plays (Law 60) after an irregularity committed by the opponent to his right.

LAW 16. UNAUTHORIZED INFORMATION

(Club Law 16 on page 151)

A player may be subject to penalty if he conveys information to his partner other than by a legal call or play.

Information conveyed by an illegal call, play or exposure of a card is subject to the applicable law in Part V or VI.

If a player conveys information to his partner by means of a remark or question or by an unmistakable hesitation, special emphasis, tone, gesture, movement, mannerism or any other action that suggests a call, lead or plan of play; and if attention is drawn to the offense immediately, (penalty) either member of the non-offending side (dummy excepted) may prohibit any call or play so suggested.

Part V

The Auction

Correct Procedure

LAW 17. DURATION OF THE AUCTION

The auction begins when the last card of a correct deal has been placed on the table. The dealer makes the first call, and thereafter each player calls in rotation. When three passes in rotation have followed any call (but see Law 34), the auction is closed.

LAW 18. BIDS

Each bid must name a number of odd tricks, from one to seven, and a denomination. A bid supersedes the previous bid if it names either a greater number of odd tricks, or the same number of odd tricks in a higher denomination. A bid that fulfills these requirements is sufficient; one that does not is insufficient. The denominations rank in descending order: no-trump, spades, hearts, diamonds, clubs.

LAW 19. DOUBLES AND REDOUBLES

A player may double only the last preceding bid, and then only if it was made by an opponent and no calls other than pass have intervened.

A player may redouble only the last preceding double, and then only if it was made by an opponent and no calls other than pass have intervened.

A player should not, in doubling or redoubling, state the number of tricks or the denomination; but, if he states either or both incorrectly, he is deemed to have doubled or redoubled the bid as it was made.

All doubles and redoubles are superseded by a subsequent legal bid. If there is no subsequent bid, scoring values are increased as provided in Law 81.

LAW 20. REVIEW AND EXPLANATION

A player who does not hear a call distinctly may forthwith require that it be repeated.

During the auction and at his own turn to call, a player (unless required by law to pass) may require a restatement of the auction in its entirety.

After the final pass, declarer before playing from dummy, or either defender at his first turn to play, may require a restatement of the auction in its entirety.

A request to have calls restated should be responded to only by an opponent (dummy, or a player required by law to pass, may so respond). All players should promptly correct errors in restatement.

A player may require an explanation of the partnership understanding relating to any call made by an opponent, but only at that player's own turn to call or play. A request for an explanation of a call should be responded to by the partner of the player making the call (see Proprieties 4).

LAW 21. CALL BASED ON MISINFORMATION

A player has no recourse if he has made a call on the basis of his own misunderstanding.

A player may, without penalty, change any call he may have made as a result of misinformation given him by an opponent, provided his partner has not subsequently called. If he elects to correct his call, his left-hand opponent may then, in turn and without penalty, change any subsequent call he may have made.

LAW 22. PROCEDURE AFTER THE AUCTION IS CLOSED

After the auction is closed:

(a) If no player has bid, the hands are abandoned and the turn to deal passes in rotation.

(b) If any player has bid, the final bid becomes the contract and play begins.

Irregularities

LAW 23. CARD EXPOSED OR LED DURING THE AUCTION
(Club Law 23 on Page 152)

Whenever, during the auction, a player faces a card on the table or holds a card so that it is possible for his partner to see its face, every such card must be left face up on the table until the auction closes; and (penalty) if the offender subsequently becomes a defender, declarer may treat every such card as a penalty card (Law 50).

In addition:

(a) If it is a single card below the rank of an honor and not prematurely led, there is no further penalty.

(b) If it is a single card of honor rank, or any card prematurely led, or if more than one card is so exposed, (penalty) the offender's partner must pass when next it is his turn to call.

LAW 24. IMMEDIATE CORRECTION OF A CALL

A player may substitute his intended call for an inadvertent call, but only if he does so, or attempts to do so, without pause for thought. If legal, his last call stands without penalty; if illegal, it is subject to the applicable law.

LAW 25. CHANGE OF CALL

(Club Law 25 on Page 152)

A call substituted for a call made previously at the same turn, when it is too late for correction as provided in Law 24, is canceled; and:

(a) If the first call was illegal, the offender is subject to the applicable law.

(b) If the first call was a legal one, the offender must either

(i) allow his first call to stand and (penalty) his partner must pass when next it is his turn to call; or

(ii) make any legal call and (penalty) his partner must pass whenever it is his turn to call.

The offender's partner will also be subject to a lead penalty as provided in Law 26 if he becomes a defender.

LAW 26. CHANGE OF CALL—LEAD PENALTIES

(Club Law 26 on Page 152)

When a player makes a call and subsequently changes it to another legal call (except as permitted under Law 24), then if he becomes a defender:

(a) if the changed call was in a suit, and the substituted call did not repeat that suit, declarer may* either require the offender's partner to lead, or prohibit him from leading, such suit when first the offender's partner has the lead (including the opening lead). A prohibition continues for as long as offender's partner retains the lead. When the irregular call artificially relates to a denomination other than the one actually named, "such suit" is the suit or suits to which the call relates.

(b) if the changed call was

(i) in notrump, and his final call at that turn was not, or

(ii) pass, double or redouble, other than an out-of-rotation call repeated in turn in accordance with Law 30 (a) or 32 (b)(i),

declarer may* prohibit offender's partner from leading any one specified suit when first the offender's partner has the lead (including the opening lead). This prohibition continues for as long as offender's partner retains the lead.

LAW 27. INSUFFICIENT BID

(Club Law 27 on Page 152)

An insufficient bid made in rotation must be corrected by the substitution of either a sufficient bid or a pass,** unless the irregular bid is accepted. Any insufficient bid may be accepted (treated as legal) at the option of the opponent on offender's left, and is accepted if that opponent calls.

If the call substituted is

(a) the lowest sufficient bid in the same denomination, the auction proceeds as though the irregularity had not occurred.***

* *Declarer specifies the suit at the time that offender's partner first has the lead.*
** *The offender is entitled to select his final call at that turn after the applicable penalties have been stated, and any call he has previously attempted to substitute is canceled, but the lead penalties of Law 26 will apply if he becomes a defender.*
*** *Offender's partner must not base any subsequent calls or plays on information gained from such a withdrawn bid.*

(b) any other sufficient bid, or pass, (penalty) the offender's partner must pass whenever it is his turn to call, and the lead penalties of Law 26 will apply if he becomes a defender.

If the offender attempts to substitute a double or redouble, it is canceled; he must pass at that turn and the offense is subject to the penalty provided in subsection (b) above.

If a player makes an insufficient bid out of rotation, Law 31 applies.

Call Out of Rotation

LAW 28. CALLS CONSIDERED TO BE IN ROTATION

A call is considered to be in rotation

(a) when it is made without waiting for the right-hand opponent to pass, if that opponent is required by law to pass.

(b) when it is made by the player whose turn it was to call, before a penalty has been imposed for a call out of rotation by an opponent; it waives any penalty for the call out of rotation and the auction proceeds as though that opponent had not called at that turn.

LAW 29. PROCEDURE AFTER A CALL OUT OF ROTATION

After a call out of rotation, the opponent to offender's left* may either:

(a) make any legal call; if he chooses to do so, the call out of rotation stands as if it were legal (but if it is an inadmissible call, see Law 35), and the auction proceeds without penalty; or,

(b) require that the call out of rotation be canceled. The auction reverts to the player whose turn it was to call. The offender may make any legal call in proper turn but is subject to penalty under Law 30, 31 or 32.

LAW 30. PASS OUT OF ROTATION

(Club Law 30 on Page 152)

When a player has passed out of rotation

(a) before any player has bid, or when it was the turn of the opponent to his right** to call, (penalty) the offender must pass when next it is his turn to call.

(b) after any player has bid and when it was the turn of the offender's partner to call, (penalty) the offender must pass whenever it is his turn to call; the offender's partner may make a sufficient bid or may pass, but may not double or redouble at that turn. The offender's partner will be subject to the lead penalties of Law 26 if he becomes a defender.

LAW 31. BID OUT OF ROTATION

(Club Law 31 on Page 152)

When a player has bid out of rotation

(a) at the turn of offender's partner to call, or before any player has called when the opponent on the offender's left was the dealer, (penalty) the offender's partner must pass whenever it is his turn to call, and the lead penalties of Law 26 will apply it he becomes a defender.

(b) at the turn of the opponent on the offender's right*** to call,

---

* *He alone exercises the option, although any player may draw attention to the irregularity.*
** *After any player has bid, a call at offender's left-hand opponent's turn is a change of call; Law 25 applies and not this section.*
*** *After any player has called, a call at offender's left-hand opponent's turn is a change of call; Law 25 applies and not this section.*

(i) if that opponent passes, the bid out of rotation must be repeated, and there is no penalty (if the bid out of rotation was insufficient, it must be corrected as provided in Law 27);

(ii) if that opponent makes a legal* bid, double or redouble, the offender may in turn make any legal call. If such call repeats the denomination of the bid out of rotation, (penalty) the offender's partner must pass when next it is his turn to call. If the substituted call does not repeat the denomination, (penalty) the offender's partner must pass whenever it is his turn to call, and the lead penalties of Law 26 will apply if he becomes a defender.

LAW 32. DOUBLE OR REDOUBLE OUT OF ROTATION

(Club Law 32 on Page 152)

When a player has doubled or redoubled out of rotation,**

(a) If it was the offender's partner's turn to call, (penalty) the offender's partner must pass whenever it is his turn to call; the offender may not thereafter, in turn, double or redouble the same bid he doubled or redoubled out of turn; and the lead penalties of Law 26 (b) will apply if he becomes a defender.

(b) If it was the turn of the opponent on the offender's right** to call:

(i) If the opponent on the offender's right passes, the double or redouble out of rotation must be repeated and there is no penalty.

(ii) If the opponent on the offender's right bids, the offender may in turn make any legal call, and (penalty) the offender's partner must pass when next it is his turn to call, and the lead penalties of Law 26 (b) will apply if he becomes a defender.

LAW 33. SIMULTANEOUS CALLS

A call made simultaneously with one made by the player whose turn it was to call is deemed to be a subsequent call.

LAW 34. RETENTION OF THE RIGHT TO CALL

A player may not be deprived of any turn to call by one or more passes following a pass out of rotation, when there has been no subsequent bid.*** All such passes—the pass out of rotation, plus the subsequent passes that would serve to end the auction—are canceled. The bidding reverts to the player whose turn it was to call before the pass out of rotation, and the auction continues as though there had been no irregularity.

Inadmissible Calls

LAW 35. INADMISSIBLE CALL CONDONED

(Club Law 35 on Page 152)

When, after any inadmissible call specified below, the opponent to the offender's left makes a call before a penalty has been assessed, there is no penalty for the offense (the lead penalties of Law 26 do not apply). If the inadmissible call was

---

* An illegal call by that opponent may be penalized in the usual way, after which this subsection, (b)(ii), applies.

** After any player has called, a call at offender's left-hand opponent's turn is a change of call; Law 25 applies and not this section.

*** After a pass out of rotation that has been accepted by a pass from the player to offender's left (it thus stands as legal), three passes in rotation may follow a call; apparently, this would end this auction, as provided by Law 17. However, a player would then be deprived of an opportunity to call, and this is not permitted.

(a) a double or redouble not permitted by Law 19, that call and all subsequent calls are canceled; the auction reverts to the player whose turn it is to call and proceeds as though there had been no irregularity;

(b) a bid, double or redouble by a player required by law to pass, that call and subsequent legal calls stand; but if the offender was required to pass for the remainder of the auction, he must still pass at subsequent turns;

(c) a bid of more than seven, that call and all subsequent calls are cancelled; the offender must substitute a pass, and the auction proceeds as though there had been no irregularity;

(d) a call after the auction is closed, that call and all subsequent calls are canceled without penalty.

LAW 36. INADMISSIBLE DOUBLE OR REDOUBLE
(Club Law 36 on Page 152)

Any double or redouble not permitted by Law 19 is canceled, and the offender must substitute a legal call: and (penalty) the offender's partner must pass whenever it is his turn to call, and the lead penalties of Law 26 (b) will apply if he becomes a defender. Further, if the bid that was inadmissibly doubled or redoubled becomes the final contract, either member of the non-offending side may specify that the contract be played undoubled.

If the right of the non-offending side to penalize is forfeited, Law 35 applies.

LAW 37. BID, DOUBLE OR REDOUBLE IN VIOLATION OF THE OBLIGATION TO PASS

A bid, double or redouble by a player who is required by law to pass is canceled, and (penalty) both members of the offending side must pass during the remainder of the auction, and the lead penalties of Law 26 will apply if they become defenders.

LAW 38. BID OF MORE THAN SEVEN
(Club Law 38 on Page 152)

No play or score at a contract of more than seven is ever permissible. A bid of more than seven by any player is canceled, and (penalty) both members of the offending side must pass during the remainder of the auction; and the lead penalties of Law 26 will apply if they become defenders.

LAW 39. CALL AFTER THE AUCTION IS CLOSED
(Club Law 39 on Page 152)

A call after the auction is closed is canceled, and:

(a) If it is a pass by a defender or any call by declarer or dummy, there is no penalty.

(b) If it is a bid, double or redouble by a defender, the lead penalties of Law 26 apply, unless the call has been condoned (see Law 35 (d)).

LAW 40. CONVENTIONS AND PSYCHIC BIDS
(Club Law 40 on Page 153)

A player may make any call or play (including an intentionally misleading call such as a "psychic bid," or a call or play that departs from commonly accepted or previously announced conventional practice) without prior announcement, provided that it is not based on a partnership understanding. But a player may not make use of a bidding or play convention unless,

(a) his side has disclosed its use of such a call or play beforehand, or

(b) it has been agreed beforehand that the use of partnership understandings be disclosed at the time they are used, and his partner does so disclose it. In this case, partner's disclosure must be confined to an indication that a convention has been used; he should not offer any explanation unless requested to do so.

Any group may, by agreement, restrict the use of conventions in its games.

Part VI

The Play

Correct Procedure

LAW 41. OPENING LEAD, REVIEW, QUESTIONS

After the auction closes, the defender on declarer's left makes the opening lead.* After the opening lead, dummy spreads his hand in front of him on the table, face up and grouped in suits with the trumps on his right. Declarer plays both his hand and that of dummy.

Declarer, before he plays from dummy, or either defender at his first turn to play, may require a restatement of the auction in its entirety.

After it is too late to have previous calls restated, declarer or either defender is entitled to be informed what the contract is and whether, but not by whom, it was doubled or redoubled.

Either defender may require an explanation of the partnership understanding relating to any call made by an opponent (see Proprieties 4), but only at that defender's own turn to play. Declarer may at any time require an explanation of the partnership understanding relating to any call or play made by a defender.

LAW 42. DUMMY'S RIGHTS

Dummy is entitled to give or obtain information as to fact or law; and provided he has not forfeited his rights (see Law 43) he may also:

    (a) question players regarding revokes as provided in Law 61;

    (b) try to prevent any irregularity,**

    (c) draw attention to any irregularity, but only after play is concluded.

LAW 43. DUMMY'S LIMITATIONS

Dummy may not participate in the play (except to play the cards of dummy's hand as directed by declarer), or make any comment on the bidding, play, or score of the current deal; and if he does so, Law 16 may apply. Dummy may not call attention to an irregularity during play except to try to prevent an irregularity before it occurs.

Dummy forfeits the rights provided in (a), (b) and (c) of Law 42 if he exchanges hands with declarer, leaves his seat to watch declarer play, or, on his own initiative, looks at the face of a card in either defender's hand; and if, thereafter,

    (a) He is the first to draw attention to a defender's irregularity, declarer may not enforce any penalty for the offense.

    (b) He warns declarer not to lead from the wrong hand, (penalty) either defender may choose the hand from which declarer shall lead.

    (c) He is the first to ask declarer if a play from declarer's hand constitutes a revoke, declarer must substitute a correct card if his play was a revoke, and the penalty provisions of Law 64 apply.

LAW 44. SEQUENCE AND PROCEDURE OF PLAY

The player who leads to a trick may play any card in his hand.*** After the lead, each other player in turn plays a card, and the four cards so played constitute a trick.

---

* After the final pass, either defender has the right to ask if it is his opening lead.
** He may, for example, warn declarer against leading from the wrong hand.
*** Unless he is subject to restriction after an irregularity committed by his side.

In playing to a trick, each player must follow suit if possible. This obligation takes precedence over all other requirements of these Laws. If unable to follow suit, a player may play any card.*

A trick containing a trump is won by the player who has contributed to it the highest trump. A trick that does not contain a trump is won by the player who has contributed to it the highest card of the suit led. The player who has won the trick leads to the next trick.

LAW 45. CARD PLAYED

Each player except dummy should play a card by detaching it from his hand and placing it, face up, on the table where other players can easily reach and see it. Dummy, if instructed by declarer to do so, may play from his hand a card named or designated by declarer.**

A card must be played:

(a) If it is a defender's card held so that it is possible for his partner to see its face.

(b) If it is a card from declarer's hand that declarer holds face up, touching or nearly touching the table, or maintains in such a position as to indicate that it has been played;

(c) If it is a card in dummy deliberately touched by declarer except for the purpose of arranging dummy's cards or of reaching a card above or below the card or cards touched.

(d) If the player who holds the card names or otherwise designates it as the card he proposes to play. A player may, without penalty, change an inadvertent designation if he does so without pause for thought; but if an opponent has, in turn, played a card that was legal before the change of designation, that opponent may, without penalty, withdraw any card so played and substitute another.

(e) If it is a penalty card, subject to Law 50.

(f) If it is a card in dummy's hand that dummy has illegally suggested as a play, unless either defender forbids the play of such card, or an equal of it, or a card of the same suit, as provided in Law 16.

A card played may not be withdrawn except as provided in Law 47.

LAW 46. PARTIAL DESIGNATION OF A CARD TO BE PLAYED FROM DUMMY'S HAND

When declarer instructs dummy to play a card from dummy's hand, as permitted by Law 45, but names only a suit or only the rank of a card, or the equivalent, without fully specifying the card to be played, declarer must complete his partial designation. Dummy must not play a card before declarer has completed his partial designation, and if dummy prematurely plays a card, Law 16 applies on that trick only, unless a defender has subsequently played.

LAW 47. RETRACTION OF A CARD PLAYED

(Club Law 47 on Page 153)

A card once played may be withdrawn only:

(a) to comply with a penalty, or to correct an illegal play, or to correct the simultaneous play of two or more cards (see Law 58);

(b) after a change of designation as permitted by Law 45 (d);

(c) after an opponent's change of play, to substitute a card for one played;***

---

* *Unless he is subject to restriction after an irregularity committed by his side.*

** *If dummy places in played position a card declarer did not name, the card must be withdrawn if attention is drawn to it before each side has played to the next trick, and a defender may withdraw (without penalty) a card played after the error but before attention was drawn to it (see Law 47).*

*** *The offending side must not base any subsequent plays on information gained from such a withdrawn play.*

(d) to correct a play* after misinformation by an opponent. A lead out of turn may be retracted without penalty if the leader was mistakenly informed by an opponent that it was his turn to lead.

Penalty Card

LAW 48. EXPOSURE OF DECLARER'S CARDS

Declarer is not subject to penalty for exposing a card, and no card of declarer's or dummy's ever becomes a penalty card. Declarer is not required to play any card dropped accidentally.

When declarer faces his cards after an opening lead out of turn, Law 54 applies.** When declarer faces his cards at any other time, he may be deemed to have made a claim or concession of tricks, in which case Law 68 applies.

LAW 49. EXPOSURE OF A DEFENDER'S CARDS

Whenever a defender faces a card on the table, holds a card so that it is possible for his partner to see its face, or names a card as being in his hand, before he is entitled to do so in the normal course of play or application of the law, (penalty) each such card becomes a penalty card (Law 50).***

LAW 50. DISPOSITION OF A PENALTY CARD

A card is a penalty card when prematurely exposed. It must be left face up on the table until it is played or until an alternate penalty has been selected.

A single card below the rank of an honor and exposed inadvertently (as in playing two cards to a trick, or in dropping a card accidentally) becomes a minor-penalty card. Any penalty card of honor rank, or any card exposed through deliberate play (as in leading out of turn, or in revoking and then correcting) becomes a major-penalty card; when one defender has two or more penalty cards, all such cards become major-penalty cards.

When a defender has a minor-penalty card, he may not play any other card of the same suit below the rank of an honor until he has first played the penalty card. (However, he is entitled to play an honor card instead of the minor-penalty card.) There is no further penalty, but the offender's partner must not base any subsequent play on information gained through seeing the penalty card.

When a defender has a major-penalty card, such card must be played at the first legal opportunity, whether in leading, following suit, discarding or trumping. If a defender has two or more penalty cards that can legally be played, declarer may designate which is to be played. The obligation to follow suit, or to comply with a lead or play penalty, takes precedence over the obligation to play a penalty card, but the penalty card must still be left face up on the table and played at the next legal opportunity.

When a defender has the lead while his partner has a major-penalty card, declarer may choose to impose a lead penalty at this point: he may require that defender to lead the suit of the penalty card, or may prohibit that defender from leading that suit (a prohibition continues for as long as he retains the lead). If declarer does impose a lead penalty, the penalty card is picked up at once. If declarer does not, the defender may lead any card; but the penalty card remains a penalty card. The defender may not lead until declarer has indicated his choice.

---

* The offending side must not base any subsequent plays on information gained from such a withdrawn play.
** Declarer should, as a matter of propriety, refrain from spreading his hand.
*** Exposure of a card or cards by a defender who is making a claim or concession of tricks is subject to Law 70.

LAW 51. TWO OR MORE PENALTY CARDS

When a defender has two or more penalty cards in one suit, and declarer requires the defender's partner to lead that suit, the defender may pick up every penalty card in that suit and may make any legal play to the trick.

When a defender has penalty cards in more than one suit, declarer may prohibit the defender's partner from leading every such suit; but the defender may then pick up every penalty card in every suit prohibited by declarer and may make any legal play to the trick.

LAW 52. FAILURE TO LEAD OR PLAY A PENALTY CARD

When a defender is required by Law 50 to play a penalty card, but instead plays another card, he must leave that illegally played card face up on the table; and

(a) declarer may accept the defender's lead or play, and declarer must accept such lead or play if he has thereafter played from his or dummy's hand, but the unplayed penalty card remains a penalty card; or

(b) declarer may require the defender to substitute the penalty card for the card illegally led or played. Every card illegally led or played by the defender in the course of committing the irregularity becomes a penalty card.

Lead Out of Turn

LAW 53. LEAD OUT OF TURN ACCEPTED

Any lead out of turn may be treated by an opponent as a correct lead. It becomes a correct lead if an opponent accepts it by making a statement to that effect, or if that opponent next to play plays a card to the irregular lead.*

However, the player whose proper turn it was to lead—unless he is the offender's partner—may make his proper lead subsequent to the infraction without his card being treated as played to the irregular lead. The proper lead stands, and all cards played in error to this trick may be withdrawn without penalty.

LAW 54. OPENING LEAD OUT OF TURN

When a defender makes the opening lead out of turn:

(a) Declarer may accept the irregular lead as provided in Law 53. Dummy's hand is spread in accordance with Law 41, and the second card to the trick is played from declarer's hand; but if declarer first plays to the trick from dummy's hand, dummy's card may not be withdrawn except to correct a revoke.

(b) Declarer must accept the irregular lead if he could have seen any of dummy's cards (except cards exposed during the auction, subject to Law 23). He is deemed to have accepted the irregular lead if he begins to spread his hand as though he were dummy** and in so doing exposes one or more cards; declarer must spread his entire hand, and dummy becomes declarer.***

(c) Declarer may require the defender to retract his irregular lead (except as provided in (b) above), and then Law 56 applies.

---

* *When such a play is made by a defender who is not next to play after the irregular lead, Law 57 applies.*

** *Declarer should, as a matter of propriety, refrain from spreading his hand intentionally.*

*** *However, if cards are so exposed from both declarer's and dummy's hands, the player who was regularly to become declarer remains declarer.*

LAW 55. DECLARER'S LEAD OUT OF TURN

When declarer leads out of turn from his or dummy's hand;
    (a) Either defender may accept that lead as provided in Law 53.
    (b) Either defender may require declarer to retract that lead. Then,
      (i) if it was a defender's turn to lead, declarer restores the card led in error to his or dummy's hand, without penalty;
      (ii) if declarer has led from the wrong hand when it was his turn to lead from his or dummy's hand, he withdraws the card led in error; he must lead a card from the correct hand, and, (penalty) if able to do so, a card of the same suit. Failure to observe this obligation in playing from his own hand is a revoke (see Law 64).

LAW 56. DEFENDER'S LEAD OUT OF TURN

When a defender leads out of turn:
    (a) Declarer may accept that lead as provided in Law 53.
    (b) Declarer may require the defender to retract that lead; the card illegally led becomes a major-penalty card (see Law 50—note that lead penalties are provided).

Irregular Leads and Plays

LAW 57. PREMATURE LEAD OR PLAY BY A DEFENDER

When a defender leads to the next trick before his partner has played to the current trick, or plays out of turn before his partner has played, (penalty) declarer may require the offender's partner to play:
    (a) his highest card of the suit led; or
    (b) his lowest card of the suit led; or
    (c) a legal card of another suit specified by declarer.

Declarer must select one of these options, and if the offender's partner cannot comply with the penalty selected he may play any card, as provided in Law 59.

When, as a result of the application of the penalty, the offender's partner wins the current trick, he leads to the next trick; and any card led or played out of turn by the other defender becomes a penalty card (Law 50).

A defender is not subject to penalty for playing before his partner if declarer has played from both hands; but a singleton or one of two or more equal cards in dummy is not considered automatically played unless dummy has played the card or has illegally suggested that it be played (Law 45 (f)).

LAW 58. SIMULTANEOUS LEADS OR PLAYS

A lead or play made simultaneously with another player's legal lead or play is deemed to be subsequent to it.

If a defender leads or plays two or more cards simultaneously, and if only one such card is visible, he must play that card; if more than one card is exposed, he must designate the card he proposes to play and each other card exposed becomes a penalty card (Law 50.)

If declarer leads or plays two or more cards simultaneously from either hand, he must designate the card he proposes to play and must restore any other card to the correct hand. If declarer withdraws a visible card and a defender has already played to that card, such defender may, without penalty, withdraw his card and substitute another.

If the error remains undiscovered until both sides have played to the next trick, Law 67 applies.

LAW 59. INABILITY TO LEAD OR PLAY AS REQUIRED

A player may play any correct card if he is unable to lead or play as required to comply with a penalty, either because he has no card of the required suit, or because he has only cards of a suit he is prohibited from leading, or because of his obligation to follow suit.

LAW 60. PLAY AFTER AN ILLEGAL PLAY

A play by a member of the non-offending side after the opponent on his right has led or played out of turn prematurely, and before a penalty has been imposed, forfeits the right to penalize the offense. The illegal play is treated as though it were legal, (except as provided in Law 53 for a play by the proper leader), unless it constitutes a revoke. If the offending side had a previous obligation to play a penalty card or to comply with a lead or play penalty, the obligation remains at future turns.

When a defender plays after declarer has been required to retract his lead out of turn from either hand, but before declarer has led from the correct hand, the defender's card becomes a penalty card (Law 50).

A play by a member of the offending side before a penalty has been imposed does not affect the rights of the opponents and may itself be subject to penalty.

The Revoke

LAW 61. FAILURE TO FOLLOW SUIT—INQUIRIES CONCERNING A REVOKE

Failure to follow suit in accordance with Law 44, or failure to lead or play, when able, a card or suit required by law or specified by an opponent in accordance with an agreed penalty, constitutes a revoke. Any player, including dummy,* may ask a player who has failed to follow suit whether he has a card of the suit led, and may demand that an opponent correct his revoke. (A claim of revoke does not warrant inspection of quitted tricks, except as permitted in Law 66.)

LAW 62. CORRECTION OF A REVOKE

A player must correct his revoke if he becomes aware of the occurrence of the revoke before it becomes established. To correct a revoke, the offender withdraws the card he played in revoking and follows suit with any card. A card so withdrawn becomes a penalty card (Law 50) if it was played from a defender's unfaced hand. The card may be replaced without penalty if it was played from declarer's or dummy's hand** or if it was a defender's faced card. Each member of the non-offending side may, without penalty, withdraw any card he may have played after the revoke but before attention was drawn to it. Except as provided in the next paragraph, the partner of the offender may not withdraw his card unless it too constituted a revoke.***

After the eleventh trick, a revoke, even if established, must be corrected if discovered before the cards have been mixed together. If the revoke was committed by a defender before his partner has played to the twelfth trick, and if offender's partner holds cards of more than one suit, (penalty) declarer may then require the offender's partner to play to that trick either of the two cards he could legally have played.

---

* *Unless he has forfeited his rights, as specified by Law 43.*
** *Subject to Law 43. A claim of revoke does not warrant inspection of quitted tricks except as permitted in Law 67.*
*** *In such case, the card withdrawn becomes a penalty card if it was played from a defender's unfaced hand.*

LAW 63. ESTABLISHMENT OF A REVOKE

A revoke becomes established when the offender or his partner leads or plays (whether legally or illegally) to the following trick, or names or otherwise designates a card to be so played, or makes a claim or concession of tricks orally or by facing his hand. The revoke may then no longer be corrected (except for a revoke after the eleventh trick—see Law 62), and the trick on which the revoke occurred stands as played.

LAW 64. PROCEDURE AFTER ESTABLISHMENT OF A REVOKE

(Club Law 64 on Page 153)

When a revoke has become established,

(a) if the trick on which the revoke occurred was won by the offending side, (penalty) after play ceases, the trick on which the revoke occurred plus one of any subsequent tricks won by the offending side are transferred* to the non-offending side (if no subsequent trick was won by the offending side, only the revoke trick is transferred).

(b) if the trick on which the revoke occurred was won by the non-offending side, (penalty) after play ceases, one of any subsequent tricks won by the offending side is transferred* to the non-offending side;

(c) there is no trick penalty for the established revoke if,

    (i) the offending side did not win either the trick on which the revoke occurred or any subsequent trick; or if,

    (ii) the revoke was a subsequent revoke in the same suit by the same player; or if,

    (iii) the revoke was made in failing to play any card faced on the table or belonging to a hand faced on the table, including a card from dummy's hand; or if,

    (iv) attention was first drawn to the revoke after all players had abandoned their hands and permitted the cards to be mixed together; or if,

    (v) the revoke was made after the eleventh trick.

N.B. When any established revoke, including one not subject to penalty, causes damage to the non-offending side insufficiently compensated by this law, the offending side should, under Proprieties 1, transfer additional tricks so as to restore equity.

Tricks

LAW 65. COLLECTION AND ARRANGEMENT OF TRICKS

The cards constituting each completed trick are collected by a member of the side that won the trick and are then turned face down on the table. Each trick should be identifiable as such, and all tricks taken by a side should be arranged in sequence in front of declarer or of one defender, as the case may be, in such manner that each side can determine the number of tricks it has won and the order in which they were taken.

LAW 66. INSPECTION OF TRICKS

Declarer or either defender may, until a member of his side has led or played to the following trick, inspect a trick and inquire what card each player has played to it. Thereafter, until play ceases, quitted tricks may be inspected only to account for a missing or surplus card. After play ceases, the tricks and unplayed cards may be inspected to settle a claim of a revoke, of honors, or of the number of tricks won or lost. If, after a claim has been made, a player on one side mixes the cards in such a way that the facts can no longer be ascertained, the issue must be decided in favor of the other side.

* For the scoring of transferred tricks, see Law 77.

LAW 67. TRICK EITHER APPROPRIATED IN ERROR OR DEFECTIVE

A trick appropriated by the wrong side must, upon demand, be restored to the side that has in fact won the trick by contributing the winning card to it. The scoring value of the trick must be credited to that side.*

A trick containing more or fewer than four cards is defective. When one player is found, during play, to have fewer or more cards than all the other players, the previous tricks should be forthwith examined, face down; if a defective trick is discovered, the player with a correspondingly incorrect number of cards is held responsible. The defective trick is inspected, face up, and—

(a) Unless all four hands have played to a subsequent trick, the defective trick is rectified as follows:

(i) If the offender has failed to play a card to the defective trick, he adds to that trick a card he can legally play:

(ii) If the offender has played more than one card to the defective trick, he withdraws all but one card, leaving a card he can legally play;

(iii) The non-offending side may, without penalty, withdraw any cards played after the irregularity and before attention was drawn to it; but the offending side may not withdraw cards that constitute legal plays, and any cards they withdraw may become penalty cards (Law 50).

(b) After all four hands have played to a subsequent trick, (penalty) the defective trick, if won by the offending side, is transferred to the non-offending side; and

(i) If the offender has failed to play a card to the defective trick, he forthwith faces and adds a card to that trick, if possible one he could legally have played to it.

(ii) If the offender has played more than one card to the defective trick, he withdraws all but one card, leaving the highest card he could legally have played to that trick. A withdrawn card may become a penalty card (Law 50); such a card is deemed to have belonged continuously to the offender's hand and failure to have played it to an earlier trick may constitute a revoke.

Claims and Concessions

LAW 68. DECLARER'S CLAIM OR CONCESSION OF TRICKS

Declarer makes a claim or a concession whenever he announces that he will win or lose one or more of the remaining tricks, or suggests that play may be curtailed, or faces his hand. Declarer should not make a claim or concession if there is any doubt as to the number of tricks to be won or lost.

LAW 69. PROCEDURE FOLLOWING DECLARER'S CLAIM OR CONCESSION

(Club Law 69 on Page 153)

When declarer has made a claim or concession, play is temporarily suspended and declarer must place and leave his hand face up on the table and forthwith make a comprehensive statement as to his proposed plan of play, including the order in which he will play the remaining cards.

Declarer's claim or concession is allowed, and the deal is scored accordingly, if both defenders agree to it. The claim or concession must be allowed if either defender has permitted any of his remaining cards to be mixed with another player's cards; otherwise, if either defender disputes declarer's claim or concession, it is not allowed. Then, play continues.

When his claim or concession is not allowed, declarer must play on, leaving his hand

* If calls have been made on a subsequent deal, see Law 78.

face up on the table. At any time, either defender may face his hand for inspection by his partner, and declarer may not impose a penalty for any irregularity committed by a defender whose hand is so faced.

The objective of subsequent play is to achieve a result as equitable as possible to both sides, but any doubtful point must be resolved in favor of the defenders. Declarer may not make any play inconsistent with the statement he may have made at the time of his claim or concession. And if he failed to make an appropriate statement at that time, his choice of plays is restricted thereby:

(a) If declarer made no relevant statement, he may not finesse* in any suit unless an opponent failed to follow in that suit before the claim or concession, or would subsequently fail to follow in that suit on any conceivable sequence of plays.

(b) If declarer may have been unaware, at the time of his claim or concession, that a trump remained in a defender's hand, either defender may require him to draw, or not to draw, the outstanding trump.

(c) If declarer did not, in his statement, mention an unusual plan of play, he may adopt only a routine line of play.

If declarer attempts to make a play prohibited under this law, either defender may accept the play, or, provided neither defender has subsequently played, require declarer to withdraw the card so played and substitute another that conforms to his obligations.

LAW 70. DEFENDER'S CLAIM OR CONCESSION OF TRICKS
(Club Law 70 on Page 153)

A defender makes a concession when he agrees to declarer's claim, or when he announces that he will lose one or more of the remaining tricks.

A defender makes a claim when he announces that he will win one or more of the remaining tricks, or when he shows any or all of his cards for this purpose. If:

(a) the claim pertains only to an uncompleted trick currently in progress, play proceeds normally; cards exposed or otherwise revealed by the defender in making his claim do not become penalty cards, but Law 16, Unauthorized Information, may apply to claimer's partner.

(b) the claim pertains to subsequent tricks, play is temporarily suspended; the claimer must place and leave his hand face up on the table and make a comprehensive statement as to his proposed plan of defense. The claim is allowed, and the deal scored accordingly, if declarer agrees to it. If declarer disputes the claim, the defenders must play on with the claimer's hand face up on the table. Those cards do not become penalty cards. However, declarer may prohibit claimer's partner, under Law 16, from making any play that could be suggested to him by seeing the faced cards.

LAW 71. CONCESSION WITHDRAWN

A concession may be withdrawn:

(a) If a player concedes a trick his side has, in fact, won; or if declarer concedes defeat of a contract he has already fulfilled; or if a defender concedes fulfillment of a contract his side has already defeated. (If the score has been entered, see Law 78).

(b) If a trick that has been conceded cannot be lost by any probable sequence of play of the remaining cards, and if attention is drawn to that fact before the cards have been mixed together.

(c) If a defender concedes one or more tricks and his partner immediately objects, but Law 16 may apply.

For these purposes, a finesse is a play the success of which depends on finding one defender rather than the other with or without a particular card.

Part VII

The Score

LAW 72. POINTS EARNED

The result of each deal played is recorded in points, which fall into two classes:

1. *Trick Points.* Only declarer's side can earn trick points, and only by winning at least the number of odd tricks specified in the contract. Only the value of odd tricks named in the contract may be scored as trick points (see Law 81). Trick points mark the progression of the rubber toward its completion.

2. *Premium Points.* Either side or both sides may earn premium points. Declarer's side earns premium points by winning one or more overtricks; by fulfilling a doubled or redoubled contract; by bidding and making a slam; by holding scorable honors in declarer's or dummy's hand; or by winning the final game of a rubber.* The defenders earn premium points by defeating the contract (undertrick penalty) or by holding scorable honors in either of their hands (see Law 81).

Each side's premium points are added to its trick points at the conclusion of the rubber.

LAW 73. PARTSCORE—GAME

The basic units of trick scores are partscore and game. A partscore is recorded for declarer's side whenever declarer fulfills a contract for which the trick score is less than 100 points. Game is won by that side which is the first to have scored 100 or more trick points either in a single deal or by addition of two or more partscores made separately. No partscore made by either side in the course of one game is carried forward into the next game.

LAW 74. THE RUBBER

A rubber ends when a side has won two games. At the conclusion of the rubber, the winners of two games are credited with a premium score of 500 points if the other side has won one game, or with 700 points if the other side has not won a game. The trick and premium points scored by each side in the course of the rubber are then added. The side with the larger combined total wins the rubber, and the difference between the two totals represents the margin of victory computed in points.

LAW 75. METHOD OF SCORING

The score of each deal must be recorded, and it is preferable that a member of each side should keep score.

Scores are entered in two adjacent columns separated by a vertical line. Each scorer enters points earned by his side in the left-hand column, and points earned by his opponents in the right-hand column.

Each side has a trick score and a premium score, separated by a horizontal line intersecting the vertical line. All trick points are entered, as they are earned, in descending order below the horizontal line, all premium points in ascending order above that line.

Whenever a game is won, another horizontal line is drawn under all trick scores recorded for either side, in order to mark completion of the game. Subsequent trick scores are entered below that line.

* *For incomplete rubber, see Law 80.*

LAW 76. RESPONSIBILITY FOR THE SCORE

When the play of a deal is completed, all four players are equally responsible for ascertaining that the number of tricks won by each side is correctly determined and that all scores are promptly and correctly entered.

LAW 77. TRANSFERRED TRICKS

A trick transferred though a revoke penalty is reckoned for all scoring purposes as though it had been won in play by the side to which it had been awarded.*

LAW 78. CORRECTION OF THE SCORE

When it is acknowledged by a majority of the players that a scoring error was made in recording an agreed-upon result (e.g., failure to enter honors, or incorrect computation of score), the error must be corrected if discovered before the net score of the rubber has been agreed to. However, except with the consent of all four players, an erroneous agreement as to the number of tricks won by each side may not be corrected after all players have called on the next deal.

In case of disagreement between two scores kept, the recollection of the majority of the players as to the facts governs.

LAW 79. DEALS PLAYED WITH AN INCORRECT PACK

Scores recorded for deals played with an incorrect pack are not subject to change by reason of the discovery of the imperfection after the cards have been mixed together.

LAW 80. INCOMPLETE RUBBER

When, for any reason, a rubber is not finished, the score is computed as follows:

If only one game has been completed, the winners of that game are credited with 300 points; if only one side has a partscore or scores in a game not completed, that side is credited with 50 points; the trick and premium points of each side are then added, and the side with the greater number of points wins the difference between the two totals.

LAW 81. SCORING TABLE

TRICK SCORE

Scored below the line by declarer's side, if contract is fulfilled:

IF TRUMPS ARE

	♣	◇	♡	♠
For each trick over six, bid and made				
Undoubled	20	20	30	30
Doubled	40	40	60	60
Redoubled	80	80	120	120

AT A NOTRUMP CONTRACT

	Undoubled	Doubled	Redoubled
For the first trick over six, bid and made	40	80	160
For each additional trick over six, bid and made	30	60	120

*Declarer plays in **3♡** and makes eight tricks. A revoke by a defender is found to have been established, with the defenders having won both the trick in which the revoke occurred and a later trick. Two tricks are transferred from the defenders to declarer, who therefore has ten tricks. Since he bid only **3♡**, he scores 90 trick points, which count toward game, and 30 premium points for the overtrick.*

The first side to score 100 points below the line, in one or more hands, wins a GAME. When a game is won, both sides start without trick score toward the next game. First side to win two games wins the RUBBER POINTS.

PREMIUM SCORE
Scored above the line by declarer's side.
RUBBER, GAME, PARTSCORE, CONTRACT FULFILLED

For winning the RUBBER, if opponents have won no game	700
For winning the RUBBER, if opponents have won one game	500
UNFINISHED RUBBER—for having won the only game	300
For having the only PART SCORE in an unfinished game	50
For making any DOUBLED or REDOUBLED CONTRACT	50

SLAMS

	Not Vulnerable	Vulnerable
For making a SLAM		
Small Slam (12 Tricks), bid and made	500	750
Grand Slam (all 13 tricks), bid and made	1000	1500

OVERTRICKS

For each OVERTRICK (tricks made in excess of contract)	Not Vulnerable	Vulnerable
Undoubled	Trick Value	Trick Value
Doubled	100	200
Redoubled	200	400

HONORS
Scored above the line by either side:

For holding four of the five trump HONORS
(**A**, **K**, **Q**, **J**, **10**) in one hand 100
For holding all five trump HONORS (**A**, **K**, **Q**, **J**, **10**) in one hand 150
For holding all four ACES in one hand at a notrump contract 150

UNDERTRICK PENALTIES
Tricks by which declarer fails to fulfill the contract; scored
above the line by declarer's opponents, if contract is not fulfilled.

	Not Vulnerable		
	Undoubled	Doubled	Redoubled
For first undertrick	50	100	200
For each additional undertrick	50	200	400
		Vulnerable	
	Undoubled	Doubled	Redoubled
For first undertrick	100	200	400
For each additional undertrick	100	300	600

Part VIII

Alternative Club Laws

When bridge is played at a club, it is often practicable to designate an impartial and experienced person as "Arbiter" for the game. The Arbiter interprets and applies the Laws after an irregularity occurs, and generally assumes the role assigned to the "Director" in duplicate bridge. When such an Arbiter is available, certain laws can be modified so as to produce greater equity.

The "Club Laws" prescribe a somewhat different procedure after attention is drawn to an irregularity, and there is a different disposition for disputed claims. The principal changes, however, lie in the authority given to the Arbiter, after specified types of irregularity, to "adjust the score" of a deal once play is over. In adjusting a score, the Arbiter assigns a new result, the result he judges would likely have been achieved had the irregularity not occurred. The Arbiter should resolve any substantial doubt in favor of the non-offending side.

The alternative laws are in force only upon advance agreement by the players, or in accordance with the standing and published policy of a club. Any game may play under these Club Laws, so long as an Arbiter is nominated in advance; when there are more than four members of a table, a non-playing member can act as Arbiter.

CLUB LAW 13

The Arbiter must be called as soon as attention is drawn to an irregularity. Calling the Arbiter does not forfeit any rights to which a player may otherwise be entitled. Any player except dummy may draw attention to an irregularity and call the Arbiter. The fact that a player draws attention to an irregularity committed by his side does not affect the rights of the opponents.

After attention has been drawn to an irregularity, no player should call or play until the Arbiter has determined all matters in regard to rectification and to the assessment of a penalty. Premature correction of an irregularity on the part of an offender may subject him to further penalty.

CLUB LAW 14

The Arbiter assesses penalties when applicable. When these Club Laws provide an option among penalties, the Arbiter explains the options available.

The Arbiter may assign an adjusted score, but only when these Club Laws empower him to do so, or when the Law provides no indemnity to a non-offending contestant for the particular type of violation of law or propriety committed by an opponent. He may not assign an adjusted score on the ground that the penalty provided in the Law is unduly severe or unduly advantageous to either side.

CLUB LAW 16

If a player conveys information to his partner by means of a remark or question, or by an unmistakable hesitation, special emphasis, tone, gesture, movement, mannerism or any other action that suggests a call, lead or plan of play; and if attention is drawn to the offense and the Arbiter is called, the Arbiter should require that the auction or play continue, reserving the right to assign an adjusted score if he considers that the result could have been affected by the illegal information.

After play ends, he should award an adjusted score to redress damage caused to the innocent side, when an opponent chose from among alternative logical actions one that could reasonably have been suggested by his partner's tempo, manner, remark, etc.

CLUB LAW 23

(Regular Law 23 stands intact but with the following addition, which applies as well to a change of call, an insufficient bid, a call out of rotation and an inadmissible call.)

When the penalty for an irregularity, under this or any other Law, would compel the offender's partner to pass at his next turn, and when the Arbiter deems that this enforced pass will necessarily* damage the innocent side, the Arbiter may reserve the right to assign an adjusted score.

CLUB LAW 25

The penalties in Club Law 23 apply.

CLUB LAW 26

Regular Law 26 stands intact, but with the following additions as sub-section (c).

(c) If the changed call related, by convention, to a denomination other than one named in the call, it is the particular denomination to which the conventional call relates, rather than the one actually mentioned, that determines which subsection the Arbiter will apply—(a) or (b)—as well as the suit to which he will apply sub-section (a).

CLUB LAW 27

Regular Law 27 stands intact but with the following addition to sub-section (a).

If the insufficient bid conveyed such substantial information as to damage the non-offending side, the Arbiter may assign an adjusted score.

CLUB LAW 30

The provisions of Club Law 23 may apply.

CLUB LAW 31

The provisions of Club Law 23 may apply.

CLUB LAW 32

The provisions of Club Law 23 may apply.

CLUB LAW 35

The provisions of Club Law 23 may apply.

CLUB LAW 36

The provisions of Club Law 23 may apply.

CLUB LAW 38

The provisions of Club Law 23 may apply.

CLUB LAW 39

The provisions of Club Law 23 may apply.

---

* *The score should not be adjusted merely because the penalty happened to result in good fortune for the offending side. The word "necessarily" restricts score adjustment to those instances in which the offender could have known, at the time of his infraction, that it would be to his advantage to require partner to pass.*

CLUB LAW 40

If the Arbiter decides that a side has been damaged through its opponents' failure to explain the meaning of a call or play, he may award an adjusted score.

CLUB LAW 47

If a card retracted under sections (c) or (d) above gave substantial information to an opponent, the Arbiter may award an adjusted score.

CLUB LAW 64

Regular Law 64 stands, except that, when after any established revoke, including those not subject to penalty, the Arbiter deems that the non-offending side is insufficiently compensated by this Law for the damage caused, he should assign an adjusted score.

CLUB LAW 69

When declarer has made a claim or concession, play ceases (all play subsequent to a claim or concession must be voided by the Arbiter). Declarer must place and leave his hand face up on the table and forthwith make a comprehensive statement as to his proposed plan of play, including the order in which he will play his remaining cards.

Declarer's claim or concession is allowed, and the deal is scored accordingly, if both defenders agree to it. The claim or concession must be allowed if either defender has permitted any of his remaining cards to be mixed with another player's cards; otherwise, if either defender disputes declarer's claim or concession, the Arbiter must be called to adjudicate the result of the deal.

The Arbiter should adjudicate the result of the deal as equitably as possible to both sides, but any doubtful point should be resolved in favor of the defenders. He should proceed as follows:

(a) He should require the declarer to repeat the statement he made at the time of his claim. The Arbiter should then require all players to put their cards face up on the table and should hear the defenders' objections to the claim.

(b) When a trump is outstanding, he should award a trick to the defenders if
   (i) in making his claim declarer made no statement about that trump, and
   (ii) it is at all likely that declarer was unaware, at the time of his claim, that a trump remained in a defender's hand, and
   (iii) a trick could be lost to that trump by any normal play (an inferior or careless play can be normal, but not an irrational play).

(c) He should not accept from declarer any proposed line of play inconsistent with his statement. If declarer did not make an appropriate announcement at the time of his original claim, the Arbiter should not accept from declarer any unusual line of play, or any proposed play that requires a finesse* in a suit, unless an opponent failed to follow in that suit before the claim or concession, or would subsequently fail to follow in that suit on any conceivable line of play.

CLUB LAW 70

A defender makes a concession when he agrees to declarer's claim or when he announces that he will lose one or more of the remaining tricks.

A defender makes a claim when he announces that he will win one or more of the remaining tricks, or when he shows any or all of his cards to declarer for this purpose. If

(a) the claim pertains only to an uncompleted trick currently in progress, play proceeds normally; cards exposed or otherwise revealed by the defender in making his claim do not

---

* For these purposes, a finesse is a play the success of which depends on finding one defender rather than the other with or without a particular card.

become penalty cards, but Club Law 16, Unauthorized Information, may apply to claimer's partner.

(b) the claim pertains to subsequent tricks, play ceases (all play subsequent to the claim should be voided by the Arbiter). The defender must place and leave his hand face up on the table and make a comprehensive statement as to his proposed plan of defense. The claim is allowed, and the deal scored accordingly, if declarer agrees to it. If declarer disputes the claim, the Arbiter must be called to adjudicate the result of the deal. He does so as equitably as possible to both sides, but should award to the declarer any trick that the defenders could lose by normal play (an inferior or careless play can be normal, but not an irrational play).

CLUB APPEALS COMMITTEE

Whenever possible, a club should establish an Appeals Committee to review decisions of the Arbiter; and any game may designate a Committee to which appeals may be taken. If such a procedure has been agreed to or published in advance, any player may appeal any decision by the Arbiter. The Appeals Committee exercises all powers assigned by these Laws to the Arbiter, and may overrule any of his decisions.

When an Arbiter's decision is overruled on appeal, only the scoring of the particular deal is affected; subsequent scores stand as recorded. If the Committee's decision results in fulfillment of a contract originally recorded as defeated, or defeat of a contract recorded as fulfilled, then,

(a) for a contract now fulfilled: in addition to the other trick score and premium score, declarer's side received a premium of 50 points for a partscore that would not then have increased the below-the-line score to 100; and for any other contract, declarer's side received a premium according to vulnerability—300 points if declarer's side was non-vulnerable, 400 points if declarer was vulnerable and the defenders not, 500 points if both sides were vulnerable.

(b) for a contract now defeated, when the original scoring resulted in a game: in addition to the other premium score, the defenders receive a premium of 50 points if they alone had scored a partscore in that game; plus a premium of 500 points if declarer's side originally won two of two games, or 200 points if the defenders side originally won two of three games.

Proprieties

1. GENERAL PRINCIPLES

These Laws cannot cover every situation that might arise, nor can they produce equity in every situation covered. Occasionally, the players themselves must redress damage. The guiding principle: The side that commits an irregularity bears an obligation not to gain directly from the infraction itself; however, the offending side is entitled to profit after an infraction, as an indirect result, through subsequent good fortune.*

* *Two examples may clarify the distinction between direct gain through an infraction and indirect gain through good luck.*

(a) South, declarer at 3 NT, will have nine tricks available if the diamond suit—ace-king-queen-sixth in dummy opposite declarer's singleton—divides favorably; and the six missing diamonds are in fact split evenly, three-three, between East and West. However, West, who holds jack-third, shows out on the third round of diamonds, revoking. Thus, declarer wins only three diamond tricks instead of six, for a total of six tricks instead of nine. The established revoke is later discovered, so one penalty trick is transferred after play ends. But declarer is still down two.

Here, East-West gained two tricks as a direct consequence of their infraction. The players should adjudicate this result, scoring the deal as 3 NT making three.

To infringe a law of propriety intentionally is a serious breach of ethics, even if there is a prescribed penalty that one is willing to pay. The offense may be the more serious when no penalty is prescribed.

There is no obligation to draw attention to an inadvertent infraction of law committed by one's own side. However, a player should not attempt to conceal such an infraction, as by committing a second revoke, concealing a card involved in a revoke or mixing the cards prematurely.

It is proper to warn partner against infringing a law of the game: for example against revoking, or against calling, leading or playing out of turn.

2. COMMUNICATION BETWEEN PARTNERS

Communication between partners during the auction and play should be effected only by means of the calls and plays themselves, not through the manner in which they are made, nor through extraneous remarks and gestures, nor through questions asked of the opponents and explanations given to them. Calls should be made in a uniform tone without special emphasis or inflection, and without undue hesitation or haste. Plays should be made without emphasis, gesture or mannerism and so far as possible at a uniform rate.

Inadvertently to vary the tempo or manner in which a call or play is made does not in itself constitute a violation of propriety, but inferences from such variation may properly be drawn only by an opponent, and at his own risk. It is improper to attempt to mislead an opponent by means of a remark or a gesture, through the haste or hesitancy of a call or play (such as hesitation with a singleton) or by the manner in which the call or play is made.

Any player may properly attempt to deceive an opponent through a call or play (so long as the deception is not protected by concealed partnership understanding). It is entirely proper to avoid giving information to the opponents by making all calls and plays in unvarying tempo and manner.

When a player has available to him improper information from his partner's remark, question, explanation, gesture, mannerism, special emphasis, inflection, haste or hesitation, he should carefully avoid taking any advantage that might accrue to his side.

3. CONDUCT AND ETIQUETTE

A player should maintain at all times a courteous attitude toward his partner and opponents. He should carefully avoid any remark or action that might cause annoyance or embarrassment to another player or might interfere with the enjoyment of the game. Every player should follow uniform and correct procedure in calling and playing, since any departure from correct standards may disrupt the orderly progress of the game.

(Note, declarer is not given a penalty trick in addition; the object is to restore equity, to restore the result likely to have occurred had the infraction not been committed.)

(b) South, declarer at **4♠**, *is entitled to require or forbid a diamond opening lead from West, because of the auction-period infraction committed by East. Declarer instructs West to lead a diamond—but West, having no diamonds, leads another suit. East, now aware that partner is void in diamonds, is able to find what would be, under normal circumstances, a most unnatural line of defense to give West two ruffs. Thereby, East-West defeat a contract that would almost certainly have been made but for the infraction.*

Here, East-West profited only indirectly through their auction-period infraction; their gain was the direct consequence of declarer's decision to require a diamond lead, and of West's lucky void. So, the players should allow the result to stand. Declarer was damaged not by the infraction itself, but by bad luck afterwards—and luck is part of the game of bridge.

As a matter of courtesy, a player should refrain from:

(i) Paying insufficient attention to the game (as when a player obviously takes no interest in his hand, or frequently requests a review of the auction).

(ii) Making gratuitous comments during the play as to the auction or the adequacy of the contract.

(iii) Detaching a card from his hand before it is his turn to lead or play.

(iv) Arranging completed tricks in a disorderly manner, thereby making it difficult to determine the sequence of plays.

(v) Making a claim or concession of tricks if there is any doubt as to the outcome of the deal.

(vi) Prolonging play unnecessarily for the purpose of disconcerting the other players.

Furthermore, the following are considered breaches of propriety:

(a) Using different designations for the same call.

(b) Indicating approval or disapproval of a call or play.

(c) Indicating the expectation or intention of winning or losing a trick that has not been completed.

(d) Commenting or behaving during the auction or play so as to call attention to a significant occurrence, or to the state of the score or to the number of tricks still required for success.

(e) Volunteering information that should be given only in response to a question.

(f) Looking intently at any other player during the auction or play, or at another player's hand as for the purpose of seeing his cards or of observing the place from which he draws a card (but it is not improper to act on information acquired by inadvertently seeing an opponent's card).

(g) Varying the normal tempo of bidding or play for the purpose of disconcerting another player.

(h) Mixing the cards before the result of a deal has been agreed upon.

4. PARTNERSHIP AGREEMENTS

It is improper to convey information by means of a call or play based on special partnership agreement, whether explicit or implicit, unless such information is fully and freely available to the opponents.

It is not improper for a player to violate an announced partnership agreement, so long as his partner is unaware of the violation (but habitual violations within a partnership may create implicit agreements, which must be disclosed). No player has the obligation to disclose to the opponents that he has violated an announced agreement; and if the opponents are subsequently damaged, as through drawing a false inference from such violation, they are not entitled to redress.

When explaining the significance of partner's call or play in reply to an opponent's inquiry, a player should disclose all special information conveyed to him through partnership agreement or partnership experience; but he need not disclose inferences drawn from his general bridge knowledge and experience. It is improper for a player whose partner has given a mistaken explanation to correct the error immediately or to indicate in any manner that a mistake has been made. (He must not take advantage of the unauthorized information so obtained).

5. SPECTATORS

A spectator, including a member of the table not playing, must not display any reaction to bidding or play while a hand is in progress (as by shifting his attention from one player's hand to another's). He must not in any way disturb a player. During the hand, he must refrain from mannerisms or remarks of any kind (including conversation with a player). He may not call attention to any irregularity or mistake, nor speak on any question of fact or law except by request of the players.

Rules for Club Procedure

The following rules, governing membership in new and existing tables, have proven satisfactory in club use over a long period of years.

A. DEFINITIONS

Member—An applicant who has acquired the right to play at a table either immediately or in his turn.

Complete Table—A table with six members.

Incomplete Table—A table with four or five members.

Cut In—Assert the right to become a member of an incomplete table, or to become a member of a complete table at such time as it may become incomplete.

B. TIME LIMIT ON RIGHT TO PLAY

An applicant may not play in a rubber unless he has become a member of a table before a card is duly drawn for the selection of players or partners.

C. NEWLY FORMED TABLES

Four to six applicants may form a table. If there are more than six applicants, the six highest-ranking ones become members. The four highest-ranking members play the first rubber. Those who have not played, ranked in their order of entry into the room, take precedence over those who have played; the latter rank equally, except that players leaving existing tables to join the new table rank lowest. Precedence between those of equal rank is determined by drawing cards, the player who draws the higher-ranking card having precedence.

D. CUTTING IN

An application establishes membership in a table either forthwith or (if the table is complete) as soon as a vacancy occurs, unless applications in excess of the number required to complete a table are made at the same time, in which case precedence between applicants is established by drawing cards, as provided in the preceding rule.

E. GOING OUT

After each rubber place must be made for any member who did not play that last rubber, by the member who has played the greatest number of consecutive rubbers at that table. Cards are drawn for precedence if necessary. A member who has left another existing table must draw cards, for his first rubber, with the member who would otherwise have played. A player who breaks up a game by leaving three players at a table may not compete against them for entry at another table until each of them has played at least one rubber.

F. MEMBERSHIP LIMITED TO ONE TABLE

No one can be a member of more than one table at the same time, unless a member consents, on request, to make a fourth at another table and announces his intention of returning to his former table as soon as his place at the new table can be filled. Failure to announce such intention results in loss of membership at his former table.

FOUR-DEAL BRIDGE

Four-Deal Bridge is a form of Rubber Bridge much played in clubs and well suited to home play. Long rubbers are avoided; extra players need wait no longer than the time (about twenty minutes) required to complete four deals. The game is also called Club Bridge or Chicago (for the city in which it originated).

A. BASIC RULES

The Laws of Contract Bridge and Rules for Club Procedure are followed, except as modified by the following rules.

B. THE RUBBER

A rubber consists of a series of four deals that have been bid and played. If a deal is passed out, the same player deals again and the deal passed out does not count as one of the four deals.

A fifth deal is void if attention is drawn to it at any time before there has been a new cut for partners or the game has terminated; if the error is not discovered in time for correction, the score stands as recorded. A sixth or subsequent deal is unconditionally void and no score for such a deal is ever permissible.

In case fewer than four deals are played, the score shall stand for the incomplete series and the fourth deal need not be played unless attention is drawn to the error before there has been a new cut for partners or the game has terminated.

When the players are pivoting,* the fact that the players have taken their proper seats for the next rubber shall be considered a cut for partners.

C. VULNERABILITY

Vulnerability is not determined by previous scores but by the following schedule:

First deal: Neither side vulnerable.

Second and Third deals: Dealer's side vulnerable, the other side not vulnerable.

Fourth deal: Both sides vulnerable.

D. PREMIUMS

For making or completing a game (100 or more trick points) a side receives a premium of 300 points if on that deal it is not vulnerable or 500 points if on that deal it is vulnerable. There is no additional premium for winning two or more games, each game premium being scored separately.

E. THE SCORE

As a reminder of vulnerability in Four-Deal Bridge, two intersecting diagonal lines should lines should be drawn near the top of the score pad, as follows:

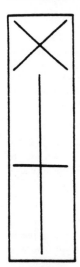

The numeral "1" should be inserted in that one of the four angles thus formed that faces the first dealer. After play of the first deal is completed, "2" is inserted in the next angle in clockwise rotation, facing the dealer of the second deal. The numerals "3" and "4" are subsequently inserted at the start of the third and fourth deals, respectively, each in the angle facing the current dealer.

A correctly numbered diagram is conclusive as to vulnerability. There is no redress for a bid influenced by the scorer's failure to draw the diagram or for an error or omission in inserting a numeral or numerals in the diagram. Such error or omission should, upon discovery be immediately corrected and the deal or deals should be scored or rescored as though the diagram and the number or numbers thereon had been properly inserted.

F. PARTSCORES

A partscore or scores made previously may be combined with a partscore made in the current deal to complete a game of 100 or more trick points. The game premium is determined by the vulnerability, on that deal, of the side that completes the game. When a side makes or completes a game, no previous partscore of either side may thereafter be counted toward game.

A side that makes a partscore in the fourth deal, if the partscore is not sufficient to complete a game, receives a premium of 100 points. This premium is scored whether or not the same side or the other side

Four-Deal Bridge Scoring

* *In a pivot game, partnerships for each rubber follow a fixed rotation.*

has an uncompleted partscore. There is no separate premium for making a partscore in any other circumstance.

G. DEAL OUT OF TURN

When a player deals out of turn, and there is no right to a redeal, the player who should have dealt retains his right to call first, but such right is lost if it is not claimed before the actual dealer calls. If the actual dealer calls before attention is drawn to the deal out of turn, each player thereafter calls in rotation. Vulnerability and scoring values are determined by the position of the player who should have dealt, regardless of which players actually dealt or called first. Neither the rotation of the deal nor the scoring is affected by a deal out of turn. The next dealer is the player who would have dealt next if the deal had been in turn.

H. OPTIONAL RULES AND CUSTOMS

The following practices, not required, have proved acceptable in some clubs and games.

(i) Since the essence of the game is speed, if a deal is passed out, the pack that has been shuffled for the next deal should be used by the same dealer.

(ii) The net score of a rubber should be translated into even hundreds (according to American custom) by crediting as 100 points any fraction thereof amounting to 50 or more points: e.g., 750 points count as 800; 740 points count as 700 points.

(iii) No two players may play a second consecutive rubber as partners at the same table. If two players draw each other again, the player who has drawn the highest card should play with the player who has drawn the third-highest, against the other two players.

(iv) To avoid confusion as to how many deals have been played: Each deal should be scored, even if there is no net advantage to either side (for example, when one side is entitled to 100 points for undertrick penalties and the other side is entitled to 100 points for honors). In a result that completes a game, premiums for overtricks, game, slam, or making a doubled contract should be combined with the trick score to produce one total, which is entered below the line (for example, if a side makes **2♠** doubled and vulnerable with an overtrick, 870 should be scored below the line, not 120 below the line and 50, 500, and 200 above the line).

DUPLICATE TOURNAMENT BRIDGE

If two pairs play a set game against each other, the outcome in a given session is determined to a certain degree by the chance distribution of aces and kings. The stronger partnership will, of course, win out in the long run. But if those same two pairs are given identical hands to play in a series of deals, their scores are likely to indicate something of their relative skill on a more consistent basis. The essential feature of duplicate pairs competition is the elimination of the luck of the deal by allowing contestants to play the same hands. Thus, whether the cards are "good" or "bad," all competitors have the same opportunity to outscore the other pairs through accurate bidding and skillful play.

During the Culbertson years in the 1930s and 1940s home games or social rubber, or contract bridge parties were very popular, especially in the United States. When Goren assumed the position of leading bridge authority, however, interest in tournament competition increased tremendously, due in part to the example Goren set as a winner of many championships who rarely played rubber bridge. From a few thousand members in the mid-1940s, membership in the American Contract Bridge League, the governing body for both contract and duplicate contract bridge in North America and Bermuda, grew to almost 200,000 by the early 1970s, and has remained at that level ever since.

EQUIPMENT

The *duplicate board* is a device for holding intact the four hands of a deal. The standard board is a plastic or aluminum tray about 9 inches long and 4 inches wide with a pocket opening from each side. On the upper face is stamped the direction of the four hands with an arrow pointing toward the North position. Above one pocket the word DEALER is stamped, and there is also a designation of the vulnerability. The letters VUL appear above the pocket of each side that is vulnerable and the bottom of the pocket itself is colored red.

A set of duplicate boards usually consists of 32 or 36 boards, and the designations on boards 1 to 16 are as follows:

Board Number	Dealer	Vulnerability
1	North	Neither side
2	East	North-South
3	South	East-West

Board Number	Dealer	Vulnerability
4	West	Both sides
5	North	North-South
6	East	East-West
7	South	Both sides
8	West	Neither side
9	North	East-West
10	East	Both sides
11	South	Neither side
12	West	North-South
13	North	Both sides
14	East	Neither side
15	South	North-South
16	West	East-West

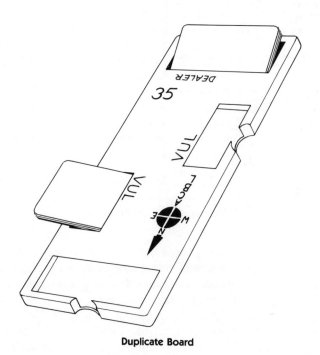

Duplicate Board

Boards 17 to 32 are marked respectively the same as 1 to 16, as are higher-numbered boards. The number of deals played by a pair over the course of a session varies widely. In club games it could be as few as 20 to 24; in championship tournaments 26 boards is standard for pair contests and up to 33 for team events.

Each board has its own pack of 52 cards, distributed in the four pockets before the boards are given out for play, although when fresh cards are

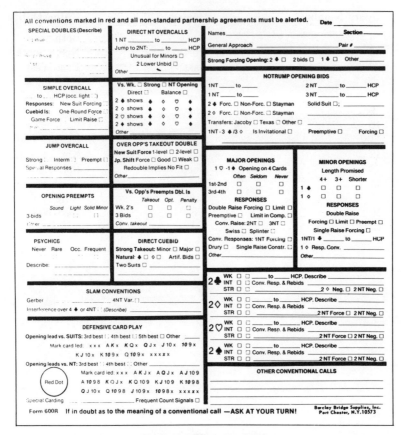

Convention Card—front side

needed, empty boards will be passed out along with new packs of cards. Before the start of a session it is customary to face the top card in the North hand to indicate that the deal has not been prepared for play.

In duplicate bridge all players have the right to know the meaning of non-standard bids or plays made by their opponents. To facilitate the exchange of information, pairs are required to fill out a *convention card*, which will then be available for inspection by the opponents. On the front face of the convention card is a list of the most generally played conventions, which can be checked off. Space is provided to write in any special bidding agreements a pair may have. There is also a section for defensive card play. If a pair is using non-standard opening leads or signals, they must describe their carding agreements as clearly as possible and attach a red dot in the indicated circle.

On the reverse side of the convention card is usually a list of boards 1 to 32 plus four blank spaces if higher number of boards are played, and

Comparison of scores or discussion of hands with other contestants during a session is ILLEGAL and a violation carries an AUTOMATIC PENALTY of a FULL BOARD of the session at which the infraction occurs. REPEATED VIOLATIONS MAY LEAD TO SUSPENSION.

Dir.	Vul.	Bd. No.	vs.	Contract & Declarer	Plus	Minus	Pts. Est.	Pts.	Bd. No.	Dir.	Vul.	Bd. No.	vs.	Contract & Declarer	Plus	Minus	Pts. Est.	Pts.	Bd. No.
N	None	1							33	N	None	17							49
E	N-S	2							34	E	N-S	18							50
S	E-W	3							35	S	E-W	19							51
W	Both	4							36	W	Both	20							52
N	N-S	5							37	N	N-S	21							53
E	E-W	6							38	E	E-W	22							54
S	Both	7							39	S	Both	23							55
W	None	8							40	W	None	24							56
N	E-W	9							41	N	E-W	25							57
E	Both	10							42	E	Both	26							58
S	None	11							43	S	None	27							59
W	N-S	12							44	W	N-S	28							60
N	Both	13							45	N	Both	29							61
E	None	14							46	E	None	30							62
S	N-S	15							47	S	N-S	31							63
W	E-W	16							48	W	E-W	32							64

INTERNATIONAL MATCH POINT SCALE

Diff. In Pts.	I.M.P.	Diff. In Pts.	I.M.P.	Diff. In Pts.	I.M.P.
20- 40	1	370- 420	9	1500-1740	17
50- 80	2	430- 490	10	1750-1990	18
90- 120	3	500- 590	11	2000-2240	19
130- 160	4	600- 740	12	2250-2490	20
170- 210	5	750- 890	13	2500-2990	21
220- 260	6	900-1090	14	3000-3490	22
270- 310	7	1100-1290	15	3500-3990	23
320- 360	8	1300-1490	16	4000 and up	24

Partnerships are required to have two convention cards identically and legibly filled out on the table throughout the session

Form 600R   PRINTED IN U.S.A.

Barclay Bridge Supplies, Inc. Port Chester, N.Y. 10573

Convention Card—reverse side

boxes opposite each number to record contract and declarer, result and the score earned on the board. Since team contests are usually scored by converting the difference in the score, if any, into International Match Points, an IMP table is included on the bottom to the left.

Each member of the partnership is obliged to have a convention card that is legible and identical with his partner's card. This regulation is rarely enforced in club games or tournaments where the number of conventions a pair may play is limited, but it is a courtesy to the opponents that should be observed. In pair, individual, or certain team events, the card must be folded in half with the convention side out so that opponents cannot see the scores a pair has achieved on previous boards.

Also required are table guide cards and score slips (see *Tournament Scoring* below). The standard table card shows the direction of each player, the number of the table and the alphabetical designation of the *section*. A section is rarely larger than 16 tables and when more than one section is

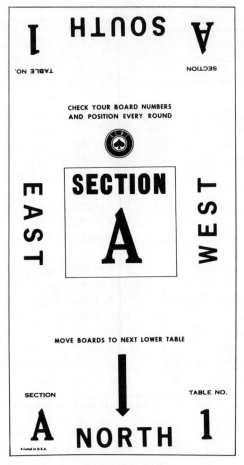

Table Guide Card

in play, different-colored table cards designate the different sections. When a Howell movement is used, the guide card indicates where a pair sits, their pair number, which boards they play, and where they move on succeeding rounds.

Mechanics of Play

After paying an entry fee, a pair receives an *entry blank* that assigns them to a particular table, section, and direction. The entry blank has space for each player's name, address, and ACBL Player number (if they are members of the League). The players must enter their full names on the entry blank. During the first round, the entry blanks will be picked up by a *caddie* and turned in to the scorer's desk.

Before the start of a game, the duplicate board is prepared for play. In small pair contests and most team events, the pack is removed from the board, shuffled, dealt into four packets of 13 cards each and then replaced in the board. In large pair tournaments, consisting of multiple sections, computer-dealt hand records are used. The deck is sorted into suits and when the *tournament director* distributes the hand records, the players duplicate the deck so that it conforms exactly with the hand record before the cards are replaced in the board. Regardless of which method is used, care must be exercised through the session to keep the four hands of each deal separate and to replace the cards in the correct pocket.

If a table has been asked to duplicate the boards from hand records, those boards will be moved down one or two tables, and the pairs will not play those deals during the course of the session. When the correct boards have been delivered to the table, the players make sure the boards are correctly aligned with the table card and then each player takes the 13 cards from the pocket in front of him. The first turn to call goes to the holder of the hand marked DEALER. Thereafter the auction proceeds as in rubber bridge, but the play is slightly different. The cards are not thrown together in tricks. Each player keeps possession of his own cards, exposing them one by one as played and turning each face down on the table in front of him after the trick is complete. Tricks won by a pair are indicated by placing the card of that trick in a vertical position. Cards of tricks lost are turned horizontally. Players should also place their cards in the order in which they were played in a row, separate from each other so that if the outcome of a hand is in dispute the play can be easily reconstructed. After the score is agreed at the end of play, each hand is returned to its pocket, so that at the conclusion of the round the boards can be passed to another table for play by the other pairs.

Alert Procedure. When a pair is using a non-standard convention, it is mandatory for a player to "alert" his opponents whenever his partner makes a bid that has a special partnership meaning. The proper procedure is for the player to say the single word, "Alert," to his right-hand opponent as soon as the bid has been made. The opponent may request an explanation of the call at that time or reserve his right to inquire at a later time when it is his turn to bid. The other opponent has the same rights; at his turn to call, he may inquire immediately as to the meaning of the bid, or wait until later in the auction. A player who gains information from his partner's alert should avoid taking advantage of it; however, if his partner has alerted in error, or given a wrong explanation, it is improper for him to correct the error or indicate in any way that a mistake has been made. Should a partnership avoid a misunderstanding or become aware of one because of an alert, the tournament director may award an *adjusted score*. Bids marked in red on the convention card must be alerted. Cue-bids of an opponent's suit, however, are not alertable.

Skip-Bid Warning. A player who is about to skip at least one level in the auction should announce: "I'm about to make a skip bid, please wait." After this warning the next player to bid is expected to pause approximately 10 seconds before making a call. The skip-bid warning is designed to prevent immediate action by the next player, which could give his partner unauthorized information and put a strong ethical burden on him. A quick pass after a skip bid, for example, could be construed as showing few if any values. The partner of the player who passed in such a manner is not entitled to that information. By requiring a player to hesitate after a skip bid, regardless of his hand, such ethical problems are usually resolved. A warning should be given for *all* skip bids, not just for those that are preemptive.

Bidding Box. This is a device for silent bidding, which, as the name implies, is a box attached to the table at the player's right. In one section of the box are cards for all possible bids. In the other section are cards for pass, double, redouble, alert and stop. To make a bid, the player detaches the card of his call and all of those behind it and places the packet on the table to his left. Subsequent bids are placed on top of, but not covering, a previous bid from left to right. To replace the cards in the box, the player first removes any pass, double, or redouble cards that may be mingled in with the bid cards, then pushes all the bid cards together, right to left, to form one packet, which is put back into the box behind the other bid cards. All bid cards are left on the table until the auction is concluded, thus avoiding the need for a review of the bidding. Another advantage of silent bidding is that the possibility of mishearing or misunderstanding a bid is eliminated. The "alert" card is used to advise the opponents of a conventional call by a player. When the bid is made, the partner of the bidder removes the alert card, places it on the table, then replaces it in the box. It is permissible to announce verbally: "Alert." The "Stop" card serves as a substitute for the verbal skip-bid warning. Prior to making a skip bid, the player places the stop card on the table, followed by his bid. After approximately 10 seconds, he removes the stop card and returns it to the bidding box. The next player should not act until the skip bidder has picked up the stop card.

Bidding boxes are used in World Championships and extensively in North American championships, and their popularity is increasing. Even some clubs utilize bidding boxes on a regular basis. The consensus is that they are a great improvement over verbal bidding.

SCORING

Each board is treated as a separate entity, and all scores for tricks and premiums are added into one total, which the players enter in their convention card as either a plus or a debit. In a pair tournament, North or South keeps the score for the table. He enters on the score slip (see Tournament Scoring below) the pair numbers, contract, and declarer, and the net plus score for North-South or East-West.

The scoring table is the same as in rubber bridge, with some important exceptions. Honors do not count. For the fourth and each succeeding doubled, non-vulnerable undertrick the penalty increases from 200 points to 300 points. The bonus for making a redoubled contract is 100 points, not 50 as in rubber bridge. There is no rubber premium; instead a premium is given for making any contract, which is in addition to any other premiums that may be due, as follows:

For making a part score	50 points
For making a non-vulnerable game	300 points
For making a vulnerable game	500 points

Types of Events

In most tournaments at the sectional, regional, or North American level, the forms of contest are limited to pairs and teams-of-four. Individual events, once popular, are still held, but on a limited basis. These contests can be played by any size group.

Pair Contests. The same two players remain partners throughout, and the method of play is generally the Mitchell Movement. After receiving a seat assignment, the entrants are divided into two groups, North-South and East-West. The North-South pairs will remain stationary throughout the session; the East-West pairs will move after each round. In a Mitchell game, the East-West pairs move up one table for the next round (from the highest-numbered table to table 1) and the North-South pairs pass the boards to the next-lowest table (from table 1 to the highest-numbered table in the section). The movement of pairs and boards continues in this fashion until the conclusion of the session, but the East-West pairs will skip a table approximately halfway through the session if there are an even number of tables in the section. For a 14-table section, for example, the moving pairs will skip a table after round seven. Comparison of final scores is made within each group, so as to determine one North-South winner and one East-West winner. The pair with the highest score is the overall winner, although in club duplicates, winners are usually declared in both directions.

Mitchell movements can be used with even a small number of tables by increasing the number of boards played each round, but for small games where it is desirable to determine one winner, a Howell movement is superior because it permits the pairs to play against all, or most, of the competing pairs. A Howell game requires special table cards to direct the movement of the boards and players.

For small games it is advantageous to avoid an odd number of pairs. If this is not possible, a *phantom pair* is necessary and play proceeds as if there were one more pair. Regardless of whether a Howell or Mitchell

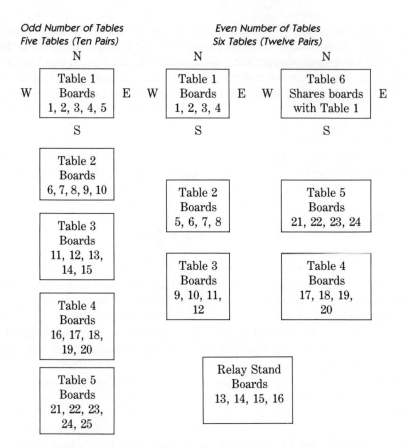

Odd Number of Tables
Five Tables (Ten Pairs)

Even Number of Tables
Six Tables (Twelve Pairs)

After all the boards at each table have been played, "the move" is called by the director of the game. The boards played at each table are moved to the next-lower numbered table (and from Table 1 to the highest-numbered table). Each East-West pair moves to the next-higher-numbered table (and from the highest-numbered table to Table 1). North-South pairs remain seated. When every East-West pair has played every North-South pair, the game is completed. With an even number of tables, a relay stand is placed between the two middle tables and holds one set of boards. The highest-numbered table uses the same boards as Table 1 in each round: When one has played a board, it passes it to the other to be played. After each round, East-West pairs and boards move as described in the column at the left, except that one set of boards always moves to the relay stand and is out of play for one round. In the illustration above, after the first round boards 17–20 move to the relay stand; boards 13–16 to Table 3; boards 1–4 to Table 5; and Tables 1 and 6 will share boards 5–8.

movement is employed, when a pair meets the phantom pair they sit out for that round and do not play the boards that are on the table.

There are a variety of pair contests in tournament bridge. Anyone may enter an Open event. Mixed, Men's and Women's Pairs are restricted by gender. Others are limited by master-point holding, such as the Life Master Pairs, which is open only to players who have achieved that rank, or Novice Pairs, open only to players with a limited number of master points. The length of a pair event can be anywhere from one session at the club level, to four or more sessions for a nationally rated competition, to more than a week for a World Championship. In multi-session contests it is usual to have the first session or first two sessions in a four-session event, designated as a *qualifying* round; only those pairs who score well in the first session go on to the final. Many two-session events, however are *play-through;* no pair is eliminated after the first session regardless of how poorly they do.

Team-of-Four Contests. Teams of four, five or six players remain as a unit throughout. They are free to rearrange their partnerships as they see fit for each session, or during a session when an opportunity presents itself. Forms of competition are knockout, Swiss, or board-a-match. A round-robin format is also possible, but it requires a complex schedule and is no longer played in the United States, although it is still popular in Europe.

A *knockout* is the same as in tennis. The teams are arranged in brackets, and each round consists of a series of matches, each between two teams. (It may be necessary to have three-way matches in the early rounds of a knockout to reduce the field to a certain number of teams; depending on the number needed, one or two teams advance from a three-way match.) The loser of the match is eliminated from the contest; the winner goes on to meet the next opponents. By successive halvings, the field is reduced to a lone survivor.

Each knockout match is played as follows:

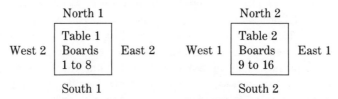

Knockout Match, order of play

After each table has played its original boards, they trade and play the remaining boards. In this case, each table will have played 16 boards. After play has been completed, the East-West pairs return to their home table to compare scores. Any difference in score is converted into International Match Points (IMPs) according to the following scale:

International Match Points

Diff. in Pts.	IMP	Diff. in Pts.	IMP	Diff. in Pts.	IMP
20–40	1	130–160	4	270–310	7
50–80	2	170–210	5	320–360	8
90–120	3	220–260	6	370–420	9

Diff. in Pts.	IMP	Diff. in Pts.	IMP	Diff. in Pts.	IMP
430–490	10	1100–1290	15	2250–2490	20
500–590	11	1300–1490	16	2500–2990	21
600–740	12	1500–1740	17	3000–3490	22
750–890	13	1750–1990	18	3500–3990	23
900–1090	14	2000–2240	19	4000 and up	24

Suppose the North-South pair at table 1 were +420 on board 1, while their teammates were only −170 because the North-South pair at table 2 did not bid game. The difference of 250 points earns 6 IMPs for team 1. Each board is IMPed in this fashion, and the team that wins the greatest number of IMPs is the winner.

As a rule, each session of a knockout is played in halves. When the comparison of scores is finished, the teams agree on the score and the second half begins. Teams may then switch their lineups. Knockout matches may consist of any number of boards, but generally not fewer than 26. In most stages of a national knockout, 64 boards are played for each match over two sessions.

Swiss Teams are similar to knockout except that the matches are much shorter and there is no elimination for losing a match. Over the course of a session, a team generally plays four 7-board matches against four other teams. After each match, the teams compare and agree on the IMP score, which is entered on a score slip. A circle is drawn around "win," "tie," or "lose" on the slip, and both score slips are turned in to the scoring table by a member of the winning team. For each succeeding round, teams with similar records are matched against each other, but a team may not play another team more than once. The winner of a Swiss event can be determined in one of two ways: wins-losses, or Victory Points (see Tournament Scoring below). Using the wins-losses formula, the team with the most wins is the victor. Ties count as one-half a win. Since this often results in ties for first overall, the Victory Point method is preferred. The IMP scores of each match are converted to Victory Points and the team that amasses the most points is the winner. Two-session Swiss teams are standard in most tournaments.

Board-a-Match Teams are considered the most difficult of all because of the accuracy required on every hand in bidding and play. In this form of competition, the East-West pairs move to play a series of teams, usually 13, over the course of a session, while their North-South teammates play the same boards against the East-Wests of the respective teams. Scores are kept in the same way as for a pairs contest. A teams wins a board if it outscores the opposing team by any margin, even 10 points. If the scores are identical, the board is a *push* (tie) and both teams receive one-half a win. The team with the most won boards is the winner. Since the strongest teams are favored in this type of contest, board-a-match teams have disappeared from most tournaments, but are still used to decide two major championships.

Individual Contests. In a perfect movement, each entrant plays once with every other as his partner, and meets him twice as an opponent. One winning individual is determined from the field. For tournaments where this movement is not possible, a number of alternatives have been designed to provide the greatest amount of mix depending on the size of the field. Although not widely played, an individual contest can be used for social functions.

Individual contests for eight or twelve players are easy to play at home. Each player is given a number. The original seating is as follows:

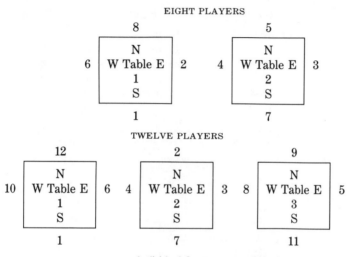

Individual Contests—seating

In the eight-player game, three or four boards are played in each round; in the twelve-player game, three boards. The cards are shuffled before each round, and the boards are traded by the tables until each table has played each board. The results of each board are scored on a traveling score slip as explained below. At the end of the round, the player of highest number remains seated; he is the *anchor*. Each other player moves to the seat just vacated by the player of next-lower number. (Player 1 follows Player 7 in the eight-player game, Player 11 in the twelve-player game.) The game ends when each player has had each other as partner; but the twelve-player game may have to be interrupted sooner, as the play of the full 33 boards may require four hours or more.

Tournament Scoring

There are two general ways of determining the winners of a tournament: International Match Point and match-point scoring.

For a knockout match, the teams agree on the IMP score and report the scores to the tournament director, who enters the totals for each side as the match progresses and the name of the winning team in the next bracket. For Swiss teams, scored by Victory Points, the tournament director converts the IMP differential into Victory Points and adds those to previous points won by a team before assigning the next round. The following scale is used for Swiss team contests with 7-board matches:

Victory Points

IMP diff.	VP split	IMP diff.	VP split
0	10–10	14–16	16–4
1–2	11–9	17–19	17–3
3–4	12–8	20–23	18–2
5–7	13–7	24–27	19–1
8–10	14–6	28 or more	20–0
11–13	15–5		

OFFICIAL (Mitchell or Howell) TRAVELING SCORE

Bid, Play & Score this board without comment and Proceed immediately to the next.

NORTH PLAYER only keeps score

SECTION _____ ENTER PAIR NO. OF EW PAIR   Board No. _____

N-S Pair No.	CON-TRACT	BY	Made	Down	SCORE N-S	SCORE E-W	E-W Pair No.	Match Points
1								
2								
3								
4								
5								
6								
7								
8								
9								
10								
11								
12								
13								
14								
15								
16								
17								
18							1	
19							2	
20							3	
21							4	
22							5	
23							6	
24							7	
25							8	
26							9	
27							10	
28							11	
29							12	
30							13	
31							14	
32							15	
33							16	
34							17	

Indulge in post-mortems, if you must, only at end of round. Play congenially. Announce or Display private conventions. Refrain from giving lessons especially to opponents. Do not make your own rulings. Call your game director that's his job. Count your cards before and after.   Form 444

Barclay Bridge Supplies, Inc.   Port Chester, N.Y. 10573

Traveling Score Slip

Match Point Capitulation Sheet

Different Victory Point scales are used in North American championships and for events with 9-board, or longer, matches.

IMP scoring can also be applied to pair contests in one of two ways: *Datum* and *IMPs-across-the-field*. In the datum method, the highest and lowest score are discarded (or the two highest and lowest scores, depending

AMERICAN CONTRACT BRIDGE LEAGUE

N—S PAIR	ALL DEALS PLAYED THIS ROUND WILL BE SCORED ON THIS CARD, CIRCLE DIRECTION OF DECLARER.						E—W PAIR
					E—W OK		
N—S SCORE	MADE	DOWN	N—S CONTRACT	BOARD NUMBER	E—W CONTRACT	MADE	DOWN	E—W SCORE
			N S		E W			
			N S		E W			
			N S		E W			

Pick-up Card

on the size of the field) and the rest of the scores are added together and divided by that number of results to produce a *mean* or datum score. The datum is posted as the North-South score, either as a plus or minus. The pairs IMP their results board by board against the datum to determine whether they won or lost IMPs on each board. IMPs-across-the-field is much more complex and generally requires the assistance of a computer. In this method, the score of each pair is IMPed against all other results in the same direction; no scores are discarded. Usually a limit is placed on the maximum number of IMPs a pair can win or lose against any opposing pair. On a given board, huge numbers of IMPs can be won or lost because of the multiplying factor of the comparisons.

Although IMP-pair contests are gaining in popularity, the vast majority of pairs contests are scored by match points. A pair is credited with 1 match point for every other pair they outscore on that board, or ½ point if the scores are the same. In club games, the North player enters the result on a *traveling score slip* (see illustration) which accompanies the board. At the end of the game, the director computes the match-point score for each pair, enters the total on the *"Match Point Capitulation"* sheet (see illustration), then adds the scores together to determine which pair earned the most match points. This is the basic way a pair contest is scored and results posted. When large fields are present, however, such as for Regional, North American and World pair championships, computers are used extensively. There are a number of advantages to computer scoring. Results come out sooner, errors are eliminated as the scores are entered, and the number of comparisons can be greatly increased by scoring across a number of sections rather than just within one section. For example, if three sections are playing the same boards which have been duplicated from hand records, a pair's score on a board can be matched not only to the 12 other results obtained in their section (assuming the board has been played 13 times), but also against the 13 results in each of the other two sections. The ability to score across the field is considered a much fairer way to decide a winner.

Since it is not desirable for pairs to see how their competitors are faring on a board, which is a disadvantage of traveling score slips, *pick-up slips* (see illustration) are used for most pair events outside of club games. At the conclusion of a round, a caddie collects the slips and delivers them to the scoring area, where the scores are entered into a computer or posted on a recap sheet.

LAWS OF DUPLICATE CONTRACT BRIDGE

American Edition

As Promulgated in the Western Hemisphere by the American
Contract Bridge League

Promulgating Bodies

The National Laws Commission
of the American Contract Bridge League

Edgar Kaplan and Edgar Theus, *Co-Chairmen*
Lee Hazen, Member Emeritus

Karen Allison

B. Jay Becker*

Easley Blackwood

Ralph Cohen

Richard Goldberg

Charles Goren

Nancy Gruver

John Guoba

Richard G. Hewitt

Amalya Kearse

Jeff Polisner

George Rosenkranz

Roger Stern

* *Deceased*

Drafting Committee for Duplicate Bridge

Edgar Kaplan, Chairman

Karen Allison

Amalya Kearse

Jaime Ortiz-Patino

Roger Stern

The Laws Commission of the World Bridge Federation

Edgar Theus, *Chairman* (United States)
Edgar Kaplan, *Vice-Chairman* (United States)
Jean Besse (Switzerland)
Carlos Cabanne (Argentina)
Grattan Endicott (Great Britain)
Santanu Ghose (India)
Colin Harding (Portland Club)
Denis Howard, *WBF President* (Australia)
Jaime Ortiz-Patino (Switzerland)
John Wignall (New Zealand)

The Scope of the Laws

The Laws are designed to define correct procedure, and to provide an adequate remedy when there is a departure from correct procedure. An offending player should be ready to pay any penalty graciously, or to accept any adjusted score awarded by the Tournament Director. The Laws are primarily designed not as punishment for irregularities, but rather as redress for damage.

Chapter 1

Definitions

Adjusted Score—An arbitrary score awarded by the Director (see Law 12). It is either "artificial" or "assigned." 1. An artificial adjusted score is one awarded in lieu of a result because no result can be obtained or estimated for a particular deal (e.g., when an irregularity prevents play of a deal). 2. An assigned adjusted score is awarded to one side, or to both sides, to be the result of the deal in place of the result actually obtained after an irregularity.

Alert—A notification, whose form may be specified by a sponsoring organization, to the effect that opponents may be in need of an explanation.

Auction—1. The process of determining the contract by means of successive calls. 2. The aggregate of calls made.

Average—The arithmetic median between the greatest and least awarded scores available.

Bid—An undertaking to win at least a specified number of odd tricks in a specified denomination.

Board—1. A duplicate board as described in Law 2. 2. The four hands as originally dealt and placed in a duplicate board for play during that session.

Call—Any bid, double, redouble or pass.

Contestant—In an individual event, a player; in a pair event, two players playing as partners throughout the event; in a team event, four or more players playing as teammates.

Contract—The undertaking by declarer's side to win, at the denomination named, the number of odd tricks specified in the final bid, whether undoubled, doubled, or redoubled.

Convention—1. A call that serves by partnership agreement to convey a meaning not necessarily related to the denomination named (for definition of conventional pass, see Law 30C). 2. Defender's play that serves to convey a meaning by agreement rather than inference.

Deal—1. The distribution of the pack to form the hands of the four players. 2. The cards so distributed considered as a unit, including the auction and play thereof.

Declarer—The player who, for the side that makes the final bid, first bid the denomination named in that bid. He becomes declarer when the opening lead is faced (but see Law 54A when the opening lead is made out of turn).

Defender—An opponent of (presumed) declarer.

Denomination—The suit or notrump specified in a bid.

Director—A person designated to supervise a duplicate bridge contest and to apply these Laws.

Double—A call over an opponent's bid increasing the scoring value of fulfilled or defeated contracts (see Laws 19 and 77).

Dummy—1. Declarer's partner. He becomes dummy when the opening lead is faced. 2. Declarer's partner's cards, once they are spread on the table after the opening lead.

Event—A contest of one or more sessions.

Follow Suit—Play a card of the suit that has been led.

Game—100 or more trick points scored on one deal.

Hand—The cards originally dealt to a player, or the remaining portion thereof.

Honor—Any Ace, King, Queen, Jack or Ten.

International Match Point (IMP)—A unit of scoring awarded according to a schedule established in Law 78B.

Irregularity—A deviation from the correct procedures set forth in the Laws.

Lead—The first card played to a trick.

Matchpoint—A unit of scoring awarded to a contestant as a result of comparison with one or more other scores.

Odd Trick—Each trick to be won by declarer's side in excess of six.

Opening Lead—The card led to the first trick.

Opponent—A player of the other side; a member of the partnership to which one is opposed (RHO, right-hand opponent; LHO, left-hand opponent).

Overtrick—Each trick won by declarer's side in excess of the contract.

Pack—The 52 playing cards with which the game of Contract Bridge is played.

Partner—The player with whom one plays as a side against the other two players.

Partscore—90 or fewer trick points scored on one deal.

Pass—A call specifying that a player does not, at that turn, elect to bid, double or redouble.

Penalty—An obligation or restriction imposed upon a side for violation of these Laws.

Penalty Card—A card prematurely exposed by a defender. It may be a major or minor penalty card (see Law 50).

Play—1. The contribution of a card from one's hand to a trick, including the first card, which is the lead. 2. The aggregate of plays made. 3. The period during which the cards are played. 4. The aggregate of the calls and plays on a board.

Premium Points—Any points earned other than trick points (see Law 77).

Psychic Call—A deliberate and gross misstatement of honor strength or suit length.

Rectification—Adjustment made to permit the auction or play to proceed as normally as possible after an irregularity has occurred.

Redeal—A second or subsequent deal to replace a faulty deal.

Redouble—A call over an opponent's double, increasing the scoring value of fulfilled or defeated contracts (see Laws 19 and 77).

Revoke—The play of a card of another suit by a player who is able to follow suit or to comply with a lead penalty.

Rotation—The clockwise order in which the right to call or play progresses.

Round—A part of a session played without progression of players.

Session—An extended period of play during which a specified number of boards is scheduled to be played before comparison of scores, and after which the ranking of contestants may be established.

Side—Two players who constitute a partnership against the other two players.

Slam—A contract to win six odd tricks (called Small Slam), or to win seven odd tricks (called Grand Slam).

Suit—One of four groups of cards in the pack, each group comprising thirteen cards and having a characteristic symbol: spades (♠), hearts (♡), diamonds (♢), clubs (♣).

Team—Two pairs playing in different directions at different tables, but for a common score (applicable regulations may permit teams of more than four members).

Trick—The unit by which the outcome of the contract is determined, regularly consisting of four cards, one contributed by each player in rotation, beginning with the lead.

Trick Points—Points scored by declarer's side for fulfilling the contract (see Law 77).

Trump—Each card of the suit, if any, named in the contract.

Turn—The correct time at which a player may call or play.

Undertrick—Each trick by which declarer's side falls short of fulfilling the contract (see Law 77).

Vulnerability—The conditions for assigning premiums and undertrick penalties (see Law 77).

Chapter II

Preliminaries

LAW 1. THE PACK—RANK OF CARDS AND SUITS

Duplicate Contract Bridge is played with a pack of 52 cards, consisting of 13 cards in each of four suits. The suits rank downward in the order Spades (♠), Hearts (♡), Diamonds (♢), Clubs (♣). The cards of each suit rank downward in the order Ace, King, Queen, Jack, **10, 9, 8, 7, 6, 5, 4, 3, 2**.

LAW 2. THE DUPLICATE BOARDS

A duplicate board containing a pack is provided for each deal to be played during a session. Each board is numbered and has four pockets to hold the four hands, designated North, East, South and West. The dealer and vulnerability are designated as follows:

North Dealer	Boards	1	5	9	13
East Dealer	Boards	2	6	10	14
South Dealer	Boards	3	7	11	15
West Dealer	Boards	4	8	12	16
Neither Side Vulnerable	Boards	1	8	11	14
North-South Vulnerable	Boards	2	5	12	15
East-West Vulnerable	Boards	3	6	9	16
Both Sides Vulnerable	Boards	4	7	10	13

The same sequence is repeated for Boards 17–32, and for each subsequent group of 16 boards.

No board that fails to conform to these conditions should be used. If such board is used, however, the conditions marked on it apply for that session.

LAW 3. ARRANGEMENT OF TABLES

Four players play at each table, and tables are numbered in a sequence established by the Director. He designates one direction as North; other compass directions assume the normal relationship to North.

LAW 4. PARTNERSHIPS

The four players at each table constitute two partnerships or sides, North-South against East-West. In pair or team events the contestants enter as pairs or teams, and retain the same partnerships throughout a session (except in the case of substitutions authorized by the Director). In individual events each player enters separately, and partnerships change during a session.

LAW 5. ASSIGNMENT OF SEATS

A. Initial Position

The Director assigns an initial position to each contestant (individual, pair or team) at the start of a session. Unless otherwise directed, the members of each pair or team may select seats, among those assigned to them, by mutual agreement. Having once selected a compass direction, a player may change it only upon instruction or with permission of the Director.

B. Change of Direction or Table

Players change their initial compass direction or proceed to another table in accordance with the Director's instructions. The Director is responsible for clear announcement of instructions;

each player is responsible for moving when and as directed, and for occupying the correct seat after each change.

Chapter III

Preparation and Progression

LAW 6. THE SHUFFLE AND DEAL

A. The Shuffle

Before play starts, each pack is thoroughly shuffled. There is a cut if either opponent so requests.

B. The Deal

The cards must be dealt face down, one card at a time in rotation, into four hands of thirteen cards each; each hand is then placed face down in one of the four pockets of the board.

C. Representation of Both Pairs

A member of each side should be present during the shuffle and deal unless the Director instructs otherwise.

D. New Shuffle and Redeal

1. Cards Incorrectly Dealt or Exposed

There must be a new shuffle and a redeal if it is ascertained before the last card is dealt that the cards have been incorrectly dealt, or that a player has seen the face of a card.

2. No Shuffle, or No Deal

No result may stand if the cards are dealt without shuffle from a sorted deck, or if the deal had previously been played.

3. At Director's Instruction

There must be a new shuffle and a redeal when required by the Director for any reason consonant with the Laws.

E. Director's Option on Shuffling and Dealing

1. By Players

The Director may instruct that the shuffle and deal be performed at each table immediately before play starts.

2. By Director

The Director may perform the shuffle and deal in advance, himself.

3. By Agents or Assistants

The Director may have his assistants, or other appointed agents, perform the shuffle and deal in advance.

4. Different Method of Dealing or Pre-dealing

The Director may require a different method of dealing or pre-dealing.

F. Duplication of Board

If required by the conditions of play, one or more exact copies of each original deal may be made under the Director's instructions.

LAW 7. CONTROL OF BOARD AND CARDS

A. Placement of Board

When a board is to be played it is placed in the center of the table until play is completed.

B. Removal of Cards from Board

Each player takes a hand from the pocket corresponding to his compass position.

1. Counting Cards in Hand before Play

Each player shall count his cards face down to be sure he has exactly thirteen; after that, and before making a call, he must inspect the face of his cards.

2. Control of Player's Hand

During play each player retains possession of his own cards, not permitting them to be mixed with those of any other player. No player shall touch any cards other than his own (but declarer may play dummy's cards in accordance with Law 45) during or after play except by permission of the Director.

C. Returning Cards to Board

Each player shall restore his original 13 cards to the pocket corresponding to his compass position. Thereafter no hand shall be removed from the board unless a member of each side, or the Director, is present.

D. Responsibility for Procedures

The North player is responsible for the proper observance of these procedures, and for maintaining proper conditions of play at the table. However, if the East-West pair alone is stationary, the responsibility becomes East's.

LAW 8. SEQUENCE OF ROUNDS

A. Movement of Boards and Players
   1. Director's Instructions
      The Director instructs the players as to the proper movement of boards and progression of contestants.
   2. Responsibility for Moving Boards
      The North player at each table is responsible for moving the boards just completed at his table to the proper table for the following round, unless the Director instructs otherwise.

B. End of Round

In general, a round ends when the Director gives the signal for the start of the following round; but if any table has not completed play by that time, the round continues for that table until play has been completed and the score of the final board of the round has been confirmed and entered on the proper scoring form.

C. End of Last Round and End of Session

The last round of a session, and the session itself, ends for each table when play of all boards scheduled at that table has been completed, and when all scores have been entered on the proper scoring forms without objection.

Chapter IV

General Laws

Governing Irregularities

LAW 9. PROCEDURE FOLLOWING AN IRREGULARITY

A. Calling Attention to an Irregularity
   1. During the Auction Period
      Any player may call attention to an irregularity during the auction, whether or not it is his turn to call.
   2. During the Play Period
      (a) Declarer or Either Defender
         Declarer or either defender may call attention to an irregularity that occurs during the play period.
      (b) Dummy (dummy's restricted rights are defined in Laws 42 and 43)
         (1) Dummy may not call attention to an irregularity during the play but may do so after play of the hand is concluded.

        (2) Dummy may attempt to prevent declarer from committing an irregularity (Law 42B2).

B. After Attention Is Called to an Irregularity

  1. Summoning the Director

    (a) When to Summon

    The Director must be summoned at once when attention is drawn to an irregularity.

    (b) Who May Summon

    Any player may summon the Director after attention has been drawn to an irregularity (for dummy, see Law 43A1).

    (c) Retention of Rights

    Summoning the Director does not cause a player to forfeit any rights to which he might otherwise be entitled.

    (d) Opponents' Rights

    The fact that a player draws attention to an irregularity committed by his side does not affect the rights of the opponents.

  2. Further Bids or Plays

  No player shall take any action until the Director has explained all matters in regard to rectification and to the assessment of a penalty.

C. Premature Correction of an Irregularity

Any premature correction of an irregularity by the offender may subject him to a further penalty (see the lead penalties of Law 26).

LAW 10. ASSESSMENT OF A PENALTY

A. Right to Assess Penalty

The Director alone has the right to assess penalties when applicable. Players do not have the right to assess (or waive) penalties on their own initiative.

B. Cancellation of Payment or Waiver of Penalty

The Director may allow or cancel any payment or waiver of penalties made by the players without his instructions.

C. Choice after Irregularity

  1. Explanation of Options

  When these laws provide an option after an irregularity, the Director shall explain all the options available.

  2. Choice Among Options

  If a player has an option after an irregularity, he must make his selection without consulting partner.

LAW 11. FORFEITURE OF THE RIGHT TO PENALIZE

A. Action by Non-Offending Side

The right to penalize an irregularity may be forfeited if either member of the non-offending side takes any action before summoning the Director. The Director so rules when the non-offending side may have gained through subsequent action taken by an opponent in ignorance of the penalty.

B. Call or Play before Imposition of Penalty

The right to penalize an irregularity is forfeited if offender's LHO calls or plays after the irregularity, and before a legal penalty has been stated and imposed.

C. Irregularity Called by Spectator

  1. Spectator Responsibility of Non-Offending Side

  The right to penalize an irregularity may be forfeited if attention is first drawn to the irregularity by a spectator for whose presence at the table the non-offending side is responsible.

2. Spectator Responsibility of Offending Side

The right to correct an irregularity may be forfeited if attention is first drawn to the irregularity by a spectator for whose presence at the table the offending side is responsible.

D. Penalty after Forfeiture of the Right to Penalize

Even after the right to penalize has been forfeited under this law, the Director may assess a procedural penalty (see Law 90).

LAW 12. DIRECTOR'S DISCRETIONARY POWERS

A. Right to Award an Adjusted Score

The Director may award an adjusted score (or scores), either on his own initiative or on the application of any player, but only when these Laws empower him to do so, or:

1. Laws Provide No Indemnity

The Director may award an assigned adjusted score when he judges that these Laws do not provide indemnity to the non-offending contestant for the particular type of violation of law committed by an opponent.

2. Normal Play of the Board is Impossible

The Director may award an artificial adjusted score if no rectification can be made that will permit normal play of the board (see Law 88).

3. Incorrect Penalty Has Been Paid

The Director may award an adjusted score if an incorrect penalty has been paid.

B. No Adjustment for Undue Severity of Penalty

The Director may not award an adjusted score on the ground that the penalty provided in these Laws is either unduly severe or advantageous to either side.

C. Awarding an Adjusted Score

1. Artificial Score

When, owing to an irregularity, no result can be obtained, the Director awards an artificial adjusted score according to responsibility for the irregularity: 40% of the available matchpoints ("average minus") to a contestant directly at fault; 50% ("average") to a contestant only partially at fault; at least 60% ("average plus") to a contestant in no way at fault (see Law 86 for team play or Law 88 for pairs play). The scores awarded to the two sides need not balance.

2. Assigned Score

When the Director awards an assigned adjusted score in place of a result actually obtained after an irregularity, the score is, for a non-offending side, the most favorable result that was likely had the irregularity not occurred, or, for an offending side, the most unfavorable result that was at all probable. The scores awarded to the two sides need not balance, and may be assigned either in matchpoints or by altering the total-point score prior to matchpointing.

LAW 13. INCORRECT NUMBER OF CARDS

When the Director determines that one or more pockets of the board contained an incorrect number of cards,* if a player with an incorrect hand has made a call, the Director shall award an artificial adjusted score, and may penalize an offender. If no such call has been made, then:

A. No Player Has Seen Another's Card

The Director shall correct the discrepancy as follows, and, if no player will then have seen another's card, shall require that the board be played normally.

1. Hand Records

When hand records are available, the Director shall distribute the cards in accordance with the records.

* *Where three hands are correct and one hand is deficient, Law 14, and not this Law, applies.*

    2. Consult Previous Players

        If hand records are not available, the Director shall correct the board by consulting with players who have previously played it.

    3. Require a Redeal

        If the board was incorrectly dealt, the Director shall require a redeal (Law 6).

  B. A Player Has Seen Another Player's Card(s)

When the Director determines that one or more pockets of the board contained an incorrect number of cards, and after restoration of the board to its original condition a player has seen one or more cards of another player's hand, if the Director deems:

    1. The Information Gained Is Inconsequential

        that such information will not interfere with normal bidding or play, the Director, with the concurrence of all four players, may allow the board to be played and scored normally.

    2. The Information Will Interfere with Normal Play

        that the information gained thereby is of sufficient importance to interfere with normal bidding or play, or if any player objects to playing the board, the Director shall award an artificial adjusted score and may penalize an offender.

  C. Play Completed

When it is determined, after play ends, that a player's hand originally contained more than 13 cards with another player holding correspondingly fewer, the result must be cancelled (for procedural penalty, see Law 90).

LAW 14. MISSING CARD

  A. Hand Found Deficient Before Play Commences

When three hands are correct and the fourth is found to be deficient before the play period begins, the Director makes a search for the missing card, and:

    1. Card Is Found

        If the card is found, it is restored to the deficient hand.

    2. Card Cannot Be Found

        If the card cannot be found, the Director reconstructs the deal, as near to its original form as he can determine, by substituting another pack.

  B. Hand Found Deficient During Play

When three hands are correct and the fourth is found to be deficient during play, the Director makes a search for the missing card, and:

    1. Card Is Found

        (a) If the card is found among the played cards, Law 67 applies.

        (b) If the card is found elsewhere, it is restored to the deficient hand, and penalties may apply (see 3., following).

    2. Card Cannot Be Found

        If the card cannot be found, the deal is reconstructed as nearly as can be determined in its original form by substituting another pack, and penalties may apply (see 3., following).

    3. Possible Penalties

        A card restored to a hand under the provisions of Section B of this Law is deemed to have belonged continuously to the deficient hand. It may become a penalty card (Law 50), and failure to have played it may constitute a revoke.

LAW 15. PLAY OF A WRONG BOARD

  A. Players Have Not Previously Played Board

If players play a board not designated for them to play in the current round:

    1. Score Board as Played

        The Director normally allows the score to stand if none of the four players have previously played the board.

2. Designate a Late Play
   The Director may require both pairs to play the correct board against one another later.

B. One or More Players Have Previously Played Board

If any player plays a board he has previously played, with the correct opponents or otherwise, his second score on the board is canceled both for his side and his opponents', and the Director shall award an artificial adjusted score to the contestants deprived of the opportunity to earn a valid score.

C. Discovered during Auction

If, during the auction period, the Director discovers that a contestant is playing a board not designated for him to play in the current round, he shall cancel the auction, ensure that the correct contestants are seated and informed of their rights both now and at future rounds, and:

1. A Player Objects
   Before a second auction begins, any player may require that the board be canceled.
2. No Player Objects
   If no player objects, a second auction begins. If any call differs from the corresponding call in the first auction, the Director shall cancel the board.
   Otherwise, play continues normally.

LAW 16. UNAUTHORIZED INFORMATION

Players are authorized to base their actions on information from legal calls or plays and from mannerisms of opponents. To base action on other extraneous information may be an infraction of law.

A. Extraneous Information from Partner

After a player makes available to his partner extraneous information that may suggest a call or play, as by means of a remark, a question, a reply to a question, or by unmistakable hesitation, unwonted speed, special emphasis, tone, gesture, movement, mannerism or the like, the partner may not choose from among logical alternative actions one that could reasonably have been suggested over another by the extraneous information.

1. When Such Information Is Given
   When a player considers that an opponent has made such information available, and that damage could well result, he may, unless the regulations of the sponsoring organization prohibit, immediately announce that he reserves the right to summon the Director later (the opponents should summon the Director immediately if they dispute the fact that unauthorized information might have been conveyed).
2. When Illegal Alternative Is Chosen
   When a player has substantial reason to believe* that an opponent who had a logical alternative has chosen an action that could have been suggested by such information, he should summon the Director forthwith. The Director shall require the auction and play to continue, standing ready to assign an adjusted score if he considers that an infraction of law has resulted in damage.

B. Extraneous Information from Other Sources

When a player accidentally receives unauthorized information about a board he is playing or has yet to play, as by looking at the wrong hand; by overhearing calls, results or remarks; by seeing cards at another table; or by seeing a card belonging to another player at his own table before the auction begins: the Director should be notified forthwith, preferably by the recipient of the information. If the Director considers that the information could interfere with normal play, he may:

---

* *When play ends; or, as to dummy's hand, when dummy is exposed.*

1. Adjust Positions
   if the type of contest and scoring permit, adjust the players' positions at the table, so that the player with information about one hand will hold that hand; or,
2. Appoint Substitute
   with the concurrence of all four players, appoint a temporary substitute to replace the player who received the unauthorized information; or,
3. Award an Adjusted Score
   forthwith award an artificial adjusted score.

C. Information from Withdrawn Calls and Plays

A call or play may be withdrawn, and another substituted, either by a non-offending side after an opponent's infraction, or by an offending side to rectify an infraction.

1. Non-offending Side
   For the non-offending side, all information arising from a withdrawn action is authorized, whether the action be its own or its opponents'.
2. Offending Side
   For the offending side, information arising from its own withdrawn action is authorized, after the payment of any penalty imposed by law. However, information arising from withdrawn actions of the non-offending side is unauthorized; then, a player of the offending side may not choose from among logical alternative actions one that could reasonably have been suggested over another by the unauthorized information.

Chapter V

The Auction

PART I: CORRECT PROCEDURE

SECTION ONE: AUCTION PERIOD

LAW 17. DURATION OF THE AUCTION

A. Auction Period Starts

The auction period on a deal begins when a player makes a call on that deal. Even if no player has called, the auction period begins for a side when either partner looks at the face of his cards.

B. The First Call

The player designated by the board as dealer makes the first call.

C. Successive Calls

The player to dealer's left makes the second call, and thereafter each player calls in turn in a clockwise rotation.

D. Cards from Wrong Board

If a player who has inadvertently picked up the cards from the wrong board makes a call, the Director may cancel the board, and must do so if any player of the non-offending side so requests (for penalty, see Law 90).

E. End of Auction Period

The auction period ends when all four players pass, or when, after three passes in rotation have followed any call, the opening lead is faced (when a pass *out* of rotation has been accepted, see Law 34).

LAW 18. BIDS

A. Proper Form

A bid names a number of odd tricks, from one to seven, and a denomination. (Pass, double and redouble are calls but not bids.)

B. To Supersede a Bid

A bid supersedes a previous bid if it names either the same number of odd tricks in a higher-ranking denomination, or a greater number of odd tricks in any denomination.

C. Sufficient Bid

A bid that supersedes the immediately previous bid is a sufficient bid.

D. Insufficient Bid

A bid that fails to supersede the immediately previous bid is an insufficient bid.

E. Rank of the Denominations

The rank of the denominations in descending order is: notrump, spades, hearts, diamonds, clubs.

LAW 19. DOUBLES AND REDOUBLES

A. Doubles

1. Legal Double

    A player may double only the last preceding bid. That bid must have been made by an opponent; calls other than pass must not have intervened.

2. Proper Form for Double

    In doubling, a player should not state the number of odd tricks or the denomination. The only correct form is the single word "Double."

3. Double of Incorrectly Stated Bid

    If a player, in doubling, incorrectly states the bid, or the number of odd tricks or the denomination, he is deemed to have doubled the bid as it was made. (Law 16—Unauthorized Information—may apply.)

B. Redoubles

1. Legal Redouble

    A player may redouble only the last preceding double. That double must have been made by an opponent; calls other than pass must not have intervened.

2. Proper Form for a Redouble

    In redoubling, a player should not state the number of odd tricks or the denomination. The only correct form is the single word "Redouble."

3. Redouble of an Incorrectly Stated Bid

    If a player, in redoubling, incorrectly states the doubled bid, or the number of odd tricks or the denomination, he is deemed to have redoubled the bid as it was made. (Law 16—Unauthorized Information—may apply.)

C. Double or Redouble Superseded

Any double or redouble is superseded by a subsequent legal bid.

D. Scoring a Doubled or Redoubled Contract

If a doubled or redoubled bid is not superseded by a subsequent legal bid, scoring values are increased as provided in Law 77.

LAW 20. REVIEW AND EXPLANATION OF CALLS

A. Call Not Clearly Heard

A player who does not hear a call distinctly may forthwith require that it be repeated.

B. Review of Auction during Auction Period

During the auction period, a player is entitled to have all* previous calls restated when it is his turn to call, unless he is required by law to pass; Alerts should be included in the restatement.

* *A player may not ask for a partial restatement of previous calls, and may not halt the review before it has been completed.*

C. Review after Final Pass
  1. Opening Lead Inquiry
     After the final pass either defender has the right to ask if it is his opening lead (see Laws 47E and 41).
  2. Review of Auction
     Declarer or either defender may, at his first turn to play, require all* previous calls to be restated (see Law 41B and 41C).
D. Who May Review the Auction
A request to have calls restated shall be responded to only by an opponent.
E. Correction of Error in Review
All players, including dummy or a player required by law to pass, are responsible for prompt correction of errors in restatement (see Law 12C1 when an uncorrected review causes damage).
F. Explanation of Calls
  1. During the Auction
     During the auction and before the final pass, any player, at his own turn to call, may request** a full explanation of the opponents' auction; replies should normally be given by the partner of a player who made a call in question (see Law 75, section C).
  2. During the Play Period
     After the final pass and throughout the play period, declarer or either defender (but Law 16, Unauthorized Information, may apply) at his own turn to play may request** such an explanation of opposing auction, and declarer may request an explanation of the defenders' card play conventions.

LAW 21. CALL BASED ON MISINFORMATION

A. Call Based on Caller's Misunderstanding
A player has no recourse if he has made a call on the basis of his own misunderstanding.
B. Call Based on Misinformation from an Opponent
  1. Change of Call
     Until the end of the auction period (see Law 17E), a player may, without penalty, change a call when it is probable that he made the call as a result of misinformation given to him by an opponent (failure to alert promptly to a conventional call or special understanding, where such alert is required by the sponsoring organization, is deemed misinformation), provided that his partner has not subsequently called.
  2. Change of Call by Opponent Following Correction
     When a player elects to change a call because of misinformation (as in 1., preceding), his LHO may then in turn change any subsequent call he may have made, without penalty (unless his withdrawn call conveyed such substantial information as to damage the non-offending side, in which case the Director may assign an adjusted score). (For unauthorized information from withdrawn calls, see Law 16C.)
  3. Too Late to Change Call
     When it is too late to change a call, the Director may award an adjusted score (Law 40C may apply).

* A player may not ask for a partial restatement of previous calls, and may not halt the review before it has been completed.
** Law 16 may apply; and sponsoring organizations may establish regulations for written explanations.

LAW 22. PROCEDURE AFTER THE AUCTION HAS ENDED

A. No Player Has Bid

After the auction period has ended, if no player has bid, the hands are returned to the board without play. There shall not be a redeal.

B. One or More Players Have Bid

If any player has bid, the final bid becomes the contract, and play begins.

PART II: IRREGULARITIES IN PROCEDURE

LAW 23. IRREGULAR PASSES CAUSING DAMAGE

Reference will be made to this Law from many other Laws that prescribe penalties for auction-period infractions.

A. Damaging Enforced Pass

When the penalty for an irregularity under any Law would compel the offender's partner to pass at his next turn, and when the Director deems that the offender, at the time of his irregularity, could have known that the enforced pass would be likely to damage the non-offending side, he shall require the auction and play to continue, afterwards awarding an adjusted score if he considers that the non-offending side was damaged by the enforced pass.

B. Damaging Pass at Partner's Turn

When a player passes out of rotation at partner's turn to call, and when the Director deems that this pass may have damaged the non-offending side, the Director shall require the auction and play to continue, afterwards awarding an adjusted score if he considers that the non-offending side was damaged by the out-of-rotation pass.

SECTION ONE: EXPOSED CARD, AUCTION PERIOD

LAW 24. CARD EXPOSED OR LED DURING AUCTION

When the Director determines, during the auction, that because of a player's action one or more cards of that player's hand were in position for the face to be seen by his partner, the Director shall require that every such card be left face up on the table until the auction closes; and (penalty) if the offender subsequently becomes a defender, declarer may treat every such card as a penalty card (Law 50). In addition:

A. Low Card Not Prematurely Led

If it is a single card below the rank of an honor, and not prematurely led, there is no further penalty.

B. Single Card of Honor Rank, or Card Prematurely Led

If the card is a single card of honor rank, or is any card prematurely led, (penalty) offender's partner must pass when next it is his turn to call (see Law 23A when a pass damages the non-offending side).

C. Two or More Cards Are Exposed

If two or more cards are so exposed, (penalty) offender's partner must pass when next it is his turn to call (see Law 23A when a pass damages the non-offending side).

SECTION TWO: CHANGES OF CALLS

LAW 25. LEGAL AND ILLEGAL CHANGES OF CALL

A. Immediate Correction of Inadvertency

A player may substitute his intended call for an inadvertent call but only if he does so, or attempts to do so, without pause for thought. If legal, his last call stands without penalty; if illegal, it is subject to the applicable Law.

B. Delayed or Purposeful Correction

If a call is substituted when section A does not apply:

1. Substitute Call Condoned

   The substituted call may be accepted (treated as legal) at the option of offender's LHO; then, the second call stands and the auction proceeds without penalty. If offender's LHO has called before attention is drawn to the infraction, and the Director determines that LHO intended his call to apply over the offender's original call at that turn, offender's substituted call stands without penalty, and LHO may withdraw his call without penalty.

2. Not Condoned

   If the substituted call is not accepted, it is cancelled; and:

   (a) First Call Illegal

   If the first call was illegal, the offender is subject to the applicable law (and the lead penalties of Law 26 may apply to the second call).

   (b) First Call Legal

   If the first call was legal, the offender must either,

   (1) Let First Call Stand

   Allow his first call to stand, in which case (penalty) his partner must pass when next it is his turn to call (see Law 23A when the pass damages the non-offending side), or,

   (2) Substitute Another Call

   Make any other legal call, in which case (penalty) his partner must pass whenever it is his turn to call (see Law 23A when the pass damages the non-offending side).

   (c) Lead Penalties

   In either case (b) (1) or (b) (2) above, the offender's partner will be subject to a lead penalty (see Law 26) if he becomes a defender.

LAW 26. CALL WITHDRAWN, LEAD PENALTIES

When an offending player's call is withdrawn, and he chooses a different* final call for that turn, then if he becomes a defender:

A. Call Related to Specific Suit

If the withdrawn call related to a specified suit or suits, and,

1. Suit Later Specified

   If that suit was later specified by the same player, there is no lead penalty.

2. Suit Not Later Specified

   If that suit was not later so specified, then declarer may (penalty) either require the offender's partner to lead the specified suit (or one particular specified suit) at his first turn to lead, including the opening lead; or prohibit offender's partner from leading the specified suit (or one particular specified suit) at his first turn to lead, including the opening lead, such prohibition to continue for as long as offender's partner retains the lead.

B. Other Withdrawn Calls

For other withdrawn calls, (penalty) declarer may prohibit offender's partner from leading any one suit** at his first turn to lead, including the opening lead, such prohibition to continue for as long as offender's partner retains the lead.

---

* A call repeated with a much different meaning shall be deemed a different call.
** Declarer specifies the suit when offender's partner first has the lead.

LAW 27. INSUFFICIENT BID

A. Insufficient Bid Accepted

Any insufficient bid may be accepted (treated as legal) at the option of offender's LHO. It is accepted if that player calls.

B. Insufficient Bid Not Accepted

If an insufficient bid made in rotation is not accepted, it must be corrected by the substitution of either a sufficient bid or a pass (the offender is entitled to select his final call at that turn after the applicable penalties have been stated, and any call he has previously attempted to substitute is canceled, but the lead penalties of Law 26 may apply).

1. Not Conventional, and Corrected by Lowest Sufficient Bid in Same Denomination
   (a) No Penalty
       If the insufficient bid was incontrovertibly not conventional, and is corrected by the lowest sufficient bid in the same denomination, the auction proceeds as though the irregularity had not occurred (but see (b) following).
   (b) Award of Adjusted Score
       If the Director judges that the insufficient bid conveyed such substantial information as to damage the non-offending side, he shall assign an adjusted score.
2. Conventional, or Corrected by Any Other Sufficient Bid or Pass
   If the insufficient bid may have been conventional, or is corrected by any other sufficient bid or by a pass, (penalty) the offender's partner must pass whenever it is his turn to call (see Law 23A when the pass damages the non-offending side; and the lead penalties of Law 26 may apply).
3. Attempt to Correct by a Double or Redouble
   If the offender attempts to substitute a double or redouble for his insufficient bid, the attempted call is cancelled; and (penalty) his partner must pass whenever it is his turn to call (see Law 23A when the pass damages the non-offending side), and the lead penalties of Law 26 may apply.

C. Insufficient Bid Out of Rotation

If a player makes an insufficient bid out of rotation, Law 31 applies.

LAW 28. CALLS CONSIDERED TO BE IN ROTATION

A. RHO Required to Pass

A call is considered to be in rotation when it is made by a player at his RHO's turn to call if that opponent is required by law to pass.

B. Call by Correct Player Canceling Call Out of Rotation

A call is considered to be in rotation when made by a player whose turn it was to call, before a penalty has been assessed for a call out of rotation by an opponent; making such a call forfeits the right to penalize the call out of rotation, and the auction proceeds as though the opponent had not called at that turn.

LAW 29. PROCEDURE AFTER A CALL OUT OF ROTATION

A. Out-of-Rotation Call Canceled

A call out of rotation is canceled (but see B following), and the auction reverts to the player whose turn it was to call. Offender may make any legal call in proper rotation, but his side may be subject to penalty under Laws 30, 31 or 32.

B. Forfeiture of Right to Penalize

Following a call out of rotation, offender's LHO may elect to call, thereby forfeiting the right to penalize.

LAW 30. PASS OUT OF ROTATION

When a player has passed out of rotation (and the call is cancelled, as the option to accept the call has not been exercised—see Law 29):

A. Before Any Player Has Bid

When a player has passed out of rotation before any player has bid, (penalty) the offender must pass when next it is his turn to call (and see Law 23B when offender's partner was dealer).

B. After Any Player Has Bid

  1. At RHO's Turn to Call

    After any player has bid, when a pass out of rotation is made at offender's RHO's turn to call, (penalty) offender must pass when next it is his turn to call (if the pass out of rotation related by convention to a specific suit, or suits, thereby conveying information, the lead penalties of Law 26 may apply).

  2. At Partner's Turn to Call

    (a) Action Required of Offender

      After any player has bid, for a pass out of rotation made at the offender's partner's turn to call, (penalty) the offender must pass whenever it is his turn to call, and Law 23B may apply.

    (b) Action Open to Offender's Partner

      Offender's partner may make any sufficient bid, or may pass, but may not double or redouble at that turn, and Law 23B may apply.

  3. At LHO's Turn to Call

    After any player has bid, a pass out of rotation at offender's LHO's turn to call is treated as a change of call and Law 25 applies.

C. When Pass Is a Convention

When the pass out of rotation is a convention, Law 31, not this Law, will apply. A pass is a convention if, by special agreement, it promises more than a specified amount of strength, or if it artificially promises or denies values other than in the last suit named.

LAW 31. BID OUT OF ROTATION

When a player has bid out of rotation (and the bid is cancelled, as the option to accept the bid has not been exercised—see Law 29):

A. RHO's Turn

When the offender has bid (or has passed partner's call when it is a convention, in which case section A2b applies) at his RHO's turn to call, then:

  1. RHO Passes

    If that opponent passes, offender must repeat the call out of rotation, and when that call is legal there is no penalty.

  2. RHO Acts

    If that opponent makes a legal* bid, double or redouble, offender may make any legal call (including pass); when this call

    (a) Repeats Denomination

      repeats the denomination of his bid out of rotation, (penalty) offender's partner must pass when next it is his turn to call (see Law 23A).

    (b) Does Not Repeat Denomination

      does not repeat the denomination of his bid out of rotation, the lead penalties of Law 26 may apply, and (penalty) offender's partner must pass whenever it is his turn to call (see Law 23A).

B. Partner's or LHO's Turn

When the offender has bid at his partner's turn to call, or at his LHO's turn to call if the offender has not previously called,** (penalty) offender's partner must pass whenever it is

---

* An illegal call by RHO is penalized as usual.

** Later bids at LHO's turn to call are treated as changes of call, and Law 25 applies.

his turn to call (see Law 23A when the pass damages the non-offending side), and the lead penalties of Law 26 may apply.

LAW 32. DOUBLE OR REDOUBLE OUT OF ROTATION

A double or redouble out of rotation may be accepted at the option of the opponent next in rotation (see Law 29), except that an inadmissible double or redouble may never be accepted (see Law 35A if the opponent next in rotation nevertheless does call). If the illegal call is not accepted, it is canceled, the lead penalties of Law 26B may apply, and:

A. Made at Offender's Partner's Turn to Call

If a double or redouble out of rotation has been made when it was the offender's partner's turn to call, (penalty) the offender's partner must pass whenever it is his turn to call (see Law 23A when the pass damages the non-offending side).

B. Made at RHO's Turn to Call

If a double or redouble out of rotation has been made at offender's RHO's turn to call, then:

1. RHO Passes

   If offender's RHO passes, offender must repeat his out-of-rotation double or redouble and there is no penalty unless the double or redouble is inadmissible, in which case Law 36 applies.

2. RHO Bids

   If offender's RHO bids, the offender may in turn make any legal call and (penalty) offender's partner must pass whenever it is his turn to call (see Law 23A when the pass damages the non-offending side).

LAW 33. SIMULTANEOUS CALLS

A call made simultaneously with one made by the player whose turn it was to call is deemed to be a subsequent call.

LAW 34. RETENTION OF RIGHT TO CALL

When a call has been followed by three passes, the auction does not end when one of those passes was out of rotation, thereby depriving a player of his right to call at that turn. The auction reverts to the player who missed his turn. All subsequent passes are cancelled, and the auction proceeds as though there had been no irregularity.

LAW 35. INADMISSIBLE CALL CONDONED

When, after any inadmissible call specified below, the offender's LHO makes a call before a penalty has been assessed, there is no penalty for the inadmissible call (the lead penalties of Law 26 do not apply), and:

A. Double or Redouble

If the inadmissible call was a double or redouble not permitted by Law 19, that call and all subsequent calls are canceled. The auction reverts to the player whose turn it is to call, and proceeds as though there had been no irregularity.

B. Action by Player Required to Pass

If the inadmissible call was a bid, double or redouble by a player required by law to pass, that call and all subsequent legal calls stand, but, if the offender was required to pass for the remainder of the auction, he must still pass at subsequent turns.

C. Bid of More than Seven

If the inadmissible call was a bid of more than seven, that call and all subsequent calls are cancelled; the offender must substitute a pass, and the auction proceeds as though there had been no irregularity.

D. Call after Final Pass

If the inadmissible call was a call after the final pass of the auction, that call and all subsequent calls are cancelled without penalty.

SECTION FIVE: INADMISSIBLE CALLS

LAW 36. INADMISSIBLE DOUBLE OR REDOUBLE

Any double or redouble not permitted by Law 19 is canceled. The offender must substitute a legal call, and (penalty) the offender's partner must pass whenever it is his turn to call (see Law 23A when the pass damages the non-offending side); the lead penalties of Law 26 may apply. (If the call is out of turn, see Law 32; if offender's LHO calls, see Law 35A.)

LAW 37. ACTION VIOLATING OBLIGATION TO PASS

A bid, double or redouble by a player who is required by law to pass is canceled, and (penalty) each member of the offending side must pass whenever it becomes his turn to call (see Law 23A when the pass damages the non-offending side). The lead penalties of Law 26 may apply. (If offender's LHO calls, see Law 35B.)

LAW 38. BID OF MORE THAN SEVEN

No play or score at a contract of more than seven is ever permissible. A bid of more than seven is canceled, and (penalty) each member of the offending side must pass whenever it becomes his turn to call (see Law 23A when the pass damages the non-offending side). The lead penalties of Law 26 may apply.

(If offender's LHO calls, see Law 35C.)

LAW 39. CALL AFTER FINAL PASS

A call made after the final pass of the auction is canceled, and:

A. Pass, or Call by Declaring Side

If it is a pass by a defender, or any call by the future declarer or dummy, there is no penalty.

B. Other Action by Defender

If it is a bid, double or redouble by a defender, the lead penalties of Law 26 may apply. (If offender's LHO calls, see Law 35D.)

SECTION SIX: CONVENTIONS AND AGREEMENTS

LAW 40. PARTNERSHIP UNDERSTANDINGS

A. Right to Choose Call or Play

A player may make any call or play (including an intentionally misleading call—such as a psychic bid—or a call or play that departs from commonly accepted, or previously announced, use of a convention), without prior announcement, provided that such call or play is not based on a partnership understanding.

B. Concealed Partnership Understandings Prohibited

A player may not make a call or play based on a special partnership understanding unless an opposing pair may reasonably be expected to understand its meaning, or unless his side discloses the use of such call or play in accordance with the regulations of the sponsoring organization.

C. Director's Option

If the Director decides that a side has been damaged through its opponents' failure to explain the full meanings of a call or play, he may award an adjusted score.

D. Regulation of Conventions

The sponsoring organization may regulate the use of bidding or play conventions. Zonal organizations may, in addition, regulate partnership understandings (even if not conventional) that permit the partnership's initial actions at the one level to be made with a hand of a king or more below average strength; Zonal organizations may delegate this responsibility.

E. Convention Card
  1. Right to Prescribe
     The sponsoring organization may prescribe a convention card on which partners
     are to list their conventions and other agreements, and may establish regulations
     for its use, including a requirement that both members of a partnership employ
     the same system (such a regulation must not restrict style and judgment, only
     method).
  2. Referring to Opponents' Convention Card
     During the auction and play, any player except dummy may refer to his opponents'
     convention card at his own turn to call or play, but not to his own.*

Chapter VI

The Play

PART I: PROCEDURE

SECTION ONE: CORRECT PROCEDURE

LAW 41. COMMENCEMENT OF PLAY

A. Face-down Opening Lead
After a bid, double or redouble has been followed by three passes in rotation, the defender
on presumed declarer's left makes the opening lead face down.** The face-down lead may
be withdrawn only upon instruction of the Director after an irregularity (see Law 47E2);
the withdrawn card must be returned to the defender's hand.

B. Review of Auction, and Questions
Before the opening lead is faced, the leader's partner and the presumed declarer each may
require a review of the auction, or request explanation of an opponent's call (see Law 20).
Declarer or either defender may, at his first turn to play a card, require a review of the
auction; this right expires when he plays a card. The defenders (subject to Law 16) and the
declarer retain the right to request explanations throughout the play period, each at his
own turn to play.

C. Opening Lead Faced
Following this question period, the opening lead is faced, the play period begins, and dummy's
hand is spread. After it is too late to have previous calls restated (see B, above), declarer
or either defender, at his own turn to play, is entitled to be informed as to what the contract
is and whether, but not by whom, it was doubled or redoubled.

D. Dummy's Hand
After the opening lead is faced, dummy spreads his hand in front of him on the table, face
up, sorted into suits, the cards in order of rank, in columns pointing lengthwise towards
declarer, with trumps to dummy's right. Declarer plays both his hand and that of dummy.

LAW 42. DUMMY'S RIGHTS

A. Absolute Rights
  1. Give Information
     Dummy is entitled to give information, in the Director's presence, as to fact or
     law.
  2. Keep Track of Tricks
     He may keep count of tricks won and lost.

---

* *A player is not entitled, during the auction and play periods, to any aids to his memory,
calculation or technique.*
** *Sponsoring organizations may specify that opening leads be made face up.*

3. Play as Declarer's Agent

He plays the cards of the dummy as declarer's agent as directed (see Law 45F if dummy suggests a play).

B. Qualified Rights

Dummy may exercise other rights subject to the limitations provided in Law 43.

1. Revoke Inquiries

Dummy may ask declarer (but not a defender) when he has failed to follow suit to a trick whether he has a card of the suit led.

2. Attempt to Prevent Irregularity

He may try to prevent any irregularity by declarer (he may, for example, warn declarer against leading from the wrong hand).

3. Draw Attention to Irregularity

He may draw attention to any irregularity, but only after play of the hand is concluded.

LAW 43. DUMMY'S LIMITATIONS

A. Limitations on Dummy

1. General Limitations

(a) Calling the Director

Dummy should not initiate a call for the Director during play.

(b) Calling Attention to Irregularity

Dummy may not call attention to an irregularity during play.

(c) Participate in or Comment on Play

Dummy may not participate in the play or make any comment, or ask any question, on the bidding or play.

2. Limitations Carrying Specific Penalty

(a) Exchanging Hands

Dummy may not exchange hands with declarer.

(b) Leave Seat to Watch Declarer

Dummy may not leave his seat to watch declarer's play of the hand.

(c) Look at Defender's Hand

Dummy may not, on his own initiative, look at the face of a card in either defender's hand.

B. Penalties for Violation

1. General Penalties

Dummy is liable to penalty under Law 90 for any violation of the limitations listed in A1 or A2 preceding.

2. Specific Penalties

If dummy, after violation of the limitations listed in A2 preceding:

(a) Draws Attention to Defender's Irregularity

is the first to draw attention to a defender's irregularity, declarer may not enforce any penalty for the offense.

(b) Warns Declarer on Lead

warns declarer not to lead from the wrong hand, (penalty) either defender may choose the hand from which declarer shall lead.

(c) Asks Declarer about Possible Irregularity

is the first to ask declarer if a play from declarer's hand constitutes a revoke or failure to comply with a penalty, declarer must substitute a correct card if his play was illegal, and the penalty provisions of Law 64 apply.

LAW 44. SEQUENCE AND PROCEDURE OF PLAY

A. Lead to a Trick

The player who leads to a trick may play any card in his hand (unless he is subject to restriction after an irregularity committed by his side).

B. Subsequent Plays to a Trick

After the lead, each other player in turn plays a card, and the four cards so played constitute a trick. (For the method of playing cards and arranging tricks see Law 65.)

C. Requirement to Follow Suit

In playing to a trick, each player must follow suit if possible. This obligation takes precedence over all other requirements of these Laws.

D. Inability to Follow Suit

If unable to follow suit, a player may play any card (unless he is subject to restriction after an irregularity committed by his side).

E. Tricks Containing Trumps

A trick containing a trump is won by the player who has contributed to it the highest trump.

F. Tricks Not Containing Trumps

A trick that does not contain a trump is won by the player who has contributed to it the highest card of the suit led.

G. Lead to Tricks Subsequent to First Trick

The player who has won the trick leads to the next trick.

LAW 45. CARD PLAYED

A. Play of Card from a Hand

Each player except dummy plays a card by detaching it from his hand and facing* it on the table immediately before him.

B. Play of Card from Dummy

Declarer plays a card from dummy by naming the card, after which dummy picks up the card and faces it on the table. In playing from dummy's hand declarer may, if necessary, pick up the desired card himself.

C. Compulsory Play of Card

1. Defender's Card

   A defender's card held so that it is possible for his partner to see its face must be played to the current trick (if the defender has already made a legal play to the current trick, see Law 45E).

2. Declarer's Card

   Declarer must play a card from his hand held face up, touching or nearly touching the table, or maintained in such a position as to indicate that it has been played.

3. Dummy's Card

   A card in the dummy must be played if it has been deliberately touched by declarer except for the purpose of arranging dummy's cards, or of reaching a card above or below the card or cards touched.

4. Named or Designated Card

   (a) Play of Named Card

   A card must be played if a player names or otherwise designates it as the card he proposed to play.

   (b) Correction of Inadvertent Designation

   A player may, without penalty, change an inadvertent designation if he does so without pause for thought; but if an opponent has, in turn, played a card that was legal before the change in designation, that opponent may withdraw without penalty the card so played and substitute another (see Law 47E).

5. Penalty Card

   A penalty card, major or minor, may have to be played, subject to Law 50.

D. Card Misplayed by Dummy

---

* *The opening lead is first made face down (unless the sponsoring organization directs otherwise).*

If dummy places in the played position a card that declarer did not name, the card must be withdrawn if attention is drawn to it before each side has played to the next trick, and a defender may withdraw (without penalty) a card played after the error but before attention was drawn to it (see Law 47F).

    E. Fifth Card Played to Trick

        1. By a Defender

A fifth card contributed to a trick by a defender becomes a penalty card, subject to Law 50, unless the Director deems that it was led, in which case Law 53 or 56 applies.

        2. By Declarer

When declarer contributes a fifth card to a trick from his own hand or dummy, there is no penalty unless the Director deems that it was led, in which case Law 55 applies.

    F. Dummy Indicates Card

After dummy's hand is faced, dummy may not touch or indicate any card (except for purpose of arrangement) without instruction from declarer. If he does so, the Director should be summoned forthwith. The Director shall rule whether dummy's act did in fact constitute a suggestion to declarer. When the Director judges that it did, he allows play to continue, reserving his right to assign an adjusted score if the defenders were damaged by the play so suggested.

    G. Turning the Trick

No player should turn his card face down until all four players have played to the trick.

SECTION TWO: IRREGULARITIES IN PROCEDURE

LAW 46. INCOMPLETE OR ERRONEOUS CALL OF CARD FROM DUMMY

    A. Proper Form for Designating Dummy's Card

When calling a card to be played from dummy, declarer should clearly state both the suit and the rank of the desired card.

    B. Incomplete or Erroneous Call

In case of an incomplete or erroneous call by declarer of the card to be played from dummy the following restrictions apply (except when declarer's different intention is incontrovertible):

        1. Incomplete Designation of Rank

If declarer, in playing from dummy, calls "high," or words of like import, he is deemed to have called the highest card of the suit indicated; if he directs dummy to win the trick, he is deemed to have called the lowest winning card; if he calls "low," or words of like import, he is deemed to have called the lowest.

        2. Designates Suit but Not Rank

If declarer designates a suit but not a rank, he is deemed to have called the lowest card of the suit indicated.

        3. Designates Rank but Not Suit

If declarer designates a rank but not a suit:

        (a) In Leading

Declarer is deemed to have continued the suit in which dummy won the preceding trick, provided there is a card of the designated rank in that suit.

        (b) All Other Cases

In all other cases, declarer must play a card from dummy of the designated rank if he can legally do so; but if there are two or more such cards that can be legally played, declarer must designate which is intended.

        4. Designates Card Not in Dummy

If declarer calls a card that is not in dummy, the call is void and declarer may designate any legal card.

5. No Suit or Rank Designated

If declarer indicates a play without designating either a suit or rank (as by saying, "play anything," or words of like import), either defender may designate the play from dummy.

LAW 47. RETRACTION OF CARD PLAYED

A. To Comply with Penalty

A card once played may be withdrawn to comply with a penalty (but a defender's withdrawn card may become a penalty card—see Law 49).

B. To Correct an Illegal Play

A played card may be withdrawn to correct an illegal or simultaneous play (see Law 58 for simultaneous play; and, for defenders, see Law 49, penalty card).

C. To Change an Inadvertent Designation

A played card may be withdrawn without penalty after a change of designation as permitted by Law 45C4(b).

D. Following Opponent's Change of Play

After an opponent's change of play, a played card may be withdrawn without penalty to substitute another card for the one played.

E. Change of Play Based on Misinformation

1. Lead Out of Turn

A lead out of turn may be retracted without penalty if the leader was mistakenly informed by an opponent that it was his turn to lead.

2. Retraction of Play

(a) No One Has Subsequently Played

A player may retract the card he has played after a mistaken explanation of an opponent's conventional call or play and before a corrected explanation, but only if no card was subsequently played to that trick.

(b) One or More Subsequent Plays Made

When it is too late to correct a play, under (a) preceding, Law 40C applies.

F. Exposure of Retracted Card by Damaged Side

If a card retracted under section C, D or E preceding gave substantial information to the offending side, the Director may award an adjusted score.

G. Illegal Retraction

Except as provided in A through E preceding, a card once played may not be withdrawn.

PART II: PENALTY CARD

LAW 48. EXPOSURE OF DECLARER'S CARDS

A. Declarer Exposes a Card

Declarer is not subject to penalty for exposing a card, and no card of declarer's or dummy's hand ever becomes a penalty card. Declarer is not required to play any card dropped accidentally.

B. Declarer Faces Cards

1. After Opening Lead Out of Turn

When declarer faces his cards after an opening lead out of turn, Law 54 applies.

2. At Any Other Time

When declarer faces his cards at any time other than immediately after an opening lead out of turn, he may be deemed to have made a claim or concession of tricks, and Law 68 then applies.

LAW 49. EXPOSURE OF A DEFENDER'S CARDS

Whenever a defender faces a card on the table, holds a card so that it is possible for his partner to see its face, or names a card as being in his hand, before he is entitled to do so in the normal course of play or application of law, (penalty) each such card becomes a penalty card (Law 50); but see the footnote to Law 68 when a defender has made a statement concerning an uncompleted trick currently in progress.

LAW 50. DISPOSITION OF PENALTY CARD

A. Definition of Penalty Card

A card prematurely exposed (but not led, see Law 57) by a defender is a penalty card unless the Director designates otherwise. The Director shall award an adjusted score, in lieu of the rectifications below, when he deems that the offender, at the time of his irregularity, could have known that exposing the card prematurely would be likely to damage the non-offending side.

B. Penalty Card Remains Exposed

A penalty card must be left face up on the table immediately before the player to whom it belongs, until it is played or until an alternate penalty has been selected.

C. Major or Minor Penalty Card?

A single card below the rank of an honor and exposed inadvertently (as in playing two cards to a trick, or in dropping a card accidentally) becomes a minor penalty card. Any card of honor rank, or any card exposed through deliberate play (as in leading out of turn, or in revoking and then correcting), becomes a major penalty card; when one defender has two or more penalty cards, all such cards become major penalty cards.

D. Disposition of Minor Penalty Card

When a defender has a minor penalty card, he may not play any other card of the same suit below the rank of an honor until he has first played the penalty card (however, he is entitled to play an honor card instead). Offender's partner is not subject to lead penalty, but information gained through seeing the penalty card is extraneous, unauthorized (see Law 16A).

E. Disposition of Major Penalty Card

When a defender has a major penalty card, both the offender and his partner may be subject to restriction, the offender whenever he is to play, the partner when he is to lead.

    1. Offender to Play

        A major penalty card must be played at the first legal opportunity, whether in leading, following suit, discarding or trumping. If a defender has two or more penalty cards that can legally be played, declarer may designate which is to be played. The obligation to follow suit, or to comply with a lead or play penalty, takes precedence over the obligation to play a major penalty card, but the penalty card must still be left face up on the table and played at the next legal opportunity.

    2. Offender's Partner to Lead

        When a defender has the lead while his partner has a major penalty card, he may not lead until declarer has stated which of the options below is selected (if the defender leads prematurely, he is subject to penalty under Law 49). Declarer may choose:

        (a) Require or Forbid Lead of Suit

            to require* the defender to lead the suit of the penalty card, or to prohibit* him from leading that suit for as long as he retains the lead (for two or more penalty cards, see Law 51); if declarer exercises this option, the card is no longer a penalty card, and is picked up.

        (b) No Lead Restriction

            not to require or prohibit a lead, in which case the defender may lead any card; the penalty card remains a penalty card.

LAW 51. TWO OR MORE PENALTY CARDS

A. Offending Player's Turn to Play

If a defender has two or more penalty cards that can legally be played, declarer may designate which is to be played at that turn.

* If the player is unable to lead as required, see Law 59.

B. Offender's Partner to Lead
  1. Penalty Cards in Same Suit
    (a) Declarer Requires Lead of That Suit
       When a defender has two or more penalty cards in one suit, and declarer requires the defender's partner to lead that suit, the cards of that suit are no longer penalty cards and are picked up; the defender may make any legal play to the trick.
    (b) Declarer Prohibits Lead of That Suit
       If the declarer prohibits the lead of that suit, the defender may pick up every penalty card in that suit and may make any legal play to the trick.
  2. Penalty Cards in More Than One Suit
    (a) Declarer Requires Lead of a Specified Suit
       When a defender has penalty cards in more than one suit, declarer may require* the defender's partner to lead any suit in which the defender has a penalty card (but B1(a) preceding then applies).
    (b) Declarer Prohibits Lead of Specified Suits
       When a defender has penalty cards in more than one suit, declarer may prohibit* the defender's partner from leading every such suit; but the defender may then pick up every penalty card in every suit prohibited by declarer, and make any legal play to the trick.

LAW 52. FAILURE TO LEAD OR PLAY A PENALTY CARD

A. Defender Fails to Play Penalty Card
When a defender fails to lead or play a major penalty card as required by Law 50, he may not, on his own initiative, withdraw any other card he has played.
  B. Defender Plays Another Card
  1. Play of Card Accepted
    (a) Declarer May Accept Play
       If a defender has led or played another card when required by law to play a penalty card, declarer may accept such lead or play.
    (b) Declarer Must Accept Play
       Declarer must accept such lead or play if he has thereafter played from his own hand or dummy.
    (c) Penalty Card Remains Penalty Card
       If the played card is accepted under either (a) or (b) preceding, the unplayed penalty card remains a penalty card.
  2. Play of Card Rejected
    Declarer may require the defender to substitute the penalty card for the card illegally played or led. Every card illegally led or played by the defender in the course of committing the irregularity becomes a major penalty card.

PART III: IRREGULAR LEADS AND PLAYS

SECTION ONE: LEAD OUT OF TURN

LAW 53. LEAD OUT OF TURN ACCEPTED

A. Lead Out of Turn Treated as Correct Lead
Any lead faced out of turn may be treated as a correct lead. It becomes a correct lead if declarer or either defender, as the case may be, accepts it (by making a statement to that

---

* If the player is unable to lead as required, see Law 59.

effect), or if the player next in rotation plays* to the irregular lead. (If no acceptance statement or play is made, the Director will require that the lead be made from the correct hand.)

B. Wrong Defender Plays Card to Declarer's Irregular Lead

If the defender at the right of the hand from which the lead out of turn was made plays* to the irregular lead, the lead stands and Law 57 applies.

C. Proper Lead Made Subsequent to Irregular Lead

If it was properly the turn to lead of an opponent of the player who led out of turn, that opponent may make his proper lead to the trick of the infraction without his card being deemed played to the irregular lead. When this occurs, the proper lead stands, and all cards played in error to this trick may be withdrawn without penalty.

LAW 54. FACED OPENING LEAD OUT OF TURN

A. A Declarer Spreads His Hand

After a faced opening lead out of turn, declarer may spread his hand; he becomes dummy, and dummy becomes declarer. If declarer begins to spread his hand, and in doing so exposes one or more cards, he must spread his entire hand.

B. Declarer Accepts Lead

When a defender faces the opening lead out of turn declarer may accept the irregular lead as provided in Law 53, and dummy is spread in accordance with Law 41.

    1. Declarer Plays Second Card

    The second card to the trick is played from declarer's hand.

    2. Dummy Has Played Second Card

    If declarer plays the second card to the trick from dummy, dummy's card may not be withdrawn except to correct a revoke.

C. Declarer Must Accept Lead

If declarer could have seen any of dummy's cards (except cards that dummy may have exposed during the auction and that were subject to Law 24), he must accept the lead.

D. Declarer Refuses Opening Lead

When declarer requires the defender to retract his faced opening lead out of turn, Law 56 applies.

LAW 55. DECLARER'S LEAD OUT OF TURN

A. Declarer's Lead Accepted

If declarer has led out of turn from his or dummy's hand, either defender may accept the lead as provided in Law 53, or require its retraction.

B. Declarer Required to Retract Lead

    1. Defender's Turn to Lead

    If declarer has led from his or dummy's hand when it was a defender's turn to lead, and if either defender requires him to retract such lead, declarer restores the card led in error to the proper hand without penalty.

    2. Lead in Declarer's Hand or Dummy's

    If declarer has led from the wrong hand when it was his turn to lead from his hand or dummy's, and if either defender requires him to retract the lead, he withdraws the card led in error. He must lead from the correct hand.

C. Declarer Might Obtain Information

When declarer adopts a line of play that could have been based on information obtained through the infraction, the Director may award an adjusted score.

* But see C below.

LAW 56. DEFENDER'S LEAD OUT OF TURN

When declarer requires a defender to retract his faced lead out of turn, the card illegally led becomes a major penalty card, and Law 50E applies.

SECTION TWO: OTHER IRREGULAR LEADS AND PLAYS

LAW 57. PREMATURE LEAD OR PLAY BY DEFENDER

A. Premature Play, or Lead to Next Trick

When a defender leads to the next trick before his partner has played to the current trick, or plays out of turn before his partner has played, (penalty) the card so led or played becomes a penalty card, and declarer selects one of the following options. He may:

1. Highest Card
   require offender's partner to play the highest card he holds of the suit led, or
2. Lowest Card
   require offender's partner to play the lowest card he holds of the suit led, or
3. Card of Another Suit
   forbid offender's partner to play a card of a different suit specified by declarer.

B. Offender's Partner Cannot Comply with Penalty

When offender's partner is unable to comply with the penalty selected by declarer, he may play any card, as provided in Law 59.

C. Declarer Has Played from Both Hands before Irregularity

A defender is not subject to penalty for playing before his partner if declarer has played from both hands, or if dummy has played a card or has illegally suggested that it be played. A singleton in dummy, or one of cards adjacent in rank of the same suit, is not considered to be automatically played.

LAW 58. SIMULTANEOUS LEADS OR PLAYS

A. Simultaneous Plays by Two Players

A lead or play made simultaneously with another player's legal lead or play is deemed to be subsequent to it.

B. Simultaneous Cards from One Hand

If a player leads or plays two or more cards simultaneously:

1. One Card Visible
   If only one card is visible, that card is played; all other cards are picked up without penalty.
2. More Cards Visible
   If more than one card is visible, the player designates the card he proposes to play; when he is a defender, each other card exposed becomes a penalty card (see Law 50).
3. After Visible Card Withdrawn
   After a player withdraws a visible card, an opponent who subsequently played to that card may withdraw his play and substitute another without penalty (see Law 47F).
4. Error Not Discovered
   If the simultaneous play remains undiscovered until both sides have played to the next trick, Law 67 applies.

LAW 59. INABILITY TO LEAD OR PLAY AS REQUIRED

A player may play any otherwise legal card if he is unable to lead or play as required to comply with a penalty, whether because he holds no card of the required suit, or because he has only cards of a suit he is prohibited from leading, or because he is obliged to follow suit.

LAW 60. PLAY AFTER AN ILLEGAL PLAY

A. Play of Card after Irregularity

1. Forfeiture of Right to Penalize

A play by a member of the non-offending side after his RHO has led or played out of turn or prematurely, and before a penalty has been assessed, forfeits the right to penalize that offense.

2. Irregularity Legalized

Once the right to penalize has been forfeited, the illegal play is treated as though it were in turn (but Law 53C applies to the player whose turn it was).

3. Other Penalty Obligations Remain

If the offending side has a previous obligation to play a penalty card, or to comply with a lead or play penalty, the obligation remains at future turns.

B. Defender Plays before Required Lead by Declarer

When a defender plays a card after declarer has been required to retract his lead out of turn from either hand, but before declarer has led from the correct hand, the defender's card becomes a penalty card (Law 50).

C. Play by Offending Side before Assessment of Penalty

A play by a member of the offending side before a penalty has been assessed does not affect the rights of the opponents, and may itself be subject to penalty.

SECTION THREE: THE REVOKE

LAW 61. FAILURE TO FOLLOW SUIT—INQUIRIES CONCERNING A REVOKE

A. Definition of Revoke

Failure to follow suit in accordance with Law 44, or failure to lead or play, when able, a card or suit required by law or specified by an opponent in accordance with an agreed penalty, constitutes a revoke (but see Law 59 when unable to comply).

B. Right to Inquire about a Possible Revoke

Declarer may ask a defender who has failed to follow suit whether he has a card of the suit led (but a claim of revoke does not automatically warrant inspection of quitted tricks—see Law 66C). Dummy may ask declarer. Defenders may ask declarer but not one another.

LAW 62. CORRECTION OF A REVOKE

A. Revoke Must Be Corrected

A player must correct his revoke if he becomes aware of the irregularity before it becomes established.

B. Correcting a Revoke

To correct a revoke, the offender withdraws the card he played in revoking and follows suit with any card.

1. Defender's Card

A card so withdrawn becomes a penalty card (Law 50) if it was played from a defender's unfaced hand.

2. Declarer's or Dummy's Card, Defender's Faced Card

The card may be replaced without penalty if it was played from declarer's or dummy's hand,* or if it was a defender's faced card.

---

* Subject to Law 43B2C, when dummy has forfeited his rights. A claim of revoke does not warrant inspection of quitted tricks except as permitted in Law 66C.

C. Subsequent Cards Played to Trick
  1. By Non-offending Side
     Each member of the non-offending side may, without penalty, withdraw any card he may have played after the revoke but before attention was drawn to it (see Law 47F).
  2. By Partner of Offender
     After a non-offender so withdraws a card, the hand of the offending side next in rotation may withdraw its played card, which becomes a penalty card if the player is a defender.
D. Revoke on Trick Twelve
  1. Must Be Corrected
     On the twelfth trick, a revoke, even if established, must be corrected if discovered before all four hands have been returned to the board.
  2. Offender's Partner Had Not Played to Trick Twelve
     If a revoke by a defender occurred before it was the turn of his partner to play to the twelfth trick, and if offender's partner has cards of two suits, (penalty) declarer may require the offender's partner to play to that trick either of the two cards he could legally have played.

LAW 63. ESTABLISHMENT OF A REVOKE

  A. Revoke Becomes Established
A revoke becomes established:
  1. Offending Side Leads or Plays to Next Trick
     when the offender or his partner leads or plays to the following trick (any such play, legal or illegal, establishes the revoke).
  2. A Member of Offending Side Indicates a Lead or Play
     when the offender or his partner names or otherwise designates a card to be played to the following trick.
  3. Member of Offending Side Makes a Claim or Concession
     when a member of the offending side makes or acquiesces in a claim or concession of tricks orally or by facing his hand (or in any other fashion).
  B. Revoke May Not Be Corrected
Once a revoke is established, it may no longer be corrected (except as provided in Law 62D for a revoke on the twelfth trick), and the trick on which the revoke occurred stands as played.

LAW 64. PROCEDURE AFTER ESTABLISHMENT OF A REVOKE

  A. Penalty Assessed
When a revoke is established:
  1. Offending Player Won Revoke Trick
     and the trick on which the revoke occurred was won by the offending player, (penalty) after play ceases, the trick on which the revoke occurred, plus one of any subsequent tricks won by the offending side, are transferred to the non-offending side;
  2. Offending Player Did Not Win Revoke Trick
     and the trick on which the revoke occurred was not won by the offending player, then, if the offending side won that or any subsequent trick, (penalty) after play ceases, one trick is transferred to the non-offending side; also, if an additional trick was subsequently won by the offending player with a card that he could legally have played to the revoke trick, one such trick is transferred to the non-offending side.

B. No Penalty Assessed

The penalty for an established revoke does not apply:

1. Offending Side Fails to Win Revoke Trick or Subsequent Trick

   if the offending side did not win either the revoke trick or any subsequent trick.

2. Second Revoke in Same Suit by Offender

   to a subsequent revoke in the same suit by the same player.

3. Revoke by Failure to Play a Faced Card

   if the revoke was made in failing to play any card faced on the table or belonging to a hand faced on the table, including a card from dummy's hand.

4. After Non-offending Side Calls to Next Deal

   if attention was first drawn to the revoke after a member of the non-offending side has made a call on the subsequent deal.

5. After Round Has Ended

   if attention was first drawn to the revoke after the round has ended.

6. Revoke on Twelfth Trick

   to a revoke on the twelfth trick.

C. Director Responsible for Equity

When, after any established revoke, including those not subject to penalty, the Director deems that the non-offending side is insufficiently compensated by this Law for the damage caused, he shall assign an adjusted score.

PART IV: TRICKS

LAW 65. ARRANGEMENT OF TRICKS

A. Completed Trick

When four cards have been played to a trick, each player turns his own card face down near him on the table.

B. Keeping Track of the Ownership of Tricks

1. Tricks Won

   If the player's side has won the trick, the card is pointed lengthwise toward his partner.

2. Tricks Lost

   If the opponents have won the trick, the card is pointed lengthwise toward the opponents.

C. Orderliness

Each player arranges his own cards in an orderly overlapping row in the sequence played, so as to permit review of the play after its completion, if necessary to determine the number of tricks won by each side or the order in which the cards were played.

D. Agreement on Results of Play

A player should not disturb the order of his played cards until agreement has been reached on the number of tricks won. A player who fails to comply with the provisions of this law jeopardizes his right to claim ownership of doubtful tricks or to claim a revoke.

LAW 66. INSPECTION OF TRICKS

A. Current Trick

So long as his side has not led or played to the next trick, declarer or either defender may, until he has turned his own card face down on the table, require that all cards just played to the trick be faced.

B. Own Last Card

Until a card is led to the next trick, declarer or either defender may inspect, but not expose, his own last card played.

C. Quitted Tricks

Thereafter, until play ceases, quitted tricks may not be inspected (except at the Director's specific instruction; for example, to verify a claim of a revoke).

D. After the Conclusion of Play

After play ceases, the played and unplayed cards may be inspected to settle a claim of a revoke, or of the number of tricks won or lost; but no player should handle cards other than his own. If, after such a claim has been made, a player mixes his cards in such a manner that the Director can no longer ascertain the facts, the Director shall rule in favor of the other side.

LAW 67. DEFECTIVE TRICK

A. Before Both Sides Play to Next Trick

When a player has omitted to play to a trick, or has played too many cards to a trick, the error must be rectified if attention is drawn to the irregularity before a player on each side has played to the following trick.

    1. Player Failed to Play Card

        To rectify omission to play to a trick, the offender supplies a card he can legally play.

    2. Player Contributed Too Many Cards

        To rectify the play of too many cards to a trick, Law 45E (Fifth Card Played to a Trick) or Law 58B (Simultaneous Cards from One Hand) shall be applied.

B. After Both Sides Play to Next Trick

After both sides have played to the following trick, when attention is drawn to a defective trick or when the Director determines that there had been a defective trick (from the fact that one player has too few or too many cards in his hand, and a correspondingly incorrect number of played cards), the Director establishes which trick was defective. To rectify the number of cards, the Director should proceed as follows.

    1. Offender Has Too Many Cards

        When the offender has failed to play a card to the defective trick, the Director shall require him forthwith to face a card, and to place it appropriately among his played cards (this card does not affect ownership of the trick); if

        (a) Offender Has Card of Suit Led

            the offender has a card of the suit led to the defective trick, he must choose such a card to place among his played cards, and there is no penalty;

        (b) Has No Card of Suit Led

            the offender has no card of the suit led to the defective trick, he chooses any card to place among his played cards, and (penalty) he is deemed to have revoked on the defective trick—he may be subject to the one-trick penalty of Law 64.

    2. Offender Has Too Few Cards

        When the offender has played more than one card to the defective trick, the Director inspects the played cards, and requires the offender to restore to his hand all extra cards,* leaving among the played cards the one faced in playing to the defective trick (if the Director is unable to determine which card was faced, the offender leaves the highest of the cards that he could legally have played to the trick). A restored card is deemed to have belonged continuously to the offender's hand, and a failure to have played it to an earlier trick may constitute a revoke.

---

* The Director should avoid, when possible, exposing a defender's played cards, but if an extra card to be restored to a defender's hand has been exposed, it becomes a penalty card (see Law 50).

PART V: CLAIMS AND CONCESSIONS

LAW 68. CLAIM OR CONCESSION OF TRICKS

For a statement or action to constitute a claim or concession of tricks under these Laws, it must refer to tricks other than one currently in progress.* If it does refer to subsequent tricks:

A. Claim Defined

Any statement to the effect that a contestant will win a specific number of tricks is a claim of those tricks. A contestant also claims when he suggests that play be curtailed, or when he shows his cards (unless he demonstrably did not intend to claim).

B. Concession Defined

Any statement to the effect that a contestant will lose a specific number of tricks is a concession of those tricks; a claim of some number of tricks is a concession of the remainder, if any. A player concedes all the remaining tricks when he abandons his hand. Regardless of the foregoing, if a defender attempts to concede one or more tricks and his partner immediately objects, no concession has occurred; Law 16, Unauthorized Information, and Law 57A, Premature Play, may apply, so the Director should be summoned forthwith.

C. Clarification Required for Claim

A claim should be accompanied at once by a statement of clarification as to the order in which cards will be played, the line of play or defense through which the claimer proposes to win the tricks claimed.

D. Play Ceases

After any claim or concession, play ceases. All play subsequent to a claim or concession shall be voided by the Director. If the claim or concession is acquiesced in, Law 69 applies; if it is disputed by any player (dummy included), the Director must be summoned immediately to apply Law 70 or Law 71, and no action may be taken pending the Director's arrival.

LAW 69. ACQUIESCENCE IN CLAIM OR CONCESSION

A. When Acquiescence Occurs

Acquiescence occurs when a contestant assents to an opponent's claim or concession, and raises no objection to it before his side makes a call on a subsequent board, or before the round ends. The board is scored as though the tricks claimed or conceded had been won or lost in play.

B. Acquiescence in Claim Withdrawn

Within the correction period established in accordance with Law 79C, a contestant may withdraw acquiescence in an opponent's claim, but only if he has acquiesced in the loss of a trick his side has actually won, or in the loss of trick that could not, in the Director's judgment, be lost by any normal** play of the remaining cards. The board is rescored with such trick awarded to the acquiescing side.

LAW 70. CONTESTED CLAIMS

A. General Objective

In ruling on a contested claim, the Director adjudicates the result of the board as equitably

---

* If the statement or action pertains only to the winning or losing of an uncompleted trick currently in progress, play proceeds regularly; cards exposed or revealed by a defender do not become penalty cards, but Law 16, Unauthorized Information, may apply, and see Law 57A, Premature Play.

** For the purposes of Laws 69, 70, and 71, "normal" includes play that would be careless or inferior for the class of player involved, but not irrational.

as possible to both sides, but any doubtful points shall be resolved against the claimer. The Director proceeds as follows:

B. Clarification Statement Repeated

1. Require Claimer to Repeat Statement

    The Director requires claimer to repeat the clarification statement he made at the time of his claim.

2. Require All Hands to Be Faced

    Next, the Director requires all players to put their remaining cards face up on the table.

3. Hear Objections

    The Director then hears the opponents' objections to the claim.

C. There Is an Outstanding Trump

When a trump remains in one of the opponents' hands, the Director shall award a trick or tricks to the opponents if:

1. Failed to Mention Trump

    claimer made no statement about that trump, and

2. Was Probably Unaware of Trump

    it is at all likely that claimer at the time of his claim was unaware that a trump remained in an opponent's hand, and

3. Could Lose a Trick to the Trump

    a trick could be lost to that trump by any normal* play.

D. Claimer Proposes New Line of Play

The Director shall not accept from claimer any successful line of play not embraced in the original clarification statement if there is an alternative normal* line of play that would be less successful.

E. Unstated Line of Play (Finesse or Drop)

The Director shall not accept from claimer any unstated line of play the success of which depends upon finding one opponent rather than the other with a particular card, unless an opponent failed to follow to the suit of that card before the claim was made, or would subsequently fail to follow to that suit on any normal* line of play.

LAW 71. CONCESSION CANCELED

A concession must stand, once made, except that:

A. False Concession

Within the correction period established in accordance with Law 79C, the Director shall cancel a concession:

1. Trick Cannot be Lost

    if a player has conceded a trick his side had, in fact, won, or a trick his side could not have lost by any legal play of the remaining cards.

2. Contract Already Fulfilled or Defeated

    if declarer has conceded defeat of a contract he had already fulfilled, or a defender has conceded fulfillment of a contract his side had already defeated.

B. Implausible Concession

Until the conceding side makes a call on a subsequent board, or until the round ends, the Director shall cancel the concession of a trick that could not have been lost by any normal* play of the remaining cards.

For the purposes of Laws 69, 70, and 71, "normal" includes play that would be careless or inferior for the class of player involved, but not irrational.

Chapter VII

Proprieties

LAW 72. GENERAL PRINCIPLES

A. Observance of Laws

1. General Obligation on Contestants
Duplicate bridge tournaments should be played in strict accordance with the Laws.

2. Scoring of Tricks Won
It is improper for a player knowingly to accept either the score for a trick that his side did not win, or the concession of a trick that his opponents could not lose.

3. Waiving of Penalties
In duplicate tournaments a player may not, on his own initiative, waive a penalty for an opponent's infraction, even if he feels that he has not been damaged (but he may ask the Director to do so—see Law 81C8).

4. Non-offenders' Exercise of Legal Options
When these Laws provide the innocent side with an option after an irregularity committed by an opponent, it is appropriate to select that action most advantageous.

5. Offenders' Options
After the offending side has paid the prescribed penalty for an inadvertent infraction, it is appropriate for the offenders to make any call or play advantageous to their side, even though they thereby appear to profit through their own infraction.

6. Responsibility for Enforcement of Laws
The responsibility for penalizing irregularities and redressing damage rests solely upon the Director and these Laws, not upon the players themselves.

B. Infraction of Law

1. Intentional
To infringe a law intentionally is a serious breach of propriety, even if there is a prescribed penalty that one is willing to pay. The offense may be the more serious when no penalty is prescribed.

2. Inadvertent Infraction
There is no obligation to draw attention to an inadvertent infraction of law committed by one's own side (but see footnote to Law 75 for a mistaken explanation).

3. Concealing an Infraction
A player may not attempt to conceal an inadvertent infraction, as by committing a second revoke, concealing a card involved in a revoke, or mixing the cards prematurely.

LAW 73. COMMUNICATION BETWEEN PARTNERS

A. Proper Communication between Partners

1. How Effected
Communication between partners during the auction and play should be effected only by means of the calls and plays themselves.

2. Correct Manner for Calls and Plays
Calls and plays should be made without special emphasis, mannerism or inflection, and without undue hesitation or haste (however, sponsoring organizations may require mandatory pauses, as on the first round of auction, or after a skip-bid warning, or on the first trick).

B. Inappropriate Communication Between Partners
 1. Gratuitous Information
    It is inappropriate for communication between partners to be effected through the manner in which calls or plays are made, through extraneous remarks or gestures, or through questions asked or not asked of the opponents, through alerts and explanations given or not given to them.
 2. Prearranged Communication
    The gravest possible offense against propriety is for a partnership to exchange information through prearranged methods of communication other than those sanctioned by these Laws. The penalty imposed for infraction is normally expulsion from the sponsoring organization.
C. Player Receives Unauthorized Information from Partner
When a player has available to him unauthorized information from his partner's remark, question, explanation, gesture, mannerism, special emphasis, inflection, haste or hesitation, he must carefully avoid taking any advantage that might accrue to his side.
D. Variations in Tempo
 1. Inadvertent Variations
    Variations of tempo, manner, or the like may violate the Proprieties when the player could know, at the time of his action, that the variation could work to his benefit. Otherwise, inadvertently to vary the tempo or manner in which a call or play is made does not in itself constitute a violation of propriety, but inferences from such variation may appropriately be drawn only by an opponent, and at his own risk.
 2. Intentional Variations
    It is grossly improper to attempt to mislead an opponent by means of remark or gesture, through the haste or hesitancy of a call or play (as in hesitating before playing a singleton), or by the manner in which the call or play is made.
E. Deception
Any player may appropriately attempt to deceive an opponent through a call or play (so long as the deception is not protected by concealed partnership understanding). It is entirely appropriate to avoid giving information to the opponents by making all calls and plays in unvarying tempo and manner.
F. Violation of Proprieties
When a violation of the Proprieties described in this law results in damage to an innocent opponent:
 1. Player Acts on Unauthorized Information
    If the Director determines that a player chose from among logical alternative actions one that could reasonably have been suggested over another by his partner's remark, manner, tempo, or the like, he shall award an adjusted score (see Law 16).
 2. Player Injured by Illegal Deception
    If the Director determines that an innocent player has drawn a false inference from a deceptive remark, manner, tempo, or the like, of an opponent who could have known, at the time of the action, that the deception could work to his benefit, the Director shall award an adjusted score (see Law 12).

LAW 74. CONDUCT AND ETIQUETTE

A. Proper Attitude
 1. Courtesy
    A player should maintain at all times a courteous attitude.
 2. Etiquette of Word and Action

A player should carefully avoid any remark or action that might cause annoyance or embarrassment to another player, or might interfere with the enjoyment of the game.

3. Conformity to Correct Procedure

Every player should follow uniform and correct procedure in calling and playing, since any departure from correct standards may disrupt the orderly progress of the game.

B. Etiquette

As a matter of courtesy a player should refrain from:

1. paying insufficient attention to the game.
2. making gratuitous comments during the auction and play.
3. detaching a card before it is his turn to play.
4. prolonging play unnecessarily (as in playing on although he knows that all the tricks are surely his) for the purpose of disconcerting an opponent.
5. summoning the Director in a manner discourteous to him or to other contestants.

C. Breaches of Propriety

The following are considered breaches of propriety:

1. using different designations for the same call.
2. indicating approval or disapproval of a call or play.
3. indicating the expectation or intention of winning or losing a trick that has not been completed.
4. commenting or acting during the auction or play so as to call attention to a significant occurrence, or to the number of tricks still required for success.
5. looking intently at any other player during the auction and play, or at another player's hand as for the purpose of seeing his cards or of observing the place from which he draws a card (but it is appropriate to act on information acquired by inadvertently seeing an opponent's card*).
6. showing an obvious lack of further interest in a deal (as by folding one's cards).
7. varying the normal tempo of bidding or play for the purpose of disconcerting an opponent.
8. leaving the table needlessly before the round is called.

LAW 75. PARTNERSHIP AGREEMENTS

A. Special Partnership Agreements

Special partnership agreements, whether explicit or implicit, must be fully and freely available to the opponents (see Law 40). Information conveyed to partner through such agreements must arise from the calls, plays and conditions of the current deal.

B. Violations of Partnership Agreements

It is not improper for a player to violate an announced partnership agreement, so long as his partner is unaware of the violation (but habitual violations within a partnership may create implicit agreements, which must be disclosed). No player has the obligation to disclose to the opponents that he has violated an announced agreement; and if the opponents are subsequently damaged, as through drawing a false inference from such violation, they are not entitled to redress.

C. Answering Questions on Partnership Agreements

When explaining the significance of partner's call or play in reply to an opponent's inquiry (see Law 20), a player shall disclose all special information conveyed to him through partnership agreement or partnership experience; but he need not disclose inferences drawn from his general knowledge and experience.

* See Law 73D2 when a player may have shown his cards intentionally.

D. Correcting Errors in Explanation
   1. Explainer Notices Own Error
      If a player subsequently realizes that his own explanation was erroneous or incomplete, he must immediately call the Director (who will apply Law 21 or Law 40C).
   2. Error Noticed by Explainer's Partner
      It is inappropriate for a player whose partner has given a mistaken explanation to correct the error immediately, before the final pass of the auction, or until play ends if he is a defender; nor is it appropriate for him to indicate in any manner that a mistake has been made. (He must not take advantage of the unauthorized information so obtained.) However, the player must inform the opponents, after calling the Director, that his partner's explanation was erroneous, at the earliest legal opportunity: after the final pass if he is to be declarer or dummy; after play ends if he is to be a defender.*

LAW 76. SPECTATORS

A. Conduct During Bidding or Play
   1. One Hand Only
      A spectator should not look at the cards of more than one player, except by permission.

---

* *Two examples may clarify responsibilities of the players (and the Director) after a misleading explanation has been given to the opponents. In both examples following, North has opened one notrump and South, who holds a weak hand with long diamonds, has bid two diamonds, intending to sign off; North explains, however, in answer to West's inquiry, that South's bid is strong and artificial, asking for major suits.*

Example 1—Mistaken Explanation

The actual partnership agreement is that two diamonds is a natural signoff; the mistake was in North's explanation. This explanation is an infraction of law, since East-West are entitled to an accurate description of the North-South agreement (when this infraction results in damage to East-West, the Director shall award an adjusted score). If North subsequently becomes aware of his mistake, he must immediately notify the Director. South must do nothing to correct the mistaken explanation while the auction continues; after the final pass, South, if he is to be declarer or dummy, should call the Director and must volunteer a correction of the explanation. If South becomes a defender, he calls the Director and corrects the explanation when play ends.

Example 2—Mistaken Bid

The partnership agreement is as explained—two diamonds is strong and artificial; the mistake was in South's bid. Here there is no infraction of law, since East-West did receive an accurate description of the North-South agreement; they have no claim to an accurate description of the North-South hands.

(Regardless of damage, the Director shall allow the result to stand; but the Director is to presume Mistaken Explanation, rather than Mistaken Bid, in the absence of evidence to the contrary.) South must not correct North's explanation (or notify the Director) immediately, and he has no responsibility to do so subsequently.

In both examples, South, having heard North's explanation, knows that his own two diamond bid has been misinterpreted. This knowledge is "unauthorized information" (see Law 16A), so South must be careful not to base subsequent actions on this information (if he does, the Director shall award an adjusted score). For instance, if North rebids two notrump, South has the unauthorized information that this bid merely denies a four-card holding in either major suit; but South's responsibility is to act as though North had made a strong game try opposite a weak response, showing maximum values.

2. Personal Reaction

A spectator must not display any reaction to the bidding or play while a hand is in progress.

3. Mannerisms or Remarks

During the round, a spectator must refrain from mannerisms or remarks of any kind (including conversation with a player).

4. Consideration for Players

A spectator must not in any way disturb a player.

B. Spectator Participation

A spectator may not call attention to any irregularity or mistake, nor speak on any question of fact or law except by request of the Director.

Chapter VIII

The Score

LAW 77. DUPLICATE BRIDGE SCORING TABLE

TRICK SCORE

Scored by declarer's side if the contract is fulfilled.

IF TRUMPS ARE	♣	◇	♡	♠
For each odd trick bid and made				
Undoubled	20	20	30	30
Doubled	40	40	60	60
Redoubled	80	80	120	120

	AT A NOTRUMP CONTRACT		
	UNDOUBLED	DOUBLED	REDOUBLED
For the first odd trick bid and made	40	80	160
For each additional odd trick	30	60	120

A trick score of 100 points or more, made on one board, is GAME. A trick score of less than 100 points is a PARTSCORE.

PREMIUM SCORE

Scored by declarer's side

SLAMS

	Not Vulnerable	Vulnerable
For making a slam		
Small Slam (12 tricks) bid and made	500	750
Grand Slam (all 13 tricks) bid and made	1000	1500

OVERTRICKS

			Not Vulnerable	Vulnerable
For each OVERTRICK				
(tricks made in excess of contract)				
Undoubled	Trick Value	Trick Value		
Doubled	100	200		
Redoubled	200	400		

PREMIUMS FOR GAME, PARTSCORE, FULFILLING CONTRACT

For making GAME, vulnerable	500
For making GAME, not vulnerable	300
For making any PARTSCORE	50
For making any doubled, but not redoubled contract	50
For making any redoubled contract	100

UNDERTRICK PENALTIES

Scored by declarer's opponents if the contract is not fulfilled:

UNDERTRICKS

(tricks by which declarer falls short of the contract)

	Not Vulnerable			Vulnerable		
	Undbld	Dbld	Rdbld	Undbld	Dbld	Rdbld
For first undertrick	50	100	200	100	200	400
For each additional undertrick	50	200	400	100	300	600
Bonus for the fourth and each subsequent undertrick	0	100	200	0	0	0

LAW 78. METHODS OF SCORING

A. Matchpoint Scoring

In matchpoint scoring each contestant is awarded, for scores made by different contestants who have played the same board and whose scores are compared with his: two scoring units (matchpoints or half matchpoints) for each score inferior to his, one scoring unit for each score equal to his, and zero scoring units for each score superior to his.

B. International Matchpoint Scoring

In international matchpoint scoring, on each board the total point difference between the two scores compared is converted into IMP's according to the following scale:

Difference in points	I.M.P.	Difference in points	I.M.P.	Difference in points	I.M.P.
20–40	1	370–420	9	1500–1740	17
50– 80	2	430– 490	10	1750–1990	18
90–120	3	500– 590	11	2000–2240	19
130–160	4	600– 740	12	2250–2490	20
170–210	5	750– 890	13	2500–2990	21
220–260	6	900–1090	14	3000–3490	22
270–310	7	1100–1290	15	3500–3990	23
320–360	8	1300–1490	16	4000 & upwards	24

C. Total Point Scoring

In total point scoring, the net total point score of all boards played is the score for each contestant.

D. Special Scoring Methods

Special scoring methods are permissible, if approved by the sponsoring organization. In advance of any contest the sponsoring organization should publish conditions of contest detailing conditions of entry, methods of scoring, determination of winners, breaking of ties, and the like.

LAW 79. TRICKS WON

A. Agreement on Tricks Won

The number of tricks won shall be agreed upon before all four hands have been returned to the board.

B. Disagreement on Tricks Won

If a subsequent disagreement arises, the Director must be called. No increase in score may be granted unless the Director is called before the round ends as specified in Law 8 (but Law 69 or Law 71 may supersede this provision when there has been an acquiescence or a concession).

C. Error in Score

An error in computing or tabulating the agreed-upon score, whether made by a player or scorer, may be corrected until the expiration of the period specified by the sponsoring organization. Unless the sponsoring organization specifies a later* time, this correction period expires 30 minutes after the official score has been completed and made available for inspection.

Chapter IX

Tournament Sponsorship

LAW 80. SPONSORING ORGANIZATION

A sponsoring organization conducting an event under these Laws has the following duties and powers:

A. Tournament Director

to appoint the tournament Director. If there is no tournament Director, the players should designate one of their own number to perform his functions.

B. Advance Arrangements

to make advance arrangements for the tournament, including playing quarters, accommodations, and equipment.

C. Session Times

to establish the date and time of each session.

D. Conditions of Entry

to establish the conditions of entry.

E. Special Conditions

to establish special conditions for bidding and play (such as written bidding, bidding boxes, screens—penalty provisions for actions not transmitted across a screen may be suspended).

F. Supplementary Regulations

to publish or announce regulations supplementary to, but not in conflict with, these Laws.

Chapter X

Tournament Director

SECTION ONE: RESPONSIBILITIES

LAW 81: DUTIES AND POWERS

A. Official Status

The Director is the official representative of the sponsoring organization.

* An earlier time may be specified when required by the special nature of a contest.

   B. Restrictions and Responsibilities
      1. Technical Management
        The Director is responsible for the technical management of the tournament.
      2. Observance of Laws and Regulations
        The Director is bound by these Laws and by supplementary regulations announced by the sponsoring organization.
   C. Director's Duties and Powers
The Director's duties and powers normally include the following:
      1. Assistants
        to appoint assistants, as required to perform his duties.
      2. Entries
        to accept and list entries.
      3. Conditions of Play
        to establish suitable conditions of play, and to announce them to the contestants.
      4. Discipline
        to maintain discipline, and to insure the orderly progress of the game.
      5. Law
        to administer and interpret these Laws, and to advise the players of their rights and responsibilities thereunder.
      6. Errors
        to rectify any error or irregularity of which he becomes aware in any manner, within the correction period established in accordance with Law 79C.
      7. Penalties
        to assess penalties when applicable.
      8. Waiver of Penalties
        to waive penalties for cause, at his discretion, upon the request of the non-offending side.
      9. Disputes
        to adjust disputes, and to refer disputed matters to the appropriate committee when required.
     10. Scores
        to collect scores and tabulate results.
     11. Reports
        to report results to the sponsoring organization for official record.
   D. Delegation of Duties
The Director may delegate any of the duties listed in 'C' to assistants, but he is not thereby relieved of responsibility for their correct performance.

LAW 82. RECTIFICATION OF ERRORS OF PROCEDURE

   A. Director's Duty
It is the duty of the Director to rectify errors of procedure and to maintain the progress of the game in a manner that is not contrary to these Laws.
   B. Rectification of Error
To rectify an error in procedure the Director may:
      1. Award of Adjusted Score
        award an adjusted score as permitted by these Laws.
      2. Specify Time of Play
        require or postpone the play of a board.
   C. Director's Error
If the Director has given a ruling that he or the Chief Director subsequently determines to be incorrect, and if no rectification will allow the board to be scored normally, he shall award an adjusted score, considering both sides as non-offending for that purpose.

LAW 83. NOTIFICATION OF THE RIGHT TO APPEAL

If the Director believes that a review of his decision on a point of fact or exercise of his discretionary power might be in order (as when he awards an adjusted score under Law 12), he shall advise a contestant of his right to appeal.

SECTION TWO: RULINGS

LAW 84. RULINGS ON AGREED FACTS

When the Director is called to rule on a point of law or regulation in which the facts are agreed upon, he shall rule as follows:

A. No Penalty

If no penalty is prescribed by law, and there is no occasion for him to exercise his discretionary powers, he directs the players to proceed with the auction or play.

B. Penalty under Law

If a case is clearly covered by a law that specifies a penalty for the irregularity, he assesses that penalty and sees that it is paid.

C. Player's Option

If a law gives a player a choice among penalties, the Director explains the options and sees that a penalty is selected and paid.

D. Director's Option

If the law gives the Director a choice between a specified penalty and the award of an adjusted score, he attempts to restore equity, resolving any doubtful point in favor of the non-offending side.

E. Discretionary Penalty

If an irregularity has occurred for which no penalty is provided by law, the Director awards an adjusted score if there is even a reasonable possibility that the non-offending side was damaged, notifying the offending side of its right to appeal.

LAW 85. RULINGS ON DISPUTED FACTS

When the Director is called upon to rule on a point of law or regulation in which the facts are not agreed upon, he shall proceed as follows:

A. Director's Assessment

If the Director is satisfied that he has ascertained the facts, he rules as in Law 84.

B. Facts Not Determined

If the Director is unable to determine the facts to his satisfaction, he shall make a ruling that will permit play to continue, and notify the players of their right to appeal.

SECTION THREE: CORRECTION OF IRREGULARITIES

LAW 86. IN TEAM PLAY

A. Average Score at IMP Play

When the Director chooses to award an artificial adjusted score of 60% (see Law 84) to a non-offending contestant in IMP play, that score is 3 IMP.

B. Non-balancing Adjustments, Knockout Play

When the Director assigns non-balancing adjusted scores (see Law 12C) in knockout play, each contestant's score on the board is calculated separately. The average of the two scores is then assigned to both contestants.

C. Substitute Board

The Director shall not exercise his Law 6 authority to order one board redealt when the final result of a match without that board could be known to a contestant. Instead, he awards an adjusted score.

LAW 87. FOULED BOARD

A. Definition

A board is considered to be "fouled" if the Director determines that one or more cards were misplaced in the board, in such manner that contestants who should have had a direct score comparison did not play the board in identical form.

B. Scoring the Fouled Board

In scoring a fouled board the Director determines as closely as possible which scores were made on the board in its correct form, and which in the changed form. He divides the score on that basis into two groups, and rates each group separately as provided in the regulations of the sponsoring organization.

SECTION FOUR: PENALTIES

LAW 88. AWARD OF INDEMNITY POINTS

In a pair or individual event, when a non-offending contestant is required to take an artificial adjusted score through no fault or choice of his own, such contestant shall be awarded a minimum of 60% of the matchpoints available to him on that board, or the percentage of matchpoints he earned on boards actually played during the session if that percentage was greater than 60%.

LAW 89. PENALTIES IN INDIVIDUAL EVENTS

In individual events, the Director shall enforce the penalty provisions of these Laws, and the provisions requiring the award of adjusted scores, equally against both members of the offending side, even though only one of them may be responsible for the irregularity. But the Director, in awarding adjusted scores, shall not assess procedural penalty points against the offender's partner, if, in the Director's opinion, he is in no way responsible for the violation.

LAW 90. PROCEDURAL PENALTIES

A. Director's Authority

The Director, in addition to enforcing the penalty provisions of these Laws, may also assess penalties for any offense that unduly delays or obstructs the game, inconveniences other contestants, violates correct procedure, or requires the award of an adjusted score at another table.

B. Offenses Subject to Penalty

Offenses subject to penalty include but are not limited to:

1. Tardiness
arrival of a contestant after the specified starting time.
2. Slow Play
any unduly slow play by a contestant.
3. Loud Discussion
any discussion of the bidding, play, or result of a board, which may be overheard at another table.
4. Comparing Scores
any comparison of scores with another contestant during a session.
5. Touching Another's Cards
any touching or handling of cards belonging to another player (Law 7).
6. Misplacing Cards in Board
placing one or more cards in an incorrect pocket of the board.
7. Errors in Procedure
any error in procedure (such as failure to count cards in one's hand, playing the wrong board, etc.) that requires an adjusted score for any contestant.

8. Failure to Comply

any failure to comply promptly with tournament regulations, or with any instruction of the Director.

LAW 91. PENALIZE OR SUSPEND

A. Director's Power

In performing his duty to maintain order and discipline, the Director is specifically empowered to assess disciplinary penalties in points, or to suspend a contestant for the current session or any part thereof (the Director's decision under this clause is final).

B. Right to Disqualify

The Director is specifically empowered to disqualify a contestant for cause, subject to approval by the Tournament Committee or sponsoring organization.

Chapter XI

Appeals

LAW 92. RIGHT TO APPEAL

A. Contestant's Right

A contestant or his Captain may appeal for a review of any ruling made at his table by the Director.

B. Time of Appeal

Any appeal for or of a Director's ruling must be made within the time period established in accordance with Law 79C.

C. How to Appeal

All appeals shall be made through the Director.

D. Concurrence of Appellants

An appeal shall not be heard unless both members of a pair (except in an individual contest), or the captain of a team, concur in appealing. An absent member shall be deemed to concur.

LAW 93. PROCEDURES OF APPEAL

A. No Appeals Committee

The Chief Director shall hear and rule upon all appeals if there is no Tournament or Appeals committee, or when a committee cannot meet without disturbing the orderly progress of the tournament.

B. Appeals Committee Available

If a committee is available,

1. Appeal Concerns Law

The Chief Director shall hear and rule upon such part of the appeal as deals solely with the law or regulations. His ruling may be appealed to the committee.

2. All Other Appeals

The Chief Director shall refer all other appeals to the committee for adjudication.

3. Adjudication of Appeals

In adjudicating appeals the committee may exercise all powers assigned by these Laws to the Director, except that the committee may not overrule the Director on a point of law or regulations, or on exercise of his disciplinary powers. The committee may recommend to the Director that he change his ruling.

C. Appeal to National Authority

After the preceding remedies have been exhausted, further appeal may be taken to the national authority (on a point of law, in the ACBL the National Laws Commission, 2200 Democrat Road, Memphis, TN 38116).

BRIDGE VARIATIONS

Chicago (Four-deal) Bridge

In bridge clubs and social home games when more than four players are present, rubber bridge is an impediment to the enjoyability of the game. Too often a hard-fought rubber can stretch to over an hour to complete, which is a wearisome time for the player or players who are waiting to cut into the game. To resolve this difficulty, American clubs have adopted Chicago in lieu of rubber bridge. Since a Chicago "rubber" consists of exactly four hands, which are usually completed within 15 to 20 minutes, players sitting out can be accommodated quickly. The rules of Chicago are on page 157.

Pivot Bridge

Pivot bridge is simply a rotation of partners when there are four or five players at the table. The game is arranged so that each player plays with each other player as a partner once and as an opponent twice. The method of play can be rubber bridge or Chicago, where the players change at the end of every four deals, each player having dealt once (or redealt if a hand was passed out).

The rotation for four players can be done two ways. Players can cut for choice of seats and cards each round. If on the second round the same players cut each other again, the player with the highest card plays with the one who drew the third-highest card. Since the third round is predetermined, the cut is for choice of seats and cards only.

A more formal movement is that the player who draws the highest card on the first round becomes the *wheel* for the pivot. He has choice of cards for the entire pivot and for seats for the first round. His partner for the first round is the player who drew second-highest card. Third-highest sits to the wheel's left and fourth-highest to his right. At the end of the first round the players rotate clockwise around the wheel, who remains stationary. After three rounds have been completed, the players cut to start a new pivot.

When five players are present, the initial cut determines the order of who sits out. Lowest card is first out; highest card is last out. The two players drawing the highest two cards become partners for the first round against the other two. Choice of cards and seats go to the player with the highest card. When the first round is over, the player entering the game replaces the next out and the two players to the right of the incoming player switch seats. This pivoting continues until five rounds are finished. Since players are constantly changing seats in a five-handed rotation, there is no wheel for the pivot. Therefore the players should decide beforehand whether to cut for dealer and choice of cards on each round, or to allow the deal to continue from the preceding round. The five-handed rotation can also accommodate six players, but if the above movement is used, all but one player will have to sit out two consecutive rounds before reentering the game.

As a matter of courtesy, the players should agree to complete a pivot once they have started it, unless a player announces prior to the start of a pivot that he is unable to do so.

Cutthroat Contract

Many have sought methods to devise a Bridge game in which the partnerships are not fixed in advance but are determined by the bidding. One such was Pirate Bridge, devised in Auction Bridge days by R. F. Foster; another was Elective Contract, the inventor of which was F. Dudley Courtenay. Of all these games, the one that came closest to becoming generally popular is the one described below, the invention of S. B. Fishburne, and called "Reject," or Cutthroat Contract—a name more often used for regular three-handed Bridge (page 225).

The Auction. After the same preliminaries as in Contract Bridge, with the 52-card pack, the four players proceed to bid as in Contract Bridge except: (1) a player is subject to penalty if he makes the opening bid without having at least 13 points in high cards and at least four cards in the suit bid; (2) the first bid may be any legal bid, from one club up, but the second bid may be no lower than three notrump (in some games, four notrump, or three notrump with no subsequent bids below game).

If the final bid is not sufficient for game, the cards are thrown in and a new hand is dealt. No doubling is permitted during the auction, so a player is always safe in making a partscore bid, no matter how unprepared he may be to play it.

If the final bid is sufficient for game, the player who made it becomes the declarer and selects any of the other players as his partner. Unless that player is already in the seat opposite declarer, he exchanges places with the player in that seat.

The partner selected may now accept the partnership, in which case the scoring will be as in Contract Bridge; or may reject the partnership, in which case declarer will collect from all three other players if he makes his contract and will pay all three other players if he is defeated.

When the partnership has been accepted or rejected, the defender on declarer's left may double, and if he does not, the other defender may double. If doubled, declarer may redouble (or dummy may redouble if he has accepted).

The Play proceeds as in Contract Bridge.

Scoring. A separate score is kept for each player, who may score both above and below the line. A player holding honors receives the only score for them. If declarer makes his contract and neither defender is vulnerable, he scores 700 points as a rubber bonus; if either defender is vulnerable he scores only 500. If dummy has accepted the partnership and is not vulnerable, he gets only 300 points for game even though declarer wins the rubber; but if he and declarer are both vulnerable, both score the rubber bonus.

If declarer is defeated, and he is vulnerable (or dummy is vulnerable and has accepted) the defenders score the undertrick penalties at vulnerable rates.

When a player has won two games, the rubber ends; all scores are totalled up and each player settles with each other player on the difference in their scores.

Irregularities. If a player passes out of turn, each of the other three players scores 50; if he bids or doubles out of turn, each of the other players scores 300. An insufficient bid must be corrected unless the player next in turn has called, but is not subject to any other penalty.

If declarer made the opening bid, and does not have the requirements, he may announce this fact before selecting his partner and in that case there is no penalty; if it is discovered after he has selected his partner, declarer pays 300 points to each player. If declarer's partner opened the bidding without the requirements, declarer may call the deal off and he and the other two players each score the 300-point penalty; or declarer may condone the offense, in which case there is no penalty.

Strategy. Every player tries to doublecross every other player. Fake bids that misrepresent the hand are frequent, the idea being to induce one's selection as a partner, and then, by rejection, to collect undertrick penalties.

Goulashes

Strictly speaking, the "goulash" hand (also called Mayonnaise, or Hollandaise) is not a game, but only a way of creating freak hands in a regular Bridge game; however, some players prefer games in which nothing but goulash hands are played.

Usually, a goulash is played only after a hand has been passed out in a regular Contract Bridge game. Every player assorts his cards into suits. Dealer places his sorted hand, face down, in the center of the table; on top of this is placed the hand of the player on his left, then his partner's hand, then the hand of the player on his right. The cards may now be dealt with or without a cut; it is preferable to have them cut. Dealer gives five cards at a time to each player, then another five cards at a time to each player, then three cards at a time to each player. The resultant hands are bid, played and scored as in Contract Bridge. The assortment of the cards almost always results in freakish hands.

Passing Goulashes. In the form of goulash play which became most popular, after picking up his goulash hand each player exchanged one card, face down, with his partner; having looked at his new card, he exchanged two cards with his partner; and having looked at these he exchanged three cards with his partner. The auction then began.

This form of the game permitted even more freakish hands to be built up.

When playing passing goulashes, it is permissible to return to partner a card previously received from him; in fact, it was often conventionally played that the first card so passed signaled the player's desire for other cards of that suit, and the card passed was supposed to be returned later.

A version of goulash is played on commuter trains in order to get in as many hands as possible before the players reach their destination. After each deal, the deck is shuffled once or not at all, and the cards are dealt out in packets of five, five, and three. The bidding, play, and scoring are as in Contract Bridge.

Towie

Essentially a three-hand game, Towie may be played by four, five, or more players, only three of whom are active at any one time. The game was invented by J. Leonard Replogle and Paulding Fosdick.

Preliminaries. As in Contract Bridge. Four hands are dealt, the one opposite dealer (between his two opponents) being dummy. Following the deal, dealer must turn up six of dummy's cards before looking at his hand. The players then bid, in turn, as in Contract Bridge, two passes following any call closing the bidding.

If the final contract is not enough for game, a goulash is next played; but the final contract is sufficient for game if fulfilling it will result in 100 trick points; that is, a contract of two spades doubled is a game contract.

When a goulash is played, dealer assorts dummy's hand. After the deal, he shuffles the new dummy hand. Six cards of dummy are turned up after a goulash deal, as after any other deal.

The Play is as at Contract Bridge.

The Scoring follows the Contract Bridge laws of 1927, which have since been revised. The Towie scoring table is as follows:

ODD TRICKS: Notrump, 35; spades or hearts, 30; diamonds or clubs, 20. If doubled, multiply by 2; if redoubled, by 4. Game requires 100 in trick points.

OVERTRICKS: Not doubled, 50 each. Doubled, 100 each if not vulnerable, 200 if vulnerable. Redoubled, 200 each if not vulnerable, 400 if vulnerable.

FULFILLING CONTRACT: Doubled, 50 if not vulnerable, 100 if vulnerable; redoubled, 100 if not vulnerable, 200 if vulnerable.

UNDERTRICKS: Undoubled, 50 each if not vulnerable, 100 if vulnerable. Doubled and not vulnerable, 100 each for 1st and 2nd, 200 each for 3rd and 4th, 400 each thereafter; doubled and vulnerable, 200 for 1st, 400 each thereafter. If redoubled, multiply doubled values by 2.

GAME, RUBBER: The winner of a game scores 500 and becomes vulnerable; when a vulnerable player makes a game he scores 1000 as a rubber bonus, and a new rubber is begun.

SLAMS, HONORS: Same as in Contract Bridge.

A separate score is kept for each player, and points he scores are entered to his credit. At the end of the game, each player settles with each other player the difference in their scores.

If declarer fulfills his contract, he scores whatever points are due him; if declarer is defeated, every other player, whether active or not, scores the undertrick penalties. Honors are scored only by the player holding them.

Precedence. An original order of precedence is established by drawing, if there are more than four players. After each deal declarer goes out and the next player in order of precedence replaces him.

A player who is not vulnerable always ranks in order of precedence ahead of a player who is vulnerable.

Irregularities. *New Deal.* Exposure of a card in dummy during the deal does not require a new deal unless more than six cards are so exposed, in which event there is a new deal and each player other than dealer scores 100 points. In case of an irregularity in the deal of a goulash, there is a regular redeal followed by a goulash deal. There must be a new deal if a player takes up and looks at another player's hand; and each of the offender's opponents scores 100 points.

Facing dummy's cards. If dealer looks at any of his own cards before turning up six of dummy's cards, each of his opponents scores 100 points; if dealer turns up any of dummy's cards in a goulash without having shuffled them, each of his opponents scores 100 points (independent of the penalty if dummy has also looked at his own cards first). An opponent who turns up any of dummy's cards, except at dealer's request, pays dealer 100 points for every opponent of dealer. If dealer turns up more than six of dummy's cards, he pays 100 points to each opponent and there must be a new deal.

Call out of turn. Successive calls by both other active players condone it. Otherwise: A pass, bid, double or redouble out of turn is void and the offender is barred thereafter.

Insufficient bid. If the offender corrects it before attention is drawn to it, he need only make it sufficient in the same denomination. If attention is drawn to the irregularity before correction, the offender must make the bid sufficient and is thereafter barred from the auction.

Revoke. The penalty for an established revoke is two tricks for the first revoke and one trick for each subsequent revoke.

Inactive players. If an inactive player advises an active player in bidding or play, he pays 100 points to every other player.

Three-hand Bridge

CUTTHROAT BRIDGE

Three players, but the preliminaries and deal are as in Contract Bridge. The hand between dealer's two opponents is left on the table untouched until the auction is completed. Dealer has the first turn to call, and the auction proceeds as in Contract Bridge until two successive passes following any call close the auction. The player at the left of the high bidder then leads, and the high bidder sorts the dummy and spreads it opposite himself and between his two opponents. Play proceeds as in Contract Bridge.

Scoring. A separate score is kept for each player. If declarer fulfills his contract, he scores the proper points; if he is defeated, each of his opponents scores the penalty points in full. If a defender holds honors, both defenders score them.

Since Contract Bridge scoring is used, the winner of the rubber scores 500 points bonus if either opponent has a game, and 700 points if neither has a game.

Irregularities. The laws of Contract Bridge should be followed for all irregularities occurring or continuing after the auction ends. During the auction there is no penalty for a bid out of turn or an insufficient bid, but either opponent may demand that an insufficient bid be made sufficient. A bid out of turn is void unless both opponents condone it. A double out of turn may be canceled by the player who is doubled, and thereafter neither opponent may double him at any contract.

EXCHANGE DUMMY

This is no different from regular Three-hand Bridge except that, at the close of the auction, declarer puts his own hand down as dummy and takes the unexposed fourth hand as his own.

Two-hand (Honeymoon) Bridge

Nearly all two-hand Bridge games are called "Honeymoon Bridge." There are several different ways of playing.

DOUBLE DUMMY

Four hands are dealt, as in Contract Bridge. The two players sit in adjoining positions at the table, not opposite each other. The hand opposite each player is that player's dummy.

Without looking at their dummies, the players bid as in Contract Bridge, dealer first, until a pass following any call closes the auction. Each player then looks at his dummy.

In one variant, the opening lead is made from the hand at declarer's left, then both dummies are exposed and the cards are played out, each hand playing in turn, each player choosing the card to play from his dummy.

In the other variant, neither player exposes his dummy to his opponent. Racks for holding the cards can be obtained and placed on the table in such position that a player cannot see his opponent's dummy but can see his own.

When the play is finished, the result is scored as in Contract Bridge.

SEMI-EXPOSED DUMMY

After the four hands have been dealt, six cards of each dummy are placed face down in a row, and the other seven cards of that dummy are turned up, one being placed on each of the face-down cards. The bidding ended, play proceeds with six cards of each dummy still face down; a player must play as he can from his dummy's exposed cards, and when a play from dummy uncovers a face-down card, that card is turned up.

DRAW BRIDGE

The players face each other across the table. Thirteen cards are dealt to each, one at a time, and the other twenty-six cards are placed face down to form the stock. Non-dealer leads first, and the cards are played as at notrump, two cards constituting a trick. After each trick, each player draws a card from the stock, the winner of the trick drawing first. The first thirteen tricks do not count. When the stock is exhausted, there is an auction as in Contract Bridge, dealer bidding first; then the last thirteen tricks are played and a record is kept of them, the result being scored as in Contract Bridge.

Plafond

One of the earliest forms of Contract Bridge, Plafond is a French game. It achieved some popularity in England, but never in the United States. It is the same as Contract Bridge except in the scoring, which is in some respects like Auction Bridge and in other respects like Contract Bridge.

The trick score is the same as in Auction Bridge except that only the value of odd tricks bid for and made can be scored below the line, as in Contract Bridge.

Any trick won in excess of the contract scores 50 points.

Fulfilling any contract, whether or not it is doubled, scores 50 points in addition to the trick score and overtricks, if any. If the contract is doubled, the bonus is 100; if redoubled, 200.

Each undertrick counts 100 points undoubled, 200 doubled, 400 redoubled; there is no vulnerability.

Four honors in one hand count 100, or 150 if partner holds the fifth; five honors in one hand, or four aces at notrump, count 200.

It is not necessary to bid a little slam (which counts 100) or a grand slam (which counts 200) in order to score for it.

Each side receives a bonus of 100 points when it wins its first game. The side which wins the rubber receives 400 points. If the rubber is unfinished, a side having the only game receives a bonus of 150.

AUCTION BRIDGE

There is no difference whatsoever between Auction Bridge and Contract Bridge, except in the scoring. Auction Bridge may be played in any form in which Contract Bridge is played, including duplicate, progressive and pivot games. The last code of Auction Bridge laws published in the United States, copyright 1926 by The Whist Club, has been superseded by the Laws of Contract Bridge (page 129) except for sections 36 to 41, 50, and 51, relating to the scoring, which are reprinted here by permission:

36. Odd Tricks. (a) Odd tricks are tricks won by Declarer after he has won six tricks. The first six tricks won by Declarer constitute his book and have no scoring value. If Declarer fail to win the number of odd tricks called for by his contract, his side scores nothing for tricks; but if he fulfill his contract, his side scores for all odd tricks, including any won in excess of his contract.

(b) When Declarer fulfills a doubled contract, his side scores the doubled value of his odd tricks in its trick score; and, for making his contract, bonus of fifty points in its honor score. If he makes more than his contract, his side scores an additional bonus of fifty points for each extra trick. When the contract has been redoubled, each bonus is one hundred points instead of fifty, and the odd tricks count four times their normal value in the trick score.

37. Odd Trick Values. Each odd trick counts in the trick score:

With Notrump	10 points
With Spades trumps	9 points
With Hearts trumps	8 points
With Diamonds trumps	7 points
With Clubs trumps	6 points

Doubling doubles these values; redoubling multiplies them by four.

38. Undertricks. (a) The book of the adversaries is seven minus the number of odd tricks named in Declarer's contract; when the adversaries win a trick or tricks in addition to their book, such tricks won are undertricks.

(b) The adversaries score in their honor score for all undertricks; fifty points for each undertrick when the contract is undoubled, one hundred points when the contract is doubled, and two hundred points when the contract is redoubled.

39. Honors. In a Notrump contract, the honors are the four Aces; in a suit contract, the honors are the Ace, King, Queen, Jack and Ten of that suit.

40. Honor Values. Honors are scored in the honor score of the side to which they are dealt; their value is not changed by doubling or redoubling. All honors held by either side are scored according to the following table.

TRUMP HONORS

0 in one hand, 3 in the other, count 30 points
1 in one hand, 2 in the other, count 30 points
1 in one hand, 3 in the other, count 40 points
2 in one hand, 2 in the other, count 40 points
2 in one hand, 3 in the other, count 50 points
0 in one hand, 4 in the other, count 80 points
1 in one hand, 4 in the other, count 90 points
0 in one hand, 5 in the other, count 100 points

NOTRUMP HONORS

0 in one hand, 3 in the other, count 30 points
1 in one hand, 2 in the other, count 30 points
1 in one hand, 3 in the other, count 40 points
2 in one hand, 2 in the other, count 40 points
0 in one hand, 4 in the other, count 100 points

One or two honors held by a side are not counted.

41. Slams. Either side winning thirteen tricks scores one hundred points for Grand Slam. Either side winning twelve tricks scores fifty points for Small Slam. Slam points are added to the honor score. When Declarers' contract is seven and he wins six-odd, he counts fifty for Small Slam although his contract fails.

50. Game. A game is won when one side makes a trick score of thirty (30) or more points. . . . No trick-points are carried over from one game to the next; each side starts a new game with a trick score of zero.

51. Rubber. The side which has won two games adds a bonus of 250 points to its honor score. The side then having the greater total of points wins the rubber.

WHIST

Four, two against two as partners.

CARDS

The pack of 52. In practice, two packs are used, having contrasting back designs, so that one pack may be shuffled while the other is being dealt. The cards in each suit rank: **A** (high), **K, Q, J, 10, 9, 8, 7, 6, 5, 4, 3, 2**.

PRELIMINARIES

Players draw cards for partnerships, choice of cards and deal; in drawing, ace is low. All the cards are dealt out, one at a time, so that each player holds thirteen. The last card must not be dealt, however; it must be turned up as the trump card, and every card of its suit becomes a trump. This card belongs to the dealer and before playing to the first trick he takes it into his hand.

THE PLAY

Eldest hand leads first; he may lead any card. Each other player in turn must play a card, and if possible a card of the suit led; the four cards so played (the lead and the cards played by the other players) constitute a trick and is won by the highest card of the suit led, or, if it contains a trump, by the highest trump. The winner of a trick leads next.

One player for each side gathers in all the tricks won by his side.

SCORING

Each odd trick (trick in excess of six) won by a side counts one point for that side. The first side to score 7 points in all wins the game.

Bid Whist

The preliminaries and deal are as in Whist, except that the last card is not turned. Eldest hand has first turn to bid, and each player may bid once. The lowest bid is one (odd trick) and the highest bid is seven. Each player in turn may pass or bid; a bid must be higher than the preceding bid. The high bidder names a trump suit and then leads first. (Some play that the bidding continues, as in Contract Bridge, until a bid is followed by three passes. Others play that each player has only one bid and that dealer may name the trump at the amount of the highest previous bid, without going over it.)

Scoring. If the bidder's side wins as many odd tricks as it bid, it scores all the tricks it makes, one point for each. If the bidder's side does not make its bid, the opponents score the amount of the bid plus one point for every trick over one that the bidder goes down; thus, if the bid is four and the bidder's side wins only eight tricks, the opponents score 5.

There is no "game" established; play may end at the finish of any hand, and settlement is by the difference in total-point scores. Partnerships do not change, though of course there may be a cut for partners by common consent. Bid Whist is quite often played on commuters' trains, where it is inconvenient to change seats and where it is desirable to be able to stop play at any time, in case the train has reached its destination.

Honors. Some play that the ace, king, queen and jack of trumps each count 1 point, and each trick counts 1 point, making a total possible score of 17 points. The lowest bid is seven, for the bidder must undertake to win the odd trick, but the highest possible bid is seventeen.

Notrump Bid. In some games, the bidder is permitted to name a notrump contract. If the hand is played at notrump, the usual score, whether the bidder makes or loses his contract, is doubled.

Norwegian Whist

The preliminaries and deal are as in Whist, but no trump card is turned. There are never any trumps in the play.

Each player in turn, beginning with eldest hand, may either pass or name a game. There are two games: *Grand*, by which is meant an undertaking to win the odd trick; and *Nullo*, an undertaking to lose the odd trick. If all four players pass, there is a new deal by the next dealer in turn. If any player names a game, play begins immediately.

If a grand is named, the player on the maker's right leads first and play proceeds as in Whist; if nullo is named, the player on the maker's left leads first. Each trick is won by the highest card of the suit led.

When a grand is played, if the bidder's side wins the odd trick, it scores four points for each odd trick it wins. If the other side wins the odd trick, it scores eight for each odd trick it wins. If nullo is named, the side losing the odd trick scores four for every odd trick its opponents win. If the first three players pass, dealer must name either grand or nullo.

Game is won by the first side to amass 50 points.

Irregularities are governed by the laws of Whist.

Solo Whist

Preliminaries. Four play, but each for himself. The deal is as in Whist, the last card being turned for trump, though another trump may supplant it. The trump card is taken into dealer's hand before he plays to the first trick.

Bidding. Eldest hand bids first, and the bidding continues until three players have passed; when a player once passes, he may not thereafter bid. The possible bids, from lowest-ranking to highest, are:

Proposal. The player says "I propose," and thus undertakes to win eight tricks with the turned-up suit as trump and with a partner, the partner being a player who *accepts the proposal.* Each player in turn thereafter, until the proposal is overcalled, may say, "I accept," after which no one else may accept the proposal, but the proposal may still be overcalled.

Solo. The bidder undertakes to win five tricks, playing alone, with the turned-up suit as trump.

Misère. To win no tricks, playing alone, at notrump.

Abundance. To win nine tricks, playing alone, and naming any trump suit.

Abundance in trumps. To win nine tricks with the turned-up suit as trump, playing alone.

Spread misère. To win no tricks, playing alone, at notrump, with all his cards exposed.

Slam. To win all tricks, playing alone, with any suit the bidder selects as trump and with the right to make the opening lead.

Eldest hand has two privileges: He always makes the opening lead, except at slam, and he alone may accept a proposal even when he has previously passed (though he may not make any other bid when he has previously passed).

The Play commences when a bid (or acceptance of a proposal) has been passed by the other three players; if all four players pass, or if no one accepts a proposal, there is a new deal. (Some, however, play that when all pass there is a "grand" played at notrump and with the player winning the last trick paying two chips to each other player.)

When an accepted proposal is the final bid, the partners retain their original seats. The other three players combine to defeat the bidder playing alone.

Settlement. Chips are usually used, a red chip being worth five whites. If the bidder fulfils his contract, and if the bid was: A *proposal,* he and his partner receive one red chip each, the opponents paying one red chip each; at *solo,* the bidder receives two red chips from each other player; at *misère,* three red chips; at *abundance,* four red chips; at *spread misère,* six red chips; at *slam,* eight red chips. If the bidder fails to fulfil his contract, payment is made to his opponents at the same rate. The white chips are used for overtricks: If the bidder makes more tricks than he needs, he collects from each opponent one white chip for each additional trick; and if he fails by more than one trick, he pays to each opponent one white chip for each additional trick.

Irregularities. The rules of Whist are followed; but in the case of a revoke, the penalty is three tricks; play continues, but the offending side must pay at least the value of the bid.

Other Whist Variants

There were once a dozen and more variants of Whist, all now obsolete. *Cayenne*, one of the early ones, perhaps inspired one feature of Bridge Whist; for the dealer could make the trump, or could pass that privilege to his partner. *Boston* was a complex game, which has survived in simplified form in Solo Whist, described in the foregoing pages; unlike most Whist-family games, Boston was usually played for high stakes. *Vint*, a Russian game, probably helped to inspire Auction Bridge.

THE
EUCHRE
FAMILY

THE EUCHRE FAMILY

Triomphe, or Triumph, or Trumps* was a "short" game in which each hand was dealt five cards, the next card was turned for trump, and the object of play was to win three tricks. The descendants of Triomphe form a large and widespread family of games. Three of them have at some time been considered "national" games; Écarté in France, Napoleon in England, and Euchre in the United States. A fourth is usually included: Spoil Five in Ireland. Besides these flourishing survivors, there is a long list of obsolescent games: Beast, La Mouche, Man d'Auvergne, das Kontraspiel, Rams, Loo.

Euchre

PLAYERS

Basically, Euchre is a game for four players, in two partnerships, as described below. Its great popularity has led to its adaptation to any number of players from two to seven. These variants are described after the four-hand game.

CARDS

The pack of 24. The rank of cards in each suit is, in general: **A** (high), **K**, **Q**, **J**, **10**, **9**. But in the trump suit, the jack (called *right bower*) is elevated to the highest trump, and the second-highest trump is the other jack of the same color as right bower (called *left bower*). *Example:* If hearts are trumps, the trumps rank: ♡**J** (high), ♢**J**, ♡**A**, **K**, **Q**, **10**, **9**. The trump suit always contains seven cards; the *next* suit (same color as the trump) contains five; the *cross* suits (opposite color from the trump) each contain six.

PRELIMINARIES

Draw cards for partners, seats, and first deal. The two lowest play against the two highest; lowest card has choice of seats and is the first dealer. In drawing, the ace is low, below the seven. Two or more players drawing equal cards must draw again. Partners sit opposite each other.

---

* The French triumph *is the origin of the English* trump, *to ruff. Triomphe is not the same, however, as the game Triumph to which Whist is traced.*

Dealer has the right to shuffle last. The pack is cut by the player at his right. The cut must leave at least four cards in each packet. It is usual to use two packs alternately, dealer's partner shuffling the still pack during the deal.

DEALING

Five cards are dealt to each player, in two rounds of 3–2 or 2–3, as dealer chooses. The cards are dealt in rotation to the left, beginning with eldest hand.

After dealing the last packet to himself, dealer places the rest of the pack face-down on the table, and turns the top card face up. This *turn-up* proposes the trump suit for the deal.

MAKING

Eldest hand may pass or may accept the turn-up for trump. The latter choice is signified by saying "I order it up" (since dealer alone has the right to take the turn-up into his hand). If eldest hand passes, the next player has the same option, and so on. If partner of the dealer wishes to accept the turn-up suit, he says "I assist." Opponent at right of dealer accepts in the same words as eldest hand, by ordering it up.

Should any player, including dealer, accept the turn-up, dealer at once discards one card from his hand. The discard is by custom placed crosswise under the undealt cards. The turn-up belongs to dealer in place of his discard. By custom the turn-up is not placed in dealer's hand, but is left on the pack until duly played.

If all four hands pass, dealer puts the turn-up, still face up, crosswise under the undealt cards, signifying that the proposed trump has been *turned down*. Eldest hand then has the right to name the trump suit, or to pass; in the latter event, dealer's partner may *make it* or pass, and so on. But no player may *make it* the suit of the rejected turn-up.

Naming the other suit of same color as the rejected turn-up is called *making it next;* naming a suit of opposite color is *crossing it.*

If all four hands pass in the second round, the cards are thrown in, and the next dealer deals.

PLAYING ALONE

The hand that makes the trump, whether in the first or second round, has the right to declare "I play alone." The partner of the *lone player* then lays his cards face down on the table and does not participate in the play, but duly shares the increased winnings if the lone player succeeds.

THE PLAY

If the maker plays alone, the opening lead is made by the opponent at his left; otherwise, the opening lead is made by eldest hand regardless of the position of the maker.

A lead calls upon each other hand to follow suit if able; if unable, the hand may play any card. A trick is won by the highest trump, or by the highest card of the suit led. The winner of a trick leads to the next.

The object of play is to win at least three tricks. If the making side fails to win three it is *euchred*. The winning of all five tricks by one side is called *march*.

SCORING

Maker of trump, if playing with partner, wins: for making 3 or 4 tricks, 1 point; for march, 2 points. Maker playing alone wins: for 3 or 4 tricks, 1 point; for march, 4 points. In any case, if making side is euchred, opponents win 2 points.

Four-hand Euchre is usually played for a game of 5 points, but this is sometimes increased by agreement to 7 or 10.

Rubbers may be played; the side that first wins two games scores a rubber, and receives a bonus of 2 *rubber points*. In addition it scores the difference between its total and opponents' total of rubber points awarded for each game separately; 3 rubber points for a game in which the losers failed to score; 2 for a game in which losers scored 1 or 2; 1 for a game in which losers scored 3 or 4.

It is customary for each side to keep track of the number of points it has won toward a game by use of two low cards, a three and a four, as shown in the illustration.

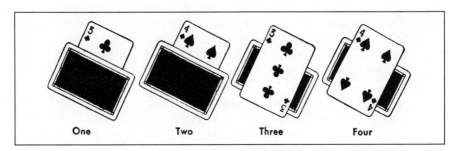

| One | Two | Three | Four |

Point Keeping in Euchre

Set Back is a method of scoring sometimes used in Euchre, Seven Up, and other games where *game* is a small number of points. At the outset each player holds a number of chips equal to *game*. Every time he wins a point he discards one chip; each time he loses a point he must take an extra chip. The first to get rid of his chips wins.

IRREGULARITIES

Misdeal. There may be a new deal by the same dealer if a card is exposed in dealing; a card is faced in the pack; or if the pack is found imperfect. When a pack is found imperfect, previous scores stand.

A deal by the wrong player may be stopped before a card is turned up; if the error is not noticed until later, the deal stands.

Error in Bidding. A player who *orders it up* when he is partner of dealer, or *assists* when he is an opponent of dealer, is deemed to have accepted the turn-up for trump. If a player names for trump the suit of the turn-up after it has been turned down, his declaration is void and his side may not make the trump.

Declaration Out of Turn. If a player makes a declaration (or turn down) other than a pass, out of turn, it is void and his side may not make the trump.

Incorrect Number of Cards. If any hand is found to have too many or too few cards, and the error is discovered before the first trick is quitted, there must be a new deal; if the error is not noticed until later, play continues and the side of the erroneous hand may not score for that deal.

If dealer has accepted the turn-up and plays to the first trick before discarding, he must play with the five cards dealt him and the turn-up card is out of play.

Lone Hand. A hand playing alone does not incur penalty for lead or play out of turn or exposing a card, but must correct the error on demand if it is noticed in time.

Lead Out of Turn. If a hand leads out of turn and all other hands play to the trick before the error is noticed, the trick stands. But if any hand has not played, the false lead must be taken back on demand of any player and becomes an exposed card. Any cards played to the incorrect lead may be retracted without penalty. An opponent of the incorrect leader may name the suit to be led at the first opportunity thereafter of the offender or his partner to lead; such call must be made by the hand that will play last to the trick.

Exposed Cards. A card is deemed exposed if it is led or played out of turn; dropped face up on the table except as a regular play in turn; played with another card intended to be played; or named by a player as being in his hand. An exposed card must be left face up on the table and must be played at the first legal opportunity.

Quitted Tricks. Each trick as gathered must be turned face down, and the tricks must be kept separate so that the identity of each can be determined. Quitted tricks may not be examined for any purpose until the end of play. If a player turns up a quitted trick at any previous time, the opponents may call a lead from his side.

Revoke. Failure to follow suit to a lead when able is a revoke. A revoke may be corrected before the trick is quitted, and if it is corrected any opponent who played after the revoke may retract his card and substitute another. If a player so mixes the tricks that a claim of revoke against his side cannot be proved, the claim must be considered proved.

Upon proof of established revoke, the non-revoking side has the option of scoring the hand as played or of taking the revoke penalty. The revoke penalty is 2 points, which may be either added to the score of the non-revoking side or subtracted from the score of its opponents. If the revoke was made by the opponents of a lone hand, the penalty is 4 points.

STRATEGY

Distribution. In four-hand Euchre, the expectation as to the number of trumps in play is about six. The maker of trump must usually hold three, leaving an average of one for each other player. But if trump is ordered up, opponents must expect to find two trumps in hand of dealer. The odds are about 7:3 against any hand's being dealt a card of each suit, but (very roughly) 2:1 against the opening side's being able to trump the first lead of a side suit.

Eldest Hand normally should not order up the trump without three fairly sure tricks. Even then, it is not always advisable to do so. If the trump should be turned down, eldest hand will have the first opportunity to make a different trump. If he can make it next, particularly through possession of a bower, he should usually pass; if dealer takes up the trump, the bower may euchre him.

But all bidding must be "to the score." A crucial situation arises when dealer's side has not more than 2 points, and the opponents are *at the bridge*, that is, have 4 points. If dealer's side makes a lone hand, it wins the game. Opponents can afford to suffer a euchre, 2 points, to avert this danger. The rule is then for eldest hand not to pass at the bridge, unless he can be fairly sure of three tricks at the turned trump; otherwise he must order it up and make the dealer a gift of 2 for euchre.

Partner of Eldest Hand should be guided by the same considerations at a low score. But at the bridge he reverses the policy of eldest hand. The pass by eldest hand shows some defensive strength, so that if partner has two trumps he should usually order it up with expectation of winning.

Dealer's Partner should normally assist with any two trumps and a side high card, or possibly with two side aces regardless of the rest of the hand. The expectation is that dealer, with help of the turn-up, will have enough trumps to outlast the opponents. At the bridge, dealer's partner should order it up with less, possibly with no tricks at all, to shut out a possible lone hand by the opponent on his left. But if a high card, especially a bower, is turned, partner should usually pass to give dealer an opportunity to call lone hand.

Dealer may risk taking up the trump on a weak hand when his side has not more than 2, and he must do so when opponents have 4 points, rather than let them name the trump. But when opponents have 3, so that a euchre of dealer will put them out, dealer should be conservative. When dealer turns it down, the practice is for eldest hand to make it next, if he has any prospects, on the theory that the dealer probably has no bower. If strong in the next suit, dealer usually turns it down for a trap.

When Trump Is Turned Down the assumption is that dealer has no bower, so that eldest hand usually makes it next or passes, while dealer's partner usually crosses or passes. But of course no hand of three very probable tricks in any suit should be passed. And if a side can afford to give the opponents 2 points for euchre, a sub-minimum hand may be bid to shut out an adverse lone hand.

Playing Alone is the indicated policy in either of two situations: (a) the player has an ironclad hand, such as two bowers and the ace of trumps, or every card either an ace or a trump; (b) the hand has reasonable prospect of three tricks, and opponents are at the bridge while own side has 1 or 2 points.

The Play does not admit of subtlety. The general policy must be to try to win everything that comes along. Aces, possibly kings, should be usually led at the earliest opportunity, so that partner may see them; otherwise he might, second hand, waste a trump on a lead destined to go to the ace. But a hand with three trumps and a side ace should usually lead trumps first, to lessen the danger that the ace will be trumped.

Three-hand (Cutthroat) Euchre

In a three-hand game, a separate score is kept for each player, but the maker of trump is always opposed by the other two playing in temporary partnership. There is no call of "alone," because the maker is necessarily a lone hand (and is so treated in applying the laws on irregularities). The scoring: Maker scores, for 3 or 4 tricks, 1 point; for march, 3 points. If maker is euchred, each opponent scores 2 points.

Two-hand Euchre

From the regular Euchre pack discard the sevens and eights, reducing it to 24 cards. All rules, including scoring, are as at four-hand, except that there is no declaring "alone," since no partnership play is possible in any case.

Railroad Euchre

A number of local features have been introduced to speed up the tempo of Euchre. The game is usually called Railroad Euchre when any such feature is adopted. Any or all of the following may be included:

Joker. The joker is added to the pack and always ranks as the best trump, above the right bower. One suit is agreed upon in advance to be the proposed trump in case the joker is turned up.

Playing Alone. A player announcing alone may discard one card from his hand and receive the best card from his partner's hand. (The selection is made by partner, without exposure of any cards.) This exchange is additional to dealer's right to take up the trump, so that dealer may make two discards. He takes partner's best before taking the turn-up, so that if the card from partner does not suit him he can discard it for the turn-up. If dealer's partner plays alone, dealer may give him the turn-up.

Opposing Alone. After a player announces a lone hand, either opponent may announce that he will oppose alone. This lone opponent is entitled to discard one card and receive partner's best card. Euchre of a lone hand by a lone opponent counts 4 points.

Laps. If a game is won by a total of more than 5 points, the excess over 5 is carried forward to the next game. The object of laps is to preserve the incentive for playing alone, whatever the score.

Slam. A game counts double if the losers did not score a point. Hence, if rubbers are played, a single game may constitute a rubber.

When the lone player is allowed to call for partner's best, it may be agreed that he can try for higher score by standing pat on his original hand. (The dealer, playing lone and pat, does not take the turn-up). The scoring is then: Maker wins, for 3 or 4 tricks, 1 point; for march, 5 points; maker is euchred, opponents win 3 points. Lone opposition is not allowed against a lone and pat hand.

Jambone is a lone hand played with the cards exposed. Either opponent may direct the card to be played from the exposed hand at each turn, but opponents may not consult. The only object in calling jambone is to try for the increased score for march, which counts 8 points. Lone opposition is not allowed against jambone.

Jamboree is simply a royalty, 16 points, for holding the five highest trumps. It may be scored only by the maker of trump. Dealer gets credit for jamboree made with the help of the turn-up.

Auction Euchre

Of several variants of Euchre adapted to more than four players, the most interesting is Auction Euchre. See also the description of Euchre.

PLAYERS

Five, six or seven. The same rules can be adapted, if desired, to any lower number of players.

CARDS

For *five-hand*, use the pack of 32 cards; *six-hand*, use 36 cards; *seven-hand*, use full pack of 52. The joker may be added, if desired; it ranks as the highest trump, over the right bower. The rank of trumps, from high to low, is: (Joker), **J** *(right bower)*, **J** (of other suit of same color as the trump, *left bower)*, **A**, **K**, **Q**, **10**, **9** . . . The rank in each plain suit is: **A** (high), **K**, **Q**, **(J)**, **10**, **9** . . .

PRELIMINARIES

All participants draw cards from a spread pack. Lowest card has first deal and choice of seats. Next-lowest sits at his left, and so on around the table. Dealer has the right to shuffle last, and the pack is cut by the player at his right. The cut must leave at least four cards in each packet.

DEALING

Cards are dealt in packets to the left, beginning with eldest hand. The widow is dealt after the first round of the deal. *Five-hand and six-hand:* Each player receives five cards, in rounds of 3–2 or 2–3, and the widow is two cards. *Seven-hand:* Each player receives seven cards, in rounds of 3–4 or 4–3, and the rest of the pack goes to the widow.

A method of scoring peculiarly suited to five-hand and seven-hand is *set-back*. All players commence with equal numbers of chips. When a player wins, he puts chips from his pile into the pool. When he is euchred, he draws chips from the pool. The first player to get rid of all his chips wins the game.

Call-Ace Euchre

Call-Ace is essentially a method for fixing the temporary partnerships in a cutthroat game of four, five, or six players, when the trump is made as described under Four-hand Euchre. The maker of trump names any suit, and the holder of the best card in that suit becomes his partner. Said partner must not acknowledge his holding, until the fall of the cards reveals it. Since not all of the pack is dealt, a player may not know until the last trick whether he is the maker's partner. If it turns out that the maker himself holds the best card of the named suit, he is deemed a lone player; the only effect on the scoring is to increase the count for march to equal the number of players in the game. If made by a partnership, march counts

2 in four-hand, 3 if there are more than four players. If the maker wishes to play alone, he may so announce, or may call a suit on the chance or certainty that he holds the best card in it.

THE AUCTION

Eldest hand declares first. Each player has one turn in which he may bid or pass. Each bid must be higher than the preceding bid. Bidding is by points alone, the intended trump suit not being named until the highest bidder is determined. The meaning of the bids is given in the table below.

BID OF	MAKER CONTRACTS TO
	Five-hand
3	take 3 tricks, with help of one partner, using widow
4, 5	take this number of tricks, with help of two partners, using widow
8	take five tricks, playing alone, using widow
15	take 5 tricks, playing alone, without widow
	Six-hand
3, 4, 5	take this number of tricks, with help of partners, using widow
8	take 5 tricks, playing alone, using widow
15	take 5 tricks, laying alone, without widow
	Seven-hand
4, 5	take this number of tricks, with help of one partner, using widow
	Seven-hand
6, 7	take this number of tricks, with help of two partners, using widow
10	take 7 tricks, playing alone, using widow
20	take 7 tricks, playing alone, without widow

Unless his bid obligates him to play without it, the highest bidder adds the widow to his hand and discards an equal number of cards. He then names the trump suit and chooses his partners.

CHOOSING PARTNERS

Five-hand and seven-hand: Maker of trumps names one or two of the other players as his partners, as entitled by his bid. He may choose any, regardless of position at the table. All players not chosen play in temporary partnership against the making side. If a player announces alone, all others combine against him. *Six-hand* is usually played in two partnerships of three on a side, the partners sitting alternately at the table. If a player announces alone, his two partners place their cards face down on the table, and the lone hand plays against the three opponents.

THE PLAY

If the maker plays alone, the opening lead is made by the opponent at his left; otherwise, the opening lead is made by eldest hand. A lead calls upon each other hand to follow suit if able; if unable, the hand may play any card. A trick is won by the highest trump, or by the highest card of the suit led. The winner of a trick leads to the next.

The object of play is to win tricks, particularly to make or defeat the contract.

SCORING

The number of points bid is credited to the making side or to the opponents, according as the contract is made or euchred. There is no credit for winning extra tricks above the contract. In five-hand and seven-hand, the score for the deal is credited to each member of the winning partnership individually.

Hasenpfeffer

This simplification of Euchre is said to have been invented by the Pennsylvania Dutch and named after their favorite dish, "jugged hare with pepper." It seems more likely, however, that the name is a corruption of the German phrase "Hase im Pfeffer"—used in the sense of "Ay, there's the rub!" For, desirable as it is to be dealt the joker, "there's a catch to it."

PLAYERS

Four, in partnerships.

CARDS

The pack of 24, made by deleting all cards below the nine from the pack of 52, plus the joker, making 25 cards in all. The joker is the highest trump; the second is the jack of the trump suit *(right bower);* the third is the jack of the other suit of same color as the trump *(left bower).* The other trumps are: **A** (fourth-best), **K**, **Q**, **10**, **9**. In plain suits the rank is: **A** (high), **K**, **Q**, **J**, **10**, **9**.

PRELIMINARIES

Cards are drawn; lowest card has choice of seats and deals first. In cutting, all suits rank in the plain order. If equal cards are drawn for low, the tying players must draw again.

Dealer shuffles last, and the pack is cut by the player at his right. The cut must leave at least four cards in each packet.

DEALING

Cards are dealt to the left, commencing with eldest hand. Each player receives six cards, dealt three at a time. The last card is placed face down on the table to form the widow.

BIDDING

Each player in turn, commencing with eldest hand, has one chance to bid or pass. A bid specifies the number of tricks the player (with help of partner) will contract to win if allowed to name the trump suit. The high bidder names the trump, takes the widow card into his hand, then discards any one card. If all four players pass without a bid, the holder of the joker must acknowledge it and must then bid three. (Should the joker be the widow, and all four pass, the deal is abandoned.)

THE PLAY

The high bidder makes the opening lead. A lead calls upon each other hand to follow suit if able; if unable, the hand may play any card. A trick is won by the highest trump, or by the highest card of the suit led. The winner of a trick leads to the next.

SCORING

If the contracting side makes at least its contract, it scores one point for each trick taken. If it fails, the amount of the bid is deducted from its score (the side is said to be *set back*). In either case, the opposing side scores one point for each trick it wins. Game is 10 points. If both sides reach 10 in the same deal, the contracting side counts first and so wins.

IRREGULARITIES

Use the laws of Euchre.

STRATEGY

As there are eight trumps, a holding of three in one hand should be counted worth one probable long-card trick. Each high trump (sufficiently guarded) is an additional trick, and each side ace should be counted a trick. The bidder is also entitled to include in his bid the expectation that partner can win one trick. The normal minimum for a bid of three is thus any three trumps and a side ace. It pays to be forward, rather than conservative, in bidding, for the right to name trump is a considerable advantage, and the widow may help. Inducing the opponents to overbid is also an important factor.

The chief problem in the play is whether to open trumps, as bidder. This must be decided by the trump length and strength, and by the question of whether an attempt is to be made to win tricks with side cards lower than aces. If partner's hand must furnish a trick to make the contract, it is usually better not to open trumps, as he may be able to ruff a plain suit.

Double Hasenpfeffer

This variant is played with the Pinochle pack of 48 cards, without the joker. Three, four, or six may play. With an even number partnerships are usually arranged, partners sitting alternately. The whole pack is dealt, with no widow. The lowest bid permitted is for half of the tricks, and the dealer must bid this number if all others pass. The high bidder may elect to play *alone*, in which case he may discard two cards and ask for the best two his partner can give him. If a lone player fails to make his contract, he is set back by as many points as there are cards per hand; if he makes contract, he scores twice this amount. If dealer fails to make a forced bid, he is set back only half. Scoring in all other cases is as in Hasenpfeffer (preceding section). Game is 62 points.

ÉCARTÉ

Écarté has been described as "Hazard played with cards." Although it retains the character of its ancestors—the hand of five cards, the play for three tricks, the turned trump—Écarté so far eliminates the element of judgment as to make the analogy with dice play very close. The Écarté player, like the dice player, must have a complete knowledge of the mathematical probabilities as applied to his game, and the coolness to be governed by them rigidly. Beyond that, there is little else.

PLAYERS

Two. But Écarté, like Craps, is usually played to afford a large group opportunity to participate in betting. In clubs, the rule is that any spectator can offer to back one player or the other. If one player covers all bets offered by the adverse gallery, he may bar all comment and advice from his own gallery. But if he allows his own gallery to cover any of the bets offered by the other, his gallery has the right to check on the correctness of the score, to give him advice, to discuss questions of fact and interpretations of law. The player is not bound, however, to act upon the advice of his gallery.

CARDS

The pack of 32. The cards in each suit rank: **K** (high), **Q**, **J**, **A**, **10**, **9**, **8**, **7**. In practice, two packs are used alternately.

PRELIMINARIES

Each player draws a card from the pack. The higher card has choice of seats and deals first. If equal cards are drawn, both must draw again.

Dealer has the right to shuffle last. Opponent cuts, and must leave at least two cards in each packet.

DEALING

Dealer gives five cards to each hand, beginning with opponent. He must deal in rounds of 3–2 or 2–3. Whichever order he adopts on the first deal must be followed throughout the game. If he wishes to change to the other order in a later game, he must so inform his opponent on presenting his pack for the cut.

The eleventh card is turned face up on the table, and the rest of the pack is set face down beside it to form the *stock*. The turn-up fixes the trump suit for that deal.

If the turn-up is a king, dealer scores one point immediately.

PROPOSAL

Non-dealer commences by saying either (a) "I stand" or "I play"; or (b) "I propose." If he *stands*, the original hands are at once played out. If he *proposes*, dealer says either (a) "I refuse" or "I play"; or (b) "I accept" or "How many?" If dealer *refuses*, the original hands are at once played out. If he *accepts*, non-dealer first and then dealer discard any desired number of cards from their hands and dealer restores each hand to five cards by dealing from the top of the stock.

When a proposal is accepted, non-dealer must draw at least one card, and may take up to five. Dealer may draw any number or none.

After the draw, non-dealer again may stand or propose, and if he proposes dealer again may refuse or accept. And so on: proposals may be made and accepted repeatedly until one player says "I play" or until the stock is exhausted. If at the end not enough cards remain to satisfy the wishes of both players, non-dealer may draw what he wants or as many as remain and dealer may take any residue, but each hand must finally hold five cards. When the stock is exhausted, the hands must be played out.

THE PLAY

The opening lead is made by non-dealer, regardless of which hand decided to play. Before leading, non-dealer must warn "I play." If either player holds the king of trumps, he scores 1 point, provided that he announces his king before the opening lead. The preliminary "I play" gives dealer a chance to declare the king.

The leader to each trick announces verbally the suit of the lead. Should he fail to do so, his opponent may not be penalized for revoke.

Upon each lead, the other hand must follow suit if able and *must win the trick* if able, by playing higher in the same suit or by trumping if he is void.

A trick is won by the higher trump or by the higher card of the suit led. The winner of each trick leads to the next.

The object of play is primarily to win three tricks, secondarily to make *vole* by winning all five.

SCORING

If the original hands are played out (without discard and draw), the player who decided to stand scores 1 point for taking three or four tricks, or 2 points for vole. If he fails to take three tricks, his opponent scores 2 points (nothing extra for vole).

If the first proposal is accepted, the score becomes simply 1 point for majority of tricks or 2 for vole, regardless of which player decided to play.

Game is 5 points. The usual method of keeping score is to provide four chips to each player; one chip is transferred from the player's left to his right for each point won.

If a player with a score of 4 receives the king of trumps, he wins at once by showing it.

Pool Écarté is chouette play among three players. All contribute equal stakes to a pool. Cards are drawn, and the lowest card stays out of the first game. The winner of the first game also plays in the second, the loser giving way to the *rentrant* previously idle. The loser pays a stake into the pool. When any player wins two games in succession, he takes the pool and all ante anew to make the next pool. Sometimes four or even five players participate in one game by the chouette method.

IRREGULARITIES

The Draw for Deal. If a player exposes more than one card in drawing for deal, he must draw again. The draw stands even though the pack be found imperfect.

The Cut. If a card is exposed in cutting, there must be a new cut. If the cut was omitted, there must be a new shuffle, cut and deal on demand of a player who has not looked at any of his cards; but if a card has been turned for trump, the deal stands.

The Deal. If a player deals out of turn or with his opponent's pack, the deal is void if the error is discovered before the turn of trump; if it is discovered later, the deal stands and if the wrong pack was used the packs remain changed.

Misdeal. If dealer gives the wrong number of cards to either hand, or departs from his chosen order of dealing, non-dealer may, if he has not looked at his hand and if trump has not been turned, demand a new deal or require the error to be rectified. If, before turn of the trump, a card is found faced in the pack, there must be a new deal. If dealer exposes any cards that go to himself, the deal stands. If he exposes any cards that go to opponent, the latter may demand a new deal if he has not looked at any other of his cards.

The Turn-up. If dealer turns more than one card for trump, non-dealer may, if he has not looked at his hand, demand a new deal or choose which card shall become the turn-up (and the others are discarded from the pack). If non-dealer has looked at his hand, there must be a new deal.

Wrong Number of Cards. If, after the turn of trump but before the faulty hand has declared, it is discovered that

    (a) non-dealer has more than five cards; he may demand a new deal or discard extra cards of his own choice (and dealer may not look at these discards);

(b) non-dealer has less than five cards; he may demand a new deal or draw additional cards from the top of the stock;

(c) dealer has more than five cards; non-dealer may demand a new deal or may rectify dealer's hand by drawing out excess cards (which he may then look at if dealer has looked at his hand);

(d) dealer has less than five cards; non-dealer may demand a new deal or permit dealer to draw additional cards from the top of the stock.

In any case where a faulty deal is rectified and allowed to stand, dealer may not score for turning up the king.

Marking the King. If a king is turned up, the dealer may mark it at any time before the turn-up in the next deal. A player holding the king of trumps is not obligated to announce it, but may not mark it if he fails to announce it before playing his first card. If a player erroneously announces the king, not having it, his opponent (if without the king) may require retraction of all cards played up to the time the error was discovered, and the hands are replayed; if the offender wins any points in the replay, 1 point is subtracted from his score.

Discards. Dealer, if required, must inform the other how many cards he has drawn. Each player must keep his discards face down and separate from the stock and the adverse discards. Cards once discarded must not be looked at.

The Draw from the Stock. If either player takes more cards than he has discarded and places any in his hand, the other may demand a new deal, or may draw excess cards out of the hand without sight thereof (but he may look at the cards so drawn if the other has seen any card of the draw).

If non-dealer asks for, or dealer takes, fewer cards than were discarded, the deficiency may be supplied from the top of the stock, unless the short hand has played any card, in which case it must continue short, and the opponent wins all final tricks to which it cannot play.

If dealer gives non-dealer fewer cards than asked for, non-dealer may demand a new deal or may supply the deficiency at any time from the top of the stock.

If during the draw from the stock, a card is found faced in the pack, it must be shown to both players and then discarded, the next card being dealt instead. If dealer exposes a card during the draw, he must accept it if it goes to himself; if it goes to non-dealer, the latter may accept it or may require that it be discarded from the pack.

Wrong Call of Suit. If a player names one suit and leads a card of another, opponent may accept the lead or may demand that it be retracted; in the latter case a card of the called suit must be substituted, and if the leader is void of the called suit his opponent may name the suit to be led.

Revoke. A player revokes if he fails to follow suit, to trump a plain lead, or to play a higher card of the same suit, when able to do so. A revoke may be corrected before the next lead is made, otherwise it stands. When an established revoke is discovered, opponent of the offender may let the play stand or may demand that all cards be retracted and replayed; if the offender wins any points in the replay, 1 point is subtracted from his score.

New Cards. A player may call for new cards at his own expense, after play of a hand is completed and before the cut for the next deal. He must then supply two packs, of which the opponent has choice.

Imperfect Pack. If the pack be found imperfect, the current deal is cancelled but all previous scores stand.

Error in Scoring. A proved error in the score may be rectified at any time during the deal in which the error was made, or before the turn of trump in the next deal.

JEUX DE REGLE

The principal problem at Écarté is when to propose or accept, when to stand or play. This is a matter of mathematical probability, and it has been completely answered for every possible hand.

The player who stands risks loss of 2 points in the attempt to win 1. Therefore he should stand only on a hand which has at least a 2-to-1 chance to win three tricks. The minimum hands that answer this description are called the *jeux de regle*, which may be translated "regulation hands."

Where only four cards are shown, any fifth card may be added.

PLAIN SUITS				PLAIN SUITS		
1ST	2ND	3RD		1ST	2ND	3RD
No trumps				*1 trump*		
K, A	K	K		K, Q, 7		
Q, J	K	K		K, 8, 7	K	
Q, J	Q, J	K		Q, J, A	J	
K, Q	K	Q		K, A	K, 7	
K, J	K, J	Q		Q, J	K, 7	
2 trumps				Q, J	Q, A	
K, 7	9			K, Q	Q	7
8	Q, 10			K, A	K	7
J, 10	10			K, 7	K	A
A, 10	A			K	K	9, 8
7	Q	Q		Q, J	J	J
A	J	Q		*3 trumps*		
J	J	J		8, 7		
				8	9	

The trumps in every case are supposed to be the lowest possible, in sequence from the seven up. *The holding of higher trumps does not, in general, decrease the side strength necessary.* Only in extreme cases is there any effect, and then it is trifling. Example, **K-Q-J** of trumps is sure for three tricks, but **9-8-7** of trumps is a *jeu de regle* unless the two other cards are in two suits and total less than 17 spots.

King of Trumps. The general rule is to stand and play the moment a *jeu de regle* is obtained, either in the original deal or by drawing. Even with a strong hand it is inadvisable to draw, in the hope of making vole, if the king of trumps has not yet appeared. But if the king was turned, or the player himself holds it, he can afford to speculate for vole, and this is practically the only situation in the game that admits of judgment.

Discarding. The general rule of discarding is to let go everything but kings and trumps. If the hand can discard no more than two cards under this rule, it is very likely to be a *jeu de regle*. After a draw of less than three cards, the opponent should usually stand and play, unless he is surely strong enough to save vole and wants to speculate on making vole himself.

Leads. The correct opening lead by non-dealer from each *jeu de regle* is the first card in each row of the table, except that from three or more trumps the correct lead is a trump. Subsequent leads depend of course on the fall of the cards; the ideal lead is a suit of which opponent has already shown void. After that, choose a long suit rather than a short, and prefer the lead from a sequence to a lead from a tenace. With the king of trumps, there can hardly be an advantage in failing to lead it at the first opportunity.

SPOIL FIVE

From two to ten may play, but the best game is for five or six. Each plays for himself.

CARDS

The pack of 52. The ♡**A** is always the third-best trump; consequently there are 13 trumps when hearts are trumps, but 14 when any other suit is trump. The rank of spot cards is different in the red and black suits; the mnemonical phrase goes "Highest in red; lowest in black."

The rank of cards in the *trump* suit is as follows:

Hearts: ♡**5** (high), **J, A, K, Q, 10, 9, 8, 7, 6, 4, 3, 2**.
Diamonds: ◇**5** (high), ◇**J**, ♡**A**, ◇**A, K, Q, 10, 9, 8, 7, 6, 4, 3, 2**.
Clubs or Spades: **5** (high), **J**, ♡**A**, **A, K, Q, 2, 3, 4, 6, 7, 8, 9, 10**.

The rank of cards in the *plain* suits is as follows:

Hearts or Diamonds: **K** (high), **Q, J, 10, 9, 8, 7, 6, 5, 4, 3, 2**, (◇**A**).
Clubs or Spades: **K** (high), **Q, J, A, 2, 3, 4, 5, 6, 7, 8, 9, 10**.

PRELIMINARIES

Players may take seats at random. Any player distributes cards around the table, one at a time face up, and the first jack marks the first dealer.

Dealer has the right to shuffle last, and the pack is cut by the player at his right. The cut must leave at least five cards in each packet.

Prior to the first deal, each player antes one chip into the pool. So long as this pool is not won, each successive dealer antes one additional chip. When the pool is taken, all hands ante one chip to form a new pool.

DEALING

Cards are dealt to the left, beginning with eldest hand. Each player receives five cards, dealt in rounds of 3–2 or 2–3. The deal completed, the next card is turned up for trump.

ROBBING

If the turn-up is an ace, dealer is entitled to take it in exchange for any card he chooses to discard. He must make his discard before the opening lead; having done so, he need not pick up the ace to establish his ownership.

If any player holds the ace of trumps, he is entitled to take the turn-up in exchange for any discard. At his first turn to play, and before playing, he must pass his discard face down to dealer, who gives him the turn-up in exchange. (Or dealer, holding the ace, puts his discard under the stock and takes the turn-up). The turn-up card so received need not be played to the current trick.

THE PLAY

Eldest hand makes the opening lead. A lead calls upon each other hand either to follow suit or trump; that is, he may trump even when able to follow suit. If unable to follow suit, the hand may play any card. A trick is won by the highest trump, or by the highest card of the suit led. The winner of a trick leads to the next.

Reneging is a privilege enjoyed by the three highest trumps. The lead of an inferior trump does not compel the holder to play the trump **5**, **J**, or ♡**A**; if he has no smaller trump, he may discard. But the lead of a superior trump always calls for the play of an inferior; if the trump **5** is led, no player may renege, even with a singleton trump **J** or ♡**A**.

Each player is for himself, and his primary object is to win at least three tricks. The second object is to win all five tricks. If unable to win three tricks, the player tries to prevent any other player from doing so. Consequently the game actually becomes a temporary partnership of the have-nots against the haves. When no hand wins three tricks, the game is *spoiled*.

Jink. When a player has won three tricks, he must immediately abandon his cards, or announce that he will *jink it*. In the latter event, play continues and he must win all five tricks, else the game is spoiled.

SETTLEMENT

A player who wins three tricks takes the pool; if he wins five tricks, he wins the pool plus an additional chip from each other player. If the game is spoiled, the pool is left intact to be won in the next or a subsequent deal.

IRREGULARITIES

If a hand is found to have the wrong number of cards, during the play, it must be returned to the stock face down, and the owner drops out of the current deal. He may not take the pool in that deal, but no change is made in the ownership of tricks already played.

If a player robs when he does not hold the trump ace, leads or plays out of turn, reneges to the lead of a superior trump, fails to follow suit or trump when able, or exposes a card after any player has won two tricks, he forfeits the right to win the current pool on that or any subsequent deal. His rights are restored after the current pool is won. In any event, he must ante to the pool whenever he is dealer.

STRATEGY

Three out of five hands are spoiled, on the average, in a five-hand game. Of the cases where one player wins three tricks, four out of five result from abnormal trump length or strength.

Little can be said of positive play with a hand that looks as though it may win three tricks. This is usually a matter of leading trumps at the first opportunity. Since only half of the pack is in play, the best card should usually be played on a plain suit lead, if no higher card has previously been played. Occasional opportunity for withholding high cards does arise, however, as for example: Second hand (left of eldest hand) holds ♣5 J ♡Q 3 ◇7, and ♣9 is turned for trump; eldest hand leads ♡9; second hand should play low. The plan is to save the ♡Q until after the hand gains the lead, as by trumping. Then the lead of the other trump may pull all outstanding trumps and give ♡Q a better chance of going through.

Most of the strategy of play is concerned with spoiling. The renege privilege should be used to save a singleton high trump for later use against any dangerous opponent.

When one opponent seems likely to win the first three tricks, and almost sure to win three tricks, it is often good strategy to conceal possession of a winning trump (as by reneging) in the hope that the opponent will decide to jink it, whereupon the winning trump will spoil the pool.

Forty-five

Forty-five is Spoil Five without the spoil. It is played two-hand, or by partnerships of two against two or three against three, seated alternately. The side that wins three tricks scores 5 points, or 10 for taking all five tricks. The side that first reaches a total of 45 wins the game.

Auction Forty-fives

Four play, two against two as partners; or six, in two partnerships of three to the side. Partners are seated alternately.

In drawing for partnerships, the cards rank from ace high to deuce low; but in the play the rank of the cards is as in Spoil Five. Each player is dealt five cards, three at a time, then two; or two at a time, then three.

Bidding. Eldest hand has first turn to bid, and thereafter the turn passes to the left. Each bid names a number of points, in multiples of 5, without specifying a suit; the highest bid is 30. Each player except the dealer must go higher than the preceding bid; the dealer, when his turn comes, may say "I hold," which means he will take the contract at the highest preceding bid, without going over. If the dealer holds, each player who has not previously passed may bid again, again provided he goes over the preceding bid. When the dealer does not hold, the highest bidder's side must play at the contract named. When the dealer holds and is not overcalled, dealer's side must play at the contract named.

Discarding and Drawing. The high bidder (or dealer, if he was allowed to hold) names a trump. Then each player in turn discards face down as many as he pleases of his original cards and dealer restores his hand to five cards from the top of the stock. (In six-hand play, some allow the dealer then to *rob the pack* as in Cinch, to replace his own discards.)

The Play. The first lead is made by the hand to the left of the player who named the trump, and play proceeds as in Spoil Five, including the requirement of following suit or trumping, and the privilege of reneging when holding one of the three highest trumps. All players of a partnership combine to fulfil their joint contract or to defeat the adverse contract.

Scoring. Each trick counts 5, and the highest trump in play counts an additional 5 (making 10 in all for the trick it wins). If the contracting side fulfils its contract, it scores all the points it makes; if it falls short of its contract, the amount of the contract is deducted from its score. The opposing side in either case scores all the points it makes.

If a side bids 30 and wins all five tricks, it scores 60.

Game is won by the first side to reach 120 points. A side having 100 points or more may not bid less than 20.

Irregularities. *New deal.* There must be a new deal by the same dealer if a card is exposed in dealing, or any player receives the wrong number of cards, or the dealer fails to adhere to the plan of dealing that he has commenced (as regards the number of cards to be dealt in each round).

Incorrect hand. If, after the first bid but before the draw, any hand is found incorrect, a short hand is supplied with additional cards from the top of the stock, and excess cards are drawn from a hand and discarded by the right-hand opponent.

If, after the draw but before the opening lead, any hand is found incorrect, it must be rectified in the same way. If in giving cards to replace discards the dealer exposes a card, the player to whom it would have gone may refuse it, and then take a replacement after all other hands have drawn.

If, after the opening lead, any hand is found incorrect, or if a player exposes one of the three highest trumps, the offender must discard his entire hand and stay out of the play for the remainder of that deal; and his side may not score in that deal. If the offender's side named the trump, it loses its contract.

If any lower card is exposed illegally, after the opening lead, it must be placed face up on the table and played by the holder at his first legal opportunity.

NAPOLEON (NAP)

PLAYERS

Any number from two to six may play; four is the best number. Each plays for himself.

CARDS

The pack of 52 is used. The cards in each suit rank: **A** (high), **K**, **Q**, **J**, **10**, **9**, **8**, **7**, **6**, **5**, **4**, **3**, **2**.

PRELIMINARIES

In drawing for deal, ace is low, below the two. Lowest card has choice of seats and deals first. Second-lowest sits at his left, and so on. Or players may take seats at random and draw merely for deal.

Dealer has the right to shuffle last, and the pack is cut by the player on his right. The cut must leave at least four cards in each packet.

DEALING

Cards are dealt one at a time, beginning with eldest hand. Each player receives five cards.

BIDDING

There is one round of bidding, commencing with eldest hand. Each hand must pass or make a bid higher than the preceding bid. Each bid is for the number of tricks that the player is willing to try to win, given the right to name the trump suit. If all other hands pass, dealer is bound to bid at least one. Except for this situation, a bid of less than two is usually barred. The bid of all five tricks is called *nap*.

THE PLAY

The highest bidder makes the opening lead, and the suit of this lead becomes trump. A lead calls on each other hand to follow suit if able; if unable, the hand may play any card. A trick is won by the highest trump, or the highest card of the suit led. The winner of a trick leads to the next.

The other players all combine in temporary partnership against the high bidder. The object of play is solely to make or defeat the bid. There is no credit for extra tricks over the bid. The moment the trick is gathered that makes or sets the bid, the winner must expose his remaining cards so that they may be examined for a possible revoke.

SCORING

Each deal is settled for immediately. If the bid is made, the bidder collects its value from each other player; if the bid is defeated, he pays the value to each other player. The value of any bid less than nap is the same as the number of tricks bid. Nap is worth 10 if made, but costs only 5 if defeated.

IRREGULARITIES

Misdeal. If a misdeal is called for any of the usual causes, the same dealer redeals.

Incorrect Number of Cards. A player dealt the wrong number of cards must announce the error before making any bid or pass, otherwise he must play on with the incorrect hand. A short hand cannot win a trick on which it has no card to play. If bidder's hand is correct, an opponent's incorrect, bidder does not pay if he loses but collects if he wins. If bidder's hand is incorrect, all others correct, bidder does not collect if he wins but pays if he loses.

Play Out of Turn. There is no penalty for a lead or play out of turn by bidder, but the error must be corrected on demand if noticed before the trick is turned and quitted, otherwise the trick stands. If an opponent of bidder leads or plays out of turn, he must pay three chips to bidder and may collect nothing if bidder loses.

Revoke. Failure to follow suit to the lead when able is a revoke. If a revoke is detected and claimed before settlement for the deal, play is abandoned and settlement made at once. A revoking bidder must pay all opponents as though he had lost. A revoking opponent must pay bidder the full amount he would have collected had he won, the other opponents paying nothing.

STRATEGY

Unless there are more than five players, more than half the pack is out of play in each deal. The bidding is therefore bound to be speculative. But the following rules of hand valuation hold in the long run. (Applicable to four-hand or five-hand play.)

TRUMP HOLDING	PROBABLE TRICKS
x x	½
K x	1
x x x	1½
J x x	2
x x x x	3

PLAIN SUIT

A or **K**	1
Q x	½

A small card accompanying a side ace or king is a "plus" value, countable in a hand holding three trumps. That is,

♡**x x x   ♣A x**

should be counted worth three tricks with hearts as trumps. Average expectation is that some other hand will hold two trumps, but that it can be forced to ruff the small club after the ace is cashed.

This table is intended to guide the first bidder, and may be applied to an overcall of a preceding bid of two. But if the player has to meet a bid of three or more ahead of him, he should count only his trump tricks plus side aces and kings, no lower and no "plus" values.

The time-honored rule of play is "Try to take every trick you can." There is rarely any point in withholding a card that can top the previous cards on a trick; the exceptions depend upon specific inferences from the first two or three tricks.

Nap Variants

The following are some of the special features introduced into Nap in various localities.

Wellington. The bid of nap can be overcalled by a bid of *Wellington*, which is also a bid to win all the tricks but doubles the stakes. (Variant. Wellington if made wins 10, but loses 10 if defeated.)

Blucher. Where Wellington is allowed, so usually is *Blucher*. This likewise is a bid to win all the tricks, with stakes trebled. Note that Wellington may not be bid unless nap is previously bid, and Blucher may not be bid unless Wellington has preceded it. (*Variant.* Blucher collects 10 or pays 20.)

Misere. The bid of *misere* overcalls a bid of three and is superseded by a bid of four. It is an offer to take no tricks, without a trump suit. It is scored as a bid of three.

Widow (Sir Garnet). An extra hand is dealt to the right of the dealer. Any player in his turn to bid may pick up the widow and discard any five cards of the ten. By so doing he bids nap. Wellington and Blucher are not allowed in this variation.

Peep. A widow of one card is dealt during the first round of the deal. At his turn to declare, a player may before passing or bidding peep privately at the widow upon payment of one chip to the pool. The highest bidder takes the widow and discards one card. The pool goes to the first player to make nap.

Pool. On the first deal, each player antes two chips to a pool. Each subsequent dealer antes two more chips so long as the pool is not won. Fines are assessed for irregularities and paid into the pool. A player who bids nap and fails must double the amount in the pool, and it may be further increased by allowing *peep*. The pool goes to the first player who bids and makes nap, after which all hands ante to start a new pool.

Purchase or Écarté Nap. This variant is played with a pool. After the deal, but before the bidding commences, each player in turn may discard any number of cards he pleases, and draw an equal number from the stock on the payment of one chip per card to the pool. There is only one round of drawing, followed by one round of bidding.

LOO

Loo was the leading card game of England in the late eighteenth and early nineteenth centuries, a favorite alike of the idle rich and industrious poor. It is probably mentioned more often in English literature than any other card game. Although Whist, Bridge, and Poker have largely displaced Loo, it is still played.

Originally Loo was called Lanterloo, from the French *lanterlu*, the refrain of a popular seventeenth-century song. The game may have developed from Rams, which has been called "the connecting link between the more strongly marked members of the Euchre family and Division Loo." Rams was popular in Germany; its variant Bierspiel was favored among students as a way to decide who should pay for the drinks.

The major variations of Loo depend upon whether the hand is of three or five cards, and whether the stake is limited or unlimited. (The form first described below is three-card limited.) Local divergences are found on the use of pam, on the recognition of flush and blaze, and on the rule of heading a trick.

PLAYERS

Theoretically, any number up to seventeen may play Three-Card Loo. Practically, the game should be limited to about nine, with not less than five. Each plays for himself.

CARDS

The pack of 52. If less than five play, the pack of 32 is preferred. The cards in each suit rank: **A** (high), **K, Q, J, 10, 9, 8, 7, 6, 5, 4, 3, 2**.

PRELIMINARIES

Players may take places at random. Any player distributes cards around the table, one at a time face up, and the first jack marks the first dealer.

Dealer has the right to shuffle last, and the pack is cut by the player at his right. The cut must leave at least two cards in each packet.

DEALING

Cards are dealt one at a time, beginning with eldest hand. Each hand receives three cards. See also *The Play*, below.

THE POOL

The dealer always antes three chips into a pool. The pool is increased by payments for loo, and also by forfeits for irregularities. All such increments are made in multiples of 3, so that the pool can always be divided evenly into three parts, one for each trick.

A deal that commences with only three chips in the pool, the dealer's ante, is a *single* (or *force*). With more chips in the pool, it is a *double*.

THE PLAY

Eldest hand makes the opening lead. A lead calls upon each other hand to follow suit if able; if void, to trump if able; and also, if able, to *head* the trick by playing higher than all previous cards. A trick is won by the highest trump, or by the highest card of the suit led. The winner of a trick leads to the next.

The cards to a trick are not gathered together; each is left face up in front of the owner.

Single Pool. The deal completed, eldest hand leads forthwith. Should all hands chance to follow suit to each of the three leads, no trump suit is fixed, since it would make no difference in the ownership of the tricks. But the first time any hand fails to follow suit, the current trick is completed, then the top card of the stock (remainder of the pack) is turned up to fix the trump suit. This trump must be reckoned in deciding the ownership of the current and any subsequent tricks.

One-third of the pool is collected for each trick won. Each hand that has failed to win a trick is *looed* and must put three chips in the next pool, thereby making it a double.

Double Pool. An extra hand, called the *miss*, is dealt just to the right of the dealer. After the deal, the next card is turned up for trump. Prior to the opening lead, dealer requires each hand in turn, beginning with eldest, to state his intentions. Each player must pass, stand, or take the miss.

If a player passes, he is out of that deal, and his hand is forthwith placed face down under the stock. To stand is to remain in play. If a player takes the miss (and so commits himself to stand), his original hand is placed under the stock. If all other players pass but dealer, or a player before him who has taken the miss, the lone player takes the pool and the cards are abandoned. If only one player ahead of the dealer stands, dealer must either stand and play for himself or take the miss and *defend the pool*.

To the usual rules of play is added the rule that the leader to each trick must lead a trump if able; further, the ace of trumps must be led at the first opportunity, or the king if the ace was turned up.

All hands that did not pass participate in the play, and the pool is divided into three parts, one for each trick. Each hand looed pays three chips to the next pool (which thus may or may not be another double).

When dealer is forced to defend the pool, he neither collects nor pays, settlement being made only by his opponent.

Flush. A flush is a hand of three trumps. The player holding a flush wins the entire pool without play, and if two or more hold flushes the elder hand wins. Flushes are announced after the dealer has declared, and all hands that have stood (or taken the miss) are looed.

IRREGULARITIES

A player forfeits three chips to the current pool for any of the following irregularities:

1. Causing a misdeal by dealing the wrong number of cards, exposing a card, etc. If the error is made by the dealer, there is a new deal by the next dealer; if it is made by another player, the same dealer deals again.

2. Turning trump, in a single, before there has been any renounce.

3. Declaring out of turn, in a double.

4. Picking up another player's hand, in a double; the player thus wronged may look at both hands concerned and take his choice.

5. Looking at one's own hand, as dealer in a double, before all other players have declared.

6. Leading or playing out of turn.

7. Failing to make payment for loo prior to turn of trump in the next deal.

A Revoke is any failure to lead or play as required by the rules. A revoke may be corrected without penalty before the next hand plays; otherwise it stands as established. The penalty for established revoke is six chips, payable to the next pool. As soon as an established revoke is discovered, the cards are abandoned, and the pool is divided evenly among all players in the deal but the offender, any odd chips being left for the next pool.

Unlimited Loo

In Limited Loo, the forfeit for loo or for an irregularity is three chips (or any agreed multiple of 3). To ginger up the game our forbears devised Unlimited Loo—the forfeit is equal to the total amount in the current pool. A series of consecutive doubles can pyramid the costs to astronomical figures. At this game "a certain Irish Lord is reported to have lost 10,000 pounds at one sitting at half-crown [ante]."

Irish Loo

In this variant, no distinction exists between single and double pools. No widow is dealt, and a card is always turned up for trump on completion of the deal. Each player in turn must stand or pass. Those who have stood may then draw cards from the stock, from zero to five, in exchange for equal discards. If all ahead of him pass, dealer wins the pool. If only one ahead of him stands, dealer must stand for himself or play to defend the pool. The rules of play are as in *Double Pool*, above.

Five-card Loo

The ante is five chips, forfeits are paid in units of five, and each hand is dealt five cards. (The deal may be in rounds of 3–2 or 2–3.) Other rules are as in Irish Loo. Optional features that may be added are:

The turn-up belongs to the dealer, and may be taken into his hand prior to discarding if he plays. He then draws one less card than he discards, to reduce his hand to five.

Pam, the jack of clubs, is always the highest trump. It may also be used as a wild card to complete a flush or blaze. (Old usage was to permit the owner of pam to withhold it on a trump lead, and require him to do so if the lead was the ace, or the king from ace-king, when the leader uttered the formula "Pam be civil!" Later this rite fell into disuse and pam had to be played to avoid revoke in trumps.)

Flush comprises five cards of one suit, or four with pam. *Blaze* is five face cards, or four with pam. The hands rank in order: Pam-flush or pam-blaze (equal and high), natural trump flush, natural plain-suit flush, natural blaze. A player dealt one of these hands wins the pool, all others who stood being looed. As between equal hands, the elder wins.

FIVE HUNDRED

The rules of Five Hundred were originally copyrighted in 1904 by the United States Playing Card Company. At that time the game most widely played in the United States was Euchre. There was demand for a game affording more opportunity for skill than Euchre, but requiring less concentration than Whist. Five Hundred fitted this description. It largely supplanted Euchre and for some years was the major social card game.

Five Hundred is by custom classed as a member of "the Euchre family," because it places right and left bowers at the top of the trump suit. But the popularity of Five Hundred rests on its vital difference from Euchre: descendants of Triomphe are all *short* games (not all the cards are in play) while Five Hundred is a *long* or full-pack game.

PLAYERS

Two to six may play. The rules below are given for three-hand, which is the most prevalent form. The four-hand partnership game (page 273) is equally good.

CARDS

(For three-hand.) The pack of 32, with the joker added. The cards in the trump suit rank: **joker** (high), **J** *(right bower)*, **J** (of the other suit of same color as the trump, *left bower*), **A, K, Q, 10, 9, 8, 7**. The cards in each plain suit rank: **A** (high), **K, Q, (J), 10, 9, 8, 7**.

The suits rank: hearts (high), diamonds, clubs, spades. For bidding purposes, *notrump* ranks above hearts.

PRELIMINARIES

Draw for first deal. Lowest card deals; in drawing, the ace ranks below the two and the joker is the lowest card.

Dealer has the right to shuffle last, and the pack is cut by the player at his right. The cut must leave at least four cards in each packet.

DEALING

Cards are dealt to the left, beginning with eldest hand. Each player receives ten cards, in rounds of 3–4–3. After the first round, three cards are dealt face down in the center to form a widow.

BIDDING

Commencing with eldest hand, each player in turn may make one bid or pass. Each bid names a number of tricks, from six to ten, together with the intended trump suit or no trump. Each bid must be for a greater number of tricks than the previous bid, or for the same number in a higher-ranking declaration. The highest bid becomes the contract, and the two other players combine in temporary partnership against the bidder.

If all hands pass without a bid, the cards are bunched and the next dealer deals. In some circles, if a deal is passed out, the hand is played at notrump, each player for himself. Eldest hand leads. Each trick won counts 10 points; there is no *set back*.

THE PLAY

Highest bidder takes up the widow, then discards any three cards. He makes the opening lead, and is free to lead any card. A lead calls upon each other hand to follow suit, if able; if unable, the hand may play any card. A trick is won by the highest trump, or by the highest card of the suit led. The winner of a trick leads to the next.

At notrump, the joker is a trump suit in itself. The joker may not be played unless one is void of the suit led, but when played, it wins the trick.

When the joker is led, the leader must specify the suit for which it calls.

The object of play is to make or defeat the contract. Although the opponents combine against the bidder, they must keep their tricks separate for scoring purposes. The bidder makes nothing extra for extra tricks over his contract, unless he wins all ten tricks and his bid was for less than 250.

SCORING

The value of every possible bid is shown in the scoring table.

TRICKS	6	7	8	9	10
♠	40	140	240	340	440
♣	60	160	260	360	460
◇	80	180	280	380	480
♡	100	200	300	400	500
Notrump	120	220	320	420	520

If the bidder makes his contract, he scores the value of his bid. If he took all ten tricks, and his bid was for less than 250, he scores 250 instead of the value of his bid. If the bidder is *set back*—fails to make contract—the value of his bid is subtracted from his running total. Thus it is possible for a player to have a minus score, and such score is usually marked by drawing a ring around it. The player is then *in the hole*.

Each opponent of the bidder, whether the contract is made or set, scores 10 for each trick taken by himself.

Game is 500. If two or more players *go out* in the same deal, bidder wins; as between opponents alone, the first to win a trick that makes his total 500 wins. An opponent may *count out* by winning a trick that gives him 500, and the hand is then abandoned unless the bidder would also go out if he made contract.

The individual score kept for each player is the running total and net of his winnings and losses.

NULLO

An additional declaration allowed in some circles is *nullo,* an offer to win no tricks at notrump. The value of nullo is 250, so that for bidding purposes it ranks higher than eight spades and lower than eight clubs. If nullo takes the contract, the bidder loses if he wins a single trick, and each opponent scores 10 for each trick taken by the bidder.

IRREGULARITIES

Misdeal. There must be a new deal by the same dealer if too many or too few cards are given to any hand, if the dealing is not in strict accordance with the rule "3-widow-4-3"; if a card is found faced in the pack or is exposed in the dealing; if the pack is found to be imperfect. But if the pack is found to be imperfect, any prior scores stand.

A deal by the wrong player or with an uncut pack may be stopped before the deal is complete; after that, it stands.

Bid Out of Turn. In a partnership game, if a player bids out of turn the bid is void and his side may make no further bid on that deal. In a game where each plays for himself, there is no penalty for a bid out of turn; the bid is void; the correct hand bids; and the erroneous bidder may bid in due turn.

Wrong Number of Cards. If, during the bidding, two hands (not including the widow) are found to hold an incorrect number of cards, there must be a new deal by the same dealer. If one hand and the widow are incorrect, the incorrect hand loses the right to bid, and any other player draws a sufficient number of cards from the excess and gives them to the deficient hand.

If, during the play, the bidder and an opponent are found to have an incorrect number of cards, there must be a new deal by the same dealer. If the bidder and widow alone are incorrect, the bidder loses at once, but the hand is played out to determine how many tricks the opponents can win. In this event some tricks at the end may be short, and in a partnership game if any hand of the bidding side cannot play to a trick it cannot win it.

If, during the play, the opponents are found to have an incorrect number of cards, the bidder and widow being correct, bidder at once wins the value of his game, and may continue play in the effort to win all the tricks. He wins any trick to which an opponent cannot play.

Exposed Cards. The following are exposed cards: a card dropped face upward on the table except in regular turn to play; additional cards dropped with one intended to be played; a card so held that partner sees any portion of its face; a card named by a player as being in his hand. There is no penalty for exposure of a card by bidder playing alone, except for a card he exposes in a corrected revoke.

A card exposed by a player who has a partner (including opponents of the bidder at three-hand) must be left face up on the table. Any adversary may call for the play of the exposed card in regular turn, and the card must be played if it can be without revoking. The card is subject to repeated call until it can be legally played. The owner of an exposed card must pause before playing in turn, to give the adversaries opportunity to call this card. If he plays without due pause, the card played also becomes exposed and subject to call.

Play Out of Turn. If a player leads out of turn, and all others play to the trick before the error is noticed, it stands without penalty. If noticed earlier, the error must be corrected; the lead becomes an exposed card; the other cards on the trick are retracted; the correct leader may lead. If the correct leader is partner of the offender, the adversary at his right may call upon him to lead or not to lead a trump, or may forbid the suit of the exposed card to be led.

If a player plays when it is the turn of the hand at his right to *play* (but not to *lead)*, the premature card stands as played without penalty; it may not be retracted.

Revoke. If a hand fails to follow suit when able, the offender may correct it before the trick is quitted and before he plays to the next trick. If it is not corrected, play ends immediately the revoke is noticed. If the revoke was by the bidder, he loses the value of his bid and the opponents score for whatever tricks they have taken up to that time. If the revoke was made by an opponent of the bidder, the bidder scores his bid and the opponents may score nothing.

Corrected Revoke. The revoke card becomes an exposed card and subject to penalty (see above) even if it is the bidder's card.

Error in the Score. If proved, an error in the scoresheet may be corrected prior to the first bid (other than pass) made on the next deal after that to which the error pertains. An error discovered at a later time must stand.

Looking at Quitted Tricks, or bidder looking back at his discard. The opponent at the offender's right may call a suit the next time the offender leads.

THE NEW COMPLETE HOYLE

Giving Unauthorized Information. The player at the offender's right may call a suit from the offender or the offender's partner, whichever leads next.

STRATEGY

Bidding. As there are 10 trumps, an average share is between three and four. The minimum trump length for a bid is four, but with only four they should include two of the three highest trumps or be heavily compensated with side strength. Most contracts go to hands with five or more trumps. The chances of improving the trump length by the widow are:

CHANCE OF FINDING AT LEAST ONE TRUMP IN WIDOW

When you hold 4 trumps	1091/1771	5:3 for
When you hold 5 trumps	955/1771	5:4 for

The chances of buying two or three helpful cards in the widow are negligible unless there are so many "places open" that the hand scarcely has a chance of taking the contract anyhow. If any one card will improve the hand sufficiently to make contract likely of fulfillment:

CHANCES OF FINDING ONE IMPROVING CARD IN WIDOW

"Places open"

1	231/1771	7:1 against
2	441/1771	3:1 against
3	631/1771	9:5 against
4	802/1771	6:5 against
5	955/1771	5:4 for

An approximate method of hand valuation is to count as a trick each trump in excess of 3, each top trump as good as the ace, and each side ace or guarded king.

Since each hand has only one turn to bid, it is important to bid the full value. With defensive strength, be conservative and do not overbid in the hope of improving. For example:

Joker ♡ **J A 8 7** ◇ **K 7** ♣ **K 8** ♠ **A**

This hand is worth a bid of seven hearts, by the rule, and might well be so bid by dealer. But if the widow is worthless, the hand may easily lose four tricks. If a bid of seven is made ahead of this hand, the safer course is to pass.

Conversely, where the strength is in the pattern, with few aces and kings, be bold. For example:

♡— ◇ **A K 8 7** ♣— ♠ **J K Q 9 8 7**

Dealer holding this hand should bid eight spades. On a hand with so little defense against bids in hearts and clubs, the bid of eight spades is a worthwhile gamble.

Discarding. The discard is not, as in Pinochle and similar games, an opportunity to lay away valuable cards. It is merely a necessity in order to reduce the bidder's hand to ten cards. The discards are almost invariably worthless low cards. There is no direct advantage in voiding the hand of a suit, but bidder often makes a void as a consequence of saving his best cards. A small card may make at the end of a holding of four or more, whereas a worthless doubleton or singleton never wins a trick.

Play. With five or more trumps, the bidder should lead trumps at once in order to draw two for one. Even with four trumps, they should be opened if the hand has stoppers in every suit. A plain suit of four or more cards, if not solid, should also be led early in the effort to establish long cards. High cards in short suits should be saved for reentries.

The opponents should try to get the bidder in the *middle* by letting the lead come from his right rather than his left. So long as the defenders have any trumps left, the general policy is for the left-hand opponent to lead a short suit rather than a long, and the opponent on the right to lead long rather than short. But specific high-card holdings may make the converse policy safer. If the bidder has shown void of a suit, opponents should lead this suit at every opportunity; the only exception to this rule arises when bidder is found to be so weak in trumps that the opponents can bail him out and then cash their suit entire.

Notrump is essentially a long-suit game by both sides, strong, short holdings being saved to stop the adverse long suit. Many a shaky notrump contract is saved by the joker, which can be used either to stop an adverse long suit or as an extra "swing" to solidify one's own long suit. Very few notrump contracts, indeed, are attempted without the joker.

Two-hand Five Hundred

The deal is the same as for three players, a dead hand being placed at dealer's left. The winning bidder takes the widow and discards three cards; then the two hands are played out. Since the ten cards of the dead hand are not in play, bidding can and must be somewhat speculative.

Four-hand Five Hundred

The four-hand game is played in two partnerships, the partners sitting alternately. The pack is of 42 cards; the joker is usually not used, but it may be if desired. Each player is dealt ten cards, and the balance of two or three cards goes to the widow. Rules are the same as at three-hand, but the play is always two against two. A single score is kept for each side.

Five Hundred for Five or Six

The full pack of 52 (to which the joker may be added) is used in five-hand. Each player is dealt ten cards and the balance goes to the widow. During the bidding, each is for himself, but the high bidder then chooses partner(s) according to either of these alternative plans:

(a) A bid of six or seven entitles him to one partner; a bid of more entitles him to two; he names the players to be his partners, regardless of their position at the table;

(b) The bidder names a specific card, and the holder thereof becomes his partner, but must say nothing to reveal his identity until the card is duly played.

For six-hand play, in two partnerships of three each, the recommendation by the proprietors of the game is to use "the 62-card pack, the regular pack of 52 plus four 11's, four 12's, and two 13's." These added cards rank in order above the ten and below the jack or queen. Each player is dealt ten cards, and the balance of two (or three, with joker) goes to the widow.

Game of 1,000 or 1,500

A variant is to set game at 1,000 or 1,500. In this case, bonus points are given for the cards won in tricks, on the following count:

Each ace	1
Each king, queen, jack or ten	10
Each lower card	pip value
Joker	0

The bonus points of course do not count toward making or defeating the bid. A bidder who is set back may not score any bonus.

THE
HEARTS
GROUP

HEARTS

The *nullo* principle—losing tricks instead of winning them—was introduced into many early card games, no doubt in order to give some defense to a player who is dealt a very poor hand for the ordinary purposes of the game. Ombre had its *nullissimo*, Schafkopf its *kleineste*, and nullo play survives in most of their descendants. It is found in Cayenne and other varieties of Whist; in Five Hundred and other varieties of Euchre.

There are many ancient games in which nullo play predominates, if not monopolizes. In most (as Slobberhannes, Polignac) the "minus" cards or points are few. Perhaps the first game with any considerable number of minus points was Reverse, or Reversis (not to be confused with the board game of similar name). The game of Hearts may have derived (by simplification!) from Reverse, in which special emphasis was placed on the heart suit. Certainly the *take-all* feature of Omnibus Hearts was taken straight from the *reversis* that gave the older game its name.

Hearts is a comparatively recent game, but has largely displaced all the older nullo games. It has developed many variants of its own, largely by borrowing features from the older games. Thus, the sweepstake settlement of straight Hearts comes from Reverse, and the diamond ten as a plus card in Omnibus Hearts from the little-known French Whist.

Hearts is a round game, which may be played in one form or another by two to eight players. "Straight" Hearts, Heartsette, Black Lady, and Domino are suitable for three to six players. Two may play Domino or the variant described as Two-hand Hearts. More than six may play Cancellation. Particularly interesting with four players are Auction and Omnibus Hearts.

"Straight" Hearts

PLAYERS

Any number from three to six may play, each for himself.

CARDS

The pack of 52. With other than four players, strip out some small cards to equalize the hands. Three players: discard ♣2. Five players: discard ♣2 and ◇2. Six players: discard ♣2, ♣3, ◇2, ♠2. (*Variant.* In Heartsette, the full pack is used whatever the number of players. The cards are dealt out evenly as far as they will go. Odd cards form a widow, which is added to the first trick and goes to the winner thereof.)

The cards in each suit rank: **A** (high), **K, Q, J, 10, 9, 8, 7, 6, 5, 4, 3, 2**. There is no relative ranking of suits and never a trump. (Hearts are often called "trumps" but do not actually have the trump privilege.)

PRELIMINARIES

Cards may be drawn for choice of seats and first deal. Low card deals. The deal rotates to the left. Dealer has the right to shuffle last, and the pack is cut by the player at his right. The cut must leave at least four cards in each packet.

DEALING

The entire pack is dealt out one card at a time, beginning with eldest hand.

THE PLAY

Eldest hand makes the opening lead. A lead calls upon each other hand to follow suit if able; if unable to follow suit, a hand may play any card. A trick is won by the highest card of the suit led. The winner of a trick leads to the next.

The sole object of play is to avoid taking hearts in tricks. Each heart counts 1 against the player taking it. (*Variant.* In Spot Hearts, $\heartsuit$**A** counts 14; $\heartsuit$**K**, 13; $\heartsuit$**Q**, 12; $\heartsuit$**J**, 11; and all other cards their index value.)

SCORING

Settlement may be made by any of three alternative methods:

Cumulative Scoring. The number of hearts taken by each player is recorded in a running total column. When play ends, the average of all scores is computed and each player is debited or credited his amount over or under the average. The players who are over the average pay out, and those who are under collect.

For example, suppose the final scores are

A	B	C	D
51	132	38	91

The total of the scores is 312, and division by 4 gives the average of 78. The net differences from average are:

A	B	C	C
−27	+54	−40	+13

Players B and D pay, A and C collect, their differences from average.

Sweepstake. After the play of a deal, each player puts in the pot one chip for every heart he took. If one player alone was *clear*—took no hearts—he wins the pot. If two players were clear, they divide the pot; if there is an odd chip, it goes into the next pot. If every player is *painted*—takes one or more hearts—the pot is a *jack* and is added to the next pot. The pot is likewise a jack if one player takes all thirteen hearts.

Howell Settlement. Each player puts in the pot, for each heart taken, as many chips as there are players in the game other than himself. Each player then takes out of the pot one chip for every heart, out of thirteen, that he did *not* take. In other words, he receives from the pot as many chips as the difference between thirteen and the number of hearts he took.

For example, in a four-hand game:

	A	B	C	D
Hearts taken	6	4	2	1
Put in pot	18	12	6	3
Receive	7	9	11	12
Net	−11	− 3	+ 5	+ 9

IRREGULARITIES

Misdeal. If dealer exposes a card in dealing, or gives one player too many cards, another player too few, the next player in turn deals.

Play Out of Turn. A lead or play out of turn must be retracted if demand is made before all have played to the trick; after all have played, a play out of turn stands without penalty.

Quitted Tricks. Each trick gathered must be placed face down in front of the winner and tricks must be kept separate. If a player so mixes his cards that a claim of revoke cannot be proved, he is charged with all 13 points for the deal, regardless of whether the alleged revoke was made by him or another player. [In Spot Hearts the penalty here and below is 104 points.]

Revoke. Failure to follow suit when able to do so constitutes a revoke. A revoke may be corrected before the trick is turned and quitted; if not discovered until later, the revoke is established, play is immediately abandoned, and the revoking hand is charged with all 13 points for the deal. If revoke is established against more than one player, each is charged 13 points. But the revoke penalty may not be enforced after the next ensuing cut after the deal in which the revoke occurred.

Incorrect Hand. A player discovered to have too few cards must take the last trick (if more than one card short he must take in every trick to which he cannot play).

STRATEGY

Little can be said in general terms of the strategy of play, which is largely a matter of keeping track of every card played, by whom, and making inferences as to the location of unplayed cards.

But there are some points on *danger suits* applicable to all nullo play. A holding is dangerous not through the presence of high cards, but through the absence of low cards. The suit **A–10–7–4–2** is usually impregnable; against any but a freak distribution of the remaining cards, it can avoid winning any trick, can provide exit, or can give the player entry if he wants it. The suit **Q–10–9–7** is dangerous; it can be and probably will be forced to win several tricks, and has little prospect of providing forced exit.

The danger from absence of low cards of course increases with the length of the suit. When saddled with such a holding as **A–K–Q–J–10**, a player can only hope and pray. But with a short danger suit (not hearts), the player can strike a blow in self-defense by leading it out early rather than waiting for it to come to him late. For example:

♠ Q 2   ♡ A 10 9 7 6   ◇ Q 10 9   ♣ A 5 4

With the opening lead, this hand should start the diamonds at once, in order to get rid of the high cards while there is the maximum of chance that no hand can discard on the suit.

A suit is distributed 4–3–3–3 only 10% of the time. In the other 90% of cases, some hand will be able to discard on the third round or earlier. With a holding that can be forced to win one or two of the first three rounds of the suit, play the high cards first, saving the low card. The hand given above will as a matter of course play ♠**Q** on the first round of spades and ♣**A** on the first round of clubs.

In *Cumulative* and *Howell* scoring, it pays to take some hearts in order to avoid taking a greater number. For example:

♠ J 9 8 4   ♡ A 3   ◇ K 9 7 6   ♣ A Q J

With the opening lead, this hand may well lead ♡**A** followed by the ♡**3**. The hand looks predestined to win many tricks, including a round of hearts. By accepting four hearts at once, the player gets in a second lead of the suit, leaving not more than five hearts at large available for discard on later tricks that he will have to win.

Such holdings as the spades and diamonds above are middling-dangerous. Leading from them for exit purposes may boomerang on the player, leaving him with one or two cards by which he can later be forced back in the lead.

Sweepstake scoring creates peculiar necessities. Taking one heart is as fatal as taking ten: all that matters is how many players are painted.

A player has to take desperate chances to stay clear, such as giving up an only low card to duck a trick containing a heart, when such play risks that he may later be "sewed in." But, once he is painted, the player cares not how many more hearts fall to him; his sole concern is to try to paint every other player as well and so create a jack. In this project he has the support of any other player that has been painted. Sweepstake is consequently a game of temporary partnerships, the "haves" conspiring together against the "have-nots."

Joker Hearts

In three-hand play, the joker may be added to the pack to avoid necessity of stripping it. Each hand receives 17 cards.

In four-hand play, the joker may be added and the ♡**2** discarded.

In any case, the joker ranks between ♡**J** and ♡**10**. It wins any trick to which it is played, unless any of the four higher hearts is also played to the trick (whether in following suit or discarding), in which case that trick is won by the highest heart it contains.

Domino Hearts

Only six cards are dealt to each player. The stock (rest of the pack) is placed face down on the table. Play is as usual, but a hand unable to follow suit must draw cards from the top of the stock until he can. When the stock is exhausted, the cards are played out with discarding permitted when a hand cannot follow suit. Each player drops out as his cards are exhausted, and if he wins a trick with his last card, the active player at his left makes the next lead. The only counting cards are the hearts, which cost one each. The player with the lowest score, when another reaches minus 31, wins.

Two-hand Hearts

The pack of 52 is used. Thirteen cards are dealt to each player. The stock (rest of the pack) is placed face down on the table. The first lead is made by non-dealer. The rules of play are as in Hearts, but after each trick the winner draws the top card of the stock and his opponent draws the next. Thus the hands are kept at thirteen cards until the stock is exhausted, whereupon the last thirteen are played out. Only the hearts count, one each, and the player with the lesser number wins by the difference.

Cancellation Hearts

This variant was devised to allow from six to ten players to participate. Two packs of 52 are used, shuffled together. The cards are dealt one at a time as far as they will go evenly, and any odd cards are left in a widow, which goes to the winner of the first trick. The play is as in Hearts, except that when two identical cards fall on the same trick they cancel each other; neither can win the trick. If all cards played to a trick cancel out, they go to the winner of the next trick.

The counting cards are the hearts, 1 each, and ♠**Q**, counting 13. Use cumulative scoring, as given under *Hearts*. A game ends when one player reaches a prefixed total, usually 100.

Auction Hearts

PLAYERS

Best for four. Each plays for himself.

CARDS

The pack of 52. Cards in each suit rank: **A** (high), **K, Q, J, 10, 9, 8, 7, 6, 5, 4, 3, 2**.

PRELIMINARIES

Cards may be drawn for choice of seats and deal. Low card deals first. Dealer has the right to shuffle last. The cut is made by the player on his right. The cut must leave at least four cards in each packet.

DEALING

The cards are dealt one at a time, thirteen to each player.

BIDDING

Commencing with eldest hand, each player in turn may make one bid, or may pass. Each bid must be higher than the preceding bid. The bid is the number of chips that the player is willing to put in the pot for the right to name the "minus" suit. Any amount may be bid from one up, but is naturally limited by the number of chips in the pot. The pot will contain 13 chips, or more if it is a jack.

The highest bidder names any one of the four suits as the "minus" suit (colloquially called "trumps," but the suit does not actually have the trump privilege).

THE PLAY

The opening lead is made by the bidder. A lead calls for each other hand to follow suit if able; if unable, a hand may play any card. A trick is won by the highest card of the suit led. The winner of a trick leads to the next.

The object of play is to avoid taking in tricks any cards of the named suit.

SETTLEMENT

At the end of play, each player pays into the pot one chip for each card of the named suit that he has taken. If only one player is *clear*—having no minus cards—he wins the entire pot. If two players are clear, they divide the pot, the odd chip if any being left in the pot. If all players are *painted*—take one or more minus cards—the pot is a *jack* and is added to the pot on the next deal. If one player takes all thirteen cards of the minus suit the pot is likewise a jack.

There is no bidding in a jack pot; the right to name the minus suit rests with the player who previously paid for it, and continues until the jack containing his contribution is won. He does not have to pay any additional chips to preserve this right, but must make due payment if he wins cards of the suit he names.

Black Lady

Black Lady has very largely supplanted "straight" Hearts. All rules of the latter apply, with the following additions:

Counting Cards. Each heart counts 1 against the player taking it in a trick, and the ♠Q (called *Black Lady, Black Maria, Calamity Jane)* counts 13. Many play that the ♠Q must be discarded the first time the holder is unable to follow suit to the card led; failure to do so is a revoke.

The Pass. Before the opening lead, each player selects any three cards of his original hand and passes them to his right-hand neighbor. Each player must pass before looking at the cards received from his left.

With five or more players, only two cards are passed.

(*Variant.* Some pass the cards to the left instead of to the right.)

Scoring. Any of the three methods of settlement may be used, but cumulative scoring is largely preferred. If one player takes all thirteen hearts and the ♠Q, no score is recorded for the deal. (*Variant.* Many play *Shoot-the-Moon;* a player who takes all the fourteen counting cards wins 26, that is, 26 is subtracted from his cumulative total.)

Strategy. All remarks on *danger suits*, under the strategy of Straight Hearts, apply with even greater force to Black Lady.

The pass gives each player a chance to mitigate the dangers of his original hand. The most dangerous holding is in spades; one or two of the three top cards, in a length of three spades or less. From all such holdings as **Q–x–x**, **K–x–x**, **A–Q–x**, the top cards must be passed, else the hand is very likely to collect the ♠**Q** on spade leads. The ♠**Q** is safer in the player's hand than out, if accompanied by enough guards—at least three other cards. With only three guards, one of them should be high enough to stop the suit: thus **Q–7–5–2** is dangerous to hold, **Q–J–5–2** is less dangerous, and **A–Q–5–2** should always be held intact.

With no danger points in the hand, the pass is usually all diamonds or all clubs, to establish a void. Such a pass is imperative when the hand was dealt only one or two small spades and is thus in danger if it receives high spades in the pass. Attempts to create a heart void are less common, because any small heart will usually be kept as insurance against receipt of high hearts. Rarest of all is a spade void after the pass; almost never can the pass of a spade lower than ♠**Q** be good.

All these considerations have bearing on what to do with a hand that has more danger points than can be cured by the pass. For example:

♠ **Q 7 5**   ♡ **K J 2**   ◇ **A Q 5**   ♣ **Q 9 8 6**

The ♠**Q** has to be passed. The heart holding almost surely will be forced to win at least one trick; the other two suits are middling-dangerous. Yet the pass of ♡**K J** cannot be recommended. If hearts are received, this pass was useless or needless. If diamonds and/or clubs are received, the chance of gathering ♠**Q** on one of these suits is greatly increased. The recommended pass, besides ♠**Q**, is ◇**Q** and ♣**9**. The hazards are lessened by the knowledge that the player holding ♠**Q** will have to follow to at least one round of each suit, diamonds and clubs. The pass of ◇**Q** instead of ♡**K** is based on the fact that a heart void in another player's hand is far less to be expected than a diamond void.

Omnibus Hearts

So called because it includes all the optional features introduced into Black Lady in various localities, Omnibus Hearts is considered by many to offer the greatest opportunity for skill among all the Hearts variants. By the use of a "plus" card it adds to nullo play (avoidance of hearts and Black Maria) the incentive to win certain tricks.

The game is best for four players, each for himself. So played, it is comparable to the games of the Whist family in profundity.

To the rules of "straight" Hearts, add the following:

COUNTING CARDS

Each heart counts 1 minus, the ♠**Q** counts 13 minus, and the ♢**10** counts 10 plus. *(Variant.* Some use the ♢**J**, some the ♢**8**, instead of the ♢**10**).

THE PASS

Before the opening lead, each player passes three cards of his original hand to his left neighbor. The player must pass before looking at the cards received from his right. *(Variant.* In a four-handed game, the pass may alternate: three to the left, three to the right, then three across.)

SCORING

Cumulative scoring is used. A game consists of an agreed number of deals, or lasts until any player reaches an agreed limit, as −100.

Each player is debited or credited for the counting cards he wins in tricks. But if one player takes all fifteen counting cards he scores +26, the others scoring nothing. (Called *take-all* or *slam.)*

STRATEGY

All remarks on *danger suits* under "straight" Hearts, and all discussion of the strategy of Black Lady, apply to Omnibus Hearts.

There are four possible campaigns of play. The cards to pass must usually be selected with one campaign in mind, but keeping open the possibility of a switch of plan according to the cards received.

Take-none is the mere effort to avoid being painted. It is "straight" Hearts. This plan is the necessary policy when the hand does not contain the right cards for a positive campaign.

Save-the-Ten is open only to the hand dealt the ♢**10** or to the hand that receives it in the pass. The ♢**10** is won by the hand holding it only in one of two ways: (a) ♢**10** becomes the master card through the early play of all higher cards; (b) ♢**10** wins an early lead, despite outstanding higher cards, through fortuitous circumstance.

Catch-the-Ten is the effort to snare ♢**10** by winning the last several tricks, after ♠**Q** is gone, or, rarely, to drop ♢**10** with top diamonds. Catch-the-ten is the natural policy of any hand with a modicum of high cards sufficiently guarded. The full-blown campaign involves four efforts: to force out the ♠**Q** on spade leads; to establish one or more long suits; to avoid diamond leads, lest ♢**10** drop prematurely; to save enough winning cards for final entry when the rest of the tricks can be claimed.

If dealt the 10, a player has to pass it if he wants to try catch-the-ten. Almost as imperative is to rid the hand of lower diamonds, if it was dealt more than one. A player may hope to sneak by no more than one round of diamonds without damage.

Since receipt of ◇ **10** kills catch-the-ten hopes, the player in passing should try to keep enough low cards and safe suits for a switch to take-none.

Shoot-the-Moon is naturally reserved for a hand of great strength, but this can be and usually is massed in two or three suits. The pass must rid the hand of these fatal weaknesses: ◇ **10**, except in a near-solid suit; low hearts, except in a solid heart suit. Low diamonds make poor prospects; with more than one such after the pass, the take-all usually has to be abandoned.

A *Shoot-the-Moon* hand must usually make a few low leads in order to solidify its long suits before the opponents discover the take-all intention and play to prevent it.

EXAMPLES OF PASSING

♠ **K 8 4**   ♡ **A J 9 5 3**   ◇ **8 4**   ♣ **K 10 7**

For take-none, pass ♠**K**, ♣**K 10**. Better, try catch-the-ten and pass ♠**K**, ◇**8 4**.

♠ **A Q 10 4**   ♡ **4 3**   ◇ **Q 10 9 8 4**   ♣ **Q 5**

With the opening lead, pass ♡**4 3**, ♣**5**, planning to lead ◇**Q** for save-the-ten. Without the opening lead, the same might be tried on the chance of receiving high cards for entries, but safer is to pass ◇ **10 9 8**, and receipt of high cards may change take-none into catch-the-ten.

♠ **Q 7 5**   ♡ **A Q J 5 3**   ◇ **10 4**   ♣ **A J 9**

Pass ♠**Q**, ◇**10 4**. The hand may turn into a take-all if helpful cards are received.

♠ **A K 4**   ♡ **K Q 10 8**   ◇ **6**   ♣ **A J 10 9 4**

Pass ♡**10 8**, ◇**6**. Bound to be painted for plenty anyhow, the hand may as well try for take-all.

Opening Lead. The "normal" opening lead is a spade. It is the indicated lead for a hand not having a dangerous holding and intent on either take-none or catch-the-ten, and these two campaigns monopolize 80% of the game. Failure to open spades may indicate: (a) possession of ♠**Q** or higher spades without sufficient guards; (b) desire to rid the hand of a short, high holding in clubs or diamonds; (c) effort to establish the suit opened, for save-the-ten or take-all; (d) rarely, spade void.

When the first spade lead is won by a hand without "spade trouble," the suit is continued, unless the hand has special operations to be executed first.

EXAMPLE DEAL

W: ♠ K 6 5   ♡ Q 7 4 2   ◇ K 8 6   ♣ Q 10 9
N: ♠ A 4 3   ♡ J 10 9 8 6   ◇ J 9 7 4   ♣ 5
E: ♠ J 7   ♡ K   ◇ A 5 3 2   ♣ A K 7 6 4 2
S: ♠ Q 10 9 8 2   ♡ A 5 3   ◇ Q 10   ♣ J 8 3

West passes ♠K, ♣Q 10. North passes ♠A, ♡J 10. Both of these players have spade trouble, as well as a dangerous side suit. East passes ♡K, ◇5, ♣7. He might instead try for take-all by passing ◇5 3 2, but decides against it as the clubs cannot be solid. South passes ◇10, ♣ 8 3. The pass of low clubs, instead of high, is made because South is not afraid of the lead, having low hearts for exit and himself holding ♠Q. He wants to get in whenever he can to direct the play toward his own catch-the-ten.

The hands after the pass are:

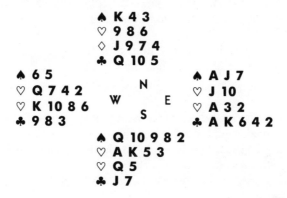

```
                   ♠ K 4 3
                   ♡ 9 8 6
                   ◇ J 9 7 4
                   ♣ Q 10 5
         ♠ 6 5              ♠ A J 7
         ♡ Q 7 4 2      N   ♡ J 10
         ♡ K 10 8 6  W    E ♡ A 3 2
         ♣ 9 8 3       S   ♣ A K 6 4 2
                   ♠ Q 10 9 8 2
                   ♡ A K 5 3
                   ♡ Q 5
                   ♣ J 7
```

The Play. The card that wins the trick is underlined. The card below it is the lead to the next trick.

TRICK	WEST	NORTH	EAST	SOUTH
1	♠ 5	♠ 3	♠ 7	♠ 8
2	♣ 9	♣ Q	♣ A	<u>♣ J</u>
3	♣ 8	♣ 10	<u>♣ 4</u>	♣ 7
4	◇ 8	<u>◇ 7</u>	◇ A	◇ 5
5	♣ 3	♣ 5	<u>♣ 2</u>	♠ Q
6	♡ 7	<u>♡ 9</u>	♡ 10	♡ 5
7	◇ 6	◇ 4	<u>◇ 2</u>	◇ Q
8	♠ 6	♠ 4	♠ J	<u>♠ 10</u>
9	◇ K	◇ 9	<u>◇ 3</u>	♠ 2
10	<u>♡ 4</u>	♡ 6	♡ J	♡ 3

East wins the last three tricks. Score: North, −13, East −3.

Polignac

Other names for this game are Quatre Valets, Four Jacks.

PRELIMINARIES

Four, five or six play, each for himself. The pack of 32 cards is used, for four-hand. If five or six play, strip out ♠7 and ♣7, reducing the pack to 30 cards.

The cards of each suit rank: **A** (high), **K, Q, J, 10, 9, 8, 7**. There is no ranking of suits, and never a trump suit.

The cards are all dealt out, making equal hands. With four players, deal in rounds of 3–2–3; with five, deal 3–3; with six, deal 3–2 or 2–3.

THE PLAY

Eldest hand makes the opening lead. The lead calls upon each other hand to follow suit if able; if unable, a hand may play any card. A trick is won by the highest card of the suit led. The winner of a trick leads to the next.

The object of play is to avoid taking in tricks any of the four jacks. The ♠**J** *(Polignac)* counts 2 against the player taking it; each other jack counts 1.

SCORING

Before the first deal, equal numbers of chips are distributed to the players. Payment for each jack taken is made to the pool, and the first player to lose all his chips loses the game.

CAPOT—(Optional)

Any player may announce, before the opening lead, that he will win all the tricks. If he succeeds, he pays nothing, while all other players pay the pool five chips each, in addition to payment for jacks. If the *capot* player fails, he pays five chips to the pool, and there is due payment for all jacks.

Slobberhannes

Follow the rules of Polignac on all points except the following: The only minus points are winning first trick, winning last trick, and taking the ♣**Q**. Each counts 1 against the player. But if one player gathers all three points, he is charged 4 instead of 3.

THE
STOPS
FAMILY

STOPS

In most of the games in the "Stops" family the object is to get rid of one's cards by playing them out sequentially—lower to higher cards. When one is "stopped" by the lack of cards that would continue a sequence, cards which may be either held by another player or be buried in an unplayed widow hand, the player loses his turn and possibly the chance of going out.

The most popular current "Stops" games are Michigan, Fan Tan, and Eights, whose descriptions, along with that of their variants, will open this section, to be followed by some of the early versions of this venerable, two-century-old family of games.

One of the earliest Stops games of which we have record is Comet, described by Abbe Bellecour in 1768 as "the new game." There is good reason to believe that the invention of the game was inspired by the return, in 1759, of the comet whose advent had been predicted by Edmund Halley fifty years previously. The fulfillment of this prophecy made a profound impression on the social as well as the scientific world, and for some years thereafter the brand "Comet" was attached to everything from merchandise to philosophic systems.

In Comet, the object of play is solely to get rid of one's cards, and there is considerable opportunity for skill. The long train of variants have been mostly concerned with enhancing the element of luck, and it was not until the invention of the modern game Eights that Comet found a peer.

One of the earliest variants, Commit, seems to have been devised by persons with only a remote acquaintance with either astronomy or spelling; we find references in early nineteenth-century game books to "Hadley's Commit."

Probably of independent origin are Snip Snap Snorem, Enflé, and Lift Smoke. They are placed here because of a certain resemblance to Stops. In the first two, the object is to get rid of one's cards, the hands being played out in tricks. The objective is reversed in Lift Smoke—the survivor is the winner.

Michigan

Michigan is also called Stops, Boodle, Newmarket, Saratoga, Chicago. See Boodle.

PLAYERS

Three to eight may play. Five or more make a better game than three or four.

CARDS

The pack of 52. The cards in each suit rank: **A** (high), **K, Q, J, 10, 9, 8, 7, 6, 5, 4, 3, 2**.

PRELIMINARIES

Players may take seats at random. Any player deals cards face up one at a time, and the player receiving the first jack is the first dealer. The game should break up only at a time when all participants have dealt an equal number of times.

Dealer has the right to shuffle last, and the player at his right cuts. The cut must leave at least five cards in each packet.

BOODLE CARDS

A layout is placed on the table, composed of four cards taken from another pack: ♡**A**, ♣**K**, ◇**Q**, ♠**J**. (Or any four cards, **A–K–Q–J**, of different suits.) Prior to the deal, the dealer antes two chips on each boodle card; each other player puts one chip on each.

DEALING

Cards are dealt one at a time to the left, beginning with an extra hand or *widow* placed between dealer and eldest hand. The whole pack is distributed, even though some hands contain one more card than others.

THE WIDOW

The dead hand or widow is the property of the dealer. He may exchange it for his original hand, if he wishes, or he may auction it to the highest bidder. If he does not take it himself, he must sell it. If all including the dealer refuse the widow, no player may look at it. In any other case, the player who takes the widow discards his original hand, which thereafter may not be looked at by any player.

THE PLAY

Disposition of the widow being decided, eldest hand leads any card, which may be of any suit but must be the lowest he holds in that suit. The hand (eldest hand or any other) holding the next-higher card in the same suit plays it, regardless of the position of the owner at the table. And so following: the sequence is built up in the suit until stopped by play of the ace or because a card of the sequence is in the dead hand. The hand that plays last before a stop may start a new sequence, provided that he can *change suit* from the previous sequence. If unable to change suit, the player must pass and the turn passes to his left. Every new sequence must be started with the lowest card of the suit in the hand of the player.

Each player plays his cards in a pile before himself. It is not permitted to spread a pile to inspect played cards. The rank of each card is stated verbally as it is played, and also the suit when a new sequence is started.

When a player plays a card that duplicates a boodle card, he takes all the chips on that card. If a boodle card is not cleared in one deal, the chips remain on it until duly won.

Play ends when any player gets rid of his last card.

SETTLEMENT

The player who *goes out* collects one chip for each card remaining in every other hand.

IRREGULARITIES

Should a player start a suit with a card not the lowest he holds in the suit, he must pay one chip to each other player and he may not collect for any boodle cards he plays subsequent to his error.

Should a player cause a stop by failing to play a card when able, play continues as usual, even though the card withheld may later enable the offender to get a stop. But the offender may not collect for any boodle cards he plays subsequent to the error; if at the end of the hand the chips are still on the boodle card of the suit of the card erroneously withheld, the offender must pay an equal amount to the player (if any) who held the duplicate; if the offender is first to get rid of his cards, he does not collect, but play continues to determine the winner.

STRATEGY

Buying the widow is always an advantage in giving the player complete knowledge of the stops in the dead hand. The price that is worth paying of course depends on several factors—the amounts on the boodle cards, the possible number of boodle cards in the widow as inferred from the number of bidders, the merits of the original hand. A hand with more than its average share of high cards (face cards and aces) should be retained even if it lacks any boodle card.

The play, so far as the player can control it, is largely a matter of keeping track of the stops. A common practice is to transfer to one end of the hand any card that has become a stop by the lead of the next-higher card. Unless done discreetly this practice gives information to the other players.

In the early play, the natural course is to start the longest suit in the hand. But with a money card in a shorter suit, one should usually prefer to lead this suit at every opportunity.

Fan Tan

The game widely known as Fan Tan should better be called Sevens or Parliament, an elaboration of the original Fan Tan, which in turn was an elaboration of Play or Pay.

PLAYERS

Three to eight may play.

CARDS

The pack of 52. The cards in each suit rank: **K** (high), **Q**, **J**, **10**, **9**, **8**, **7**, **6**, **5**, **4**, **3**, **2**, **A**.

PRELIMINARIES

Players may take seats at random. Any player deals cards face up one at a time, and the player receiving the first jack is the first dealer. The dealer has the right to shuffle last, and the pack is cut by the player at his right. The cut must leave at least four cards in each packet.

THE POOL

Equal numbers of chips are distributed to all players, and before the deal each player antes one chip into the pool.

DEALING

Cards are dealt one at a time to the left, beginning with eldest hand. The whole pack is dealt out; it does not matter if some hands have one more card than others. (An optional rule is that each hand with fewer cards must ante an extra chip.)

THE PLAY

The turn to play rotates to the left, beginning with eldest hand. The characteristic feature of the game (indeed, of the whole Play or Pay group of games) is that a player unable to play in turn must pay a chip to the pool.

All sevens are *set* cards, corresponding to foundations in Solitaire. A seven is always playable, and until the first seven is laid on the table no other card can be played. Once a seven is down, the six and eight of the same suit are playable, and thereafter cards in suit and sequence with them. The four sevens, as played, are laid in a row in the center of the table; the four sixes are laid in a row on one side, and the four eights in a row on the other. Thereafter, the suits may be built in sequence, on the eights up to the king, and on the sixes down to the ace. Only one card may be played in any turn.

Play ends when any player gets rid of his last card. Each other player puts one chip in the pool for each card remaining in his hand, and the winner then takes the entire pool.

IRREGULARITIES

If a player passes when able to play, he must pay a penalty of three chips to the pool (additional to the chip already paid for the pass). If he passed when able to play a seven, he must in addition pay five chips each to the holders of the six and eight of the same suit.

STRATEGY

There are no "stops" properly speaking—cards whose play gives opportunity to play a second time. However, every card is a stop in the sense that until it is played no other cards of the suit beyond it in sequence can be played. Hence the player can rarely do better than play from his longest suit, whenever any choice offers, in order to preserve the greatest chance of not passing later. Exception arises only when it can be inferred that withholding the natural play will postpone the time when another hand goes out.

Five or Nine

Eldest hand, or the first after him able to play at all, has choice of playing a five or a nine as the first *set*. The first card played fixes the rank of the four set cards for that deal. In all other respects the game is identical with Fan Tan.

Play or Pay

Eldest hand may lead any card. The player at his left must play the next-higher card of the same suit, or pass. And so following: all thirteen cards of the suit must be played before a new suit is begun. The sequence in the suit is continuous, that is, **Q**, **K**, **A**, **2**, etc., and must be built *up* only, not down. The player of the thirteenth card of the suit leads any card for a new sequence. In all other respects the game is identical with Fan Tan. (Play or Pay is actually the older game. In the original Fan Tan, elaborated from it, the first lead fixed the rank of the four *set* cards, which were then built both up and down in *continuous sequence*. The further elaboration Parliament, now called Fan Tan, eliminated eldest hand's free choice of the set and limited the building to the king on one side and the ace on the other.)

Eights

Eights, played by two, is the best game of the Stops family so far as concerns the opportunity for skill. It is also called Swedish Rummy, but is neither Rummy nor Swedish; the alternative name is strong evidence that the game originated in the United States, where it is customary to attribute a foreign origin to any new variant. In "Crazy Jacks," "Crazy" Sevens, Aces, etc., another card is the wild card.

PLAYERS

Two, three, or four playing in two partnerships.

CARDS

The pack of 52. Usually two packs are used alternately.

PRELIMINARIES

Draw for deal. Low deals, the cards ranking as in Bridge. Dealer shuffles and player on his right cuts. The cut must leave at least four cards in each packet.

DEALING

Cards are dealt one at a time to the left. With two players, give each seven cards; with three or more, give each hand five cards. The remainder of the pack after the deal is placed face down to form the *stock*. The top card is turned over and placed beside it to form the *starter*.

THE PLAY

Eldest hand plays first. He must lay on the starter a card of the same suit or rank. If it is of the same rank, the suit switches to that of the card played. The play continues in turn in the same way: each card played (other than an eight) must match the top of the *talon* pile in suit or rank.

A hand unable to play must draw cards from the top of the stock until able. A player may draw from the stock even if able to play. After the stock is exhausted, a hand unable to play passes, and the turn passes to the left.

All eights are *wild*. An eight may be played at any time, even though the hand could follow with another card. The player of an eight designates a suit, any suit, and the next hand must follow with that suit or play another eight. (An eight may never be designated as calling for a rank.)

Play ends when any player gets rid of his last card, if the game is cutthroat. In four-hand partnership play, play ends when both hands of a partnership have gone out.

A hand must play in turn if able, whether before or after drawing from the stock. If the stock is exhausted and no hand can play, the game ends in a *block*.

SCORING

The player or side that goes out collects for all cards remaining in hands of the opponents: 50 for each eight, 10 for each face card, 1 for each ace, index value for all other cards.

If play ends in a block, the player or side with lowest total count collects the difference of counts from the opponents. If two players tie (in three-hand play) they split the winnings.

Score may be kept on paper. A running total is then kept for each player or side, and the first to reach 100 or more wins a game. The winner scores 100 for the game, plus the difference of final totals.

IRREGULARITIES

Misdeal. There must be a new deal by the same dealer if a card is exposed in dealing; if the wrong number of cards is given to any hand; or if the pack is found imperfect. Previous scores made by an imperfect pack, however, stand.

Wrong Number of Cards. If, after the first lead but before the first draw from the stock, it is found that any hand was dealt the wrong number of cards, the hand must be rectified and play continues. A short hand draws extra cards from the stock. A hand with too many cards is spread face down, and any other player draws the extra cards, which are buried in the middle of the stock.

False Block. When play ends in a block, all hands should be faced for inspection. If it is then found that any player passed when able to play, play must be continued upon demand of any other player. A hand that so causes a false block and consequent exposure of cards by a false pass is barred from winning, but must play on to determine the winner among the other players.

STRATEGY

The principal point to remember is to save eights for emergencies; when no other hand is near to going out, it is worthwhile digging into the stock to avoid giving up an eight. Keeping track of the cards played, at least to the extent of counting the number in each suit, is of course vital. Many opportunities arise to "corner" the remainder of a suit, as by willfully taking the whole stock when it is low. A "corner," especially when fortified by one or two eights, may enable a hand with twenty or thirty cards to go out before a hand that holds only a few.

It is permissible for the player who plays the last eight to cause a block deliberately by calling for a suit which has been exhausted.

Craits

Craits, whose name is an amalgamation of "Crazy" and "Eights," is a whimsical variation of Eights, popular among Bridge players. Practices differ in various sections of the country, but the first principle is that a kibitzer is not allowed to be taught the rules of the game! He learns by watching, or by joining the game without knowing the rules (except for the "one card" announcement; see *Rules and Customs*).

PLAYERS

Four, playing as individuals. With fewer, Eights is preferred.

CARDS

A pack of 52 cards.

DEALING

Cards are dealt clockwise. For the first deal, each player receives eight cards. Play for that deal ends when any player gets rid of all of his cards. The deal then rotates to the left, and seven cards are dealt to each player, followed by six cards, on down to one card, then back up to eight. A game consists of 15 deals, eight to one to eight. For each deal, one card from the stock is turned face up to start the play.

THE PLAY

The player to dealer's left plays first, unless a ten is turned up. As in Eights, he is obliged to play a card of the same suit or rank as the up card. If it is of the same rank, the suit switches to the card played. What makes the game so zany is the effect different cards have on the play:

Ten—Changes direction of play.

Nine—Permits a player to change the suit played to the other suit of the same *color*. (Diamonds to hearts, clubs to spades, etc.)

Eight—Wild card. The player calls the suit.

Seven—Forces the player sitting opposite to pick a card.

Six—The player must go again. If he cannot, he draws a card from the stock.

Five—Requires the other three players to draw a card.

Four—The next player loses his turn.

Two—Starts *the count*.

When a deuce is played, the player announces "two" and each subsequent player must continue the count by following with an ace or two and call out the new total as the count progresses. Thus, on the play of a two, ace, two the count is five. If a player cannot continue the count by following with an ace or a deuce, he picks the number of cards equal to the count from the stock.

A hand must play if he is able. Otherwise he draws one card from the stock. When the stock is exhausted, the player who is required to pick a card incurs a *shuffle pressure*. He leaves the last card played face up and shuffles the rest of the cards to form a new stock, from which he draws as many cards as required.

SCORING

Separate totals are kept for each player. For the hand that goes out, he subtracts 10 points from his total. More than one hand may go out if it happens during "the count," but only the first to do so subtracts 10 points. Cards remaining in a player's hand are counted as follows:

King, queen, or jack—10 points each

Ten—25 points each

Nine, six, or five—30 points each

Eight—50 points each

Seven, or deuce—20 points each

Four—15 points each

Ace—1 point each

Treys are valuable cards to retain in hand when another player goes out. Their count is 3, but each trey can be used to cancel another card, except an eight or another trey. If a player is left with only treys, he reduces his score by 50 points for each trey held. *Example:* If a player is left with **K, K, 3, 3**, his count is 6 (the two treys cancel the two kings). **Ace, 3, 3** also counts 6 because treys cannot cancel each other.

A player who is subject to a shuffle pressure scores 5 points for the first time he has to shuffle. Thereafter the total keeps doubling for every time he is required to shuffle throughout the game, not per deal.

RULES AND CUSTOMS

A player who is about to reduce his hand to one card *must* announce "one card" before the penultimate card is placed on the table. If the last card played is a six, which requires him to draw from the stock, he must make the same disclosure as he is picking a card. Failure to declare "one card" results in lost of turn and the draw of two *idiot* cards from the stock at the next turn.

When a player goes out during *the count*, play continues until the count is broken. Should it come back to the player who is out, he must draw cards equal to the count. A player who has failed to announce "one card" participates in the count, but it is not considered a turn.

At the start of a deal, the facing of an eight permits dealer to name a suit before he has looked at his hand. A nine allows him to select the other suit of the same color. If dealer fails to make a designation before looking at his hand, the suit remains as is. Dealer distributes penalty cards to the other three players when a five is turned up and to the player across from him if a seven is faced.

The penalty for all errors is an idiot card. Possible infractions include dealing of the wrong number of cards; plays or picks out of turn (for cards drawn in error, the player keeps only those cards); incorrectly advising another player it is his turn to play (if he plays, both get idiot cards). For all blunders, the offender draws one card from the stock. Since the game should be played as briskly as possible, there is no penalty for a *renege* (picking a card when a legal play was available). A player is allowed to correct a renege and play a card or cards out of his hand, but he keeps the card he has drawn by mistake. Habitual renegers, however, are rarely welcomed back into the game.

Comet

PLAYERS

Any number from two to five may play.

CARDS

Two special packs are made up from two regular packs of 52. First discard all aces; next place all black cards together and all red cards together; then exchange ♣**9** and ♢**9**. The result is two packs of 48, one all black but for the red **9**, the other all red but for the black **9**. The two packs are used alternately. The off-color **9** in each pack is the *comet*.

The cards rank: **K** (high), **Q**, **J**, **10**, **9**, **8**, **7**, **6**, **5**, **4**, **3**, **2**. Suits are ignored in the game.

PRELIMINARIES

Players may take seats at random. Draw cards for deal; low card deals first. Dealer shuffles last, and the pack is cut by the player at his right. The cut must leave at least four cards in each packet.

DEALING

The manner of dealing is given in the following schedule. The cards remaining after all hands are dealt out are put aside face down, to form a dead hand. Cards are distributed to the left, beginning with eldest hand.

NUMBER OF PLAYERS	EACH RECEIVES	DEAD HAND	CARDS DEALT EACH ROUND
2	18	12	3
3	12	12	3
4	10	8	2
5	9	3	3

THE PLAY

Eldest hand begins by leading any card in his hand. He continues play so long as he can add cards in ascending sequence. All cards played by all players are stacked in one pile in the center of the table. Spreading this pile to inspect played cards is not permitted.

The rank of each card is announced as it is played. When unable to continue, the player says "without" the next-higher rank. *Example:* A player lays down **4, 5, 6**, saying "Four, five, six, without seven." The turn then passes to the player on the left, who must continue the sequence from the point where it was interrupted. Lacking any card of the required rank, the player says "Pass," and the next hand plays.

A hand must play in turn if able, and must continue play so long as possible, except that if his only playable card is the comet the player may pass in order to reserve it.

Whoever plays a king effects a stop (originally, hoc), and he starts a new sequence, beginning with any card he chooses. Likewise, if one player calls "without," and all others pass for lack of the same rank, the first may commence a new sequence, playing any card.

The object of play is to get rid of all the cards in the hand. As soon as one player succeeds, play ends and settlement is made.

Four of a Kind. In general, only one card of a rank may be played at a time, but if a player holds all four cards of a rank he may play them simultaneously if he wishes. Also, any three nines, with or without the comet, may be played at one time.

The Comet. The ♠**9** or ◇**9**, as the case may be, is a wild card. It may be played as a card of any designated rank and always acts as a stop. That is, upon playing the comet the owner is entitled to start a new sequence with any card he chooses. But the comet may be played only in turn; nothing abridges the right of the previous player to continue a sequence until forced to call "without." The comet has special scoring value.

SCORING

When the comet is played, the owner immediately collects 2 chips from each other player. The base value 2 is increased by 2 for every consecutive deal in which the comet is found in the dead hand. *Example:* If dealt three times in succession to the dead hand, the comet is worth 8. After it has been dealt to an active hand and duly paid for, the comet reverts in the next deal to the base value 2.

When one player *goes out* by getting rid of his last card, he collects for the cards remaining in each other hand—10 for each face card and the index value for all other cards. If caught with the comet in his hand, a player pays double its value at that time, and double the count of all his other unplayed cards.

When a player goes out by playing the comet for his last card (not as a nine), he collects double from every other hand; if he plays the comet last and as a natural nine (after play of an eight) he collects quadruple. He also collects the bonus for playing the comet, doubled or quadrupled in the same way.

Opera. If eldest hand goes out on his first turn, no other hand playing a card, he collects double for *opera* (additional to any doubles for play of the comet). This feature is best waived when three or more play; in two-hand, it is usually agreed that dealer can nullify the deal if in turn he also can make the *opera*.

IRREGULARITIES

Illegal Pass. If a player passes when able to play a card other than the comet, he may not thereafter play any card of the rank refused.

Play Out of Turn. No penalty, but cards played out of turn must be retracted and the turn reverts to the rightful player. But if after a play out of turn and call of "without" the player at the left has duly played a card, the play stands as regular.

Settlement. A proved error in scoring or settlement must be corrected at any time prior to the cut for the next deal, but not thereafter.

STRATEGY

In the early play, the natural plan is to try to get rid of duplicated ranks first, reducing the hand if possible to only one card in each rank. As play progresses, more important becomes the matter of creating and utilizing stops. The player must keep track of what ranks each other player is "without." Only at the end, when another hand is on the verge of going out, is it advisable merely to get rid of as many cards as possible by starting with the lowest of the longest sequence in the hand.

Commit

Players. Three to seven may play.

Cards. The pack of 52, with the ◇ **8** discarded. The cards rank as in Comet and likewise suits are ignored.

Preliminaries. As in Comet.

Dealing. Deal cards one at a time, beginning with eldest hand, as far as they go evenly. Set aside extra cards face down as a dead hand. (With three players, give each 15 cards and put 6 in the dead hand.)

The Ante. Before the deal, all players ante an equal number of chips to a pool.

The Play. As in Comet—except for the comet. Here the ◇**9** is the comet; the holder may choose to play it when otherwise he would have to say "without." The next hand able to play must continue either with ◇**10** or with the card next above that for which the comet was substituted. First option goes to the owner of the comet.

Scoring. He who plays the comet collects 2 chips at once from each other player. The player of any king collects 1 chip from each other player. The hand that goes out first wins the pool, plus 1 for each king remaining in the other hands, plus 2 from a player still holding the comet.

Irregularities. See Comet.

Boodle

This game is also known as Newmarket; and the names Boodle and Newmarket are frequently applied to the more popular game Michigan.

PLAYERS

Three to eight may play.

CARDS

The pack of 52. The cards in each suit rank: **K** (high), **Q**, **J**, **10**, **9**, **8**, **7**, **6**, **5**, **4**, **3**, **2**, **A**.

PRELIMINARIES

Players may take seats at random. Any player deals cards face up one at a time, and the player receiving the first jack is the first dealer. The game should break up only at a time when all participants have dealt an equal number of times.

Dealer has the right to shuffle last, and the pack is cut by the player at his right. The cut must leave at least four cards in each packet.

BOODLE CARDS

A layout is placed on the table, composed of four cards taken from another pack: ♡**A**, ◇**K**, ♠**Q**, ♣**J**. (Or any four cards, **A–K–Q–J**, of different suits.) Prior to the deal, the dealer announces the number of chips that all players must ante upon the layout, usually from 4 to 10. Each player may distribute his chips as he pleases, all on one card or some on all, etc. The layout cards are called *boodle* or *money* cards.

DEALING

The cards are dealt one at a time, and the cards remaining after the deal are set aside face down as a dead hand, according to this schedule:

NUMBER OF PLAYERS	EACH RECEIVES	DEAD HAND
3	15	7
4	12	4
5	9	7
6	8	4
7	7	3
8	6	4

(*Variant.* Originally, the ◇**8** was discarded from the pack, and the ◇**9** was a comet, as in Commit. The dead hand then contained one less card.)

THE PLAY

Eldest hand begins by leading any suit, but must lead the lowest card he holds of that suit. The hand holding the next-higher card in the same suit plays it, regardless of the position of the owner at the table; if it is eldest hand who has the next-higher card, he must play it. And so following: the sequence is built up in the suit until *stopped* by play of the king or because a card of the sequence is in the dead hand. The hand that plays last before a stop may start a new sequence, provided always that he plays the lowest card in his hand of the chosen suit (which may be the same as that just stopped).

When a player plays a card that duplicates a boodle card, he takes all the chips on that card. If a boodle card is not cleared in one deal, the chips remain on it until duly won.

Play ends when any player gets rid of his last card.

SETTLEMENT

The player who *goes out* collects one chip for each card remaining in every other hand. (If ◇**9** is used as a comet, it is paid one chip by every other hand when played, and costs 2 chips if left in the hand when another goes out.)

IRREGULARITIES AND STRATEGY—See Michigan

Spinado (or Spin)

Same as Boodle except that ◇**A** has special privilege: It may be played together with a regular card in sequence, and then is a stop. The player is entitled to start a new sequence (even though he himself could continue the former sequence).

Saratoga

Same as Boodle except that every player antes the same amount on each boodle card. This variant developed into Michigan.

Snip Snap Snorem

PLAYERS

Four to eight.

CARDS

The pack of 52.

DEALING

The cards are dealt out one at a time as far as they will go. It does not matter if not all hands are equal.

THE PLAY

All players are provided with equal numbers of chips. (An optional rule is that each hand with the lesser number of cards, when hands are not even, must ante one chip into the pool.)

Eldest hand leads any card. Each hand in turn must then either play a card of the same rank or pass. Whenever two consecutive hands play (not pass), the first of the two is *snipped* if he was the leader, or *snapped* if he played the second card of the rank, or *snored* if he played the third card. For snip the player pays 1 chip to the pool; for snap, 2 chips; for snorem, 3 chips. *Example:* West leads ◇**5**; North plays ♠**5**, and West must pay a chip; East passes; South plays ♡**5**; West plays ♣**5**, and South must pay three chips; North escapes snap through East's pass.

The hand that plays the fourth card of a rank makes a new lead; he may lead any card. The play ends when any player gets rid of his last card. Each other hand pays one chip to the pool for each remaining card, and the winner takes the pool.

Variants. It is usual to call attention to the forfeit imposed on the previous player by saying "snip," "snap," or "snorem." In a juvenile variant, Earl of Coventry, the leader is supposed to improvise a line of verse, and each other card of the rank is supposed to be accompanied by a rhyming line. No payment is made for snip, etc., the sole object being to get rid of all cards. Similar in object is the German *Schnipp-Schnapp-Schnurr-Burr-Ba-silorum*, probably the parent game; but here each lead is built up in suit and sequence by *four* additional cards, and "play in turn" is meaningless as in Michigan. In an English variant, Jig, play is likewise in upward sequence but only three cards are added to the lead. Neither of these obsolete sequence games can be played under the surviving rules, which do not state whether the sequence in a suit goes "around-the-corner" nor what happens when there are not enough cards left unplayed in a suit to make a complete sequence of four or five.

Enflé

An alternative name for this game is Schwellen.

PLAYERS

Four, five, or six may play, each for himself.

CARDS

From the pack of 52 strip out enough cards so that there remain eight for each player in the game. The cards in each suit rank: **A** (high), **K**, **Q**, **J**, **10**, and so on. The cards deleted should be from the deuces up, an equal number from each suit.

PRELIMINARIES

Players take seats at random. Cards may be drawn for the first deal; highest card deals. The entire pack is dealt out into hands of eight cards, either one card at a time or in packets of two and three.

THE PLAY

Eldest hand leads any card. Each successive hand must follow to the lead if able; if all follow, the trick is won by the highest card. The winner of a trick leads to the next. Tricks are of no value in themselves: they are simply cards no longer in play. All tricks may therefore be thrown into a common pile. A hand unable to follow suit must pick up all cards already played to the trick, and then lead to the next trick. He may, if he wishes, lead the suit which he just renounced. Normal policy is always to lead from the longest suit in the hand, so as to keep some cards of each suit so long as possible.

The first player to get rid of all his cards wins the game. When Enflé is played for a stake, all players ante to make a pool, before the deal, and the winner takes the pool.

Lift Smoke

PLAYERS

Four to six, not more.

CARDS

The pack of 52. The cards in each suit rank: **A** (high), **K, Q, J, 10, 9, 8, 7, 6, 5, 4, 3, 2.**

DEALING

Cards are dealt one at a time to the left, beginning with eldest hand. Each player receives as many cards as there are players in the game. The last card dealt to the dealer is turned up to fix the trump suit. The rest of the pack is placed face down on the table to form the stock.

THE PLAY

Eldest hand leads any card. A lead calls upon each other hand to follow suit if able; if unable, the hand may play any card. A trick is won by the highest trump, or by the highest card of the suit led. The winner of a trick draws the top card of the stock and leads to the next trick.

When a player's cards are exhausted, he drops out of the deal and the others continue. The last survivor to have any cards left wins the deal. If several hands are exhausted by the last trick, the winner thereof wins the deal.

SCORING

The usual method is to require equal antes from each player before the deal. The winner takes the entire pool.

THE
ALL
FOURS
FAMILY

All Fours is our name (the correct name) for the game best known in the United States as Seven-up, and sometimes as High-Low-Jack, or Old Sledge, or by other names. The name Seven-up meant simply that it took 7 points to win. From Seven-up were developed many of the most popular card games, such as Auction Pitch (page 316), Cinch (page 321), and the other variants described on the pages immediately following this one. Charles Colton wrote in 1674, "All-Fours is a game very much play'd in Kent, and very well it may, since from thence it drew its first original." American colonists took it with them and for a hundred years, until displaced by Poker, it was the favorite of the American gamester; the writings of Bret Harte, Mark Twain, O. Henry and similar annalists of the middle classes refer repeatedly to games of the All Fours family.

ALL FOURS—THE BASIC GAME

PLAYERS

Two or three may play, each for himself, or four in partnerships of two each.

CARDS

The pack of 52. The cards in each suit rank: **A** (high), **K, Q, J, 10, 9, 8, 7, 6, 5, 4, 3, 2**.

PRELIMINARIES

Cards are drawn; the highest card deals first. The draw may also be used to determine choice of seats, and partnerships. Players drawing equal cards must draw again.

Dealer has the right to shuffle last, and the pack is cut by the player at his right. The cut must leave at least four cards in each packet.

DEALING

Each player receives six cards, dealt in rounds of three at a time, beginning with eldest hand. The deal completed, the next card is turned for trump. If the turn-up be a jack, dealer immediately scores 1 point. When more than two play, only eldest hand and dealer may look at their hands until the turn-up is accepted or rejected.

BEGGING

Eldest hand commences by *standing* or *begging*. If he stands, thereby accepting the turn-up for trump, all players pick up their hands and play begins. If he begs, dealer then has the option of insisting on the turned trump or agreeing to choose a new trump.

If dealer wishes to play the turn-up suit as trump, he says "Take it" and eldest hand scores 1 point for *gift*. If satisfied to choose another trump, dealer *refuses gift*. Dealer is compelled to refuse gift if eldest hand is only 1 point short of game.

RUNNING THE CARDS

When gift is refused, dealer *runs the cards*, that is, he deals another round of three cards and turns a new trump (the first having been discarded face down). If the second turn-up is of a different suit from the first, it fixes the trump suit and play begins; should it be a jack, dealer scores 1 point. But if the second turn-up is in the same suit, it must be discarded, another round of three cards must be dealt, and a third card turned up. And so following—the cards are run until a new suit is turned up. If the pack is exhausted without the turn of a new suit, the deal is abandoned, and the same dealer deals again. (Dealer never scores for the turn of a jack in the suit of the first rejected turn-up.)

THE PLAY

If the pack has been run, each player discards enough cards to reduce his hand to six. Eldest hand makes the opening lead. A lead calls upon each other hand to follow suit or to trump; if able to follow, the hand has the option of doing so or of trumping. If unable to follow suit, a hand may play any card, trump or plain. A trick is won by the highest trump, or by the highest card of the suit led. The winner of a trick leads to the next.

The object in play is to score any or all of the four points from which the game derives its name, as below.

THE FOUR POINTS

All members of the All Fours family agree on the following constants in scoring. Each is worth 1 point.

High is the highest trump in play; it is scored by the holder.

Low is the lowest trump in play. In the basic All Fours, here described, low is scored by the player to whom it was dealt. In some descendant games, low is scored by the player who takes it in a trick.

Jack is the jack of trumps, and is scored by the player who takes it in a trick.

Game is a plurality of points for cards won in play, reckoned:

each ace	4
each king	3
each queen	2
each jack	1
each ten	10

In two-hand and four-hand play, the side with a majority of points for cards wins 1 for game. In three-hand play, one player having a plurality wins the 1 point; if dealer ties for high total with one opponent, the latter wins; if the two non-dealers tie for high total, *game* is not scored.

The points are always scored in the given order: high, low, jack, game. (The jack will not always be in play, in the variants where not all the cards are dealt out, but the other three points are always scored. If there is only one trump in play, it scores both as high and low.)

SCORING

Each player or side is credited with the points it wins in play, scored in the given order. The first to reach a total of 7 wins the game. If a player "counts out" during a deal, it is played out only if an opponent could win enough points superior in precedence to go out ahead of him.

IRREGULARITIES

Revoke is failure to follow suit or trump, when able to follow suit. A revoke may be corrected before the trick is turned and quitted or the next lead is made, otherwise it stands as established. Penalty for established revoke: Revoker may not win the game in that deal, and may count only to 6; if jack was not in play, 1 point is deducted from revoker's score; if jack was in play, 2 points are deducted.

Exposed Card is one dropped on the table, played or led with another, withdrawn in correction of revoke, or otherwise seen by partner of the owner not in regular course of play. There is no penalty for exposure when two or three play, but in four-hand an exposed card must be left on the table and played on demand of an opponent when such play is legal.

California Jack

The basic All Fours is a "short" game; comparatively few of the cards are in play. The results are largely determined by the luck of the deal. California Jack provides for putting all the cards into play, and therefore increases the opportunity for skillful play.

PLAYERS

Two.

CARDS

The pack of 52. The cards in each suit rank: **A** (high), **K, Q, J, 10, 9, 8, 7, 6, 5, 4, 3, 2**.

PRELIMINARIES

Cards are drawn; the higher deals first. Before each deal, non-dealer lifts a packet (at least four cards) from top of pack and turns it over; the bottom card of this packet fixes the trump suit for the ensuing deal. The cards are then shuffled. Dealer has the right to shuffle last. Opponent cuts; the cut must leave at least four cards in each packet.

DEALING

Each player receives six cards, dealt one at a time, beginning with non-dealer. The rest of the pack is placed face up on the table to form the *stock.* (In the variant **Shasta Sam** the stock is placed face down, eliminating the principal element of skill in the game.)

THE PLAY

Non-dealer makes the opening lead. After each trick, the winner thereof takes the top card of the stock, and opponent takes the next. The stock must at all times be kept squared, so that only the top card can be identified. The hands are thus restored to six cards before each lead. After the stock is exhausted, the last six cards are played out.

Formerly the rule was that second player could either follow suit to the lead or trump, as in All Fours. Now the rule is preferred that second hand *must* follow suit if able. The chief skill of the game lies in keeping track of what the opponent has drawn, so as to force him to win the trick when the top of the stock shows a valueless card or to win the trick by force when it is desired.

SCORING

At the end of play, each player examines the cards he has taken in tricks and scores whatever they contain. The four points to be scored, worth 1 point each, are: *High*, ace of trumps; *low*, two of trumps; *jack*, jack of trumps; *game*, majority of points when each ace is counted 4, king 3, queen 2, jack 1, ten 10.

The usual game is 7 points. A player may "count out" during a deal, which is then not played out unless opponent could win enough points of superior precedence to go out ahead of him. The points are scored in the given order.

All Fives

This is a variant of California Jack, for a game of 61, scored on a cribbage board. During the play, for taking any of the following trump cards in a trick, a player pegs:

ace	4
king	3
queen	2
jack	1
ten	10
five	5

At the end of the play, the high cards are counted to fix the winner of 1 point for game.

PITCH

Auction Pitch

A nineteenth-century development, Auction Pitch (usually called Pitch, or Setback) became the most popular member of the All Fours family. It yielded first place to Cinch for ten years or so, and then returned to favor. It is the most popular game of the All Fours family being played today.

PLAYERS

From two to seven may play, but the game is best for four, each for himself.

CARDS

The pack of 52 is used, the cards of each suit ranking: **A** (high), **K, Q, J, 10, 9, 8, 7, 6, 5, 4, 3, 2**.

PRELIMINARIES

Players may take seats at random. Cards are drawn for first deal; highest card deals. Dealer has the right to shuffle last, and the pack must be cut by the player at his right, the cut leaving at least four cards in each packet.

DEALING

Each player in rotation receives six cards, dealt in rounds of three at a time, beginning with eldest hand.

BIDDING

Each player in rotation, beginning with eldest hand, has one turn to bid. The lowest bid is one, the highest four. Each bid must be higher than the preceding bid. The high bidder names the trump.

THE PLAY

The high bidder leads first; this is called *pitching*, and the suit of the card pitched becomes trump. Since a bid of four cannot be overcalled, no one bothers to bid it; he merely pitches a trump when his turn comes. If able to follow suit to the card led, each player in turn must either follow suit or trump. If unable to follow suit, he may play any card. A trick is won by the highest trump, or by the highest card of the suit led. The winner of a trick leads to the next.

SCORING

One point each is scored for winning in play: *high*, highest trump card in play; *low*, lowest trump card in play; *jack*, jack of trumps; *game*, plurality of points when each ace is counted 4, king, 3; queen, 2; jack, 1; ten, 10.

High and low are always counted; jack may not be in play, and game is not scored if two players tie for it.

If the pitcher scores at least as many points as he bid, he adds to his score all the points he makes. If he falls short of his bid, the amount of the bid is subtracted from his previous score (which may put him in the hole). In either case, any opponent of the pitcher always scores as many points as he makes.

Game. An individual score is kept for each player (or chips are used). The first player to reach a score of 7 wins the game. If two or more players could reach 7 on the same deal, the pitcher's points are counted first and as among other players the points are scored in order high, low, jack, game. Expert players usually count the score by the number of points still needed to win: A player who has scored 6 points is "One," while a player who has not scored is "Seven."

Some play a game of 10 points.

SETTLEMENT

The winner collects from each other player: one chip for game; plus one chip for each time the loser was set back; plus one chip from any player who was in the hole when the game ended.

Smudge. If a player bids four and makes it, he wins the game immediately, unless he was in the hole at the time, in which case his score becomes 4. (Some play that any player wins the game in the one deal when he makes all four points, regardless of the bid.)

VARIATIONS

Bunch. In two-hand play the dealer may offer "bunch"—meaning that his opponent must choose whether to let dealer play at a contract of two, or have a new deal by the same dealer. This is not often played except when the dealer has the right to assume the contract without bidding over.

Bidding Over. At one time, eldest hand (or, in some games, dealer) had the right to assume the contract at the highest previous bid, without "bidding over." When eldest hand was given this privilege, the player at his left had the first turn to bid. In modern play, every player must bid over to get the contract.

Joker. The 53-card pack, including the joker, may be used. The joker is a trump but ranks below the lowest trump in play and does not count as *low*. If the joker is pitched, spades become trump. There are 5 points in play, 1 point being scored by the player who wins the joker in a trick. In counting out, this point ranks between low and game. Usually 10 points are game.

Double for Smudge. Some count smudge as 8 points, whether or not the player was in the hole at the time.

IRREGULARITIES

Misdeal. It is a misdeal if an ace, jack or deuce is exposed in dealing. Since the deal is an advantage, a misdeal loses the deal.

Revoke (failure to follow suit or trump, when able to follow suit). A play once made cannot be withdrawn, so a revoke stands and play continues to the end. If the pitcher revokes, he cannot score and is set back the amount of his bid, while each other player scores what he makes. If any player except the pitcher revokes, all players except the revoker score what they make (including the pitcher, even if he does not make his bid). The revoking player cannot score, and has the amount of the bid deducted from his score.

Error in Bidding. An insufficient bid, or a bid out of turn, is void and the offender must pass in his turn to bid.

Error in Pitching. Once the pitcher plays a card, the trump cannot be changed.

If a player pitches before the auction closes, he is assumed to have bid four and play proceeds; except that any player in turn before him who has not had a turn to bid may himself bid four and pitch, whereupon the card illegally pitched, and any card played to it, must be withdrawn.

If the wrong player pitches after the auction is closed, the pitcher may require that card and any card played to it to be withdrawn; and, when first it is the offender's turn to play, the pitcher may require him to play his highest or lowest card of the suit led or to trump or not to trump; except that if the pitcher has played to the incorrect lead, it cannot be withdrawn and the pitcher must immediately name the trump, which he must then lead the first time he wins a trick.

STRATEGY

Not all the cards are dealt in Pitch, and it is often necessary to compute the probability that a certain card is in play. Holding

$$♡ \text{ K Q J} \qquad ◇ \text{ 6} \qquad ♣ \text{ 5 2}$$

and with a bid of two ahead of him, a player can bid three and almost surely make it if ♡**A** is among the undealt cards, but will almost as surely be set back if another player holds ♡**A**, since he may get jack and perhaps low, but can hardly expect game (having only two winning tricks). In fact, he is unlikely to make low, because other players normally combine against the pitcher and an opponent holding low will prefer to play it on another opponent's ♡**A** if he can do so.

With three in the game, 18 cards are dealt and 34 remain undealt; it is nearly two to one that ♡**A** is not in play and on the hand shown a bid of three is wise. With four in the game, 24 cards are dealt and the odds are 28 to 24 in favor of finding ♡**A** undealt and making the bid of three. With five in the game, there is a 30-to-22 chance that some other player *does* hold ♡**A** and the opposing bid of two should be passed.

It should be noted that no thought is given to the danger of finding an opponent with more than three trumps, including low, and thus losing low. All the outstanding trumps can usually be pulled in two rounds and almost invariably in three.

While all opponents usually conspire to defeat the pitcher, the score is a more pressing consideration. A player holding the deuce of trumps will usually try to keep the pitcher from taking it. Let the pitcher be several points away from winning, however, while another player is within a point of going out, and low will promptly be thrown to the pitcher so that the more dangerous player cannot get it.

Bidding is almost always based on trump length. Since a player need not follow suit if he can trump, the pitcher cannot count even on aces as winning tricks unless he has first drawn trumps.

The play for game is usually a matter of conspiracy against the pitcher, and all opponents often try to throw their tens to some one opponent who seems to have the best chance to cost the pitcher that point.

Commercial Pitch, or Sell Out

During the nineteenth century, American players of All Fours quite generally abandoned the turning of trump, begging, and running the cards. The rule became to let eldest hand name the trump suit, with proviso that his first lead must be a trump. The game in this form was called Blind All Fours, or Pitch. Then bidding was added, making the original Auction Pitch. It differed from the modern game only in the bidding, which was as follows:

Eldest hand has the vested right to name the trump if he is willing to bid as high as any bidder. The bidding therefore starts with the player at his left. Each in turn must pass or make a bid higher than the preceding bid. The only possible bids are 1, 2, 3, 4. After dealer has declared in turn, eldest hand may either (a) lead, signifying that he names the trump by assuming the highest bid as his contract, in which case the high bidder immediately scores the amount of his bid; or (b) *sell*, signifying that he yields to the highest bidder, in which case eldest hand immediately scores the amount of this bid as his compensation for selling his rights. If eldest hand leads before the bidding is ended, he is committed to play a contract of 4.

Eldest hand must sell if refusal to do so would put the high bidder out. No bidder is permitted to bid a number that, if accepted by eldest hand, would give him the game. (This old rule leads to the absurdity that if eldest hand needs only 1 for game, none can bid against him. One alternative adopted to circumvent this difficulty was to place no limit on bidding, but limit eldest hand to one-less-than-game whatever the bid at which he sold out. The better alternative is the modern bidding practice, explained under Auction Pitch.)

Pedro

Pedro is a collective name for a number of elaborations of Auction Pitch, all based on the addition of the five of trumps *(pedro)* as a counting card.
Pedro Sancho. Four to seven players. Each receives six cards. Eldest hand bids first. There is one round of bidding. Dealer has the privilege of taking the contract at the highest previous bid. The contracting player pitches the trump. All points scored are for trump cards won in tricks, counted in order:

High, highest trump in play	1
Low, lowest trump in play	1
Jack, the jack	1
Game, the ten	1
Pedro, the five	5
Sancho, the nine	9

The maximum of points per deal is thus 18. Game is usually set at 100.
Dom Pedro, or Snoozer is the same as Pedro Sancho with the addition of two more counting cards: the three of trumps, worth 3, and the joker (called *snoozer*) worth 15, bringing the total per deal up to 36 maximum. The trump three counts after the ten (game), and snoozer counts after the nine (sancho). Snoozer is always a trump, ranking below the two.

CINCH

It is believed that Cinch (Double Pedro, High Five) originated in the neighborhood of Denver, Colorado, about 1885. It spread to Chicago and became a favorite among Whist players there. The publication of several books on the game carried it into card clubs throughout the country, and for a decade it was a serious contender with Whist and Euchre for supremacy. Although both gave way to Auction Bridge, Cinch remains one of the top-ranking games of skill.

PLAYERS

Four, in two partnerships of two each. Although it is often stated that Cinch may be played by any number from two to seven, to play cut-throat instead of partnership misses the essence of the game.

CARDS

The pack of 52. The cards in each suit rank: **A** (high), **K**, **Q**, **J**, **10**, **9**, **8**, **7**, **6**, **5**, **4**, **3**, **2**. The five of trumps is called *right pedro*. The five of the other suit of same color as the trump is called *left pedro;* it is also a trump, ranking lower than right pedro, higher than the trump four.

Each pedro counts 5 points for the hand winning it in tricks. In addition, each of the following trumps counts 1 for the winner: *high* (the ace), *jack* (the jack), *low* (the two), and *game* (the ten). The total of scoring points per deal is 14.

PRELIMINARIES

Cards are drawn; the two highest play as partners against the two lowest, and the highest has choice of seats and is the first dealer. Players drawing equal cards must draw again.

Dealer has the right to shuffle last, and the pack is cut by the player at his right. The cut must leave at least four cards in each packet.

DEALING

Each hand receives nine cards, dealt in rounds of three at a time, beginning with eldest hand.

BIDDING

Each player in turn, beginning with eldest hand, makes a bid or passes. Each bid must be higher than the preceding bid. Each bid names a number of points, up to 14, that the bidder is willing to contract to take in play, with help of partner. The intended trump suit is not named in bidding. When the round of bidding is completed, the highest bidder names the trump suit, without consulting his partner in any way.

Should the first three hands pass, dealer must name the trump suit, but he need not assume a contract. The deal is played for whatever points each side can make.

DISCARDING

The trump suit having been named, each player discards from his hand all cards that are not trumps. (A player may keep one or more plain cards, if he wishes, though he thereby lessens his chances of drawing additional trumps. But he must not discard a trump.) Each in turn, beginning with eldest hand, announces the number of cards he needs to bring his hand up to six, and dealer gives him cards from the top of the pack. Dealer, in his turn, *robs the pack*. Instead of drawing from the top, he looks through the pack and takes out all remaining trumps. If not enough remain to give him six cards, he takes any plain cards he pleases. If more than six trumps remain in his hand and the pack, he must take six and place the remainder face up on the table, so that all may know what trumps are out of play. Dealer must always announce how many cards he needs to fill out his hand.

THE PLAY

The player who named the trump suit makes the opening lead. A lead calls upon each other hand to follow suit or trump, if able to follow suit. If unable to follow suit, the hand may play any card, trump or plain. A trick is won by the highest trump, or the highest card of the suit led. The winner of a trick leads to the next.

SCORING

After play ends, each side counts the number of points it has won in tricks. There are 14 points in every deal, except when dealer has found more than six trumps in robbing the pack. If the total is short, due to the improper discard of a trump, this trump belongs to the side that made the trump.

If the contracting side made at least the number of points bid, the side having the higher total wins the difference of totals. Example: If a side bids and makes just 8, it wins 8 minus 6, or 2. It is possible for opponents of the bidder to score, even though contract was made. *Example:* A side bids and makes just 6; opponents win 2.

If the contracting side fails to make contract, opponents score all the points they took in tricks, plus the amount of the bid. *Example:* A side bids 9 but takes only 8; opponents win 6 + 9 = 15.

Game is usually fixed at 51. If score is kept on a cribbage board, game is 61.

IRREGULARITIES

Misdeal. If a card is found faced in the pack, there must be a new deal by the same dealer. If dealer exposes a card in dealing, opponents may consult and may let the deal stand or call for a new deal by the same dealer. If dealer gives the wrong number of cards to a hand, there must be a new deal by the next dealer. If a player deals out of turn or with the wrong pack, the error must be corrected on demand made before the deal is complete, otherwise it stands as regular.

Bid Out of Turn. Is void, and both partners of the offending side must pass thereafter, but any legal bid made previous to the error stands.

Naming Trump in Bidding (when it is not certain that bidder has won the right) bars partner of the offender from bidding.

Wrong Number of Cards. During bidding: A hand found to be short continues short, and may bid; it is rectified by the draw. A hand with too many cards may not bid; the excess cards are drawn out by an opponent and placed at bottom of the pack.

During play: A hand found to be short draws cards from the discard, without penalty. A hand with too many cards continues play as it is, but the offending side may not score in that deal.

Exposed Card is one dropped on the table, played or led with another, or otherwise shown to partner except in legal play; it must be left face up on the table and played on demand of either opponent when such play is legal.

Lead Out of Turn. If it was an opponent's turn to lead, the erroneous lead becomes an exposed card. If it was partner's turn to lead, either opponent may require or forbid him to lead a trump.

Play Out of Turn. If leader's partner plays before second hand, fourth hand also may play before second hand, either of his own volition or at request of second hand. If fourth hand plays to a lead when neither intervening hand has yet played, leader's side may claim the trick, but the hand that actually wins it makes the next lead. No penalty for playing fourth hand when it is third hand's turn.

Revoke is failure to follow suit or trump, when able to follow suit. A revoke may be corrected before the next lead. If revoke becomes established, revoking side is deemed to have won no points in play, and opponents score accordingly.

STRATEGY

A side making its bid scores at most 14 points. A side defeating an adverse bid scores at least 15 points. Consequently there is nothing to be gained (as there is in Bridge) by willful overbidding.

There are 14 trumps, and the bidding side should usually aim to hold a majority. But there are many more exceptions than are met in games (as Bridge) where a player may not trump if able to follow to a plain-suit lead. The bidding side frequently is able to make high contracts with 7 or 6, or even 5 trumps. What is more important than the number of trumps is the rank. A holding of **A–K–Q–3** has good prospect of winning a majority of the points, while **10–8–7–6–5–2** needs abnormal help from partner to make more than 7.

Since the player has only one chance to bid, the first bidder on a side should think more of giving information than of trying to buy the contract cheaply. The game lends itself to elaborate systems of informatory bidding; for example:

Holding any pedro, bid five in the suit to show it.
Holding an ace at the top of three or four cards, bid six.
Holding ace and king, even without any more cards in the suit, bid seven.
Holding **A–K–J–x–x** bid eleven.
Holding **A–K–Q–x** bid eleven or twelve.

The partner of the first bidder should try to infer the intended trump suit, and should raise the bid when he holds adequate support. For example, a player holds

♠ K 8 5   ♡ K 7   ♣ 5   ♢ A 9 4

His partner opens the auction with a bid of 7, showing **A–K**. His suit must be clubs. This hand should jump to eleven, name clubs, and lead ♣**5**. The jump surely can be read to show both pedros, and ♣**A K** can be cashed at once to gather 11 points, even if the opponents take the rest of the tricks.

The play focuses principally on catching the pedros. Until both pedros have been played (or located), both sides are wary of letting a lead ride to the fourth hand without a trump in it as good as the 6, for otherwise the last player will be able to make a pedro if he has it. Third hand—if no previous player has done so—usually *cinches* such a trick, by playing a trump, 6 or higher.

ILLUSTRATIVE DEAL

```
                    ♠ 8
                    ♡ 7 5 4
                    ♣ Q
                    ◊ 9
        ♠ —                    ♠ —
        ♡ A J          N       ♡ 8 6 3 2
        ♣ 10 6    W        E   ♣ A
        ◊ 8 5          S       ◊ 4
                    ♠ 3
                    ♡ K Q 10 9
                    ♣ —
                    ◊ K
```

South bid six and named hearts. In the draw, West took 4 cards, North 4, East 2, South 2.

TRICK	SOUTH	WEST	NORTH	EAST
1	♠ 3	◊ 8	♡ 7	♣ A
2	♡ Q	♡ A	♡ 5	♡ 3
3	◊ K	♣ 6	♣ Q	♡ 6
4	♡ 10	♣ 10	◊ 9	◊ 4
5	♡ K	♡ 5	♡ 4	♡ 8
6	♡ 9	♡ J	♠ 8	♡ 2

North-South win six points, making the contract. East-West score 2.

Trick 2. The lead of the pedro looks best, since if South has the ace, contract can be made at once. The trump lead also tends to warn that North cannot cinch any more tricks.

Trick 3. South must resist the temptation to take ♡ 10. He needs all his trumps to catch left pedro, without which he will lose contract.

Trick 4. A bad mistake would be the play of ♡ 9. This might, and in fact would, lose the contract. South would be happy to see his ♡ 10 fall to the jack, for then he would take the last two tricks, catching left pedro and low.

Trick 5. The sole remaining hope is that ♡ J and ◊ 5 are in the same hand. Since they are, South catches ◊ 5, which is enough with ♡ 10 to make the contract.

Auction Cinch (Razzle Dazzle)

This is a variant for five or six players, each for himself. Only six cards are dealt to each hand, in rounds of three at a time. Bidding is as in Cinch;

highest bidder names the trump suit. All cards but trumps are discarded, and dealer gives cards to restore each hand to six. The high bidder then names a trump not in his hand; the holder of this card must acknowledge it, and he becomes the partner of the bidder. The two play for a joint contract against the rest. (Partners keep their seats, so that they may chance to play consecutively.) If they make their contract, each scores separately the amount earned by his side (see scoring of Cinch). If they lose, each opponent scores the amount of the bid plus whatever points he individually took in tricks.

THE BIG
BÉZIQUE
FAMILY

PINOCHLE

The original game of Pinochle is for two players, is almost identical with Bézique and is unquestionably derived from that game. Legends of an earlier and independent origin for Pinochle are hardly trustworthy unless Pinochle was merely a Scandinavian and Teutonic name for the game which came to be known as Bézique in France and England. Both games, in their relatively modern version, date from the 1860s.

The most plausible account of the origin of the name Pinochle is as follows: The word *bézique*, as pronounced in French, is much like the word *besicles*, which in French means eyeglasses; *binocle* also means eyeglasses, in both French and German. The spelling *binocle* is one of the many earlier spellings of the word *pinochle*, now generally employed.

The most popular forms of Pinochle—Auction Pinochle and Partnership Pinochle—are purely American, though they were developed by European (chiefly German) immigrants who combined elements of Bézique and Skat.

Pinochle was for many years the principal game of American Jews, but was and is almost equally popular with the Irish people of the larger cities and in Middle Atlantic and midwestern states is a family game among the entire population.

Auction Pinochle

PLAYERS

There are three active players in each deal. The game is better for four, the dealer taking no cards; five often play in the same game, and sometimes even six.

CARDS

The pack has 48 cards, two each of **A, K, Q, J, 10** and **9** in each of four suits, spades, hearts, diamonds and clubs. The cards in each suit rank **A** (high), **10, K, Q, J, 9**.

PRELIMINARIES

The Draw. Each player lifts a portion of the pack, taking no more than half the cards remaining. The last player must leave the bottom card on the table. When all have cut, each shows the bottom card of the portion he cut. Lowest has choice of seats and is the first dealer; next lowest sits at dealer's left, and so on. If two players draw cards of equal rank they cut again to determine precedence as between the two.

The Shuffle. Dealer shuffles the pack and places it on the table, face down, at his right.

The Cut. The player at dealer's right lifts a portion of the pack, leaving at least five cards in each packet. Dealer picks up the remainder of the pack, and places it on top of the portion lifted off by the player at his right.

Rotation. Each player's turn, in dealing, bidding and playing, comes to him in rotation to the left, i.e., he acts in each case immediately after the player seated to his right.

DEALING

When there are four players, dealer receives no cards; when there are five players, dealer and the player second from his left receive no cards; when there are six players, these players and the player at dealer's right receive no cards. Players who receive no cards are *inactive* and may give neither advice nor information to the active players.

Dealer gives cards to each active player in turn, either three at a time throughout or four at a time for the first three rounds and three at a time for the last round. After the first round of dealing, dealer must give three cards face down in the center of the table to the *widow*. The whole pack being dealt, each player has fifteen cards.

OBJECTS OF THE GAME

The objects of the game are to score points by melding and by winning in tricks cards having scoring values.

The melds, and their values, are as follows:

SEQUENCES

A - **K** - **Q** - **J** - **10** of trump (flush)	150
K - **Q** of trump (royal Marriage)	40
K - **Q** of any other suit (Marriage)	20

GROUPS

♠**A** - ♡**A** - ◇**A** - ♣**A** (100 aces)	100
♠**K** - ♡**K** - ◇**K** - ♣**K** (80 kings)	80
♠**Q** - ♡**Q** - ◇**Q** - ♣**Q** (60 queens)	60
♠**J** - ♡**J** - ◇**J** - ♣**J** (40 jacks)	40
♠**KQ** - ♡**KQ** - ◇**KQ** - ♣**KQ** (round house)	240

SPECIAL

♠**Q** - ◇**J** (pinochle)	40
9 of trumps (*dix*, pronounced deece)	10

A card which is part of a meld under one heading may be counted as part of a meld under another heading but may not be counted as part of another meld under the same heading.

The scoring values of cards taken in tricks, and of the last trick are: Each ace, 11; each ten, 10; each king, 4; each queen, 3; each jack, 2; last trick, 10. The nines have no scoring value when taken in tricks. Some players simplify the count by counting aces and tens 10 each, kings and queens 5 each, jacks and nines nothing. Other players count aces, tens and kings 10 each, queens, jacks and nines nothing. In any case, the last trick counts 10 and the total of points scored in each deal is 250.

BIDDING

Each active player in turn, beginning with the player at dealer's left, must make a bid or must pass. A bid is expressed in points only, in multiples of ten points, and each successive bid must be higher than the last preceding bid. The player at dealer's left must bid 300 or more; though in some games a minimum bid of 250 is permitted, in other games a minimum bid of 200, and in still other games the first player is not required to bid, whereupon a deal may be passed out.

Having passed, a player may not thereafter bid. When two players have passed, the auction is closed. The highest bid becomes the contract, and the player who made the highest bid becomes the Bidder. The other two players jointly are the *opponents*.

THE KITTY

A separate score, or a separate pile of chips, is maintained for an imaginary extra player called the *kitty*, which is the joint property of all players in the game. If the kitty has a deficit, they must supply it equally. When any player leaves the game, each player takes his proportionate share of the kitty's score or chips.

In all games, the kitty solely collects when the Bidder concedes defeat without exposing the widow. The kitty also shares in the settlement of other bids, the bids depending upon agreement among the players: In most games, the kitty pays or collects the same as any other player when the bid is 350 or more, and in many games the kitty collects if a bid of less than 350 is played and not made (double bete) although in such games the kitty does not pay when a contract of less than 350 is made.

THE WIDOW

If the Bidder obtained the contract at 300 (or such other minimum bid as is determined by the rules of the game), the Bidder may decline to expose the widow and pay to the kitty a forfeit equivalent to the value of a 300 or other minimum bid, after which the deal passes to the next player in turn.

In any other case, the Bidder, immediately after the bidding is closed, turns the three cards of the widow face up on the table so that all players may see them. After this he takes them into his hand.

MELDING

Only the Bidder may meld. Melding consists in announcing or showing combinations of cards which have values according to the table previously given. If the Bidder merely announces his melds, he must show them at the request of any player, and it is customary for the Bidder to show them without being asked.

Having shown his melds, the Bidder takes them back into his hand; but, on demand, he must show his melds again at any time before either opponent has played to the first trick.

The Bidder may change his meld at any time before he has led to the first trick.

BURYING

After melding, and preferably before picking up any cards he shows on the table, the Bidder must *bury* or lay away, face down, any three cards which he has not melded, to reduce the number of cards in his hand to fifteen. The cards laid away will count to the credit of the Bidder after the cards are played. It is not necessary for the Bidder to announce the fact when he lays away a trump, an ace, or any other card.

At the same time, the Bidder announces the trump suit. He may change his meld, the cards he buries and the trump suit as often as he wishes before he leads to the first trick, but not thereafter. If the Bidder names the trump suit and both opponents concede, he may not then change the trump suit.

CONCESSION

The Bidder may concede defeat without leading to the first trick, whereupon he pays to each other active and inactive player the basic unit value of his bid. This is a *single bete*.

Either opponent may propose that the Bidder's contract be conceded to him, and if the other opponent agrees, the contract is made; but if the other opponent declines to concede the Bidder must commence play.

THE PLAY

The Bidder always leads to the first trick. He may lead any card.

The card led and two cards, one each played in turn by the other two active players, constitute a *trick*. Any trick containing a trump is won by the player who played the highest trump; any other trick is won by the player who played the highest card of the suit led. Of two cards of identical suit and rank, the one played first is the higher. The winner of each trick leads to the next, and may lead any card.

Each player must follow suit to the card led if able. If he is unable to follow suit, but holds a trump, he must play a trump. If another player has previously played a trump to the same trick, he may play any trump—he need not win the trick.

If the card led is a trump, each player must, if able, play a higher trump than any previously played to the trick. This is called *playing over*.

The Bidder gathers all tricks he wins into a pile, face down, the cards he buried being at the bottom of the pile and counting for him in the final settlement. One opponent gathers in all tricks won by his side. At the end of the play, the two sides agree on the number of points each has taken in.

If the Bidder has scored, in melds and tricks, at least as many points as he named in the contract, his contract is made. If he has scored fewer points, he is *double bete*.

SCORING

It is most convenient to use chips, so that each player pays or collects after each deal, settling separately with each other player. A satisfactory score may also be kept with pencil and paper.

In settlement, the Bidder pays to or collects from every other player, active or inactive, and including the kitty if the contract was 350 or more. If the Bidder made his contract, he collects by any one of the following schedules, each of which is in use in one or another locality to establish the basic unit values of contracts:

Basic Unit Values

Contract	A	B	C	D
300–340	3	3	1	1
350–390	5	5	2	3
400–440	10	10	4	7
450–490	15	20	6	10
500–540	20	40	8	13
550–590	25	80	10	16
600 or more	30	160	12	19

If the Bidder leads to the first trick and then does not fulfill his contract, he is double bete and pays twice the basic unit values shown in whichever schedule is adopted.

In nearly all circles, the basic unit values are doubled if spades are trumps. In some circles, the basic unit values are tripled if hearts are trumps.

In no case does the Bidder score more than the amount of his contract, regardless of how many points he actually scores.

Play for 1,000 Points. Some do not play each deal as a separate game, but play until any player has scored 1,000 points, when that player wins the game. If a Bidder fails to fulfill his contract, the amount of the bid is subtracted from his score, even if it gives him a net minus score.

OPTIONAL LAWS

290 or 320. In some games, when the first player is permitted to pass, although the minimum bid for the first two players is 250, the third player, after two passes, may not make any bid in the 250 range of less than 290; nor any bid in the 300 range of less than 320.

Bonus Payments. If the Bidder melds 100 aces without the help of the widow, he receives an additional chip from each other player if he makes his contract, but pays nothing additional if he is bete. This is called "in the mitt."

Graduated Aces. Some who play bonus payment for aces "in the mitt," also play that the bonus payment increases with the amount of the bid: If it is one chip at a 300 bid, it is two chips at a 350 bid, three chips at a 400 bid, etc.

Exposed Widow. In some games some card of the widow is exposed after the first round of bidding. In other games, one card of the widow is exposed before the bidding begins.

Players who use these rules sometimes add an additional rule that after a deal in which there was a 400 bid, two cards of the widow are exposed for the next deal, but each player has only one bid.

IRREGULARITIES

The following laws covering irregularities are reprinted, by permission, from the Laws of Auction Pinochle, copyright 1946.

Misdeal. There must be a new deal by the same dealer:

(a) If the pack was not properly shuffled or was not cut, and if a player calls attention to it before the widow has been dealt;

(b) If, in dealing, the dealer exposes more than one card of any player's hand;

(c) If any card of the widow is exposed in dealing;

(d) If at any time before the cards are shuffled for the next deal the pack is found to be imperfect. Scores made with the same pack in previous deals are not affected.

Exposure of the Widow. (a) If a player sees a card in the widow before the auction closes, he may not make another bid.

(b) If at any time before the auction closes a player handles the widow and in so doing exposes a card, there must be a new deal by the next dealer in turn, and (penalty) the offender must pay to each other player, including the kitty and every inactive player, the unit value of the highest bid last made prior to his offense.

Incorrect Hand. If any player or the widow has too few cards and another player, or the widow, has too many:

(a) If it is discovered before the widow has been properly exposed by the Bidder, the hand with too few cards draws the excess, face down, from the player or widow having too many. A player who held too many cards, and who looked at all of them, is barred from further bidding on that hand.

(b) If it is discovered at any time after the widow has been properly exposed by the Bidder, and if the Bidder's hand (including the widow) contains the correct number of cards, the Bidder's contract is made; if the Bidder's hand contains an incorrect number of cards, he is single or double bete, depending on whether or not he has led to the first trick.

(c) If the widow has too few cards, there must be another deal by the same dealer.

Exposure of One Card. If a player drops, or names, or otherwise exposes his possession of any one card, except in leading or playing it:

(a) If that player is or becomes the Bidder, there is no penalty;

(b) If that player is or becomes an opponent, then when first he can legally lead or play that card he must so announce and the Bidder may either require or forbid him to play it. Pending such time the card must be left face up on the table.

Exposure of More Than One Card. If the opponents of the Bidder, or either of them, expose more than one card, the Bidder's contract is made.

Bid Out of Turn. A bid out of turn is void without penalty; but the other two players (or either of them, if the other has passed) may treat it as a correct bid by bidding or passing over it.

Insufficient Bid. If a bid in turn is not high enough to overcall the last preceding bid it is considered a pass; except that the other two players (or either of them, if the other has passed) may treat it as a correct bid by bidding over it.

Impossible Bid. If a player bids less than 300 (or whatever is the agreed minimum, such as 250); or more than 680; or any figure not expressed in multiples of 10 points, his bid is void without penalty and he is deemed to have passed.

Played Card. A card is played when its holder places it upon the table with apparent intent to play, or when he names it as the one he intends to play. A card once played may not be withdrawn, except as provided in Section 37.

Improper Burying. If the Bidder leads before burying, or buries a card he has melded, or buries too many or too few cards and as a result has an incorrect number of cards in his hand, he is double bete.

Information As to the Auction and Meld. (a) Until an opponent has played to the first trick, the opponents may ask or state the number and nature of the cards melded by the Bidder, the point value of the meld, the amount of the bid and the number of points the Bidder needs to win in cards.

(b) After either opponent has played to the first trick, any player may ask what the trump suit is; but if an opponent names the trump suit except in response to such a question, or if an opponent asks or gives any information as to the amount of the bid, the nature or value of the meld, the number of points the opponents have taken in, play ceases and the Bidder's contract is made.

(c) A player has no redress if he acts on incorrect information given in response to a question, or if he does not know what suit is trump, whether or not the Bidder announced the trump suit.

Looking At Turned Card. (a) The Bidder may turn and look at the cards he buries, at any time before he leads or plays to the second trick. If he does so thereafter, he is double bete.

(b) Any player may turn and look at a trick until his side has played to the next trick. If the Bidder turns and looks at a trick thereafter, he is double bete; if an opponent does so, the contract is made.

Trick Appropriated in Error. A trick taken in by the side not winning it may be claimed and must be restored at any time before it is covered by cards taken in on a subsequent trick; unless so claimed and restored it remains the property of the side which took it in.

Revoke (Renege). A player revokes, if, when able to play as required by law, he:
(a) Fails to follow suit;
(b) Fails to play over on the lead of a trump;

(c) Fails to play a trump when he has no card of the suit led;

(d) Fails to play a card previously exposed when directed by Bidder to play it, or plays such card when directed by Bidder not to play it.

A revoke may be corrected before a member of the revoking side has led or played to the next trick, and if the offender is the Bidder, the opponents may withdraw any cards played to the next trick, but there is no other penalty; if the offender is an opponent, play continues but the Bidder does not pay if he fails to fulfill his contract.

A revoke becomes established when either member of the revoking side has led or played to the next trick, and if the offender is the Bidder, he is double bete; if the offender is an opponent, the contract is made.

If both sides revoke, the penalty applies to the offense to which attention is first called; if attention to both revokes is drawn simultaneously, the penalty applies to the offense which was committed first.

Lead Out of Turn. (a) If the Bidder leads when it was an opponent's turn to lead, there is no penalty; the opponent whose lead it was may choose to treat the lead as a correct one, or may require that the card be withdrawn.

(b) If an opponent leads when it is not his turn to lead, it is treated as a revoke (Section 36).

Claim or Concession. If at any time after the first lead is made:

(a) The Bidder concedes that he is bete, or an opponent exposes or throws in his cards or expressly concedes that the contract is made, play ceases and the concession is binding;

(b) An opponent suggests concession, as by saying to his partner, "Shall we give it to him?", the concession is not valid, and play must continue unless said partner agrees;

(c) The Bidder claims that the contract is made, or an opponent claims that the Bidder is bete, play ceases and all unplayed cards are taken by the side which did not make the claim.

Error in Count of Meld. (a) If, after the Bidder leads to the first trick, he is found to lack a card essential to a meld he announced but did not show, he is double bete.

(b) If an incorrect point value was agreed upon for the Bidder's meld, correction may be made at any time before settlement is completed.*

---

* Example: *The contract is 350. Bidder shows* ♠A K Q J 10 9 *and* ◇K Q J. *The agreed value is 210; Bidder plays and takes in 134. Before paying, he recalls that his melds as shown actually totaled 220. The contract is made.*

Error in Settlement. (a) Chips paid and collected as a result of an erroneous agreement on the result of a bid, or its unit value, are not returned.

(b) A score entered by a scorekeeper based on an erroneous agreement by all active players as to the result of a bid, or its unit value, may not be corrected after the cards have been mixed for the next shuffle.

(c) A score incorrectly entered by the scorekeeper—that is, not entered in accordance with the agreed result or value of the bid—may be corrected whenever it is discovered.

STRATEGY

Conservatism in bidding is the primary requirement for winning at Auction Pinochle. Except in unusual cases, a player should bid only upon values already held in his hand. He should not expect to find an extra meld in the widow, although he can count on adding about 20 points to the playing strength of his hand through the cards he finds in the widow. It is almost invariably bad tactics to stretch a sure 300-hand to a doubtful 350, or a sure 350-hand to a doubtful 400.

Altogether there are 5,456 possible three-card buys. The following table gives the figures on the various chances:

CHANCES	FAVORABLE CASES	ODDS
1	961	5 to 1 against
2	1802	2 to 1 against
3	2531	23 to 20 against
4	3156	1½ to 1 for
5	3685	2 to 1 for
6	4126	3 to 1 for

If, as in many Pinochle games, you must pay the kitty on betes of under 350, but do not collect from the kitty if you make a bid of under 350, you are giving 4 to 3 odds that you will make your contract when you bid in the 300 range. You need at least four places open to make your bid a good bet if you are counting on help from the widow to make your bid.

Pushing. There are many hands on which you would be willing to bid 350 but would not care to risk 370. Most Pinochle players would bid 350 on the following hand:

♠ A 10 Q 9 9   ♡ A 10 9   ◇ A 10 K Q J 9   ♣ J

However, this is a better 300 bid. It is absolutely sure to make 300, and might conceivably be safe at 350; since 150 points in cards would still be needed and a bad buy or a bad break might prevent making them. If a bid of 350 is pushed by another player who bids 360, it is impossible safely to bid 370; while if you start in the 300 range and permit yourself to be pushed to 350, you will probably be permitted to play it; the fact that you did not start with 350 will indicate that you do not have a sure 350 hand.

The odds must be better than 2 to 1 in favor of making a 350 bid for you to bid it. Here is how it works out: Suppose there are three cases in which you hold the same hand. In each case you are safe for 300 but the odds are 2 to 1 in favor of making 350.

If you bid 300 all three times, at a value of three chips per player each time, you will make it each time and collect 27 chips top in all.

If you bid 350 each time, at a value of five chips per player including the kitty, you will make it twice and collect twenty chips each time, for a total of forty chips; but once you will not make it and even if it is only a single bete you will pay out twenty of those chips, leaving yourself with a net gain of only twenty chips for the three times, as against the twenty-seven you would have had by stopping at 300.

This conservatism in bidding has two other good effects: First, it permits you to push an opponent by overbidding him when he goes to 350 or more, since he cannot be sure but that you have underbid your hand in the first place, and may keep on bidding rather than let you have it; and such tactics will discourage the opponents from pushing you, since they will learn that when pushed you can very likely go one step higher and have an excellent chance of making your bid.

When to Play. Assuming that spades are double, and that no other suit has any premium value, the mathematical considerations in deciding whether or not to play are as follows: If spades are trumps, play if you have at least an even chance to make the contract. If any other suit is trumps, play even if the odds are as much as 2 to 1 against your making it.

Suppose diamonds are trumps and you figure that the odds are 2 to 1 against your making it. That is, if you play the hand three times you would make it only once and be double bete twice. The bid is 300. Here is how it works out:

If you concede all three times you lose 3 × 9, or 27 chips in all.

If you play all three times you collect 9 chips the time you make it, but lose 18 + 18 the two times you are double bete. You will have taken in 9 and paid out 36, losing 27 chips in all.

In other words, you break even when the odds are 2 to 1 against you. If the odds against you are any less, you show a clean profit by playing. If the odds are any greater against you, you lose by playing.

When spades are trumps you should have an even chance to make the contract because if you decide not to play you can name another suit as trumps and lose only a single bete, whereas if you play at spades and are double bete it costs you four times the value of the contract.

Counting Losers. Before playing, a player counts the cards in his hand that he expects the opponents to win, and credits the opponents with the maximum number of points they might win on each of his losing tricks. It is true that if two aces are outstanding, both may be in the same hand and cannot fall on the same losing trick; nevertheless, a player holding a nine must expect to lose 22 points on the trick containing his nine. To a certain extent this slight pessimism compensates for unexpected bad suit breaks that may be encountered.

So, a player holding ♣K Q and no other club expects to lose two tricks in clubs, each trick containing three cards, and the six cards altogether comprising the six highest clubs in the pack—two aces, two tens, the king and the queen, comprising 49 points in all.

Discarding. Before discarding (burying) his three cards, the Bidder imagines his hands in various forms in which he might eventually play it. It is quite legitimate to remove the three-card discard from the hand, study the resultant playing hand, restore the discard to the hand and try removing three other cards, and so on until the best possible playing hand is achieved.

It is traditional and entirely sound to strive for a two-suited hand— the long trump suit plus the longest possible side suit. It is equally traditional, and equally sound, to void a three-card or shorter suit in which no ace is held.

♠ A 10 K K Q J 9 ♡ A A 10 ◇ A Q Q 9 9 ♣ 10 K J

The normal discard from this hand is the three clubs. The opponents cannot then win a club trick and are likely to lose both their aces of clubs; burying the clubs retains a five-card diamond suit to act as a second long suit; and the three hearts, unless one of them is trumped, will win tricks when held in the hand and therefore will count in the hand as well as they would if buried.

The opponents' cards in a long suit may be expected to break as follows:

SUIT BREAKS IN AUCTION PINOCHLE

IF THE OPPONENTS HOLD	THEY WILL BREAK		
7 cards	4–3	61	% of the time
	5–2	31	%
	6–1	7⅓%	
	7–0	⅔%	
6 cards	4–2	47⅓%	
	3–3	34⅓%	
	5–1	15	%
	6–0	3⅓%	
5 cards	3–2	67	%
	4–1	29	%
	5–0	4	%

IF THE OPPONENTS HOLD	THEY WILL BREAK	
4 cards	3–1	50 %
	2–2	40 %
	4–0	10 %
3 cards	2–1	77½%
	3–0	22½%
2 cards	1–1	51¾%
	2–0	48¼%

The advantage of the long side suit is that it may be led before trumps are drawn and if one opponent is short in that suit he must trump when he cannot follow suit. If he must trump it means he cannot smear (schmier, or fatten) his partner's winning tricks in that suit by discarding aces and tens of other suits. If he wishes to avoid the burden of trumping, his side must lead trumps and that will make it easier for the Bidder than if he had to lead trumps himself. Therefore the strategy of playing a two-suit hand is to lead the side suit and reserve the trumps, except in such cases as when the side suit consists almost entirely of winning cards, when it becomes desirable to lead trumps and thereby exhaust the opponents' trumps before leading the side suit.

Leading Trumps. The Bidder's first lead may be any card of any suit, and it is usually neither necessary nor desirable to lead trumps. Sometimes, however, trumps should be led first; as in such a hand as the following:

♠ A A 10 10 Q J   ♡ A 10 K Q J 9   ◇ A J 9   ♣ —

Playing for 150, with hearts trumps, it is desirable to exhaust the opponents' trumps, so that six solid spade tricks may be run. But the opponents have six hearts and they may be expected in most cases to break 4–2 or worse. If hearts are led immediately Bidder may expect to lose two heart tricks, two diamond tricks and last—and the opponents cannot win enough points on those tricks to get the 101 they need. Trumps may be led immediately. From a holding such as this, the best first lead to limit the trump loss to two tricks is the queen.

Occasionally it is necessary to play such a trump suit to lose only one trick. In such a case the ace should be led first, followed immediately by another trump lead—the nine if the ten fell on the first round (for then the only hope is that one opponent held **A-10** alone), and otherwise the queen, unless the queen dropped on the first round.

Defensive Play. The following pointers will guide the opponents' play in most cases:

When the Bidder needs 100 or more points, lead his shortest suit and make him trump as often as possible.

When the Bidder is playing for fewer than 100 points, especially when he is playing for only 50 or 60 points, lead trumps at every opportunity, even if it means leading into the Bidder's hand.

When declarer leads a side suit without drawing trumps, judge from partner's play whether or not he can win the final tricks in that suit. If partner has winning tricks in the suit, lead trumps, and if partner has no winning tricks in the suit do not lead trumps.

When the Bidder runs winning cards, discard all the cards from your shortest suit first. It permits you to smear later on partner's winning cards in that suit. This advice does not apply, of course, to discarding aces or winning tens.

ILLUSTRATIVE DEAL NO. 1

In each of the following hands, when the play is tabulated, the winning card of each trick is underscored; the card immediately below it is the lead to the next trick.

Dealer

```
                          N
♠ 10 K J J 9 9                    ♠ K Q
♡ J 9                 W       E    ♡ 10 K Q 9
◇ 10 Q Q J 9                       ◇ 10 K
♣ A 10                S           ♣ A 10 K Q J J 9

                ♠ A A 10 Q
                ♡ A A 10 K Q J
                ◇ A A J
                ♣ K Q
```

The auction:

	EAST	SOUTH	WEST
1st Round	350	360[1]	Pass
2nd Round	370	380	
3rd Round	Pass		

The widow: ◇ **K 9** ♣ **9**
The discard: ♣ **K Q 9**[2]
The meld: 190   *Points needed:* 190   *Trumps:* hearts

NOTES:

[1] A jump to 370 might be considered, for it would force East to go 380 or pass; South might make such a bid if he were willing to play 370 but not 380. In this case, however, South's playing strength suggests that he might buy the contract at 360.

[2] It is rarely wise to bury a marriage rather than meld it; but if

South buries ◇ **K 9** ♣ **9** and melds 210, he will need 170. The opponents, needing 80, can win 49 in clubs, 22 in diamonds, 17 in spades, or 88 in all, even if no heart trick is lost. By discarding **K Q 9** South needs 190, but the opponents now figure to win only 37 in diamonds (assuming that an ace will be smeared on one trick) and 17 in spades, only 54 points, or 6 less than they will need.

The playing hands:

♠ **10 K J J 9 9**		♠ **K Q**
♡ **J 9**	W E	♡ **10 K Q 9**
◇ **10 Q Q J 9**		◇ **10 K**
♣ **A 10**	S	♣ **A 10 K Q J J 9**

♠ **A A 10 Q**
♡ **A A 10 K Q J**
◇ **A A K J 9**

The play:

	SOUTH	WEST	EAST	SOUTH POINTS	E-W POINTS
1.	◇ **A**	◇ **9**	◇ **K**	22[1]	
2.	◇ **J**	◇ **Q**	◇ **10**		15
3.	♡ **A**	♡ **9**	♡ **9**	11	
4.	◇ **9**	◇ **Q**	♡ 10		13
5.	♡ **K**	♡ **J**	♡ **Q**	9	
6.	♡ **A**	♠ **9**	♡ **K**	15	
7.	♡ **10**	♠ **9**	♣ **9**	10	
8.	♡ **Q**	♣ **10**	♣ **J**	15	
9.	♡ **J**	◇ **J**	♣ **J**	6	
10.	◇ **A**	◇ **10**	♣ **Q**	24	
11.	◇ **K**	♣ **A**	♣ **K**	19	
12.	♠ **10**	♠ **J**	♠ **Q**	15	
13.	♠ **A**	♠ **K**	♠ **K**	19	
14.	♠ **Q**	♠ **10**	♣ **A**		24
15.	♠ **A**	♠ **J**	♣ **10**	33	
				198	52

NOTES ON THE PLAY:

[1] Including the 7 points buried.

Trick 2. Leading the card which was melded; for the opponents already know South holds it.

Trick 6. East is marked with another heart—the king—for his bidding could have been based only on a club flush and 80 kings. With six or more clubs, four hearts, and probably ◇ **10 K** alone, East can have at most three spades. By running his trumps, South can force West to come down to four spades and three diamonds; then West can be thrown in on a fourth round of spades and must lead a diamond away from his 10.

Trick 9. West could not win a trick with the ◇ **10** anyway.

Trick 13. A falsecard, to make South believe the spades were divided 5–3 and that each opponent now has one left. South does not fall for it.

ILLUSTRATIVE DEAL NO. 2

South holds:

♠ **A 10 K Q J** ♡ **K Q J 9** ◇ **A K Q J 9** ♣ **K**

South bids 350; West pass; East 360; South 400; East pass.
The widow: ♡**10 9** ◇**10**
The discard: ♡**10 J 9**
The meld: 310   *Points needed:* 90
Trumps: Spades (South should make diamonds trumps, melding 320; but he tries for the double collection at spades)

The playing hands:

```
        ♠ 10 9 9              ♠ A K Q J
        ♡ K Q J         W  E  ♡ A A 10
        ◇ K Q J 9             ◇ A 10
        ♣ 10 Q Q J 9     S    ♠ A A 10 K J 9

              ♠ A 10 K Q J
              ♡ K Q 9
              ◇ A 10 K Q J 9
              ♣ K
```

	SOUTH	WEST	EAST	SOUTH POINTS	E-W POINTS
1.	◇ A	◇ 9	◇ 10	33	
2.	◇ 9	◇ K	◇ A		15
3.	♣ K	♣ 10	♣ A		25
4.	♠ Q	♣ 9	♣ A	14	
5.	◇ J	◇ Q	♠ K		9
6.	♠ K	♣ J	♣ 9	6	
7.	◇ Q	◇ J	♠ Q		8
8.	♠ J	♠ 10	♠ A		23
9.	♠ 10	♣ Q	♣ J	15	
10.	◇ K	♠ 9	♠ J		6
11.	♠ A	♣ Q	♣ K	18	
				86	

NOTES ON THE PLAY:

Trick 1. South hopes to find the diamonds split 3–3, so that he can force two trumps at once by later diamond rounds. Although the split is 4–2, he cannot do better than continue the suit.

Trick 8. If East led another club before cashing ♠**A**, South would trump; cash his own ♠**A**; and then force out East's ♠**A** with a diamond lead. South would still make a trump trick with ♠**10**. The extra trump trick would give South 90 points and his contract.

Trick 11. South cannot win another trick, since West has ♠**9** to trump a diamond lead and East has the high hearts. South is double bete.

Two-hand Pinochle

PLAYERS
Two.

CARDS
As in Auction Pinochle.

PRELIMINARIES
Dealer is decided as in Auction Pinochle. Non-dealer may shuffle, then dealer shuffles last and non-dealer cuts, leaving at least five cards in each packet.

The winner of each hand deals next, if each hand is played as a separate game; when the game of 1,000 points is played, the deal alternates.

DEALING
Dealer gives twelve cards to each player, three at a time face down. He turns the next card up; it is the trump card and every card of its suit is a trump. The undealt cards are placed so as partly to cover the trump card, which is face up in the center of the table; this forms the stock.

OBJECTS OF THE GAME
The object is to score points, either by melds or by winning tricks containing counting cards.

A player melds by placing the necessary cards face up on the table before him, immediately after winning a trick in the play, and before drawing from the stock. The following are the combinations which constitute melds:

SEQUENCES

A - **K** - **Q** - **J** - **10** of trump (flush)	150
K - **Q** of trump (royal Marriage)	40
K - **Q** of any other suit (Marriage)	20

GROUPS

♠**A** - ♡**A** - ◇**A** - ♣**A** (100 aces)	100
♠**K** - ♡**K** - ◇**K** - ♣**K** (80 kings)	80
♠**Q** - ♡**Q** - ◇**Q** - ♣**Q** (60 queens)	60
♠**J** - ♡**J** - ♡**J** - ♣**J** (40 jacks)	40

SPECIAL

♠**Q** - ◇**J** (pinochle)	40
9 of trumps (*dix*, pronounced deece)	10

The following rules apply to melding:

1. Only one meld may be made in each turn;

2. For each meld, at least one card must be taken from the hand and placed on the table, but a card or cards may be taken from the hand and combined with one or more cards already on the table;

3. The same card may not be used twice in the same meld, nor in any two melds of the same class unless the second is higher-scoring than the first. Thus, **K-Q** of trumps may be melded for 40 and **A-J-10** added for 150, but if **A-K-Q-J-10** are melded first the marriage may no longer be counted, nor may another king or queen be added to make a marriage.

It should be noted that there are two identical cards of each suit and rank, and though one of them has been used in a meld, the other may be used in an identical meld composed, however, entirely of cards not used in the first meld.

Values of Tricks. Each ace taken in on a trick counts 11; each ten, 10; each king, 4; each queen, 3; each jack, 2. The winner of the last trick counts 10. Nines count nothing in tricks.

A simplified count is commonly used to speed up the scoring. Each ace and ten are counted as 10 points; kings and queens are 5 points each. Jacks and nines have no value. The winner of the last trick is awarded 10 points. The total count should come to 250 points.

The Dix. After winning a trick, a player may exchange the trump nine for the trump card (or for a nine previously exchanged for it), taking the trump card into his hand and leaving the nine there, and counting 10 points. If dealer turns the nine as a trump card, he scores 10 immediately.

THE PLAY

Non-dealer leads to the first trick, and dealer plays a card to the lead, the two cards constituting a trick; thereafter the winner of each trick leads next. The card led loses the trick to a higher card of the same suit, or to a trump if the lead was not a trump; but otherwise wins.

After each of the first twelve tricks, each player draws a card face down from the stock, non-dealer drawing first. After the twelfth trick, the winner must show the card he draws, while the loser takes the trump card or the dix exchanged for it.

In the first twelve tricks, it is not necessary to follow suit to the card led, nor is the choice of plays in any way restricted. After the stock is exhausted, the last twelve tricks are played and it is necessary to follow suit to the card led if able to do so; to win the trick if possible when a trump is led; and to trump if possible when unable to follow suit to a lead of any other suit. Except for these restrictions, any card may be played.

SCORING

Use of Chips. Each player may be supplied with a stack of chips, and as he scores points he removes chips from the stack. If each deal counts as a separate game, the player who in the course of the deal has removed the greatest number of chips is the winner, scoring 1 point. If game is 1,000 points, each player is originally supplied with chips of 1,000 points in value, and the first player to get rid of all his chips is the winner of the game.

The most common way to keep score is with pencil and paper. Whenever a meld is made, the points for it are written down on the score pad immediately.

Count of Cards. The points for cards won in tricks are not scored until the last trick has been played. The winner of the last trick counts the points he has won in cards and adds 10 for last trick. If his opponent disputes the count, his opponent's tricks are also counted. The total of points must be 250. Scores are always entered in even tens, and a fraction of six points or less does not count. A fraction of seven points or more counts as a full ten.

Declaring Out. At any point in the game, a player who believes he has scored 1,000 points, including melds and cards won to that point, may declare himself out. Play ceases and his cards are counted and their total added to his previous score. If he has 1,000 points, he wins the game. If he has less than 1,000 points, he loses the game.

When the game is more than 1,000 points, as explained below, a player may declare himself out if he believes he has enough points for game.

Inconclusive Game. If neither player declares himself out, and at the end of the play each player has 1,000 points or more, the game is undecided and becomes 1,250. Play continues until one player reaches 1,250, or declares himself out at 1,250 under the rule given above. If the game is undecided at 1,250, the winning total becomes 1,500; if undecided at 1,500, it becomes a game of 1,750; and so on. Whatever the number of points required for game, a player may declare himself out at any time he claims to have reached that total.

IRREGULARITIES

Misdeal. A misdeal does not lose the deal. If the dealer exposes one of his opponent's cards in dealing, the opponent may demand a new deal or may let the deal stand. If either player was dealt too many or too few cards, either player may call for a new deal before he has led or played to the first trick; thereafter, it stands and is corrected as described below. When there is a new deal, there is a new shuffle and a new cut.

Exposed Card in Stock. If dealer exposes more than one card in turning the trump card, the cards exposed are shuffled in with the stock, non-dealer may cut, and a trump card is then turned. If at any later point a card is found exposed in the stock, dealer shuffles the stock (except for the trump card or the dix exchanged for it), non-dealer cuts and play is resumed.

Exposed Card. If a player carelessly drops a card, or exposes it in any way except in legally leading or playing, he may restore it to his hand without penalty.

Played Card. A card is considered played when the player detaches it from his hand with apparent intent to play it and releases it on the table. A card once played may not be withdrawn, except by direction of the opponent as explained in the next paragraph.

Lead Out of Turn. The opponent may treat it as a regular lead and play to it, or may require that it be withdrawn and restored to the hand of the player who led it.

Wrong Number of Cards. A player with the wrong number of cards may not meld until he has corrected his number of cards and then won a trick. If he has too few cards, he draws enough cards to restore his hand to the proper number; if he has too many cards, he does not draw until, at the end of any trick, his hand has been reduced to eleven cards.

Drawing Out of Turn. When a player draws out of turn, his opponent may let the draw stand as regular, but in that case it does not change the lead to the next trick; or may demand the card illegally drawn, in which case the offender must show the card he next draws from the stock.

Drawing More Than One Card. If a player draws more than one card at a turn, he keeps the top card but must show it, and each other card he drew, to his opponent. Each card illegally drawn must be then replaced on top of the stock.

Stock Incorrect. If at any time it is found that the number of cards in the stock is odd when it should be even, both hands being correct, and the pack being correct, play continues. When only two cards remain in the stock, the player whose turn it is to draw may elect to take the trump card or the other. If he takes the trump card, the other is then exposed. The rejected card is in either case dead and does not count.

Revoke. A player who, during the last twelve tricks, fails to observe the rules regarding following suit, trumping and winning a trump trick, has revoked. If each deal is a game, he loses the game. When game is 1,000 points, the offender may score nothing for cards; but play continues to determine the winner of last trick and the number of points taken in cards by the non-offender.

Error in Scoring. A player may correct, or demand correction of, an erroneous score at any time before he leads or plays to the next trick; thereafter it stands.

STRATEGY

Melding. The play of the first twelve tricks is planned with two objectives in mind: melding, and building up the strongest possible hand for the final twelve tricks. Counting cards taken in tricks during this period count as much as when they are taken later, of course, but nevertheless are not one of the principal considerations in play. Melding is far more important than winning counting tricks immediately or later. It is desirable to take the opponent's lead of a ten with an ace, because it counts 21 points; but the prospect of using that ace later to count 100 aces is so much more important that it is usually wise to save the ace. When it becomes apparent that 100 aces can no longer be melded, then the ace cannot be put to better use than to win an opponent's lead of the ten. In the opening stages, each player tries desperately to hold cards which he may turn into melds by future draws from the stock. Therefore, holding a "safe" flush or 100 aces, early in the play, it is well to delay melding them so as not to discourage the opponent from holding cards he may be saving for an identical meld. Such a meld is safe, however, only when it is obtained early enough so that there is fairly sure to be a later opportunity to meld it even though the opponent may try to prevent it by leading cards which cannot be taken without breaking up the meld.

Until about half the stock has been drawn, a player holding a flush should first meld his royal marriage, scoring 40, and add the remaining cards for the flush on a later turn. After half the stock is gone, it is safer to meld the flush unless, of course, the player holds two aces or two tens of trumps and cannot be prevented from winning a future trick without disturbing his flush. He must at all times keep in mind the danger that if he melds the royal marriage he will not thereafter win a trick which will entitle him to meld the flush. He must also count at all times the probable winning tricks (which means opportunities to meld) he will still have. It may be well to forget about a marriage if the hand holds 80 kings, 60 queens or anything better.

The Early Play. Leads should usually be made from the longest suit; the opponent is least likely to be able to cover such a card without breaking up a possible meld. Discards made to relinquish an unwanted trick should not be made from the longest suit, as that should be saved for leading; a discard of a nine, and sometimes a jack, from a shorter suit, is preferable. If the opponent leads ♡**9** on the first trick and you hold:

♠ **10 K Q 9 9**   ♡ **A J**   ◇ **K 9**   ♣ **A K 9**

Hearts being trumps, either ◇**9** or ♣**9** is a better discard than one of the space nines. Since you are long in spades, the opponent is probably short; whenever you get in, you will wish to lead a spade, and you should save all available spades for that purpose so long as you can discard any other worthless or nearly worthless card (such as a jack, or a melded queen).

It is essential to keep track of cases in which duplicate cards are unavailable to the opponent—either because both of them have been played, or both are in your own hand, or one has been played and the other is in your own hand—because melds involving those cards are closed to the opponent. As the stock is depleted, it is advisable to try to prevent the opponents from winning tricks if there are valuable melds still open to him, but if it is apparent that there is nothing of value he can meld, one may safely disregard all but the higher scoring tricks and devote the rest of his attention to building up a good playing hand for the last twelve tricks.

Play of a Hopeless Hand. Occasionally a hand is so poor that it offers very little hope of building up melds. When playing a game of 1,000 points, it is wise to devote one's attention to winning as many points in the play as possible. Aces should be taken, particularly when the opponent leads a ten. Tens should be used for winning tricks when a king or queen is led. Such aces and tens, if held, may not win tricks in the later play because the opponent may void his hand of those suits; and it is unnecessary to save them for later trick-winning possibilities if there is nothing to meld anyway.

When each deal is a separate game, it is better to save cards which may turn into melds, even though miraculous draws from the stock will be required. It is almost impossible to win a single hand on cards won in the play alone.

64-card Pinochle

The most serious players of two-hand Pinochle usually play with a 64-card pack consisting of two 32-card packs mixed together. The game is exactly the same as the one previously described, except that each player receives 16 cards, four at a time, in the deal; the seven of trumps is the dix; nines, eights and sevens do not have any value when won in tricks.

Three-hand Pinochle

The 64-card pack is used, and the rotation is to the left. Each player is dealt twelve cards. Each plays to every trick, and when identical cards are played the one played first outranks the other. Only the winner of the trick may meld, then all three draw from the stock, the winner first. Each player keeps a separate score, and the first to win 1,000 wins the game. Other rules are as in two-hand Pinochle. This game has been supplanted by Auction Pinochle.

Partnership Pinochle

PLAYERS

Four play, in two partnerships, each player facing his partner and having an opponent at each side.

CARDS

The pack of 48 cards, as described on page 329, with the cards in each suit ranking ace (high), **10, K, Q, J, 9**.

PRELIMINARIES

A pack is spread on the table and each player draws a card, but not one of the four cards at either end of the pack. The players drawing the two highest cards play as partners against the other two. There is no rank of suits, and if two players draw cards of the same rank they draw again to determine which of the two is higher.

Any player may shuffle the cards, the dealer having the right to shuffle last. The player at dealer's right must cut the pack.

DEALING

The dealer distributes the cards in rotation, beginning with the player at his left, three at a time face down, until he comes to the last three cards; of these, he gives himself the two top cards and turns up the last, which was the bottom card of the pack. This is the *trump card*. This card, and every other card of its suit, is a trump.

Exchange for the Trump Card. If the trump card is a nine, dealer's side scores 10 points. If it is any other card, each player in turn, beginning with the player at dealer's left, may exchange the nine of trumps for the trump card. The trump card, or the card exchanged for it, then becomes part of the dealer's hand.

MELDING

Each player then places on the table his melds, as follows:

SEQUENCES

A - K - Q - J - 10 of trump (flush)	150
Double flush	1,500
K - Q of trump (royal flush)	40
K - Q of any other suit (Marriage)	20

GROUPS

♠**A** - ♡**A** - ◇**A** - ♣**A** (100 aces)	100
All 8 aces	1,000
♠**K** - ♡**K** - ◇**K** - ♣**K** (80 kings)	80
All 8 kings	800
♠**Q** - ♡**Q** - ◇**Q** - ♣**Q** (60 queens)	60
All 8 queens	600
♠**J** - ♡**J** - ◇**J** - ♣**J** (40 jacks)	40
All 8 jacks	400

SPECIAL

♠**Q** - ◇**J** (pinochle)	40
Double pinochle	300
9 of trumps (*dix*, pronouned deece)	10

A player holding a dix scores for it whether or not he exchanges it for the trump card. Dealer does not score for the dix exchanged for the trump card. The same card may be used as part of melds under different headings, but may not be used in two melds under the same heading.

A side loses the melds of both its members unless either member wins a trick during the play of the cards. Winning a trick is said to make the melds "official."

THE PLAY

When all melds have been shown, each player restores the cards to his hand and play begins. Eldest hand leads to the first trick; he may lead any card. Each player in turn thereafter must play a card to the trick, and must observe the following rules: If holding a card of the suit led, he must follow suit; having no card of the suit led, but having a trump, he must play a trump but need not try to win the trick; if the card led was a trump, each player in turn must try to win the trick by playing a higher trump than any previously played to that trick, if he has one. If unable to play according to these rules, a player may play any card.

The four cards so played constitute a trick. A trick is won by the highest-ranking card of the suit led; or, if it contains a trump, by the highest trump it contains. A member of the side winning the trick gathers it in and turns it down in front of him. The winner of each trick leads to the next. (Some play that each player must try to win every trick, whether or not a trump was led. This is not, however, a natural rule of games of the Pinochle family, and reduces the opportunities for the exercise of skill in the play.)

When the rules require a player to try to win a trick, he must do so even when the highest card previously played was his partner's.

Values of Cards. When the play is completed, each side counts 10 points for each ace or ten it won in a trick, and 5 points for each king or queen it won in a trick. Jacks and nines have no scoring value. The side winning the last trick scores 10. (Some further simplify the count by making all aces, tens and kings count 10 each and no other cards count anything. Some, however, use the original Pinochle count of 11 for each ace, 10 for each ten, 4 for each king, 3 for each queen, and 2 for each jack.) The total score by cards, including last trick, is 250.

SCORING

Only two scores are kept, one for each side, and all points scored by either partner on one side are entered together. Game is 1,000, and is won by the first side to reach that figure; if at the end of the play of a hand each side has 1,000 or more, game becomes 1,250; and if both sides pass 1,250 on the same hand, game becomes 1,500, and so on.

Declaring Out. A player may declare his side out (that is, claim sufficient points to win the game, whether it is 1,000, 1,250, or a higher figure) at any point during the play. When such a claim is made, play ceases and the points of the claiming side are counted. If, including tricks won up to the time of the claim, it has at least the number of points claimed, it wins the game even though the other side has more points; if it does not have enough points, it loses the game.

A side may not claim the game before the play of the cards begins, for it must win a trick to make its melds official.

IRREGULARITIES

New Deal. If any rule governing the shuffle, cut or deal has been omitted or disregarded, a player who has not looked at his hand may demand a new deal at any time before the last card is dealt; thereafter, the deal stands.

If more than one card is exposed in dealing, there must be a new deal.

If dealer neglects to turn the trump card, either opponent may call for a new deal. If no new deal is demanded, a trump card is drawn, face down, from the dealer's cards before melding begins.

When there is a new deal, it is by the same dealer.

Wrong Number of Cards. If one player has too many cards and another too few, and if it is discovered before these players have looked at their hands, the player with too few cards draws the extra cards from the player with too many. If the irregularity is not discovered before the players have looked at their hands, they proceed to meld, after which the player with too few cards draws the excess from the unmelded cards of the player with too many.

If it is discovered, after the play of the cards has begun, that any player has an incorrect number of cards, play continues unless it is found that the pack is incorrect; the side of the player with the incorrect hand may not score any points for cards in that deal, but does not necessarily lose its melds; a player with too few cards does not play to the last trick, while any card remaining in the hand of a player after the last trick is dead.

Incorrect Pack. If the pack is discovered to be incorrect or imperfect, play ceases, and no points either for cards or for melds score in that deal, but the results of previous deals are not affected.

Revoke. If a player fails to follow suit, trump, or play over on a trump lead, when able, his side may not score anything for cards in that deal, but does not necessarily lose its melds.

Exposed Card. If a player illegally exposes a card, he must leave it on the table and play it at his first legal opportunity to do so; and either opponent may call a lead from the offender's partner the next time it is his turn to lead. (Many, however, penalize an exposed card as a revoke.)

Lead or Play Out of Turn. The penalty is the same as for an exposed card.

Error in Count or Scoring. A player is entitled to the full value of any melds he shows on the table, even if he announces their value incorrectly, but no correction may be made after the final score of the deal has been agreed upon by both sides and entered on the score sheet (or settled in chips). The same rule is followed when a player overstates the value of his melds or of cards won in play.

Partnership Auction Pinochle

This is the same game as Partnership Pinochle, except that no trump card is turned. Each player in turn may make one bid, or may pass. Eldest hand bids first. The lowest possible bid is 100, and each bid must at least overcall the last previous bid. Bids must be in multiples of 10 points.

The highest bidder names the trump, after which melding and play proceed as in Partnership Pinochle, except that the high bidder leads to the first trick.

Scoring. The non-bidding side always scores whatever it makes in melds and cards. The bidding side scores whatever it makes, provided this is at least as much as it bid; if it makes less than it bid, the entire amount of the bid is subtracted from its score, which may give it a net minus score. **Game** is 1,000 points, as in Partnership Pinochle, but the score of the bidding side is always counted first and if it equals or passes 1,000 it wins the game even though its opponent's score, if it were counted, would be more. There is no declaring out.

Irregularities are the same as in Partnership Pinochle, except for the revoke penalty, which is: If a player corrects his revoke before he or his partner has led or played to the next trick, play continues but if the offender was an opponent of the bidding side, the contract cannot be defeated; if the offender was a member of the bidding side, the bidding side may not score but is not set back if it fulfills its contract. If the revoke is not corrected in time, the penalty is as in Partnership Pinochle. An insufficient bid, or a bid out of turn, counts as a pass.

Partnership Auction Pinochle, Continuous Bidding

This game differs from Partnership Auction Pinochle only in that each player may continue to overbid the last previous bid until he has passed, after which he may not reenter the auction.

Partnership Auction Pinochle with a Widow

Only eleven cards are dealt to each player, three at a time on the first three rounds and two at a time on the last round; the four other cards are placed face down in the center of the table. There is bidding as in Partnership Auction Pinochle (either with one bid to each player, or with continuous bidding, as the players prefer). The highest bidder picks up the widow, takes one card for himself, and gives one card to each of the other players, without showing the cards. Melding and play then proceed as in Partnership Auction Pinochle.

Six-hand Partnership Pinochle

Three play as partners against the other three. Members of the opposing sides are seated alternately, so that each player has an opponent at his right and at his left. Two 48-card Pinochle packs are mixed together to make a 96-card pack, of which each player receives sixteen cards, dealt four at a time.

The rules of either Partnership Pinochle or Partnership Auction Pinochle, in any variant, may be followed; but it is customary to add the following bonus melds to the table shown on page 352:

Two kings and two queens of same suit	300
Three kings and three queens of same suit	600
Four kings and four queens of same suit	1200
Triple pinochle	600
Quadruple pinochle	1200
12 aces	2000
12 kings	1600
12 queens	1200
12 jacks	800
Triple royal sequence	3000
15 of same denomination, as 15 aces, etc.	3000

Eight-hand Partnership Pinochle is the same as the six-hand game except that only twelve cards are dealt to each player, three at a time.

Double-pack Pinochle

PLAYERS

Four, two against two as partners.

CARDS

80 cards, four each of **A**, **10**, **K**, **Q**, **J** (the cards ranking in that order) in each suit. Mix two regular Pinochle packs together, discarding all nines.

PRELIMINARIES

The draw for partners, the shuffle and the cut are as in Partnership Pinochle (page 351).

DEALING

All the cards are dealt out, no more than 5 and no fewer than 4 cards at a time, so that each player holds 20 cards.

BIDDING

(a) Beginning with the player at dealer's left, each player in turn must make a bid, announce a meld, or pass. Having once passed, a player may not reenter the auction.

(b) The minimum bid is 500. Each bid must be higher than any previous bid. Bids are in multiples of 10 points. When a player bids, he may announce that he has a trump sequence, or a long trump suit, but may not name a suit, may not say that he has more than one strong suit, and may give no information about his playing strength.

(c) A player in turn may announce a meld in points; he may have more than he announces. Before any player has bid, a player announcing a trump sequence or long suit is deemed to have bid 500, but announcement of a meld in points does not constitute a bid. After a bid has been made, any announcement constitutes an overcall of 10 points for each 100 points (or fraction thereof) of meld announced. (Thus: over a bid of 500, announcing a meld of 140 constitutes a bid of 520.)

(d) If no one bids in the first round, the hands are thrown in and the next player deals.

VARIATION

Only bids and passes are allowed, no announcement of melds or long suits.

MELDING

The high bidder names the trump before melding begins. (If he does not, the first card he melds, or the bottom card—the one touching the table—of several cards melded at once, fixes the trump suit.) All players then meld, according to the following values:

SEQUENCES

A - **K** - **Q** - **J** - **10** of trumps (flush)	150
K - **Q** of trumps (royal marriage)	40
K - **Q** of any other suit (marriage)	20

(No extra score for duplicated sequences;
e.g., double flush counts 300.)

GROUPS

♠**A** - ♡**A** - ◇**A** - ♣**A** (100 aces)	100
Double aces	1000
Triple aces	1500
♠**K** - ♡**K** - ◇**K** - ♣**K** (80 kings)	80
Double kings	800
Triple kings	1200
♠**Q** - ♡**Q** - ◇**Q** - ♣ **Q** (60 queens)	60
Double queens	600
Triple queens	900
♠**J** - ♡**J** - ◇**J** - ♣**J** (40 jacks)	40
Double jacks	400
Triple jacks	600

(A quadruple group counts as two doubles;
e.g., sixteen aces count 2000.)

SPECIAL

♠**Q** - ◇**J** (pinochle)	40
Double pinochle	300
Triple pinochle	450
Quadruple pinochle	3000

Each partner melds separately; the melds of partners may not be combined.

A side's meld does not count unless it wins at least one scoring card in the play.

THE PLAY

The high bidder leads, and the play follows the rules of Partnership Pinochle (page 351). A player must follow suit if able, play over if a trump is led, and trump if unable to follow suit. Of duplicate cards, the one played first ranks higher.

SCORING

Cards won in tricks count 10 each for aces, tens, and kings; nothing for queens and jacks. (Some count aces and tens 10 each, kings and queens 5 each, jacks 0.) Last trick counts 20. The total score in cards is 500.

If the bidding side, in melds and cards, makes at least the amount of its bid, it scores whatever it makes; if it makes less than it bid, the amount of the bid is subtracted from its score. The non-bidding side in any case scores whatever it makes.

Game is 3,550 and the score of the bidding side is counted first.

IRREGULARITIES

Follow the rules of Partnership Pinochle for Misdeal and Incorrect Hand (pages 353–54); except that any player may demand a new deal if two players have incorrect hands and have looked at their hands.

Revoke. A revoke may be corrected (by withdrawing such cards as are necessary) until the revoking side has led or played to the next trick. If it is too late for correction: the bidding side is set back the amount of its meld. Its opponents score their meld. No points are scored for cards.

Illegal Information. During the bidding, if a player names his suit, or says he has two suits, or gives any other illegal information, the opponents may call it a misdeal.

Wipe-Off

This is Double-pack Pinochle with the proviso that a side must score 200 or more points in cards to count either its meld or its cards.

Three-hand Double-pack Pinochle

There are two methods of dealing:

(a) 25 cards to each player and 5 to a widow; the high bidder must announce the trump *before* seeing the widow.

(b) 26 cards to each player and 2 to a widow; the high bidder may announce the trump *after* seeing the widow.

Game is 4,550. The minimum bid is 500, and if the first two pass, dealer must bid 500. There are no announcements of melds or suits in the bidding. Each player melds, and must win a scoring trick to make his meld count. The high bidder gets the widow cards and must discard that many before picking up his meld; his discard counts for him, but he must still win a trick to score his meld. Any irregularity in discarding is a revoke.

The high bidder may concede defeat before leading, in which case each opponent scores his meld plus 100, while the bidder is set back the amount of his bid.

Firehouse Pinochle

This is Partnership Auction Pinochle with Continuous Bidding (page 355) with the following special rules: The minimum bid is 200. The high bidder must meld a marriage (or flush) in the trump suit he names. (Therefore no player may bid without a marriage.) Eldest hand bids first and leads first. Game is 1,000 and the score of the bidding side is counted first.

Check Pinochle

Four play, in two partnerships, and preliminaries are as in Partnership Pinochle, but it is usual to have two packs of cards, so that one may be shuffled while the other is in play.

Each player receives twelve cards, three at a time, but no trump card is turned.

Bidding. Eldest hand bids first, or may pass. The lowest bid is 200. To bid, a player must have a marriage, except the dealer ("man in the seat"), who must bid 200 if the other three pass and who may bid more than 200 if he has a marriage. Until he has passed, a player may continue to bid in turn provided he overcalls the last previous bid, bids being in multiples of 10 points. The high bidder names the trump suit.

Melding and Play are as in Partnership Pinochle, with the high bidder always leading to the first trick.

Scoring. If the high bidder's side scores at least the amount of its bid, it scores all it makes; if it does not equal its bid, the amount of the bid is subtracted from its score. Its opponents always score all they make. It is not necessary to win a trick for melds to count.

An odd 5 points won in cards does not count.

Game is 1,000 points, with the score of the bidding side counted first. When a game is ended, there is a new draw for partners and a new game is begun.

Settlement is made in *checks* (chips), and when a side or either member of that side earns a check award, each member of that side immediately collects the appropriate number of checks from the opponent at his right. Checks are paid in accordance with the following table:

FOR MELDING

Round trip	4 checks
Flush	2 checks
100 aces	2 checks
80 kings, 60 queens or	
40 jacks	1 check
Double pinochle	1 check

IF CONTRACT IS	FOR MAKING CONTRACT	FOR DEFEATING OPPONENTS' CONTRACT
200–240	2 checks	4 checks
250–290	4 checks	8 checks
300–340	7 checks	14 checks
350–390	10 checks	20 checks
400–440	13 checks	26 checks
	and 3 additional	and 6 additional
	checks for each	checks for each
	series of 50 points	series of 50 points

For slam (winning all 12 tricks) 4 checks
For winning game 7 checks, plus

1 check for each 100 points, or fraction thereof, by which winners' score exceed losers'; and if the losers have a net minus score, the winners receive an additional 4 checks.

IRREGULARITIES

Misdeal. There must be a new deal by the same dealer with the same pack if any card is faced in dealing, or if it is discovered at any time before the cards have been mixed that one player has been dealt too many cards and another too few. If one hand is short a card and the other hands are correct, and if the missing card can be found, the deal stands; the card is restored to the player's hand, and is considered to have been part of his hand all the time, and he is liable for any revoke due to failure to play it.

Exposed Card. Any card exposed, except in legally melding or playing it, becomes a penalty card and must be left face up on the table and played at the holder's first legal opportunity. If a player has more than one penalty card, the opponent at his left shall decide which he shall lead or play first. If a player exposes a card before the auction closes, his partner is barred from bidding thereafter.

Bid Out of Turn. A bid out of turn is void; the correct player in turn may bid, and the offender's partner must pass thereafter.

However, if the offender's partner is the dealer, and all other players pass, the dealer must still bid 200.

Pass Out of Turn. Both the offender and his partner must pass thereafter, except that nothing relieves the dealer of his obligation to bid 200 if all other players pass.

Bidding Without a Marriage. This must be discovered before the play begins, due to the offender's failure to meld his marriage; and his opponents, after consultation, may either (a) call off the deal; (b) decide to play the hand themselves at any bid they made during the auction; (c) force the offending side to play the hand at the highest bid it made during the auction.

Revoke. If a player fails to play as required by law, he may correct his revoke at any time before he or his partner has led or played to the next trick, and the only penalty is that the card played in error becomes a penalty card. After either member of the offending side has led or played to the next trick, the revoke is established and when it is discovered play ceases; the offending side keeps all tricks it won prior to the revoke trick, but all other cards go to its opponents.

OTHER GAMES OF THE BÉZIQUE FAMILY

Besides the perennially popular Pinochle, the Bézique family includes Bézique itself, Piquet, which dates back to the fifteenth century, Klaberjass or Klob, and Sixty-Six. The original game of Bézique was invented in the 1860s and is seldom played today; however, some of its derivatives, such as Rubicon Bézique and Chinese or Six-pack Bézique, are still enjoyed.

Bézique

PLAYERS

Two play in most variants. There are Bézique games for three and for four, but they are far less popular.

CARDS

The pack of 64 cards, consisting of two 32-card packs shuffled together. The cards in each suit rank ace (high), **10, K, Q, J, 9, 8, 7.**

PRELIMINARIES

Each lifts a portion of the shuffled deck and shows the bottom card; if the cards are of the same rank they cut again, and continue to do so until the lower of the two cards determines the first dealer. Either player may shuffle, the dealer last. Non-dealer must cut the pack.

DEALING

Each player receives eight cards, dealt face down, three at a time, then two at a time, then three at a time, non-dealer receiving cards first.

The next card is turned face up as the trump card; every card of its suit becomes a trump. The remaining cards are placed face down so as partly to cover the trump card, and becomes the *stock*.

OBJECT OF THE GAME

The first player to amass 1,500 points wins the game. Each ace or ten (called a *brisque*) taken in a trick counts 10; dealer counts 10 if he turns a seven as the trump card, and thereafter either player, upon winning a trick, may exchange a seven of trumps for the trump card, or merely show a seven of trumps and score 10 for it; and winning the last trick counts 10.

Declarations. Upon winning a trick, a player may place on the table in front of him any of the following combinations of cards and score for them as indicated:

Marriage (**K**, **Q** of the same suit),
    in trumps 40
    in any other suit 20
Sequence (**A**, **K**, **Q**, **J**, **10** of trumps) 250
Bézique (**♠Q** and **◇J**) 40
Double bézique 500
Any four aces 100
Any four kings 80
Any four queens 60
Any four jacks 40

THE PLAY

Non-dealer leads first. He may lead any card and (until the stock is exhausted) his opponent may play any card. The card led and the card played by opponent constitute a trick and are won by the higher card of the suit led, or by the higher trump; when identical cards are played to the same trick, the one led wins the trick. The winner of each trick leads to the next, after declaring and after drawing from the stock to restore his hand to eight cards, the winner drawing first and his opponent next.

A declaration is made after winning a trick and before drawing, by placing the required combination of cards face up on the table. Once declared, the cards remain there until the stock is exhausted, unless the holder wishes to lead or play them, which he may do as though they were in his hand. Only one declaration may be scored in each turn.

A card may be used in different declarations, but not twice in the same declaration; for example, **♠Q** may be used in a marriage, sequence, bézique and four queens; but if four queens have been declared and one of them has been played, another queen may not be added for the same score. Four different queens would be required.

A king or queen of trumps which has been declared in a sequence may not be later declared in a royal marriage.

Bézique may be declared as 40, and a second bézique added for 500, but if double bézique is declared at the same time it counts only 500.

The Final Play. When only one face-down card and the trump card remain in the stock, there may be no more declaring. The winner of the next trick takes the face-down card, and his opponent the trump card; each picks up all declared cards he has on the table, and the last eight tricks are played. In this play, a player is required to follow suit to the card led, and to win the trick, if he is able to do so.

GAME

If one player reaches 1,500 points before his opponent has 1,500 points, he wins the game. If both players reach or pass 1,500 points on the same deal, the higher score wins; if they have exactly the same score, they continue play and game becomes 2,000.

IRREGULARITIES

Incorrect Deal. It may be rectified by mutual agreement, but either player may demand a new deal. There must be a new deal if either player is dealt too many cards and it is discovered before a card is played.

Incorrect Hand. If it is discovered at any time that each player has too many cards, there must be a new deal. If it is discovered, after both players have drawn from the stock, that a player has too few cards, play continues and the player with fewer cards than his opponent cannot win the last trick. If one player has too many cards and his opponent the right number, the opponent may either demand a new deal or permit the offender to rectify his hand by not drawing.

Exposed Card. Non-dealer may demand a new deal if one of his cards is exposed in dealing. There must be a new deal if a card of the pack is found exposed before a play has been made; if discovered thereafter, the card is shuffled into the stock.

Illegal draw. If a player, in drawing, sees a card he is not entitled to, his opponent at his next draw may look at the two top cards of the stock and select either.

Lead Out of Turn. It must be withdrawn on demand, but may not be withdrawn without permission.

Odd Number of Cards in Stock. The last card of the stock (trump card) is dead.

Error in Declaring. If a player shows and scores for cards which do not in fact constitute the declaration claimed, the score stands unless the opponent demands correction before playing to the next trick.

Error in Scoring. May be corrected at any time before the final score for the deal has been agreed.

Revoke. If a player fails to play according to law after the stock is exhausted, his opponent scores last trick.

Imperfect Pack. If it is discovered before the final score has been agreed, the deal is void; except that if the imperfection consists of a shortage due to cards found on the floor or in the vicinity of the table, the deal stands and such cards are dead.

Bézique Without a Trump

No trump card is turned; the first marriage declared establishes the trump suit. Otherwise Bézique is played, as described above.

Bézique for Three

Use a 96-card pack composed of three 32-card packs shuffled together. The turn to deal, to play to a trick, and to draw from the stock, rotates to the left, the player at dealer's left leading to the first trick. All three play to each trick, and the winner draws first from the stock and leads to the next trick. Triple bézique counts 1,500, and a player having already counted for double bézique may add the third and count 1,500. Game is 2,000.

Bézique for Four

Use a 128-card pack (four 32-card packs shuffled together). Each plays for himself, as in the three-hand game, and game is 2,000. If a player holds all four béziques he counts only 1,500 for having the fourth, the same as for the third.

Partnership Play. When four play, they may play as partners, two against two. The winner of each trick may either make a declaration or pass that privilege to his partner. Partners may not consult on which shall declare. A player may combine one or more cards from his own hand with declared cards exposed on the table by his partner to form a declaration, except that he cannot use any card of his partner's in a declaration his partner would not be entitled to make.

Rubicon Bézique

Two play, using a 128-card pack (four 32-card packs shuffled together). Each player receives nine cards in the deal, three at a time. No trump is turned, the first marriage declared establishing the trump suit.

Carte Blanche. When a player's hand as originally dealt to him does not contain any face card (that is, is composed entirely of sevens, eights, nines and aces), he may show it and declare *carte blanche*, scoring 50. Each time thereafter that he draws he may show the card drawn and if it is not a face card he may score 50 again. Once he has drawn a face card, he may not thereafter declare carte blanche.

Declarations. In addition to the declarations listed on page 363, a sequence in a non-trump suit (called a "back door") counts 150; triple bézique counts 1,500, quadruple bézique counts 4,500. There is no count for the seven of trumps.

Method of Declaring. The same cards may be used more than once in the same declaration, as follows: A declaration is made and scored exactly as in Bézique. If a card of that declaration is then played from the table, and the player (after winning a trick) adds a card which restores the declaration, he counts in full for the declaration again. *Example:* A player declares four queens and scores 60. He plays one of the queens. Later he wins a trick and puts down one other queen from his hand. He scores 60 again. Another example: Diamonds are trumps. A player declares **A-K-Q-J-10** of diamonds and scores 250. He plays the queen of diamonds, and later replaces it with another queen of diamonds, scoring 250 again.

To score a declaration, all cards required for the declaration must be on the table at the time the score is made.

The Play. It is customary to let the cards played accumulate in the center until any brisque is played, whereupon the winner of that trick takes in all the cards. Brisques are not counted except to determine whether or not there is a rubicon, explained below. The last trick counts 50 for the winner.

Rubicon. Each deal is a game. If the loser (player with the lower score for that deal) has less than 1,000 points, including his brisques, he is *rubiconned;* the winner receives all the points scored by both players, plus 320 for all the brisques.

Bonus for winning game is 500; or, in a rubicon, 1,000.

The rubicon counts even though the winner himself has less than 1,000 points; if he wins by 800 to 600, his margin for the game is 2700 points (2720 in all, but in settlement fractions of 100 are disregarded).

Six-pack Bézique, or Chinese Bézique

This is a development of Rubicon Bézique and is the most popular form of the game. The rules are similar to those of Rubicon Bézique, with the following exceptions:

Six 32-card packs are used, shuffled together to make a pack of 192 cards. It does not matter if the packs used differ in back design or color.

Twelve cards are dealt to each player.

Declarations. In addition to all the declarations used in Rubicon Bézique, four aces of trumps count 1,000; four tens of trumps, 900; four kings of trumps, 800; four queens of trumps, 600; four jacks of trumps, 400.

Carte blanche counts 250.

Winning the last trick counts 250.

Brisques are never counted, and all the played cards accumulate in the center, untouched.

Players are permitted to look back at played cards, and to count the stock to see how many cards remain.

The Béziques. Most people play that cards making up the bézique vary in accordance with the trump suit: ♠**Q** and ◇**J** are bézique if spades are trump; ◇**Q** and ♠**J** if diamonds are trump; ♡**Q** and ♣**J** if hearts are trump; ♣**Q** and ♡**J** if clubs are trump. However, there are many who play with ♠**Q** and ◇**J** always serving as bézique.

Dealer's Pack. Before dealing, dealer lifts off a portion of the total pack, trying to lift off exactly 24 cards. Without touching or counting the cards lifted off, his opponent tries to guess how many he took. If dealer took exactly 24 cards he scores 250; if his opponent guessed the number correctly, his opponent scores 150.

Game. Each deal is a game, the winner adding 1,000 to his score. If the loser has failed to reach 3,000, he is rubiconned and the winner scores the total of both players. Fractions of 100 points are disregarded except to determine the winner of the game.

Eight-pack Bézique

The eight-pack game is exactly the same as the six-pack game except that eight 32-card packs are used, and each player originally receives fifteen cards. Quintuple bézique counts 9,000, five trump aces count 2,000, five trump tens 1,800, five trump kings 1,600, five trump queens 1,200 and five trump jacks 800. The loser is rubiconned if he fails to reach 5,000.

Bézique Strategy

The declarations are relatively far more important in Bézique than are, for example, the melds in Pinochle; and the brisques are less important than are the cards won in Pinochle, for the brisques in any one deal total only 160 points. Last trick, which counts 10, is always worth playing for, but melding opportunities should not be sacrificed to build up a hand which will win last trick. The principal thought throughout is to retain chances for declarations.

Thus each player tries desperately to hold on to cards which figure in declarations, at least until he is reasonably sure that he will not be able to complete the declaration (either because the cards essential to it have been played or because there will not be time to score it even if it is completed). Of opportunities to declare, that of scoring 40 for jacks is abandoned first because four cards are required to get 40 points; that of making a marriage in a non-trump suit is abandoned next; the chance of getting 100 for aces or a sequence in trumps is not abandoned until the bitter end.

In addition to the necessity for forming combinations which can be declared, there is the necessity for winning a trick before a declaration can be made. Thus, cards which do not figure in declarations but are of value for winning tricks are carefully retained until the opportunity to use them will pay best; such cards are tens and the low trumps, sevens, eights and nines.

Of all cards, those which form béziques are held to the end, queens of spades and jacks of diamonds. The score of 40 for single bézique is sufficiently desirable in itself, since for two cards 40 points are declared; no declaration short of aces and sequence is more lucrative. Beyond this, there is the opportunity to score 500 for double bézique, and while this occurs rarely it is so valuable a score that it is kept in mind so long as a possibility remains that it will be made.

Leads are designed to force the opponents to relinquish cards which might form declarations in the future if retained. Plays are designed to retain the opportunities for future declarations; to retain maximum length in some non-trump suit in which the opponent may be forced by future leads; to retain trump length both for trick-winning power once declarations are ready to be put down, and secondarily for playing strength at the end in the effort to win last trick; and finally, to save cards which offer hope of declarations. If the opponent leads a card to which you have no desirable play, and if there is a choice between throwing to him one of three kings or a ten which will give him an immediate brisque, the ten can more easily be spared.

Rubicon Bézique, Six-pack Bézique. Here the early effort is to establish the trump suit. It is of extreme value to establish the trump suit, especially in that form of Six-pack Bézique in which it is the queen of trumps which will determine what cards form bézique. The big scores for double, triple and quadruple bézique are the prime objectives of the game.

Therefore, the first player who has a marriage should hasten to declare it and establish its suit as trump. Even if that player has five or six strong cards in another suit, but lacking a marriage; and only the two cards constituting the marriage in the suit in which he can declare, he should hasten to win a trick by any means, declare the marriage, and make that suit trump. This may prevent the opponent from establishing as trump a suit in which he has a readymade sequence; it at least assures the player who establishes trump of having at least a start toward a bézique and a sequence; and it limits the risk, in that there is at least one bézique-forming queen which the opponent can never draw. Since there is no trump suit until the marriage is declared, the player holding it should make sure of winning the trick by leading an ace if he has one; lacking an ace he should lead a ten on the hope (which more often than not is justified) that his opponent will not have an ace of the same suit; and if it is his opponent's lead, he should win the trick at almost any cost. Perhaps the one exception to this is that if you hold ♡**K Q ♣J**, which constitute a marriage and a bézique if you can make hearts trump; and if your opponent leads ♣**9**, which you can win only by playing ♣**J**, it is not well to sacrifice ♣**J** to win the trick. The opponent probably does not yet have a marriage or he would have led a higher card. You can take a chance that he will not draw a marriage on this turn, or that you can win the next trick and declare the heart marriage even if he does.

In any form of Bézique, it is wise at times to postpone a declaration when the exposure of its cards would tell the opponent that he need not continue to hope for certain declarations. This is particularly true of declaring four jacks if they include one or two of the bézique jacks.

When the stock nears exhaustion, one should plan his play carefully to assure himself of scoring the more important declarations he has, and of preventing his opponent from scoring such declarations as he might have or be able to make; the strategy here is identical with that of Two-hand Pinochle, which see.

Sixty-six

PLAYERS

The principal game is for two. There are variants for three and four, but they are not much played.

CARDS

A pack of 24 cards is used, from the ace to the nine in each suit, ranking **A** (high), **10**, **K**, **Q**, **J**, **9**.

PRELIMINARIES

Each lifts a portion from a shuffled pack and shows the bottom card; if these cards are of the same rank they cut again. The player cutting the higher card deals first, shuffles the pack and has it cut by his opponent, and gives six cards to each player, three at a time, beginning with his opponent.

The next card is turned up as the trump card, and every card of its suit becomes a trump. The undealt cards are placed face down so as partly to cover the trump card, and become the *stock*.

THE PLAY

Non-dealer leads to the first trick. A trick consists of the card led and a card played to it by the opponent. Until the stock is *closed* (see below) it is not necessary to follow suit. The card led wins the trick unless a higher card of the same suit, or a trump on the lead of any other suit, is played by the opponent; in the latter case the opponent wins the trick. The winner of each trick leads to the next, after each player has drawn a card from the stock, the winner drawing first.

Exchange for the Trump Card. Provided he has won any previous trick, a player holding the nine of trumps may exchange it for the trump card. However, if the last card drawn face down from the stock is the nine of trumps, it may not be exchanged for the trump card, which the opponent draws.

Melding. A player holding king and queen of the same suit may count 40 for them (if in trumps) and 20 in any other suit, by showing both cards and then leading one of them.

Closing. The game is *closed* when the last card of the stock has been drawn; or either player, when it is his turn to lead, may declare the game closed before leading. This is done by turning down the trump card, and thereafter no cards will be drawn from the stock and the play will be ended when the six cards in each player's hand have been played out. In the play after the stock is closed, each player must follow suit to the card led if possible. Closing does not affect the right of the players to score for marriages.

SCORING

In addition to the count for marriages, each player counts for cards won in tricks as follows: ace, 11; ten, 10; king, 4; queen, 3; jack, 2. The player winning the last trick scores 10 unless the stock was closed by either player, in which case last trick does not score. The total number of points in play by cards is 130, whereupon the game is won by the first player to reach 66.

Game Points. The game is won by the first player to score 7 game points. A player who scores 66 in any deal before his opponent does gets 1 game point. If his opponent has scored fewer than 33 points *(schneider)*, the winner scores 2 game points; if his opponent has not won a trick *(schwarz)*, the winner scores 3 game points.

A player who closes must win 66 or more points or his opponent scores 2 game points; if his opponent had not won a trick at the time of closing, but wins, he scores 3 game points.

If a deal is played out, and neither player has 66 points, or both players have 66 points and neither has declared himself out, neither scores for that deal but 1 game point is carried over and added to the score of the winner of the next deal.

Declaring Out. A player may at any time declare that he has won 66 points or more. At that point play ends and if the claim is justified, the claimant wins; but if he has not 66 points, his opponent scores 2 game points.

If the score for a marriage will put a player over 66, he may simply show the marriage and declare himself out; it is not necessary in this case to lead a card from the marriage.

IRREGULARITIES

Misdeal. The same dealer redeals. If one of non-dealer's cards is exposed in the deal, he may call for a new deal provided he has not looked at any other card dealt to him. If a card is exposed in the stock, or if either player has too few cards, non-dealer may either have it rectified or demand a new deal until he has played to the first trick; thereafter the deal stands. There must be a new deal if before both players have played to the first trick it is discovered that either has too many cards.

Incorrect Hand. A player with too many cards plays without drawing; a player with too few cards draws enough from the top of the stock to correct his hand.

Exposed Card. A card carelessly dropped or led out of turn may be restored to the hand without penalty, except that the opponent may choose to treat a lead out of turn as regular. If a player illegally exposes or sees a card in drawing, he must show his opponent the card he drew.

Incorrect Stock. If three cards remain in the stock at the end, the winner of the trick draws the top card and the loser may choose between the other two, without looking at the face-down card; the card rejected is dead.

Revoke. (failure to follow suit, when able, after the stock is closed or exhausted). Any cards won or scores made after the revoke occurs count for the offender's opponent.

Sixty-six for Three Players

The turn to deal rotates and the dealer takes no cards, but scores as many points as the winner of the deal scores. In the case of a tie game, dealer scores the 1 point and the other players nothing. Game is still 7 points, but the dealer cannot win the game; on his deal he may score no points which put him above 6.

Klaberjass

A much publicized game, "Klob" is less known and played in the United States than in European countries. It has several forms: R. F. Foster reported one of these as a popular Swiss game, named Jass, in 1916; the French call a slightly different form Belotte; Americans have for years played still another variant, calling it Clabber. In the thirties the game had a brief popularity in the New York bridge clubs, where its name was confused with that of the dissimilar Hungarian game Kalabriás, under which name it has frequently appeared in books and magazine articles. Various spellings of its name, in addition to those previously cited, are: Clob, Clab, Klab, Kalaber.

PLAYERS
Two.

CARDS

The pack of 32. In the trump suit, the cards rank: **J** (high), **9**, **A**, **10**, **K**, **Q**, **8**, **7**. The jack of trumps is called *jasz* (pronounced yahss), and the nine is *menel'*. In plain suits the rank is: **A** (high), **10**, **K**, **Q**, **J**, **9**, **8**, **7**.

PRELIMINARIES

Cards are drawn and the lower card deals first. If equal cards are drawn both players must draw again. Dealer has the right to shuffle last, and the other cuts. The cut must leave at least three cards in each packet.

DEALING

Cards are dealt three at a time, beginning with non-dealer. Each player receives six cards. The thirteenth card is turned face up and placed partly underneath the stock.

BIDDING

The turned card, often called *the trump*, proposes the trump suit for the deal. Non-dealer begins the bidding by making one of three declarations: *take*, *schmeiss*, or *pass*. To take is to accept the suit of the turn-up for trump. To schmeiss is to propose that the deal be abandoned; if the opponent refuses, the turn-up is trump and the schmeisser (not the refuser) is the *maker* of trump. Refusal of a schmeiss is therefore usually expressed by saying "Take it."

If non-dealer passes, dealer has the option of the same three declarations. If he too passes, there is a second round of bidding. Non-dealer may schmeiss, pass, or name a suit for trump (other than that rejected). If he declares schmeiss, and dealer refuses, non-dealer must name the trump suit and become the maker. If non-dealer passes again to commence the second round, dealer may name the trump or abandon the deal.

The player who voluntarily or by compulsion (refusal of his schmeiss) accepts the turn-up or names the trump suit is the trump *maker*.

ADDED CARDS

The trump suit being fixed, dealer gives three more cards to each hand from the top of the stock. The bottom card of the stock is then exposed and placed face down on top. The exposed card does not enter into the play.

SEQUENCES

The hands being filled to nine cards each, any *sequences* held are declared. A sequence is a group of three or more cards of adjacent rank in the same suit, with the rank (for this purpose alone) fixed as: **A** (high), **K**, **Q**,

J, 10, 9, 8, 7. A sequence of three cards counts 20; of four or more cards, 50.

Only the player holding the best sequence may score it. One worth 50 beats any worth 20; one of higher rank beats one of lower rank when both count the same; of two equal in the foregoing respects, a trump sequence beats a plain, and if both are plain, non-dealer's beats dealer's. There is no tie.

If non-dealer holds a sequence, he announces "Fifty" or "Twenty." Dealer responds "Good," "Not good," or "How high?" and so on, pursuing inquiry only until he has received enough information to pronounce "Good" or "Not good." The object of making comparison in this way is to protect the non-scorer from divulging anything more than is necessary to settle who may score. The hand entitled to score for best sequence may also score any additional sequences he holds. All sequences that score must be exposed to the opponent, after the first trick is complete.

THE PLAY

Non-dealer makes the opening lead. The other hand must follow suit to a lead, if able, and if unable must play a trump if able. On a trump lead the other must play higher if able. A trick is won by the higher trump, or by the higher card of the suit led. The winner of a trick leads next.

The combination of the king and queen of trumps in one hand is *bella*, and it scores 20 if the holder announces "Bella" on playing the second of the two cards. (The holder may keep silent, and avert the extra loss, if he sees that he must go *bete*.)

If the turn-up card is accepted for trump, either player holding the seven of trumps (called *dix*, pronounced deece) may exchange it for the turn-up, provided that he does so before playing to the first trick. There is not, as in Pinochle, a score for the dix. The object of the change is solely to obtain a higher trump.

The Objects in Play are to win cards of counting value, and to win the last trick, which counts 10.

SCORING

The high cards have *point values* as follows:

Jasz (trump jack)	20
Menel (trump nine)	14
Each ace	11
Each ten	10
Each king	4
Each queen	3
Each other jack	2

After the play, each player totals what he has scored in sequences, bella, last trick, and points for cards won in tricks. If the trump maker has the higher total, both players score their totals in the running record. If the totals are the same, the maker scores nothing, while non-maker scores his own total. If the non-maker has the higher total, he scores both his own and the maker's total. In the last case, the maker is said to go *bete*.

The first to reach 500 points wins the game. The usual practice is to play out every deal, and if both players reach 500 in the same deal the higher total wins. But by agreement "counting out" during the play may be allowed as in Pinochle, (page 347).

IRREGULARITIES

Misdeal. Before bidding, non-dealer may either require a new deal or require correction if any of his cards is exposed in dealing, if a card is exposed in the pack, or if either player has the wrong number of cards. When correction is demanded, a hand with too many cards is offered face down to the opponent, who draws the excess; a short hand is supplied from the top of the pack.

Incorrect Hand, if discovered after the bidding has started, must be corrected.

A Revoke is: failure to follow suit, to trump, or to play over on a trump lead, when required by law to do so; announcing a meld not actually held (as, for example, by saying "how high?" when not holding a sequence of equal value); having too few or too many cards after leading or playing to the first trick. The non-offender receives all points for melds and cards on that deal.

A player may not exchange the dix for the turned-up card after playing to the first trick, nor score 20 for the trump king-queen if he does not announce "Bella."

STRATEGY

The average number of points counted by both players together per deal is about 110. To undertake the obligation of trump maker, a player therefore should expect to score about 60 points with his nine cards, or 40 with his first six cards. Naturally, this requirement is elastic. Many hands with which experienced players will take total only 35 in the usual method of valuation.

In reckoning the probable value of a hand of six cards, count jasz, menel, bella, and any sequence at face value. To the argument that menel *might* fall to the jasz, or that a sequence might not be good, the answer is that these exceptions are so rare as to be of no weight in the average. Also, count any ace as 11. But the combination ace-ten cannot be counted for 21 unless the hand is strong enough to lead trumps. In other circumstances, count the ten as 5, for a half chance to make. A ten not accompanied by the ace is problematical.

The principal reason for taking, or for naming a suit as trump, is to promote a jack to jasz. (The calculation of the average deal takes account of the fact that the jasz is almost always in play.) The jasz alone is often enough in trumps to warrant taking. For example, if ♠8 is turned, non-dealer should take with

♠ J   ♡ A 8   ♣ A 8   ◇ 8

Lacking jasz, the hand should hold at least two trumps for a take, together with a solid expectation of winning 40. Here it is dangerous to shade, for the opponent may hold or receive the jasz. Similarly, a trump length of three or more cards is alluring, yet without jasz or menel must reckon with the chance that the opponent holds one or both.

For example, suppose that ♠8 is turned. Non-dealer should take, holding

♠ 9 Q   ♡ A 10   ♣ A 7   ◇ 8

but should pass holding

♠ 10 Q 7   ♡ A   ♣ J   ◇ A

With this hand the idea is of course to name clubs if dealer also passes.

The effect of the schmeiss is to deprive the opponent of opportunity to name the trump suit. It thus is a powerful weapon for the dealer in the event non-dealer commences by passing. The typical hand for a schmeiss is one not strong enough to take, but better prepared to play the turned trump than any other. For example, if ♠8 is turned and non-dealer passes, dealer should schmeiss holding

♠ Q 7   ♡ A 8   ♣ 10 8   ◇ 8

He would rather take his chance as the forced maker in spades than hear non-dealer name another suit.

Non-dealer should never schmeiss on the first round. If he is not strong enough to take, he stands only to lose by the schmeiss. Dealer, having a hand with which he would take, becoming the maker, could then refuse and force non-dealer to become the maker. Thus dealer would stand to win all the points in play instead of only those won by himself. But non-dealer can use the schmeiss to advantage on the second round, to prevent dealer from naming his own suit.

The rules of play leave little choice except as to leads.

The jasz should usually be led at first opportunity. Rarely can it do better service than pull an adverse trump. A trump suit of exceptional length—four or more—may be led as a measure of protection for side cards. Aside from these two cases, early trump leads are generally useless or unsafe or both. Non-dealer, whoever is the maker, usually does best to open his longest suit. With no suit of four or more cards, it is better to lead from sequences, or from worthless cards, than to lead away from tenaces, as **A K**, **10 Q**.

ILLUSTRATIVE DEAL

The turn-up is the ♠ **8**. Non-dealer holds the hand given on page 375 as worth a take. After the additional cards are dealt, the hands are:

Non-dealer ♠ **J** ♡ **A Q 8** ♣ **A 10 8** ◇ **J 8**

Dealer ♠ **10 K 7** ♡ **K 9** ♣ **J** ◇ **A 10 Q**

In the play below, the card underlined wins the trick, and the card below it is the lead to the next.

TRICK	NON-DEALER	DEALER	MAKER WINS	OPPONENT WINS
1	♠ J	♠ 7	20	
2	♣ A	♣ J	13	
3	♣ 10	♠ 10		20
4	◇ 8	◇ A		11
5	◇ J	◇ 10		12
6	♡ 8	◇ Q		3
7	♡ A	♡ K	15	
8	♣ 8	♠ K		4
9	♡ Q	♡ 9	13	
			61	50

Note that the non-dealer has made, although the only valuable card he drew, the ♣**10,** proved a liability.

Jass

PLAYERS

Two, three or four. See below for special rules in which two-hand differs from the game with three or four. In four-hand, each plays for himself.

CARDS

The pack of 36, made by adding the sixes to the Klaberjass pack. The rank of cards is the same, 6 low. The trump jack is *jass*, the trump nine is *nell*.

DEALING

All the cards are dealt out, three at a time, into four hands of nine cards each. The last card, which goes to the dealer, is turned up and fixes the trump suit for the deal. (The trump cannot be changed.)

In three-hand, the extra hand is a widow which may be taken by any player in exchange for his original nine cards. First option on the widow goes to the dealer, and thence in turn to his left.

MELDING

Before the opening lead, any player holding the trump six may exchange it for the turned card held by dealer. The exchange may be made with the discarded hand, if dealer has taken the widow. But a player who holds the trump six in his original hand, and then discards it for the widow, loses the chance to obtain the turn-up.

Any hand, after playing to the first trick, may *meld* (place on the table) any of the following combinations:

Four jacks	200
Four aces, tens, kings or queens	100
Five-card sequence	100
Four-card sequence	50
Three-card sequence	20
King and queen of trumps	20

As in Klaberjass, a sequence is a group of cards of the same suit and adjacent in rank, the rank for this purpose only being: **A** (high), **K, Q, J, 10, 9, 8, 7, 6**.

A player loses the score of his melds if he fails to win at least one trick in the play.

THE PLAY

Eldest hand makes the opening lead. The rules of play are as in Klaberjass, except that jass may renege—it need not be played when a trump is called for, if the hand has no other trump. The objects of play are also the same. Last trick counts 5.

SCORING

Each player scores whatever he has made in melds (if he has won a trick), in *point values* of high cards won in tricks (see Klaberjass), and last trick. The first to reach 1,000 wins a game. It is usual to allow "counting out" during the play.

Two-hand Jass

This is played like two-hand Pinochle. Each hand receives nine cards at the outset, and after each trick the winner draws the top card of the stock, his opponent taking the next. Until the stock is exhausted, there is no obligation to follow suit to a lead. Melds may be made, only one per turn, by the winner of a trick before leading to the next. After the stock is exhausted, it is obligatory to win any lead if able, as well as to follow suit, except that jass may renege.

MISCELLA-
NEOUS
CARD
GAMES

SKAT

Skat is one of the few games of whose origin we can be perfectly certain. (See the introduction to Schafkopf.) It was first played at Altenburg in 1811. The first use of the word *skat* as the name of the game appears to be in an article in the *Osterländer Blättern*, 1818. As the name of the widow, *skat* was borrowed from Tarok, an Italian game still widely-played. The term derives from the Italian *scartare*, to discard, or *scatola*, a place of safe-keeping. In early books, the term is spelled *scat*, as in Tarok.

After the accretion of various features derived from Schafkopf, Tarok, and Calabrasella, the new game Skat was codified at a congress of more than a thousand players convened at Altenburg on August 7, 1886. Skat leagues were formed in Germany, and the American Skat League was founded at a congress held in St. Louis, Mo., on January, 1898. The principal variants or modifications that have come into being since the first codification are the elimination of the lowest game *frage*, the introduction of *passt mir nicht*, and the displacement of tournee by *Räuber Skat*.

PLAYERS

Skat is a game for three. More than three frequently participate in a game, but only three hands are dealt. With four, the dealer does not give cards to himself. With five, dealer omits himself and the third player at his left.

CARDS

The pack of 32 is used, **A** to **7** inclusive.

The suits rank: clubs (high), spades, hearts, diamonds.

The four jacks are always the four highest trumps, ranking: ♣**J** (high), ♠**J**, ♡**J**, ◇**J**. The remaining cards of the trump suit rank: **A** (high), **10**, **K, Q, 9, 8, 7**. This is also the rank of the cards in each plain suit. When there is no trump suit, the cards in every suit rank: **A** (high), **K, Q, J, 10, 9, 8, 7**.

PRELIMINARIES

If cards are drawn for seats and deal, lowest card has first choice. Between cards of the same rank, the rank of suits decides.

In many circles the custom is for one player to be appointed scorekeeper and for the player at his left to deal first.

Dealer has the right to shuffle last. The cut must leave not less than three cards in each packet.

DEALING

Each active player is dealt ten cards, in rounds of 3–4–3. After the first round of the deal, two cards are dealt face down for the skat (widow).

DESIGNATION OF PLAYERS

In order to left of the dealer, the three active players are known as Vorhand (forehand or leader), Mittelhand (middlehand), and Hinterhand (endhand or rearhand). The highest bidder, who names the game to be played, is called the Player, and the other two, who combine against him, are the opponents.

BIDDING

The first declaration is made by Mittelhand, for the reason that Vorhand is entitled to name the game unless another player makes a bid which he is unwilling to meet. If Mittelhand wishes to try for the contract, he makes his bid, and Vorhand may either pass or say "I stay," "I retain," "Yes," or similar words indicating that he is willing to name a game of value at least as great as Mittelhand's bid. When Vorhand stays, Mittelhand may increase his bid, until one of the two eventually drops out. The survivor then settles in the same way with Hinterhand for the right to name the game.

If Mittelhand and Hinterhand both pass without a bid, Vorhand MUST name the game, but in this case he has the additional option of naming *ramsch*.

A bid is for a number of points, without reference to any intended game or trump suit. With the elimination of Simple Game, formerly played, the lowest possible bid is 10. Mittelhand, if he bids at all, starts with 10 and increases no more than he has to in order to force out Vorhand, if he can do so at all. The rules state that each bid must be for a number of points that can be scored in some game, e.g., 10 and 12 are possible, but 11 is not. The bidding is very largely in even numbers.

THE GAMES

The high bidder, now the Player, forthwith names the game he will play. As Skat is played today, there are fifteen different "games" from which a bidder may choose. They are classed in four categories, as follows:

Tournee. A card is turned up from the skat to determine the trump suit.

Solo. The Player names the trump suit, and plays without use of the skat.

Grand. Only the four jacks are trumps. In some grand declarations, the skat is used; in others, it is not.

Null. There are no trumps. The skat is not used.

Full explanation of the games is given in succeeding sections. The *base value* of all games is given in the following table.

TRUMPS	$\Diamond$	$\heartsuit$	♠	♣	JACKS TRUMPS		NO TRUMPS	
Tournee	5	6	7	8	Tournee grand	12	Simple null	20
Solo	9	10	11	12	Gucki grand	16	Null ouvert	40
					Solo grand	20		
					Grand ouvert	24		
					Ramsch	10		

Tournee. If the Player names *tournee*, he looks at the top card of the skat without showing it to the opponents. Should it satisfy him as the trump suit, he faces it, then picks up both skat cards without showing the second. Then he discards two cards face down to restore his hand to ten cards. His discards are counted toward his point score after the play.

If dissatisfied with the first card of the skat, the Player may place it in his hand without showing it. The second card is then faced and fixes the trump suit. Rejection of the first card is called *passt mir nicht*—"It does not suit me"—or, in the American laws for Skat, Second Turn. If the Player loses the game at Second Turn, his loss is double what he would have won had he made it. In Second Turn, as when the first card is accepted, the Player picks up both skat cards and discards two.

If either card turned up from the skat is a jack, the Player may either accept its suit as trump or declare grand—in which only jacks are trumps. The game *grand tournee* thus can arise only through the accident that a jack is turned after a declaration of simple tournee.

Solo. The Player forthwith names the trump suit, or declares grand (jacks trumps), and play begins. The skat cards are not touched, but are added to the Player's tricks at the end of the hand.

Gucki Grand. This is also called *guckser*. The Player declares grand (jacks trumps) and forthwith picks up the skat. (Taking both cards of the skat, without any remark, is equivalent to declaring gucki grand.) He discards two cards, which will be added to his tricks after the play. When a gucki contract is not fulfilled, the loss is doubled.

Simple Null. There are no trumps, and the cards rank as at Bridge. The Player contracts to win no tricks at all. The skat is set aside untouched.

Ouvert. In declaring ouvert (open), the Player contracts to play with his entire hand exposed to inspection by the opponents. Such exposure must be made before the opening lead. Declaration of ouvert may be made only at grand or null, and precludes use of the skat.

Null Ouvert is the same as simple null with the addition that the Player faces his hand.

Grand Ouvert is a contract to win *all the tricks*, with jacks trumps and the Player's hand exposed.

Ramsch. This game may be declared only by Vorhand, if he so chooses, when Mittelhand and Hinterhand pass without a bid. Jacks are trumps, and the object of play is to take in as few points as possible. Each hand plays for himself. The skat is not touched, but is added to the last trick and goes to the winner thereof.

THE PLAY

Vorhand invariably makes the opening lead. He may lead any card. A lead calls upon the other two hands to follow suit if able. When unable to follow suit, a player may play any card in his hand, trumping or discarding as he pleases. Each trick is won by the highest card of the suit led, or by the highest trump if it contains one. The winner of a trick leads to the next.

Except at ramsch, the Player is opposed by the two others acting in partnership. Their object is to prevent the Player from taking the number of points or tricks called for by his game.

The object in play is described below.

Point Values of Cards. The higher cards have a *point value* as follows:

Each ace	11	Each queen	3
Each ten	10	Each jack	2
Each king	4	(No count for 9, 8, 7)	

There are 30 points in each suit, and 120 in the pack.

In any tournee, solo, or gucki, the Player contracts to win in tricks (plus the skat or his discards) cards that total at least 61 points. If he fails, he loses the value of his game (doubled in case of gucki and Second Turn). If he succeeds, and also if the value of his game is at least equal to his bid, he wins this value.

Schneider and Schwarz. If the Player wins 91 or more points in play, he is said to *schneider* the opponents and the value of his game is increased. If he wins all the tricks, he wins a further increase for *schwarz.*

If the Player fails to win 31 points in play, he is schneidered and his loss is increased. Similarly he loses more if he suffers schwarz, by taking no trick.

Prediction. The Player may, in an effort to increase his winnings, announce that he will win schneider or schwarz. Such announcement is permitted only in solo games (skat not used), and it must be made before the opening lead. Of course he loses if he does not fulfill the prediction.

Matadors. The Player who holds the ♣J is said to be *"with"* so many *matadors*—as many top trumps as he holds in unbroken sequence from the ♣J down. For example, a top holding of ♣J, ♠J, ◇J is "with two," because the ♡J is missing.

The Player who lacks the ♣J is said to be "without" as many matadors as there are trumps outstanding higher than his highest. For example, if his highest trump is ◇J, the Player is "without three."

COMPUTING THE GAME

The *value of a game* is the product of two factors, of which the first is the base value of the game as given in the table under *The Games*. The second factor is the sum of all applicable *multipliers*, and can never be less than 2. (Hence 10 is the lowest possible bid.)

The first item reckoned under the multipliers is the number of matadors that the Player is either "with" or "without." This number can vary from 1 to 11. The usual way of reckoning is then to count "1 for game," plus any increments for schneider, schwarz, and prediction. A less confusing way is: To the number of matadors ("with" or "without"), add *one* item below.

Player makes "game" (61–90 points in play)	1
Schneider made, without prediction (91 up by Player; 90 up by opponents)	2
Schwarz made (by either side) without prediction	3
Schneider announced and made by Player	3
Schneider announced, schwarz made, by Player	4
Schwarz announced and made by Player	5

At either null game, no multipliers apply. The base values are invariable. Therefore a player is not permitted to declare simple null if he has bid more than 20, nor null ouvert if he has bid more than 40.

Ramsch has a special scoring as described below.

Here are some example hands showing the computation of their value.

♣ J ◇ J
♣
♠ A 10 K 9
♡ 8
◇ A 10 Q

A good spade solo. Value, 2 × 11 = 22.

♣ J ♠ J
♣ A
♠ 10 7
♡ A 10
◇ 10 Q 8

Playable as diamond solo. Value, $3 \times 9 = 27$.
But preferable bid is gucki grand. Value, $3 \times 16 = 48$.

$$\diamond \ \textbf{J}$$
$$\clubsuit \ \textbf{Q 8}$$
$$\spadesuit \ \textbf{A 9}$$
$$\heartsuit \ \textbf{A 10 7}$$
$$\diamond \ \textbf{10 Q}$$

A risky tournee. Value if a heart is turned, $4 \times 6 = 24$.

SCORING

If the Player makes his contract, and if the value of his game is at least equal to his bid, he wins the full value.

If the Player fails to win the required number of points in play, he loses the value of his game. If the game was gucki grand or Second Turn in a tournee, the loss is doubled.

If the value of the Player's game is less than his bid, he is said to have *overbid* and he loses regardless of whether he wins the required number of points in play. The amount he loses is that multiple of the base value of his game which is the first higher than his bid. For example, a player bids 18 and plays a spade tournee; he makes game but not schneider and is found to be "without one." His game is worth only $2 \times 7 = 14$. He loses 21, the next multiple of 7 higher than 18. If the tournee was a Second Turn, his loss would be 42.

Ramsch has a special scoring. The player who gathers the least points in tricks wins 10, or 20 if he takes no tricks at all, and the others score nothing. If each player takes 40 points in tricks, Vorhand is deemed the winner and scores 10. If two players tie for low score, the one who did not take the last trick as between these two scores 10. If one player takes all the tricks, he loses 30 points and the others score nothing.

SETTLEMENT

The score kept for each player is the running net of his winnings and losses. Some or all of these nets can be minus.

At the end of a session, the final scores are added (algebraically) and divided by the number of players, to determine the average. Those who are minus pay out, and those who are plus collect.

For example, suppose the final scores to be

A	B	C	D	E
119	92	76	35	−12

The total is $322 - 12 = 310$. Dividing by 5 gives the average as plus 62. The differences from average are:

	A	B	C	D	E
	+57	+30	+14	−27	−74

If the scorer finds minus signs in the final scores confusing, he can eliminate them by adding to each score the numerical value of the lowest score. This step does not alter the final result. Thus:

	A	B	C	D	E
	119	92	76	35	−12
add	12	12	12	12	12
	131	104	88	47	0

Total, 370; average, 74.

net	+57	+30	+14	−27	−74

Strategy of Bidding

Solo. The minimum trump length normally required for a solo is five. Since there are eleven trumps, the Player should have enough so that more than 50% of the time he will have the longest trump holding in the three hands. With four trumps, there is too large a chance that an opponent will hold four or more trumps, so that such a hand should be declared a solo only if very strong in side cards.

With five trumps, the classic rule of thumb states that the player should have three side cards which are aces and tens (including at least one ace). In other words, he should have no more than two cards lower than ten in the side suits.

Experience shows that this minimum is needlessly high. Tournament players are satisfied with two side aces or a side ace and a ten (in a different suit) if the hand has some "plus" value, such as a king with the ace.

Each extra trump over five may be deemed to take the place of a side card in the minimum requirement, so that six trumps with a side ace "plus" is a minimum solo bid. But with a suit of extra length, as with all freaks, it is usually simpler to calculate directly what can be lost in the play. For example:

♡ J ◇ J
♣ A K Q 9
♠ —
♡ A 9 7
◇ 8

At a club solo this hand may lose two trump tricks, two hearts, and a diamond. Barring a bad trump break, it will be able to catch everything else. The loss may be 18 points in trumps (the ten and four jacks), 17 in hearts, and 21 in diamonds, a total of 56. The hand is certainly worth a bid. (There is of course a chance that on a heart trick won by an opponent the other will be able to smear the spade ace or ten. But this chance is more than offset by the chance that the Player will be able to discard one or two hearts on worthless tricks in spades and diamonds.)

Or count the hand from the point of view of what it can win. It should be able to take in at least the **A, K, Q** of clubs and **A** of hearts, for a total of 29. Game is then dependent on catching all the spade honors (28) plus any red card as good as a king.

With two suits of equal length, the weaker should be declared for trump. As example:

♣ **J**
♣ **A**
♡ **A 10 K 9**
♢ **10 9 8 7**

Barring bad breaks, the ace and ten of hearts will be made whatever the trump. But the diamond ten is much surer to make as a trump, by ruffing, than as a plain card. At heart solo the hand probably will not win any diamond tricks; at diamond solo it may get two or three ruffs.

Position of the Bidder. In an unfavorable position, a minimum hand usually should not be bid.

Tournee. The object in declaring tournee, in preference to solo, is twofold: (a) to obtain an additional trump card; (b) to be able to lay away some cards. As to (b), the advantage may be in saving a ten that otherwise might go to the opponents in play, or in getting rid of a short worthless holding.

The chance of buying a valuable card in the skat, as an ace or ten, is too slight for inclusion in evaluation of a hand. The odds against finding a helpful card in the skat are as follows:

ODDS AGAINST BUYING ONE CARD

When only one card will serve	10 to 1
When either of two cards will serve	5 to 1
When any of three cards will serve	3 to 1
When any of four cards will serve	2 to 1
When any of five cards will serve	3 to 2
When any of six cards will serve	even

But this is not the whole story. The buy of an ace is no help if neither skat card proves to be of a suit that the hand is prepared to play as trump. Gambling on the skat for a high card is really a two-card buy. Here are the chances.

ODDS AGAINST BUYING TWO CARDS

When any of three will serve	76 to 1
When any of four will serve	38 to 1
When any of five will serve	22 to 1
When any of six will serve	14 to 1
When any of seven will serve	10 to 1
When any of eight will serve	7 to 1
When any of nine will serve	5 to 1

The tournee is enough of a gamble as it is, since few hands are prepared to play any of the four suits as trump.

The general rule is that a hand must be ready to play any of three suits. The odds are favorable that both of the skat cards will not be of the fourth suit. If the normal requirement of five trumps for a playable suit is adhered to, the declaration of tournee is limited to two types of pattern:

(1) One jack, and three suits of three cards each. (2) Two jacks, and at least two cards in each of three suits.

With one of these classical patterns, the minimum strength may be less than for a solo bid, since the Player will have a chance to save a doubtful ten and to improve his pattern by discarding.

Here are some examples of tournees:

1. ♣ J	2. ♠ J ♡ J	3. ♣ J ◇ J
♣ 10 8 7	♣ A 8	♣ 7
♠ A 9 8	♠ 10 8	♠ A 10 8
♡ A 8 7	♡ A 7	♡ K 7
◇ ——	◇ 9 7	◇ A 8

Grand. A convenient rule for weighing the merits of a hand for a grand is to reckon each jack or ace as one, and position as Vorhand as one; grand should not be bid with less than 5 of these possible 9 points.

With only four trumps in play, the Player can rarely count on catching adverse aces and tens by ruffing. His game must be made largely by aces and tens in hand, plus whatever he can catch with them. Even a minimum hand is usually solid enough so that a direct count can be made of points that will be lost. For example,

♣ J ◇ J
♣ ——
♠ Q 7
♡ A 8
◇ A 10 K 9

Vorhand should declare solo grand in preference to diamond solo. Unless both other jacks are held by one opponent, Vorhand can cash seven tricks at once. On the last three, the opponents cannot possibly take in more than two aces, three tens, a king, and the ♠**Q**, for 59 points.

Change the ♡**A** for the ♡**10** and the solo grand will probably be beaten. But the hand would be worth a bid of Gucki grand, for then the ♡**10** could be laid away if the skat furnished no help in the suit.

Null. A bid to take no tricks is naturally possible only with a hand liberally supplied with low cards. Such a holding as **K–J–9–7** is unassailable, since it can always underplay any lead and remain with the lowest card of the suit. A holding of **10–7** doubleton is fairly safe, but **J 10 8** or any other combination of three or more cards lacking the **7** is risky. As there are only eight cards in each suit, one opponent must have less than three cards, and it is not uncommon to find one hand void. If the other opponent has the **7**, such a holding can be forced to win a trick with the **8**. Either other position is preferable to Vorhand for a null, since the lead is no advantage and may be a positive disadvantage.

Discarding

The advantages to be sought in discarding, after the Player has taken up the skat are (a) saving cards that might be lost in play, especially tens, (b) improving the pattern of the hand. For example,

♣ **J**
♣ **A Q 7**
♠ **A 9 8**
♡ ——
◇ **10 Q 9**

In skat: ♡ **7,** ♠ **Q**

At Second Turn in a tournee, spades become trumps. Player will of course discard ♡**7**. His other discard should be ◇**10**, which would be difficult to make in play. With ◇**10**, ♣**A** and ♠**A**, the Player need catch only the top hearts (**A, 10, K**) to make game.

♡ **J** ◇ **J**
♣ **A K**
♠ **K 8**
♡ **A 10**
◇ **K 9**

In skat: ♣ **Q,** ♡ **8**

The ♣**Q** is turned first and accepted for a club tournee. If the Player discards ♠**K** and ◇**K**, he can lose 21 points on the first round of each suit, or 42. Normal expectation is to lose at least 32 in these two tricks.

If the Player discards both cards of one suit, he stands to lose all 28 points in the other, but to win most of the points in the suit of which he is void. Obviously it is better to void the hand of one suit.

Strategy of Play

Says an old maxim: *Fordern ist die Seele des Spiels*, leading trumps is the soul of the play.

The only question with the Player is usually what trump to lead, when he does not hold solid tops. He must bear in mind that, the later a trump round won by an opponent, the greater is the chance that the other will be able to *smear* (discard a valuable card). For example,

♣ J   ♡ A 10 9 8

To start with ♣J will almost surely let an opponent win the third round. It is better to start with ♡8. If forced to trump to regain the lead, play ♡10. Then continue with ♡9 or ♣J according to how the trumps fell on the first round.

The lead of ♣J would be proper from this holding if the Player needs only to protect his own side cards from being trumped, to make game. If he can afford to let the opponents smear, he should be sure to get two trump rounds in before losing the lead.

With two or more jacks, there is rarely anything to be gained by failing to start with a jack, even from a minor tenace. For example,

♠ J   ◇ J   ♣ A 9 8

The plan is to lead both jacks, possibly losing both, but clearing the ace. If one opponent holds up a jack, perhaps in the hope of catching the Player's ace, the Player's chance of dropping the ten from the other opponent is increased. In fact, the opponents save their ten only if the distribution is right for them and if they find the right defense.

With four or less trumps (as may happen in an unlucky tournee), the Player usually is not strong enough to lead trumps, but must try to use his trumps for ruffing.

When only jacks are trumps, a jack is never led unless the play is absolutely safe, or unless the only chance is a desperate gamble. The hand on page 391 shows a safe lead of the ♣J, because if it does not drop both ♠J and ♡J the Player can force out the other by leading his diamonds. With

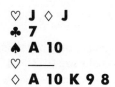

391

at a grand solo, the Player would be foolish to lead a jack. With both other jacks in one adverse hand, he would probably lose all the tricks. By starting his diamonds at once, he stays one trump longer than any opponent, who will have to ruff to gain the lead. The Player is thus sure of seven tricks against any possible break.

The Player is "in the middle" when the lead is made by opponent at his right. The effort of the opponents is naturally to put the Player in the middle as often as possible. The advantage of this position may be utilized in three ways: (a) to play through the Player's two- or three-card plain suit up to a guarded high card in third hand, so as to catch the Player's ten or clear third hand's ten; (b) force the Player to trump or let third hand win with ace or ten; (c) let third hand trump a valuable card forced from the Player.

When Mittelhand is the Player, Vorhand should usually open a long plain suit, in the effort to give Hinterhand immediate or eventual ruffs. When Hinterhand is the Player, Vorhand should usually open his shortest plain suit, to put himself in a position to over-ruff.

The opponents must be on the alert at all times for opportunities to smear, and also wary of traps that an experienced Player will lay to induce a smear on a trick he will win. An essential part of defense is attention to the fall of the cards, and the avoidance of false-carding, so that an opponent playing first or second to a trick may infer which side will win it. For example, in following suit with **9–8** play the **8**, not the **9**; in leading from **K–Q** lead the **K**, not the **Q**.

It goes without saying that each side must keep accurate count of the points taken in by at least its side, trick by trick. The governing factor throughout the play is the constant calculation of how the cards must lie.

ILLUSTRATIVE DEAL

In skat: ♣ **9**, ◇ **K**

Mittelhand bids for a heart solo, worth 2 × 10 = 20. But Vorhand stays on 20, having a club solo worth 2 × 12 = 24. Mittelhand might well pass and expect to defeat the Player, but instead buys the contract at 26 and declares gucki grand, worth $2 \times 16 = 32$. He finds no help in the skat, and indeed his best discard is these same two cards. His only chance is to find his hearts solid, but even that is not enough. Since he does not have the lead, his jacks may be forced out by club leads, ahead of the adverse jacks forced by his hearts. He then must hold his possible side entries; to bury the ♠10 would be suicidal. He can be fairly sure that Vorhand holds all missing aces and tens, for his stay at 20, so that at least his ♠10 is over the ♠A.

TRICK	V	M	H	TO PLAYER	TO OPPONENTS
1	♣ A	◇ J	♣ 7	13	
2	♡ 9	♡ A	♡ 7	11	
3	♡ J	♡ 10	♡ K		16
4	♣ Q	♠ J	♣ 8	5	
5	◇ 10	♡ Q	♣ J		15
6	♠ A	♠ 8	♠ 7		11
7	♣ 10	◇ 7	♠ Q		13
8	♣ K	♡ 8	♠ 9		4
9	♠ K	♠ 10			
10		◇ A		28	
				57	59
				skat 4	
				61	

Trick 4. The notion of letting Vorhand win his ♣Q K, saving ♠ J for the ♣10, is inviting but unsound. What is Mittelhand to discard? After ◇7 he can only let go a high heart or the guard to his ♠10. To let go even ◇7 at this stage risks warning the opponents that he is holding up a spade tenace.

Trick 5. The smear of ◇10 shows Hinterhand that Vorhand does not have ◇A.

Trick 6. Hinterhand may toy with the idea of leading a diamond, letting Mittelhand in at once but forcing him to lead away from his spades at the end. But there is no assurance that Mittelhand has any spades at all. He may have buried ♠10 and Vorhand may have ♠8.

Note that Mittelhand wins his game by reason of the buried ◇K. Had he held it, it would have gone to the opponents.

Seventh Prize. For a Tournee won against the greatest number of matadors.

(If two or more players have a game without an equal number of matadors, the rule stated at third prize shall govern.)

(In deciding the relative value of different Tournee plays, where there is a tie, the same rank as given in the case of Solo games applies, always considering Tournee as a separate class.

Räuber Skat

In the original game of Skat, the Player may not pick up the skat cards unless he is willing to let them fix the trump suit, or to declare only jacks trumps. The essential idea of the variant Räuber (*German:* pirate, brigand) is to let the Player pick up the skat and then name any game he chooses, after the manner of Pinochle. The differences from the original game, consequent of this principle, are given below.

THE GAMES

Any one of the four suits as trump; grand (only jacks trumps); null or nullo (no trump); ramsch or reject (a grand in which the object is not to win points).

All rules for ramsch are as in Skat. Any other game may be played either with use of the skat cards or without. Playing solo without the skat is called *handplay.* In handplay with a trump, the Player has the right to try for increased score by announcing that he will win *little slam* (same as schneider) or *grand slam* (same as schwarz). If he chooses to use the skat cards, the Player need not name the trump until he has seen them.

At nullo, the Player may try for increased score by playing *open* (same as ouvert), either with or without use of the skat. Nullo is a contract to lose all the tricks.

BASE VALUES

TRUMPS		NULLO		HANDPLAY	
◇	9	Simple	23	(open) 59	
♡	10	Open	46		
♠	11				
♣	12	Ramsch	10		
Jacks	20				

MULTIPLIERS

Following is the list of all possible multipliers.

Matadors	from 1 to 11
Game	1
Handplay	1
Little Slam	1
Big Slam	1
Announced Little Slam	1
Announced Big Slam	1

As in Skat, matadors are counted whenever there is a trump and "1 for game" is always counted (except ramsch).

The multipliers for slams are cumulative, that is, having earned any one of the four listed, the Player is entitled to all preceding it. For example, if he announces and makes little slam, he adds 3 for it to matadors and game.

SCORING

If the Player fails to make his game or his overbid, he loses the value of his game at handplay, or double the value if he has used the skat. The opponents may count slams, if made by them, but of course may not announce slams. If the Player picks up the skat and believes he cannot make game, he has the right to abandon his cards in order to save slam. When he does so he must name some game, so that the amount of his loss can be computed.

When the Player is found to have overbid, the value of his game is fixed at the multiple of the base value next higher than his bid. (As in Skat.) The value is then doubled if he has picked up the skat.

SCHAFKOPF

Schafkopf, or Sheepshead, is of Wendish origin and is believed to be at least 200 years old. According to a well-documented story, in 1811 a certain coachman traveling in the Sachsischen Erzebirges learned the game from the peasants of the region. On returning to his master, a resident of Altenburg, the coachman explained the game to him. The master, an enthusiastic card player, carried Schafkopf into the Tarok Club of the town, where it was soon a favorite. Among its early adherents was advocate F. F. Hempel, who had much to do with the addition of features borrowed from Tarok and Kalabriàs, through which the game of Skat was eventually evolved. In 1848 was published the first book on Skat, written by Professor J. F. L. Hempel, a cousin of the advocate.

While Schafkopf thus gave birth to the highly-codified Skat, the progenitor has continued to be played in many forms and has spread to many countries, without having achieved any standard set of rules. All that can be attempted by way of description of the game is to list the more prevalent variations as to number of players, cards, bidding, scoring, and so on.

PRELIMINARIES

Players. Three. In some variations four or more play. See page 399.

Cards. The pack of 32. All queens, jacks, and diamonds are permanent trumps, ranking: ♣Q (high), ♠Q, ♡Q, ◇Q, ♣J, ♠J, ♡J, ◇J, ◇A, **10, K, 9, 8, 7**.

In each plain suit the cards rank: **A** (high), **10, K, 9, 8, 7**.

Point values. The high cards have point values as follows:

Each ace counts	11	Each queen counts	3
Each ten	10	Each jack	2
Each king	4	(No count for lower cards.)	

Dealing. Each player receives ten cards, dealt in rounds of 3–4–3. After the first round of the deal, two cards are dealt face down on the table to form the *skat* or widow.

The Player. Vorhand (eldest hand) has first right to pick up the skat; then Mittelhand and Hinterhand in turn have the right to pick it up, if the preceding players have passed. The first to take the skat becomes the Player, and contracts to win at least 61 points by cards taken in tricks. If all three pass, the deal is played at *least*.

THE PLAY

When the skat has been picked up, the Player discards two cards face down. He is opposed in play by the other two.

The opening lead is invariably made by Vorhand. A lead calls upon each other hand to follow suit if able; if unable, the hand may play any card. A trick is won by the highest card of the suit led, or by the highest trump. The winner of a trick leads to the next.

SCORING

If the Player takes 61 to 90 points in tricks, he scores 2 *game points*. If he takes 91 or more, he scores 4 (making *schneider*); if he wins all the tricks (schwarz) he scores 6. The points in the Player's discard are counted for him at the end of the play.

If the Player takes only 31 to 60 points, he loses 2 game points. If he takes less than 31 he loses 4 (schneider), or, if he loses all the tricks (schwarz), he loses 6.

A running total of game points is kept for each player, and the first to reach 10 wins a game.

LEAST

When all three pass, the skat is set aside, but is added to the tricks of the player who wins the last trick. Vorhand makes the opening lead, and the rules of play are as usual. But the object is to win as few points in tricks as possible. Each plays for himself.

If every player takes a trick, the one with the least points scores 2 game points. If two tie for least, the one who did not take the last trick as between the two wins the 2 points. If each takes 40 points, dealer wins the 2 game points.

If one player takes no tricks, he scores 4 game points. If one player takes all the tricks, he loses 4 points, the others scoring nothing.

IRREGULARITIES

Follow the laws of Skat (page 381).

STRATEGY

There are 14 trumps, leaving only 16 plain cards in play. The chief requirement to pick up the skat is a long strong trump suit, about seven including four of the eight top trumps. With fewer trumps, or less top strength, the hand should hold one or two side aces. The odds are roughly 2 to 1 against picking up a trump in the skat. There are only 6 cards in each plain suit, so that **A–10** cannot be counted upon to win two tricks, unless the hand is strong enough to take out the adverse trumps first. When trumps are long and strong enough for a bid, tens are better out of the hand than in. Contrast the two example hands:

ILLUSTRATIVE DEAL

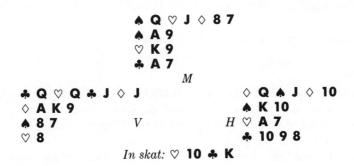

♠ Q ♡ J ◇ 8 7
♠ A 9
♡ K 9
♣ A 7

        M

♣ Q ♡ Q ♣ J ◇ J   ◇ Q ♠ J ◇ 10
◇ A K 9   ♠ K 10
♠ 8 7   V   H ♡ A 7
♡ 8   ♣ 10 9 8

In skat: ♡ **10** ♣ **K**

Vorhand picks up skat, having a strong suit of seven trumps. The skat cards are best discarded, so as to save ♡ **10** and void the hand of clubs. The play is as follows. The card that wins the trick is underlined; the card below it is the lead for the next trick.

TRICK	VORHAND	MITTEL-HAND	HINTER-HAND	OPPONENTS WIN	PLAYER WINS
1	◇ J	◇ 7	♠ J	4	
2	♡ 8	♡ K	♡ A	19	
3	♠ 7	♡ 9	♡ 7		
4	♠ 8	♠ A	♠ 10	40	
5	◇ A	♠ K	♠ 8		15
6	♣ J	◇ 8	◇ Q	45	
7	◇ K	♣ 7	♣ 9		19
8	♣ Q	♡ J	◇ 10		34
9	◇ 9	♠ Q	♣ 10	58	
10	♡ Q	♣ A	♣ 9		48
				discard	14
					62

The Player makes game.

Trick 1. The Player plans to lead jacks, so as to shut out ◇ **10**.

Trick 3. If the spade ace and ten were in the same hand, this discard would assure the player of catching one of them. The defense plays perfectly to make trouble.

Trick 6. If Mittelhand happened to put up ♠**Q**, Hinterhand could smear ◇ **10**. But then the Player's top trumps would drop the rest, and he would catch ♣**10** in compensation. The given play still leaves him a guess.

Trick 8. There being only three trumps out, Player sees that swinging ♣**Q** will win game if ◇**10** or ♠**Q** is blank, or if they are both in one hand.

Trick 9. Player's care in saving ◇**9** for a losing lead now pays dividends. Opponents win 13 on this trick, but still fall short of their 60.

Schafkopf Variations

Local variations are found in every phase of Schafkopf. A few of these are:

Players. Four players, in two partnerships, use the pack of 32 and deal out all the cards, each hand receiving eight. Five players, each for himself, use the pack of 40. Six players use two packs of 24 shuffled together, and play as two partnerships of three each, partners being seated alternately. Seven or eight players use two packs of 32 shuffled together.

Permanent Trumps. The four jacks only; or, the two black queens followed by the four jacks; or, the queens and jacks, with or without the addition of a suit named by competitive bidding.

The Player. The hand holding the highest trump announces it and becomes the Player; the hand holding the second-highest trump becomes Player's partner, but does not reveal his identity until he plays this card. Or, a hand holding the two highest trumps names an ace, and the holder thereof becomes his partner. Sometimes the hand holding highest trump may announce solo and play alone against all the rest.

In partnership play (four or six players), the players bid for the number of points over 60 that they will undertake to win in play, and the highest bidder takes the contract for his side.

No Contract. No player undertakes a contract. Every deal is played at cutthroat, each player trying to win as many tricks as he can. The cards have no point value. A player is debited 1 point for every trick less than two that he takes, or credited with 1 point for every trick over two.

Frog

This game has been known under a great variety of names—Tapp, Solo, Heart Solo, *sans prendre*, wurttembergischer Tarok, Bayerischer Tarock, Slough, Sluff. It probably was not derived directly from Tarok, but from Skat, which is based on Tarok. The name Frog is the anglicization of the German *frage*. In Tarok, Skat, and other three-hand games the Vorhand begins the bidding with "Ich frage!"—"I ask" (whether any wishes to bid against me for the right to name the trump or game). Frage came to mean the lowest-scoring game that could be played, as in Skat.

PRELIMINARIES

Frog is identical with Six-bid Solo except in the bids and settlement.

THE BIDS

There are only three possible bids, Frog (lowest), Chico and Grand.

Frog (also called Rana). Hearts are trumps. The bidder picks up the widow and then discards any three cards face down.

Chico. The bidder names any suit but hearts as trumps. The widow is not used during play, but is added to the bidder's tricks afterward.

Grand. Hearts are trumps. The widow is not used during play, but is added to the bidder's tricks afterward.

SETTLEMENT

The bidder collects or pays for every point won in play, over or under 60. If the points are split 60–60, there is no payment. The value per point in settlement is: Frog 1, Chico 2, Grand 4. All other rules are as in Six-bid Solo.

STRATEGY

Frog, because of its scoring, give more scope than any other member of the Skat family for forward bidding. In fact, willful overbidding, within reasonable limits, is a lucrative policy. It pays to bid frog and chico on weak hands, and incur small losses on three hands out of four, for the sake of the big killing made by a lucky widow or lucky play on the fourth.

The normal requirement for grand is about the same as for a heart solo in Six-bid Solo. Chico may be bid with about four trumps and three side cards as good as ace or ten. Frog should be bid with about a side ace less. Even those "normal requirements" are shaded by sporty bidders— much depends upon how accurate the opponents are in defense. Many a frog has been bid and made with only three trumps, and two ace-tens on the side.

Six-bid Solo

Developed in the western United States, Six-bid Solo is an elaboration of Frog (q.v. for historical notes).

PLAYERS

Only three may play at a time, but four or five may sit at a table.

CARDS

The pack of 36. The cards in each suit rank: **A** (high), **10**, **K**, **Q**, **J**, **9**, **8**, **7**, **6**. The cards have a *point value* as in Skat:

Each ace counts	11	Each queen counts	3
Each ten	10	Each jack	2
Each king	4	(No count for lower cards.)	

PRELIMINARIES

Follow the same procedure as in Skat. The deal gives 11 cards to each hand, in rounds of 4–3–4. After the first round of the deal, three cards are dealt for a widow.

THE BIDDING

Eldest hand must make a bid or pass. If he bids, next hand may overcall or pass. If he overcalls, eldest hand may name a still higher game, and so on. The first two players settle as to the highest bidder between them, and then the third settles with the survivor. Each bid must name one of the six possible declarations, as given below.

THE GAMES

The six possible bids are as follows:

> Simple Solo (lowest)
> Heart Solo
> Misère
> Guarantee Solo
> Spread Misère
> Call Solo

Simple Solo. If this bid takes the contract, the bidder names any suit other than hearts as trumps. He undertakes to win 60 points or more in counting cards.

Heart Solo. Hearts are trumps. In all other respects, this game is like Simple Solo.

Misère. The bidder undertakes to take no counting card at all. There is no trump suit.

Guarantee Solo. If the bidder names hearts as trumps, he undertakes to win 74 or more points in play. With any other suit as trump, he must win 80 or more.

Spread Misère. The bidder plays a misère, exposing his whole hand face up on the table just prior to playing to the first trick. The opening lead is made by the player at his left.

Call Solo. The bidder undertakes to win all 120 points (not necessarily all the tricks). He is entitled to name any card not in his hand, and the holder of this card must give it to him in exchange for any card the bidder wishes to discard. If the called card is not in play (being in the widow), the exchange may not be made. After calling a card, the bidder names the trump suit. He may name any one of the four, but at hearts the game is worth more.

THE WIDOW

To all intents, the widow is a dead hand: it is never picked up and used in play. If there is a trump suit, the widow cards are added to the bidder's tricks after the play. At either misère game, the widow is not even counted.

THE PLAY

The opening lead is made by eldest hand, at every game except Spread Misère. Rules of play are as in Skat. The lead calls on other hands to follow suit; if unable to follow suit, a hand may play any card. A trick is won by the highest card of the suit led, or by the highest trump. The winner of a trick leads to the next.

The bidder plays alone against the other two, who play in partnership. The object in play is always to win (or, at misère, to avoid winning) counting cards.

SCORING

The higher games have a fixed value as follows:

Call Solo, hearts trumps	150
Call Solo, another trump	100
Spread Misère	60
Guarantee Solo	40
Misère	30

The bidder wins or loses the value of the game, according as he makes or fails to make his contract.

In Heart Solo and Simple Solo, the bidder collects or pays for each point won in play, over or under 60.

Heart Solo	3 per point
Simple Solo	2 per point

If the counting cards are split 60–60 there is no score for the deal.

IRREGULARITIES

Use the laws of Skat, page 381.

STRATEGY

There are nine cards in each suit. Normal expectation is that a plain suit will go two rounds without being trumped, if the player holds no more than three cards. For a trump bid the normal minimum trump length is four cards, with two of the three top trumps, or greater length with weaker top strength.

In hand evaluation, the Pinochle rule-of-thumb is useful: Count each trick that must be lost in plain suits as worth 15 points.

Since even a Simple Solo undertakes to lose not more than 60 points in tricks, the normal minimum for any trump bid is a hand that will not lose more than three plain-suit tricks.

Expectation of cards in the widow can be taken in account only as a "plus value." For example, if the player can win around 50 points in aces and tens, he may expect to go over 60 by face cards caught with his tops, plus the chances of finding a few points in the widow.

For all bids higher than Heart Solo, the hand must be so far "ironclad" that their evaluation is simple.

The following examples show minimum holdings for various bids:

$$\heartsuit \ \text{A 10 J 8} \qquad \spadesuit \ \text{A K 7} \qquad \diamondsuit \ \text{A 10 6} \qquad \clubsuit \ \text{8}$$

Bid Heart Solo. The hand takes 52 points minimum against normal breaks; the tops should catch some face cards.

$$\heartsuit \ \text{7} \qquad \spadesuit \ \text{A 10 K 8 7} \qquad \diamondsuit \ \text{8} \qquad \clubsuit \ \text{A 10 Q}$$

Bid Guarantee Solo in spades. There is evident risk, for 21 points might be lost in each red suit, and the club swings might not drop ♣**K**. But the gamble is worth taking.

$$\heartsuit \ \text{9 7} \qquad \spadesuit \ \text{Q 9 6} \qquad \diamondsuit \ \text{J 8 7} \qquad \clubsuit \ \text{K 7 6}$$

Bid Misère. If having to make the opening lead, lead ◇**8**. Of course all misère bids are safer if the hand does not have to lead.

SOLO (MODERN OMBRE)

In the fourteenth century, while Tarok was developing in Italy, the game of Ombre was developing in Spain. Both games spread throughout Europe, and for more than four hundred years were the two major card games. Ombre became the favorite of the fashionable. But the phenomenal rise of the Whist family in the last hundred years swept Ombre and many other ancient games into obsolescence.

Ombre was originally played with the Spanish pack of 40 cards. Then it was adapted to the French pack of 52. In its travels through many lands it acquired a lengthy and polyglot terminology: from Spanish, *hombre* (the man, i.e., the high bidder), *spadille, manille, basto, casco, matador;* from French, *respect, obscur, sans prendre, forcee, vole;* from Italian, *grandissimo, nullissimo;* from German, *frage.* Ombre like Tarok is basically a game for three players, but a four-hand variant Quadrille (so-called) largely superseded it, especially in France and England. It is notable that Quadrille is one of the five games covered by Edmond Hoyle in his "Treatise on Games," 1743 (the others being Whist, Piquet, Chess, and Backgammon).

Ombre and Quadrille are largely forgotten, but the simplification which follows, called Solo, still flourishes. The name is unfortunately ambiguous; it has been given also to variants of Tarok and Whist. Solo is also known as GERMAN SOLO.

PLAYERS

Four play, each for himself, but the nature of the game provides for temporary partnerships.

CARDS

The pack of 32. The ♣Q, called *spadille* or *spadilla,* always ranks as the highest trump. The ♠Q, called *basto* or *basta,* always ranks as the third-best trump. The second-best trump, called *manille* or *manilla,* is the **7** of the trump suit. The rank in all suits, except for the promotion of these three cards to the top of the trumps, is: **A, K, (Q), J, 10, 9, 8, (7)**.

(The three top trumps are customarily called matadors. Formerly the matadors had special privileges in addition to their high rank, but these privileges have disappeared from Solo.)

It should be noted that when a red suit is trumps, there are ten trumps, but when a black suit is trumps, there are only nine.

PRELIMINARIES

Choice of seats may be decided by any agreed method. To fix the first deal, any player deals cards around, one at a time face up, and the first club dealt marks the first dealer. The dealer has the right to shuffle last. The pack is cut by the player at his right, and the cut must leave not less than five cards in each packet.

DEALING

Each player receives eight cards, dealt in rounds of 3–2–3.

THE COLOR

The suit clubs is called *the color*. Any bid of clubs for trumps is *in color*. A bid of spades, hearts or diamonds for trumps is *in suit*. (In some localities, there is no prefixed color. The game is begun with all suits on a parity, but the suit named for trumps in the first successful contract thereafter becomes the color.)

DECLARATIONS

There are three types of game that may be proposed: frog, solo, and tout. Since each may be bid either *in suit* or *in color*, there are in all six bids, ranking as follows:

> Frog in suit (lowest)
> Frog in color
> Solo in suit
> Solo in color
> Tout in suit
> Tout in color

Frog (or Simple Game). If this bid wins, the bidder names the trump suit and then names an ace that he does not hold himself. Whoever holds that ace becomes his partner, but must say nothing to indicate the fact until the play of the ace broadcasts it. If the bidder was dealt all four aces, he may call for a king.

Solo. The bidder, if high, names the trump suit and plays alone against the other three.

Tout. This is a solo in which the bidder undertakes to win all the tricks.

BIDDING

Eldest hand declares first. If he bids, the next player to the left may try to overcall him, and these two battle it out until one passes. The survivor then settles with the third player, should the latter care to enter into competition. And so on; the dealer competes, if at all, with the survivor of the bidding among the other three. Once a player has passed, he is out of the auction.

The highest bidder is not bound to the bid which won him the contract. He may name any game he pleases, equal to or higher than his bid. It is, therefore, to the advantage of each player to bid as little as is necessary to overcall the last previous bid. The auction then takes the form of a sparring match, thus:

The first bidder usually starts with "I ask"—equivalent to the *ich frage* of Skat, meaning "I am willing to undertake a contract. Does any wish to bid against me?" If none dispute, the asker stands committed to play at least a frog in suit. The first bid against him takes the form "Is it in color?" meaning a frog in color. If the answer is "Yes"—meaning that the first bidder will play a game at least that high—the second may continue, "Will you play solo?" . . . "In color?" and so on. If the first bidder says "No" or passes at any time, the second stands committed to play a game at least as high as he mentioned in questioning the intentions of the first bidder.

Note that a bid *in suit* does not name the intended trump suit, which is specified only when the highest bidder is determined.

If a player holds both spadille and basto (the black queens), he is not permitted to pass a bid of frog. He must himself declare a least a solor or induce the previous bidder to declare it. The compulsion is called *forcee*.

If all four players pass without a bid, the holder of spadille (♣**Q**) must show it and then play a frog.

THE PLAY

Eldest hand always makes the opening lead. A lead calls upon each other hand to follow suit if able; if unable, a hand may play any card. A trick is won by the highest card of the suit led, or by the highest trump. The winner of a trick leads to the next.

The bidder's object in a frog or solo is to win five tricks; in tout, to win all eight tricks. On taking his fifth trick in a frog or solo, the bidder must at once abandon his cards without further play, else he stands committed to try for tout, and is penalized if he fails just as though he had bid tout.

In frog, the bidder has a partner. In solo or tout, he plays alone against the other three.

SCORING

The following table gives the values of the games:

Frog in suit	2
Frog in color	4
Solo in suit	4
Solo in color	8
Tout in suit	16
Tout in color	32

In frog, the bidder and his partner each win or lose 2 from each opponent. In solor or tout, the bidder collects from, or pays, each of his three opponents, the full value from or to each.

IRREGULARITIES

A player who fails to follow suit when able loses the game and must pay the entire loss for his side. If an opponent of the Player leads or plays out of turn, or exposes a card, his side loses and the offender must pay the entire loss. No penalty against the Player for similar errors; the error must be corrected if possible and play continued. (*Variant.* Where there is a pool, if a penalizable error is made in a Simple Game the offender also pays a *bete* to the pool. The bete is 16 chips, or as many as are needed to double the amount already in the pool.)

STRATEGY

At frog, the bidder has the help of a partner, who surely has an ace. Any hand that can lay down four tricks is therefore a sound frog bid. But the normal minimum is three tricks, for (a) nearly half the time, partner will hold two tricks; (b) the tactical advantage of making a bid is worth the risk.

The average share trumps is between two and three cards per player. The frog bidder should therefore hold at least three cards in his intended trump suit, and if he has only three they should include at least one of the three tops. Any such minimum holding as **7** (manille), **9, 8** should be counted worth one trick, not two, although it often wins two, because the three-trick requirement is "shaded" anyhow. Each extra trump over three may be counted a trick.

A red plain suit contains eight cards; a black plain suit, only seven. In either case, a plain suit should not be counted on to furnish more than one trick, the ace, unless the hand is strong enough to be able to lead trumps and so save its lower side tricks from being trumped. The countable tricks in bidding are therefore, normally, only the trumps and side aces.

$$\clubsuit \text{ A 8} \qquad \heartsuit \text{ J 9} \qquad \spadesuit \text{ Q} \qquad \diamondsuit \text{ K J 8}$$

This is a typical near-minimum hand for frog. The intention is to name diamonds and call for one of the red aces.

At solo, the bidder plays alone against three other hands. His chances of "picking up something in the play" are even less than at such three-hand games as Skat and Pinochle. A solo bid therefore requires an almost "ironclad" holding of five tricks, such as three sure trump tricks and two side aces. The trump length should be at least four cards.

$$\clubsuit \text{ Q 7 K 8} \qquad \heartsuit \text{ A 7} \qquad \spadesuit \text{ K J} \qquad \diamondsuit \text{ ——}$$

This is a typical minimum solo in color. The bidder plans to capture the lead quickly, as by trumping a diamond lead, cash spadille and manille, then lead his spade king. If the trumps do not break badly, he will then make his spade jack. He might even make all four trumps.

A hand worth a bid of tout is so rare that it does not merit discussion.

ILLUSTRATIVE DEAL

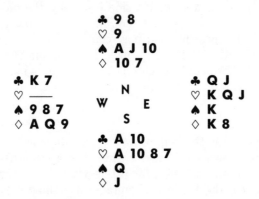

```
                    ♣ 9 8
                    ♡ 9
                    ♠ A J 10
                    ◇ 10 7
        ♣ K 7              N          ♣ Q J
        ♡ ___                         ♡ K Q J
        ♠ 9 8 7       W       E       ♠ K
        ◇ A Q 9           S           ◇ K 8
                    ♣ A 10
                    ♡ A 10 8 7
                    ♠ Q
                    ◇ J
```

South deals. West says "I ask," and the others in turn declare "No." (If South fell into the temptation of calling heart solo, he would be massacred.) West names spades and calls the club ace.

In the play below, the card underlined wins the trick, and the card below it is the lead to the next.

TRICK	WEST	NORTH	EAST	SOUTH
1	♣ 7	♣ 8	♣ J	♣ A
2	◇ A	◇ 7	◇ 8	◇ J
3	◇ 9	◇ 10	◇ K	♠ Q
4	◇ Q	♡ 9	♡ J	♡ A
5	♣ K	♣ 9	♠ K	♣ 10
6	♠ 8	♠ 10	♡ K	♡ 7
7	♠ 9	♠ J	♣ Q	♡ 8
8	♠ 7			

West and South win five tricks, making the bid.

Trick 1. West leads a club to find out at once who his partner is.

Trick 2. South wants to make basto by trumping a diamond.

Trick 5. Although South knows that the club lead will surely be trumped by some hand, probably an opponent, this is his best play to assure West the one trump trick needed for contract.

CASINO

Early writers state that Casino is of Italian origin, and that its name means precisely what it says—a public gaming hall. The word appears as *Cassino* in most English manuals, the extra *s* having been inserted, it is said, by a whimsical printer.

An ancestor of Casino may have been Papillon (butterfly), described in *The Academy of Play* (1768). Three or four players are dealt three cards each, and seven or four are dealt to the table. The object of play is to win cards by pairing or building. It is interesting to note that *sweeps*, contemned by some Casino players as a "modern vice," were counted in Papillon.

Much the same game as Papillon is described in the Anton *Encyclopedia of Games* (Leipzig, 1884) under the name Callabra. (Callabra, Calabrasella, and Kalabriàs are three entirely different games, but all may have derived from the province of Calabria, the toe of Italy.)

PLAYERS

Two. Casino can be played by three, each for himself (not a very good game), or by four, two against two in partnerships (described later).

CARDS

The pack of 52. Ace counts 1, other cards from 2 to 10 count as their index numbers; jacks, queens and kings have no numerical value.

PRELIMINARIES

Dealer has the right to shuffle last. Opponent cuts; the cut must leave at least four cards in each packet.

DEALING

In the first deal, dealer gives two cards to his opponent, then two face up to the table, then two to himself; then he deals a second round in the same manner as the first. Each player thus receives four cards, and four are placed face up on the table. The hands are played; then dealer gives each player four more cards, in rounds of two at a time. And so on following: the hands of four cards are dealt and played until the pack is exhausted. After the first deal, no more cards are dealt to the table. The dealer must announce "Last" on commencing the last deal.

THE PLAY

Each hand in turn, beginning with non-dealer, must play a card to the table and thereby *take in*, *build*, or *trail*.

Taking In. The general object of play is to win or take in cards from the table. A card from the hand may be used to take in another of the same rank on the table. *Example:* A player may use ♣8 from his hand to take ◇8 on the table. (Suits are immaterial.) Such *pairing* is the only way face cards (kings, queens and jacks) can be taken in. Other cards may also be won by building.

Building. A card from the hand may be used to take in two or more cards of the same total of pips. *Example:* A player may use ♠9 to take ♡4 and ♣5.

A card from the hand may be placed on another on the table, to be taken later by a second card from the hand. *Example:* A player may place ♣7 from his hand on ◇2, and later take them with ◇9 from his hand.

Such a play is a *build*, and on placing the first card the player must announce "Building (nine)." The announcement prevents the opponent from splitting the build and using any of the cards separately. *Example:* Non-dealer puts ♡5 on ♡3 and says "Building eight"; dealer may not then take in either of the cards by pairing.

No build may be made unless the player holds in hand a card of the rank necessary to take it. When a build is left on the table (as it has to be when it includes a card from the hand), the opponent of the builder may take it in. *Example:* Non-dealer plays ♣A on ♡5, building six. Dealer may take the build with any six.

If a player has made a build, and it is not taken by opponent, the player at his next turn may not *trail;* he must *duplicate* or *increase the build* or *take in*. But he need not take in that build; if he prefers and can, he may instead take in a pair or take an adverse build.

Duplicating a Build. The same card from the hand may be used to take in two or more groups of cards, each of which totals the like number of pips. *Example:* ♣9 from the hand may be used to take in ♡6, ♣3 and ♠A, ◇8, at the same time.

A build left on the table may be duplicated as many times as there are cards available. *Example:* Dealer builds seven with ♡4 and ♣3; at his next turn, he finds ♠5 and ♡2 also on the table; he may take them with his build. Or suppose that at his next turn only ♠5 is on the table besides his build; he may add ♡2 from his hand and ♠5 from the table to his build, to be taken in at his following turn.

Single cards, of rank ten or lower, can be built in the same way. *Example:* A player holds ♣9, ♠9, while ♡9 is on the table; he may place ♣9 on ♡9, saying "Building nines," and take the build later with ♠9. All four cards of a rank can thus be gathered in one build. Note that *face cards* may never be built, but only paired.

Increasing a Build. A player may increase a build so that it requires for capture a higher card than originally announced. *Example:* Non-dealer places ♣3 from his hand on ♣6 on the table and says "Building nine"; dealer may add ♡A and say "Building ten," provided that he has a ten in hand with which to take the increased build.

A player may increase either his own or his opponent's build. But a build that is duplicated may never be increased. *Example:* A player puts ♡4 from his hand on ♠3 on the table, and adds ◇7 from the table, building sevens; the build may not be increased.

Note that the same limitation applies to builds of pairs. *Example:* A player puts ♣4 on ♠4, and says "Building fours"; his opponent may not add ♡A and say "Building nine," because the original announcement overrides, and marks the build as double.

A build may be increased only by a card from the hand, *not* by a card from the table. (Consequently such a build cannot be taken in on the same turn when it is increased, but must be left on the table for one turn. The opponent always has an opportunity to take an increased build, or to increase it yet again.)

Trailing. If unable or unwilling to *take in*, the player in turn simply places a card from his hand face up on the table. This is called *trailing*. A player may trail if he wishes, even if able to take in by pairing. *Example:* The table shows ♡J and ♠5. Non-dealer holds ◇5, his last card of the next-to-last deal. He may trail with ◇5 instead of taking in ♠5. (The object may be to avert the chance of a sweep or to leave a combination of ten in case he is dealt ◇10 in the last deal.)

COUNTING CARDS

The object of play is to take in cards and combinations of cards of scoring value. The points to be scored are as follows:

Cards, majority of the 52 cards	3
Spades, majority of the 13 spades	1
Big Casino, the ◇10	2
Little Casino, the ♠2	1
Aces (each counting 1)	4
Total	11

Sweeps count 1 each.

A player makes a *sweep* when he takes in all the cards on the table. (In some localities sweeps do not count.)

Each player places the cards he *takes in* in a pile face down. A sweep is recorded by turning a card of this pile face up.

After the last card is played out, any cards remaining on the table go to the player who was last to *take in* any card. Gathering cards by virtue of this rule does not count as a sweep.

If each player takes in 26 cards, there is no score for *cards*.

411

SCORING

After the whole pack is played out, each player counts the number of points in his cards. If desired, each deal may be treated as a separate game for the majority of the 11 (or more) points. Much more common, however, is the fixing of game at 21 points. Players deal alternately until one "counts out." If during a deal a player claims correctly that he has reached a total of 21 points, he wins, even though his opponent has "gone out" earlier (but failed to claim the game).

If "counting out" is not allowed, and if both players reach 21 in the same deal, the points are counted in the order given under *Counting Cards* to determine the winner.

IRREGULARITIES

In two-hand play, when each deal constitutes a game, any irregularity loses the game.

Misdeal. If the dealer deals with an unshuffled or uncut pack, his opponent may call it a misdeal before making his first play, and may decide whether the dealer shall deal again or lose his deal. If the dealer fails to announce the final round, his opponent may call the deal off or let it stand.

Irregularities in Dealing. If the dealer gives any player too few cards, he must supply the deficiency from the top of the pack. If any card is exposed in dealing before the first four cards are dealt to the table, that card goes to the table and is replaced from the top of the pack. If a card is exposed in dealing after the table has its four cards, dealer must take the exposed card and give the opponent another card; if the dealer has already looked at his own four cards, he supplies the opponent from the top of the pack, the exposed card goes to the table, and on the next round the dealer plays with fewer cards than the opponent. If dealer gives any player too many cards, and it is discovered before that player looks at his hand, the excess may be drawn from the hand and restored at the top of the pack; if the player has looked at his hand, he may put the excess among the cards on the table, choosing the cards he will put there, and on the next round of dealing the dealer plays with fewer cards than his opponent.

If on the final round there are not enough cards to give every player four, the dealer receives fewer cards than the opponents (unless the pack is shown to be imperfect, in which event the entire deal is void).

Taking in Wrong Cards. If a player takes in a card to which he is not entitled, it must be restored to the table upon demand at any time before an opponent next plays a card; after that, the error may not be corrected.

Counting or Looking Back at Cards. If a player counts or looks back at any cards taken in and turned, except at cards taken in since he last played, his opponent may either add one point to his own score or deduct one point from the offender's score.

Not Taking in Builds. If a player trails when he has a build standing on the table, he must on demand take in the build; but the card with which he trailed remains on the table, and he does not play in his next turn. If a player has not the appropriate card with which to take in a build he made, his opponent may add one point to his own score or deduct one point from the offender's score.

Play Out of Turn. A card played out of turn must remain on the table, as though the offender had trailed with it, and the offender does not play in his next turn; in partnership play, his partner may not take in that card.

Exposed Card. If two or three hands play, no penalty. In partnership play, the card exposed is immediately placed upon the table and the offender does not play in his next turn. The offender's partner may not take in the card which was exposed.

STRATEGY

Casino is one of the easiest of games to *play at*—it has been a juvenile favorite for many generations—and it is also one of the hardest to play well. The expert keeps track of every card played, so that in the last deal he knows exactly the four cards held by his opponent. Naturally much practice and constant attention are required for this feat of memory.

But even the beginner can and should keep track of the aces, big and little casino, and spades. The number of cards taken by each side can be roughly estimated from the size of the piles, but the expert counts them as they are taken in.

In making ordinary plays, try to take as many cards as possible with each card in the hand. Combine this with trying for *spades*. Prefer pairings that include spades to those that do not; prefer builds that include spades. But it is better to take in three cards including no spade than two cards both spades, until such time as it can be assumed that you are sure or nearly sure to win 27 cards anyway; or until the opponent has cards won, but there is still a chance to save the point for spades.

When you are dealt an ace or a casino, concentrate on trying to save this *cash point*. If unable to pair it or build with it, non-dealer saves it for the final trail, to minimize the chance of losing it to opponent, for he will play first in the next deal.

Trail with face cards rather than low cards useful for building, until the final deal, at which time dealer is sure to take in any unpaired face card in his hand, while non-dealer is sure not to, and each can judge his play accordingly.

Three-hand Casino

Each player receives four cards on each deal, as in two-hand; four cards are dealt to the table on the first round, but no cards thereafter. Eldest hand plays first and the turn to play passes in rotation. If there is a tie for the most cards or spades, the respective points do not count for anyone. Usually a game of 11 points is played; if it is attempted to make each deal a game, there are too many ties. Three-hand Casino is not often played because eldest hand and dealer have a great advantage over the player "in the middle."

Partnership Casino

Four play, in two partnerships, partners being seated alternately. The dealing, turn to deal, and turn to play rotate to the left. Cards taken in by each pair of partners are combined and counted together, and partners try to help each other, but each player must observe the rules of the game. *Example:* One partner is known to hold a nine. The other partner has a four and there is a five on the table; but he has no nine in his hand. Therefore he cannot build a nine, even though he knows the first partner could take it in.

A game of 21 points may be played, or each deal may represent a game.

For *irregularities*, see under Casino, above.

Royal Casino

This variant has largely supplanted the game as previously described, and in the opinion of many experts it is superior as a test of skill. It is also much preferred by children, since it is more colorful and offers more opportunity for building.

In Royal Casino, face cards are used in building and duplicating builds, just like the lower cards. Jack is counted as 11, queen as 12, king as 13, while the ace may be used as 1 or 14 at the option of the player. (In juvenile play, little casino may be used as 2 or 15, and big casino as 10 or 16.) All other rules remain the same.

Spade Casino

In this variant, there is no count for majority of spades, but each spade taken in is itself worth 1 point, except jack and two, which are each worth 2. The rest of the count is the same, so that there are 24 points to be won, exclusive of sweeps. Scoring is best done on a cribbage board, with game fixed at 61. First player to "count out" during play wins the game.

Draw Casino

After the first deal of twelve cards (four to each hand and four to the table), the rest of the pack is placed face down to form the *stock*. After each play, the player restores his hand to four cards by drawing the top of the stock. After the stock is exhausted, the hands are played out as usual. This method of bringing cards into play may be used in any of the above variants.

PIQUET

Much ink has been spilled in speculation on the ultimate origin of Piquet and the etymology of the name. A writer in 1823 stated that "Of all the games at cards *Piquet* is the most ancient . . . Its origin is somewhat singular; a great *Ballet* executed in the Court of Charles VI (1380–1422) suggested the idea of it." About the only certainty is that this account is false in every particular, although it continues to be quoted. Piquet was certainly well established by 1535, for it is listed by Rabelais in the games known to Gargantua. The same list includes *La Ronfle* and *le Cent*, variant names for Piquet. There is some question whether the game is of Spanish, rather than French, origin. It spread to England under the name Cent (one hundred), and is alluded to by the Elizabethans in a wide variety of spellings, as Sant, Saunt, Saint.

PLAYERS

Two. Variants for three and four players are described later, but are comparatively little played.

In France, the terms *majeur* and *mineur* are used for the non-dealer and dealer respectively, and in England *major* and *minor* are usually used.

CARDS

The pack of 32. Usually, two packs are used alternately. There is never a trump, and no ranking of suits. The cards in each suit rank: **Ace** (high), **K**, **Q**, **J**, **10**, **9**, **8**, **7**.

PRELIMINARIES

Cards are drawn and the lower card deals first. If equal cards are drawn, both must draw again.

Dealer has the right to shuffle last, and the other cuts. The cut must leave at least two cards in each packet.

DEALING

Cards are dealt two at a time, beginning with non-dealer. Each player receives twelve cards. The remaining eight cards are spread fanwise face down on the table, forming the *stock* (in France, *talon*). It is considered courteous on the part of the dealer to separate the top five cards of the stock from the bottom three, but this rite is often omitted. (The rule is given in some books that the upper five must be placed crosswise on the lower three. No experienced players do this, because of the danger of facing lower cards in taking the upper.)

DISCARDING

Non-dealer commences by discarding any number of cards from one to five. He must discard at least one. Then he takes an equal number of cards from the upper packet of the stock. If he leaves any of the first five on the stock, he may look at them without showing them to dealer.

Dealer is entitled to take all cards left in the stock, after discarding an equal number of cards. He need not take any. If he leaves one or more, he may decide whether they shall be turned face up for both to see or left face down.

Each player keeps his discards separate from his opponent's, for he is allowed to look at his own discards during the play.

CARTE BLANCHE

A hand without a face card (king, queen or jack) is *carte blanche*. A player dealt such a hand scores 10 points for it immediately. Non-dealer should announce carte blanche on picking up his original hand; but dealer should not make the announcement until non-dealer has discarded.

CALLING

After the draw from the stock, the hands are compared to decide scores for *point*, *sequence*, and *triplets* or *fours*. The three types of combinations are scored in that order.

Point. Non-dealer states the number of cards in his longest suit, as "Five." If dealer has no suit as long, he says "Good," and his opponent scores for point. Having a longer suit, dealer so states and scores. With a suit of the same length, dealer asks "How much?" Non-dealer then computes the pip value of his suit: ace counts 11, each face card 10, each other card its index value. Between suits of equal length, the one of higher pip value scores for point; if pip values are equal, neither player scores.

The score for point is 1 for each card in the suit.

Sequence. Non-dealer announces the number of cards in his longest sequence in the same suit provided that it contains at least three cards. The French terms *tierce, quart, quinte,* etc., are often used for sequence of three, four, five, etc. Dealer responds with "Good," "Not good," or "How high?" Between sequences of equal length, the one with the higher top card wins. If the two best sequences are equal in all respects, neither player scores. The score for sequence is: three, 3; four, 4; five or more, 10 plus 1 for each card.

The player who scores for best sequence may also score for all additional sequences he holds.

Triplets or Fours. Non-dealer announces the number and kind of his highest set of three or four of a kind, provided that the rank is not lower than 10. Any four of a kind is higher than any three of a kind. Between sets with the same number of cards, the higher rank wins.

The score for sets is: three of a kind, 3; four of a kind, 14. The player who scores in this class may also score all lower sets which he holds, always provided that the rank is 10 or higher.

EXAMPLE OF CALLING

After the draw, non-dealer holds

♠ K 7   ♡ A K Q J   ♣ A   ◇ A K Q

Dealer holds

♠ A Q J 10   ♡ 10   ♣ K J 10   ◇ J 10

NON-DEALER: Four.
DEALER: How much?
NON-DEALER: Forty-one.
DEALER: Equal. (Neither scores for point.)
NON-DEALER: Quart.*
DEALER: Good.
NON-DEALER: I also have a tierce. Three aces.
DEALER: Not good. Four tens, also three jacks.
NON-DEALER: I start with 7.
DEALER: I start with 17.

Proving. The player who scores for any combination is bound to *prove* it on demand of his opponent. The simplest way to prove a set would be to expose it, but this is rarely done. The custom of the game is for the opponent to demand only the minimum of information he needs to calculate, from his own hand and discards, what the precise cards must be. For example, non-dealer calls and scores three aces, then also announces three queens; dealer never had a queen, and therefore knows that non-dealer must have discarded one; dealer asks "Which queen did you discard?" Another example: Non-dealer calls his point and dealer says "How much?"; non-dealer says "Thirty-seven"; dealer says "Thirty-nine" instead of "Not good," since the other would surely ask for the figure if it were not volunteered.

Sinking. A player need not declare a combination, even when he knows that it is high. Failure to announce a scorable holding is called *sinking* it. The object in sinking is to withhold information that might be valuable to opponent in the play.

---

* *The term* quart *has been criticized as bad French. However, it is widely used in English, instead of* quatrième.

THE PLAY

Play begins as soon as all combinations have been announced and scored. Non-dealer makes the opening lead. A lead calls upon opponent to follow suit if able; if unable, the hand may play any card. A trick is won by the higher card of the suit led. The winner of a trick leads to the next. (Formerly each lead had to be accompanied by a verbal announcement of the suit, as in Ecarté. The rule has happily died of neglect.)

The objects in play are to score points for leads and plays, as below; to win a majority of the tricks; to win last trick; to win all the tricks. Winning the majority of the tricks counts 10 points. (No count when tricks are divided six and six.) Winner of last trick gets 1 extra point. Winner of all the tricks makes *capot*, worth 40 points (and in this case there is no extra count for last trick or for majority of tricks).

A player scores 1 point for each lead of a card higher than 9, and 1 point for each adverse lead won with a card higher than 9. (Modern practice is to dispense with this distinction of rank, counting 1 for every lead and 1 for every adverse lead won.)

Counting. Since scores accumulate fast during the calling and play, each player counts his own score aloud and announces the new total after each new increment.

EXAMPLE OF COUNTING

To continue the example of calling:

Non-dealer starts with 7; Dealer with 17. Non-dealer leads his four hearts and three diamonds, counting "Eight, nine," etc. and so reaching 15. Dealer saves, for his last three cards, ♠A and ♣K J. Non-dealer leads ♠7, counting nothing for it (old style). Dealer wins, counting 18, then leads ♣J counting 19. Non-dealer wins, counting 16, then leads ♠K for last trick, counting 18 (extra point for last).

Non-dealer announces final score of 28 (10 for majority of tricks). Dealer has 19.

REPIC AND PIC

If in one deal, before the opening lead, a player amasses 30 points or more before his opponent scores a point, he adds 60 for *repic*. *Example:* Non-dealer scores 6 for point, plus 16 for a sequence of six, making 22, and 14 for four aces, making 36, plus 60 for repic, making 96. Because of repic, points must always be counted in the prescribed order: carte blanche, point, sequence, triplets or fours.

If in one deal a player reaches 30 or more, after the opening lead, before his opponent scores a point, he adds 30 for *pic*. For example, non-dealer scores 5 for point, 4 for sequence, 14 for four queens and 3 for three aces, making 26; he leads three aces, reaching 29, and then leads a queen, jumping to a total of 60. Observe that non-dealer can never suffer pic, since he has the opening lead; he must have a card higher than 9 to lead.

SCORING

To recapitulate the scoring points:

IN HAND	Carte blanche	10
	point, per card	1
	sequence of three or four	3 or 4
	sequence of five or more, 1 per card plus	10
	triplet	3
	fours	14
	repic	60
IN PLAY	lead of 10 or higher	1
	winning adverse lead with 10 or higher	1
	majority of tricks	10
	last trick	1
	capot (includes majority and last)	40
	pic	30

Game is usually fixed at 100, but there are several ways of computing the final result of a game.

Piquet au Cent. Formerly this was the almost universal method of scoring. Play continues by alternate deals until one (or both) players reach 100. There is no "counting out" during a deal; the last deal is played out. The higher then wins the difference of the two total scores, but if the loser has failed to reach 50 points this difference is doubled.

Rubicon Piquet has almost entirely supplanted Piquet au cent. A game comprises six deals, so that both players have the advantage of being major three times. If both players reach 100 or more, the higher total wins by the *difference*, plus 100 for more. If either or both fail to reach 100, the loser is *rubiconed*, and the winner scores the sum of the final totals, plus 100 for game.

The classical laws of Cavendish for Rubicon permit *undercalling*. In Piquet au cent, if a player sinks a combination he may never score it, and all combinations scored must (in theory) be proved before play begins. But in Rubicon a player need call only enough of his hand to assure the right to score in a given category; he may conceal part of the combination, or another of the same class, and score the excess after play. He need prove only what he announced. *For example:* If non-dealer calls point of four, dealer with five may ask "How much?" (thus declaring only four) and later get credit for the full five, provided that the top four totaled more than non-dealer could hold with any cards outside non-dealer's hand

and discard. *Another example:* Non-dealer holds two aces, four kings, three queens, and has discarded a jack and a ten. Knowing that dealer cannot best them, he may announce three queens, concealing the four kings until the end of play.

Many clubs, however, prohibit undercalling and enforce the Piquet au cent rule.

Four-deal Game. The desirability of shortening games in club play has led to the adoption in some clubs of four deals per game; the scores made in the first and last deal are doubled. Other rules of scoring are as in Rubicon.

IRREGULARITIES

New Deal (by the same dealer). Compulsory if a card is exposed in dealing; at option of non-dealer if either player receives the wrong number of cards.

Erroneous Discard. If a player discards more or less cards than he intended, he may not change his discard after touching the stock. If there are not enough cards available to him in the stock to replace all his discards, he must play with a short hand.

Erroneous Draw from Stock. If a player draws too many cards from the stock, he may replace the excess if he has not looked at them and if the correct order of the cards is determinable; otherwise the following rules apply. If non-dealer draws more than five cards from the stock he loses the game. If he draws less than five he should so announce; if he fails to do so, dealer is entitled to draw all that are left, even should dealer discard three and then touch the stock. If dealer draws any card from the stock before non-dealer has made his draw, dealer loses the game.

Concession. Once a player concedes an adverse combination to be good he may not claim a superior combination.

False Declaration. If a player claims and scores for a combination that he does not hold, he may announce his error before playing a card and the scoring in that class is corrected. Should a player play a card before announcing his error, he may not score at all in that deal; his opponent may declare and score all combinations he holds, even if they are inferior, and may score for all tricks he wins in play.

Wrong Number of Cards. If, after the opening lead, one hand is found to have an incorrect number of cards, play continues. A hand with too many cards may not score for play in that deal. A hand with too few cards may score for play, but cannot take the last trick. If both hands are incorrect the deal is abandoned and there is a new deal by the same dealer.

STRATEGY OF DISCARDING

There are several excellent books on the principles of discarding at Piquet. The following summarizes advice on which all agree.

Problems of discarding should be decided by reference to the following factors:

1. *Am I dealer or non-dealer?* Non-dealer has the first lead, and can win majority of tricks with one solid suit alone. Also, he can draw five cards to dealer's three; therefore he has the better chance to fill any specific combination, as point, sequence, triplet or four. Except with a very poor hand, his discarding is offensive, designed to run up as large a score as possible.

Dealer cannot afford to be so free in the discard of shortsuit stoppers. He has to think of saving majority of tricks, capot, even repic. His discarding must usually be defensive.

2. *What is against my hand?* That is, what combinations can my opponent hold, from the 20 cards not in my hand? If opponent can hold six or more cards of a suit, or four of a kind, the question arises whether to discard to try to beat his holding or offset it by scoring in another category or winning majority of tricks.

3. *What is the state of the score?* Certain situations in advanced score may dictate a more conservative or more desperate policy than would be correct at love score.

ILLUSTRATIVE HANDS FOR DISCARDING

♠ Q J 9 7   ♡ A Q   ♣ Q 10 7   ◇ K 9

Non-dealer should discard ♣Q 10 7 and ◇K 9. A typical instance of trying for point and tricks at the same time. It is not worthwhile to save the three queens in a try for four.

Dealer should discard ♠J 9 7. The chance of making point is too little to justify giving up any stopper. Best is to try for tricks, and incidentally for four queens.

♠ K J 8 7   ♡ 7   ♣ A K 10 9   ◇ K Q 8

Non-dealer should discard ♠J 8 7, ♡7, ◇8. Like the previous case, a normal try for points and tricks.

Dealer should discard ♠8 7, ◇8, keeping all protection he can against loss of tricks.

♠ A 8   ♡ K Q 10 9   ♣ A Q 10 9   ◇ J 9

Non-dealer should discard ♠8, ♣10 9, ◇J 9. With two suits of equal length and equal trick-winning prospects, if only one can be saved for point prefer that with the better chances of making sequence.

♠ A 9   ♡ Q 10 9   ♣ K Q 9 8 7   ◇ Q J

Non-dealer should discard ♠9 and ♣K 9 8 7. To save the clubs for point would necessitate giving up red stoppers, and would probably lose majority if the draw did not produce the ace. Better is to play for majority and possible four queens.

♠ K Q J 10   ♡ K Q J   ♣ A K J   ◇ K 10

Non-dealer should discard ♡**Q J**, ♣**A J**, ◇**10**. He is sure to count the spade quart and the four kings; he should take all five cards to minimize the chances of dealer to draw aces or make point. It is worthwhile to give up the three jacks in order to leave no cards.

♠ A K Q J 8 7   ♡ K 9   ♣ K 10   ◇ 10 9

Non-dealer should discard ♡**9**, ♣**10**, ◇**10 9**, leaving one card. The hand cannot be beaten in point and tricks, so can afford to try for four kings.

♠ K 10 7   ♡ Q 9 8   ♣ A K J   ◇ A K J

Dealer should discard ♠**7**, leaving two. By so doing, he is almost sure to divide the tricks, and he may easily win majority. It would be foolish to give up this prospect to increase the chance of getting the fourth king.

♠ A K Q J 10 9 7   ♡ A 9   ♣ A   ◇ A 9

An extreme example of the effect of the score.

At 0–0 or any low score, non-dealer should discard ♠**7**, ♡**9**, ◇**9**. Although the spades, originally sure for point, may not be good after the discard of ♠**7**, it is advisable to take three cards instead of two to increase the chance of breaking up the possible adverse sequence of seven clubs, which would be good against the spade six.

In the last hand of a game, if pic and cards are enough to win, non-dealer should discard the same three cards plus any ace but the spade, leaving only one card. This further increases chances of breaking up the possible adverse holding of seven clubs. If non-dealer can surely win if not beaten for sequence, and must lose if dealer counts the 17, he should let go all five cards outside of spades.

If non-dealer has 58 or more, dealer less than 80, non-dealer should discard the two nines, leaving three cards. He is then sure to win, as his hand can be laid down for point of 7, 14 aces, 11 leads (modern count), and 10 for tricks. Dealer can count no more than 17 for sequence, 2 tricks won and 1 for last.

STRATEGY OF PLAY

Much of the play at Piquet can be exactly calculated from information obtained in the calling. The basic principles are the same as in any other game where all or most of the cards are in play: Establish long suits by driving out adverse stoppers; save short-suit stoppers to hold the adverse long suit; watch the fall of the cards; lose the lead through adverse top cards that must make in any event, rather than through low stoppers, if you have no long suits to establish. A very frequent play is the throw-in, to make the last trick or to avoid losing an extra trick. For example:

NON-DEALER

♠ **K J 9 8** ♡ **A K Q 8 7** ♣ **A Q** ◇ **K**
Discard: ♣ **J 8** ◇ **10 9 7**

DEALER

♠ **A Q 10** ♡ **J** ♣ **K 10 9 7** ◇ **A Q J 8**
Discard: ♠ **7** ♡ **10 9**

Non-dealer cashes five hearts, on which dealer plays ♡ **J**, ♠ **10**, ♣ **10 9**, ◇ **8**. Non-dealer now knows that his opponent discarded two hearts. It is unlikely that the other discard was the queen of spades. He therefore exits with ◇ **K**, knowing that dealer can win only three tricks in the suit. Non-dealer discards ♠ **9 8**. Then dealer must open a black suit, giving non-dealer the extra trick needed for majority.

Dealer should assure himself of last trick by leading a club. Non-dealer can do no better than win and return a spade, which dealer wins and returns the other club, taking last trick with the other spade.

Three-hand Piquet (Piquet Normand)

Each player is dealt ten cards, leaving two for the *talon*. The dealer may discard any two cards and take the talon. Combinations are called in turn, beginning with eldest hand; only one player may score in any category.

Scoring is as in two-hand except that only 20 is needed to make repic and pic, though repic jumps to 90 and pic to 60. Plurality of trick counts 10; if two players tie for most tricks, each scores 5. Capot by one player is 40; if two players win 5 tricks each, they each score 20. The usual settlement is to make a pool which is won by the first player to reach 100.

Four-hand Piquet (Piquet Voleur)

Four-hand is played in two partnerships, partners sitting opposite each other. All the cards are dealt out, each player receiving eight cards.

Eldest hand commences by announcing whatever he holds in the categories: carte blanche, point, sequence, threes or fours. No point of less than 30 is announced. Each other hand in turn then declares any combination that will supersede that previously declared in the category. A side entitled to count for highest combination in a category may count all other holdings of the same class. Thus, if one player holds a sequence of four, and it is good, his partner may count a tierce.

Scoring is as in three-hand, with 20 necessary for repic or pic and jumping respectively to 90 or 60. (Note that if both partners of a side hold carte blanche, they score 90 for repic.)

Eldest hand makes the opening lead, and all rules of play and scoring are as in two-hand.

IMPERIAL

Imperial is sometimes described as "Piquet with a trump." This is as accurate as calling Pinochle "Whist with a double-deck." Imperial and Piquet probably developed independently from the same basic idea of comparing the hands for certain scoring combinations: this idea generated a host of games in the eighteenth century, such as Ambigu, Hoc, Poque, Romestecq, Gillet.

The early rules of Imperial do not include *carte blanche* and *point* as scoring combinations. They were probably added by Piquet players.

PLAYERS

Two. A three-hand version is described in early books, but is conceded to have been little played.

CARDS

The pack of 32. The cards in each suit rank: **K** (high), **Q, J, A, 10, 9, 8, 7**.

PRELIMINARIES

Cards are drawn for deal; higher card deals first. Dealer has the right to shuffle last. His opponent cuts, and must leave at least two cards in each packet.

DEALING

Each player receives twelve cards, dealt in rounds of two or three at a time. The twenty-fifth card is turned for trump.

COUNTERS

Score is kept with chips of two colors, as white and red. One red chip is worth six whites. A common stock of ten whites and eight reds suffices. For each increment to his score the player draws and sets before him chips of the appropriate kind and number.

HONORS

In the trump suit, as fixed by the turn-up card, there are five *honors:* king, queen, jack, ace, seven. If the turn-up is an honor, dealer at once scores 1 white chip.

CALLING

Non-dealer commences by showing any *imperials* he may hold. An imperial is any one of the combinations described below. He next announces his point, as below; then makes the opening lead. Dealer, before playing to the lead, shows his own imperials, shows a superior point or concedes that non-dealer's is good. In the last case, non-dealer must show his point, the rule being that every combination scored must be exposed to inspection by opponent.

The prescribed order of calling must be strictly observed. Neither may score for combinations in hand after playing to the first trick. If either calls his point before his imperials, he loses the latter.

Chips won for imperials are taken from the pool immediately upon showing. The chip for point is taken after dealer has settled which player has the superior point.

The several types of imperials, which must be announced in the given order, are as follows:

Carte Blanche is a hand containing no king, queen or jack. Score, 2 reds. (Some play that if either holds carte blanche, only this and other imperials are scored for the deal. Point is omitted, and the hand is not played out.)

Sequence is the four top cards of any suit: **K, Q, J, A**. There is no extra credit for additional cards in the sequence. Score, 1 red. (Some count the sequence in trumps as 2 reds.)

Fours are four cards of any rank except nine and eight.

Dealer (alone) may include the turn-up card as part of his hand in making sequences and fours.

Point is the holding in any suit that has the greatest total value, reckoning the ace as 11, each face card as 10, each other card its index value. Non-dealer announces the total count of his best suit, not the number of cards in the suit. Dealer must concede "Good" if his best suit is of less or equal total (non-dealer wins a tie). To prove "Not good," dealer need show only enough cards of his own suit to exceed non-dealer's point.

Example: Non-dealer announces "Thirty nine." Dealer holds ♠**A, Q, J, 10, 8**; he may show the four top cards and score point, concealing the fact that he has a fifth card in the suit. But he must show from the top of the suit, omitting only the lowest cards.

Score for point, 1 white chip.

THE PLAY

Non-dealer makes the opening lead. A lead calls upon the other to follow suit if able; and if void, to trump if able; and in either case, to win if able. A trick is won by the higher trump, or by the higher card of the suit led. The winner of a trick leads to the next.

The objects in play are to capture trump honors and to win as many tricks as possible. Cards are not gathered in tricks; each plays his own cards face up before himself, and may examine them at any time.

SCORING

At the end of play, the results are scored in the following order:

Imperial Tombee. For the four highest trumps in tricks, including at least one originally dealt to opponent, 1 red chip. (This "imperial in play" should be scored only by prior agreement. If it is omitted, trump honors are more conveniently scored as they are played, instead of after the twelfth trick.)

Honors. For each trump honor taken in tricks (regardless of whether originally held or caught from opponent), 1 white chip.

Tricks. For winning majority of the tricks, 1 white chip for each won in excess of six (often misstated as "for each won in excess of opponent"); but for *capot*, the winning of all twelve tricks, 2 red chips.

When a player amasses six or more white chips, he returns six of them to the pool and takes one red in exchange, thereby marking an imperial.

Whenever one player marks an imperial (either in calling or in playing), his opponent must return all white chips to the pool. The one exception to this rule is that an adverse imperial called before the play does not cost a player his white chips if he holds one or more imperials himself. This is the only category in which scoring is construed to be done simultaneously. In every other case, one player is bound to score before the other. To recapitulate the order of scoring:

> Honor turned for trump
> Imperials in hand
> Point
> Imperial in play (if allowed)
> Honors in tricks
> Majority of tricks

Examples of scoring:

1. Each has five whites when play begins. The first to catch a trump honor in tricks will mark an imperial and force the return of opponent's whites.
2. Player has five whites as deal begins. He wins point, but the only imperial is four jacks held by opponent. Player loses his five whites, as the imperial counts first, but then regains one for his point.

Game is five imperials. The first to amass five red chips wins forthwith and the current deal is not played out.

IRREGULARITIES

The laws of Piquet (page 416) may be applied, except as to revoke. In Imperial, a revoke is failure to follow suit when able, or to trump when able, or to win when able. A revoke may be claimed at any time before the cut for the next deal. The cards are replayed from the trick where the revoke occurred; the revoker may not score for tricks won, while his opponent scores all to which he is entitled by the replay.

CALABRASELLA

PLAYERS

Three. Four may participate, with the dealer giving no cards to himself.

CARDS

The Spanish pack of 40, made by discarding eights, nines, and tens from the pack of 52. The cards in each suit rank: **3** (high), **2**, **A**, **K**, **Q**, **J**, **7**, **6**, **5**, **4**. The six highest cards have scoring values: the ace counts 3 points, **3**, **2**, **K**, **Q**, **J** each count 1 point.

DEALING

The lowest of cards drawn deals first. Twelve cards are dealt to each hand, two at a time. The remaining four cards form a widow.

BIDDING

Eldest hand must declare "I pass" or "I play." If he passes, the next hand has the same option, and so on. If all pass, the deal is abandoned. If any says "I play," the play commences forthwith.

THE PLAY

The Player (he who elected to play) names the three of any suit, provided it is not in his hand; or, if he has all the threes, any two that he does not hold. The holder (if any) of the named card must surrender it to the Player, receiving in exchange any card the Player wishes to give. The latter card must not be exposed to the third player.

Next the Player discards a number of cards from his hand, from one to four—he must discard at least one. The widow is turned face up, and the Player selects what cards he wishes to restore his hand to twelve. The four cards then set aside are added to the last trick and go to the winner thereof.

After the exchange and the draw, the hand at left of the Player makes the opening lead. He may lead any card. A lead calls upon each other hand to follow suit if able. A trick is won by the highest card of the suit led, there being no trump suit. The winner of a trick leads to the next.

The two others play in temporary partnership against the Player. The object of each side is to win cards of counting value in tricks. Each suit contains 8 points, and winning the last trick counts 3 (apart from any counting cards in it and from the widow cards), so that there are 35 points in the game.

SCORING

The Player collects from or pays to both opponents the difference between the total of points won in play by each side. *Example:* The Player takes 19 points, opponents 16; each opponent pays the Player 3. But if either side takes all 35 points, the other pays 70 each.

IRREGULARITIES

If there is any misdeal, the same dealer deals again.

Looking at the widow before declaring or discarding costs 35 points, payable to each other player. If an opponent looks at any card of the widow before the Player has discarded, the Player may also look at the card and discard accordingly.

If an opponent leads out of turn, the Player may halt play, put the rest of his cards and the widow with his tricks, count 3 for last trick, and settle the deal, with the opponents counting only the points won prior to the error.

A revoke by either side costs 9 points, deducted from the revoking side at the end of play and added to the other.

STRATEGY

The natural tendency is to elect to play on hands that are too weak. The opportunity to improve the hand by the exchange and the draw appears to give license to play on a mere average hand—in fact, old manuals recommend this course. But against competent defense an "average hand" plus the three gained by the exchange will be butchered. See the example deal.

The fact is that considerable strength is needed to offset the disadvantage of playing against two opponents. As there is no trump suit, the Player must usually hold at least one stopper in every suit, and if the defense finds his weak suit on the opening lead his hand may be ruined by this suit when the defense regains the lead to cash it. A solid suit in the Player's hand is a great comfort to him—but to capture all 8 points in one suit avails little if the hand then has to lead away from tenaces in the remaining suits.

The possible improvement from the widow should not be overrated. If the Player has adequate protection in all suits, he rarely can afford to discard more than two cards, and normal expectation is that the widow will not hold more than two desirable cards.

There are ten cards in each suit; if all of a suit are in play, some hand has at least four. When a hand holds four, the probability is better for a 4-2 than for a 3-3 split of the rest of the suit. The Player has to reckon with the chances that the opponents will make a long card in a suit of which he holds three cards or less, and that his own four-card suit will not yield a long card. Perhaps the most consistent advantage gained from the widow is knowledge of what cards will not be in play—what suits will be short of ten cards.

Much depends upon the ability of the players in defense. Calabrasella is comparable with Whist in its opportunity for *throw-ins*, *squeezes*, and such like complex plays. An expert playing with two tyros has perhaps a greater "edge" than in any other three-hand game.

EXAMPLE DEAL

After two passes, the dealer elects to play, holding

♠ 3 2 5
♡ A Q 5
♣ 2 K Q
◇ 2 K 6

This hand is worth playing, in any position. The Player calls the ♡3, which is given up by eldest hand in exchange for the ♠5. The Player discards the ◇6 and ♣Q. The widow is: ♠J 7 ♣A ◇4. The Player takes the ♠J and ♣A.

In the play below, the card underlined wins the trick. The card below it is the lead to the next trick.

♠ Q 6 4
♡ J 6
♣ 3 J 7
◇ 3 Q 7 5
OB

♠ A K 5		♠ 3 2 J
♡ 2 K 7 4		♡ 3 A Q 5
♣ 6 5 4	*OA* *P*	♣ 2 A K
◇ A J		◇ 2 K

Discard: ♠ 7 ♣ Q ◇ 6 4

TRICK	OPPONENT A	OPPONENT B	PLAYER	P WINS	O'S WIN
1	♣ 4	♣ 3	♣ K		2
2	♡ K	♡ 6	♡ Q		2
3	♣ 5	♣ 7	♣ A	3	
4	♣ 6	♣ J	♣ 2	2	
5	♡ 4	♡ J	♡ 3	2	
6	♡ 7	♠ Q	♡ 5		1
7	♡ 2	◇ Q	♡ A		5
8	◇ A	◇ 3	◇ K		5
9	◇ J	◇ 5	◇ 2	2	
10	♠ 5	♠ 4	♠ 3	1	
11	♠ K	♠ 6	♠ 2	2	
12	♠ A	◇ 7	♠ J		4
			last trick		3
			discard		1
			Total	12	23

The Player loses 11 points.

Trick 5. Although *P* suspects that the hearts were split 4–2, all he can do is continue the suit and use the fourth round for a throw-in if he cannot win it.

Trick 8. *OA* can be fairly sure that *P* does not have both ◊**3** and ◊**2**, else he would have used this suit for a throw-in rather than hearts (if he also had a third diamond), or would have tried to drop the ace—since at least one diamond is in the discard. If *P* has ◊**3** he will undoubtedly try to save it for ◊**A**. Therefore *OA* leads ◊**A** to clarify matters in case *OB* has the ◊**3**.

Trick 11. As the cards lie, *P* would do better to lead the ♠**J** and take the last trick. But naturally he hopes to drop the ace doubleton from *OB*'s hand.

CRIBBAGE

According to John Aubrey (*Brief Lives*), Cribbage was invented by Sir John Suckling (1609–1642). Recent research tends to confirm this assertion. Probably it is an elaboration of an older game, Noddy, for which a special scoring board was sometimes used. A jack in the crib, of same suit as the starter, was formerly called *Knave Noddy* (as in Cotton's *Compleat Gamester*, 1674). The term has become *His Nobs*.

The original game was played with hands of five cards. The modern game gives each player six. That is virtually the only change from Suckling's directions.

PLAYERS

Two. The variants for three and four players are equally popular.

CARDS

The pack of 52. The cards in each suit rank: **K** (high), **Q**, **J**, **10**, **9**, **8**, **7**, **6**, **5**, **4**, **3**, **2**, **A**. The *counting values* are: **K**, **Q**, **J**, **10**, each 10 (wherefore these are called *tenth cards*); ace, one; all other cards, their index value.

CRIBBAGE BOARD

Indispensable to scoring is the device known as the *cribbage board*. This is a rectangular panel, long and narrow, in which are four rows of 30 holes each. (See illustration.) At one end, or in the center, are two or four additional holes, called *game holes*. The board is placed between the two players, and each keeps his own score on the two rows of holes nearest himself. Each is supplied with two *pegs*. Before the first hand, the pegs are placed in the game holes. On making his first score, the player advances one peg an appropriate number of holes (one per point) away from the *game end*

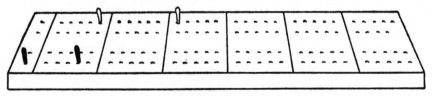

Cribbage Board

of the board. The second score is recorded by placing the second peg an appropriate distance ahead of the first. For each subsequent increment, the near peg is jumped ahead of the other, the distance between the two pegs always showing the amount of this last increment.

The traditional mode of scoring is down (away from the game end) the outer row, and up the inner row. "Once around" is a game of 61 points. "Twice around" is a game of 121 points.

PRELIMINARIES

Cards are drawn; the lower deals first. If cards of equal rank are drawn, both players draw again. Dealer has the right to shuffle last. Non-dealer cuts, and must leave at least four cards in each packet.

DEALING

Each player receives six cards, dealt one at a time face down, beginning with non-dealer. The turn to deal alternates. The dealer has an advantage.

LAYING AWAY

After seeing his hand, each player *lays away* two cards face down. The four cards laid away, placed in one pile, form the *crib*. The crib counts for the dealer. Non-dealer therefore tries to lay away *balking cards*—cards that are least likely to create a score in the crib.

THE STARTER

After both hands have laid away, non-dealer lifts off a packet from the top of the stock (the rest of the pack). Again, each packet must contain at least four cards. Dealer turns up the top card of the lower packet, which is then placed on top of the stock when the packets are reunited. The card thus turned up is called *the starter*. If it is a jack, dealer immediately pegs 2, called *2 for his heels*.

THE PLAY

Non-dealer begins the play by laying a card from his hand face up on the table, announcing its *counting value*. Dealer then shows a card, announcing the total count of the two cards. Play continues in the same way, by alternate exposures of cards, each player announcing the new total count. The total may be carried only to 31, no further. If a player adds a card that brings the total exactly to 31, he pegs 2. If a player is unable to play another card without exceeding 31, he must say "Go," and his opponent pegs 1, but before so doing, opponent must lay down any additional cards he can without exceeding 31. If such additional cards bring the total to exactly 31, he pegs 2 instead of 1.

Whenever a *go* occurs, the opponent of the player who played the last card must lead for a new count starting at zero. Playing the last card of all counts as a *go*. (Since non-dealer makes the opening lead, dealer is bound to peg at least 1 in play.)

Besides pegging for 31 and go, the player may also peg for certain combinations made in play, as follows:

Fifteen. Making the count total 15 pegs 2.

Pair. Playing a card of same rank as that previously played pegs 2. Playing a third card of same rank makes *pair royal* and pegs 6. Playing the fourth card of the same rank makes *double pair royal* and pegs 12.

The tenth cards pair strictly by rank, a king with a king, a queen with a queen, and so on. (King and jack do not make a pair, although each has the counting value 10.)

Run. Playing a card which, with the two or more played immediately previously, makes a sequence of three or more cards, pegs 1 for each card in the *run*.

Runs depend on rank alone; the suits do not matter. Nor does the score for run depend upon playing the cards in strict sequence, so long as the three or more last cards played can be arranged in a run. *Example:* **7**, **6**, **8** played in that order peg 3 for run; **5**, **2**, **4**, **3** played in that order score 4 for run.

Any of the foregoing combinations count, whether the cards are played alternately or one player plays several times in succession in consequence of a go. *Example:* N (non-dealer) leads **4** and says "Four"; D (dealer) plays **Q** and says "Fourteen"; N plays **Q**, says "Twenty-four and two for pair," and pegs 2 for pair; D plays **3** and says "Twenty-seven"; N says "Go"; D plays **2** and **A**, pegging 3 for run and 1 for go; N then lays down two jacks and pegs 2 for pair and 1 for last.

But a combination does not score if it is interrupted. Any go is an interruption. *Example:* If one player gains a go by play of a **9**, the other cannot score for pair by lead of a **9**.

Another kind of interruption is a foreign card in a sequence. *Example:* **8**, **7**, **7**, **6** are played in that order; dealer pegs 2 for fifteen, and non-dealer pegs 2 for pair; but dealer does not score for run because the extra **7** breaks it.

SHOWING

After the play, the hands are *shown*, i.e., counted. Non-dealer shows first, then dealer's hand, then crib.

The starter is deemed to belong to each hand, so that each hand includes five cards. Combinations of scoring value are as follows:

Fifteen. Each combination of two or more cards that total fifteen scores 2.

Pair. Each pair of cards of the same rank scores 2.

Run. Each combination of three or more cards in sequence scores 1 for each card in the run.

Flush. Four cards of the same suit in hand score 4; four cards in hand or crib of same suit as the starter score 5. (No count for four-flush in crib.)

His Nobs. Jack of same suit as the starter, in hand or crib, scores 1.

It is important to note that every separate grouping of cards that makes a fifteen, pair, or run counts separately. Three of a kind, *pair royal*, count 6 because three sets of pairs can be made; similarly, four of a kind, *double pair royal*, contain six pairs and count 12. Other examples:

The highest possible hand is **J, 5, 5, 5**, with starter the **5** of same suit as the jack. There are four fifteens by combining the jack with a five; four more by combinations of three fives; a total of 16 for fifteens; the double pair royal adds 12 for a total of 28; and *his nobs* adds 1 for maximum score of 29. (The score of 2 for *his heels* does not count in the total of the hand, since it is pegged before play.)

A hand (with starter) of **8, 8, 7, 7, 6** contains four fifteens (either eight with either seven) for 8; plus four runs of three (the residue after each fifteen is picked out) for 12; plus two pairs for 4; a total of 24.

A *double run* is a run with one card duplicated, as **4, 3, 3, 2**. Exclusive of fifteens, a double run of three cards counts 8; of four cards, 10. A *triple run* is a run of three with one card triplicated, as **K, K, K, Q, J**. Exclusive of fifteens, it counts 15. A *quadruple run* is a run of three with two different cards duplicated, as the example **8, 8, 7, 6, 6** previously given. Exclusive of fifteens, it counts 16.

No hand can be constructed that counts 19, 25, 26, or 27. A time-honored way of showing a hand with not a single counting combination is to say "I have nineteen."

The customary order in showing is to count fifteens first, then runs, then pairs, but there is no compulsion of law. *Example:* A hand (with starter) of **9, 6, 5, 4, 4** will usually be counted "Fifteen 2, fifteen 4, fifteen 6 and double run makes 14," or simply "Fifteen 6 and 8 is 14."

MUGGINS

The hands and crib are counted aloud, and if a player claims a greater total than is due him, his opponent may require correction. In some localities, if a player claims less than is due, his opponent may say "Muggins" and himself score the points overlooked. It is advisable to come to an understanding, before a game begins, whether or not the *muggins* privilege shall be allowed.

SCORING

The usual *game* is 121, but it may be set at 61 by agreement. Since the player wins who first returns to the game hole after going "twice around," the scores must be pegged strictly in order: his heels, pegging in play, non-dealer's hand, dealer's hand, crib. Thus, if non-dealer goes out on showing his hand, he wins, even though dealer might have gone out with a greater total if allowed to count his hand and crib.

When a game of 121 is played for a stake, a player wins a single game if the loser makes 91 points or more. If the loser fails to reach 91, he is *skunked* and the other wins a double game. If the loser fails to reach 61 points, he is *double skunked* and loses a quadruple game.

IRREGULARITIES

Misdeal. There must be a new deal by the same dealer if the cards are not dealt one at a time, if any hand receives the wrong number of cards, if a card is found faced in the pack, if a card is exposed in dealing, or if the pack be found imperfect.

Wrong Number of Cards. If one hand (not crib) is found to have the wrong number of cards after laying away for the crib, the other hand and crib being correct, the opponent may either demand a new deal or may peg 2 and rectify the hand by drawing out excess cards of dealing additional cards from the pack to supply a deficiency. If the crib is incorrect, both hands being correct, non-dealer pegs 2 and the crib is corrected by drawing out excess cards or dealing added cards from the pack. If more than one hand (including crib) is found incorrect, there must be a new deal, and if either player held the correct number in his hand he pegs 2.

Erroneous Announcement. There is no penalty for announcing a wrong total of cards or a wrong count, but the error must be corrected on demand. If an error in announcing the total is not noticed until the next card is played, it stands as announced. If an error in counting a hand is not noticed until the opponent commences counting, or until the cut for the next deal, it stands.

No player is entitled to help from another or from a bystander in counting his hand. Scores overlooked may not be taken by the opponent unless there has been previous agreement to enforce *muggins*.

Erroneous Play. A player who calls "go" when able to play may not correct his error after the next card is played. A player who gains a go and fails to play additional cards when able may not correct his error after the next card is played. In either case, the card or cards erroneously withheld are dead as soon as seen by the opponent, and the offender may not play them nor peg with them, and the opponent of the offender pegs 2 for the error.

Error in Pegging. If a player places a peg short of the amount to which he is entitled, he may not correct his error after he has played the next card or after the cut for the next deal. If he pegs more than his announced score, the error must be corrected on demand at any time before the cut for the next deal and his opponent pegs 2.

STRATEGY

Non-dealer should try to give the crib balking cards. The best cards are kings and aces, because they have the least chance of producing sequences. Tenth cards are generally good, provided that the two cards laid away are not too *near*. Good combinations are king with ten, nine, eight, seven, or six; less good is queen and ten. When nothing better offers, give two *wide* cards—at least three apart in rank.

Dealer of course should give his crib the best cards he can, while retaining the best hand he can. A sequence of three should almost never be broken, since the turn of a card of one of the ranks will add at least 5 to the count. Naturally a double run is kept intact, even if some fifteens have to be abandoned. With a poor hand, keep cards in hand for pegging. The best pegging cards are **5, 7, 8, 6, 9** in about that order. With an excess of high cards, keep an ace or deuce for a possible 31.

Examples of laying away:

K, 9, 7, 6, 4, 2. Either player should lay away **K, 4**. With only 2 points in the whole hand, the best chance is to keep cards for pegging.

Q, 8, 8, 6, 5, 3. Non-dealer should give **Q, 3**. Dealer should give **8, 8**; this will cost 3 points if a **7** is turned, but has a much better chance of producing additional scores in crib.

J, 8, 5, 3, 3, A. Non-dealer should give **8, A**. Dealer should give **J, 5**. When feasible, give the crib a **5**, because non-dealer is likely to give a tenth card.

9, 7, 4, 3, 2, A. Non-dealer should give **7, A**. This keeps 5 points in his hand and is the best chance to balk the crib. Dealer should give **9, 7**, keeping only **4** in his hand, but increasing the chances of improvement in both hand and crib.

Proverbially the safest lead is a **4**. The next card cannot make a 15. Lower cards are also safe from this point of view, but are better treasured for go and 31. The lead of a tenth card is fairly good, especially if it saves lower cards for pegging. The most dangerous leads are **7** and **8**, but may be made to trap the opponent when they are backed with other close cards. Thus from **8, 7, 7** lead a **7** regardless of the rest of the hand; if dealer plays **8** for a fifteen, you play **8** for a pair, while if he plays **7** for a pair your other **7** makes pair royal.

Generally speaking, play *on* (toward a sequence) when you have close cards and *off* when you do not. *Example:* Non-dealer leads **4**, and dealer holds **J, 9, 9, 6**. It would be very poor to play the six, since non-dealer would score with **5** or **6** and dealer could not counter with a score. Dealer should play off with a **9**.

However, the state of the score is a consideration. If far behind, play on when there is any chance of building a score for yourself; if well ahead, balk your opponent by playing off unless you will surely peg as much as he by playing on. When both players are close to game, dealer may have to throw caution to the winds and try to peg out, since non-dealer shows first. *Example:* Non-dealer needs 10 points for game and dealer 5. Dealer's hand is **8, 7, 7, 6, 5, 5**. He should lay away **7, 5**, keeping one card of each rank, and play for every possible peg, no matter how much he may give opponent.

Experienced players watch the score at all times. The average value of a hand is about 7 points; of the crib, about 5. The average amount pegged in play is between 4 and 5. In two consecutive deals, giving each player two hands and a crib, plus the play, a player is said to be *at home* (up to average expectation) if he reaches 29 points. (But Pasquin gives average expectation as only 25.) If short of the 29th hole after two deals, a player will play *on*, make risky discards, and otherwise try to recoup. If at home, the player will try to balk his opponent rather than take risks to run up a large score for himself.

Five-card Cribbage

This is the original game. Its points of difference from the six-card modern variant previously described are as follows:

Each hand receives five cards. Two are laid away to the crib, leaving only three for play. In showing, each hand thus comprises (with the starter) only four cards, but the crib includes five.

Game is 61 points. (The average value of a hand is less than 5, of the crib, 5. The expectation of pegging is 2 for dealer, 1½ for non-dealer. The importance of the *go* is proportionately greater.) A player is considered *at home* if he makes 17 in two consecutive deals. To offset the advantage of the deal, non-dealer in the first hand at the beginning of a game is given a start of 3 points.

In the five-card game, the average value of the crib is greater than of a hand. (The converse is true in the six-card game.) Consequently it is the more urgent for non-dealer to lay away so as to balk the crib, rather than to preserve his own prospects.

Three-hand Cribbage

Each player receives five cards, and one card is dealt to start the crib. Each hand lays away one card to the crib, which belongs to the dealer. The cut for starter is made by eldest hand, who then makes the opening lead. The turn to play is to the left. When one player says "Go," the hand at his left must play if able, and if he does play, the third hand must also play if able. The point for go is scored by the last to play. Eldest hand shows first, then the player at his left, then dealer's hand, then crib. The turn to deal passes to the left.

Four-hand Cribbage

Cards are drawn; the two lowest play as partners against the two highest. Alternatively, each can play for himself. Lowest card has choice of seats and deals first. Partners sit alternately. Five cards are dealt to each player. Each hand lays away one card to the crib, which belongs to dealer. Eldest hand cuts for the starter, and makes the opening lead. After a call of "Go," each succeeding player in turn has opportunity to play and thus to score for the go. The scores made by both partners of a side, in play and in showing, are pooled. Non-dealing side shows first, then dealer's side, finally crib. Game is 121.

Expectation for a hand or crib is respectively 7 or 5, as in six-card two-hand play, but here the average per side in play is about 9 points. A side is *at home* if it makes about 48 points in two consecutive deals.

If four are playing as individuals and a stake is involved, the game is over as soon as a player reaches 121. The winner collects the difference in score from each of the other players. The runner-up pays the winner, but collects the score differential from those below him. Similarly, the third finisher wins from the fourth, and the loser pays all above him. Only the player who has won the game is entitled to a skunk or double skunk bonus.

SCOTCH WHIST
(CATCH THE TEN)

PLAYERS

From two to eight may play, each for himself, but the best game by far is for four, in partnerships, as described as follows.

CARDS

The pack of 36, made by deleting fives, fours, threes and deuces from the pack of 52. The cards in each plain suit rank: **A** (high), **K, Q, J, 10, 9, 8, 7, 6**. The rank of trumps is the same except that the jack is above the ace.

PRELIMINARIES

Partnerships are determined in any agreed manner. Partners sit alternately. Cards are drawn; highest deals first. The dealer has the right to shuffle last. The pack is cut by the player at his right. The cut must leave at least four cards in each packet.

DEALING

The cards are dealt one at a time in rotation to the left, commencing with eldest hand. The entire pack is dealt, each hand thus being nine cards. The last card, belonging to the dealer, is turned, and fixes the trump suit.

THE PLAY

Eldest hand leads any card. A lead calls upon each other hand to follow suit if able; if unable, the hand may play any card. A trick is won by the highest trump, or by the highest card of the suit led. The winner of a trick leads to the next.

The object of play is to win tricks and also to capture the five highest trumps, especially the ten.

SCORING

When won in tricks, the top trumps have the point values; jack 11, ace 4, king 3, queen 2, ten 10. The side that wins the majority of the tricks also scores one point for each card over 18 (its original share). For example, the side winning five tricks scores 2 points for *cards*. At the end of play, the points are counted in order: ten of trumps, *cards*, ace, king, queen, jack. The first side to reach 41 points wins a game.

IRREGULARITIES

If a side revokes, it loses the game at once. (For this traditional rule is better substituted: the revoking side scores no points in that deal, while the opponents score all that they make.) All other cases may be settled by the rules of Whist.

STRATEGY

As is implied by the name of the game, the play centers chiefly around catching the ten of trumps, since all other points are awarded largely by the luck of the deal.

The player dealt the ten usually tries to void himself of his shortest plain suit, so as to be able to ruff with the ten. With the ten singleton or doubleton, the player usually does best to lead it, in case his partner has the ace; if the opponents hold the ace, at least the partnership knows that it has to concentrate on winning tricks. A player dealt the ace of trumps must give consideration to leading it in case his partner has the ten; if dealt the ace and king, the hand should lead the ace at earliest opportunity.

A low trump lead usually shows that the hand has the ten and three other trumps, but it may have been made to clear out trumps so as to cash established plain cards. Some of the conventions of Whist play may well be employed, notably the *echo* or *Blue Peter*—the play of an unnecessarily high plain card, followed by a lower card of the same suit, to indicate a desire to have partner lead trumps.

OH HELL (BLACKOUT)

All that we know of the history of this game is that it began to be played in New York clubs in 1931, and it was said to have come from England. Popular throughout the United States, it has the rare merit of being extremely simple to learn and play at, while affording extraordinary opportunity for skill in bidding and play.

PLAYERS

Any number from three to seven may play. The best game is with four. Whatever the number, each plays for himself.

CARDS

The pack of 52. The cards in each suit rank: **A** (high), **K, Q, J, 10, 9, 8, 7, 6, 5, 4, 3, 2**.

PRELIMINARIES

Cards are drawn, and the highest has choice of seats and deals first. If equal cards are drawn, the tying players must draw again. The other players should take places to left of dealer, in descending rank of cards drawn.

Dealer shuffles last and the pack is cut by the player at his right. The cut must leave at least four cards in each packet. The cards are dealt one at a time to the left, beginning with eldest hand.

DEALING

A game comprises a series of deals. For the first deal, each player receives one card; for the next, two; and so on to the point where the entire pack is dealt. The hands must be equal; therefore any extra cards left over in the last deal are put aside unseen. (Some play that the extra cards are exposed for all to see.) With four players, a game is thus 13 deals; with five, 10 deals; with six, 8 deals; with seven, 7 deals. With only three players, 17 deals are likely to become tedious; the game is better limited to 15.

The deal rotates to the left during the game. When more than one game is played without reseating, the first dealer should be changed in each game, since the last dealer in a game has an advantage.

After every deal in a game but the last, the next card of the pack is turned up for trump. No card is turned for the last deal, which is played at no trump.

BIDDING

Each player in turn, commencing with eldest hand, must make a bid. This bid is the precise number of tricks that the player believes he can win. The minimum bid is "zero," often signified by "pass"; the maximum is the number of cards in the hand. Thus on the first deal the only alternatives are "zero" and "one." It is important to note that each player contracts to win exactly the amount of his bid—neither less nor more.

All the bids must be recorded on paper. The duty should be assigned to an agreed scorekeeper, and after the bidding is completed he should announce "over," "under," or "even," according as to the total tricks bid exceed, fall short of, or equal the number of cards per hand. This information is essential to each player in guiding his strategy.

THE PLAY

Eldest hand makes the opening lead. A lead calls upon each other hand to follow suit if able; if unable, the hand may play any card. A trick is won by the highest trump, or by the highest card of the suit led. The winner of a trick leads to the next. The objective of each player is primarily to make his own contract; if he "busts," he tries to "bust" as many others as he can, to protect his own interests.

SCORING

A player who exactly makes his contract scores 10 plus the amount of his bid. A player who "busts" by winning more or less tricks than his bid scores nothing. The player with the highest total score at the end of a game wins.

Various methods of settlement are used. The winner may collect from every other player, according to the difference of respective totals. Or the winner may receive a game bonus of 10 points, and then each player may settle with every other upon the difference of scores.

(There is also variation in the scoring of a "zero" contract. Some circles allow only 5 points; others allow 5 plus the number of cards per hand in the deal. The latter method takes account of the fact that zero contracts are easier to make when there are fewer cards in play.)

IRREGULARITIES

Bid Out of Turn. There is no penalty for a bid out of turn, but such a bid must stand. The turn to bid reverts to the rightful player. A player may change his bid without penalty before the player at his left bids.

A Lead or Play Out of Turn must be retracted on demand of any player, and the card played in error must be left face up on the table and played at the first legal opportunity. A card exposed in any way but by legal play in turn becomes exposed and is dealt with in the same way.

Information. A player is entitled to be informed at any time how much any other player has bid, and how many tricks each player has won. Each player should keep his tricks arranged in an orderly fashion so that they may be counted by inspection.

Etiquette. By far the most important rule is one solely of etiquette. When a player sees that he is "busted"—unable to make his bid—he should refrain from communicating this fact to the table. Much of skill in the play rests upon estimating the probable holdings of the other players from their bids and the fall of the cards.

STRATEGY

It must be conceded that the first few deals are largely a matter of lucky guessing. With so few cards in play, "hand valuation" can have little meaning. Yet experience lays down some useful hints. When eldest hand has a high plain card, on the first deal, he should bid "one." It is true that he will "bust" if a trump is dealt, but the bid may induce the holder of a low trump to bid zero, and eldest hand will at least carry one of his opponents down with him. On the second deal, eldest hand with two high plain cards should bid one, as the chances are that one card will be trumped or overtaken. Following players should of course be guided by the bids of preceding players.

As a general principle, it is safer to underbid than overbid. The chances are usually better for losing a trick by force than winning a trick by force. For example, on the third deal eldest hand holds ♠A 2 ♡A, with spades trumps. To bid three, planning to lead the ♠A, is inferior to bidding two, planning to lead the ♡A and then the ♠2.

Ideal are holdings with which the hand can at will win or lose a trick, as ◇A 5 3. Dangerous are unguarded high or intermediate cards, as ♡Q 9. If forced to bid on a dangerous hand before other players have disclosed their intentions, strike a median between the maximum the hand might be forced to take, and the minimum it can take by force. With ◇A 5 3 ♡Q 9,
spades trumps, eldest hand should bid one, and lead ♡Q. If this wins, he should switch to ◇5. If ♡Q loses, he has ◇A in reserve.

Correct bidding all around the table sums to a total that is "under" in at least a plurality of cases. "Even" ranks next, with "over" a poor third. The dealer, of course, has an advantage in bidding last. Usually he should try to keep "under," but if he is leading the field and has a doubtful hand the right course is to make it "even"—then he enlists the aid of all players in helping him make his contract. Conversely, when dealer is far behind he should make it "uneven" whatever the looks of his hand. (In some circles the rule is that dealer *must* make the total uneven. While this is a good rule to preserve interest in play, it occasionally crucifies a dealer caught with an inflexible hand.)

The normal policy in play is to try to jettison dangerous holdings as early as possible. Thus, a high plain card, singleton or doubleton, is usually led at once, to ascertain whether any other hand can or will take it. A hand that has bid less than its trump length should lead small trumps, lest all outstanding trumps disappear by plain-suit ruffs.

CHILDREN'S
CARD
GAMES

Although the games in this section are simple enough to be understood by the very young, they are not without interest to adults. On the contrary, several of them are favorite "minor" games among expert Poker and Bridge players, notably Authors and I Doubt It, while Concentration is, of all card games, that which most nearly eliminates all element of luck.

All of these games are perennial favorites among children. In connection with each are given the limits of the age group to which experience has assigned it. Naturally these limits are not hard and fast.

Each of the games is played with one pack of 52 cards. Except where otherwise specified, the rank of cards in each suit is: **A** (high), **K, Q, J, 10, 9, 8, 7, 6, 5, 4, 3, 2**.

Slapjack

Age Group. Four to nine.

Players. Two to eight.

Dealing. The cards are dealt out one at a time as far as they will go. It does not matter if some players have more cards than others.

The very young who have not learned to deal need not do so. The pack is simply cut into packets of approximately equal size, one for each player. The original packets are kept separate from those won by slapping, and when one packet is exhausted the player borrows cards from any of the other original packets, until all are exhausted.

The Play. Each player keeps his cards in one pile face down. Each in turn beginning with eldest hand turns up one card from the top of his stock and places it in a common pile in the center of the table. Whenever a jack is turned, the first player to slap it takes all the cards in the common pile, and the next hand begins a new pile. The object of play is to win all 52 cards.

Cards won by slapping are put by the winner at the bottom of his stock. (Older children with good memories should shuffle the cards into their stocks.)

If a player loses all his stock, he stays in the game until the next jack is turned. If he slaps it first, he continues in play with the cards won, but if he fails, he is out of the game. The final winner is thus determined by a "freezeout" process. (*Alternative.* The player who has the most cards in his stock when another loses his last card is the winner.)

Rules important to enforce are:

1. Cards must be turned up from the stock *away* from the owner, so that he does not get a peek before the others.
2. Turning cards and slapping must be done with the same hand.

3. When several slap at once—and they always do!—the lowermost hand, nearest to the jack, wins.
4. If a player slaps a card that is not a jack, he must give one card from his stock, face down, to the player of the card. The penalty card is placed at the bottom of the receiver's stock.

Old Maid

Age Group. Five to ten.

Players. Two or three.

Dealing. One queen is first discarded from the pack. Then the pack is divided into packets approximately equal, one for each player. It does not matter if the distribution is unequal.

Discarding. Each player spreads his packet of cards and picks out all pairs, which he discards face up in the center of the table. There is no necessity for concealing the hand from the other players; it can be placed face up on the table, and players can help each other pick out the pairs.

The Play. When all hands have been reduced to non-paired cards, one at least is sure to hold an odd queen. This player (and usually the others too) mixes his cards behind his back and then holds them face down toward his left-hand opponent, who draws out one card. If it pairs with a card in his hand, he discards the pair, then shuffles his hand and presents it face down to his left neighbor. Play continues in the same way, each player drawing a card from the hand at his right, paired cards being discarded, until only the odd queen remains.

The player stuck with the queen is "Old Maid" and loses the game.

If before the first draw all three queens are still in play, eldest hand draws first, from dealer's hand. Otherwise the first draw is from the hand holding the one queen.

It is quite permissible, not to say obligatory, for the holder of Old Maid to coffeehouse in every way in order to cajole his left neighbor into drawing that card.

Pig

Pig is a modern simplification of an old game, *vive l'amour*, which was a four-handed game with the object of getting all thirteen cards of a suit.

Age Group. Six to ten. Also played by adults, with special cards, in parts of the United States where regular playing cards are deemed "the Devil's picture book."

Players. Three to thirteen. Best for four to seven.

Dealing. The pack comprises sets of four cards of a kind, as many sets as there are players. *Example:* Four players use 16 cards, which may be the face cards and aces, or any other four ranks.

Four cards are dealt to each player, one at a time. All look at their hands. Then, simultaneously, each places one card face down to the left, then picks up the card discarded from the right. Play continues by such simultaneous exchanges, the object of each player being to get the four cards of any one rank. As soon as any player so collects a *book*, he stops exchanging and puts his finger to his nose. Each other player, on noticing this action, must stop play and likewise put his finger to his nose. The last to do so is the Pig, and loses the deal.

Cuckoo (Ranter Go Round)

This is an ancient game, said to be of Cornish origin. While it was originally designed to accelerate the redistribution of wealth, the stakes can be left out, and it makes an easy introduction to the use of counters.

Age Group. Seven to fourteen.

Players. Five to about twenty.

Counters. Each player is provided with three counters, which represent three "lives." On losing all of his lives, a player drops out of play, and the winner is the lone survivor. The "freezeout" feature is not boring to children, because the game goes very fast if there are not too many players.

Dealing. One card is dealt to each player.

The Play. The object of play is not to be left with the lowest card at the table. The king is high, while the ace ranks below the two. Suits have no rank.

Eldest hand commences the play. If satisfied with his card, he says "Stand" and the turn passes to his left. If not satisfied with his card, he proffers it to his left neighbor, saying "Change." The call of "Change" compels this player to make the exchange of cards, unless he has a king, in which case he says "King." The announcement of "King" compels the suppliant to keep his unwanted card, and the turn passes to the left of the hand with the king. But when an exchange is forced, the player on the left of the pair who exchanged cards may demand an exchange with *his* left neighbor, and so on.

On giving an ace, two or three, in response to a demand for "Change," a player must announce the rank. This often has the effect of determining the loser without further play, since all holders of higher cards thereafter will naturally stand; only holders of equal or lower cards will ask for exchange.

When the turn reaches the dealer, he may stand on his original card, or on that received from his right, or he may discard his card, cut the stack, and take the top card of the lower packet. As soon as dealer has played, all players turn their cards face up.

The lowest card at the table loses a life—he must pay one chip into the pool. If two or more tie for lowest card, all lose a life. But if dealer has a king, obtained by drawing from the stock, he alone loses a life.

On losing all three lives, a player drops out of the game, and the rest play on to determine the winner. The last to have any lives left wins.

Authors

Authors is the proprietary name of a game for which special cards are manufactured. But it can as well be played with regular playing cards.

Age Group. Eight to sixteen. But it is also played by adults, sometimes for high stakes. The rules on irregularities are for adult play and should not be applied to juvenile games.

Players. Three to six. Best for four or five.

Dealing. The cards are dealt out, one at a time, as far as they will go. It does not matter if some players receive more cards than others.

The Play. Each player in turn, beginning with eldest hand, calls another by name and requests a card, by suit and rank, as "John, give me the six of clubs."

The card requested must be in a rank of which the asker holds at least one card, but must be of a different suit. (That is, a player may not ask for a card which he himself holds.)

If the player addressed has the card specified, he must give it and the asker has another turn. He may continue asking so long as he is successful in getting cards. When he fails, the turn passes to his left.

As soon as any player gets all four cards of one rank, he must show them and place the book on the table before him. The one who collects the most books wins the game.

When the game is played for a stake, a player on completing a book collects one chip from each other player.

Irregularities.

Misdeal. There must be a new deal by the same dealer if any card is exposed in dealing, or if any player has too few cards and calls attention to it before he has looked at his hand.

Exposed Card. When a player drops or otherwise exposes his possession of a card, he merely restores it to his hand. If a player exposes another player's possession of any card except by legally asking for and receiving it, he must pay one chip to each other player in the game.

Playing Out of Turn. If a player asks for a card when it is not his turn, he may not thereafter score for making a group in the denomination for which he called.

Failure to Show a Group. Unless a player shows a group before the end of the turn in which he makes it, he may no longer score for it.

Illegal Call. If a player asks for a card which he already holds, or asks for a card when he does not hold another card of the same denomination, he pays one chip to each other player in the game.

Failure to Give Up Card. If a player fails to hand over a card he has when properly asked for it, he pays a chip to each other player in the game and he may not score for making a group in that denomination.

Go Fish

This is a simpler form of Authors, suitable to a younger age group.

Age Group. Six to ten.

Players. Two to six.

Dealing. Cards are dealt one at a time. Each player receives: in two-hand, seven cards; with more players, five cards. The rest of the pack is placed face down in the center of the table to form the *stock*.

The Play. Commencing with eldest hand, each player in turn calls another by name and requests cards of a specified rank, as "David, give me your aces."

The card requested must be of a rank in which the asker holds at least one card. Having one or more cards of the specified rank, the player addressed must give up *all* of them. With none of the specified rank, the player replies "Go fish!" and the asker draws the top card of the stock.

A player's turn to ask continues so long as he is successful in getting the cards specified. If he is told to *go fish*, and he chances to draw a card of the rank he named, he may show this card, and his turn continues.

As soon as any player gets all four cards of one rank, he must show them and place the books on the table before him. The one who collects the most books wins the game.

If the draw from the stock completes a book in the hand, the book must at once be shown. Strictly, the player's turn does not continue unless the book is of the rank he last asked for, but among younger children this distinction is best eliminated: let the player's turn continue so long as he is successful in any way.

Stealing Bundles

This game is essentially Casino with the builds left out. It forms an easy introduction to Casino, which itself is a perennial favorite in the age group ten to sixteen.

Age Group. Six to ten.

Players. Two.

Dealing. Cards may be dealt one or two at a time. Each player first receives four cards, and four are dealt face up on the table. Thereafter, each time the hands are played out four more cards are dealt to each player, but none to the table. The game ends after the pack is exhausted.

The Play. Non-dealer plays first, and thereafter the hands play alternately. The player may either *trail* by placing a card face up on the table, or *take in* a card from the table with a card of the same rank from the hand. Cards taken in must be placed in a pile face up, forming the *bundle*. A player may *steal* his opponent's bundle by taking it in with a card of the same rank as its top card.

The player who has the greater number of cards in his bundle by the time the pack is exhausted wins the game.

Beggar-Your-Neighbor

Age Group. Eight to twelve.

Players. Two.

Dealing. Each player receives half the pack. It is not necessary to deal the cards one by one. It is simpler to shuffle thoroughly, then count off the first 26 cards for the non-dealer.

The Play. Each player holds his packet face down. Non-dealer turns up a card from the top and places it on the table. Dealer then turns a card from his packet and places it upon the other. Play continues in the same way, by alternate contributions to the common face-up pile, until interrupted by the appearance of a face card or ace.

When one player turns such a high card, the other must place upon it: four cards for an ace, three for a king, two for a queen, one for a jack. If the high card draws its quota in *lower* cards (ten or lower), the player of the high card takes up the entire common pile, places it face down under his packet, and leads for a new series of plays. But if a face card or ace appears in the course of playing the quota upon an adverse high card, the obligation is reversed, and the adversary must give a quota. The excitement of the game comes when high cards follow each other in close order, so that the last in effect "captures" all the rest.

The player who gets the entire pack into his hands wins. Naturally there is no opportunity for skill. The outcome is decided by the chance of the shuffle, and a game may end in one "run through" or may continue for a long time.

Go Boom

This game makes an easy introduction to the principles of trick-winning, following suit, and rank of cards.

Age Group. Eight to thirteen.

Players. Two to six.

Cards. The pack of 52. Ace is high in each suit. For children of minimum age, the pack should be stripped to 40 cards by discarding the face cards; the ace then ranks below the two. After the children are thoroughly familiar with the game, the face cards may be restored.

Dealing. Each player receives seven cards, dealt one at a time. The rest of the pack is placed face down to form the *stock*.

The Play. Eldest hand makes the opening lead. A lead calls upon each other hand either to follow suit or to play a card of same rank as the lead. When unable to comply, a player must draw cards from the top of the stock until able to play. After the stock is exhausted, a player unable to follow in suit or rank does not play to the trick at all.

A trick is won by the highest card of the suit led. The winner of a trick leads to the next. Since tricks in themselves have no scoring value, they need not be gathered and segregated by the winners, but may be thrown into a common discard pile.

The player who first gets rid of all his cards wins the game.

Scoring. In first learning Go Boom, children should play each deal as a separate game. Later they may adopt the following play: Cards left in the hand when one player *goes boom* (gets rid of his hand) are counted at 10 for each face card, 1 for each ace, and other cards their index value. The count of each hand is charged against the other. The player with the lowest score, when another reaches 100, wins the game.

I Doubt It

Age Group. Nine to ninety. This is one of the easiest of games to "play at," and at the same time it offers as much opportunity for skill as Poker— and of the same character. The game is an excellent "ice-breaker" for large adult parties.

The rules can be understood by children younger than nine, but the game is scarcely feasible for small hands, since the player sooner or later will have to hold a great many cards.

Players. Four to twelve. Best for six to nine.

Cards. Four or five players should use one pack of 52 cards. Six or more should use two packs shuffled together. The game is much better with two packs than with one.

Dealing. The cards are dealt out as far as they will go. It does not matter if some players receive more cards than others. Dealing should be in packets of convenient size, from two to four cards, except in the last round or two, when they should be dealt one at a time.

The Play. Eldest hand begins by placing any number of cards from one to eight (four with a single pack) face down in the center of the table, saying "Three aces"—or whatever the number of cards happens to be. Each hand in rotation thereafter must discard cards face down on the same pile, announcing the number of cards and their rank.

The rank is rigidly fixed: eldest hand must commence with aces, next hand must play kings, and so on in descending rank to deuces, then aces again, kings again, and so on in circular sequence.

The player must state correctly the number of cards he puts out, but none need be of the announced rank. The object of play is to get rid of one's entire hand; it is often advisable or necessary to add some cards not of the specified rank to the packet played.

Following a play, any other player may say "I doubt it!" Then if the last player discarded any card other than the specified rank, he must take all the cards on the table into his hand. But if the discard was strictly in accord with the announcement—as is proved by turning the last discard face up—the doubter must take up the whole discard pile.

It often happens that several players doubt the same discard. Paradoxically, this is most likely to occur when the discard is correct, the object of doubting being to obtain cards of certain ranks. The following rules as to precedence in doubting should be rigidly enforced:

1. I doubt it *may not be declared until the player's hand has quitted his discard.* A premature doubt is void, and the doubter loses his right to doubt that discard. (Announcement should be made before the cards are placed on the discard pile, to give due notice to would-be doubters.)

2. *The first to doubt takes precedence when his lead over the second doubter is clear.*

3. *When none has a clear lead in being the first to doubt, the doubter nearest the player's left in rotation has precedence.*

Scoring. The first player to get rid of all his cards wins the deal. Each deal should be treated as a separate game. Or the number of cards left in the hands may be charged against the owners, and the player with lowest score when another reaches 100 may be deemed the winner of a game. If the game is played for a stake, each other player pays the winner of a deal one chip for each card remaining in his hand.

Irregularities. There is no misdeal; any irregularity in dealing must be corrected as equitably as possible, as by transferring cards from one hand to another, even though the players have looked at their hands.

A player is bound to discard from one to eight (with the double pack) cards and announce the rank due in his turn; he may not say "I haven't any jacks" or put out more than eight cards, as a method of gaining possession of the discard pile.

If a player announces the wrong rank, he must correct the announcement on demand, but he may not change his discard if already completed. (It is legitimate to name the wrong rank deliberately, to try to trap opponents into doubting a correct discard.) If a wrong announcement of rank is not challenged before the next hand has completed his discard, it stands as regular. (Thus it may convict the next hand of wrong announcement, if that player has followed the original sequence of ranks instead of the changed sequence.)

Strategy. The player should arrange his cards by ranks, and the ranks in the order in which he will be called upon to play them. *Example:* In a seven-hand game, eldest hand should arrange the ranks: **A, 7, K, 6, Q, 5, J, 4, 10, 3, 9, 2, 8**. He should decide at once at what turn he will go out. Thus, if eldest hand in this example decides to finish with threes, he must get rid of all nines, twos, and eights early, by *cheating* in his discards. The hand is bound to be doubted when it has few cards; the plan should be to finish with as long a sequence as possible of *honest* discards. Thus, eldest hand might have decided to finish with threes because he was dealt no nines. He should plan to get rid of twos and eights in his first four or five turns, and then be strictly honest from about queens or fives to the end.

The plan may have to be modified, by extension of the finishing point, if one of the early cheating discards is doubted. It is no calamity to have to pick up a great many cards; barring occasional accidents, a hand with an unduly large share of the cards has the best chance at the table of winning. Possession of most of the cards in several ranks, and particularly a *corner* on all eight cards of a rank, enables the player to block other hands from going out. An expert player sometimes tries to get most of the pack at once, then block all other hands while he discards in huge and honest packets. The important point in this process is to keep track of who gets these packets in the doubting. When the "big hand" player is near to going out, he will have to depend on his memory of how his cards were distributed, or else he may doubt what proves to be an honest discard.

Concentration (Memory, Pelmanism)

As its various names suggest, this game is an excellent exercise for the development of visual memory.

Age Group. Nine to ninety. With children under sixteen, the contestants should be of nearly the same age or the older will have a pronounced advantage which is likely to be resented by the younger.

Players. Any number up to six can play; but the best game is for two.

The Layout. A pack of 52 cards is shuffled and then dealt face down on a table so that no two cards touch. No effort should be made to put the cards into orderly rows and files; the greater the irregularity, the better.

The Play. Each player in turn turns two cards face up, one at a time, without moving either away from its position in the layout. If the two cards are a pair, he removes them to his own pile of pairs won, and turns up two more cards. When he turns up two cards which are not a pair, he turns the cards face down, and the turn passes to his left.

The player who gathers a plurality of the cards wins the game.

While there is some luck in the game, victory goes consistently to the player who more accurately remembers the location of unpaired cards previously turned.

Persons who find the game too easy—and some do—should turn up four cards at a time and require that a player turn all four cards of a rank to win a *book*.

War

An old family favorite, this game is also known as "Everlasting," especially among adults who do not have the stamina or patience to play through the long game sessions that their children love.

Age Group. Four to nine.

Players. Usually two, although three or more can play as well.

The Deal. The cards are dealt face down into two equal packs.

The Play. Each player turns over his top card and the highest value wins. Both cards are then taken by the winner who adds them to the bottom of his pack. Play continues in this fashion until cards of equal value are faced, at which point war is declared. The two cards are placed in the center of the table, and each player makes a pack of three cards placed face down and a fourth face up. The player whose face-up card has the highest value wins both the cards in the center and his opponent's war pack. If the two cards faced up are once again of equal value there is another war until a winner is determined. Regular play is then resumed and continues until one player wins all his opponent's cards.

Three or more can play this game by combining two or more packs of cards. If two players turn up cards of equal value, all players are included in the war face-off, as above, with the next highest card taking all. A player drops out when he has lost all of his cards, and play continues until one player wins all the cards.

SOLITAIRE

Solitaire Basics

By Solitaire or Patience is meant any card game that can be played by one person. His opponent is the luck of the shuffle—or any personification thereof he chooses to pose, as Beelzebub. It is logical to suppose that Solitaire pastimes antedated games for two or more. But historical research into the origin of particular Solitaires meets a blank wall; the scribes for many centuries scorned these pastimes, and the rules were handed down only by word of mouth. Not until the nineteenth century did the first manual devoted to Patience appear.

There are probably more Solitaires than all other card games together, and certainly there is less uniformity in their appellations. Some few have achieved universally known names, like Canfield, though even here the name is mistakenly given by many to a different game, Klondike. But the reader must not take umbrage if he finds his favorite Solitaire described below under a name unknown to him.

The very term Solitaire, preferred in the United States to Patience, is borrowed. Formerly it belonged to the European version of a puzzle found among the American Indians (if, indeed, it does not go back to the Pachisi of ancient India). Pegs are placed in all but one of 33 (or 37) holes in the form of a cross, and the puzzle is to jump the pegs as in checkers, removing them from the board until only one remains.

Cards. Almost every Patience uses one or two packs of 52 cards each, the cards ranking: **K** (high), **Q, J, 10, 9, 8, 7, 6, 5, 4, 3, 2, A**. Sometimes the sequence is continuous, the ace and king being of adjacent rank.

To Win the game is to get the entire pack into a certain prefixed order, such as: the four suits segregated and each suit in sequence. This is also called *making* the game, or *breaking* it.

The Layout is the array of cards first dealt on the table, comprising usually the tableau, and sometimes a stock and some foundations also.

The Tableau is dealt in some distinctive arrangement; many Patience games differ only in the form of the tableau. Horizontal lines of cards are *rows*, while lines extending vertically away from the player are *columns*.

The Foundations are usually all the cards of a certain rank. The object in play is to build cards onto the foundations, and the game is won when all foundations are completely built up.

The Stock is a special pile of cards, a part of the layout in some games.

The Hand is the rest of the pack, if the layout does not use all the cards.

The Talon is a pile into which cards turned up from the hand are placed, when they cannot be immediately built onto the tableau or foundations.

Available Cards are those of the tableau, stock, etc. which may be transferred to other parts of the layout. Usually, certain cards of the tableau are not available until *released* by the transfer of covering cards.

A Space in the tableau, created by transferring all cards of one pile elsewhere, is often very helpful in building.

Building is specifically the manipulation of the tableau so as to release additional cards, aid in getting cards onto the foundations, and save cards from being buried in the talon.

Waste Piles are talon piles; usually they may be spread so that all cards are visible, while the talon proper must usually be kept squared up so that only the top card is visible.

Accordion

CARDS—ONE PACK

Deal cards one by one in a row from left to right, not overlapping. Whenever a card matches its immediate neighbor to the left, or matches the card third away to the left, it may be moved onto that card. Cards match if they are of the same suit or same rank. After making a move, look to see if it has made additional moves possible. Deal out the whole pack, combining piles toward the left when possible. The game is won if the pack is reduced to one pile.

Klondike

CARDS—ONE PACK

Tableau. Deal one card face up, then six face down in the same row toward the right. Deal one face up on the card just to right of the first face-up, then add another face down on each card to the right. Continue in the same manner, dealing one less card each round, turning the first face up, the rest face down. The result is seven piles, comprising 1, 2, 3, 4, 5, 6, 7 cards in order left to right. The top card of each pile is face up; the rest are face down.

Foundations. Aces, which must be put in a row above the tableau as they become available. Each foundation must be built up in suit and sequence to the king. A card once placed on a foundation may not thereafter be moved.

Building. On the uppermost card of a tableau pile may be placed a card of next-lower rank and opposite color. (The sequence of rank ends with the king, high.) All face-up cards on a tableau pile must be moved as a unit (onto a card of next-higher rank and opposite color to the bottom card of the unit). When such a transfer is made, the top face-down card of the pile is turned face up, and becomes available. The top card of the talon is always available. The top card of a tableau pile or of the talon may be played onto a foundation. It is not compulsory to build on a foundation when able, except that aces may not be built or built upon in the tableau.

FOUNDATIONS

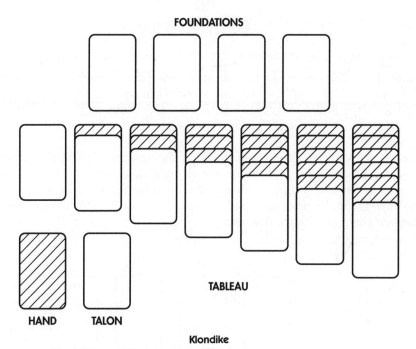

TABLEAU

HAND   TALON

Klondike

Spaces may be filled only by kings.

The Hand is turned up one card at a time and is run through only once. Any card that cannot be built or played to a foundation is placed face up on the talon.

Double Klondike

CARDS—TWO PACKS

Many solitaires can be played as games by two players. Klondike (usually miscalled Canfield) is a favorite for this purpose. Each player has a pack and makes his own Klondike layout. If one has an ace showing and the other has not, the former plays until he cannot use a card turned from his hand, whereupon the turn passes to his opponent, and so on. When neither original layout shows an ace, the player with the lowest card at the left of his tableau has precedence; if these are tied, the next card to the left decides. All aces are placed between the two players and form common foundations.

The first to get rid of all his cards onto the foundations wins the game. Or, if play comes to a standstill, the one with the most cards played to the foundations wins. It is not compulsory to play on a foundation when able; withholding a card may block the opponent from getting rid of a greater number of cards.

465

Canfield

CARDS—ONE PACK

Layout. Deal thirteen cards face down in one pile; turn the pile face up and place it at the left to form the stock. Deal the fourteenth card face up; this is the first foundation. Place it in a row above and to the right of the stock. Deal four cards face up in a row to right of stock, forming the tableau.

Foundations. All cards of the same rank as the first foundation. Such cards must be placed in the foundation row as soon as available: they may not be built or built upon in the tableau. Each foundation must be built up in the same suit and ascending sequence, the sequence in the suit being continuous, ace going on king, and so on.

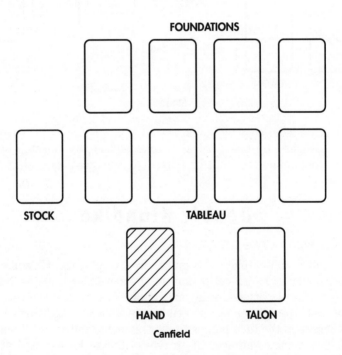

FOUNDATIONS

STOCK   **TABLEAU**

HAND   **TALON**

Canfield

Building. On the uppermost card of a tableau pile may be placed a card of next-lower rank and opposite color. A tableau pile must be moved as a unit (onto a card of next-higher rank and opposite color to the bottom card of the unit). The top card of the talon is always available. The top card of a tableau pile or of the talon may be played onto a foundation.

(Some play the rule that the top card of a tableau pile is always available.

466

Example: ♡**7** ♣**6** ♢**5** may be moved as a unit, under the regular rule, or ♢**5** may be moved onto ♠**6**, and then ♣**6** onto ♢**7**.)

Spaces must be filled by cards from the top of the stock, which should always be kept squared up so that only the top card is identifiable. After the stock is exhausted, spaces may be filled from the talon.

The Hand is turned up in packets of three cards at a time. Each packet is placed face up on the talon. The top card is available, and others below as released. After the hand is exhausted, turn over the talon, without shuffling, to form a new hand. The hand-talon may be run through any number of times, so long as any plays can be made. (Some play that the hand may be run through only three times.)

Spider

CARDS—TWO PACKS

Tableau. Deal ten cards face down in a row. Deal three more rows face down on the first. Next deal one card face down on each of the first four piles at the left. Finally deal a row of ten cards face up on the piles. The tableau thus comprises 54 cards.

Building. All building is done in the tableau, there being no separate foundations. On the uppermost card of a pile may be placed a card of next-lower rank, regardless of suit. Available for transfer is the top card of a pile, together with any or all below it which form an ascending sequence in the same suit. *Example:* The top card is ♡**5**, and below it in order are ♡**6**, ♡**7**, ♣**8**. The first one, two or three cards may be moved as a unit. But if the second card is ♢**6**, then ♡**5** must be moved before ♢**6** can be moved.

When all face-up cards have been removed from a pile, the top face-down card is turned up and becomes available.

Spaces may be filled by any available cards or units. All spaces must be filled before additional cards are dealt.

The Hand. When building on the original tableau comes to a standstill, an additional row of ten cards is dealt face up on the tableau piles. Similarly, each time all possible or desired plays are completed, an additional row is dealt, until the hand is exhausted. There is no redeal.

The Object of Play is to assemble thirteen cards of a suit, in sequence from ace to king (top to bottom). When a suit is so assembled, at the top of a tableau pile, the thirteen cards may be lifted off and discarded from play. It need not be discarded at once, however; it may be used to aid in further operations on the tableau. The game is won if the pack is discarded in eight sequences of suits.

Scorpion

CARDS—ONE PACK

Tableau. Deal a row of seven cards, the first four face down and the others face up. Deal two or more rows in the same way, overlapping the first. Then deal four more rows overlapping the first four, but all cards face up. The tableau thus comprises seven piles of seven cards each, spread so that all cards are identifiable, but with the bottom three cards of the first four piles face down.

The remaining three cards, forming the *merci*, are set aside to be used later.

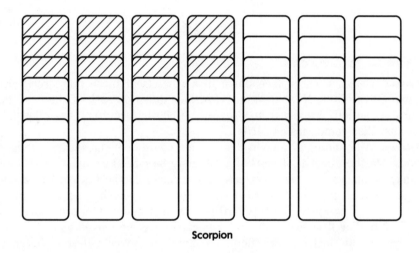

Scorpion

Building. All building is on the tableau, there being no separate foundations. On the top card of a pile may be placed the next-lower card of the same suit. Any number of cards from the top of a pile downward may be moved as a unit, provided that the bottom of the unit can be matched with the next-higher card of the same suit at the top of another pile. When all face-up cards on any of the first four piles are removed, the top of the face-down cards is turned up and becomes available. *Spaces* may be filled only by kings.

The Object of Play is to assemble all thirteen cards of a suit in order from king to ace (top to bottom) on top of a tableau pile. When any suit is so gathered, it is lifted off the tableau and discarded from play. The game is won if all four suits are assembled and discarded.

The Merci. After all operations on the tableau have come to a standstill, the three last cards of the pack are dealt face up on the first three piles. It is not obligatory to fill all spaces before dealing the *merci*. If the merci does not enable the player to win the game, a new game is in order; there is no redeal.

(Scorpion is bound to be won unless either of the following situations exist: 1. The next-lower card of same suit as a card buried face down in the tableau lies above it in the same pile, either face down, or as the first card face up. 2. There is a "criss-cross." The simplest case is illustrated by four cards in two piles, as ♣**8** on ♢**Q** in one, and ♢**J** on ♣**9** in the other. A criss-cross may involve any number of cards and any number of piles. If one is perceived in the tableau, the deal may as well be abandoned.)

The Four Seasons (Corner Card)

CARDS—ONE PACK

Layout. Deal five cards face up in the form of a cross. Deal the 6th card in the upper left corner of the cross; this is the first foundation. As other cards of same rank as the first foundation come up, place them in the other corners, making eventually a square 3 × 3.

The five cards or piles in the cross are the tableau. On the top of a tableau pile may be placed a card of next-lower rank and opposite color. Only the top card of a pile is available for transfer. A space may be filled by any available card from tableau or talon. Foundation cards may not be built nor built upon in the tableau, but must be moved to the corners at once.

Foundations are built up in suit and sequence, the sequence being continuous. *Hand* cards are turned up one at a time. Cards that cannot be built on foundations or tableau are placed face up in a talon. The top of the talon is always available. A space may be used for exchanges among the piles of the tableau, but must eventually be filled by the top of the talon before the next card is turned from the hand. The hand is run through only once.

A variant game is to deal only the five cards of the cross, placing the aces in the corners for foundations as they show up. This variant is very difficult to win.

Napoleon at St. Helena
(Forty Thieves, Big Forty)

CARDS—TWO PACKS

Tableau. Deal ten cards in a row, face up. Deal three more face-up rows overlapping the first, making 40 cards in all.

Foundations. Aces, which must be placed in a row above the tableau as soon as available. Each foundation must be built up in suit and sequence to the king.

Building. Only the uppermost card of a tableau pile is available. An available card may be played on a foundation, or on a tableau card of next-higher rank in the same unit.

Spaces may be filled by any available cards. Note that a king on a tableau pile may be moved only to a space or to a foundation.

Hand cards are turned up one at a time, and are placed in a talon pile which may be spread out so that all cards are identifiable. The top card of the talon may be played onto foundations or tableau. The hand is run through only once.

Calculation

CARDS—ONE PACK

Foundations. Place in a row one ace, one two, one three, and one four, regardless of suits. Each foundation must be built up in arithmetic sequence as follows:

> on the ace: **2, 3, 4, 5, 6, 7, 8, 9, 10, J, Q, K**
> on the two: **4, 6, 8, 10, Q, A, 3, 5, 7, 9, J, K**
> on the three: **6, 9, Q, 2, 5, 8, J, A, 4, 7, 10, K**
> on the four: **8, Q, 3, 7, J, 2, 6, 10, A, 5, 9, K**
> Suits are ignored throughout the play.

Hand cards are turned up one by one. A card that cannot be played on a foundation must be placed in one of four *waste piles* in a row below the foundations. Waste piles may be spread so that all cards are identifiable. Once on a waste pile, a card may be removed only if it can be played on a foundation. The uppermost card of a pile alone is available. The hand is run through only once.

La Nivernaise (Tournament)

CARDS—TWO PACKS

Layout. Deal two columns of four cards each, widely separated. These columns are *the flanks.* If no ace or king appears in the flanks, the chance of winning is so slight that the cards are best gathered, reshuffled, and redealt.

Deal a row of six cards face up between the flanks, in about the center of the table. Add three more rows overlapping the first, thus making six piles of four cards each. These piles constitute *the line.* (Old rules state that the line piles must be kept squared up, and that as many cards below the top in each pile may be examined as there are spaces in the flanks. This refinement substitutes luck for occasional opportunity for skill, and adds manual labor to a game already full of action.)

FLANK   FOUNDATIONS   FLANK

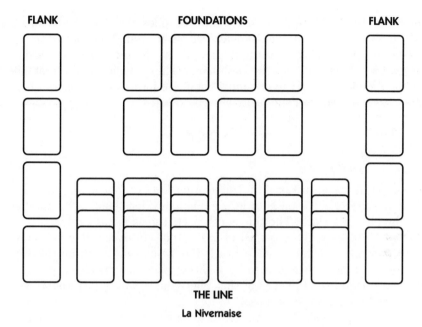

THE LINE

La Nivernaise

Foundations. Four aces of different suits and four kings of different suits must be assembled in two foundation rows above the line. It is not obligatory to play up the first card of each suit and denomination that becomes available. At the beginning of the game, an ace or king must be removed from the flanks, to make a space. (Else, as noted, the chance of winning is slight.)

Building. The only building is on the foundations, in suit and sequence. The four aces must be built up to the kings, and the four kings down to the aces. When the two foundations of the same suit meet in sequence, either can be reversed onto the other, to any desired extent. Such reversal is frequently a powerful aid in facilitating further plays. Once the sequences have passed each other, reversal is no longer possible.

Cards available for building are the flanks and the top cards of the line piles. A space in the flanks may be filled by any available card. Except as a last resort of desperation, the last space in the flanks should never be filled. Without this opportunity for maneuver, the game is almost sure to end quickly in a blockade. Of course the last space is frequently filled to initiate a train of plays making another space.

Redeals. Each time plays from the flanks and line come to a standstill, four more rows of cards are dealt upon the line piles. If at any time one line pile is entirely cleared away a column of four cards is dealt in the space, the cards overlapping.

After the hand is exhausted, the line piles may be picked up, and redealt as before. Two such redeals are permitted. Line piles should be picked up in order, with the rightmost pile at the top when the cards are turned face down to form the new hand. They should not be reshuffled. Each replenishment of the line must comprise four complete rows of cards (so far as the cards in hand last).

Clock

CARDS—ONE PACK

Tableau. Deal the entire pack in thirteen packets of four cards, face down. Place the first twelve packets in a circle; consider them to be numbered like the face of a clock. The thirteenth packet goes in the center.

The Play. Turn over the top card of the 13-pile. Suppose it to be a seven. Place it face up, halfway underneath the 7-pile, and turn up the top of that pile. Suppose this card to be a three; place it partially under the 3-pile and turn up the top card of that pile—and so on. A jack counts as 11, queen as 12, king as 13, ace as 1.

The game is won if all other cards are turned face up before the fourth king is reached. The game ends when the fourth king turns up, because then the 13-pile does not furnish a card with which to continue play.

Pyramid

CARDS—ONE PACK

Tableau. Deal 28 cards in the form of a triangle, comprising seven rows increasing from one card in the first row to seven in the last. The end cards of each row should overlap the end cards of the previous row, while the interior cards should each overlap two adjacent cards of the preceding row.

The Play. Turn up cards one at a time from the hand, and place those which cannot be used in a talon pile. The top of the talon, as well as a card just turned from the hand, is always available to be *matched* with an available card in the tableau.

A tableau card is available if it is not covered by another. At the outset, only the seven cards of the last row are available. The removal of any two adjacent cards in a row releases one card in the row below.

Two cards *match* if they total 13, counting ace as 1, jack 11, queen 12, other cards their index value. Kings, counting 13, are removed singly whenever they are released in the tableau or turned up from the hand.

Any two available cards that match, provided one is from the tableau and the other from hand or talon, are removed together and discarded from play (in a separate waste pile, not on the talon).

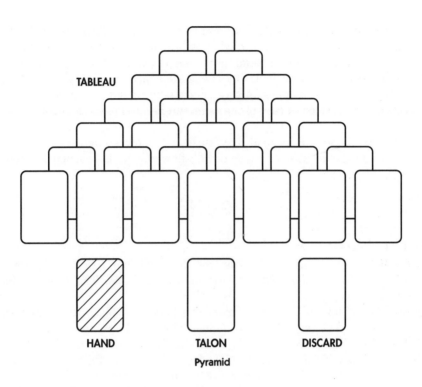

TABLEAU

HAND   TALON   DISCARD

Pyramid

The Object of Play is to clear away all cards of the tableau. If this is not achieved by the time the hand is exhausted, the game is lost; there is no redeal.

La Belle Lucie
(Clover Leaf, Midnight Oil)

CARDS—ONE PACK

Tableau. Deal the whole pack face up in trios of overlapping cards, in any convenient array. The last card of the pack is single.

Foundations. Aces, which must be removed and set in a foundation row as soon as available. Foundations are built up in suit and sequence to the kings.

Building. On the top card of a tableau pile may be placed the next-lower card of the same suit. Only one card at a time from the top of a pile is available for transfer. If an available card can be played on a foundation, it should be at once; no advantage can be gained by withholding it.

Redeals. When play comes to a standstill after the first deal, the tableau is gathered (not foundations), shuffled, and redealt in trios. After play again comes to a standstill, the tableau may similarly be dealt a third time.

The Merci. After the third deal, any one buried card may be pulled out and played. This *merci* is almost always necessary to win the game, since a single king above a lower card of the same suit in the same trio will otherwise defeat the player.

A variant game is to deal only once, but allow sequences to be built both up and down. The *merci* may be allowed, but is scorned by many players.

Golf

CARDS—ONE PACK

Tableau. Deal a row of seven cards face up. Deal four more rows face up on the first, spread so that all cards are identifiable. The tableau thus comprises 35 cards.

The Play. Turn up the first card from the hand and place it to start the talon. Any card at the top of the tableau pile may be removed and placed on the talon if it is in sequence with the top card there—*either up or down.* A series of cards may be played off the tableau talon, in one turn, provided that each pair of adjacent cards is in sequence, either way. *Example:* Top card of talon is a **4**; this may be built **4, 5, 6, 5, 4, 3**, or **4, 3, 2, 3, 2, A**, etc. Suits are ignored. But the sequence is not continuous; only a two may be placed on an ace, and a king *stops* the sequence (no card may be played on a king).

Cards are turned up from the hand and put on the talon, one at a time, until the stock is exhausted. There is no redeal.

The Object of Play is to remove all cards from the tableau into the talon. Since a tableau card may be moved only into the talon, a space has no special use.

A game is won if the tableau is completely cleared. Another way of scoring is to try to beat "par" of 36 "strokes" in nine "holes." Each deal is a hole; each card left in the tableau at the end of a deal is a stroke; par is a total of 36 in nine deals. If the tableau is cleared, any cards remaining in the hand count one "minus stroke" each, and are subtracted from the running score.

Multiple Golf

Golf Solitaire may be played as a contest among several participants. It is especially popular for two. Each is provided with a pack. Each plays nine "holes" of Golf Solitaire, and the "strokes" required for each hole are recorded on paper. A player wins 1 point for each hole he beats his opponent ("match play"), and the player with the smaller total for the nine scores 5 points ("medal play"). "Minus strokes" are duly subtracted from the final total.

The Beleaguered Castle

CARDS—ONE PACK

Foundations. Remove the four aces and place them in a column at the center. These foundations must be built up in suit and sequence to the kings.

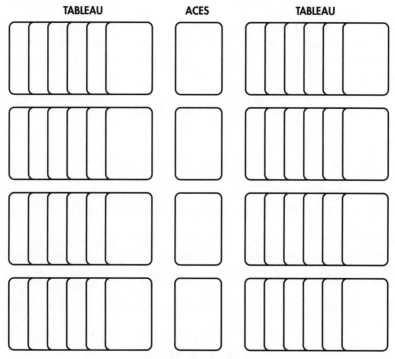

The Beleaguered Castle

Tableau. Deal four cards in a column at the extreme left, to commence the left wing. Deal a column of four just to right of the aces, to commence the right wing. Continue by dealing the whole pack in additional columns on the first, overlapping toward the right, giving cards alternately to left and right.

Building. Only the uppermost (extreme right) card of each row is available. An available card may be moved onto another of next-higher rank, regardless of suits. Spaces may be filled by any available cards.

Fortress

CARDS—ONE PACK

Tableau. Deal five cards face up in a column at the extreme left, to commence the left wing. Deal a column of five at right center, to commence the right wing. Continue by dealing the whole pack in additional columns on the first, overlapping toward the right, giving cards alternately to left and right wings. The two extra cards at the end go to the top row, one to each wing, which thus comprises a row of six cards and four rows of five.

Foundations. Aces, which must be moved to foundation column between the wings of the tableau, as soon as released. Foundations are built up in suit and sequence to the kings.

Building. Only the uppermost (extreme right) card of each row is available. An available card may be moved to another of the same suit with which it is in sequence, either up or down. Spaces may be filled by any available cards.

Virginia Reel

CARDS—TWO PACKS

Layout. Take from the pack a two, a three, and a four of different suits; place them in a column at the extreme left. Deal seven cards face up in a row to the right of each card. The 24 cards so placed will be called the tableau. Deal a fourth row of eight cards below the tableau, forming the talon.

Foundations. All twos, threes, and fours are foundations. Each must be put into its own row of the tableau, as indicated by the three foundation cards first placed. Card by card, the "tableau" must be transformed into foundation piles.

Each foundation must be built up in the same suit, by the addition of three cards, as follows:

2, 5, 8, J
3, 6, 9, Q
4, 7, 10, K

Building. The only building is upon foundations. Building may begin only when the foundation is in its proper row. All twos must go into the row of the first two, and so on. The uppermost card of any talon pile is available for building. Any tableau card is available, but with the proviso that no space may be made in the tableau unless it can immediately be filled, and a space may be filled only by a foundation of appropriate rank. Hence a tableau card may be moved to a foundation only when the talon contains an available replacement.

However, the replacement may be indirect. *Example:* A space in the 2-row is filled by a two moved from the 3-row, and the new space is filled by a three from the talon.

Furthermore, foundation cards originally dealt may be exchanged, provided that each lands in its proper row and no space is left. *Example:* A four is dealt in the 2-row, a three in the 4-row, and a two in the 3-row. A circular exchange may be made putting all three cards in their proper rows.

Talon. After all possible or desirable plays are made, deal another row of eight cards on the talon piles, which may be spread so that all cards are identifiable. Continue in the same way until the entire pack is dealt. There is no redeal.

Aces are dead cards. Any ace appearing on a talon, after the row of eight is dealt, is discarded from the game. An ace in the tableau may be discarded as soon as it can be replaced.

Poker Solitaire

CARDS—ONE PACK

Tableau. Deal the first 25 cards one by one, placing them in five rows of five cards each, with columns aligned. Each card may be placed anywhere with respect to those previously placed, so long as all remain within the limits of a "square" 5 × 5. (Some play that each card must be adjacent, if only at a corner, to some card previously placed.) Once put in position, a card may not be moved.

The Object of Play is to score as high a total as possible when each row and each column of the tableau is reckoned as a Poker hand.

Scoring. The English system of scoring is in accord with the relative difficulty of making the hands in Poker Solitaire. The American system preserves the ranking of the hands at Poker, ignoring the conditions of Solitaire play.

HAND	ENGLISH SYSTEM	AMERICAN SYSTEM
Royal Flush	30	100
Straight Flush	30	75
Four of a Kind	16	50
Full House	10	25
Flush	5	20
Straight	12	15
Three of a Kind	6	10
Two Pairs	3	5
One Pair	1	2

Variant Game. Count off 25 cards, examine them at leisure, and make the best possible count by placing them in a 5 × 5 square.

Poker Squares

This is a multiple way of playing Poker Solitaire. Any number of players may participate. Each is provided with one pack.

One player is appointed *caller* in each round (or the caller may be a non-player). Caller shuffles his pack, then turns up the first 25 cards one by one, announcing each aloud. All other players sort their packs into suits. When a card is called, each player finds it in his pack and places it in his own tableau. The player with the tableau of highest count wins the round or game.

As Poker Squares is intended to be a game of skill, the English system of scoring should be used.

Cribbage Solitaire (Domino)

CARDS—ONE PACK

Deal three cards to hand, two cards to crib, then three to hand. Look at the hand and lay away two cards to the crib. Turn up the top card of the stock for the starter. Using a cribbage board, score the hand as in Cribbage (see page 437), then discard it. Turn up the crib, score it, and discard it. Place the starter on the bottom of the stock. Deal again in the same way, and repeat until the stock is exhausted. At the end, there will be four cards left; turn them up and score them as a hand.

A jack turned as starter counts 2 for his heels. A jack in hand or crib or same suit as starter counts 1 for his nobs.

This Solitaire is recommended to beginners at Cribbage as an excellent way to learn scoring, and strategy of laying away. Average score for a game is said to be 85. A score of 121 may be considered to "win."

Cribbage Solitaire (Square)

CARDS—ONE PACK

Deal the first 16 cards one by one, placing them in four rows of four cards each. A card may be placed anywhere with reference to those previously placed, so long as all remain within a square 4 × 4. Turn up the 25th card as the starter. Count each row and column of the tableau, with the starter, as a Cribbage hand. (See page 486.) A jack turned as starter counts 2 for his heels; a jack in the tableau of same suit as starter counts 1 for his nobs (once only, not once for the row and once for the column).

The game may be considered "won" if the total is 61 or more.

Cribbage Solitaire (Accordion)

This Patience is the invention of Bill Beers, best-known as a composer of chess problems.

Deal cards face up in a row from left to right. On a cribbage board, score for each of the following combinations that is formed by either two or three adjacent cards:

One pair 2
Three of a kind 6
Three cards of the same suit 3
Three cards in sequence 3
Three-card straight flush 6
Two or three cards that total 15 2

When two adjacent cards are a pair, a third card may be turned before the pair is scored, to see if three of a kind can be scored instead.

A sequence counts even if the cards do not lie in order. *Example:* **J 9 10** is a valid sequence.

By reason of the rules of play, double runs and multiple fifteens cannot be scored.

Each combination must be scored when it shows, and then two of the adjacent cards concerned must be put together in one pile. The player may choose which to put on top. If the amalgamation creates any listed combination in two or three adjacent cards, it too may be scored. *Example:* Cards dealt are **7**, **3**, **8**, **5**, **4**, **3**. The last trio scores 3 for sequence. Put the **4** on the **5**; then the last three piles score 2 for fifteen. Put the **4**-pile on the **3**, and again there is a score of 2 for fifteen. Put the **8** on the **3**, and the first two of the three piles makes another fifteen. Finally join the first two piles, leaving **7**, **4**, or **8**, **4**.

The game is won if a total of 61 is reached by the time the pack is all dealt out.

RUSSIAN BANK
(CRAPETTE)

Russian bank, a popular pastime for two players, is often called a "game," but is really a double solitaire.

CARDS

Two packs of 52, with different backs. Each of the two players has his own pack. (A variant using one pack is described later.) The cards in each suit rank **K** (high), **Q, J, 10, 9, 8, 7, 6, 5, 4, 3, 2, A**.

PRELIMINARIES

One pack is spread face down, and each player draws a card. The lower card has choice of packs and seats, and plays first. Each player then shuffles the pack to be used by his opponent.

Each deals cards from his own pack to make the *layout*. First, twelve cards are dealt face down in a pile at the player's right; these are the *stock*. Next, four cards are dealt face up in a column above the stock, extending toward the opponent. The two columns are the *tableau*. The rest of the pack, called the *hand*, is placed face down at the player's left.

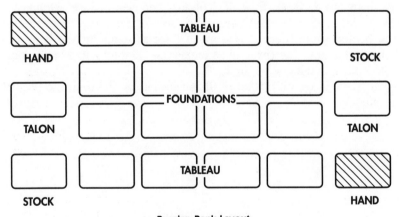

Russian Bank Layout

The players sit at left and right of this diagram. Each has his stock at his right and hand at his left. The stock (as well as hand) is dealt face down, but the top card remains face up after the player has begun his first turn.

THE PLAY

The first player must begin by moving all available aces, if any, into the space between the columns of the tableau. At the outset, only the tableau cards are *available* (for play). Later, any card turned up from the stock or the hand is available. When any build has been placed on a tableau card, only the uppermost is available. (See diagram, page 480.)

FOUNDATIONS

The eight aces are the *foundations*, which means that when any ace becomes available it must be moved to the *center* before any other play is made. The aces are arranged in two columns, and the tableau columns must be dealt far enough apart to accommodate them.

Foundations must be built up in suit and sequence, from ace to king. If any available card can be played on a foundation, this play must be made before any other. In short, a play *to the center* has priority over all others.

Plays in the Tableau. Having satisfied the center, the first player may then manipulate the tableau. On a tableau pile may be placed a card of next-lower rank and opposite color to the uppermost card, e.g., either red seven may be placed on ♣8. When *spaces* are created in the tableau, by removal of one entire pile (of the eight), the player may use them to make changes within the tableau. Any uppermost card may be moved into a space, to make lower cards available. Eventually, however (before turning a card from the *hand*), the player must fill all spaces in the tableau with cards turned up from his stock. On turning up a card, he must be careful to see whether it is playable on a foundation, before putting it in the tableau.

Before manipulating the tableau, the player is entitled to turn up the top card of his stock, as a possible guide to his play. After his first turn, he may do this even before satisfying the center (from the tableau). For example, if he plays ♡J off his stock onto ♡10 on a foundation, and ♡Q is available in the tableau, he is entitled to turn his next stock card before playing the ♡Q. The reason for this rule is that a play to the center from the stock takes priority over a play from the tableau. But at his *first* turn only, the player must satisfy the center from the tableau, before turning his first stock card.

Cards from the stock are available to be played on foundations or built onto the tableau. Having come to a standstill, and having filled all spaces in the tableau, the player next turns up a card from his hand. This card likewise is available for play on foundations or stock. If its play makes the stock card playable, or allows additional moves in the tableau, all such plays may be made, with the proviso that an unplayable card must show on top of the stock before another card is turned from the hand.

If the card from the hand is unplayable, it is laid face up directly before the player, on the *talon* or wastepile. The act of placing the card there ends the player's turn.

Loading. The first player having concluded his first turn, the second player turns up the top of his stock and commences (but first satisfies the center if the first player has overlooked such a move). He may make manipulations under the foregoing rules, but now there is an added possibility. He may build available cards (from tableau, his stock, or his hand) *upon the adverse stock and hand.* The building here is in suit and sequence, but the sequence may go up or down. For example, if ◇**9** lies on a player's stock, his opponent may cover it successively with ◇**8**, ◇**9**, ◇**10**, ◇**J**, ◇**10**, etc. Of course there is no object in *loading* the opponent with uppermost cards from the tableau, unless some change is made therein which prevents his returning the cards at his next turn.

Each player in turn makes all possible or desirable plays until compelled to place an unplayable card from his hand upon his talon, or until *stopped* as below. When a hand is exhausted, the talon is turned over and becomes a new hand. Play continues until one player gets rid of all his cards from stock and talon onto the foundations and tableau, and thereby wins the game.

STOPS

The rules as to priority of play must be strictly observed. If a player violates a rule, his opponent is entitled to call "Stop!" On demonstration of the error, the offender's turn ends. The rules are as follows:

1. Play to the center takes priority above all else, except that after his first turn a player is entitled to see one card face up on his stock before making any play. The uppermost card of a tableau pile, being available, must be played to a foundation if possible. But there is no compulsion to make lower, playable, cards available (by manipulations to remove the covering cards).

2. Among possible plays to the center, play from the stock takes priority over play from the tableau or hand. There is no priority among plays from the tableau, e.g., if the first player finds ♡**A**, ♡**2**, and ♠**A** in the layout, he may place ♡**A** and build ♡**2** before placing ♠**A**. (Play from the hand naturally takes precedence over play from the tableau, since a card turned from the hand must be placed somewhere, and to put it on the talon ends the turn.)

3. All spaces in the tableau must be filled, from the stock, before a card is turned from the hand. After the stock is exhausted, spaces may be filled from the hand. (Some circles add the rule that a

player may be stopped for overlooking that he could create additional spaces by manipulation of the tableau.)

4. Cards are turned from the hand one by one, and the player's turn continues so long as he can play each card. If such play makes possible additional plays to the center, the foregoing rules must be satisfied before the next card is turned up from the hand. An unplayable card from the hand must be placed on the talon, and it is then no longer available; the turn ends.

SCORING

The winner scores 30 points for the game, plus 1 point for each card left in his opponent's hand and talon, and 2 points for each card in his stock.

IRREGULARITIES

Any cards may be touched for the purpose of arranging, if expressly stated; otherwise, a player who touches one card when another should be played first under the rules may be stopped.

A stop may not be called for a move not in priority, if the offender has been allowed to complete another play thereafter. But attention may be drawn to the error, and the omitted play (if still possible) thereafter takes its due priority.

If a player makes an incorrect build, as ♡**7** on ♣**9**, the move must be retracted on demand, but the player may not be stopped.

If a player exposes or sees a card of his hand or stock, other than one regularly turned, he may complete a move but then his turn ends. *Example:* If he turns up two cards from his stock, he may play the uppermost if playable, but the second stays on his stock and his turn ends.

A player may spread his talon for the purpose of examining the cards, but may not spread his opponent's talon without permission. When a talon is so examined, both players are entitled to see the cards.

When a stop is called for a play out of order, the play must be retracted. When a stop is called for turning a card from stock or hand out of order, the opponent may direct whether such card shall be left up or turned down. (He may wish it up for the opportunity to load it.)

Russian Bank with One Pack

This is a double solitaire akin to Russian Bank, but without the "stops." An error of procedure must be corrected on demand, but the error does not cost the player his turn.

The cards in each suit are in circular sequence: **Q, K, A, 2** and so on. Half of a shuffled pack is dealt to each player, in 13 rounds of two at a time or any other agreed plan. Each player keeps his packet or *hand* face down before himself. The first player deals four cards in a row in the center, commencing the *tableau*. He builds in accordance with the rules below, and continues to turn cards up from his hand so long as he can play them. When he turns an unplayable card, he places it aside face up in a talon or wastepile.

The second player, at his first turn, likewise deals four cards in the center, completing the tableau of eight piles. Play continues by alternate turns; when his hand is exhausted, a player turns over his talon to form a new hand; the first to get rid of all his cards from hand and talon into the tableau wins.

There are no foundations. All building is in the tableau and upon the opponent's talon. In both cases the builds must be in suit and sequence, and may be started either up or down. Once started, the builds must necessarily continue in the same direction. Spaces may be used in the usual way. The uppermost card of a tableau pile is always available to be moved into a space. It is permissible to reverse the sequence in a tableau pile, by use of spaces. Before the player ends his turn he must fill any space in the tableau from his hand. The adverse talon may be *loaded* with cards from the hand, but not with cards from the tableau.

Spite and Malice

A two-handed game of recent origin, Spite and Malice is popular as a husband vs. wife game and has supplanted Russian Bank in some areas. The original rules are given first, followed by variations developed by Easley Blackwood in his book *Spite & Malice*, which also incorporates many suggestions for skillful play. Where the Blackwood version differs from the original rules, the original rules have been asterisked (*).

PLAYERS
Two

CARDS
There are two decks. Deck A contains the standard 52 cards. Deck B includes four jokers. The packs should be of different back designs or colors. Rank of the cards is **K** (high), **Q, J, 10, 9, 8, 7, 6, 5, 4, 3, 2, A** (low).

PRELIMINARIES
Deck A is shuffled and divided into two 26-card stacks, which become the *payoff piles* for the two players. Each player turns up the top card of his payoff pile and the higher card designates the first player; if the cards are of the same rank* the piles are shuffled and a new card is faced. Pack B

is shuffled by the opponent of the first player, who deals five cards face down, one at a time, to each player. Pack B is then put in the center of the table as the *stock*.

The Object To get rid of the payoff pile.

THE PLAY

Every ace, from a payoff pile or concealed hand, must be played immediately to form a *center stack;* there may be any number of center stacks. Every available two must be played on an open ace in a center stack.* Center stacks are built up in ascending order without regard to suit—any three on any four, any four on any five, and so on. Both players play to the center stacks.

Each player may have four *side stacks*. These are discard piles, and may be started with any card. Side stacks are built downward (any queen on any king) or with a card of the same rank (a king on a king). A player may play only to his own side stacks and only from his hand.

The top card of the payoff pile may be played only to the center, after which the next card is faced. A card from the hand or from a side stack may be played to the center. Only one card from one's hand may be played to a side stack during a turn. A player may make as many legal plays to the center as he wishes, but a play to a side stack ends his turn. Cards may not be moved from one side stack to another, or to fill a space.

A joker is wild and may be played in place of any other card except an ace. An available joker in a side stack may be played to the center. At the beginning of a turn, a player draws from the stock sufficient cards to restore his hand to five cards.* If a center stack is built up through the king, it is shuffled into the stock.

SCORING

The player who gets rid of all of the cards in his payoff pile wins, and the margin is the number of cards left in the opposing payoff pile. If cards are left in both piles because neither player can or will play, the winner is the player with the fewest cards and he scores the difference. It is not legal to count the cards in a payoff pile.

STRATEGY

The primary goal is to get rid of the top card in the payoff pile while endeavoring not to help the opponent lay off. Discard piles should be maintained to permit the greatest flexibility in discarding, and discards should be selected to permit one or more discards for the next turn. It is rarely wise to block a discard pile by doubling up with two or more cards of the same rank. If doubling up is necessary, try to limit such plays to cards that head the pile—i.e. kings and queens. Starting all discard piles with cards of the same or high rank is not desirable.

485

Occasionally it may be prudent to claim a freeze rather than foul a promising discard pile. Other times you may announce a freeze rather than play a card to the center that will permit your opponent to get rid of a card in his payoff pile. Even though a player cannot draw a card from the stock until he has reduced his hand to fewer than five cards, winning tactics demand such strategy.

Blackwood Variations

PRELIMINARIES

A tie in rank of the cards first faced in the payoff pile is broken by rank of suit, spades (high), hearts, diamonds and clubs (low).

The Play: An ace or deuce on the payoff pile or a discard pile must be played on a center stack, but a player does not have to play an ace or deuce from his concealed hand unless both players claim to be *frozen* (unable to make a play or discard). A player is not required to play a joker from his hand to a discard pile. He may also declare himself frozen even when he has a playable card. If both players announce that they are frozen, voluntarily or not, the center piles, discard piles and concealed hands are shuffled together to form a new stock; five cards are dealt to each player, and the game continues. The original payoff piles remain intact.

During a turn, if a player lays off his entire concealed hand on the center stacks, he draws five more cards from the stock and continues his turn. He may not discard on a side stack.

If a joker becomes available in a discard pile, it may be played to the center and designated any rank. It does not necessarily retain the same rank for which it was used in the discard pile.

Complete center stacks are not added to the stock until it is about to become depleted. If that condition exists and no center stacks have been completed, all cards in the center are shuffled to form a new stock.

A player may count his own payoff pile and require his opponent to do the same and announce the total.

SCORING

In addition to one point for each card in the opposing payoff pile, the winner receives a 5-point bonus for going out. Since an average win is 11 points, the players may decide that the first to attain a series total of 25, 50, 100, etc. points is the winner. Since games can be lengthy, high series totals are unlikely to be reached in one session.

SOCIAL
GAMBLING
GAMES

Red Dog (High-card Pool)

Essentially a gambling game, though it is more often played by family groups for meaningless stakes than by serious gamblers and is not seen in gambling houses, Red Dog is basically one of the simplest of games. Two cards are compared and the higher wins.

PLAYERS

Any number up to ten may play.

CARDS

The 52-card pack is used. In each suit, the cards rank: **A** (high), **K, Q, J, 10, 9, 8, 7, 6, 5, 4, 3, 2**. There is no rank of suits.

PRELIMINARIES

Each player puts up some agreed number of chips, which may be as few as one per player in large games and as many as ten per player when only three or four are playing. These chips form a pool which is the common property of all participants, in equal shares.

Anyone picks up a shuffled pack, has it cut by any other player, and deals one card face up to each player in rotation. The player receiving the highest card is the first dealer and thereafter the deal rotates to the left. If two or more players tie for high, cards are dealt to them to determine which is highest among them.

Any player may shuffle, the dealer last. The player at dealer's right must cut the cards, leaving at least four cards in each packet.

DEALING

The dealer distributes the cards, face down, one at a time to each player in rotation to his left, beginning with the player at his left, until each player has five cards. The dealer places the remaining cards face down before him to serve as the *stock*.

When there are nine or ten players in the game, only four cards are dealt to each player.

THE PLAY

The Object of Play Each player in turn is to beat whatever card is on top of the stack when his turn comes. To beat this card, he must have in his hand a card of higher rank in the same suit.

Betting. Each player in turn makes a bet against the pool, not against the other players. The eldest hand has first turn, which then passes in rotation from player to player to his left.

Each player must bet at least one chip; the maximum bet is the number of chips in the pool at the time. The pool constitutes the pile of chips in the center of the table. When a player's turn comes, he places just outside the pool the number of chips that he bets.

Settlement of Bets. Dealer then turns face up the top card of the stock. If the player's hand contains any card to beat it, he shows that card and withdraws his bet; the dealer then removes from the pool and pays him an equivalent amount. The player's other cards are placed aside unseen.

If the player cannot beat the card shown, the chips he bet are added to the pool and he shows his entire hand, face up, after which (when every player has had an opportunity to see it) it is turned over and laid aside for the next deal.

If a player prefers, he may pay a one-chip forfeit to the pool instead of placing a bet.

Renewal of Pool. If a player's winning bet leaves no chips in the pool, each player contributes the amount originally required to form a new pool, and play continues. If at the beginning of any deal the pool has an insufficient number of chips, by agreement among the players it is replenished, each player contributing the same number of chips. If a player leaves the game, the pool must be divided and each player takes an equal share, an odd chip remaining in the pool for continuation of the game. If there is more than one odd chip, or if the game is ending, ownership of the odd chips is decided by lot in any way.

Betting to Lose. Some play that each player in turn may choose to bet either that he can beat the top card of the stock, or that he will lose to the top card of the stock. If he bets that he will lose, he must show his entire hand after the card is turned, even though he has a card that would beat it.

IRREGULARITIES

If a player is dealt too few cards, he may choose whether to play on with the cards dealt him or to withdraw, in which case he is not forced to bet when his turn comes. He may not, however, withdraw any chips from the pool in recompense for the error in dealing.

If a player is dealt too many cards, the dealer must draw the excess from his hand, offered face down after being shuffled; and play continues.

If a player pays the pot, thinking he has lost, when in fact he could beat the exposed card, the transaction is final; chips once placed in the pool may not be removed. However, an erroneous announcement of the result is not valid until chips are placed in the pool or until a card has been turned for the next player.

If a player names the amount he is betting without actually putting up the chips, he must stand by his announcement. If he names an amount greater than the number of chips in the pool, he is deemed to have bet the amount of the pool (called "betting the pot").

STRATEGY

A player should evaluate his hand before betting. That is, he should consider the number of cards (including those he knows have been dealt to other players and are dead) which he can beat; and the number of cards which can beat him. If there are more cards that he can beat than can beat him, he has a good bet; if the converse is true, he has a poor bet and should bet the minimum or forfeit one chip. A player forfeits one chip when his hand is so weak that he has almost no chance to win, and would rather pay the forfeit and keep his hand unexposed than let the other players see how many low cards are thus put out of play.

The simplest way to determine the chances of winning and losing is to consider every suit a sequence from 2, which is low, up to 14, representing the ace. Assuming that five cards have been dealt to each player, there are 47 unknown cards at the start. Subtract the highest card held in each suit from 14, counting a void suit as 1; the sum of the differences will be the number of cards which one's hand cannot beat. Since there are 47 unknown cards altogether, if there are 23 or less such cards outstanding, the player has a better than even chance to win; if there are 24 such cards or more, he has a less than even chance. As each additional card shows up, either from the top of the stock or in the hand of a player whose turn has come up earlier, that card should be deducted from the number of possible winning or possible losing cards, as the case may be.

Theoretically, a player should either "bet the pot" (make the maximum bet), if he has a better than even chance; or make the minimum bet, if he has a less than even chance. Psychologically, it is preferable to bet the pot if there are only one-third of the unknown cards that will beat you; make a medium bet if slightly less than half the unknown cards can beat you; and make the minimum bet if more than half the unknown cards will beat you.

Blackjack (Twenty-one)

Nearly two hundred years ago a French book commented, speaking of a game called "The Farm," that the game was very ancient but was still played in the provinces (from which we might infer that it had already passed out of fashion in Paris). Yet The Farm and games of the same type are still among the most widely played, internationally, of all games. The principal game of this family is called Blackjack when it is played in American homes and among American soldiers who have made it one of their two favorite games (the other being Poker). The game is also known by Americans as Twenty-one; the French know it as Vingt-et-un ("twenty-one"); and the English as Van John, an obvious corruption of Vingt-et-un. See page 513 for Blackjack as played in the gambling casinos.

PLAYERS

Any number can play, but five to nine make the best game.

CARDS

The pack of 52 cards is used, often with a joker or blank card which does not figure in the play. When there are many players, it is desirable or permissible to use a double pack of 104 cards, consisting of two 52-card packs shuffled together, plus one joker or blank card.

Values of Cards. The cards have no rank, but have numerical value as follows: Any ace counts 1 or 11, at the option of the holder. Any face card or ten counts 10. Any other card counts its index number.

PRELIMINARIES

There may be a permanent dealer, or the right to deal may pass from player to player. When it does, any player picks up a shuffled pack and deals the cards out face up, one at a time to each player, until a jack shows up. The player to whom the jack falls is the first dealer.

Any player may shuffle the cards, but the dealer shuffles last. He offers the shuffled pack to any other player, who cuts them, and dealer completes the cut. If a joker or blank card is used, dealer places this face up at the bottom of the pack to mark the end of the shuffled cards. If no such card is used, dealer turns up the top card of the pack, shows it to all players and (unless it is an ace) places it face up at the bottom of the pack. This is called *burning* a card. If the card so turned up is an ace, the pack must be reshuffled, cut again, and the same process gone through.

DEALING

Dealer gives one card face down to every player in rotation, beginning with eldest hand and including himself. He then gives each other player, in the same rotation, one card face down; and gives himself a card face up.

BETTING

If there is a permanent dealer, each player must place a bet, at least one chip and no more than the maximum established by the dealer at the beginning of the game, before any card is dealt.

If the game is played with a changing dealer, each player may look at the first card dealt to him and then place a bet from one chip up to the maximum; the dealer may then look at his card and, if he wishes, double all such bets; and then each other player may redouble.

Each player bets only with the dealer.

THE PLAY

When each player, including the dealer, has two cards, each player in turn, beginning with the eldest hand and including the dealer, has the right to draw additional cards one at a time.

Object of the Game. Each player's object is to have cards whose numerical values total 21, or as close to 21 as possible without exceeding 21.

Naturals. If a player's first two cards count exactly 21—that is, if they are a face card or ten and an ace—he has a *natural* or *blackjack* and wins the amount of his bet immediately, unless dealer also has a natural.

If there is a permanent dealer, he pays such a player one and one-half times the player's bet, but if the dealer has a natural he collects only singly from each other player. If a permanent dealer and any other player both have naturals, the bet between them is a stand-off.

If there is a changing dealer, and any other player has a natural, he pays that player twice the amount of that player's bet, doubled or redoubled as the case may be; if only the dealer has a natural, he collects from each other player twice the amount of that player's bet, doubled or redoubled as the case may be; and if the dealer and any other player both have naturals, dealer collects the amount of the bet, but only singly.

When there is a changing dealer, any player opposed to the dealer who gets a natural becomes the next banker (after all bets of the current deal have been settled) unless the dealer also has a natural, in which case he remains the dealer. If dealer has no natural, but two or more other players have, the one of them closest to the dealer's left becomes the next dealer.

The dealer may not look at his face-down card to see if he has a natural unless his face-up card is an ace, face card or ten.

Hitting. If dealer has no natural, when all bets on naturals have been settled, each player in turn, beginning with eldest hand, may draw additional cards until he chooses to *stand*, which means that he has a count of 21 or less and does not desire any more cards; or until he *busts*, which means that he has a count of more than 21. In the latter case, he pays the amount of his bet to dealer immediately.

A player who wishes an additional card says "Hit me." Dealer then gives him one card face up. There is no limit to the number of cards a player may so draw, except that he may not draw a card after his count equals or passes 21.

When a player wishes no more cards, he says "I stand," whereupon dealer proceeds to serve the next player to his left.

Play of Dealer's Cards. When all other players have been served, dealer turns up his face-down card. A permanent dealer must now stand if his count is 17 or more, and must hit himself if and so long as his count is 16 or less. A changing dealer may choose whether to stand or to take another card at any count.

If dealer goes over 21, he pays the amount of any bet not previously settled. If dealer stands at a figure of 21 or less, he settles with each other player who has stood: A permanent dealer pays any higher count, collects from any lower count, and is at a stand-off with any player having the same count; a changing dealer pays any higher count but collects from any player having the same or a lower count.

REDEALING

As each bet is settled, dealer takes the cards which are thus put out of play and places them face up on the bottom of the pack. When the deal brings the dealer to a face-up card, all face-up cards in the pack are shuffled by the dealer, any player in the game cuts them, and the deal continues. Dealer may also choose at the beginning of any deal to shuffle all cards, if in his opinion there will not be enough to complete the deal.

Changing the Bank. In addition to the methods described above—that the player holding a natural against the dealer becomes the next dealer—there are various other methods for changing the dealer:

(a) Each player in turn may deal one hand;

(b) each player as he becomes dealer may name an amount which constitutes his bank, and when he loses it all or doubles it he ceases to be the dealer and the next player in turn deals;

(c) the first dealer may be decided by auction, the privilege going to the player who bids the largest amount as the size of his bank, and each player in turn beginning with eldest hand may bet all or any part of the established bank until it has all been taken, players lower down in precedence being unable in that case to bet and receiving no cards. When the last-named method is used, dealer remains dealer until he has lost the full amount of his bank, or until at the end of a deal he withdraws; and dealer may not at any time reduce the amount of his bank, which includes the original amount plus any winnings which have been added to it.

Whenever the dealer changes, there is a new shuffle of all the cards for the next deal.

PLAYER'S OPTIONS

Splitting a Pair. If a player's first two cards are the same—as two sixes, or two queens—he may place the same bet on each card that he placed originally on his single hand, and play them as two different hands. When his turn comes, he announces this, whereupon he exposes both cards and dealer gives him one card face down to go with each of them. He then plays each as a separate hand, hitting or standing independently of the other. Dealer settles with each hand separately, as though they were played by different players.

One Down for Eleven. If a player's first two cards have a numerical value of eleven, as a six and a five, or a seven and a four, he may turn them both face up when his turn comes, double his bet, and receive one card from the dealer face down. He may not ask for an additional card. Later, dealer will settle with him on the total count of the three cards.

BONUS PAYMENTS

If a player has a total of five cards and his total is still 21 or under, he may show his cards, collect double his bet, and cannot be beaten by dealer even if dealer later gets a total closer to 21; or the player may draw another card and try to get six cards with a total of under 21.

If a player gets six cards and his total is under 21, he collects four times the amount of his bet, and cannot be beaten, as described in the preceding paragraph. This bonus for "five cards and under" or for "six cards and under" is played in most social games.

IRREGULARITIES

If dealer fails to burn a card, he must, on demand, shuffle the remainder of the pack and burn a card before continuing the deal.

If dealer fails to give any player a card on the first round of dealing, he must on demand supply that player from the top of the pack unless attention is called to the error after dealer begins the second round of dealing, in which case the player lacking a card stays out for that deal.

If dealer gives any player his first card face up, that player must still make his bet, but dealer must give him his next card face down. If dealer fails to give him his next card face down, the player may withdraw his bet and drop out for that deal.

Any player who stands must expose his face-down card as soon as dealer has stood or gone over. If that player has in fact a total of more than 21, he must pay dealer double the amount of his bet even if dealer has gone over.

If the dealer gives a player two cards on the first round of dealing, that player may choose which card to keep and which to discard; or may keep both cards, play two hands, and place a bet on each. He may not, however, play both cards as belonging to the same hand.

If dealer gives a player two cards on the second round of dealing, the player may choose which to keep and must discard the other.

If dealer gives a card to a player who did not ask for it, that player may keep the card if he chooses, or may refuse it, in which case it is a discard and is placed face up at the bottom of the pack. The next player in turn may not claim it.

If a card is faced in the pack, the player to whom it would fall may accept it or refuse it.

An irregularity must be corrected if discovered before the bet has been settled; after the bet has been settled, there can be no correction.

If dealer has a natural, but fails to announce it before dealing an additional card to any player, his hand constitutes a count of 21 but can be tied by the hand of any other player whose total is 21 in three or more cards.

STRATEGY

A player should not ordinarily take another card when his total is 15 or more; although it is wise for the dealer to hit 16, wherefore gambling houses adopt the rule that he must, it should be remembered that dealer is drawing only against players who have stood and thus may be assumed to be satisfied with their totals, whereas the player against the dealer is drawing against an unknown hand which may total 12, 13 or 14.

The option of splitting pairs should be exercised in the case of aces (and, for this reason, some gambling houses do not permit aces to be split); tens and nines should never be split, since the total of 20 or 18 respectively will probably win; lower pairs should not be split for a different reason, which is that the chance of winning will be less than even in any case and splitting the pair requires increasing the bet.

Doubling the bet and drawing one card to a count of 11 decreases the player's chance of winning.

When dealer's face-up card is lower than an eight, it is often advisable to stand on a count of 14 and even, in the opinion of many players, 13.

The Farm (Farmer)

PLAYERS

Any number may play, but it is best for six to twelve players.

CARDS

The pack contains 45 cards, consisting of **A, K, Q, J, 10, 9, 7, 5, 4, 3, 2** in spades, diamonds and clubs; and **A, K, Q, J, 10, 9, 7, 6, 5, 4, 3, 2** in hearts.

Each ace counts 1, each face card or ten counts 10, and each other card counts its index figure.

PRELIMINARIES

Each player antes one chip to form a pool. The players then engage in an auction to determine which will be the *farmer*. The highest bidder adds the amount of his bid to the pool, shuffles the cards and has them cut by the player at his left, and deals one card to each player in rotation, face down, beginning at his left. The farmer should be careful not to expose the bottom card of the pack. The undealt cards constitute the *stock*.

THE PLAY

Each player in turn, beginning with eldest hand, must draw one or more cards. After drawing each card, he may decide to stand or to draw another card. All such cards are served by the dealer from the bottom of the stock, and turned up as they are served.

Object of the Game To reach 16 or as close thereto as possible without exceeding 16.

SETTLEMENT

If any player makes exactly 16, in two or more cards, at the end of the deal he takes the entire pool and becomes the next farmer. If two or more players have 16, and one has the six of hearts, he wins; if neither has the six of hearts, but one has fewer cards than the other, he wins; and if each has the same number of cards, the one nearest the dealer's left in rotation wins.

When a player's count passes 16, he does not show his hand; but after every player has drawn, he pays to the farmer one chip for every point by which his count exceeds 16.

If no player has 16, the pool remains for the next deal; but the player having closest to 16 without exceeding 16 is the winner and collects one chip from each other player except the farmer. If two or more players tie for this position, and one has the six of hearts, he wins; if none has the six of hearts, but has fewer cards than any other, he wins; and if two or more have the same number of cards, the one nearest the dealer's left in rotation wins.

STRATEGY

When choice of plays is possible, it is wise to play to avoid loss rather than to win. One should not draw to a total of more than 9, since at 9 he may lose nothing (if some other player reaches 16 and takes the farm) and can lose at most one, while by drawing he is likely to go over 16 and have to pay two or more. The strategy thus is to wait for a lucky hand and to reduce the danger of loss on poorer hands.

Seven and One-half

This is the same game as Blackjack except that it is played with a pack of 40 cards, **A, K, Q, J, 7, 6, 5, 4, 3, 2** of each suit, face cards counting as ½ point each, aces as 1 point each, and every other card its index value.

The object is to reach a total of 7½ or as nearly as possible, without going over 7½. Each player receives one card face down, and may then bet as in Blackjack with a changing dealer; dealer may double these bets after looking at his card, but the bet may not be redoubled. A player may stand on the one card dealt to him, or may draw one or more additional cards. Seven and one-half in two cards is a natural. Ties pay the dealer.

Macao

This is similar to Blackjack, the count of cards being the same except that tens and face cards each count zero and the object is to reach a count of 9 in one or more cards. Each player places a bet before a card is dealt, and receives one card face down. If it is a nine, he is paid three times the amount of his bet; if it is an eight, he is paid twice; if it is a seven, he is paid singly, except that dealer ties a nine with a nine, beats an eight with a nine, beats a seven with an eight or nine, and ties if he has the same number. If dealer has no seven, eight or nine, then when bets involving those numbers are settled each player in turn may draw one or more cards as in Blackjack, the object being to reach 9 or as close thereto as possible without going over 9. When dealer and any other player tie, the bet between them is called off.

Stock Market

PLAYERS
Any number up to eleven. Best for more than five.

CARDS
The pack comprises four times as many cards as there are players. The cards in each suit are: **A** (counting **1**), **2**, **3**, etc. up to a number one less than the number of players. *Example:* In a seven-hand game, the highest cards in play are the sixes. Besides these cards, the pack includes any four face cards, each counting zero.

DEALING
Anyone may deal. The pack should be thoroughly shuffled and cut without exposing any card. Each player receives two cards, usually dealt one at a time.

TRADING
The players now trade *ad lib* in a supposititious stock, whose *market price* is the total of pips on all the cards dealt.

Since exactly half of the pack is in play, the "expected" market price is half of the pips in the entire pack. This is equivalent to the number of players times the rank of the highest card in the pack; in a seven-hand game the expected price is 42.

No player knows what the actual *market price* will prove to be, but has some clue to whether it will be above or below expectations, from his own two cards. His "operations" are guided by this clue, and also—the essence of the game—by what he can infer as to the beliefs of the other players from their operations.

Any player may offer an unlimited number of "shares" in the supposititious stock, for any price he can get. Each player notes his own transactions on paper. Trading is suspended by general agreement, when no more buyers are found. Then all cards are turned face up, and they are summed to determine the actual market price; then settlement is made.

A player, the net of whose transactions is the sale of stock below the market price, pays the difference due into a pool. Likewise a player who in the net bought above the market price pays into the pool. Then those who sold above the market price or bought below it collect their due shares from the pool.

Speculation

PLAYERS

Any number up to about nine. Best for five or more.

CARDS

The pack of 52. The cards in each suit rank: **A** (high), **K, Q, J, 10, 9, 8, 7, 6, 5, 4, 3, 2**.

PRELIMINARIES

As the deal is an advantage, the first dealer should be determined by lot. Thereafter the deal rotates to the left.

A pool is formed by antes from all the players, the dealer contributing a double share.

Cards are dealt one at a time to the left, commencing with eldest hand. Each player receives three cards, which he must keep in a pile face down, stacking them in the order received. After the deal is complete, the next card is turned up to fix the "trump" for that deal. This turn-up is the property of the dealer (who thus in effect has four cards).

THE SPECULATION

The pool goes eventually to the player holding the highest card of the trump suit. If the turn-up is an ace, dealer takes the pool at once and the cards are gathered for the next deal. When the turn-up is any other card, dealer may elect to keep it or sell it. He need not accept a bid, but must sell if at all to the highest bidder. The purchase price of the turn-up goes to the dealer, not to the pool. The player who buys it places it face up on his cards.

The disposition of the turn-up decided, eldest hand (unless he bought the turn-up) turns up the top of his three cards, and the other players in rotation to the left do the same, excepting the purchaser of the turn-up, until some player turns a trump higher than the turn-up. The owner may sell this card, or decide to keep it, any payment for it being his property.

The game continues in the same manner until all cards are turned up. Each time a new card appears which is higher than the last preceding apparent winner, it becomes the subject of "speculation" at the owner's pleasure. The disposition of the card being decided, players in rotation to the left turn up one card at a time until a higher trump shows.

It is usually permissible for players to bargain with one another for the sale of unturned cards. For example, the holder of the highest trump may decide to try to buy in all remaining unturned cards, so as to assure his winning of the pool. When unturned cards are sold, they must be placed face down under the buyer's cards, not exposed to any participant.

DICE GAMES

Dice are the oldest gaming implements known to man, but it is only during the twentieth century that a game played exclusively with dice has become the principal gambling game of an occidental country. That game is Craps, or Crap-shooting, which is not only an informal gambling game but is also, in American gambling houses, the layout game (see page 535) which attracts the largest betting. The modern game of Craps developed from an old English game called Hazard, which was not, however, the game described as Hazard in this book (page 93).

Craps

PLAYERS

As many may play as are accorded space by the room or area in which the game is held.

EQUIPMENT

Two dice, of the same size, color and markings. Each die should be a cube in the strictest sense, except that the corners may be uniformly rounded; each side should be approximately ⅝ inch, and no smaller than ½ inch. Each face of the die is marked with one to six dots, opposite faces representing reciprocal numbers adding to seven; if the vertical face toward you is 5, and the horizontal face on top of the die is 6, the 3 should be on the vertical face to your right.

When the game is played in a club or with a fixed bank, a player has the privilege of calling for a change of dice at any time.

THE PLAY

The players form a ring around the playing surface, which in an informal game may be a floor or ground, and is known as the *center;* in a gambling house it is a table marked with a layout on which bets are placed.

In a small game, each player may roll the dice once and the one rolling the highest number *shoots* first. In a larger game, the first shooter is usually the one who picks up the dice and offers a bet.

The shooter places some sum of money in front of him, and announces the amount. That is his *center* bet and other players are invited to *fade* it. The shooter is betting he will win; the players who fade him are betting he will lose.

The shooter takes the dice in his hand and rolls them out, preferably so that they hit a wall and bounce back, if the playing area affords the means to enforce this rule. The faces which are upmost when the two dice come to rest determine the number thrown.

Any one of five numbers thrown on the first roll settles the bets immediately:

Seven or **eleven** is a *natural* and the shooter wins.

Two, three or **twelve** is *craps* and the shooter loses.

When any one of these numbers is thrown, bets are settled, the shooter announces the amount he is betting, and the game continues as previously described.

Points. If the shooter's first number is four, five, six, eight, nine or ten, the bets are not settled. The number thrown becomes his *point.* He picks up the dice, shakes them and rolls them out again, and continues to do so until either (a) he shoots the same number again, in which case he wins, collects his bets, and announces his next bet; (b) he rolls a seven, in which case he loses his bets in the center and the next player in turn to his left becomes the shooter.

So long as the shooter wins, he remains the shooter. But he may voluntarily pass the dice to the man at his left when the current bets are settled.

When the shooter wins it is known as a *pass;* when he loses, it is known as a *miss.*

BETTING

Players place bets with one another. (In the gambling-house game, all bets must be placed with the house; that method of betting will be described later.) There are many bets in addition to the bets in the center between the shooter and the players who fade him.

Come Bets. On the shooter's first roll, or any other roll, one player may bet with any other player that the shooter "comes"—that is, that he will win in a series of rolls beginning with the next, as though the next roll were the first. The player who takes this bet is betting that the shooter "don't come." Also, the former, who is betting that the shooter will win, is said to bet *right;* the other player is betting *wrong.*

Side Bets. Once the shooter has thrown a point, he and other players may bet that he will (or will not) make his point. If his point is six or eight, the odds are 6-to-5 that he will not make it; if his point is five or nine, the odds are 3-to-2 that he will not make it; if his point is four or ten, the odds are 2-to-1 that he will not make it. Bets on five, nine, four and ten are usually placed at the correct odds, but bets on six or eight are usually placed at even money, so that anyone betting that the shooter will not make his point has a considerable advantage.

Hardway Bets. If the shooter's point is four, the odds are 8-to-1 that he will not make it by throwing 2–2 (because there are eight combinations of the dice which will give him 3–1 or a seven, as against only one combination which will give him 2–2); making the four with 2–2 is called making it the *hard way*. The odds are also 8-to-1 against making a ten the hard way; and the odds are 10-to-1 against making six or eight the hard way.

There are innumerable other methods of betting on what number or combination of numbers will or will not appear on the next roll or in the next two or three rolls; many if not most of these are "hustlers' bets," offered by someone who knows he has the best of it mathematically if his bet is accepted. It is easy to calculate what the proper odds should be (see pages 661–63).

IRREGULARITIES

If either die is resting against any object which causes any uncertainty as to which face is upward, it is "cocked dice" and the throw is void.

If either die rolls outside the playing surface in such a way that it cannot clearly be seen, the throw is void.

If a player picks up one of the dice before either die has stopped rolling, the throw is void.

In case there is disagreement as to which player has faded all or any portion of the shooter's bet, precedence is given to (a) the player who has faded the entire bet; (b) if it is the shooter's first roll, to the player who last lost the dice; (c) if it is not the shooter's first roll, to the player who faded the largest portion of the shooter's previous bet.

The shooter may withdraw any unfaded portion of his bet at any time, but may not withdraw any portion of his bet after it has been faded unless he withdraws his entire bet and passes the dice.

STRATEGY

Skillful play at Craps consists solely of knowing the proper odds and not making or accepting any bets which are mathematically unsound. A table of odds in the most common cases is given following pages 661–63.

Barbudi

Eastern Europeans play a game with two dice in which the shooter and his opponent roll the dice against each other, alternately. The shooter names the game: 6–6, 5–5 and 3–3 are always winning numbers, and 1–1, 2–2 and 4–4 are always losing numbers, but he may decide whether or not 6–5 shall also be a winning number and 1–2 also a losing number. His opponent names the stakes for which they shall roll. The shooter has the first chance to cover it all; if he leaves any part untaken, other players at the table may take it. The shooter rolls the dice; if no decisive number appears, his opponent rolls them back; and this continues until a decisive number appears, all other numbers being meaningless. The player rolling the dice wins his bet if he rolls a winning number, and loses if he rolls a losing number; bets are settled, and if the shooter won he keeps the dice and the next player in turn becomes his opponent; if the opponent won, the dice pass to the player at the shooter's left.

In this game there is no advantage to either side. It is played principally in clubs or gambling houses devoted entirely to Barbudi, and in the latter case the gambling house deducts 5% of the losing bets, giving the remainder to the winner. This amounts to 2½% of all the money bet.

Four-Five-Six

Three dice are used. One player is chosen by lot to be the first banker, and he states the amount of his bank. Each other player, in order of precedence beginning at the banker's left, may take all or any part of the bank, or of whatever remains of it, until it is all faded; any unfaded portion is withdrawn by the banker. The banker then rolls the dice once.

If he rolls 4–5–6, or any triplet, he wins all bets.

If he rolls 1–2–3, he loses all bets.

If he rolls any pair plus six, he wins; any pair plus one, he loses.

If he rolls any pair plus two, three, four or five, the latter number is his *point*.

The banker continues to roll until one of these numbers appears. If it does not settle the bets, instead giving him a point, the dice pass to the player at his left.

This player then rolls to settle his bet with the banker; he wins if he rolls a winning number, loses if he rolls a losing number, and wins, loses or ties when he rolls a point number, depending upon whether his point is respectively higher, lower, or the same as the banker's. His bet having been settled, the dice pass to the next player at his left, and so on until all bets are settled.

The banker has an advantage in Four-Five-Six, because he rolls first and there are more automatic winning numbers than losing numbers. His advantage amounts to about 2½% of all money bet against him. As usually played, the bank changes from player to player: either when the banker loses his bank, in which case it passes to the player at his left; or when any player gets a Four-Five-Six or triplet against the banker, in which case that player becomes the next banker.

Poker Dice

Strictly speaking, the set of poker dice should consist of five cubes whose markings are of playing cards instead of the dots seen on standard dice: The six faces of each die bear representations of an ace, king, queen, jack, ten and nine. As in Poker, the faces rank from highest to lowest in the order stated.

Any number may play, each having one turn. The dice are cast from a dice cup. In his turn, a player may cast the dice once, twice, or three times. His object is to get the best possible poker hand. The hands rank: Five of a kind (high), four of a kind, full house (three of a kind and a pair), three of a kind (straights do not count, and as there are no suits there can be no flush), two pair, one pair, high card. Ties are broken as in Poker (page 12).

After his first cast, a player may pick up one or more dice and cast them again; after his second cast he may do the same; his third cast determines his hand. After any cast he may stand on what he already has and end his turn.

The highest hand wins. If two or more players tie for high, each of them gets three more rolls to break the tie as among those who tied.

Poker Dice games are usually played with five standard dice, in which case aces rank highest, then sixes, fives, fours, threes, deuces.

Twenty-one with Dice

Any number may play. Only one die is used, each player in turn rolling this die as many times as he wishes. The object is to get to 21, or as close as possible, without going over 21. After any cast, a player may stand on his total.

A player going over 21 pays one chip to the pot. When every player has had his turn, the player closest to 21 wins this pot plus one chip from every player who did not go over. If two or more tie for the winning total, the one who used the least number of rolls wins. If there is still a tie, those who tied play another game to determine the winner.

High Dice

Five dice are used, and any number may play. Each player in turn has a maximum of five casts. From each cast he must keep at least one die, and may keep as many as he chooses, and may then roll the other dice again.

The object is to have as high a total of spots as possible on the final five faces showing. After any cast, he may stand on the total he has.

Once having let a die stand, a player may not pick it up and recast it on a later cast.

The player with the highest total wins. If two or more players tie, they play another game among themselves to determine the winner.

High Dice may be played with almost any number of dice, and with any number of turns per player from one up.

Yacht

Any number may play. Five dice are used. Each player in rotation may cast the dice three times in each round, and there are twelve rounds in all.

After each of his first two casts in each round, a player may pick up and cast over as many of the dice as he wishes. The faces of the five dice showing on the table at the end of his third cast (or at the end of a previous cast, if he chooses to stand on what he has) must be scored in whichever of the following categories the player chooses:

Yacht (five of a kind) scores 50.

Big Straight (2, 3, 4, 5, 6) scores 30.

Little Straight (1, 2, 3, 4, 5) scores 30.

Full House (three of one kind and two of another); *Four of a Kind*, and *Choice* (any five dice); each scores the total number of pips showing on the five dice cast in that turn.

Sixes scores as many times six as there are sixes among the five dice; likewise with *Fives*, *Fours*, *Threes*, *Twos* and *Aces*.

In each turn a player must select a category not previously selected; therefore at the end of the game he will have selected each category once. He may select a category even though it will make his score zero for that turn; thus, having tried for Little Straight and missed, he may select Aces even though his dice show 2–2–3–4–5, because the most he could ever score for Aces would be 5 and it is the cheapest category to forgo. Having wound up with 6–6–5–4–3 when trying for Big Straight, he may select Choice and score 24, which is close to the maximum he could make with five dice in any case.

Some play that in his first turn a player must select Yacht, and keep on rolling till he gets five of a kind; if he has to use more than three casts, 5 points are deducted from his score for every cast over three.

A special score sheet is usually ruled off, to keep track of the categories each player has previously selected and the scores he has made:

CATEGORY	MAXIMUM SCORE	A	B	C	D	E
Yacht	50					
Big Straight	30					
Little Straight	30					
Four of a Kind	29					
Full House	28					
Choice	30					
Sixes	30					
Fives	25					
Fours	20					
Threes	15					
Twos	10					
Aces	5					

Crag

The same type of game as Yacht, Crag is played with only three dice and in each turn a player may cast the dice only twice (or may stand on his first cast).

There are thirteen categories in all: *Crag*, which is a pair plus a third die which makes the total of the spots on all three dice 13; this counts 50. *Thirteen* consists of any three dice whose spots total 13, and counts 26. *Three of a kind* counts 25. *High Straight* (6, 5, 4), *Low Straight* (1, 2, 3), *Odd Straight* (1, 3, 5) and *Even Straight* (2, 4, 6) count 20 each. *Sixes, Fives, Fours, Threes, Twos* and *Aces* count as in Yacht—the total of the selected numbers showing in that turn. A special score sheet is used as in Yacht.

Double Cameroon

Ten dice are used, and the principle of play is as in Yacht, but after his third cast in each turn the player must divide his ten dice into two groups of five and select a category for each group. There are ten categories, so each player has five turns in all. The categories are:

Five of a kind, scoring 50; *Large Cameroon* (2, 3, 4, 5, 6), scoring 30; *Little Cameroon* (1, 2, 3, 4, 5), scoring 21; *Full House, Sixes, Fives, Fours, Threes, Twos, Aces,* each scoring the total number of spots on the five dice selected which match that category. A special score sheet is ruled off, as in Yacht.

Liar Dice

In Liar Dice, as in Poker, it is possible for the inferior hand to win. In fact, of all the dice games based on Poker hands, this is the only one that allows for play comparable with the card game.

Two play, each having five dice and a dice cup. A light screen, a panel about a foot square with brackets along one edge so that it will stand upright, is set up between the players, and each rolls his dice against it. Neither player should be able to see the rolls of the other.

After each roll, the entire five dice are read as a poker hand, ace ranking above the six in every combination except a straight, where it always ranks below the deuce. The rank of hands is: Five of a kind (high); four of a kind; full house; high straight (6 high); low straight (5 high); three of a kind; two pairs; one pair.

To begin a game, each player throws a single die, and higher becomes the first *caller*. Thereafter the winner of each *deal* is caller in the next. A game is two out of three deals, or three out of five, as agreed.

To begin a deal, each player rolls all five dice simultaneously. The caller may then state he is satisfied or that he is not; in the latter case the opponent has the same alternatives. If either is satisfied, the deal is played out. If both are dissatisfied, the dice are picked up and the deal is begun again. (This option of beginning again is merely an added psychological weapon. It is used largely to give the opponent a false impression as to what one considers a good hand. The caller often passes the buck by saying "Either way," meaning that he expresses no preference but will let the opponent decide.)

When the first roll stands, the caller must announce his (supposed) hand, giving the spots on all five dice. (When the announcement is as low as one pair, the rest of the hand is usually skipped. But "aces up" is not a sufficient announcement. The player must say "aces and sixes and a five-spot.")

The cardinal rule of the game is that *a player may announce any hand he pleases, regardless of what his roll actually is.*

In reply to any announcement, the other player must do one of two things: (a) lift the screen; or (b) announce a higher hand.

The act of lifting the screen is equivalent to saying politely "You're a liar!" If the hand is as good or better than announced, the player who lifts the screen loses the deal, but if it is inferior, he wins.

Each player is entitled, after his first roll, to make two additional rolls of some or all of his dice. For example, having cast 4, 4, 2, 5, 6, he may save the pair of 4's and roll the other three dice; if he then rolls 4, 1, 3, he may add the third 4 to the pair and roll the remaining two dice. Dice that are saved should be placed against the screen at one end, and the remaining dice should be rolled against the other end.

If a player does not at once lift the screen following his opponent's announcement, he must call a higher hand, but before doing so he is entitled to make one or both of his additional rolls. (Having made an additional roll, he may not change his mind and lift the screen.)

If a player rolls five aces, he so announces and raises the screen. Since the opponent cannot call higher, he can only roll to try to make five aces himself; if he does so, the deal is a tie.

Strategy. A straight on the first roll should be announced correctly. This is the worst hand to try to improve. The best chance is to force the opponent to roll for a full house; and, once he has announced, raise the screen whatever he announces.

If you bluff after making a roll, beware of calling so high that your opponent is bound to lift the screen. Leave him something to roll for. For example, if he called three 4's and a pair of 5's, and your roll does not beat the call, announce a better full house or (more convincing) four of a kind of rank 3 or 2; he may roll two dice to try for another 4, but certainly will not roll three dice to try for two 5's.

Announce an actual good hand (full house or better) correctly. If you "sink" it by a few spots, and your opponent chances to reply by calling your exact hand, you are stuck.

If opponent announces four of a kind, and you have a better four of a kind, with a roll to go, here is an opportunity to establish that you are "lucky"—hence that your opponent must in the future be more cautious in lifting the screen. Concede that his call is good, roll your odd die, and call your better four of a kind. He is then bound to look. (The swindle cannot work if the equipment is such that he can hear that only one die was cast instead of two.)

Most of the effective jockeying and bluffing takes place in the call of three of a kind after the first roll. Such a call lays the ground for convincing the opponent later that you have a full house or four of a kind.

CASINO
GAMBLING
GAMES

♣

♦

♥

♠

BLACKJACK

Blackjack is one of the world's most popular card games. It is also the favorite game of casino patrons around the globe. At any given time, a crowded casino may have thirty or more tables with seven card players at each. Blackjack is second only to Bank Craps in amounts of money won and lost.

The history of the game, known commonly as *Twenty-one*, can be traced back to Italian, Spanish, or French card games of similar nature. History books from the eleventh century make references to such card games where players attempted to reach certain totals.

By its French name, *Vingt-et-un* (21 in English), it was the parlor game of fashion in the eighteenth century. Its popularity spread throughout the world, and the French name became corrupted into various forms: in England, *Van John*, and in England and Australia, *Pontoon*.

Blackjack gained enormous popularity in the first half of this century, thanks in part to the U.S. Army. Along with poker, this was the American soldier's favorite card game. In just the last few decades, the rise in popularity has changed it into a big money game, where betting limits have increased from $25 to $1000—and higher in many casinos.

THE SYSTEM

Blackjack players have been bombarded with information, books, and pamphlets claiming that the game may be beaten with a "system," making the player a consistent winner if he follows certain rules unwaveringly. Such claims are usually made by non-gambling mathematicians and are entirely misleading.

Blackjack is an exciting game because, from one deal to the next, the odds vary perceptibly; the player who can maintain an estimate of the cards that have already been dealt (known as card counting) takes full advantage of this fact. The recommendations in the section on strategy (page 519) are formulated to reduce the House's 5.8% advantage against the blackjack player by a considerable amount.

PLAYERS

From one to six or seven players, depending on the size of the table.

PERSONNEL

The dealer, who also banks the casino's chips. He is the permanent dealer throughout the game.

A casino official who supervises the game. It is his responsibility to see that the dealer behaves fairly and that he pays off and collects wagers correctly. He also has the final word on any arguments between the dealer and a player. He is known as the pit boss, the supervisor, or the inspector.

Blackjack Table Layout

EQUIPMENT

CARDS

From one to eight standard decks, each containing 52 cards.

THE SHOE

A box made of wood or plastic, from which the cards may easily be removed one at a time by the dealer (if more than two decks are used).

A HORSESHOE-SHAPED TABLE

Seating six or seven players, the table is covered in green baize cloth, and has printed upon it boxes in front of each player's chair plus such directives as "The dealer must stand on all 17's."

A RACK

Containing betting chips or currency.

TWO JOKER OR INDICATOR CARDS

Used as part of the shuffle (to be explained later).

CARDS

The suits have no value in Blackjack. The cards 2 through 9 are valued at the number on the face. Tens and all picture cards (jacks, queens and kings) are equally valued at 10.

The ace may be counted as either 1 or 11 by the player. The dealer's freedom to count the ace as either 1 or 11 is limited by the rules of the casino; these vary from casino to casino.

It has become nearly standard practice in legitimate casinos to use multiple decks when dealing blackjack. Between two and eight decks are employed. Half of the cards have blue backs and half have red backs. The different colors help to protect players from being dealt a card other than the top one by the dealer (known as dealing "seconds") when a shoe is not being used.

THE SHUFFLE

The dealer shuffles the cards. When the game is played with multiple decks, the dealer splits the cards into two piles; he then takes a third of each deck and shuffles them together. The process is repeated twice more. The dealer then cuts the deck in several places. He hands one of the players a blank or joker. The player inserts the indicator card into the deck and the dealer cuts the deck at that point. The indicator card becomes the last card in the deck. The dealer inserts another indicator card fifty cards or so from the bottom. When this indicator card appears during play, that deal is finished, and then the deck is reshuffled, following the procedure just explained.

The second indicator card is inserted to reduce the value of card counting. A skilled card player will attempt to make note of the cards that have been dealt, so he can gain an idea of the cards that remain. The card counter tries to keep tabs on how "rich" the deck is in certain cards, most notably the cards that count 10: tens, jacks, queens, and kings. This information is most useful toward the end of the shoe. By ending play and reshuffling the deck before the last section of the deck is dealt, the card counter is robbed of such information.

In casinos where blackjack is dealt from a single deck, the official in charge may order the dealer to reshuffle the deck at any time during play. Again, this is a tool the casino uses against card counters. If, with few cards remaining in the deck, a player greatly increases his wager, the pit boss may order the dealer to reshuffle the deck.

BETTING

Before any card is dealt, each player must place his wager in the space in front of him. Each player is betting against the dealer and not against the other players. The dealer then checks to see that all wagers fall within the minimum and maximum amounts allowed. In most of the larger American casinos the minimum bet is usually $5; however, on weekends or in peak periods the minimum may be raised to $15. The maximum wager can go as high as $1,000 to $3,000. A bettor may ask the permission of the pit boss to place a bet higher than the limit. The pit boss can either grant or deny that request. A player at times will neglect to make a bet, and thus will be dealt out for that hand.

Some casinos permit players to hold more than one hand at a time. If a player sits at a table with three players and the other four player spaces are empty, he may place wagers in more than one space. The dealer will then deal him additional hands. Each hand must be played to completion beginning on the player's right before he may move left to play the next hand.

DEALING

After all bets have been placed for the first deal with a new shoe, the dealer removes the top card without showing it to anyone and places it in a box reserved for discards. At the end of each round all the cards used in each hand also go in the discard pile. Removing the top card is known as *burning* the card. The top card is burnt to prevent the first player from making a large bet on the chance that he'd seen it when the deck was cut.

The dealer gives one card face up to the player on his extreme left (whose place at the table is known as *first base*), and deals each player one card face up, moving in a clockwise direction. He gives one card to himself, face up. He repeats the deal, giving each player, starting on his left, a second card face up, and one more to himself, face down. Since the cards are dealt face up to the players, they have no need to touch them.

OBJECT OF THE GAME

Each player wins by having a higher total of points than the dealer, equaling or coming as close to 21 as possible without exceeding it. Any player holding less than or equal to 21 when the dealer goes over 21 also wins. If a player goes over 21 he has *busted* and so loses his bet.

THE PLAY

If the dealer's face-up card is an ace or a card valued at 10, he must look at his other card (his face-down card is known as the *hole card*). In some areas, the dealer must look at his hole card immediately after the deal of the first card. In other areas the dealer may wait until it is his turn to draw before looking at the hole card.

In most casinos, when the dealer draws an ace face up, the players are invited to *insure* their bets (more on this later). If he has a natural 21 or blackjack (an ace and a 10-count card), he turns the hole card over and announces: "Twenty-one." Play ceases and the bets are collected. If a player also has blackjack, his wager is considered a standoff and remains in the player's possession. A blackjack beats all other hands except another blackjack.

When a player has a natural 21 and the dealer does not, he wins one and a half times his bet and is paid immediately. A player who bets $10 and receives blackjack wins $15 above his original wager, for a total of $25. Conversely, when the dealer has blackjack he is not paid off at 3–2 odds, but collects the original wager made by the losing player.

If the dealer does not have blackjack and he has paid off any player with blackjack, that round continues. Starting on the dealer's extreme left, each player either stands (or sticks) on the count he has received or asks to be *hit* for an additional card (or cards) in an effort to improve his score. Casinos require players to ask for cards non-vocally. That is done either with a scraping motion of the fingers or as when motioning someone to come over to you. Using a hand motion negates possible confusion, amidst the ruckus of a crowded casino, as to whether or not the player has called for a card.

Each player must draw until satisfied with the final count before the dealer can move to the next player. When a player stands, he indicates it by passing his hand horizontally over his cards.

If a player busts, meaning going over 21 in the count, the dealer immediately removes his cards, placing them on the discard pile, and collects his wager.

THE DEALER'S TURN

When all of the players' hands are completed, the dealer flips over his hole card and either takes cards or stands on his hand according to fixed rules:

If his hand is a 17, 18, 19, or 20, he must stay.

If his hand is less than 17 he must draw a card—and continue to draw until his hand reaches 17 or more (the rule on whether or not the dealer hits on a so-called soft 17 varies, and will be explained in a moment).

The dealer has no freedom within the rules on drawing and standing. These rules are standard for each casino. The player has the advantage of knowing ahead of time which route the dealer is going to take.

HARD AND SOFT HANDS

Players can count the ace as either 1 or 11. For this reason, a hand of 5-A (a 5 and an ace) may be counted either as a *soft* 16 or a *hard* 6.

A player can draw on a soft 16, hoping for a 5-count or less. If he apparently busts, he continues to draw, now counting the ace at a value of 1.

In casinos where the dealer has to hit on soft 17s, it works against the player.

SETTLEMENT

When the dealer stands, he pays off all winning players—those with a higher total than his own. Bets are paid at 1–1 odds. If a player has the same total as the dealer, no money changes hands. If a player has a lower total than the dealer, he loses his wager.

If the dealer has bust, he pays off all players who have not bust.

After chips have been collected and paid out, the dealer puts all the cards into the discard pile and starts the next hand.

SPLITTING PAIRS

When a player receives two identical cards (perhaps two 3s or two queens—the suits of the cards are ignored), they are considered a pair. The player then has the option to divide the pair and treat each as if it were the first card dealt in a hand. Splitting pairs requires that an additional wager of the same amount as the original wager be placed on the new hand; and he indicates his desire to split the pair by placing a second wager beside his first.

The player must draw or stand on the card to his right and complete it before drawing on the second card. If the third card dealt to him is identical to the others, he may again split this hand, into a third one, and a third wager is required. However, aces cannot be split this way in most casinos; and if they may be split, only one card can be drawn to each ace.

If the hand, once split, yields a count of 21 with two cards, it's considered a normal 21, not blackjack. If the hand is a winner, it pays off at 1–1 and not 3–2 odds.

DOUBLING DOWN

Once a player is dealt his two cards, he may *double down*. The player places a wager equal to the original bet in the box before him, and is then allowed to draw one card only. This last card is dealt face up.

The best opening hand for a player to take advantage of the double-down rule is a two-card count of 11, as it is impossible to bust and the odds are greatest that a 10-value card will be drawn, yielding 21 (there are sixteen 10-count cards in each deck, more than any other).

Most casinos allow the double down on any two-card total; some, however, restrict this bet only to 9-, 10-, and 11-count totals.

INSURANCE

When the dealer's face-up card is an ace, the player has the option to place an insurance bet. This is done before the dealer looks at his hole card. A bet half the amount of the player's opening wager is placed on the insurance line.

Insurance bets pay off at 2–1 odds, thus "insuring" against the dealer's blackjack. If the dealer does not have a 10-count card in the hole, the player loses his insurance bet but keeps his original wager until final settlement of the hand.

In Atlantic City, where the dealer can't look at his hole card until all of the players have acted, insurance bets are paid off or collected at the end of the round.

SURRENDER

This option is offered in some casinos. It allows a player to drop out of a hand after seeing his first two cards. He forfeits half of his original bet and the dealer removes his cards from the table. This action has to be taken before the player takes any cards other than the original hand.

The surrender bet is in effect in Atlantic City casinos and a few casinos in Las Vegas. It is a terrible bet for the player, and gives the House more than a 20% advantage in most cases.

Strategy

In blackjack, the House has a considerable mathematical advantage. A player can combat the House percentage by utilizing certain tools and card-counting skills (to gain knowledge of the contents of the deck). He must exploit his ability to deviate from the dealer's rules of hitting and standing; the competitive blackjack player should also double down and split pairs when the odds dictate. Lastly, he must bet wisely.

The House gains its advantage through the order in which the hand is played. In every case, the player must draw or stand before the dealer can complete the action on his own hand. If the player busts, that hand is over. The dealer collects his cards and wager. The dealer wins automatically, without continuing to see whether he, too, would have busted. The rules in blackjack about all ties ending in a standoff do not hold in the case of the player's bust. The dealer's percentage advantage works out to be 8.33%.

The player's 3–2 payoff on blackjack gives him an advantage of 2.4% over the House. By subtracting the player's advantage from the House advantage, the dealer ends up with a net advantage of 5.8%.

HITTING STRATEGY ON HARD HANDS

It is a given that on any hand of 11 or below, the player will hit. On any hand of 17 or above, he will stand. The dealer must hit on all counts of 16 or below, and stand on all counts of 17 and above.

The situation, then, that the player must master is whether to stand or hit on counts of 12, 13, 14, 15, and 16. These hands are known as *stiff* hands.

In general, the player will draw to a stiff hand when the dealer's face-up card is high, and stand on a stiff hand when the dealer's face-up card is low.

The following recommendations were calculated using a single deck of 52 cards. It was assumed that the hands appeared exactly as probability predicted from a full deck, and that the dealer and one player only were involved. It was found that this is statistically reliable; there is no need to use eight decks and several players. However, if you own a computer, you might like to write a program to confirm (or refute!) these rules.

RULES FOR HITTING AND STANDING

When the player holds a count of 12 and the dealer's face-up card is a **2**, **3**, **4**, or **7** or higher, he should ask to be *hit*. When the dealer's face-up card is a **5** or **6**, he should stand.

As there are more 10-count cards in the deck than any other, it is always most likely that the dealer will have a hole card valued at 10. If he does, a face-up card of **5** or **6** puts him in the dangerous position of having to hit on 15 or 16. As the dealer has no choice but to hit below 17, he is likely to hit and go bust. That is what the player hopes for when employing this strategy. The dealer's chance of busting outweigh the player's chance of hitting to a final count of between 17 and 21.

Whether the player holds a 13, 14, or 15, he should always stand when the dealer shows a **2** through **6**. If the dealer's face-up card is higher than **6**, the player should always hit.

When the dealer's face-up card is a **7**, **8**, or **9**, the player holding a 16 should ask to be hit; otherwise he should always stand.

It's difficult sometimes for the player holding a count of 16 to hit, only to see the dealer bust right after. In the long run though, the player holding a 16 must take the risk and hit when the dealer holds a **7**, **8**, or **9**.

The following chart simplifies the many rules for standing and hitting on hard totals:

Table 1
Strategy for Hitting and Standing on Hard Hands

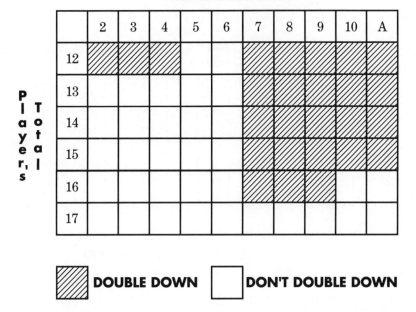

Dealer's First Card

DOUBLE DOWN   DON'T DOUBLE DOWN

SOFT HAND HITTING STRATEGY

A soft hand is any one in which the ace is counted as 11 instead of 1. A hand of **A-3** can be totaled as a soft 14 or a hard 4; **A-7** is totaled as a soft 18 or a hard 8.

An opening hand with an ace can never total more than 11 or 21, so it's impossible to bust taking one card on a soft total. The advantage of a soft hand is that the smart player has two chances to better his score: If he hits on, for example, a soft 17 and receives a **4**, he stands pat with a soft 21. If he receives a **7**, he now counts the hand not as 24 but as a hard 14 and hits or stands according to the rules of hard hand strategy. It is better, at this point, to be stuck with hard 14, having tried to improve the soft 17, than never to have risked it by standing on the soft 17 and hoping the dealer ties or busts. In the long run, a 16 or 17 is not a winning hand, and a tie in blackjack is not a desirable outcome. The longer a player sits and waits for his numbers or cards to appear, the stronger are the odds against him. Hands that end in a tie just drag out the process.

A player should never stand on a soft 17 or less. If the player holds a soft 18 and the dealer's face-up card is a **7** or below, it's best to stand; when it's an **8** or higher, hit on the soft 18. It's better to hit the soft hand, or bust and try again with a hard total, than to stand pat and hope the dealer busts or ties.

The player should always stand on a soft 19 or higher.

Table 2
Strategy for Hitting and Standing on Soft Hands
Dealer's First Card

Player's Total		2	3	4	5	6	7	8	9	10	A
	17	▨	▨	▨	▨	▨	▨	▨	▨	▨	▨
	18							▨	▨	▨	▨
	19										

▨ **HIT**   ☐ **STAND**

SPLITTING PAIRS

Any two cards of the same value are considered a pair. When splitting a pair into two new hands, an additional wager equal in amount to the first must be placed beside the new split hand. Although all pairs can be split, it is not in a player's best interests to do so randomly. As will be seen, not all pairs are equal.

For example, a player is dealt a pair of **5**s, which total 10. A **5** is harder to make into a good hand than one totaling ten. The player who splits a pair of **5**s is making more trouble for himself than he who keeps the hand as a pat 10.

The rest of the rules are as follows:

Split **2**s and **3**s when the dealer's face-up card is **7** or lower;

Split **7**s when the dealer holds a **5**, **6**, or **7**;

Split **8**s unless the dealer holds a **9**, a 10-count, or an ace;

Split **9**s unless the dealer's face-up card is 10-count or an ace;

Split aces always, even though most casinos only allow one card to be drawn to a split ace.

Do not split **4**s, **5**s, **6**s, or 10-counts.

Aces and **8**s are both recommended as pairs to be split, but for different reasons. The best possible hand to start with is 11, so two chances of starting with 11 are far better than one chance of hitting on a count of 2 or 12.

Table 3
Strategy for Pair Splitting

Dealer's First Card

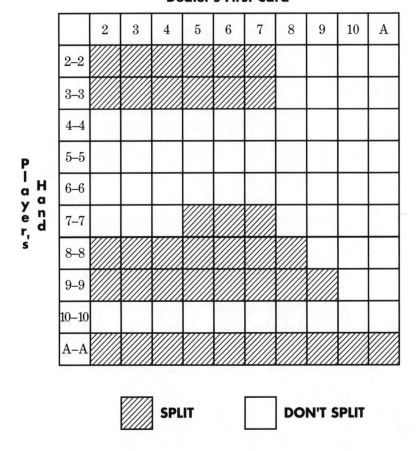

	2	3	4	5	6	7	8	9	10	A
2–2	▨	▨	▨	▨	▨	▨				
3–3	▨	▨	▨	▨	▨	▨				
4–4										
5–5										
6–6										
7–7				▨	▨	▨				
8–8	▨	▨	▨	▨	▨	▨	▨			
9–9	▨	▨	▨	▨	▨		▨	▨		
10–10										
A–A	▨	▨	▨	▨	▨	▨	▨	▨	▨	▨

Player's Hand

▨ SPLIT   ☐ DON'T SPLIT

Split **8**s because together they make sixteen, a terrible hand. In this case, splitting the hand yields the lesser of two evils. Rather than hit on 16, it's wiser to start over and hit on two hands of 8.

DOUBLING DOWN STRATEGY

The player has the option, in almost all casinos, to double his wager after the opening deal (sometimes he is restricted to doubling down only on the 10- or 11-count). The player is then allowed one card only to complete the hand. Many gamblers turn this asset into a liability by ignoring the basic strategy for this type of play. A player might double down his hand simply because he sees another player doing so, or because the dealer asks. Neither of these methods is recommended.

Table 4a
Strategy for Doubling Down on Hard Hands
Dealer's First Card

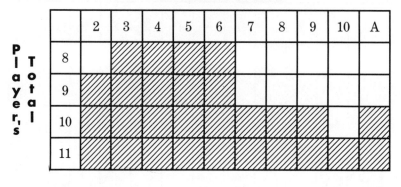

Table 4b
Strategy for Doubling Down on Soft Hands
Dealer's First Card

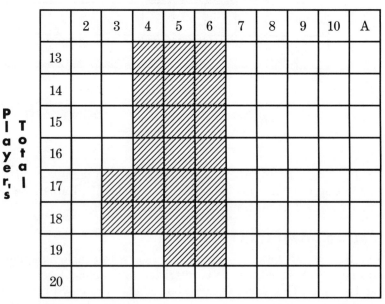

Player totals of 10 and 11 are excellent hands on which to double down, even when the dealer's face-up card is an ace. (As mentioned, in Atlantic City, the dealer is not allowed to peek at his hole card until he acts upon his own hand.) This doesn't affect the double down or additional wager in a split hand; if the dealer does in fact have blackjack, only the original wager is lost, and not the extra amount doubled down or wagered for a split hand.

Think of a double down bet this way: Pretend that the dealer's face-up card is a **6**; with a **6** the dealer has the lowest probability of reaching a hand of 17 to 21 and the greatest chance of busting. If you as a player knew this, you'd wager more, especially if you knew what your hand would be. That's the advantage doubling down gives the player.

The exact cases of when to double down and when not to are as follows:

Double down on a soft 13 through 16 when the dealer's face-up card is a **4**, **5**, or **6**. Even though soft 13s, 14s, 15s, and 16s are weak hands, the player is wagering that the dealer showing a **4**, **5**, or **6** will probably bust.

Double down on a soft 17 or 18 or a count of 8 when the dealer's face-up card is a **3**, **4**, **5**, or **6**.

Double down on a soft 19 when the dealer's face-up card is a **5** or **6**.

Double down on a 9-count when the dealer's face-up card is a **2**, **3**, **4**, **5**, or **6**.

Always double down on a 10-count, except when the dealer's face-up card is a 10-count card.

Always double down on a count of 11, regardless of the dealer's face-up card.

This is the only maneuver allowed the player in which the betting limit may be exceeded, in this case by up to twice the original wager. A wise player can make excellent use of this option.

STRATEGY ON INSURANCE BETTING

When the dealer's face-up card is an ace, the player has the option to place an insurance bet, wagering that the dealer has blackjack.

Before the dealer looks at his hole card, a bet of half the amount of the player's opening wager is placed on the insurance line. Insurance bets pay off at 2–1 odds, though the original wager that the player opened with is lost when the dealer has blackjack. If the dealer does not have a 10-count card in the hole, no blackjack, the player loses his insurance bet but his original wager remains until the hand is settled.

A 52-card deck holds sixteen 10-count cards. The odds with the deck untouched are 35–16 that the hole card is a **10**. Of course once a few cards are dealt, the chemistry of the deck changes. But for purposes of estimation we use the deck's original count. The odds that the dealer's hole card is a **10** (35–16 or 2.1875–1) yields greater than 2–1 odds by almost

6% on any given hand. So that generally, on any given hand, it would be unwise for the player to make an insurance bet.

However, if the player is counting cards and has noted, for example, that only two 10-count cards have passed in 26 cards dealt, he will know that more than half of the remaining deck will be made up of 10-count cards. In this case it is in the player's favor to make an insurance bet, as the odds are that the dealer holds a 10-count card.

When the player is counting cards and knows the deck to be poor in 10s, the chances are less likely that the dealer's hole card is a 10-count card, making it foolhardy to place an insurance bet.

Players also misuse the insurance bet when the dealer holds an ace and the player holds blackjack. Fearing a tie, he figures that by making an insurance bet he can at least win that bet. But if the dealer holds something besides blackjack, the player's paid off at 3–2 odds for the blackjack, and loses the insurance bet. The 50% loss negates the blackjack odds payoff. It is recommended to risk a tie with the dealer rather than to forfeit the 3–2 blackjack payoff.

Many gamblers know little or nothing of the germane ratios when making an insurance bet. They make this bet when their hand is very bad, hoping the dealer will have blackjack and save them; or they throw money away on an insurance bet when they have a very strong hand, such as a 19 or 20, and don't want to see it lose to the dealer's blackjack. Either way they buck unknown odds, which almost always spells disaster.

ADVANCED CARD COUNTING STRATEGIES

Expert blackjack players do not lose, on the average. They profit by taking advantage of this important fact: At any time throughout play, and more so as the cards left in the shoe decrease, the cards will favor either the dealer or the player, often by a clear margin.

For that reason an expert blackjack player will often deviate from the rules discussed on hitting and standing, splitting pairs and doubling down. As was already mentioned, these rules are formulated upon a complete deck. Once the first card is dealt, the balance of the deck is altered.

Blackjack experts have trained themselves to remember the number of key cards that have already been dealt. They know that on a particular hand, the deck may be rich or poor in certain cards of value to either the player or the dealer.

For example, a card counter holds a 15 to the dealer's face-up **4**. He knows, from keeping track of the discards, that the deck is very rich in **5**s and **6**s, yet all of the 10-count cards save one have been dealt. He chooses to hit, knowing that the chances of finishing with a hand of 20 or 21 are great, and his chances of busting, with few **10**s and many **5**s and **6**s, are small. His move corresponds to the cards in the deck at that moment.

Counting cards is more difficult than it used to be. At one time all games were dealt from a single deck. By dealing from two, four, six or eight decks of cards, reshuffled well before all the cards have been dealt, the card counter is robbed of a considerable mathematical advantage.

In a casino that deals from a single deck (if one still exists!), pit bosses know what to look for in a card counter. Any gambler who increases or decreases his bets dramatically, and, if a shuffle is called, removes the wager, is a sure card counter. A player who attracts the pit boss's attention, either by increasing bets tenfold every so often or by appearing consumed with concentration, will invite close scrutiny. A casino official may attempt to distract the player by standing at his elbow or by calling for a reshuffle after every hand. Even with all of the hindrances and safeguards against card counting, a general impression of the contents of the deck is important and will alter the smart player's betting strategy.

COUNTING

Roughly speaking, 10-count cards favor the player and 5-count cards favor the dealer. This is because 10-count cards favor doubled-down hands (9s, 10s, and 11s) and bust the dealer's stiff hands of 12 through 16 (with which he must hit).

On the other hand, 5-count cards favor the dealer when he hits on those stiff hands, giving him a count of 17 or better. They don't do much for the player's doubled-down 9s, 10s, and 11s.

To a lesser extent, **2**s, **3**s, **4**s, and **6**s also favor the dealer. Aces favor the player. Since there are only four aces per deck, keeping track of them isn't too difficult.

A simple method of keeping track of the high and low cards is as follows: Consider **2**s through **6**s low cards. When one appears, count it as plus one. When any 10-count card or ace appears, count minus one. There are five low cards (**2**s, **3**s, **4**s, **5**s, and **6**s) and five high cards (**10**s, jacks, queens, kings and aces). At zero, the deck favors neither the player nor the dealer. If the deck tallies plus eight, that means many more low than high cards have been dealt, and the player should increase his bet. If the deck tallies minus four, the deck holds more low cards than high, and the player should make note. With some practice this method can become second nature and will yield a general idea of the cards not yet dealt.

ROULETTE

Roulette is the casino game of glamour all over the world. There are two distinct versions of the game, American and European Roulette; each is conducted in a wholly unique manner. The European game is more elegant and affords the player better odds, while the American version is faster and more straightforward.

Roulette is thought to be of French origin. It's said to have been created by monks bored with the drudgery of monastic life. They marked off sections of a cartwheel, and wagered, using comestibles to place bets as to where the wheel would come to a stop. Evidence supports the game's existence, beginning in the eighteenth century, in various forms throughout Asia and the Western Hemisphere.

Roulette, upon its introduction to American casinos at the turn of the century, used a wheel with a total of 30 numbers ranging from 1 to 27, alternating in red and black, as well as a 0 (zero) and 00 (double zero), and a third space picturing an eagle or an American flag. Number bets were paid off at considerably less than true odds, giving the House an advantage of between 10% and 12%. When the ball landed in any of the zeroes and flag spaces, all even money bets lost.

European casinos originally used a wheel with 36 numbers and a 0 and 00. Bets on any of the number spaces were paid off at 34–1 odds. In the 1860s, Monte Carlo switched to a wheel with only the single 0, paying off straight bets at 35–1. Most other casinos that played roulette in the European fashion followed suit.

PLAYERS

As many players as can reach the table to place bets.

PERSONNEL

Two casino officials are required: the dealer, known as a *croupier* in European games (the European game is conducted entirely in French, whether the game takes place in San Remo, Italy, Nice, France, or Rio de Janeiro in Brazil) and his assistant. The dealer spins the wheel, "throws" the ball round the groove, and handles the chips on the layout. The dealer exchanges cash for chips and pays off winning bets. In American Roulette the dealer uses his hand, not a wooden rake, to remove bets from the layout. When the ball has dropped into a space and comes to rest there, the dealer calls out the number.

His assistant stacks the chips into piles of twenty, making them readily available for payouts. If the table is very crowded, the assistant can also act as cashier for players entering the game. When a table has betting layouts on each end, a third assistant is required.

Often, two roulette tables will be situated end to end in a casino, with an overseer or pit boss positioned between them. The pit boss is on hand to make sure personnel perform according to policy, and to settle any disputes that might arise between the dealer and a player.

EQUIPMENT

A table with a roulette wheel built into its center or at one end. The wheel is wooden, and is approximately 2½ feet wide. It spins in a smooth motion on a center spindle, upon a single ball bearing. On the outermost edge of the wheel, a groove has been cut in the wood. The groove runs the entire circumference of the wheel, and it is from here that the dealer spins the roulette ball. The ball is always thrown in the opposite direction as the wheel is rotating. Below that, toward the center, is an area with metal buffers inserted to upset the ball's fall as it slows and drops into the middle. These buffers, set at horizontal and vertical angles, are present to insure the randomness of the ball's fall. Around the next ring toward the center spindle are the numbers 1 through 36, 0, and 00, painted in gold. The background colors red and black alternate with each number, except for 0 and 00; those spaces have a green background. In front of each number, the spaces, called *canoes*, are divided by steel frets. The ball falls into one of the thirty-eight canoes and stays there until the dealer removes it.

To space the numbers out evenly, the 0 and 00 are situated opposite each other; the numbers on either side of the 0 are black; 00 has red pockets on either side; odd and even numbers alternate.

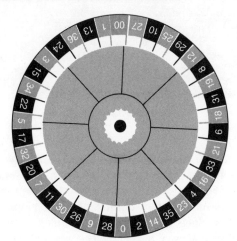

Roulette Wheel

The arrangement of numbers on the wheel appears to follow no apparent pattern. Actually, pairs of numbers of like color in succession add up to 37. Two exceptions are 9 and 28, and 10 and 27; each of these pairs is made up of a black and a red pocket.

A white ball, of either ivory or plastic, a half inch in diameter.

Stacks of betting chips. Each table has six or seven stacks of different-color chips. The chips are of equal value and each player is given a different color. The value of the chips is determined by the *buy-in.* So, for example, a player can buy 20 chips and pay the dealer $10, $20, or $100. Roulette chips are good only at the roulette table, although other betting chips may be used as well.

A baize layout on which bets are placed. All thirty-six numbers are listed in numerical order in three columns of twelve numbers each, starting at the end nearest the wheel. At the head of the layout are the 0 and 00, but they don't fall into any of the columns. At the foot of each column is a space that is either blank or says *2 to 1*. Along the edge of one side are the bets *1st 12, 2nd 12* and *3rd 12;* these bets allow the player to wager that 1 through 12, 13 through 24, or 25 through 36 will appear on the next spin. Alongside these bets are the spaces marked *1 to 18, Even, Red, Odd, Black,* and *19 to 36.*

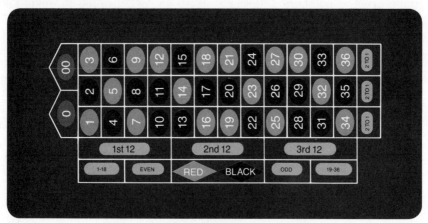

Roulette Table Layout

THE PLAY

Bets may be placed before or while the wheel is spinning. The dealer spins the wheel and the ball in opposite directions. After the ball begins to slow down and is ready to drop off the track into the center of the bowl, the dealer will say, "No more bets." Until that time, chips are placed on the layout. The players place their own chips, unless the bet is too far to reach. If the dealer places a bet, it is the player's responsibility to see that it's put on the right spot.

When the ball comes to rest in a particular space, the dealer announces the winning number and points to it on the layout. He then clears away all losing chips with his hand. Following the first round of betting, the dealer always spins the wheel from the preceding winning number.

As soon as bets have been paid off, and while the collected chips are being restacked, the wheel and ball are again put into motion, both being spun in the opposite direction from the preceding time.

The Bets Available in Roulette, the Odds, and the House Percentages

Chips may be placed in such a way on the layout as to signify a single number, a column, a dozen, an even money choice, or a combination of numbers. For instance, a chip placed squarely on the 5 signifies a bet that the number 5 will appear next. If the player wins his bet, he's paid off at 35–1 odds. If he places his chip across the line that divides the 5 and the 6, he's wagering that either the 5 or the 6 will appear on the next spin. If he wins, the bet pays off at 17–1 odds. A chip placed at the intersection of four numbers covers all four numbers and pays off at 8–1 odds. The following explains all of the available bets in detail.

BET A—STRAIGHT BET

A wager on any single number is called a *straight* or *straight-up* bet. The House pays off winning bets, should the chosen number come up on the next spin, at 35–1 odds. The wheel has 36 numbers plus the 0 and 00, making a total of 38 possible spaces as the outcome on any one spin. The difference between the House odds and the true odds gives the casino a 5.26% advantage. A player can make multiple straight bets at one time, or a straight bet (or bets) together with other types of bets. The straight-up wager can be placed on numbers 1 through 36, as well as the 0 and 00.

BET B—COLUMN BET

A bet made on any of the three groups of twelve numbers is known as a column or twelve number bet. The payoff is made at 2–1 odds. The true odds on 12 of 38 numbers appearing are 2.166–1. The House advantage is the same as on the straight-up bet, 5.26%.

Should the ball land in the 0 or 00 pocket, any column bet loses.

BET C—DOZENS BET

This is a wager made on the outside section of the layout, and it refers to the boxes marked *1st 12*, *2nd 12* and *3rd 12*. As you can guess, these mean the numbers 1 to 12, 13 to 24, and 25 to 36 inclusive and respectively.

The House pays off winners at 2–1 odds, and reaps a 5.26% advantage. Any time the ball falls into the 0 or 00 pocket, all dozens bets lose.

BET D—BLACK OR RED BET

The chips to be wagered are placed on the spot marked *Red* or *Black*. The winning color bet is paid off at 1–1 odds. Because this is an even money bet, it's a very popular choice. The true odds are actually 1.11–1. The player bucks a House advantage of 5.26%.

When 0 or 00 appears, depending upon location, one of two things happens: According to Nevada rules, even money bets, including Odd-Even and High-Low bets, lose automatically. In Atlantic City, when 0 or 00 appears, the player must forfeit half his wager immediately, and the other half is returned. With this rule in force, the advantage against the player is halved.

BET E—ODD OR EVEN BET

The player who puts his or her wager on the box marked *Odd* or *Even* bets that either an odd or even number will appear on the next spin of the wheel. The true odds are 1.11–1. The House pays off at 1–1 odds and its advantage is 5.26%.

BET F—HIGH OR LOW NUMBER BET

This bet covers the boxes numbered 1–18 and 19–36. The winner is paid off at 1–1 odds. The true odds are 1.11–1. The House gains a 5.26% advantage.

BET G—TWO-NUMBER OR SPLIT BET

A chip placed on the line that divides any two adjacent or contiguous numbers is a *split bet*. The player wagers that one of the two numbers will appear on the next spin, and is paid off at 17–1 odds. As the correct odds are 18–1, the House's advantage is 5.26%.

The player can bet the 0 and 00 as a split also. If the 0 and 00 are at the opposite end of the table, the player may place a chip between the second and third column of 12 to signify a split bet on the 0 and 00, and the dealer will recognize it as such.

BET H—ROW OR STREET BET

The player puts his wager on the outside line of the three columns. His bet covers the three numbers going across the column. If any of the three numbers appears on the next spin, the House pays off at 11–1. The true odds are 11.66–1, giving the casino a 5.26% advantage.

BET I—CORNER OR SQUARE BET

A chip placed at the intersection of four squares covers those four numbers. The House pays off the winner, in case any of the four numbers appears, at 8–1 odds. The true odds are 8.5–1, giving the House—you guessed it— a 5.26% advantage.

BET J—FIVE-NUMBER BET

The bet may be made only on the five numbers 1, 2, 3, 0, and 00. A chip is placed on the outside line intersecting the 3 and 00 boxes. The House pays off at 6–1 odds, while the true odds are 6.6–1. The House has a 7.89% advantage in this case, making it the worst bet in roulette.

BET K—SIX-NUMBER BET

A chip placed on the transversal between two rows of three numbers covers all six numbers. If any of the six numbers wins, the player is paid off at 5–1 odds. The actual odds are 5.33–1. The House has a 5.26% advantage.

BETTING LIMITS

The minimum chip value may be 5, 10, 25, or 50 cents. Regardless of the value of the chip, the minimum bet is often four chips. The four chips can be spread out anywhere on the layout, excluding 1–1 and 2–1 odds bets. The minimum bet of $1 is required on those boxes.

Always in roulette, the bets that pay off at higher odds have lower maximum limits, to prevent the casino from being hurt too badly in one spin. With a 5.26% advantage, it's safer and easier for a casino to grind out its profits over time than to risk big wins and losses in one spin.

The maximum varies from casino to casino, but the fairly standard limits are as follows:

MAXIMUM BETTING LIMITS

One-to-six-number bets: $100.

Twelve-number bets (columns and dozens): $500.

Even-money bets (high-low, black-red, odd-even): $1000.

ROULETTE BETTING SYSTEMS

Countless systems for winning at roulette have been devised. It would be fruitless to explain them here, because none of them really works. Every few years someone writes a book or appears in the media publicizing a system that has won them hundreds of thousands of dollars. The claim is almost surely due to an amazing hot streak of luck, or is the work of colleagues playing a system together.

Progressive betting systems have received attention from various magazines and books in the past. These systems dictate that the bettor increase his wager each time he loses. When he wins, the payoff makes up for all of his losses and adds a profit. The problem is that casinos know about progressive betting systems and set betting maximums with these systems in mind. After a string of ten or eleven losses, the player would have to go over the House maximum to place his next bet and retrieve his losses. Even if he could do so, he'd be risking an enormous amount of money to make a relatively meager final profit. In his favor, the bettor using a progressive system of betting knows the odds are against his losing so many bets in a row.

Other types of gambling systems are built upon the law of averages. In one system, if there are a number of red wins in succession, the player is instructed to bet on black on the next spin. The idea behind this strategy is that if red comes up three or four—or twenty—times in a row, the odds against its coming up one more time are very high. The same idea is applied to any bet on the table. For instance, if a lot of high numbers have appeared, the system dictates that more than likely a low number is due, and so a low-number bet should be made.

The error in this reasoning is based on the short and long run of averages. It is true that over the long run, red and black should appear equally. But from one turn to another, no single spin depends on the spin before it. Each turn allows almost a 50–50 chance of either black or red appearing (don't forget the 0 and 00 canoes). The number 15 can appear five times in a row and it's still a 37–1 shot that it will come up on the next spin. Every bet has the same likelihood of appearing on the first or the fiftieth spin.

For the same mistaken reason, many gamblers back off a winning streak because they believe the odds against the streak continuing increase with each win.

Money Management

The most important thing to remember in a casino is that gambling is supposed to be fun. Never gamble with money you can't afford to lose. Never gamble when drunk or under great stress. Do not make bets in an attempt to win back your losses; the gambler who does so will lose the remaining bankroll that much quicker.

Set a limit, before starting the night's gambling activities, of how much money you'd like to win or be willing to lose. When that limit is reached, get up and cash in your chips. The longer a player sits, the less likely are his chances of profiting.

CRAPS—THE BANKING GAME

Casino craps is not just an extremely popular game of chance, it is also the game with the best odds a gambler can find. A Line Bet plus the Free Odds (to be explained later in this section) gives the House about an 0.8% advantage—the smallest percentage advantage of any casino bet.

The players stand around a table covered with a baize layout. It is the approximate size of a large billiards table. A wooden retaining wall ten inches high runs along the edge of the table, to enclose the playing surface and to keep the players and chips from disturbing the action on the table. A groove is often made within the railing for players to store chips.

In a casino, gamblers are required to exchange cash for chips. Chips make it easier for dealers to handle and identify, and allow the establishment to operate with less cash on hand than is actually in use.

The layout of the table (see below) is in three sections, with the two side sections identical. Proposition bets are placed in the center section. Two dealers, a stickman, and one boxman (sometimes two boxmen) are required as personnel to run a casino craps table. The dealers pay and collect bets, each responsible for one half of the layout. The boxman sits between the dealers and is the official in charge of the table. He watches the game, the bets paid out, the players, and the dice. The boxman makes sure that the players and dealers don't work together in collusion.

The stickman handles the dice, retrieving them with a long curved stick, and announces the numbers thrown. He also places proposition bets for players in the proper betting boxes.

The shooter is chosen at random by the stickman, and bets by the shooter and all other players are placed on the table. The shooter will be required to throw the dice so that they bounce off the retaining wall. In some cases the table is too long to make this practical, so a string is stretched

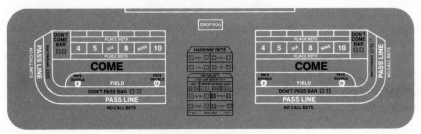

Casino Craps Table Layout

across the table and the dice must be thrown over it. The shooter chooses two dice from a group of six, and usually keeps these dice as long as he throws. However, he may ask for new dice at any time.

The Betting

The *Win* or *Pass Line* is a bet that the shooter will pass, on either his first throw or a series of throws. This is one of the best bets available, allowing the house a minimal 1.4% advantage. Certain *free odds* bets allow the House an even smaller advantage, to be explained later. The win or pass line bet pays off at even money (1–1 odds). This is a very common bet, although inexperienced gamblers are often attracted to bets with greater payoffs (and larger House percentages).

As in private craps, if on his first roll the shooter throws a natural (7 or 11), he wins; if he throws a crap (2, 3, or 12), he loses. Any other number thrown becomes a point that must be repeated before the shooter throws a 7 in order for the player to win his pass line bet. At this stage the odds favoring the House increase—dramatically, in most cases. If, for example, the shooter throws a 4 on the come-out roll, which then becomes his point, the odds (of his repeating the 4) against his rolling a 7 are 2–1, though the House still pays off winners at 1–1 odds. Refer to Table 5 for a complete list of the odds.

The *Don't Pass* (or lose bar) is an equally good bet, the player wagering before the come-out that the shooter will miss on the next roll or series of rolls. The player wins his bet if the shooter *misses* either by throwing a crap (2, 3, or 12) on the come-out, or by establishing a point and throwing a 7 before he repeats his point. This bet also pays off at even money and allows the house the same small 1.4% advantage. This advantage is maintained by *barring* either the 2 or 12.

The term *bar* is borrowed from roulette. In some cases certain slots, usually the 0 and 00, are barred and neither win nor lose. In the case of banking craps, if the shooter throws a 6–6 or 1–1, the don't-pass bet is undecided. If a barred number is thrown on the come-out, the bettor may

Table 5
Odds on Throwing the Point

Point	Ways	Correct odds that the number will repeat itself before a 7 is rolled
4	3	2–1
5	4	3–2
6	5	6–5
8	5	6–5
9	4	3–2
10	3	2–1

withdraw his bet or leave it to be settled by subsequent rolls of the dice. Either way, a barred number is not a losing roll for the House.

If the House were to allow don't-come bets without the barred 1–1 or 6–6, the wrong bettor would have a 1.414% advantage. With one number barred, a seemingly minuscule change, the wrong bettor suddenly faces a 1.402% disadvantage.

In some cases, the House will bar the 1–2. This roll appears twice as often as the 1–1 or 6–6. Players may think that since the barred roll is a tie, two ties are no different from one—a fallacious assumption. The ways in which the House can win remain constant, but the ways in which it can lose are reduced in this case, thus more than tripling its percentage advantage against the don't-lose player.

Come bets are made only when the point has been established. The player making a come bet wins or loses his wager in accordance with the rules of a pass bet. For example, the shooter throws a 9 on the come-out roll. A come bet is then made by putting a bet on the area marked *come*. The point 5 is then thrown, establishing it as the come point. The dealer moves the player's chip(s) to the box marked 5. Now the 5 must repeat before the 7 for the come bet to pay off. The bet is paid off at 1–1 odds, and suffers the same 1.4% disadvantage as pass and don't-pass bets.

Don't-come bets correspond to don't-pass or -lose bets in the same way that come bets correspond to pass bets. A don't-come bet is made after the come-out roll. The player wagers that the shooter will throw a crap on the next roll, or a 7 will appear before the come point. To allow the House a favorable percentage, either the 2 or 12 is barred. If a barred point is rolled, no decision is levied.

Free Odds bets can only be made after a player makes a pass, don't-pass, come, or don't-come bet. Once the point has been established, the player may back up his line bet with an additional wager on the point in which the House lays correct odds. Some casinos allow the player to make an odds bet equivalent to the line bet; some allow half that amount. By laying correct odds, the House advantage has been eliminated, though the original line or come bets must be invested first. Taking that fact into account, the House advantage is reduced to about 0.8% on an odds bet. This bet is highly recommended as it is the best bet to be found in the casino, on any gaming table.

Once a point has been established, the bettor hands additional chips to the dealer and says, "Odds on the point" or "Odds on the come." The additional chips are placed offset on the original bet. The line bet pays off at 1–1 odds; the odds bet pays off at the true odds for each point.

For example, a pass line bet of $20 is made. The point 8 is established. The bettor hands the dealer another $20-worth of chips and says, "Odds on the point." The correct odds on the 7 appearing before the point 8 are 6–5. On the next roll the shooter throws a 9, then a 6, and a 9 again. The

9, having appeared again, does not qualify as a pass, because the point 8 has already been established. On the following roll, the shooter throws an 8. At this point the pass line bet pays off at 1–1 odds, or $20, and the odds bet pays off at 6–5 odds for $24. If the 7 had been rolled any time before that, both bets would have been lost.

When the pass line point established by the shooter is different from the player's come point, it may happen that the shooter passes, bringing up a new come-out roll before the player's come point appears. In that case the odds bet is "off," but the come bet is still "working." The player must specify, if he so desires, that his odds bet is also "working" on the come-out roll.

When the player making the odds bet is betting the lose or don't-come line, it is the player who lays the odds. The free odds bet is limited by its intended payoff. The payoff can be no greater than the original line bet.

For example, a $10 lose or don't-come bet is made and the point 5 is established. The casino will pay off, on the free odds bet, an amount equal to the original $10 bet. Since the odds are 3–2 in the player's favor that the 7 appears before the point 5, he must risk $15 to win $10. Though it sounds foolish, this is a better bet than most so far discussed, with the House percentage advantage a mere 0.8%. This information appears on the far right column of the following chart:

Table 6
Free Odds Table

Point	Ways	Odds	PASS OR COME BET Payoff when taking odds on a $10 bet	LOSE OR DON'T-COME BET Amount wagered to receive $10 payoff
4 or 10	3	2–1	$20	$20
5 or 9	4	3–2	$15	$15
6 or 8	5	6–5	$12	$12

Buy bets are ones for which the House lays the correct odds on a place or point bet, similar to a free odds bet. The House lays true odds in return for a 5% commission on the winnings. They work like pass line bets in that the point must appear before the 7 to be a winner. The House advantage ranges from 2.4% to 4.8%.

Lay bets are buy bets in which the player lays the odds, as with lose bets, hoping the 7 appears before the point. In this case the player is laying odds predetermined by the House (not the true odds) so as to maintain an advantage over the player. The House advantage is 1.8% when the player lays 5–4 odds on the 6 or 8; the true odds, as you know, are 6–5 that the 7 will appear before the 6 or 8. When the player lays odds of

11–5 on the 4 or 10, as directed by the House, he bucks a 3% disadvantage. The true odds are 2–1.

Big 6 and *Big 8* are bets that can be made at any time. The player wagers that the number will appear before the 7, and the House pays off at 1–1 odds. The true odds are 6–5 that the 7 appears first. The House advantage is 9.09%.

One-roll bets, often called *proposition* bets, are made in the center area, usually by the stickman.

Field bets are wagers in which the player backs the numbers 2, 3, 4, 9, 10, 11, and 12 against the numbers 5, 6, 7, and 8. This gives the bettor sixteen ways to win and twenty to lose on a bet that pays off at 1–1 odds. Sometimes the House pays double on the 2 and 12, which, as Table 7 below explains, reduces the advantage from 11% to 5.5%.

Hardway bets are often suggested by the dealer, who may be mistakenly identified as an adviser to the players. He isn't, and will consistently encourage foolhardy bets. Hardway bets leave players at a considerable disadvantage, giving the House anywhere from a 9% to 22% head start. When the odds say "7 for 1" or "9 for 1" that really means 6 to 1 (6–1) or 8 to 1 (8–1) odds, respectively. This word play is one additional way to catch the inexperienced gambler. Many layouts will use the word *for* in place of *to* as in "15 for 1" instead of "15 to 1" odds. The bettor who wins a "15 to 1" odds bet receives fifteen times the amount he bet plus the bet itself. A $1 bet will yield a profit of $15. For the same bet on "15 for 1" odds, the bettor receives $15 in exchange for his $1, for a $14 profit. This is equivalent to "14 to 1" odds.

Table 7
Odds on Hardway Bets

BET	TRUE ODDS	HOUSE ODDS	HOUSE % ON $1
Hardway, 4 or 10	8–1	7–1	11.11%
		7 for 1	22.22%
Hardway, 6 or 8	10–1	9–1	9.11%
		9 for 1	18.09%

Come-out bets, called *Horn* or *Horn High* bets, allow the player to bet simultaneously that one of four different numbers (2, 3, 11, or 12) will appear on the next roll. The player's wager is split among the four numbers, and a winning number pays off at the same odds as a normal center or proposition bet (2 and 12 at 30–1 or 30 for 1 odds, and the 3 and 11 at 15–1 for 1 odds). In any case, the House has from an 11% to 16% advantage.

Any Craps gives the player a chance to bet that on the following roll, a 2, 3, or 12 will appear. Craps can be made four of thirty-six possible ways the dice can roll. The true odds on this happening are 8–1. The House gives, at best, 7–1 odds. The House advantage is 11%.

In the following table, the most common bets in banking craps are shown along with the amount the House should expect to keep out of every dollar bet against it; this is known as the house percentage. This arrangement is maintained either by laying less than the true odds on certain bets, or by charging a percentage on specific wagers or winnings.

Table 8
Craps Odds and House Payoffs

Bet	Chances against		Chances for	House pays	For every $1 bet the house keeps
Line (bet that shooter passes)	251	to	244	Even	1.40¢
Don't pass (barring 1–1 or 6–6)	976	to	949	Even	1.40¢
Don't Pass (barring 1–2)	488	to	447	Even	4.40¢
8 or 6 before 7	6	to	5	Even	9.00¢
Craps (2, 3 or 12 on next roll)	8	to	1	7–1	11.00¢
Hardway, 4 or 10	8	to	1	7–1	11.00¢
				7 for 1	22.00¢
Hardway, 6 or 8	10	to	1	9–1	9.00¢
				9 for 1	18.00¢
7 on next roll	5	to	1	4–1	16.67¢
Field (2–3–5–9–10–11–12)	19	to	17	Even	5.50¢
Field (2–3–4–9–10–11–12)	20	to	16	Even	11.00¢
Field (2–3–4–9–10–11–12, paying double on 2 or 12)	380	to	340	Even	5.50¢
Any Double on next roll	5	to	1	4–1	16.67¢
3 or 11 on next roll	17	to	1	15–1	11.00¢
				15 for 1	16.67¢
2 or 12 on next roll	35	to	1	30–1	14.00¢
Under 7 (or over 7)	7	to	5	Even	16.67¢

BACCARAT

*B*accarat–Chemin-de-fer originated from the Italian game of *Baccara*. The name, which means zero, stems from the fact that picture cards (jacks, queens, and kings) and 10-count cards are valueless. Outside the United States, where Baccarat is still making inroads with the gambling public, the game is associated with high stakes and elegant dress; it is one of the most popular casino games in Europe and Latin America. Baccarat was the choice of the *bon vivant* kings of eighteenth-century Europe, and is still the favorite of the card-playing nobility.

Baccarat was introduced to the French upper class during the reign of Charles VIII, in the late 1400s, and found a home in the country's many illegal gambling dens. The game fell prey to widespread cheating and suffered spotty popularity until legalization helped to rescue it at the turn of the century.

Early in this century, *Chemin-de-fer*, a version of Baccarat, became a hobby of the Prince of Wales, the future King Edward VII. He brought it back to British casinos, where it became the rage. Until 1960, this version was also played in American casinos. Today's Baccarat, as it is played presently in Nevada and Atlantic City, is the same game played in Monte Carlo, Deauville and San Remo, with slight exceptions, and is referred to as *Punto Banco* in Britain and elsewhere.

Since the 1920s, a game called *Baccarat à deux tableaux* has attracted gamblers of the highest order of wealth and fame. Its popularity is limited primarily to France. The game is banked by a casino or independent syndicate that pays the casino a percentage of its profits.

Regardless of where it is played and what it is called, Baccarat is essentially the same simple card game. The major differences are in who deals the cards and who bets against whom.

The American game of Baccarat came into existence in 1959 at the Sands Hotel in Las Vegas. While the basic rules are both lengthy and complicated, the play from the gambler's point of view is really very straightforward. Baccarat is a card game be tween two players, and all of the inactive players for that hand are allowed to bet on either the *player* hand or the *bank* (or *banker*) hand.

There are no options in Baccarat, and the percentage difference in either of the two available bets is extremely close. Bets on the player hand buck a House advantage of 1.34%; bets on the bank hand fight a 1.19% House advantage. All wagers are paid off at even money.

A 5% commission is extracted from winning bets on the bank hand, because the bank hand wins more often than the player hand. The 1.19% House advantage takes this 5% commission into account. Winning bets on the player's hand pay no commission.

It is also possible to bet that the two hands dealt will tie. Depending on the odds offered, the House advantage is between 4.5% and 15%. Not a wise move!

PLAYERS

From one to as many players as there are spaces in the layout—usually fourteen with the number thirteen skipped.

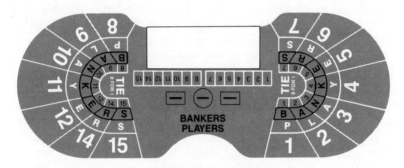

Baccarat Table Layout

EQUIPMENT

A kidney-shaped Baccarat table covered with a green baize layout.

A discard box for the cards used in each round.

A money box to hold chips from the House's 5% commission.

A shoe to hold multiple decks of cards.

Eight decks of 52 cards. The decks are equally divided into four red- and four blue-backed decks.

Two jokers or indicator cards to be used in the shuffle.

Three long, thin paddles to be used by the dealers for wagers too far to reach by hand.

PERSONNEL

Three casino employees run the game. Two dealers, one on each end, service either half of the layout. They collect all losing bets, pay off all winners, and tally commissions on each bank hand won. When the deck is reshuffled, the dealers collect these commissions from each player.

The caller, or callman, stands in the center and calls for the cards to be dealt. He places both hands in front of him and announces the totals. He then calls for additional cards to be dealt to either or both hands according to the strict rules. The caller announces the winner and oversees the payouts and collections.

A ladderman, who functions as an overseer, is also on hand in most casinos. He makes sure the personnel behave according to protocol, and settles any disputes that might arise between a player and the dealer.

OBJECT

Two two-card hands are dealt, one to the player and one to the bank. In some cases a third card is drawn, as dictated by strict rules. The object is to hold a hand valued at 9, or as close to 9 as possible.

VALUE OF THE CARDS

Tens and picture cards are valued at 10, though they are really worth nothing. The ace is counted as 1. The cards 2 through 9 are counted at their face value.

In Baccarat, the first digit of any total greater than 9 is discounted. For instance, the hand 7–4, totaling 11, is valued at 1. The hand 7–6–9, totaling 22, is valued at 2; K–6 is valued at 6, not 16. Now you see why the tens and picture cards really count zero, not ten.

SHUFFLE

At the start of play, eight new decks of cards are unwrapped and shuffled by the three casino personnel. The collection of 416 cards is split into thirds, shuffled, and then placed together. A player is handed an indicator card or joker, and one of the dealers will ask the player to cut the deck. All of the cards forward of the indicator are moved to the back, with the indicator card as the last card in the deck. The cards are then placed in the shoe, and another indicator card is inserted 10 to 20 cards from the last card. When this card is reached, the dealer will announce, "One more hand please," after which he will reshuffle the decks.

It was traditional after the shuffle that the dealer would face the top card and, depending on its value, *burn* that number of cards. He removed these cards and placed them into a discard pile. For example, if the top card were an eight, he'd discard the next eight cards; if the top card were a queen, he'd burn the next ten cards. Nowadays, the dealer usually burns the top three, four or five cards.

BETTING

A player places his wager, known as *fading*, on either the space marked *player* or the space marked *banker*.

Because Baccarat was originally played with cash, the minimum bet was $20, and still is in many places. Bets higher than the maximum of $2,000 are often allowed when a recognized high roller requests it.

THE PLAY

The shoe is passed to the player in seat number one so that he may deal the first hand. To become the first dealer, a player must place a bet of at least the minimum on either the player or the banker. Since he is the banker for this hand, he usually bets on the banker.

After the banker either loses a hand or relinquishes the right to deal, the shoe moves to the player in seat number two, on the banker's immediate right. Any player can refuse the right to deal at any time, in which case the shoe moves to the next player. Usually, though, every player takes his or her turn dealing.

Two hands are dealt. One is referred to as the player hand, and the other as the banker hand.

The first and third cards are dealt to the caller, the second and fourth cards are dealt to the banker. All cards are dealt face down. Once the hands are dealt, the caller slides the player hand, as a ritual, to the bettor placing the largest sum on the player hand. The bettor faces them and slides them back to the caller. If no one has placed a bet on the player hand, the caller faces the hand himself. Then the caller asks for the banker's hand. The banker faces them and hands them to the caller. To turn the bank hand over before the caller asks is considered bad form.

Now the caller has both hands in front of him. If either hand totals 8 or 9, and the other does not, that hand wins and bets are paid off and collected accordingly. A two-card count of 8 or 9 is known as a *natural*. A natural 9 beats a natural 8. If neither hand is a natural, one or both hands must draw a third card. The rules are as follows:

WHEN THE PLAYER'S
HAND TOTALS:

0 to 5	player draws one card
6 or 7	player must stand

The banker then draws according to his own hand total or to the card the player has drawn. At times the rules seem contrary to logic, but they've been carefully devised to give the banker a slight edge.

When the player stands, the banker hand follows the same rules of drawing and standing:

0 to 5	banker draws one card
6 or 7	banker must stand

When the player draws, and the banker hand totals:

0 to 2	banker must draw

When the player draws, and the banker hand totals 3, 4, 5, or 6, the banker must draw or stand depending upon the card just drawn by the player.

WHEN THE BANKER HAND TOTALS:	BANK DRAWS WHEN PLAYER HAND DREW	BANK STANDS WHEN PLAYER HAND DREW
3	1-2-3-4-5-6-7-9-10	8
4	2-3-4-5-6-7	1-8-9-10
5	4-5-6-7	1-2-3-8-9-10
6	6-7	1-2-3-4-5-8-9-10

When the banker holds a 7, he must stand.

Let's look at some examples. The banker deals the cards, and the caller announces each hand's total. The player hand is 3–A, and the bank hand is 6–2. The caller announces, "Eight, a natural for the bank. Banker wins eight over four."

On the following deal, the hands are:

PLAYER	BANKER
A–K	**7–4**

Both hands total 1. According to the rules, the player hand must draw a card. He draws a Jack, so his total is still 1. When the player holds anything other than a natural **8** or **9**, the banker must draw a card when he holds 1. He draws a **6**, giving him a total of 7. The banker wins, 7 over 1.

PLAYER	BANKER
2–3	**K–10**

The player hand totals 5, the bank hand totals 0. When the player holds a hand valued at 5, he must draw a card. He receives a **9**. His total is now 4. The bank must draw a card whenever his total is between 0 and 2, unless the player holds a natural. The banker draws a **3**, making his total 3. The player wins, 4 over 3.

PLAYER	BANKER
Q–K	**5–5**

Both hands total 0. When the player holds a hand valued at 0, he must draw a card. He draws an **8**. His total is now 8. This is not a natural 8, however, since it is a three-card hand. The banker must draw when his total is between 0 and 2. He draws a **9**. The banker hand wins, 9 over 8.

PLAYER   BANKER

A–A   **6–Q**

The player hand totals 2, the banker hand totals 6. The player draws a card, and receives a **5**, for a total of 7. When the banker holds a 6 and the player draws a 1 through 5 or 8 through 10, the banker must stand. The player drew a **5**, so the banker stands. The player hand wins, 7 over 6.

PLAYER   BANKER

4–4   **A–9**

The player hand totals 8, and the banker hand totals 0. Since the player hand is a natural, no more cards may be drawn to either hand. The player hand wins, a natural 8 over 0.

PLAYER   BANKER

2–4   **9–4**

The player hand totals 6, and the banker hand totals 3. The player must stand on a hand of 6. When the player stands, the banker must draw to a **3**. He draws a **3**, making his total 6. The hands tie, and no chips are exchanged (except when someone makes the bet to tie).

PLAYER   BANKER

8–2   **7–8**

The player hand totals 0, and the banker hand totals 5. The player draws an **8**, bringing his total up to 8. When the bank holds a hand valued at 5, and the player draws an **8**, the bank must stand pat. The player wins, 8 over 5.

THE ODDS IN BACCARAT

Some gamblers believe, because of the 5% commission extracted from winning bets on the bank hand, that the House has a 5% advantage over the players. Others believe that since the House takes 5% from winning bank bets and nothing from winning player bets, that the gambler's disadvantage on the player bet must be even worse than 5%.

These gamblers are wrong on both counts. As was previously mentioned, the bettor bucks a 1.34% disadvantage on player bets, and a 1.19% disadvantage on banker bets.

The bank wins 50.67% of all hands, and the player wins 49.33% of all hands. So the player stands 1.34% less chance of winning versus the bank.

The bank hand is then taxed 5%. The House commission reduces the plus 1.34% to minus 1.19%.

Were a gambler to bet $10,000, over the long run he should expect to lose $134 betting on the player hand, and to lose $119 betting on the bank hand.

Anyone who chooses to frequent a casino, no matter which game is played, will take the worst of it in the long run. But Baccarat's even-money bets on the player and banker are some of the least unfavorable odds found in a casino, and will stretch a gambler's bankroll further.

Chemin-de-fer

Chemin-de-fer is the version of Baccarat played in most gambling houses in Europe and England. The name means "railroad" in French, and refers to the eight-deck shoe, called a *sabot*, as it slowly makes its way around the table. The main differences between Chemin-de-fer and Baccarat are the standing and drawing options and the betting process. In American Baccarat, players bet against the House. In Chemin-de-fer, the players bet among themselves. The House "rents" the equipment and personnel necessary to play the game, in return for a 5% commission on the banker's winnings. The banker for each hand stakes his or her own money, which then becomes the bank. Usually only one croupier is required. He acts as a caller and watches to make sure the game proceeds fairly and according to the strict Baccarat rules. The game is conducted entirely in French, or using French terminology. A natural 9 is known as *la grande*, and a natural 8 is known as *la petite*. A hand in Baccarat is referred to as a *coup*.

The first dealer is determined by an auction. The player who stakes the highest amount becomes the banker, and may remain so until he either loses a hand or forfeits the bank voluntarily. When the bank hand loses, the shoe passes to the banker's right. If the banker simply forfeits the bank, another auction is held. The shoe again goes to the highest bidder.

After the banker has been determined, the sum offered by that player is handed to the croupier, who verifies the amount and places it in the center of the table. Players are then allowed an opportunity to *fade* all or part of that amount. The player who makes the largest bet against the bank is the *active player* for that hand. A player who wishes to fade the entire amount calls "Banco." If more than one player wishes to banco, the player closer to the dealer's right has priority; that privilege is known as *banco prime*. A banco bet has precedence over any smaller bet. If no one bancos, then smaller bets are accepted. Any amount of the bank that isn't faded is returned to the banker or set aside.

The player who bancos has the right of *banco suivi* if he loses the coup. *Banco suivi* means he wishes to fade against the entire bank, and has priority over any other player. If the player does not exercise this right, then fading the bank reverts to the above rules. If no one fades the entire amount, then the player who makes the largest bet is determined by the croupier to be the active player for that hand. Once the entire bank has been faded, any player who has not placed a bet does not take part in that coup.

The banker deals in an identical manner to American Baccarat. The active player then examines his cards, and, if he holds an 8 or 9, calls "*la grande*" or "*la petite*" and faces them. If he does not, he says "*passe*" and leaves his cards face down. If the banker holds a natural 8 or 9, he faces them and play ceases. If he does not, the active player draws or stands on his hand. The rules for drawing and standing are similar to American Baccarat. He must draw on 0–4, stand on 6 and 7. There is one option allowed the player: he may either stand or draw on a card with a count of 5.

WHEN THE PLAYER'S
HAND TOTALS:

0 to 4	player draws one card
5	player may draw or stand
6 or 7	player must stand
8 or 9	both hands stand

The banker then acts on his hand. He must stand with a hand totaling 7, draw with 0–2, and follow these rules with a count of 3–6:

WHEN THE BANKER HAND TOTALS:	BANK DRAWS WHEN PLAYER HAND DREW	BANK STANDS WHEN PLAYER DREW	BANKER'S OPTION WHEN PLAYER DREW
3	1–2–3–4–5–6–7–10	8	9
4	2–3–4–5–6–7	1–8–9–10	
5	5–6–7	1–2–3–8–9–10	4
6	6–7	1–2–3–4–5–8–9–10	

Exercising these options from the banker's point of view makes only a small difference. When the banker hand totals a 3 and the player's third card is a **9**, the banker may either stand or draw. If he stands, the banker will win six out of ten hands; if he draws, that figure is reduced to 5.9 out of ten hands. When the player's third card is a **4** and the banker holds a 5, drawing another card will give the banker a 0.5% advantage over standing.

Each time the banker wins, the banker's profits, minus the House's 5% commission, must go into the bank for the next coup. With every hand the banker wins, the risk and excitement of *Chemin-de-fer* increases. He may opt to pass the deal to another player, but he cannot remove part of the winnings and continue to deal.

TILE
GAMES

♣

♦

♥

♠

DOMINOES

Dominoes are believed to have a common origin with dice, and dice are believed to be the first gaming tools devised by man.

The bones came to be called dominoes from their fanciful resemblance to the style of half-mask called *domino*.

The term domino has been borrowed to describe a feature of certain card games, as in Domino Hearts. In most games with dominoes, not all the bones are distributed originally: some are left in a "boneyard," from which a player must draw additional bones if unable to play in turn. Card games that use this device are conveniently called *domino* games.

THE DOMINO SET

Dominoes are rectangular pieces of bone, ivory, wood, etc. Each *bone* is divided, by a line through the center, into two *ends*, and each end is marked by dots such as are used in marking dice. The commonest set of dominoes comprises 28 bones, as follows:

6–6, 6–5, 6–4, 6–3, 6–2, 6–1, 6–0
5–5, 5–4, 5–3, 5–2, 5–1, 5–0
4–4, 4–3, 4–2, 4–1, 4–0
3–3, 3–2, 3–1, 3–0
2–2, 2–1, 2–0
1–1, 1–0
0–0

Any domino set includes every possible combination of two numbers, from *blank* (0), one, two, etc., up to its maximum, allowing for repetitions. A set sometimes used extends to 12–12, and therefore comprises 91 bones.

The bones whose two ends are alike are called *doublets*. Each doublet belongs to one *suit* alone, while every other bone belongs to two suits. In the set up to 6–6, there are seven bones in each suit, but *eight ends* of any one number.

As between two bones, one is *heavier* than the other if it has more dots, the other being *lighter*.

The Draw Game

Most of the characteristic domino games are elaborations of the basic *draw game*. This is best for two players, but can be played by three or even four.

SHUFFLING

The bones are turned face down, and are shuffled with due care that none becomes exposed.

DRAWING THE HANDS

When there are two players, each draws seven bones and so places them that the faces cannot be seen by his opponent. The bones may be held in the hand, but they are usually made thick enough to stand on edge with fair stability, so that they can be placed on the table before the player.

Three or four players draw five bones each.

THE SET

The first bone played is called *the set*. Rules vary as to the set in the draw game and all its derivatives. A common practice is to allow the player having the highest doublet to set it. A better rule is to alternate in playing first, and allow any bone to be set.

MATCHING

After the set, the two players play alternately. (If there are more than two, the turn passes to the left.) A play consists in placing a bone adjacent to one already on the table. The cardinal rule is that a bone so played must *match* that upon which it is played—the adjacent ends must show like numbers. *Example:* First player sets 6–6. Second can play only another bone of the 6-suit; suppose he plays 6–4. First player may then follow with a bone of the 6-suit or the 4-suit.

DOUBLETS

In the basic draw game, each doublet must be placed *crosswise. Example:* First player sets 4–3. Second plays 3–3; this must be placed so that its side, not its end, is adjacent to the previous 3. The next 3 played must be placed against the opposite side of the 3–3.

In the basic game, this placement of doublets does not alter the fact that there are always exactly two *open ends* in the layout. The sides of doublets are open: the ends closed; whereas the ends of non-doublets are open, the sides closed.

THE BONEYARD

The bones remaining of the original stock, after the original hands are drawn, constitute the *boneyard*. If unable to play in turn, a player must draw bones one by one from the boneyard until able to play. If he exhausts the boneyard and still cannot play, the turn passes.

Rules sometimes met are: Not all of the boneyard may be drawn; a player must play as soon as he is able; he may not dig deeper into the boneyard in hopes of getting a better bone. Neither of these rules is appropriate to the basic draw game.

DOMINO

The first to get rid of his whole hand wins the deal. The winner customarily calls "Domino!" to signify the end of play.

SCORING

The winner scores as many points as there are dots on the bones left in the hands of his opponents. *Game* may be fixed at 50 or 100, or each deal may be treated as a separate game.

If the game ends in a block, with the boneyard exhausted and no player able to play, the one with the lightest total in his hand wins.

IRREGULARITIES

If a player draws less than the correct number of bones for his original hand, he must fill his hand from the boneyard whenever the error is discovered.

If a player draws more than the correct number for his original hand and looks at them, he must keep them all.

If a player exposes a bone, in drawing for his original hand or later, he must take it into his hand.

If a bone is played that does not match, the error must be corrected on demand before the next hand has played, but if the error is not noticed until later it stands as regular.

STRATEGY

A doublet should usually be played in preference to another bone, as it is harder to get rid of.

An effort should be made to keep as extensive an assortment of suits as possible. *Example:* Having to play a 6 from 6–5, 6–4, 5–3, choose the 6–5, so as to keep a bone of the 4-suit, as well as 5 and 3.

Watch for opportunity to block the game when your hand is light, and try to prevent the opponent from blocking when your hand is heavy. Try to force him to draw by making both open ends the number of your most extensive suit.

The bones in any set can be arranged in an endless chain. But this does not mean that with all the bones in play a block is impossible. The following example illustrates how a block arises. After five turns, the layout is:

6–3, 3–5, 5–6, 6–6, 6–4, 4–2, 2–6, 6–0, 0–1.

The first player is left with two bones, and the second with three. The latter holds 6–1. For his fifth turn, this player can play the 6–1 on either end. If he plays it on the 6, the game is still open. But if he plays it on the 1, both ends are 6, and there are no more 6's in the set. This play will force the first player to draw the 14 pieces in the boneyard, and the game will end with the second player an easy winner.

With four or more bones of the same suit in the original hand, play to force the opponent to draw. *Example:* First player sets 6–6. Second player holds: 6–5, 6–0, 5–4, 4–4, 4–3, 4–2, 2–1. He plays 6–5. First plays 6–3. Second plays 5–4. First plays 3–2. Second plays 2–4, making both ends 4. First player has to draw, and eventually plays 4–0. Second plays 6–0. (Not 4–4, because opponent will be compelled to play 6–2 or 6–1 next.) First plays 6–2. Second plays 2–1. Now, unless first player digs into the boneyard for the 6–4 or 4–1, second player is sure to go out on next turn with his 4–4.

Muggins (All Fives, Sniff)

Muggins, especially the variant Sniff, is considered by many the best of domino games. It is essentially the draw game, plus the rule that if a player makes the open ends of the layout total 5 or a multiple of 5 he scores that number. Sniff adds some special rules about the set.

To the rules of the draw game (page 552) add the following:

FIRST TURN

To commence a game, shuffle the bones. Each player draws one, and the heavier bone will play first in the first deal. Thereafter the turn to play first rotates. The bones so drawn should be shuffled back so that they cannot be identified.

THE HAND

In two-hand, each player draws seven bones for his hand. With three or four players, each takes five bones.

THE SET

First player may play any bone. The first doublet played, whether set or played later, is *sniff*.

SNIFF

The sniff doublet is open *four ways*. There is free choice of which way to place it (when it is not set) or of how to play on it (when it is set). All other doublets must be placed crosswise.

MUGGINS

There may be two, three or four *open ends* in the layout, dependent on whether branches have been started on the side of sniff. A player scores the total of all open ends when his play makes the total a multiple of 5.

Care must be taken to count *all* the dots at the open ends, including the whole of a doublet. In illustration:

FIRST PLAYER	SCORE	SECOND PLAYER	SCORE
6–4	10	6–6 (a)	10
4–4 (b)		6–2 (c)	10
6–0 (d)	10	6–5 (e)	15
5–5	20	0–0	20

(a) Placed endwise; permissible because this doublet is sniff.
(b) Must go crosswise.
(c) On the end of sniff.
(d) Off the side of sniff.
(e) Off the side of sniff.

Points scored in play are called *muggins* points. Some follow the rule (as in Cribbage) that if a player overlooks a score his opponent may call "Muggins!" and takes the score himself. But this rule applies only by advance agreement. However, when score is kept by pencil and paper (instead of a cribbage board), a player (including the scorekeeper) must announce a score on making his play in order to receive credit for it.

SCORING

Muggins points are scored when made. The play ends when one hand goes *domino*, or when the boneyard is exhausted and neither can play. The player with the lighter hand remaining wins the difference of total points in the two hands, taken to the nearest five. (That is, 2 becomes 0, 3 and 7 become 5, 8 becomes 10.)

The first to reach a total of 200 points wins the game, and if he reaches game during play, the deal is not finished out.

IRREGULARITIES

Same as on page 553, except that if a player originally draws too many bones and looks at them, his opponent (before playing) may draw one of them, look at it, and then shuffle it into the boneyard. Once the opponent has played, the irregular hand stands.

STRATEGY OF SNIFF

Most of the time it is more lucrative to play for muggins scores than for domino. Keeping a variety of suits is less important than scoring when able. Often it is worthwhile to dig into the boneyard for a certain bone, to score, even when able to play without digging.

Some players prefer to curb this opportunity by the rule that a player may draw only one bone per turn from the boneyard; if he cannot then play, he must pass.

When a player scores, he increases his chances of scoring on his next turn. Occasionally one player scores in each of three or four successive turns, while his opponents make nothing. To break this "losing tempo" certain bones are particularly valuable:

5–5, 5–0 and 0–0 always make a score if played just after opponent has made a score.

6–1 makes a score if played endwise after opponent has made a score. It can also (uniquely) make a score, without prior score by opponent, when played off the side of sniff.

6–4, 4–1, 3–2, together with 5–5 and 5–0, are the bones that score when set.

6–3, 4–2, 2–1 make a score after opponent has scored by play of a doublet (not sniff) of the lower number.

Any of these valuable bones drawn in the original hand should be saved, if possible, to be used in the appropriate situation.

All Threes

All Threes is in all other respects the same as Muggins, but scores are made by bringing the total of open ends to a multiple of 3.

Bergen

Follow the rules of the draw game (page 552) with the following additions:

The highest doublet must be set. A player who makes both open ends of the layout alike scores 2 points for *double-header;* if there is a doublet on one end when both ends are alike, he scores 3 for *triple-header.* The player who wins the deal, either by going domino or having lightest hand in a block, scores 1 point. Game is 15 points.

Matador

Matador is the draw game (page 552) with a different way of *matching.* Here ends match if they total 7.

Nothing can be played on a blank but a *matador.* There are four matadors: 0–0, 6–1, 5–2, and 4–3. These bones are "wild"; they may be played at any time, and with either end abutting the layout. The play of 0–0 leaves the end open only to another matador. Doublets are placed endwise, not crosswise, and are counted singly in matching: e.g., 2–2 matches with a 5, not with a 3.

The Block Game

The Block Game is in all other respects like the draw game (page 552), but there is no drawing from the boneyard. A player unable to play in turn passes. If none goes domino, and none can play, the lightest hand remaining wins the total of all other hands. The two-hand block game is little played, since there is virtually no opportunity to overcome the luck of the draw, but with more players block is preferred to draw.

Domino Pool is the block game for three, four or five players. With three, each hand is seven bones; with four, five bones; with five, four bones. Each plays for himself. When the game ends in a block, the lightest hand wins the difference of totals from each other hand. Each deal may be settled at once, or game may be fixed at 100 points.

Sebastopol is played by four, each taking seven bones. The 6–6 is set by the holder, and no other plays may be made until four 6's have been played four ways off this doublet. Then there is free choice of plays on the four open ends. The game is scored like Domino Pool.

Tiddly-Wink

Tiddly-Wink is one of the few games for a large number of players. It is best for six to nine. Each draws three bones. The highest doublet is set. Each hand in turn must play or pass; there is no drawing from the boneyard. There are two peculiarities in the play. There is only one open end—on the bone played last previously. Anyone playing a doublet, including the set, has the right to play again if able. The usual mode of settlement is for all players to ante before the draw; the player who goes domino wins the pool.

Card Games with Dominoes

Many card games, such as Euchre, Poker, Quinze, Vingt-et-un, Pitch, have been adapted to play with dominoes. These games were particularly popular in sections of the United States where playing cards were considered "the Devil's picture book," but dominoes were rated genteel. There is nothing else to be said in favor of these domino games, which are far inferior to the original card games. With the evaporation of the old prejudices they have largely disappeared, but the following two still flourish.

Forty-two

Forty-two is an adaptation of Auction Pitch. It was invented by W. A. Thomas during his boyhood at Garner, Parker Country, Texas, about 1885. It spread throughout the Southwest.

PLAYERS

Four, in two partnerships.

COUNTERS

In the 6–6 set, there are five bones that total 5 or 10 dots: 5–5, 5–0, 6–4, 4–1, 3–2. These bones are counters, and together they make up 35 of the game points.

DEALING

Each player draws 7 bones.

BIDDING

The holder of 1–0 calls first. Each player in turn makes a bid or passes. There is only one round of bidding. There are 42 points to be divided by the play; each bid must be a number from 30 to 42, or one of the two special bids 84 and 168. The highest bidder names the trump suit.

THE PLAY

Highest bidder makes the opening lead, and must *pitch* a trump. Since each non-doublet bone belongs to two suits, the leader specifies which he intends as trump. A lead calls upon each other hand to follow suit if able. A trump lead calls for trumps; a non-trump lead calls for the higher suit on the bone. If unable to follow suit, a player may play any bone. A trick is won by the heaviest bone of the suit led, or by the heaviest trump. The winner of a trick leads to the next. The object in play is to win the counters and all tricks.

SCORING

Each trick counts 1. (The total for tricks is 7; together with the 35 for counters, this makes up the 42 points in play which gave the game its name.) After the play, each side totals its points in tricks and counters. If the contracting side fulfils contract, both sides score their totals. If the contracting side fails, it scores nothing, and its opponents score their total won in play plus the amount of the bid. *Example:* Contractors bid 36 but win only 29. Opponents score 13 plus 36, or 39.

Game is 250.

Bids of 84 and 168 contract to win all 42 points. Such a contract, if made, wins only 42, but if lost, loses the amount bid plus the opponents' total won in play.

Bingo

Toward the close of the 19th century Bingo was rated as "the king of the Domino games, requiring a deal of skill and a good memory to play well." It is based on Bezique, and is still popular wherever Pinochle has not supplanted the parent game.

PLAYERS
Two.

SCORING BONES
The 0–0, bingo, is used like the joker in card play: it wins any trick to which it is played. It is worth 28 when blanks are trumps, but 14 when another suit is trumps. The doublet of the trump suit counts 28; all other doublets and trumps count their total of dots. The 6–4 and 3–0 count 10 each, whatever the trump suit.

The total of points in the scoring bones depends upon the trump suit, as follows:

TRUMPS	TOTAL POINTS
0	143
1	135
2	138
3	131
4	134
5	129
6	140

DEALING
Each player draws 7 bones.

TURN UP
The turn to play first is decided by lot in any agreed manner (as by drawing for heavier bone before the deal). After the deal, the non-leader turns up one bone from the boneyard, and the higher number on it fixes the trump suit.

THE PLAY

Leader may play any bone, and opponent may play any bone, up to the time the boneyard is exhausted. A trump wins any non-trump bone; the lead wins if opponent neither follows suit or trumps; the heavier bone wins if the two bones played to a trick are of the same suit. The winner of a trick leads to the next.

After a trick is completed, each player draws one bone from the boneyard, the winner of the trick drawing first.

DOUBLETS

A player holding two or more doublets in his hand at any stage of the game may try for extra score by leading one of them, and announcing how many he holds. If the lead wins the trick, he shows the doublets announced, and scores extra points, additional to the count of doublets he wins in tricks. The usual form of announcement, and the extra value for declared doublets, are as follows:

Two doublets, "double," 20; three, "triplet," 40; four, "double double," 50; five, "king," 60; six, "emperor," 1 *game point*; seven, "invincible," 3 game points.

Observe that the same stock of doublets (depleted by one on each occasion) may be made the basis for repeated announcements and separate scores each time the doublet led wins a trick.

FINAL PLAY

The turn-up must not be drawn from the boneyard until all other bones are gone; it then goes to the last player to draw. In the last seven tricks, each lead requires the opponent to follow suit if able; he must follow to a trump with a trump, or to a non-trump in this order of precedence: the higher suit, the lower suit, a trump. Only if unable to follow to either suit and unable to trump may be discard.

CLOSING

At any previous stage of the game, a player who believes he can reach 70 points may turn down the turn-up bone, whereupon the hands are played out under the above rules without further drawing. The privilege of turning down may not be exercised, however, before the player has won his first trick.

SCORING

At the end of the play, each player totals the counting bones he has won in tricks, with any points gained for "king" or any lesser number of doublets declared. If the total is 70 or more, the player scores 1 game point, or 2 if opponent totals less than 20, or 3 if opponent did not win a single trick.

Both players may score game points in the same deal. Points for "emperor" and "invincible," being *game points* directly, do not figure in the count of totals won in play.

If a player who has turned down the trump bone fails to reach 70, his opponent wins 2 game points, or 3 if he had not won a trick before the turndown, additional to what he may earn by reaching 70 himself.

Game is 7 game points. If a player *counts out* during play of a deal, he wins at once; the deal is not played out.

MAH JONGG

Many fanciful tales are told of the origin of the Chinese game variously known as *ma chiao, mo tsiah, ma chiang, ma cheuk*, but none is accepted by the antiquarians. Probably the game developed by contributions from many sources, commencing with the very use of playing cards or dominoes. Dominoes, precursors of the Mah Jongg "tiles," are believed to have been devised in China; Chinese annals record that dominoes were standardized in 1120 A.D. They must have originated considerably earlier.

Even today there is little uniformity in the way Mah Jongg is played in the various provinces of China. Little has been written about the rules, which have descended from generation to generation by word of mouth.

Prior to 1920, an American traveler in China, Joseph P. Babcock, made a study of the Chinese game, in its many variants, and devised a set of rules for Occidental play. He retained such features as he found common to the Chinese versions, and added others borrowed from Western card games. He invented a complete terminology, including some rough transliterations of the sound of Chinese terms, but few a translation of the sense. Having obtained patents for his game under the trademark "Mah-Jongg," in 1920 he commenced the importation of Mah Jongg sets to the United States and other countries. On the Chinese "tiles" were imposed arabic numerals, to identify the various ranks for players who could not read the Chinese characters.

Mah Jongg enjoyed one of the most remarkable booms in the history of games. Many books were published which reported to American players the various local practices of Chinese players, and these localisms began to be adopted at a rate which threatened the popularity of the game. In 1925 a committee composed of Babcock, R. F. Foster, Milton C. Work, Lee Foster Hartman, and John H. Smith published "An American Code of Laws for Mah Jong" (in the *Auction Bridge and Mah Jong Magazine*), which endeavoured to meet the popular demand for "color" while preserving some semblance of uniformity.

In essence, Mah Jongg is identical with Rummy, a game of "structures." This character was not given to it by Babcock; it is the feature common to all Chinese variants. One wonders whether Conquian, the ancestor of the Rummy family, was devised by players familiar with the Chinese game.

EQUIPMENT

The Mah Jongg set comprises 144 *tiles*—small rectangular blocks of wood with ivory or bone faces. Of this total, 108 are *suit* tiles, 28 are *honors*, and 8 are *flowers* (also called *seasons*).

Suits. The three suits are *bamboo* (also called *sticks*), *circles* (also called *dots*), and *characters* (also called *cracks, actors*). Each suit comprises four duplicates each of tiles numbered from one to nine, inclusive.

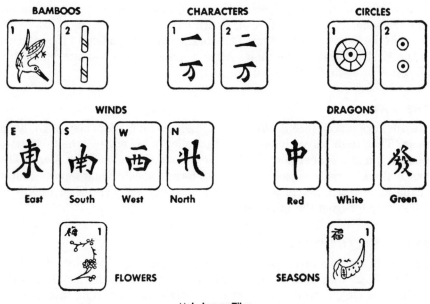

Mah Jongg Tiles

Honors. There are four duplicates each of *East wind, West wind, North wind, South wind, red dragon, green dragon,* and *white dragon.*

Flowers. These are all individually marked, but are assigned in pairs to the four winds. In Chinese play, the flowers are often discarded, as they are not used in play but merely add lucky bonuses to the score.

Accessory equipment usually furnished with the set includes two dice, a quantity of tokens (colored sticks) used for scorekeeping, and four racks. The rack is a device on which 14 tiles can be placed, so tilted that they are visible only to the owner of the hand.

PLAYERS

The game is played by four, each for himself. To commence a game, one player is selected by chance as *East*. He has choice of seats. The others may take seats as they please. They are called West, North, and South, in proper compass orientation. East collects or pays double, according to whether he or another player *woos*. If East wins, the compass designations remain the same for the next game. When East loses, each compass title passes to the player at the right.

WINDS

During the first deal, East wind *prevails*. This means that a player who obtains a set of tiles of the prevailing wind scores more therefor than for another wind. In the second deal, South wind prevails; in the third, West wind; in the fourth, North wind. This rotation is independent of the rotation of the East position at the table. After a round of winds—four deals—the players cast again for the positions at the table.

THE WALL

The tiles are placed face down on the table, and all players help in shuffling them. Then each player builds a wall parallel to his edge of the table, two tiles high and eighteen long. Each pile of two tiles is called a *stack*. The four walls are finally pushed together to form a hollow square in the center of the table. Each player sets a rack before himself. (The East rack is of different color from the other three.)

BREAKING THE WALL

East casts the two dice and totals the two numbers. Counting himself as one, South as two, and so on clockwise, he counts to this total, and the position on which the last number falls marks the wall to be first broken. The player at that position then casts the dice again, and the total is added to the previous total to determine which stack of the wall shall be taken first. The count of stacks begins at the right end, and continues around the corner to the next wall at the left if the grand total exceeds 18.

The selected stack is lifted out, and the two tiles are set face down on the wall just to the right of the break. The lower tile is placed adjacent to the break, and the upper tile at its right. The two are called loose tiles; whenever both have been drawn, another stack from the right side of the break is set on the wall to make a new supply.

DRAWING THE HANDS

Beginning with East, each player in turn to the left takes two adjacent stacks (four tiles) from the left side of the break, until each has twelve. Then each in turn takes one more tile, and finally East takes one extra tile. East thus draws 14 tiles, and each other player 13.

Flowers. The flowers are not counted as part of a hand of 13 tiles. On drawing a flower, the player immediately places it face up before him and takes a loose tile to fill his hand. After the original hands are drawn, any flowers in the hands are so *grounded*, and the players draw loose tiles in rotation beginning with East.

Kong in Hand. Any player who holds a *kong* (see below) in his original hand may at once ground it. The two end tiles should be turned face down to indicate that it counts as a concealed set (see below). The player draws a loose tile, in turn, to fill his hand.

SETS

The object in play is to obtain *sets* of tiles. The sets are of three kinds: *chow, pung, kong.*

Chow is a sequence of three tiles in numerical order in the same suit.

Pung is three like tiles, of the same suit and rank, or three dragons of the same color, or three winds of the same direction.

Kong is a pung plus the fourth like tile.

A Complete Hand comprises four sets and a pair of like tiles—14 tiles. Since the hand during play contains 13 tiles, the 14th must be obtained by draw or taking a discard. The first player to show a complete hand wins the deal.

Whenever a kong is grounded (placed on the table), the owner draws a loose tile, thus maintaining 13 tiles in his hand exclusive of flowers and fourth tiles in kongs.

A set is *concealed* if it was obtained entirely by drawing from the wall. A kong so obtained must nevertheless be grounded to score as a concealed group hence it is marked by turning the end tiles face down. A set is *from table** if it was completed by use of a discard. All sets from table are necessarily grounded.

THE PLAY

East commences the play by discarding one tile, reducing his hand to thirteen. Except as noted below, each hand plays in turn, the rotation being to the right, counterclockwise. In his turn, a player must either draw one tile from the wall (to left of the break), or must use the last discard. He ends his turn by discarding one tile.

Discarded tiles are placed face up within the wall. Grounded sets are placed between the wall and the owner's rack.

Discards. A discard may be used if it can at once be grounded as part of a set. To be used, it must be claimed immediately, before the next hand

---

* *The usual term antithetical to* concealed *is* grounded, *but it is incorrect in case of a kong.*

plays. Any player who can use the discard can claim it, regardless of whether it is his turn to play. If there are several claims, they take precedence in order: for woo (first claim), for pung or kong, for chow. Among claims for the same purpose, the first hand in order to play has precedence. The player who obtains the discard grounds it with his set, then discards, and the turn passes to his right neighbor; intervening hands between the discarder and the claimer lose their turns.

Grounding Sets. After commencement of play, a concealed kong may be grounded only after the player has drawn (from wall or table) and before he discards. A kong in the hand, not grounded before another player woos, counts only as a concealed pung.

A player holding a concealed pung, and obtaining the fourth tile from the table, may ground only three of the tiles if he wishes, holding the fourth in hand. But if it is still in hand when another player woos, the set counts only as a pung. A player who holds or draws from the wall the fourth tile to match his grounded pung may, in turn, add it to the set to make a kong, and draw a loose tile. But a discard may not be claimed to be added to an already grounded pung.

WOO

On making his hand complete, four sets and a pair, a player may *woo* by showing his whole hand; he is the winner of the deal and play ends.

The tile needed to complete the hand, whether it fits with a chow, a pung, or the pair, may be obtained by drawing from the wall or claiming a discard or *robbing a kong*. To rob a kong is to claim (for woo only) a tile that another player has just added to his grounded pung.

The last fourteen tiles of the wall may not be drawn. If no player woos after the fifteenth tile from the end is drawn, the deal is a draw, there is no score, and East retains his position for the next deal. The player who draws the last available tile duly discards, and play continues so long as each successive discard is used, but ends when a discard is not claimed.

SCORING

The value of the winner's hand is first computed, and each other player pays him this amount. If the winner is East, he collects double from each other player. Then the values of the three other hands are computed, and the players settle among themselves according to the difference of their scores. If East is one of the three, he pays or collects double the difference.

The value of a hand is the sum of points for sets, its *basic count*, doubled one or more times for sets of special character.

BASIC COUNT FOR ALL HANDS

CHOW	FROM TABLE	CONCEALED
Pung of simples (suit ranks 2 to 8)	2	4
Pung of terminals (suit ranks 1 and 9)	2	4
Pung of honors (winds or dragons)	4	8
Kong of simples	8	16
Kong of terminals	16	32
Kong of honors	16	32
Pair of dragons	2	2
Pair of prevailing wind	2	2
Pair of player's own wind	2	2
Pair of player's own wind, when prevailing	4	4
Each flower	4	

DOUBLES FOR ALL HANDS

The number given is the actual factor by which the basic count is to be multiplied.

	FACTOR
Each pung or kong of dragons	2
Pung or kong of prevailing wind	2
Pung or kong of player's own wind	2
Player's own flower	2
Bouquet of four flowers	16
(includes the double for player's own flower)	

BONUSES FOR WOO HAND ONLY

	ADD TO BASIC COUNT
For going woo	20
For drawing winning tile from wall	2
For filling the only place to complete hand	2

	FACTORS
Winning with last available tile or a subsequent discard	2
Winning with loose tile drawn after a kong	2
No chows	2
All chows and a worthless pair	2
All one suit, with honors	2
All terminals, with honors	2
All one suit, without honors	8
All terminals, without honors	Limit
All honors, without suits	Limit

LIMIT HANDS

In the American code, the limit that a hand may collect or be forced to pay another is 500 (for East, 1,000). In the Chinese game, certain exceptional

567

complete hands are recognized as *limit hands*—the owner collects the limit, whatever it may be. Both the limit and the list of limit hands vary from locality to locality in China. The colorful names of these hands—Three Small Scholars, Four Small Blessings, Nine United Sons, Thirteen Unique Wonders—made great appeal to the American public during the boom of 1920–1926. The committee that formulated the laws made grudging recognition of a few of these hands, although it is patent that limit hands, like flowers, enable the luck of a few draws to rob a player of all the benefits of skillful play. But American players went far beyond the Chinese in inventing limit hands, to the point where it did not pay to go woo with an ordinary hand. The simple requirement of four sets and pair for woo was stiffened by many with the *cleared hand* rule—the woo hand may contain tiles only of one suit, besides honors. Finally, the death blow to the popularity of the game was struck when a school of players exalted the limit hands above all else, requiring that the woo hand be one of a small and exacting list; to avert the large proportion of draws that such a rule would entail, the flowers were made *wild*.

IRREGULARITIES

Incomplete Set. If the set is found to be incomplete, the current deal is void unless a player has wooed, but scores made in all previous deals stand.

Exposed Tile. If a tile is exposed in building the wall, the tiles must be reshuffled. If a tile is exposed in the act of drawing another, it must be shuffled with six adjacent stacks and that section of the wall must be rebuilt.

Incorrect Hand. A player who draws less than the correct number of tiles for his original hand may draw the balance before East's first discard; otherwise he must play with a short hand. If a player draws too many for his original hand, but does not look at any of them before the error is noted, the excess may be drawn out by the player sitting opposite him and placed in the open end of the wall; but if the player has looked at any of the tiles, or the error is not noted until East has made his first discard, the player must play with a long hand.

If a player fails to draw a loose tile to replace a flower or the fourth tile of a kong, or discards two tiles, or otherwise renders his hand incorrect, he may correct his error before the next hand has played (or before East's first discard); otherwise he must play on with an incorrect hand.

Incorrect Set. If a player grounds an incorrect set, he may retract it or otherwise correct his error before the next hand has played; otherwise he must play on with a foul hand. If he erroneously claimed a discard that he cannot use, and corrects his error in time, the discard is open to claim by the other hands.

Short, Long, and Foul Hands. A hand that is short or foul may not woo; it is counted as usual for non-winners, except that double for flowers and for sets may not be applied. A long hand may not woo and is scored as zero.

False Woo. If a call of woo is found to be incorrect, the hand being incomplete, short, long, or foul, the false call ends the deal. The offender must pay the limit to East and half the limit to each other player, or, if he is East, must pay the limit to all. There is no settlement among the other three players. East retains his position for the next deal, if he was not the offender; otherwise the positions rotate.

Rules and Penalties*

1. All tiles must be turned face down and thoroughly mixed before the game starts.
2. No looking ahead. Players are not permitted to pick the fourteenth tile, or working tile (sometimes referred to as the "future" tile) from the wall before the player to the left discards a tile.
3. Thirteen tiles must be in the hand at all times, including the exposed part of the hand.
4. Fourteen tiles are needed to complete a winning hand.
5. After winning hand or wall game, the position of East moves to the player to the right of east.
6. A tile cannot be claimed until correctly named. If a miscalled tile is wanted for a Pung, Kong or Quint in an exposed hand it cannot be claimed, no penalty. If a miscalled tile is wanted for "Mah Jongg," game ends. Miscaller pays four times the value of claimant's hand. Other players do not pay. If no one claims "Mah Jongg," miscalled tile must be correctly named. It then may be called for Pung, Kong or Quint for exposure, or the final tile needed for a Run, Pair, Pung, Kong or Quint for Mah Jongg.
7. Once a tile is discarded and named, it cannot be taken back by the discarder. Down is down!
8. If a player incorrectly assumes East position, the player continues to finish the game. The next game reverts back to rightful East and the round continues, skipping East for the player who erred.
9. Should any player's hand contain the wrong number of tiles before the Charleston, the tiles are thrown in and the wall is broken again. If the player to the left of East has only twelve tiles after picking of tiles from the wall or after the Charleston, only this player may rightfully pick the thirteenth tile before the Charleston or before East has discarded the first tile.

Reprinted from Mah Jongg Made Easy with the permission of the National Mah Jongg League, Inc.

10. (a) Should a player's hand contain the wrong number of tiles after East has discarded the first tile, or if an incorrect number of tiles are exposed, the player's hand is "dead." "Mah Jongg" cannot be called. Dead Hand ceases to pick and discard. Pays same as other players.

    (b) Should two players have the wrong number of tiles, the other players may continue playing.

    (c) Should three players have the wrong number of tiles, the game is replayed.

11. A player shall not be permitted to call a tile for an Exposure or Mah Jongg, after player to the right of the discarder has drawn a tile from the wall and discarded.

12. When two discards of the same tile are thrown in rapid succession and a player wishes to claim said tile, for either Mah Jongg or Exposure, the second discard must be taken, except when the second discard is a Joker. In this case **only,** the first tile must be claimed and the Joker remains on the table as a dead tile.

13. (a) When two players want the same tile for an Exposure, the player nearest in turn to the discarder gets the preference.

    (b) When two players want the same tile, one for an Exposure and the other for Mah Jongg, the Mah Jongg declarer always gets the preference.

    (c) When two players want the same tile for Mah Jongg, the player nearest in turn to the discarder gets the preference.

14. If an incorrect exposure is made, the hand may be declared dead by any of the other three players. Bettor must remain silent. If the exposure goes unnoticed, the erring player does not have to announce it and continues to play. Of course, Mah Jongg cannot be made.

15. When Mah Jongg has been declared and exposed, no tile previously discarded may be called for an Exposure or Mah Jongg by any other player.

STRATEGY

Three objectives should be kept constantly in view: (a) to complete the hand as quickly as possible; (b) to block the opponents by retaining tiles useful to them; (c) to build up a hand of large count. The beginner is prone to concentrate on the third; the expert is ever ready to sacrifice it to further either of the others.

The decision to try for one of the combinations that score double must rest upon a good start in the original hand. For example, Hartman says that the idea of clearing the hand (limiting it to one suit, with or without dragons) should not be entertained unless the original hand contains at least nine clear tiles. With the great majority of hands, the early discards are governed by the following considerations:

Single tiles of winds, not the player's own wind, and single terminals, ones and nines, should be discarded as early as possible, when the chance that they can be purged or chowed by opponents is at a minimum. One's own winds and dragons are usually kept, on speculation. After terminals, twos and eights are desirable discards. Threes and sevens stand on the borderline; they are best retained if the hand as a whole has little prospect of woo and defensive play is therefore indicated. The best suit tiles to keep are naturally the middle series, fours, fives, and sixes, since they stand the best chance of improvement (chow) by the draw.

The foregoing refers to isolated tiles. Pairs are naturally kept, also two tiles of the same suit in sequence. With these two-tile sequences should be kept the tiles one or possibly two ranks removed, as 4–5–7 or 4–5–8. With more than four such groups, it is evident that some will eventually have to be abandoned if the hand is to woo. Consideration should be given to choosing the victims early; especially when a tile drawn increases the prospects elsewhere. *Example:* The player holds the 5 of bamboo and draws the 7. If no 6 has been discarded, any of four tiles will complete a set. This "inside draw" is better than holding a pair, which can be filled only by one of two tiles; hence the 7 should be kept even at a sacrifice of an (isolated) pair in another suit.

At the beginning of the game, what to keep may be decided chiefly by the number of tiles outstanding that will fill each possible set. But as the play progresses, other considerations rapidly increase in importance. Apropos of the last example above, when a hand lacks only one or two tiles of completion, a pair is better kept than a part-sequence, even a "two-ender," for the pair is a wooing set in itself, and may develop into a pung, while a sequence is nothing unless complete.

The American code allows any player to claim a discard for any kind of set. The Chinese rule excepts the chow, which is the easiest kind of set to complete. Only the player at the right of the discarder may take a discard to complete a chow. This rule creates the chief opportunity for skill in the Chinese game—defense. Hartman pictures the experience of an American tyro against three expert Chinese players in these words:

"Somehow the adversary on his left will persistently discard tiles which are of no earthly use to him, while the adversary on his right will repeatedly bury in the discard the very tiles he wishes to chow—but can't. Even if he has a run of good luck in the draw and gets his hand down to two pairs, he may sit waiting for either a four or six of Bamboos, let us say, to match either of his pairs, when presently his left-hand adversary will lay down a completed hand—all in Characters except for a four-five-six Bamboo sequence, which contains both the tiles which the American is calling. Hard luck, doubtless. What our American fails to understand is that his seemingly scattered and meaningless discards have been a succession of revelations of what tiles he doesn't want until his watchful adversaries, by an intricate series of deductions, know perfectly well what he does want, and refuse to discard it. The amazing skill which some Chinese have developed in this business of inference and deduction, until after eight or nine rounds of the draw they can read with amazing accuracy the make-up of all three opposing hands, is the whole art of Mah Jong."

BOARD
GAMES

BACKGAMMON

There is much historical evidence for the belief that games of skill played with counters on a board were preceded by games in which the movement of pieces was governed by chance throws of dice. Backgammon would thus seem to be older than Chess. In fact, the theory that a primitive ancestor, of which Backgammon and Pachisi (Parcheesi) are the nearest living prototypes, was the source of Chess, Checkers, Mill, Ticktacktoe, and many Oriental and African games.

Backgammon was certainly played by the Greeks and the Romans. Plato alludes to a game in which dice are thrown and the men are placed after due consideration. That this was similar to modern Backgammon is probable from the Roman name, *ludus duodecim scriptorum*, "twelve-lined game."

Of course, there have been many variant games played on the Backgammon board. Among those whose heyday is past were Irish, Tric-Trac, Jacquet, Puff, Revertier, Tokkadille. In England the rules of Backgammon were codified by Edmond Hoyle about 1750 and, except for the addition of the doubling cube, remain virtually intact today. The game we call Backgammon is occasionally referred to as Tric-Trac in France.

Starting in the late 1960s, the game enjoyed a worldwide resurgence that far eclipsed the great Mah Jongg craze of the 1920s and the Canasta fad of the 1950s. Thousands of clubs devoted exclusively to Backgammon opened; millions learned to play the game. Tournaments were organized and an attempt was made to establish a governing body to regulate and promote the game, much as the American Contract Bridge League does for Contract Bridge. Although the Backgammon boom had waned somewhat by the end of the 1980s, the game still enjoys widespread popularity, especially in clubs where other games are played.

PLAYERS

Two.

EQUIPMENT

The board is square or rectangular, consisting of 24 triangles, called *points*, divided into four quadrants of six triangles each. Separating the quadrants is the spine of the board, known as the *bar*. The quadrants are referred to as a player's *home* or *inner* board and his outer board, and the opponent's home and outer board. The 24 triangles alternate in color.

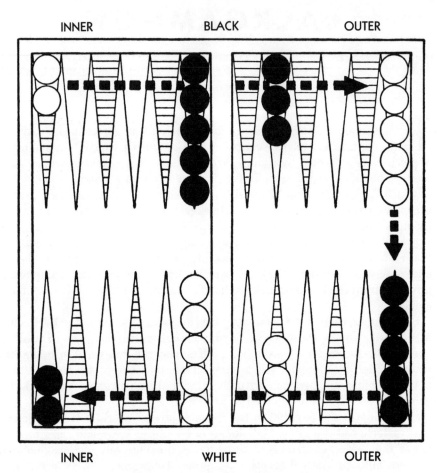

Backgammon Board—Initial Position—Notation
The arrows show the direction in which White moves. Black moves in the opposite direction.

The players sit opposite each other, and each is provided with 15 checkers (or *men*) of different colors. For the purpose of this discussion, the checkers will be designated white (W) and black (B), although many different color combinations are used. Four dice and two dice cups are also necessary.

DESIGNATION OF POINTS

In the modern game, all 24 points are numbered. The innermost point of each player's home board is the one-point. The outermost is the 24-point, which is the opponent's one-point. In the diagram above, the points have been numbered from W's position. The corresponding numbers for B would be 1 for W's 24, clockwise around the board to 24 for W's 1. Each player's 7-point is known as the *bar point*.

COMMENCEMENT OF PLAY

The checkers are placed as in the diagram, i.e., five checkers on a player's 6-point, three on his 8-point, five on the 13-points (known as the *midpoint*) and two on the 24-point. (Turn the board 180° and an acceptable mirror image of the starting position would exist.)

Each player rolls one die. The player with the higher number moves first, and he must use the two numbers cast by him and his opponent. If equal numbers are rolled, both must roll again until different numbers turn up. By agreement, an initial tie roll may result in an *automatic double* (doubling the stakes of the game). After the first roll, the players cast two dice, alternating turns.

OBJECT OF THE GAME

Each player endeavors to move all of his checkers into his home board and thence off the board. The first to *bear off* all of his checkers wins the game. The direction of W's checkers in the above illustration is clockwise (from his 24-point to his home board); B's checkers move in the opposite direction, counterclockwise.

MOVEMENT OF THE CHECKERS

A player's throw of the two dice indicates how many points, or *pips*, he can move his checkers forward (checkers cannot be moved backward). The following rules apply:

1. A checker may be moved only to an *open point*, one that is not occupied by two or more opposing checkers.

2. The two numbers on the dice constitute separate moves. If, for example, a player rolls 5 and 4, he may move one checker 5 pips, then 4 pips, or he may move one checker 5 pips and another 4 pips. The cumulative total on the dice may not be taken unless one of the numbers lands on an open point. Suppose that on the first roll W has to play 6 and 1. He moves W 13 to W 7 and W 8 to W 7, thereby placing two men on the 7-point. B now throws 6 and 5. He may not move one of his men off W's 1-point because the point 5 pips away is occupied by five opposing checkers and the point 6 pips away is covered by two.

3. A player who rolls doubles plays the number shown on the dice twice. A cast of 6 and 6 means that he has four sixes to play, and he may move any combination of checkers he feels appropriate to complete this requirement.

4. A player must play both numbers of the roll if legally possible (or all four numbers of a double). He may not move a checker in such a way that the other number on the dice cannot be played if some other move is possible. He may not forfeit his turn. When only one number can be played, he must use the higher. When neither can be played, he loses his turn. Numbers that cannot be played are forfeited.

MAKING POINTS

One of the objects of the game is to make points to impede the movement of the opponent's checkers and to provide safe landing spots for one's own checkers as they are moved around the board. A point is made when a player places two checkers on the same point. Thereafter he may place additional checkers on points he *owns*, but piling up too many men on one point is not desirable. Try not to *strip* (reduce to two checkers) your 6-point, 5-point, or bar point if you have made those points. A third checker on those points allows you to build additional points in your home board without giving up a key point. An extra man on the 6-point is especially advantageous.

BLOTS

A single checker on a point is called a *blot*. A blot does not constitute a point—on the contrary, if an opponent is able to move a checker to that same point, the blot is *hit* and is temporarily removed from play by literally being placed on the bar.

ENTERING

When one or more checkers are on the bar, the first obligation of a player is to enter his checker(s) into the opposing home board. Until all checkers are entered, a player may not move another checker. A checker may be entered only if one number on the dice corresponds to an open point in the opponent's board. *Example:* W is on the bar and B has made his 6-, 5-, and 3-points. To enter B's home board, W must cast a 1, 2, or 4 on one of his dice. Each time he fails to do so, the turn passes to B, for W may make no other move as long as one of his checkers is on the bar. The sum of the dice cannot be used for entering. Once a checker is back in play, the second number on the dice must be played, with either that checker or some other checker.

If a player has made all six points in his inner board, he has a *closed* board. Any opposing checkers on the bar are unable to enter, so the opponent has no move. He continues to pass his turn until such time as a point is opened and offers opportunity for entry.

BEARING OFF

As soon as a player has moved all of his 15 checkers into his home board, he may commence bearing off. To remove a checker, the player must roll a number that carries a checker pass the 1-point in his inner board. Thus a 6 allows the player to remove a checker from his 6-point (5 pips to the 1-point and 1 pip off the board). If a number is rolled higher than on any point where a checker is located, a checker on the next lowest point is borne off instead. *Example:* W, with no men on his 5- and 6-point, rolls

6–5. He takes two men off his 4-point. He may not take men off lower-number points until higher-number points are cleared unless he rolls a specific number that allows him to do so. A throw of 1 permits a player to bear a man off his 1-point, but a 2 must be played by some other checker if possible. A player is under no obligation to bear off men if he feels it is strategically advisable to move men within his inner board. On a roll of 3 and 1, it may enhance later bear off prospects to move a checker from the 6-point to the 3-point and a checker from the 2-point to the 1-point rather than to take one checker off the 4-point.

A checker borne off does not return to play. A player, however, must always have all of his active checkers in his home board before he can bear off. If a checker is hit during the bear-off process, the player must enter that checker and bring it back into the inner board before he can continue to take other checkers off the board. The first player to bear off all 15 checkers wins the game.

DOUBLING

Backgammon is played for an agreed stake per point. Initially the game starts at one point, but the stake may be increased manyfold during the course of play by doubling and redoubling. For this purpose a *doubling cube* is used. The doubling cube, which is placed on the bar between the two players, is essentially a large die with the numbers 2, 4, 8, 16, 32, and 64 printed on its six sides. Automatic doubles, gammons, and backgammons also increase the stake of a game.

If identical numbers are thrown for the first roll, the doubling cube is turned to 2, thereby doubling the stakes of the game, but it remains in the middle. Players must adopt this agreement prior to beginning of play. There is no rule that requires a player to accept an automatic double unless he has made a previous commitment to do so. Generally, only one automatic double is permitted per game, so additional tie rolls do not continue to double the stakes.

When a player feels he has an advantage in the play, he may double the stakes by turning the cube to 2, or the next highest number, such as 4, after an automatic double. This may be done only before he has rolled and only when the cube is in the middle, or if his opponent has previously doubled him. The same player may not double twice consecutively. The opponents may *take* the double (agree to play for higher stakes), in which case he *owns* the cube and is the only player who may later redouble, or he may *pass* (concede the game and the number of points on the cube). When a player takes a double, the cube is removed from the center of the board and placed on his side of the table. In most stakes games in the United States, particularly in clubs, *beavers* are permitted. When a player is doubled, he may immediately redouble (beaver) while retaining possession of the cube. Beavers are optional, and must be agreed to in advance.

GAMMONS AND BACKGAMMONS

If the loser has borne off at least one checker, he loses the single value of the game as shown on the doubling cube. If he has not taken off any checker when his opponent goes out, he is *gammoned* and loses a double game. If he has borne off no men and still has a checker on the bar, or in the opposing inner board, he is *backgammoned* and loses triple the amount on the doubling cube. (Outside the United States there is no distinction between gammons and backgammons; both pay double.) A popular variation on the gammon and backgammon scoring is the Jacoby Rule, which states that gammons and backgammons are scored as single games unless a player has been doubled. The Jacoby Rule does not apply in tournament play.

IRREGULARITIES

1. The dice must be rolled together inside the right-hand section of the board.

2. The dice must land flat on the board. A reroll is required if a die lands outside the right-hand board, on a checker, or is "cocked" (not flat).

3. A move is not completed until a player has picked up his dice.

4. If a player rolls his dice before his opponent has completed a move by picking up the dice, the roll is voided. In bear-off positions where no further contact is possible, or when a move is forced, this rule is generally waived.

5. Errors in the setup of the board or illegal moves may be corrected by either player before the next player rolls. Errors not corrected in time stand as played.

Strategy

The first task of a beginner is to familiarize himself with the board so that he can see moves at a glance instead of having to count them out. The alternating colors of points is very helpful, because a move of an even number keeps a checker on a point of the same color, while a move of an odd number lands a checker on a different color. Corresponding numbers on the inner and outer boards are 6 pips away. Thus a man on the 24-point is 6 away from the opponent's bar point.

The importance of making points cannot be overstated, but some points are more significant than others. In your board, the 5-point is the most valuable point you can have, followed by the bar point, then the 4-point. A chance to make any of these points should be seized, but lower-numbered points are not as significant. However, do not wait for ideal numbers to make points. In the early stages of a game, it is usually correct to move men singly from your 13-point onto your outer board in order to increase your chances of subsequently rolling a number that will make a key point. For example, a *builder* (checker) placed on the 9-point will allow you to make the bar point with a 2–1, the 5-point with 4–1 or 4–3, or your 4-point with 5–2 or 5–4 on your next roll. The fact that you may be leaving one or two blots is unimportant. Even if your opponent is able to hit, he will rarely have more than two points in his home board, so you should be able to enter your checkers easily from the bar.

Points impede the progress of opposing checkers, especially when they are made in a row. Six points in sequence are known as a *prime*, which almost always leads to a winning position. Five points in a row will often prove just as effective.

As desirable as it is to make points, there are other considerations. If you can hit an advanced opposing checker, it is usually right to do so since it gives you an edge in the race to get your checkers around the board. Hitting too many of the opponent's blots, though, is not wise, as it will allow him to make additional points in your home board, making it more difficult for you to bring all your checkers to the bear-off position. Do not leave your checkers exposed unnecessarily. If you have to leave a blot, an *indirect* shot (7 or more pips away) is preferable to a *direct* shot (6 pips or closer). Despite this assertion, there are occasions when it is necessary to *slot* (place) a single checker within direct firing range of an opposing checker in the hope of making a critical point on the next roll. Decisions of when to leave blots and when to play safe must always be taken in light of how many points your opponent has made in his inner board. Four or five dictates that you should play safely, unless you are hopelessly behind in the race and have an *anchor* (point) in his home board where you can enter a hit checker. Finally, the two men on your 24-point must be moved around the table. You cannot wait for two 6 and 5s to land those men safely on your midpoint, or doubles so that they can be moved in pairs. Usually you will have to *split* those men, moving one to another point. Splitting the back men has several advantages. It gives you more numbers to move your men to safety, or to make an advanced point in the opponent's home board. If you can make his 5-point (the "golden" point), you are in a very advantageous position. Checkers on the opposing 5-point have direct shots on all blots your opponent may leave in his outer board and are much easier to move to the relative safety of your outer board. Owning the opponent's 4-point is almost as good.

OPENING MOVES

White has won the opening roll. The standard move is shown first. Any alternative move that follows is asterisked (*) and is deliberately venturesome. However, the risky moves mobilize men quickly, make important points early in the play, and are part of the modern opening move theory.

ROLL	MOVE
6 and 5	W 24 to W 13
6 and 4	W 24 to W 14
	*W 24 to W 18, W 13 to W 9
6 and 3	W 24 to W 15
6 and 3	*W 24 to W 18, W 13 to W 10
6 and 2	W 24 to W 16 or
	W 13 to W 5
	*W 24 to W 18, W 13 to W 11
6 and 1	W 13 to W 7, W 8 to W 7
5 and 4	W 24 to W 15
	W 13 to W 8, W 13 to W 9
	*W 24 to W 20, W 13 to W 8
5 and 3	W 8 to W 3, W 6 to W 3 or
	W 13 to W 8, W 13 to W 10
5 and 2	W 13 to W 8, W 13 to W 11
5 and 1	W 13 to W 8, W 24 to W 23 or
	W 13 to W 8, W 6 to W 5
4 and 3	W 13 to W 9, W 13 to W 10
	*W 24 to W 20, W 13 to W 10
4 and 2	W 8 to W 4, W 6 to W 4
4 and 1	W 24 to W 23, W 13 to W 9 or
	W 13 to W 9, W 6 to W 5
3 and 2	W 13 to W 11, W 13 to W 10
	*W 24 to W 21, W 13 to W 11
3 and 1	W 8 to W 5, W 6 to W 5
2 and 1	W 13 to W 11, W 6 to W 5 or
	W 13 to W 11, W 24 to W 23

The player who moves first can never play doubles, but the next to play might. The correct way to play doubles is shown next. (These moves would apply throughout the early play, assuming points were open.) In all cases the player moves two men at a time, indicated by the numerical 2 in front of the move.

ROLL	MOVE
6 and 6	2/B 24 to B 18, 2/B 13 to B 7
5 and 5	2/B 13 to B 3
4 and 4	2/B 24 to B 20, 2/B 13 to B 9
3 and 3	2/B 24 to B 21, 2/B 8 to B 5 (best) or
	2/B 8 to B 5, 2/B 6 to B 3
2 and 2	2/B 24 to B 20 or
	2/B 13 to B 11, 2/B 6 to B 4
1 and 1	2/B 8 to B 7, 2/B 6 to B 5

To slot a single man on the opponent's bar point, as a modern expert would do on an opening roll that includes a 6 (except for 6 and 1), may seem dangerous, but is not. If the checker is hit, the opponent will usually have to leave a single checker on his bar point. This gives you a number of *return shots*. If you come in with any number that includes a 6, or any 7, you will hit his blot. In the exchange you will lose 6 pips for getting hit, but gain 18 pips for sending an advanced checker back. The concept of return shots plays an important role throughout the game. Sometimes it is too dangerous to hit a blot because your opponent has too many return shots on your exposed checker.

THE FORWARD GAME

Although Backgammon is essentially a race, the strategic value of positioning your men to make points and to block opposing moves holds more interest. Nevertheless, eventually you do have to move all of your men into your home board. Some principles of forward play are:

1. Keep track of the pip count. In the early going, this is unimportant because a few lucky rolls or an indirect hit can easily turn an unfavorable race into an auspicious one. As the end game nears, knowledge of how many pips you are ahead or behind is the key to determining whether you should move exposed checkers to safety or hold back in the hope of getting a shot at an opposing blot. To count pips, multiply the number of checkers the opponent has on a given point by the number of that point. Thus if he has five men on his 6-point, his pip count is 30. An easier method of counting is to offset men on the same point, so if you also have five checkers on your 6-point, the count is zero.

2. Don't allow your back men to languish on your 24-point. Try to bring them forward to make a point on the opponents inner or outer board. It's much easier to free your men from an advanced point than from the 24-point. If the opponent has run both of his back men to safety, it may be wise to stay on the 24-point unless you can move forward with doubles. You are sure to get several indirect shots at a blot, and if your opponent is unlucky, he may have to leave you a direct shot.

3. Be wary of hitting blots if you are way ahead in the race. It is in your interest to let the opposing forces go by your checkers so that they aren't poised to hit as you enter your home board.

4. When the opponent has a strong inner board, or when you are ahead in the race, avoid leaving blots if you can. The following table indicates the odds of getting hit from each distance, assuming all numbers can be played. The probabilities are expressed as the number of shots that are available out of 36, which is the number of possibilities on the dice.

ODDS OF HITTING A SINGLE BLOT

DISTANCE TO THE BLOT IN NUMBER OF PIPS	SHOTS AVAILABLE
1	11/36
2	12/36
3	14/36
4	15/36
5	15/36
6	17/36
7	6/36
8	6/36
9	5/36
10	3/36
11	2/36
12	3/36
15	1/36
16	1/36
18	1/36
20	1/36
24	1/36

5. The opponent's bar point is a liability. If you make it, you should break it early before the opponent has built up his inner board. If you move from his bar late in the game, you will often have to leave him one or more direct shots.

6. When the armies are past each other, cross your checkers from his outer board to your outer board, using the minimum number of pips possible, and bring your men into your inner board as economically as possible. However, do not stack your men on your 6-point. Try to place them equally on the 4- and 5-points. Too many checkers on the 6-point can turn a possible win into a sure loss.

7. When you have a closed board and an opposing checker is on the bar, try to keep an even number of men on the higher-number points to handle all adverse rolls of the dice. If you roll 6 and 1 and have four men on your 6-point, take one checker off and move one checker from the 6-point to the 5-point. Otherwise a roll of 6 and 5 next could leave a blot. In this situation, it is also correct to bear men off the higher-numbered points first, even when an even position can be maintained and other checkers can be removed. *Breaking* the back points minimizes the risk of getting hit by an entering checker.

THE BACK GAME

The natural progression of the checkers is forward, but a series of poor early rolls or opposing hits may compel a player to try a different tactic. A back game is characterized by having an unusual number of men in the opponent's inner court while holding two or more points, preferably the lower-numbered. It is designed to grant the opponent a long lead in the race in the expectation of getting a shot or series of shots (almost always realized) as the opponent brings his men home or bears them off and can no longer rebuild his board.

To execute a back game it is essential to establish a second point in the opposing inner board. Once that has been accomplished, blots can be left randomly around the board in hope of getting hit. By being sent back, you *slow down* your game (limit the number of moves you have to make); it is actually advantageous not to enter a checker from the bar. The object of a back game is to wait patiently until the opponent has ruined his inner board and leaves a blot. If a shot is missed, there will invariably be other shots. Once a blot is hit, all efforts are made to create a prime (six points in a row), which the opposing checker cannot get past. The prime is then *walked* (each lower point being made in order) until the inner board is closed and the opposing checker is on the bar. A single checker trapped behind a walking prime usually costs the game.

The ideal way to walk a prime is to lay a spare checker just ahead of it and wait for a six to cover it, which can be played from the back of the prime while keeping the prime intact. It does not matter if the blot is hit because the checker will be entered and brought around to work on extending the prime. Two catastrophes can happen to a walking prime. You may have one or two checkers idle in your home board or trapped in the opposing inner board, in which case an unlucky series of rolls could force you to break the prime. Also, high doubles play havoc with a prime. Since these numbers have to be played twice over, the prime will often be reduced to four points in sequence instead of six.

Back games are exciting, but also very dangerous. If you do not get a shot, or miss the blots as they appear, you will almost surely be gammoned or backgammoned. A similar fate may befall if you prematurely have to break a point in the opponent's home board to play a high number. The strategy to prevent a back game from developing is not to hit too many opposing checkers (three back is sufficient), and if an opponent does establish a second beachhead in your home board, to cease hitting altogether and force him to play his full move.

DOUBLING

Backgammon has been rejuvenated by the addition of the doubling cube. The introduction of doubling privileges not only shortens the length of the average game—an important consideration in club and Chouette play— but it also allows a player to capitalize on a superior position. Heretofore, superiority at any stage was meaningless because the game went on and any advantage a player might have had could be undone by subsequent rolls.

Sound doubling is based on strategic advantages, specifically a position that is likely to endure or improve. Five points in sequence or excellent prospects of making five in a row is a strong strategic advantage, especially when two men are trapped behind what may quickly become a full prime. When a player doubles in these circumstances, he is offering his opponent a 3 to 1 proposition: he expects to win three out of four games from that position. If those are the true odds, (which is always difficult to determine), the other player should accept. If he drops all four games, he will lose 4 points. If he accepts and wins one 2-point game and loses three 2-point games, he loses exactly the same, but on that one game he wins he may be able to redouble and win a 4 game, which cuts his overall losses for the four games to 2 points.

In a racing game, the general rule of thumb is that a player should double if he is on roll and ahead 10% of his total pip count. Thus, if he has 100 pips on his board and is leading by 10, he should double. These doubles should also be accepted, even if the doubler is ahead by as much as 13% of his total pip count. In a dice game, one poor roll followed by a good roll could promptly even the race.

Tournament Backgammon

A natural outgrowth of the Backgammon boom has been the organization of tournaments so that expert players can test their skill against each other. In any given game, a novice might beat the finest player in the world on a fortunate roll of the dice, but over a series of games the luck of the dice will even out and the more able player will triumph. In tournaments, *matches* are played. A match is designated as a certain number of points (a 7-point match, 11-point match, etc.) and may be any length, but they rarely exceed 25 points. The first player to reach the point total wins the match.

Tournaments are generally divided into an Open division and an Intermediate division, although Beginners, Pairs, and Mixed Pairs events are occasionally held. Since there is no national or international body to rank the players, any player may enter the Open series, but players who have won a certain amount of money in previous tournaments are usually required to enter the Open division and not some lower-rated event. Tournaments are staged as a knockout. Players are seeded into brackets (or drawn randomly for position in casual tournaments) and play head-to-head matches. The loser is eliminated from the championship; the winner goes to meet the next opponent until only one survivor remains.

Common to most tournaments for both the Open and Intermediate divisions is a Second Chance event to accommodate players who are eliminated in the early rounds of the championship. The losers, in effect, compete in a separate, albeit secondary, event of their own. For players no longer active in any other event, there may be a Last Chance event, which requires an additional entry fee.

Unlike bridge, Backgammon tournaments are played for prize money. Large tournaments that attract an international field may be sponsored by a corporation. For those that are not sponsored, a portion of the players' entry fees is retained by the organizing unit to cover expenses; the remainder is split between the championship and second-chance events (the main event usually gets 70 or 75% of the available prize money) and awarded to the top finishers in those series. Backgammon tournaments have raised substantial amounts of money for charity. When a charity is involved, the players are auctioned off, either singly or in *fields* (three or four players sold as a unit) or a combination of the two, to the highest bidder prior to the start of play. The charity shares in the proceeds from the auction; the balance is returned to the owners of the successful players or fields.

Tournament Backgammon is played the same as the stakes game, except that there is no automatic double on a tie opening roll, and double and triple games can be won without a player being doubled. Beavers are not allowed. When a player is 1 point from winning a match, the Crawford Rule is in effect: The losing player may not double for one game.

Backgammon Variants

Chouette

Although only two may play at a time, other players can join a game by forming a Chouette. To determine the order of play, each player casts one die. In the event of a tie, there is a reroll. The player who rolls the highest number becomes the *man in the box* and competes against the other players, who form a team. The player who has cast the next highest number becomes the *captain* of the team and rolls against the man in the box. Notation of the rotation of the players should be made from the first roll of the individual die.

Team members may advise the captain freely, but in the event of a dispute the captain has the final decision. If the man in the box wins the game, he retains the box, and the captain is replaced by the next player and goes to the bottom of the rotation. If the box loses, the captain becomes the man in the box and the former box joins the team as last in rotation.

When doubling the man in the box, the team acts as a unit: all double at the same time or not at all. (In some games separate cubes are used and each individual may double the box as he chooses.) If the man in the box doubles, however, each team member has the option of accepting the double or passing. Those who drop out each lose to the man in the box the number of points on the doubling cube, and no longer participate as team advisers. If the captain drops while others wish to play on, the captaincy is assumed by the next player in rotation who accepts the double, and the previous captain is dropped to the bottom of the rotation. A player does not lose his place in the rotation if he drops.

The player who wins the game is always the next man in the box. The original man in the box may win one point each from three players, then lose a two-point game to one player for a net plus of one, but once he loses the game he forfeits the box.

Acey-Deucey

Acey-Deucey was and perhaps still is the favorite Backgammon variant in the U.S. Navy, Marine Corps, and Merchant Marine. There are of course some local variations, but the following rules are fairly standard, according to Captain F. G. Richards, U.S.N., and Commander Everett W. Fenton, U.S.N.R.

For the sake of uniformity, the rules are here given in the traditional terminology of Backgammon. But, of course, the Navy has its own lingo— to roll one die for first play is to *piddle* or *peewee*, the bar is the *fence*, the opponent's inner table is the *starting quarter* or *entering table* while one's own inner table is the *finishing quarter*, a blot or single man is *kicked* rather than hit.

1. Each player rolls one die, and the higher plays first. (Ace is high.) For his first play, winner picks up both dice and rolls them again.

2. All stones are originally off the board, as though on the bar. They must be entered in the adverse inner table in the usual way.

3. Having entered one or more stones, the player may use subsequent rolls to move these stones, or to enter additional stones, or for both purposes.

4. A blot may be hit and sent to the bar in the usual way and must be reentered before the player may make any other move.

5. Doublets are used twice over, as usual.

6. On roll of 1 and 2 (*acey-deucey*), the player (a) moves the 1 and 2; (b) names any doublet he wishes, and moves accordingly; (c) rolls again. If the player is unable to use any part of the roll, he forfeits the rest. *Example:* The player can move 2 but cannot use the 1. He may not name a doublet nor roll again.

It is permissible to name a doublet, only part of which can be used, although the player could name and use another doublet entire. *Example:* The player moves 1 and 2, and names 6 and 6, being able to move only three 6's. He loses the fourth 6 and does not roll again, even though he could have named 5 and 5, used all four 5's, and taken a second roll.

Some place a limit upon the number of successive rolls of 1 and 2 which a player may use, for example, that upon rolling a third 1 and 2 in succession a player must place his most advanced man on the bar and the 1 and 2, with all its privileges, belongs to his opponent.

7. Rules as to making points, hitting blots, and bearing off, are as in regular Backgammon.

8. *Settlement.* Here there is widest divergence of practice. Many play that the loser owes 1 point for every stone he has left on the board when opponent bears off his last stone. Others pay for each remaining stone its distance from the bearing-off edge. Some double the stake each time 1 and 2 is rolled. Some allow voluntary doubles, besides the automatics. Doubling for gammon and tripling for backgammon are usually eliminated.

European Acey-Deucey

This variant differs markedly from the Acey-Deucey game described above. The stones are all placed on the board, just as for regular Backgammon. The points of difference in the rules from the regular game are:

1. A roll of 1 and 2 (*acey-deucey*) doubles the stake automatically, and the player may use the roll 1 and 2; then name any doublet and move accordingly; then move in accordance with the *complementary doublet;* then roll again.

The complement of a number is its difference from 7. (Opposite faces of a die total 7.) Thus, having named 3 and 3, the player next uses 4 and 4.

If the player is unable to use any part of the roll, he loses the rest. *Example:* A player rolls 1 and 2, moves, names 5 and 5, moves, but can then move only three 2's. He loses the fourth 2 and does not roll again.

2. At any time when all his stones are in his home table, the player may not move any of them down (toward the 1-point); he may only bear off the points corresponding to the dice. *Example:* The player rolls 6 and 2, having stones on all points but 6-point and 2-point. He has no move.

Russian Backgammon

All stones are originally off the board. Both players enter in the same home table, and move around the board in the same direction toward the same bearing-off edge. Other rules:

1. Having entered at least two stones, a player may use subsequent rolls to move them, to enter additional stones, or for both purposes.

2. When a blot is hit, the owner must reenter it before he makes any other move. But at any other time a player must move stones already entered, to use his full roll, even if unable to enter any additional of the original 15 off the board.

3. Doublets are used twice over, and then (except on his first roll)

the player uses the *complementary doublets*. (The complement of a number is its difference from 7.) Provided that he can use all the eight numbers, in the given order, he may then roll again. If he is unable to use any portion of the roll, he loses the rest and may not roll again.

Dutch Backgammon

All stones are originally off the board. Each player enters in the adverse inner table, and the two forces move in contrary directions, as in regular Backgammon. A player must enter all 15 of his stones before he may commence to move. He may not hit a blot until he gets at least one stone into his own inner table. All other rules are as in regular Backgammon.

Snake

Black places his fifteen stones in the usual initial position; five on B6, three on B8, five on W12, two on W1. White places two stones on each of B1, B2, B3, and his other nine stones on the bar. First turn is decided in the usual way. White must enter all his stones before he can commence moving. All other rules are as in regular Backgammon.

Snake is primarily intended to give practice in how to play, and how to play against a back game. It also gives an easy method of handicapping. The stronger player may take White, and may commence with three, two, one, or no points already made in the Black home board. At best (with three points made), the odds against White are about two to one. Or the weaker player may take White and commence with three, four or five points in the Black inner table.

The correct policy for Black is to try to make points in his home board at any cost. He should strew blots there, and also near his bar when White is completely entered, for his game is better if sufficiently delayed to avoid piling up all stones on the 6-, 5-, 4-points. If White gets all his stones entered while Black still has a sufficiency of stones outside his home board, Black should let some White stones emerge, then hold a blockade against the rest.

CHESS

The ultimate origin of Chess is a question of scholarly controversy. In 1694 Dr. Thomas Hyde of Oxford *(De Ludis Orientalibus)* said that the game was invented by Nassir Daher in India about 500 A.D. In 1801, James Christie in his essay on the Mill game (see "The Mill") said that Hyde's conclusions were wrong on his own evidence, and that Chess probably was known in Homeric times. In 1850, N. Bland *(Persian Chess)* attributed the game to Persia, stating that from there it spread to India. In 1860, Prof. Duncan Forbes *(A History of Chess)* reversed the flow, making Persia learn the game from India. In 1874, van der Linde *(Geschichte und Litteratur des Schachspiels)* fortified this view, showing that Chess was known in Hindustan in the 8th century, but rejecting Forbes' other conclusions. In 1913, H. J. R. Murray *(A History of Chess)* said that Chess is descended from an Indian game played in the seventh century.

In 1783–89, Sir William Jones pointed out the likeness between modern Chess and an Indian game *chaturanga*, which is still played in India and Persia under the corrupted name *shatranj*. Four players compete in two partnerships, around a board 8 × 8. Each is provided with eight pieces; the *rajah*, *elephant* and *horse* have the same powers respectively as the Chess king, rook and knight. The *footmen* are equivalent to pawns, and the *ship* is identical with the Arabian *alfil* whence came the modern bishop. The moves are governed in part by casting dice. Sir William showed that *chaturanga* is repeatedly mentioned in the *Bhawishya Puranas*, historical and theological poems dating back to about three thousand years B.C. The *chaturanga* theory was strongly espoused by Forbes, who labeled it the basic game from which Chess was derived. Van der Linde reversed the relationship: *chaturanga* is a comparatively recent offspring of Hindu Chess. He denied that there is any proof for the great antiquity of Chess. Forbes was also criticized by Stewart Culin (1898), who said that his theory "has not been generally accepted by students of the game. The antiquity of the Purana in which it is described has been questioned, and the game asserted to be a comparatively modern adaptation of the primal Hindu game." But Culin parted company with van der Linde as to placing the origin of Chess as late as the eighth century. He went on to say, "Apart from this discussion the relation of Chess to an earlier dice game, such as Pachisi, appears to be evident. The comparative study of games leads to the belief that practically all games as Chess, played upon boards, were preceded by games in which pieces were animated by dice, cowries or knuckle bones, or by staves . . ."

To sum up: Most scholars believe Chess to have originated in India, at least as early as the seventh century A.D. Whether it is older depends largely on how you choose to define Chess. Certainly it was preceded by similar games of movement upon a board, the ancestors of Pachisi, Backgammon, etc.

What may be called the modern era of Chess dates from about the fifteenth century, when the pieces reached their present form. The king, rook and knight have had their present powers from earliest times. The same pieces exist (under different names) in the Chinese and Japanese variants. The pawn acquired the right to make a double jump on its first move, a privilege that necessitated the rule of *en passant capture*. The all-powerful queen replaced the *fers* (also *ferz, farzin, wazir*), which moved like the king, though with some special privileges. It is said that "by philological error" the *fers* in France became the *vierge*, and then, more politely, the *dame*. At all events, the queen is the *dame* in virtually all European languages other than English. The bishop replaced the *phil*, or in Arabic, *alfil*, which moved diagonally to the next square but one, hopping over any intervening piece. The move *castling* was adopted in the sixteenth century. (The term *castle* as an alternative to *rook* is obsolescent. The modern player understands *castle* to mean *perform the act of castling*, and calls the piece *rook*, a term derived from the Indian *rukh*.)

The literature of this modern period may be said to commence with the *Bonus Socius*, a huge and anonymous collection of the principal (van der Linde said flatly, *of all*) medieval Chess problems or *mansubat*. The first writer to merit the name of analyst was a Spaniard, Ruy Lopez de Segura (1561), who gave his name to an opening still one of the most-played. In the seventeenth century notable contributions were made by the Calabrian, Giacchino Greco. A new era was precipitated by the publication of *Analyse des echecs* in 1749, by François Philidor, who made a great name both in Chess and in operatic composition. This work went through many editions, was translated into many languages, and stimulated many others to undertake rigorous analysis of Chess play. The literature of Chess grew rapidly until it surpassed that of any other game and of most other activities.

PLAYERS
Two.

THE CHESS BOARD
The Chess Board is a large square composed of 8 × 8 = 64 smaller squares, colored alternately "white" (any light color) and "black" (any dark color).

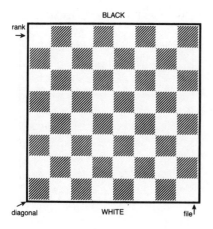

Fig. 1. The Chess Board   *Fig. 2. The Initial Position*

The two players are conventionally called "White" and "Black," after the color of the pieces used by each, initial capitals being used to distinguish the players from the squares. (Fig. 1.)

The players sit on opposite sides of the board, which is so placed that each finds a white square at the corner near his right hand. In printed diagrams, Black by convention sits above and White below. Rows of squares are designated by the following terms:

File. Any row of 8 squares extending from White's side of the board to Black's.

Rank. Any row of 8 squares parallel to the White and Black sides.

Diagonal. Any row of squares parallel to a diagonal of the square board. The diagonals vary in length from 8 squares to one.

THE CHESS PIECES

Each player is provided with sixteen pieces, as follows:

one king

one queen

two rooks

two bishops

two knights

eight pawns

593

*Fig. 3. The White Knight attacks
all the Black Knights*

Fig. 4

(a) *The Pawn attacks both
    Knights*

(b) En Passant *capture*

(c) *Stopped Pawns*

(d) *The Pawn promotes*

The initial position of the pieces for the commencement of a game is shown in Fig. 2. The powers of the pieces are explained below. (The term *piece* is often used in a restricted sense to mean a man other than a pawn.)

The King (♔) may move one square at a time in any direction, on the rank, file, or diagonal. (See also *Object of Play*. The king may not move to a square attacked by an enemy piece.)

The Rook (♖) may move on the file or rank, any distance so far as the line is unobstructed by any other piece.

The Bishop (♗) may move on either diagonal radiating from its square, any distance so far as the line is unobstructed. A bishop is thus tied to squares of one color throughout the game. As can be seen in Fig. 2, each player commences with one "white" and one "black" bishop.

The Queen (♕) combines the powers of rook and bishop, moving on any file, rank, or diagonal, any distance so far as the line is unobstructed.

The Knight (♘) has a peculiar move, best described as "from corner to diagonally-opposite corner of a rectangle three squares by two" (Dr. Lasker). Fig. 3 shows that a knight in the center of the board may move to any of 8 squares. From the edge of the board, the knight can reach only 4 squares, and from a corner only 2.

The knight move is a jump from point to point, not a line move, and cannot be obstructed by nearby pieces. In Fig. 2 any of the knights can at once leap out to the rank in front of the pawns.

The Pawn (♟) in general moves forward on the file (away from the player) one square at a time. But from its original square on the second rank it has the option of advancing one or two squares. The pawn has some other peculiarities described in the next three sections.

PROMOTION

If a pawn reaches the eighth rank (farthest from the player) it *promotes*. See Fig. 4 (d). That is, it is replaced by a queen, rook, bishop or knight, at the option of the owner. Since the player usually chooses a queen, the strongest piece, promotion is often called *queening*. Promotion is permitted even though the player has not lost a single piece by capture; it is possible for three or more queens to be on the board at the same time.

CAPTURE

All pieces, but not pawns, capture in the same way as they move. If any square that a piece can reach is occupied by an enemy unit, that unit can be captured. It is removed from the board and replaced by the captor. (Capturing is optional; there is no compulsion to capture when able.)

The pawn cannot capture a piece ahead of it on the file, and therefore can be *stopped* by an adverse obstruction. The pawn captures on either square that is diagonally adjacent and forward of it. See Fig. 4 (a) and (c).

En Passant Capture. An advancing pawn is liable to capture by the adverse pawns on both adjacent files. A pawn is not permitted to escape this attack by use of the double-jump. In Fig. 4 (b) the White pawn has just moved up two squares from its original square. Had it moved only one square, it would have been attacked by both Black pawns. The attack is deemed to exist "in passing," so that either Black pawn can execute the capture, by moving diagonally to the square skipped over by the White pawn. The rules governing *en passant* capture are:

1. If a pawn makes a double-jump, it can be captured by an adverse pawn that could have captured it had it advanced only one square.

2. The *en passant* capture must be executed immediately or not at all; it may not be made at any later turn.

CASTLING

Once during a game a player may make a special move called *castling*. This is actually a simultaneous move of two pieces: the king and a rook. See Fig. 5. The circumstances in which castling is legal are:

(a)   BLACK

(b)   WHITE   (c)

Fig. 5

(a) Black can Castle
 on either side White has Castled
(b) on Queen side
(c) on King side

1. Both the king and rook stand on their original squares, neither having moved since the beginning of the game.

2. The squares on the rank between king and rook are vacant, and neither of the two adjacent to the king is attacked by an adverse unit.

3. The king is not in check.

The move *castling* is executed by first moving the king on the rank, two squares toward the rook, then placing the rook on the square passed over by the king. (Do not move the rook first, for if it is relinquished before the king is touched a legal move has been completed, and in strict play the transfer of the king can be barred. Moving the king first indicates clearly the intention to castle, since at no other time may the king move two squares.)

OBJECT OF PLAY

The object of play is to capture the adverse king. If a move directly attacks the king, the player announces "Check!" (The warning is customary but not obligatory.) His opponent must parry the attack or forfeit the game. The ways in which the attack may be met are: moving the king, capturing the attacker, interposing a piece on the line of attack.

When a check cannot be parried by any means, the king is said to be checkmated (or simply mate) and the game ends. The capture of the king is not actually carried out. A large proportion of games reach a decision without checkmate, one player resigning because he is satisfied that he cannot escape eventual checkmate.

DRAWN GAMES

A draw may result in any of the following ways:

Stalemate. If a player in turn to move cannot make any legal move, but is not in check, the position is a *stalemate* and is at once abandoned as a draw.

Insufficient Force. If the pieces remaining on the board are too few and too weak to be able to administer checkmate by force, the game is abandoned. See *Minimum Forces*.

Perpetual Check. If a player demonstrates that he can check the adverse king without surcease, he can claim a draw.

Recurrent Position. If a position recurs three times in a game, identical as to the disposition of all pieces, and with the same player to move in each case, this player may claim a draw. (The draw is not automatic.)

Fifty-move Rule. If during fifty consecutive moves no unretractable change has occurred (pawn move, capture, or castling), either player may call upon the other to demonstrate a forced win or to agree to a draw.

Agreement. A draw may occur by agreement between the players, neither being inclined to continue play. In tournament play, draw by agreement is permitted only after Black's thirtieth move.

LAWS OF CHESS

Laws of Chess are promulgated by an international organization, *Federation Internationale des Échecs* (known as F.I.D.E.). The principal provisions of the present code are as follows:

Touch and Move. If a player touches one of his own men, he must move it if he can legally do so. If he touches an adverse man, he must if legal capture it. If a player touches several men, his opponent may choose which is to be moved or which is to be captured, provided that a legal move is available.

Adjusting. A player may touch his own pieces in order to adjust them, provided that he gives verbal notice of his intention, as by saying "I adjust." A player must not touch an adverse piece for purpose of adjusting, but may request his opponent to adjust and such request must be complied with.

Completed Move. A completed move, if legal, may not be retracted. A simple move is completed when the player removes his hand from the piece; a capturing move is completed when the adverse piece is taken from the board and the player removes his hand from the capturing piece; a promoting move is completed when the pawn is taken from the board and the player removes his hand from the piece that replaces it.

Illegal Move. If a player makes an illegal move, and his opponent draws attention to the fact before touching any of his own men, the illegal move must be retracted, and the player must if possible make a legal move with the same piece, or, if the illegal move was a capture, must if possible make a legal capture of the same piece.

Erroneous Position. If during play it is proved that an illegal move was made and not retracted, or that the number or position of the men was altered illegally, the position just prior to the illegal move or alteration must be restored, and the game continued from that point.

If during play or immediately afterward it is proved that the pieces were initially placed on the board incorrectly, or the board was turned wrong, the game is annulled.

Erroneous Checkmate. An erroneous announcement of checkmate, on the move or in several moves, is void without penalty and the game must be continued.

Deportment. A player may not take advice from spectators, nor refer to or have at the table any written notes other than the record of the game. A player should not comment on any of the moves to his opponent, nor in any way annoy or distract his opponent. A player forfeits the game if he willfully upsets the board or disarranges the men, refuses to comply with a legal requirement, arrives more than an hour late for commencement or resumption of play, or exceeds the time limit.

TIME LIMIT

Tournament Chess is played under a time limit. Each player must make 30 moves in the first two hours of his own time, 45 moves in the first three hours, and so on. (This is the standard rate prescribed in the laws. In some tournaments it is stepped up to 20 moves per hour.) Time is kept by a device comprising two clocks in one case, with a lever whereby one clock may be stopped and the other started simultaneously. The player switches the lever after making and recording his move, so as to stop his own clock and start his opponent's.

In what is called "rapid transit" play, only ten seconds is allowed for each move. A rapid transit tournament is timed by a referee, who strikes a bell every ten seconds, whereupon a move must be made at every table in the game.

MINIMUM FORCES

If one side is reduced to king alone, the other can force checkmate if he has, besides his king, any of the following: one queen, one rook, two bishops, or a bishop and a knight. Insufficient to force checkmate are: one bishop, one knight, or two knights. (Queens and rooks are called *major pieces* because of their superior power; bishops and knights are *minor pieces*.)

A queen wins against a rook and usually against a rook and a pawn, but can draw only against a rook and a minor piece. Two bishops can usually draw against a queen, but bishop and knight or two knights usually lose.

A rook and a minor piece against a rook usually can only draw, and likewise a rook against one minor piece can usually only draw.

A single pawn cannot win unless it can be promoted. If the lone king can occupy the square in front of the pawn (before it has reached the seventh rank), the game is a draw, but it does not follow that the pawn can be queened in all other cases.

RELATIVE VALUES

The fighting power of the pieces is estimated to be in ratio: pawn 1, knight 3, bishop 3, rook 5, queen 9. More precisely, the following are shown by experience to be equivalent:

$$\text{Queen} = B + B + Kt + P = R + B + P$$
$$R + R = Q + P = B + B + Kt$$
$$\text{Rook} = B + P + P$$
$$B + B = R + P + P$$
$$\text{Knight} = P + P + P = \text{Bishop}$$

. The more disparate the pieces involved in exchange captures of unlike pieces, the more likely is it that the relative strength of the remaining forces will depend upon the exact position. For example, an ending of king and rook against king and five pawns cannot be discussed in general terms; there is no "typical position."

The knight and bishop are about equal, but the latter is more often favored by the position than the former. Two bishops together are usually stronger than an opposing bishop and knight, and stronger still against two knights. The bishop can operate at a distance and is thus less vulnerable to attack; it can operate at long range in two directions; it is therefore markedly superior in any ending against a knight when there are pawns

BLACK

QR1 / QR8	QKt1 / QKt8	QB1 / QB8	Q1 / Q8	K1 / K8	KB1 / KB8	KKt1 / KKt8	KR1 / KR8
QR2 / QR7	QKt2 / QKt7	QB2 / QB7	Q2 / Q7	K2 / K7	KB2 / KB7	KKt2 / KKt7	KR2 / KR7
QR3 / QR6	QKt3 / QKt6	QB3 / QB6	Q3 / Q6	K3 / K6	KB3 / KB6	KKt3 / KKt6	KR3 / KR6
QR4 / QR5	QKt4 / QKt5	QB4 / QB5	Q4 / Q5	K4 / K5	KB4 / KB5	KKt4 / KKt5	KR4 / KR5
QR5 / QR4	QKt5 / QKt4	QB5 / QB4	Q5 / Q4	K5 / K4	KB5 / KB4	KKt5 / KKt4	KR5 / KR4
QR6 / QR3	QKt6 / QKt3	QB6 / QB3	Q6 / Q3	K6 / K3	KB6 / KB3	KKt6 / KKt3	KR6 / KR3
QR7 / QR2	QKt7 / QKt2	QB7 / QB2	Q7 / Q2	K7 / K2	KB7 / KB2	KKt7 / KKt2	KR7 / KR2
QR8 / QR1	QKt8 / QKt1	QB8 / QB1	Q8 / Q1	K8 / K1	KB8 / KB1	KKt8 / KKt1	KR8 / KR1

WHITE

Fig. 6

599

on both wings. The short-stepping knight has to be brought closer to its targets and thus is more easily repelled; it is superior only in positions where lines are blocked, or, in an ending against a single bishop, where its ability to reach squares of both colors can be capitalized.

NOTATION

English Notation. The notation largely used in England and the United States to record games is illustrated in Fig. 6. Each square has two alternative designations, according to the color of the moving piece. The abbreviation Kt for knight is sometimes replaced by N or S.

An example game record:

SICILIAN DEFENSE

WHITE	BLACK
1 P - K4	P - QB4
2 Kt - KB3	P - Q3
3 P - Q4	P x P

The position after these three moves is shown in Fig. 7.

The initial of the piece moved is written before the hyphen, and the square moved to is written after. More data is added, if necessary to avoid ambiguity, as Kt(2) - Q4, "knight on the second rank to queen's fourth," in a position where the other knight also could move to Q4.

The symbol x, read "takes," indicates a capture. Black's third move above is "pawn takes pawn." Symbols commonly used are:

BLACK

WHITE

Fig. 7

x   takes
ch check
!   "Best" (of a move)
?   "not the best" or "bad"

Algebraic Notation. The notation preferred everywhere else, and used by problemists even in England and the United States, is illustrated in Fig. 8. Each square has a single designation: the letter of its file and number of its rank, as f5. Besides avoiding ambiguity, this notation is more condensed, especially in the linear style. The moves leading to Fig. 7 are written (columnar form):

SICILIAN DEFENSE

WHITE	BLACK
1 e2 - 24	c7 - c5
2 Ng1 - f3	d7 - d6
3 d2 - d4	c5 - d4:

The abbreviation of the piece is pre-fixed to each move except for pawn moves. Before the hyphen comes the square from which the piece is moved, and after, the square moved to. Linear writing is abbreviated by omission of the former square: *Sicilian.* 1 e4, c5; 2 Sf3, d6; 3 d4, c5 : d4.

The symbols !, ?, are used in algebraic as in English notation; in addition the following are used:

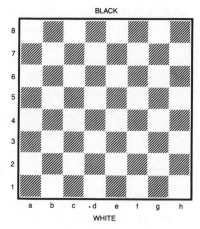

Fig. 8. The Algebraic Notation

:	takes
†	check
††	checkmate
0 - 0	castles on king side
0 - 0 - 0	castles on queen side

Strategy

MOTIVES OF THE OPENING

The two broad objectives at the outset of a game are (a) development and (b) control of the center.

Development is the process of getting pieces into action. At the beginning of a game, the player guards squares no farther forward than his third rank; only the eight pawns and the two knights are free to move. The bishops, rooks, and queen must be liberated and some or all of them must be moved to posts from which they guard more advanced ranks and attack the adversary's pieces. A piece is said to be *developed* if it has left its original square. The development is usually construed to be complete when the rooks are *connected*, i.e., "attack" each other on the first rank. It thus involves at least one move by each minor piece and the queen, a move by the king (usually castling), plus at least two pawn advances to liberate the bishops.

It has been abundantly demonstrated that any serious loss of time in developing can lead to quick defeat. It is therefore desirable (a) to avoid developing one piece where it will hinder the development of another; (b) to post each piece at once on its most effective square, usually the most

601

advanced square from which it cannot be driven without loss of time to the opponent; (c) to avoid moving any piece more than once in the opening, unless its later moves involve an equal loss of time to the opponent.

Control of the Center is important in the opening simply because it is important throughout the whole game. Technically, the *center* comprises the four squares d5, e5, d4, e4. The center is the focus of much of the battle because (a) a long-range piece (queen, rook, bishop) standing in the center has the maximum of mobility; (b) control of the center tends to split the adverse army into wings and hinder its communications.

Control of the center, or of a center square, does not necessarily mean its *occupation* by a pawn or a piece. Rather, it means the *guarding* of the center so that the adversary cannot effectively post and maintain a piece there. Since the pawn is a short-range piece, however, it must reach at least the *subsidiary center* (the eight squares adjacent to the center) in order to guard the center.

It is convenient to classify as *regular* all openings that commence 1 P - K4 or 1 P - Q4, and all defenses by Black that involve the immediate advance of a center pawn to the fourth rank. (But standard positions of regular openings are frequently reached by irregular preparatory moves, such as 1 Kt - KB3 or 1 P - QB4.)

Virtually all of opening play revolves about the effort of each side to follow up the double-advance of one center pawn by a double-advance of the other. When the effort is not opposed by the adversary, it should usually be executed at once. (For example, 1 P - K4, P - K3; White's best move is 2 P - Q4.)

KING'S PAWN OPENINGS

From 1 P - K4, P - K4 stem the following openings:

RUY LOPEZ. 2 Kt - KB3, Kt - QB3; 3 B - Kt5. (*Morphy Defense,* 3—P - QR3. *Berlin Defense,* 3—Kt - KB3. *Steinitz Defense,* 3—P - Q3.)

GIUOCO PIANO. 2 Kt - KB3, Kt - QB3; 3 B - B4, B - B4. (*Evans Gambit,* 4 P - QKt4. *Max Lange Attack,* 4 O - O, Kt - B3; 5 P - Q4.)

TWO KNIGHTS DEFENSE. 2 Kt - KB3, Kt - QB3; 3 B - B4, Kt - B3. (*Prussian Attack,* 4 Kt - Kt5.)

FOUR KNIGHTS GAME. 2 Kt - KB3, Kt - QB3; 3 Kt - B3, Kt - B3. (*Double Ruy Lopez,* 4 B - Kt5, B - Kt5.)

SCOTCH GAME. 2 Kt - KB3, Kt - QB3; 3 P - Q4. (*Scotch Gambit,* 3—P x P; 4 B - B4.)

PONZIANI ATTACK. 2 Kt - KB3, Kt - QB3; 3 P - B3.

PHILIDOR DEFENSE. 2 Kt - KB3, P - Q3.

PETROFF DEFENSE. 2 Kt - KB3, Kt - KB3.

KING'S BISHOP OPENING. 2 B - B4. (*Classical Defense,* 2—B - B4. *Berlin Defense,* 2—Kt - KB3.)

CENTER GAME. 2 P - Q4. (*Danish Gambit,* 2—P x P; 3 P - QB3.)

VIENNA GAME. 2 Kt - QB3. (*Vienna Gambit*, 2—Kt - QB3; 3 P - B4.)

KING'S GAMBIT. 2 P - KB4. (*King's Gambit Declined*, 2—B - B4. *Falkbeer Counter Gambit*, 2—P - Q4. After acceptance of the gambit by 2—P x P may follow: *Bishop's Gambit*, 3 B - B4. *Pernau Gambit*, 3 Kt - QB3. *Knight's Gambit*, 3 Kt - KB3, which can lead to 3—P - KKt4, and: *Muzio Gambit*, 4 B - B4. *Allgaier Gambit*, 4 P - KR4, P - Kt5. *Kieseritzki Gambit*, 4 P - KR4, P - Kt5; 5 Kt - K5.)

Among the irregular replies to 1 P - K4 are:

FRENCH DEFENSE. 1—P - K3.
SICILIAN DEFENSE. 1—P - QB4.
CARO-KANN DEFENSE. 1—P - QB3.
CENTER COUNTER. 1—P - Q4.
KING'S FIANCHETTO. 1—P - KKt3.
ALEKHINE DEFENSE. 1—Kt - KB3.
NIMZOWITSCH DEFENSE. 1—Kt - QB3.

QUEEN'S PAWN OPENINGS

The openings that follow 1 P - Q4 or 1 P - QB4 are as fertile in variations as the king's side openings, but are less simple to classify. Their distinguishing characteristics lie in later positions, not in the early play leading to them, for there is much scope for transposition of the order of early moves.

The positions are divided broadly into two types: *Queen's Gambit*, in which White pawns stand on Q4 and QB4 and a Black pawn on Q4; *Queen's Pawn*, in which there is some other configuration (but a White pawn on Q4).

Queen's Gambit. After the opening moves 1 P - Q4, P - Q4; 2 P - QB4, the gambit may be *accepted* with 2—P x P, but is more often *declined*, as follows:

ORTHODOX DEFENSE. 2—P - K3; 3 Kt - QB3, Kt - KB3. (*Pillsbury Attack*, 4 B - Kt5. *Cambridge Springs Defense*, 4 B - Kt5, QKt - Q2; 5 P - K3, P - B3; 6 Kt - B3, Q - R4.)
TARRASCH DEFENSE. 2—P - K3; 3 Kt - QB3, P - QB4.
SLAV DEFENSE. 2—P - QB3.
ALBIN COUNTER GAMBIT. 2—P - K4.

Queen's Pawn. After the opening moves 1 P - Q4, P - Q4; 2 Kt - KB3, Kt - KB3 may follow:

COLLE SYSTEM. 3 P - K3, P - B4; 4 P - B3.
CATALAN OPENING. 3 P - KKt3.

After 1 P - Q4, P - Q4, White may inaugurate:

STONEWALL. 2 P - K3.

The opening 1 P - Q4, Kt - KB3; 2 P - B4 may lead to:

TCHIGORIN DEFENSE. 2—P - Q3.
BUDAPEST DEFENSE. 2—P - K4.
QUEEN'S INDIAN. 2—P - K3; 3 Kt - KB3, P - QKt3.
KING'S INDIAN. 2—P - KKt3. (*Gruenfeld Defense*, 3 Kt - QB3, P - Q4.)
NIMZO-INDIAN DEFENSE. 2—P - K3; 3 Kt - QB3, B - Kt5.

Irregular replies to 1 P - Q4 are:

DUTCH DEFENSE. 1—P - KB4. (*Staunton Gambit*, 2 P - K4.)
BENONI COUNTER. 1—P - QB4.

IRREGULAR OPENINGS

Some of the openings here called irregular are in fact an effort to reach an advantageous position of a regular opening. This is especially true of the lines branching from 1 Kt - KB3.

BIRD'S OPENING. 1 P - KB4.
VAN'T KRUYS OPENING. 1 P - K3.
ENGLISH OPENING. 1 P - QB4. (*From Gambit*, 1—P - K4.)
POLISH OPENING. 1 P - QKt4.
SARAGOSSA OPENING. 1 P - QB3.
ZUKERTORT OPENING. 1 Kt - KB3. (*Reti System*, 1—P -Q4; 2 P - QB4. *Nimzowitsch Attack*, 1—Kt - KB3; 2 P - QKt3.)

TACTICAL ELEMENTS

Among the tactical possibilities to be reckoned with throughout a Chess game are the following:

Attack. The term is here used in the narrow sense of a threat to capture an adverse piece or pawn. Since any gain of material, of so little as a pawn, is as a rule sufficient for victory, all such attacks have to be met.

Guard. An attack may be met by defending the attacked piece. *Example:* 1 P - K4, P - K4; 2 Kt - KB3. White attacks the KP. Black can defend it by 2—Kt - QB3 or P - Q3. Such guard is adequate if the attacked piece is worth no more than the attacker.

Withdrawal. After 1 P - K4, P - K4; 2 Kt - KB3, Kt - QB3; 3 B - Kt5, P - QR3 Black attacks the bishop. White can guard it by 4 Kt - B3, but to do so would be to give up a bishop for a pawn. To maintain equality White must withdraw the bishop, as by 4 B - R4, or exchange it for the (approximately) equal knight by 4 B x Kt.

Obstruction. An attack by a bishop, rook or queen may be met by interposing a piece on the line of attack. *Example:* 1 P - K4, P -K4; 2 Kt - KB3, Kt - QB3; 3 B - B4, Kt - B3; 4 Kt - Kt5. White attacks the KBP twice, and it is only once defended. The correct defense is 4—P - Q4, obstructing the bishop. Under obstruction may be included also the prevention of a pawn advance by placing a piece on the file ahead of the pawn. *Example:* 1 P - Q4, P - Q4. Black at once blocks the further advance of the White pawn.

Counterattack. The term is here used in the same restricted sense as attack. The adversary's threat to capture a unit may be met by threatening to capture an equal unit elsewhere on the board. *Example:* 1 P - K4, P - K4; 2 Kt - KB3, Kt - KB3. Instead of guarding his KP, Black threatens to gain the White KP in compensation for loss of his own.

The standard openings are replete with counterattacks, which the beginner must learn in order to understand why certain moves are made and others avoided. *Example:* 1 P - K4; P - K4; 2 Kt - KB3, Kt - QB3; 3 B - Kt5, P - QR3. Black apparently loses a pawn by 4 B x Kt ch, P x B; 5 Kt x P. But this 5th move is regularly avoided, since by 5—Q - Q5 Black attacks both the knight and the KP and so will win the latter. *Example:* 1 P - Q4, P -Q4; 2 P - QB4, P - K3; 3 Kt - QB3, Kt - KB3; 4 B - Kt5, QKt - K2. Black apparently loses a pawn by 5 P x P; P x P; 5 Kt x P. But this 6th move is fatal; Black can play 6—Kt x Kt! After 7 B x Q, B - Kt5ch White's only move is 8 Q - Q2, and after 8—B x Qch; 9 K x B, K x B Black is a piece ahead.

Sacrifice. It is said that "all attacks have to be met," but this does not mean that a player can never afford to submit to material loss. Pieces or pawns may be sacrificed for an equivalent *positional superiority.* The superiority must be sufficient to enforce either checkmate of the adverse king or eventual recovery of the sacrificed material. *Example:* 1 P - K4, P - K4; 2 Kt - KB3, P - KB3? This defense is unsound; White wins at once by the "sacrifice" 3 Kt x P; for after 3—P x Kt; 4 Q - R5 ch Black can avert mate only by returning more than his loot, e.g., 4— P - Kt3; 5 Q - K5 ch followed by 6 Q x R.

Pin. Suppose the opening moves 1 P - K4, P - K4; 2 Kt - KB3, Kt - QB3; 3 B - Kt5, P - Q3; 4 P -Q3, Kt - B3; 5 B - Kt5. (See Fig. 9.) The Black knight at QB3 is *pinned,* that is, it is prevented from moving since its move would illegally expose the Black king to check. The Black knight at KB3 is also pinned in the sense that to move it would expose the queen to capture by the lesser piece, the bishop. These two kinds of pin are sometimes distinguished as absolute or complete pin, and relative,

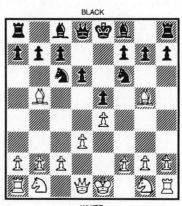

Fig. 9. Pinning

virtual, or dynamic pin. The object of pinning an adverse piece may be to nullify its attack on certain squares, or to prevent its withdrawal while additional pieces are moved to attack it.

Fork. A fork is a simultaneous attack by one piece on two or more others. *Example:* 1 P - K4, P - K4; 2 B - B4, Kt - B3; 3 Kt - QB3. Black can now capture the guarded KP, because after 3—Kt x P; 4 Kt x Kt, P - Q4 the fork by the QP is bound to regain the piece sacrificed. Particularly fitted to make forks is the knight. *Example:* (not good play) 1 P - K4, P - K4; 2 P - Q4, P x; 3 Q x P, Kt - QB3; 4 Q - R4, P - Q4; 5 Kt - QB3, B - Q2; 6 P x P, Kt - Kt5; 7 Q - Kt3, P - QR4; 8 P - QR3? P - R5; 9 Q - B4, Kt x Pch. The knight forks the king and rook, winning the latter and the game.

It is stated by a leading American master that every combination* is based upon simultaneous attack on two or more units or squares.

Discovered Check. After the opening moves 1 P - K4, P - K4; 2 Kt - KB3, Kt - KB3; 3 Kt x P, Kt x P? 4 Kt - 2, Kt - KB3?? Black is lost, for 5 Kt - B6ch wins the queen for a knight. This illustrates the prime danger in submitting to a check by *discovery;* the unmasking piece is momentarily immune from capture, since the check has to be met. When this piece, also, delivers check, there is *double-check,* to which the only possible answer is a move of the king. See Fig. 10.

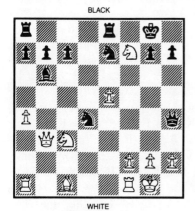

BLACK

WHITE

Fig. 10. "Philidor's Legacy"
White mates in three:
1. Kt–R6 dbl. check, K–R1;
2. Q–Kt8ch, R × Q; 3. Kt–B7
"Smothered mate."

STRATEGICAL OBJECTIVES

Among the strategical elements to be considered are:

Pawn Structure. The slowest-changing element of a position is the configuration of the pawns. In end-play the pawn structure is the controlling factor.

---

* The term combination *is much used. It means the exertion of a threat and the calculation of specific continuations to be followed after every possible defense to the threat. The beginner may believe that all Chess play must be of this order, but not so. Capablanca, late world champion, when asked how many moves "on average" he calculated ahead, replied "One." Much of Chess is* positional play, *for the achievement of very limited objectives, or "small advantages." A combination has been defined as "the discharge of accumulated advantages." In other words, a combination is an effort to turn positional superiority into an immediate decision, by mate or gain of material.*

Therefore even in the opening the expert is cautious of incurring any irremediable weakness in his pawn structure. Certain weaknesses are shown in Fig. 11.

Black's QP is *isolated*, since both pawns on the adjacent files have disappeared; if attacked, the isolated pawn can be defended only by pieces. Black's QKt pawn is *backward;* it is prevented from advancing from its original square by the White QRP, and the pawns originally at Black's QR2 and QB2 have advanced or disappeared. White has *doubled* pawns on the QB file; neither pawn can defend the other and both can be stopped by a single Black piece on QB5. The Black kingside formation has *holes* at KB3 and KR3— squares on the third rank in which enemy pieces can settle without being repelled by pawns. (The hole is more likely to be a mid-game than an end-game weakness.)

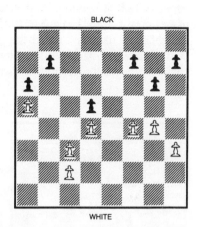

BLACK

WHITE

Fig. 11. Pawn formations

The strongest formation of adjacent pawns for offense is the *phalanx*, two on the same rank, as White's KBP and KKtP, commanding the maximum of squares. The strongest defensive formation is the *chain*, the diagonal arrangement of the KKtP and KRP on both sides.

Opening of Lines. If a player is better developed than his opponent, he should try to open lines by forcing exchanges of obstructing pawns. Then his long-range pieces can be brought to bear on the adverse side of the board. Conversely, the player with inferior development strives to avoid opening of lines until he has completed the preliminary posting of his pieces.

An *open file* is one from which both pawns have disappeared. A file is *half-open* for a player when his own pawn has disappeared but the adverse pawn remains. The rooks participate in the mid-game either through backing up pawn advances or emerging from the first rank through open files. It has been said that "an open file cries aloud for a rook." An important objective of development itself (getting the knights, bishops and queen off the first rank, and castling) is to make both rooks available to occupy any file that may be opened.

Outpost Knight. The knight has to be placed close to the adverse forces to bear upon them at all. In the early game the knight cannot be advanced far without being repelled by the adverse pawns. But as soon as a *hole* appears in any part of the adverse pawn structure, it invites the posting of a knight there, supported by as many pawns and pieces as are necessary to maintain equality of material. Such an *outpost* can seriously cripple the opponent by limiting the mobility of his king, queen, and rooks.

Centralization. A pervasive principle is to post pieces as far as possible toward the center of the board rather than the sides, or so that they command central rather than side squares. It is important to strive for at least equal command of the center, and also to give the pieces their maximum range of action (through the center) in the event that obstructing pawns disappear. Knights are usually moved first to B3, so as to command two of the four center squares; rarely is the deployment of R3 to be recommended. In a choice of capturing either of two pawns on the same square, the general rule (with few exceptions) is "Capture toward the center." *Example:* 1 P - K4, P - K4; 2 B - B4, B - B4; 3 Kt - KB3, Kt - KB3; 4 P - Q3, P - Q3; 5 B - K3, B - Kt3; 6 B x B. Now Black should play 6—RP x B; much inferior would be BP x B.

A corollary is the principle of *overprotection:* When your command of the center depends upon maintaining a unit on a certain key square, bring up more guards than are necessary to the defense of this square. *Example:* 1 P-K4, P-K3; 2 P-Q4, P-Q4; 3 P-K5. The safety of the pawn at K5 depends primarily on the maintenance of the pawn at Q4; the latter square is vital. This game usually continues by a Black attack through such moves as P-QB4, Kt-QB3, Q-Kt3, countered by White overprotection of Q4 through P-QB3, B-K3, Kt-K2, and sometimes Kt-Q2-Kt3 or Q-Q2 and the move of a rook to Q1.

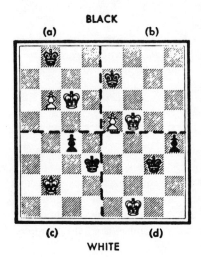

BLACK

(a)   (b)

(c)   (d)

WHITE

Fig. 12

(a) *White to move wins*
    Black to move draws

(b) *Either to move, draw*

(c) *Either to move, Black wins*

(d) *Either to move, draw*

END PLAY

When the pieces remaining on the board are insufficient to force checkmate, but pawns remain, the objective becomes to force a pawn to the eighth rank and make a new queen. (The *end-game* is usually deemed to commence when the queens disappear by capture, but there are "queen endings" as well.)

In the end-game, *accuracy* is at a premium; a single error may lose the game. The outcome often hinges on a seemingly slight advantage, such as a king one step nearer the center than the adverse king. Of constant importance is the *opposition*—the relative position of the kings, in conjunction with the pawn configuration. See Fig. 12, in which four possible positions are shown.

Odds Chess

In social play between players of disparate caliber, it is usual for the stronger to grant odds to his opponent. Many chess clubs rank their members according to the odds which each should be given by the club champion. The common types of odds are given below, in order of weight, from slightest to heaviest.

The draw. A draw counts as a win for the weaker player.

Pawn and move. The stronger player takes Black and removes his KBP.

Pawn and two. The stronger player takes Black and removes his KBP, and White commences with two moves, but may not go beyond his fourth rank. The usual opening by White is P - K4 and P - Q4.

Knight. The stronger takes White and removes his QKt.

Rook. The stronger takes White and removes his QR; the odds are sometimes mitigated by allowing White to place his QRP (otherwise unprotected) on QR3.

Rook, pawn, and move. The stronger takes Black, and removes his QR and KBP.

Rook and knight. The stronger takes White and removes his QR and KKt.

Queen. The stronger takes White and removes his queen.

Capped pawn. The stronger takes White, and loses if he fails to give mate with his KBP (unpromoted).

Kriegspiel

Analogy is often drawn between Chess play and the grand tactics of warfare. Useful as the analogy may be for some purposes, it is notably false in several particulars. One is that in Chess the position of the adverse forces is entirely known, whereas in warfare these are always imponderable elements.

Kriegspiel is a way of playing Chess devised to approximate more nearly the conditions of warfare.

It requires three boards, three sets of men, and the services of a third person. Each party has his own board, and the two players must be so placed that neither can see the other's board. (The players may be placed in different rooms, but usually agree to play in the same room so that each may hear what passes between the other and the referee.)

On his board, the player moves the pieces of his chosen color and must at all times keep them in the actual position to which they have been brought by his moves and captures by his opponent. The pieces of opposite color he may distribute on the board as he sees fit, in order to keep track of what he has discovered about the adverse position.

The referee announces alternately, "White has moved," "Black has moved," and so on, but does not state what the move is. But he says "No" whenever a player tries to make a move which, in view of the adverse position, is illegal. The referee therefore has to keep the actual position of both forces on his own board, to perceive and forbid illegalities.

Each player has the following source of inference as to the adverse position:

(a) The referee says "No" to any illegal try; therefore by trying long-range moves of bishop, rook, queen, or pawn advances, etc. the player may detect the presence of obstructing adverse pieces. But if any such try proves to be legally playable, it stands as the player's move.

(b) When a move gives check, the referee states the fact and also the direction of the check, which must be one of: on the rank, on the file, by the knight, on the long diagonal, on the short diagonal. (In explanation of the last two: From every square of the board radiate two diagonals, one of which is longer than the other. From K1, the long diagonal extends to QR5, the short diagonal to KR4. From White's K3, the long is QR7 - KKt1 and the short is QB1 - KR6.)

(c) Whenever a move is a capture, the referee so announces, as by "White captures at his K5," but he does not state what was captured or by what.

(d) If the capture of a pawn by a pawn is *en passant*, the referee so states.

(e) At his turn to move, a player may ask the referee "Any?" meaning "Can any of my pawns make a capture?" The reply "Try" is affirmative, and the player must then make at least one try. Should his try be correct, it stands. Should it be incorrect, he may continue trying until he finds it, or he may at any time abandon the hunt and make another move.

(f) When the two players are in the same room, each may learn something from what the referee says to the other. *Example:* When the referee says "No" to a player on his third move, the likelihood is that he has moved a bishop to Kt2 or Kt5 and is trying to move it to the eighth rank to annex a rook or queen. In strict rules, the referee must nullify the effort of a player to deceive the other by trying moves he knows to be illegal, such as moving a knight like a bishop; in such case the referee says "Impossible" instead of "No."

The following is a typical Kriegspiel brevity:

	WHITE	BLACK
1	P - QR4	P - Q3
2	R - R3	P - QB4
3	R - K3	Kt - QB3
4	Kt - QB3	P - K4
5	Kt - K4	Kt - R3
6	P - KB4	P x P
7	Kt - B6 mate	

Chess Derivatives

Many games, especially of a frolicsome character, have been derived from Chess. Few of them can be called *variants* in the usual sense; they use the chessboard, the pieces with their usual powers, but so far modify the rules or objectives as to go far afield from regular Chess.

Battle Chess is a very old variation in the way of commencing a game. A screen is placed between the two players, bisecting the board. Each player then disposes his forces as he wishes, limited by the rules:

1. No piece may be placed beyond the third rank.

2. No pawn may be placed on the first rank.

3. Bishops must be placed on squares of opposite color.

4. (sometimes abrogated by agreement.) There must be one pawn on every file.

When the warriors have finished their strategical dispositions, the screen is removed and play begins.

Reversed Minor Pieces. A simple way to "get out of the books" in opening play is to reverse the initial positions of knights and bishops. A tournament was held in the 80s to test this change. In recent times, the late J. R. Capablanca (world champion) suggested the change as a way of lifting tournament Chess from the stagnation into which it fell for a time, and he played a number of games to test it.

The "Little Game of Chess" is an exercise in end-play. The initial position is shown in the illustration. While exhaustive analysis proves that White wins, the inexperienced player is likely to make many mistakes playing either White or Black.

The "Little Game of Chess"

The Peasants' Revolt

The Peasants' Revolt is another exercise in end-play. The initial position is shown in the illustration. It probably can be demonstrated that the knights win, but with less than expert management they are hard put to draw.

Bughouse Chess commences with the pieces in the usual initial array. The only difference from the regular game is that each piece captured is immediately replaced on the board, wherever the captor wishes, except that a pawn may not be put on the first rank, and a bishop must be kept to squares of its original color.

Each player strives to denude the adverse king of defenders, especially pawns; to place adverse pawns so that they enclose holes; to put adverse heavy pieces into such holes.

Giveaway Chess commences from the usual initial array, but the object is to get rid of all one's own pieces. The first side to be eliminated from the board wins. The rules are:

1. If able to make a capture, the player must do so. But he may choose any when he has a choice of more than one.

2. A pawn that reaches the eighth rank must be promoted to queen.

3. If the player in turn to move cannot make a move (but has at least one piece on the board), the game is drawn.

4. The king has no special privileges or obligations; like any other piece, it may be captured. (*Variant:* The king must be protected, checks must be met, as in regular Chess. But a player loses if he checkmates the adverse king. The first to get rid of all his pieces other than the king wins.)

It has been demonstrated that the plausible opening move P - Q3 loses. The main line of the analysis is as follows:

WHITE	BLACK	WHITE	BLACK
1 P - Q3?	P - KKt4	9 Kt x Kt	R - Kt1
2 B x P	B - Kt2	10 Kt x K	R x P
3 B x P	B x P	11 B x R	P - B3
4 B x Q	B x R	12 B x P	R x B
5 B x P	B - B6	13 Kt x P	R - Kt1
6 B x Kt	R x B	14 Kt x P	R - Kt8
7 Kt x B	P - Q4	15 Q x R	B - Kt2
8 Kt x P	Kt - B3	16 Q x B	P - R3
			and wins

CHECKERS (DRAUGHTS)

In his history of Chess, A. van der Linde held that the game of Checkers was developed from medieval Chess problems. He said "The earliest plain accounts of the game are in the Spanish books of the middle ages." The first of these books was by Antonio Torquemada, and was published in Valencia in 1547. But the study of Oriental games tends to indicate that Checkers had a common origin with Pachisi, Chess, The Mill and other board games.

It is true that not until relatively recent times has Checkers received the same serious consideration that has been bestowed from ancient times on Chess. The first scientific study of its possibilities known is a manual by Peter Mallet, a French professor of mathematics, published in 1668. Mallet stated flatly that Checkers was played throughout the world, and was probably as old as Chess.

The first English publication was *Instruction to the Game of Draughts*, by William Prynne, 1756. Eleven years later W. Painter published his *Companion for the Draughts Player*. The most important early contribution to theory was made by Joshua Sturges in *Guide to the Game of Draughts*, 1800. This remained the standard English guide throughout the nineteenth century, being revised from time to time by later editors.

In early times, it was fashionable to deprecate Checkers as "Chess for ladies." This evaluation has persisted in the name for the game, in many countries—in France, *jeu des dames;* in Germany, *Damenspiel;* in Italy, *il giuco delle dame;* in Portugal, *o jago das damas;* in Persia and Turkey, *Daama.* But the development of far-flung Checkers leagues and of national and international championship tournaments throughout the world contradicts the notion that Checkers is not a game of very considerable skill. It has been rated the equal of Chess by some who have mastered both games (e.g., James Pillsbury, American Chess champion, and Newell Banks, American Checkers champion).

National variants exist (see page 626), but English Draughts as played throughout the English-speaking world is by far the most popular member of the Checkers family.

EQUIPMENT

The Checker Board is identical with the Chess board—a large square composed of 8 × 8 smaller squares colored alternately dark and light. The board is set between the two players in the same orientation as for Chess; all play is conducted on the dark squares; consequently each player finds a *double corner* near his right hand. The distinction between *double corner* and *single corner* may be seen in Fig. 1. Notice that in the diagram the pieces are represented on the light squares instead of the dark; this invariable

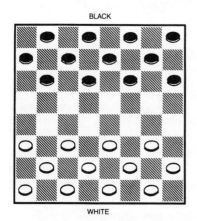

BLACK

WHITE

Fig. 1. The Initial Position

practice is necessary for clarity. But the "white" squares of the printed diagrams are actually the "black" squares of the board.

The Checker Pieces are of uniform shape— wooden or composition disks at least one inch in diameter and a little less than half as thick. Each player is provided with twelve pieces, of his own color. (Actually, black and white checkers are rarely seen. The usual combinations of colors are black and red, or green and white. A set of Checker men always comprises fifteen pieces of each color, so that it will serve also for Backgammon.) The initial position of the pieces is shown in Fig. 1.

PLAYERS

The players sit on opposite sides of the board. They are designated as Black and White, in accordance with the (approximate) color of the pieces used by each. There is unfortunately no uniformity of style in printing diagrams, as to whether the Black or White side is turned uppermost. In some books, Black is always uppermost; in others, White; in many periodicals, the side whose turn it is to move is placed at the bottom. The stipulation, such as "Black to move and win," thus indicates which way the board is turned.

Black invariably makes the first move, and thereafter the players move alternately.

THE PLAY

The movement of the pieces is simple. A piece may move diagonally forward one square, if that square is vacant. Or it may *capture* an adverse piece which is adjacent, diagonally forward, if the square next beyond that piece is vacant. The capture is executed by jumping over the adverse piece to the vacant square and removing the enemy from the board. If the capturing piece lands on a square from which another adverse piece is attacked in the same manner, it continues jumping, in the same turn, to capture all adverse pieces it can. A *single man* can capture a maximum of four pieces in one turn.

Away from the edge of the board, a piece can move in either of two directions. In a series of captures, a piece may change direction at will from each landing spot.

The primary rule of play is that, if able to do so, a player must capture rather than make a non-capturing move. Among several possible captures, a player may make a free choice. He is not compelled (as in Spanish Checkers) to capture two pieces in preference to one. But a capturing piece may come to rest only when unable to make any additional capture.

Crowning. All pieces on the board at the outset are *single men*. A single man may move only forward. The row of squares at the Black or White edge of the board is called the *king row*. On reaching the adverse king row, a single man is *crowned* and becomes a *king*. Its promotion is indicated by placing upon it a second checker of the same color. A player is required by law to crown the adverse pieces that reach his king row.

A *king* has the same powers of move and capture as a single man, plus the right to move backward as well as forward. If a single man reaches the king row by capture, it has to stop to be crowned; it may not continue capturing (as a king) in the same turn.

OBJECT OF PLAY

The object of play is to deprive the opponent of the ability to move in his turn. This is usually accomplished by capturing all twelve of his pieces, but it can also result from blocking his remaining pieces. The first player to find himself unable to move in turn loses the game.

A Draw results only by agreement, each player being satisfied that he has no prospect of winning. If one player proposes a draw and the other refuses to abandon play, the latter must within forty moves demonstrate an increase in his advantage, or else concede the draw.

NOTATION

The notation used in recording games is based on numbering the squares as in Fig. 2. A move is denoted by the number of the square moved from, followed by the number of the square moved to, often joined by a hyphen. For example, the seven moves open to Black at his first turn are: 9–13, 9–14, 10–14, 10–15, 11–15, 11–16, 12–16. Moves may be written linearly, as in this example, or in a column. No mark is attached to show whether a move is made by Black or White. So long as there are no kings on the board, the numbers themselves show the color of the move, for Black moves up and White down. An example of opening moves:

Fig. 2. The Notation

$$11–15$$
$$23–19$$
$$8–11$$
$$22–17$$
$$9–13$$
$$17–14$$
$$10–17$$
$$21–14$$

The last two moves are captures. No mark is used to indicate a capture; the fact of capture is (except in long king tours) evident from the difference between the numbers. No non-capturing move can carry a piece to a square differing by more than 5.

A symbol much-used in annotation is the *star* (*). A *starred move* is the only one to win or to hold the draw.

RESTRICTION PLAY

Checkers tournaments were formerly conducted in "go as you please" style—the contestants could play what openings they chose. The inordinately high proportion of draws resulting among experts led to the adoption of "restriction play."

Two-move Restriction. Black and White each have seven possible first moves, so that there are 49 combinations for the first two moves. Two of these combinations are *barred* because they lead to loss of a piece without compensation: 9–14, 21–17 and 10–14, 21–17. Four others were also barred, but in recent times have been shown to be playable for White. In the two-move restriction, each of the 47 playable combinations is written on a card, and the opening to be played in each match is decided by drawing a card at random. Each match comprises two games, each player being required to play both the Black and White side of the selected opening.

Three-move Restriction. Even the two-move restriction having been largely exhausted by top-flight players, the American championship tournaments now use a three-move plan. The number of combinations of the first three moves used at present for the field of chance selection is around 150.

LAWS OF CHECKERS

The following are the principal provisions of the standard laws, as revised by the American Checkers Association:

Colors. The pieces shall be placed on the black squares, on the three ranks nearest each player. The player of the Black pieces moves first. At the beginning of a contest the players shall toss for colors. Thereafter the colors shall alternate in each succeeding opening balloted.

Time Limit. At the end of five minutes (if a move has not been previously made) "Time" shall be called by the person appointed for that purpose; and if the move is not completed on expiry of another minute the game shall be adjudged lost through improper delay. When a "jump" must be made, and there is only one way to "jump," "Time" shall be called at the end of one minute.

Touch and Move. At the beginning of a game each player shall be entitled to arrange his own or his opponent's pieces properly on the squares. After a move has been made, should either player touch or arrange any piece, without giving intimation, he shall be cautioned for the first offense, and shall forfeit the game for any subsequent offense of this kind.

Should the person whose turn it is to play touch one of his own playable pieces, he must play it or forfeit the game.

If any part of a playable piece be moved over an angle of the square on which it is stationed, the play must be completed in that direction. Inadvertently removing, touching or disturbing from its position a piece that is not playable, while in the act of making an intended move, does not constitute a move, and the piece or pieces shall be placed back in position and the game continued.

Jumps. The old laws of Checkers included the rule of "huff or blow"; if a player failed to capture when able, his opponent could either insist on the capture or remove the remiss piece from the board. The American laws now provide that all captures must be executed. All "jumps" must be completed, and all jumped pieces must be removed from the board.

Crowning. When a single piece reaches the king row it becomes a king, and that completes the move or jump. The piece must then be crowned by the opponent by placing a piece on top of it. If the opponent neglects to do so and makes a play, then any such play shall be put back until the piece that should have been crowned is crowned. "Time" does not start on the player whose piece has reached the king row until it is crowned.

Draws. A draw is declared when neither player can force a win. A player who has what is apparently the inferior position may request the Referee for a "count of moves." If the Referee so decides, the opponent must then complete a win, or show an increased advantage, within 40 more of his own moves, failing which he must relinquish the game as a draw.

Leaving the Table. After an opening is balloted (or the first move has been made in unrestricted play), neither player shall leave the table without permission of the Referee. If permission is granted, his opponent may accompany him, or the Referee may designate a person to accompany him. "Time" shall be deducted accordingly from the player whose turn it is to move.

Conduct. Anything that may tend to annoy or distract the attention of the opponent is strictly forbidden, such as making signs or sounds, pointing, or hovering over the board either with the hands or the head, or unnecessarily delaying to move a piece touched. Any principal so acting, after having been warned of the consequences and requested to desist, shall forfeit the game.

Any spectator giving warning either by signs or sound or remark on any of the games, whether playing or pending, shall be ordered from the room during the contest. Spectators shall not be allowed to smoke or talk near the playing boards.

Strategy

The end play of Checkers is very intricate. While some principles of general application can be discerned, the end play must be learned largely by study of a great number of specific positions.

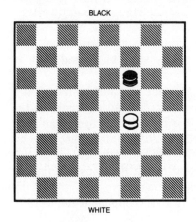

BLACK

WHITE

Fig. 3
Black to move, loses;
White to move, draw

THE MOVE

Of fundamental importance is the move (opposition). In Fig. 3, if it is Black's turn, he must give way before the enemy and is eventually trapped at the edge of the board. White to play similarly would have to retreat, but escapes loss by reaching the double-corner. Whoever has to move in this case is said to have *the move* against him.

The rule for calculating the move, when the two sides are even in pieces is: Consider four alternate files as a *system;* count the number of pieces in either system; if the total is odd, the player in turn has the move; if the total is even, the player in turn finds the move against him.

If one player has fewer pieces than the other, his hope of avoiding loss is usually to reach one of classic drawn positions. For this purpose, "Patterson's Rule" is useful: If you are a piece down, and it is your turn to move, count the pieces in *your own* system; if the total is even, hold an adverse single man on your single-corner side; if the total is odd, hold an adverse single man on your double-corner side. The application of this rule is seen in Fig. 4. White to play should hold the man on 13; if it is Black's turn, White holds the man on 20.

White to play: 19–23, 20–24, 23–26, 24–27, 26–30, 27–31, 30–25, 2–6, 25–30, 6–10, 30–25, 10–14, 25–21, 31–27, 21–25, 27–24, 25–30, 24–19, 30–26, 19–15, 26–23 reaches "Payne's Draw" (Fig. 7).

Black to play: 2–7, 22–26, 13–17, 26–31, 17–22, 19–23, 22–25, 31–27, 25–30, 27–31, 7–10, 23–19, 10–14, 19–23, 14–17, 31–27, 17–22, 27–31 reaches "Roger's Draw." The draw here depends on the fact that if the single man advances he becomes locked in the corner, e.g.: 20–24, 23–27, 24–28, 27–32; now White moves the king from 31 along the diagonal to 20 perpetually, and cannot be driven out or exchanged.

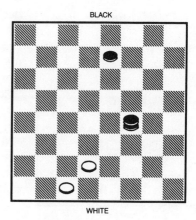

Fig. 4
Either to move, draw

Fig. 5
Either to move and win

The move is changed by an ordinary *cut*, an exchange of captures in which the first capturing piece is itself captured. In Fig. 5, if White to move plays 26–23, a cut ensues: 19–26, 30–23. In the initial position, *the move* was against White, but the cut has changed it, and White wins. Black to play finds the move against him, but wins because he can likewise force a cut. Thus: 7–10, 30–25 (if 26–22, 10–14, followed by 14–18), 10–14, 25–21, 19–24, 26–23 (or 26–22, 24–19, 22–17, 19–15), 24–27, 23–19, 27–23, 19–15, 23–18, 15–10, 14–17.

There are other forms of capture which do not change the move. In opening play, the move is rarely important, as it is destined to be changed many times by cuts. But from the moment the first king is crowned the move is likely to be a factor.

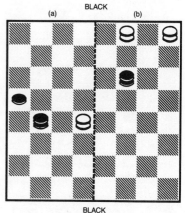

Fig. 6
Black moves, draw
White moves, draw

DRAWS

Fig. 6 (b) shows the only position in which one king can draw against two. If 3–8, Black moves 11–7 or 11–16, and returns to 11 next move. As with most piece-down draws, this one depends on the fact that if the stronger side sacrifices a piece to gain freedom he leaves his opponent with the move or lets him gain the double-corner.

All other piece-down draws depend upon regaining the piece or on holding

BLACK

WHITE

Fig. 7. "Payne's Draw"
Black to move, White to draw

back a single man of the stronger side. Thus in Fig. 6 (a) Black cannot advance the piece on 13 after 17–21, 18–22; sacrificing a piece will leave White with the move. This position is seen to be the embryo of "Payne's Draw," Fig 7. The principal line of this important ending is: 14–17, *23–26, 17–21, 26–23, 15–10, *23–26, 10–14, *26–30, 14–17, *22–18, *17–14 (forced, since 17–22 loses). As indicated earlier, the star (*) indicates a move that is the only one that will win or hold the draw.

SACRIFICES

The temporary sacrifice of a piece is often seen in early-game play; it is usually made with prospect of regaining the piece with superior position. How a lesser force can triumph over a greater is shown in many problems, as Fig. 8. Here White appears to be in trouble, for after 30–26, 7–11 White is lost. But the immediate sacrifice 18–15 wins, for after 10–26, 30–23, 7–11, 23–19, Black can continue only by giving up two pieces. The beginner should note the undesirable formation of the Black pieces at the left, where three are held back by two.

THE "POSITIONS"

Certain endings upon which many others depend are given the names of First Position, Second Position, etc. The most important is First Position,

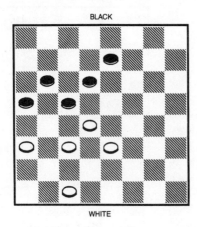

BLACK

WHITE

Fig. 8
White to move and win

BLACK

WHITE

Fig. 9. First Position
White to move and win

Fig. 9. Here it is demonstrated that two kings win against king and single man if (a) the single man is forced to the double-corner side; (b) the accompanying king is held in the double-corner where the single man must crown; (c) the stronger side has the move. The necessity for the last proviso is seen from the diagram. Black to move would actually win by 12–16. But if the double corner is not invaded by White the Black king can shuttle there perpetually.

The principal variation of the solution of Fig. 9 is: 24–27, 28–32, 19–23, 32–28 (or 12–16, 27–24, 16–20, 24–28), 27–32, 28–24, 23–18 (else Black cuts by 24–19), 24–28, 18–15, 28–24, 32–28, 24–27, 15–18, 12–16, 28–32, 27–24, 18–15, 16–20 (or 16–19, 32–27), 15–18, 24–19, 32–28, 19–16, 18–23, 16–11, 23–19, 11–8, 28–32, 8–11, 32–27, 11–8, 27–23, 8–11, 23–18, 11–8, 18–15, 8–12, 15–11.

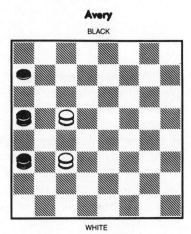

Avery

BLACK

WHITE

Fig. 10. Third Position
Black to move and win

Third Position, Fig. 10, should be compared with Fig. 7. Black must exercise the utmost care to prevent the forcing of "Payne's Draw." The main line of the solution is: 13–9, 22–18, 9–6, 18–22, 6–1 (not 6–2, 14–10, 5–9, 10–6, 9–13, 6–10, 21–17, 22–18 and White draws as in Fig. 6), 22–18, 21–25, 18–15, 1–6, 14–17, 6–2, 17–14, 25–22, 15–10, 22–26, 14–18, 5–9, 10–6, 9–13, 6–10, 26–31, 10–14, 31–27, 18–22, 27–23 (imperative to stop 14–18, which would secure Payne's Draw), 22–25, 2–7, 25–22, 7–11, 22–25, 11–15, 25–22, 23–27, 22–26, 27–24, 26–22, 24–20, 22–26, 20–16, 26–22, 16–12 (16–11 would be a mistake, for then with 14–17 White gets the king to 21 and secures the draw; 14–17 is useless so long as Black can reply with 15–18), 22–26, 12–8, 26–22, 8–3, 14–9 (to avoid the cut by 15–10), 15–10, and with the White kings split the win is easy.

THE BRIDGE

Black pieces on 1 and 3 constitute the Black *bridge*, a formation that offers as much opposition as two pieces can to the entry of White single pieces seeking crowns. The maintenance of one's own bridge, the breaking of the adverse bridge, are focal points of many Checker games. Much study has been expended on *bridge* problems. Fig. 11 shows the basic strength of the formation. White pieces appear to have reached safety, but fall for lack of space: 14–9, 6–2 (or 7–2, 3–8 and wins a piece), 1–5, 10–6, 3–10, 6–1, 10–15, 1–6, 9–13, and Black wins by Third Position after crowning 15.

BLACK

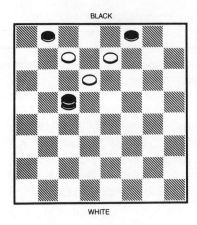

WHITE

Fig. 11
Black to move and win

BLACK

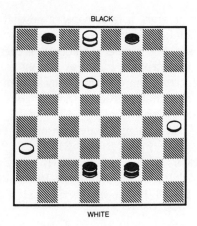

WHITE

Fig. 12
"Petterson's Drawbridge"
White to move and draw

"Petterson's Drawbridge," Fig. 12, shows what White has to do to draw against the bridge. The man on 10, without which White cannot crown, is threatened with capture. It is true that if Black moves a king to 15, White can put his king on 2, accept the cut, and relieve his worries. But by placing the other king on 9, before moving 18–15, Black would threaten to win 10 outright. In the diagrammed position White is saved by his pieces on 20 and 21, which prevent a Black king from reaching 9 or 11 (because the only routes attack 10 first). It is vital to keep the pieces on 20 and 21 until Black has broken his bridge.

BLACK

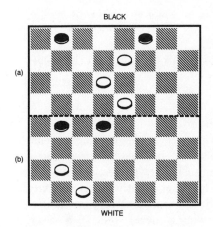

(a)

(b)

WHITE

Fig. 13. Two-for-one shots

SHOTS AND STROKES

A shot is the forcing of exchanges to reach a won position or avoid impending loss. A professional Checkers player once said, "Almost everybody knows how to play Checkers—just well enough to fall into every two-for-one shot." Fig. 13 shows two typical formations that allow shots. In (a) White has moved 11–7, thinking to run the piece through to crown. But Black "knocks out the middle man" by 1–6 and wins two for one. In (b) Black plans to play 17–22 and get through to the king-row. But White gets there first with 25–22.

BLACK

BLACK

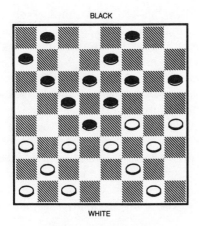

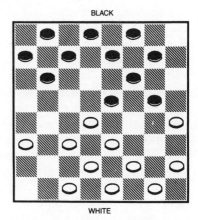

WHITE

WHITE

Fig. 14. "The Big Stroke"
Black to move

Fig. 15. "The Goosewalk"
White to move

In the opening and mid-game, constant vigilance is required to avoid falling into strokes. Analysts have compiled a long list of such traps that lurk in all the common formations. The next two diagrams are typical instances.

Fig. 14 arises from the opening "Old Fourteenth," as follows:

11–15, 23–19, 8–11, 22–17, 4–8, 17–13, 15–18, 24–20, 11–15, 28–24, 8–11, 26–23, 9–14, 31–26, 6–9, 13–6, 2–9, 26–22.

At this point 9–13 looks like a good move for Black, but it leads to what is called "the big shot": 9–13 (?), 20–16, 11–20, 22–17, 13–22, 21–17, 14–21, 23–14, 10–17, 25–2 and White wins.

Fig. 15 arises from the "Single Corner," as follows:

11–15, 22–18, 15–22, 25–18, 8–11, 29–25, 4–8, 24–20, 10–15, 25–22, 12–16.

Now 27–24 looks good, as it threatens to win two for one by 24–19, but it allows a stroke called "The Farmer" or "The Goosewalk": 27–24 (?), 15–19, 24–15, 16–19, 23–16, 9–14, 18–9, 11–25, and takes the piece on 9 next move, winning.

PRINCIPLES

Few Checkers theorists will commit themselves so far as to utter any principle for the guidance of opening and mid-game play. The reason is that exhaustive analysis of specific positions has repeatedly exploded various "theories of play." The prime maxim of early nineteenth-century players was, "Never move a piece off your king row until you have to"; modern opening variations flout this idea. It is true that there remains a strong tendency to preserve the *bridge* so long as possible—the Black men on 1

623

and 3, the White men on 30 and 32. But this too is at times erroneous. The Second Double Corner, for a long time considered to be a White loss, has been rehabilitated by the discovery that White can draw by breaking his bridge promptly.

In the present stage of Checkers knowledge, it seems that opening play must focus upon occupation or control of squares 14 and 19. A piece on either square tends to cramp the enemy forces on that side of the board. But this conception of "key squares" is insufficient to explain the why and wherefore of all early tactics. Likewise only partial in scope is the counsel to "Mass your pieces toward the center." Forces creeping up the sides of the board occasionally strangle the solid enemy phalanx in the center.

The only course to mastery of Checkers appears to be an extensive knowledge of "the book" combined with the ability to analyze rapidly and accurately over the board.

OPENINGS

All of the 47 playable two-move openings are given in the following tabulation, together with variations frequently arising from each. The variations given are not necessarily the best, but are selected to show different formations that may arise in early play. The names given to some of these formations in the pioneer days of the game are noted in parentheses.

CONTINUATIONS FROM 9–13 (Edinburgh)

21–17, 5–9, 25–21, 11–15, 29–25, 9–14, 23–18, 14–23, 27–11, 8–15.
22–17, 13–22, 25–18, 6–9, 29–25, 11–15, 18–11, 8–15, 25–22, 4–8.
22–18, 12–16, 24–20, 8–12, 18–14, 10–17, 21–14, 16–19.
23–18, 5–9, 26–23, 11–16, 24–19, 10–14, 30–26, 8–11, 28–24, 16–20.
23–19, 11–15, 22–18 (Will o' the Wisp).
24–19, 11–15, 28–24, 6–9, 22–18, 15–22, 25–18, 9–14, 18–9, 5–14.
24–20, 11–15, 22–17 (Wagram), 13–22, 25–11, 8–15, 21–17, 5–9, 17–13,
 9–14.

CONTINUATIONS FROM 9–14 (Double Corner)

22–17, 11–15, 25–22, 15–19, 24–15, 10–19, 23–16, 12–19, 17–10, 6–15.
22–18, 5–9, 25–22, 11–16, 24–19, 8–11, 22–17, 9–13, 18–9, 13–22, 26–17,
 6–22, 30–26.
23–18 (formerly *barred*), 14–23, 27–18, 12–16, 18–14, 10–17, 21–14.
23–19, 5–9, 22–17, 11–15 (Fife), 26–23, 9–13, 24–20, 15–24, 28–19, 13–22,
 25–9, 6–13.
24–19, 11–15, 22–18, 15–24, 18–9, 5–14, 28–19, 8–11, 25–22, 11–15.
24–20, 11–15, 22–18, 15–22, 25–9, 5–14, 29–25, 7–11,22, 6–9.

CONTINUATIONS FROM 10–14 (Denny)

22–17, 7–10, 17–13, 3–7, 25–22, 14–17, 21–14, 9–25, 29–22, 11–15.
22–18, 11–15, 18–11, 8–15, 24–19, 15–24, 28–19, 6–10, 25–22, 4–8.

23–18 (formerly *barred*), 14–23, 27–18, 12–16, 32–27, 16–20, 26–23, 6–10.
23–19, 11–16, 26–23, 9–13, 22–17, 13–22, 25–9, 5–14, 29–25, 7–11.
24–19, 6–10, 22–17, 9–13, 28–24, 13–22, 25–9, 5–14, 26–22, 11–15.
24–20, 11–15, 22–18, 15–22, 25–18, 6–10, 26–22, 8–11, 27–24, 10–15.

CONTINUATIONS FROM **10–15** (Kelso)

21–17, 11–16, 22–18, 15–22, 25–18, 16–20, 17–13, 8–11.
22–17, 11–16, 23–18, 15–22, 25–18, 9–14, 18–9, 6–22, 26–17, 8–11.
22–18, 15–22, 25–18, 6–10, 18–14, 9–18, 23–14, 10–17, 21–14, 1–6.
23–18 (Kelso-Cross), 12–16, 26–23, 8–12, 30–26, 16–20, 21–17, 9–13.
23–19, 6–10, 22–17, 1–6, 25–22, 11–16, 17–13, 16–23, 26–19, 7–11.
24–19, 15–24, 28–19 (Kelso Double Corner), 6–10, 22–17, 9–14, 25–22, 11–15.
24–20, 15–19, 23–16, 12–19, 27–24, 7–10, 24–15, 10–19, 21–17, 11–15.

CONTINUATIONS FROM **11–15**

21–17 (Switcher), 9–13, 25–21, 8–11, 17–14, 10–17, 21–14.
22–17 (Dyke), 15–19, 24–15, 10–19, 23–16, 12–19, 25–22, 8–11, 27–23, 4–8.
. . . , 8–11, 17–14 (White Dyke).
. . . , 8–11, 25–22 (Pioneer).
. . . , 8–11, 17–13, 15–18 (Maid of the Mill).
. . . , 8–11, 17–13, 4–8, 25–22 (Douglas).
. . . , 9–13, 24–20 (Wagram).
. . . , 9–13, 17–14 (Boston).
22–18 (Single Corner), 15–22, 25–18, 8–11, 29–25, 4–8, 25–22, 12–16.
23–18 (Cross), 8–11, 27–23, 4–8, 23–19, 10–14, 19–10, 14–23, 26–19, 7–14.
. . . , 8–11, 18–14 (Waterloo).
23–19 (Orthodox), 9–13 (Will o' the Wisp), 22–18, 15–22, 25–18, 10–14, 18–9, 5–14.
. . . , 9–14, 27–23 (Defiance), 8–11, 22–18, 15–22, 25–9, 5–14.
. . . , 9–14, 22–17, 6–9 (Souter), 17–13, 2–6, 25–22, 8–11.
. . . , 9–14, 22–17, 5–9 (Fife), 26–23, 9–13, 24–20, 15–24, 28–19.
. . . , 9–14, 22–17, 7–11 (Whilter), 25–22, 11–16, 26–23, 5–9, 17–13, 3–7.
. . . , 7–11, 22–18 (Whilter Exchange).
. . . , 8–11, 22–17, 11–16 (Glasgow), 24–20, 26–23, 27–11, 7–16, 20–11, 3–7.
. . . , 8–11, 22–17, 4–8 (Old Fourteenth), 17–13, 15–18, 24–20, 11–15, 28–24, 8–11.
. . . , 8–11, 22–17, 15–18 (Center).
. . . , 8–11, 22–17, 3–8 (Alma), 25–22, 11–16, 26–23, 7–11, 30–26, 15–18.
. . . , 8–11, 22–17, 9–13, 17–14, 10–17, 19–10, 7–14 (Black Doctor).
. . . , 8–11, 22–17, 9–13, 17–14, 10–17, 21–14 (Laird and Lady), 15–18, 19–15, 4–8, 24–19, 13–17.
. . . , 8–11, 26–23 (Nailor).

. . . , 8–11, 22–18 (Tillicoultry), 15–22, 25–18, 11–16, 27–23, 16–20, 32–27, 10–14.

24–19 (Second Double Corner), 15–24, 28–19, 8–11, 22–18, 11–16, 25–22, 16–20.

24–20 (Ayreshire Lassie), 8–11, 28–24, 4–8, 23–19, 15–18, 22–15, 11–18.

CONTINUATIONS FROM **11–16** (Bristol)

21–17, 9–13, 23–18, 5–9, 25–21, 10–15, 18–11, 8–15, 24–19, 16–23, 27–11, 7–16.

22–17, 9–14, 24–19, 8–11, 25–22, 11–15, 17–13, 15–24, 28–19, 4–8.

22–18, 16–19, 24–15, 10–19, 23–16, 12–19, 27–24, 9–14, 18–9, 5–14, 24–15, 7–10.

. . . , 10–14, 25–22, 8–11, 24–20, 16–19, 23–16, 14–23, 26–19 (White Doctor).

23–18 (Bristol-Cross), 16–20, 26–23, 8–11, 30–26, 10–14, 22–17, 7–10.

23–19 (formerly *barred*), 16–23, 26–19, 9–14, 27–23, 8–11, 22–17, 11–15.

24–19 (Paisley), 8–11, 22–18, 10–14, 26–22, 16–20, 22–17, 7–10.

24–20, 16–19, 23–16, 12–19, 22–18, 9–14, 18–9, 5–14, 25–22, 10–15.

CONTINUATIONS FROM **12–16** (Dundee)

21–17, 9–13, 24–20, 11–15, 20–11, 7–16, 25–21, 5–9.

22–17, 16–19, 24–15, 11–18, 23–14, 9–18.

22–18, 8–12, 24–20, 16–19, 23–26, 12–19, 27–23, 4–8, 23–16, 8–12.

23–18, 16–19, 24–15, 10–19, 18–15, 11–18, 22–15.

23–19 (formerly *barred* and still in question), 16–23, 27–18, 11–16, 26–23, 16–20, 32–27, 8–11.

24–19, 8–12 (Paisley), 22–18, 4–8, 25–22, 10–14, 22–17, 9–13.

24–20, 8–12, 28–24, 9–14, 24–19, 11–15, 20–11, 15–24, 27–20, 7–16, 20–11, 3–7.

National Variants

Spanish Draughts is like the English game with the following differences:

1. With a choice of captures, a player must capture the maximum possible of adverse pieces.

2. The king may move any distance along an open diagonal, and captures by jumping to the adjacent vacant square beyond an adverse piece, any distance away.

3. The double corner is placed at the player's left.

Italian Draughts is like the English game with the following differences:

1. A single piece cannot capture a king.

2. With choice of captures, the player must capture with a king rather than with a single man, and must take the maximum of adverse pieces, and must take the most powerful if the number of adverse pieces concerned in the choice is the same.

3. The double corner is placed at the player's left.

Polish Draughts is little known in Poland. It probably was named in the same spirit as "Chinese Checkers"—to invoke the lure of the exotic. It is known to have been played in Paris as early as 1723. The board is 10 × 10, and each side has twenty pieces, set initially on the first four ranks. The rules are:

1. A single piece moves only forward (diagonally), but captures both forward and backward.

2. A single piece that reaches the king row by capture and finds an adverse piece adjacent (with a vacant square beyond it) must continue jumping in the same turn.

3. A single piece is crowned and becomes a king (actually it is called a queen) only when it reaches the king row and can legally stop there.

4. With a choice of captures, the player must take the maximum possible number of adverse pieces.

5. A king (queen) moves any distance along an open diagonal, and captures an adverse piece any distance away by landing on *any* vacant square beyond it on the same line. But the landing point must be chosen so as to enable the king to continue jumping, and with the maximum of captures, when there is any choice.

6. Each captured piece is removed from the board before the captor continues jumping; its removal may therefore open up additional captures previously impossible.

German Draughts is Polish Draughts played on the 8 × 8 board, with twelve pieces on each side.

Turkish Draughts differs from all other variants in that all 64 squares of the 8 × 8 board are used. Each player has sixteen pieces, which are placed initially on the second and third ranks. The rules are:

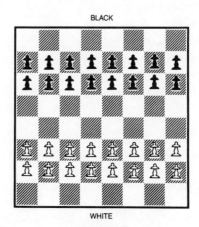

Turkish Draughts

627

1. A single man may move one square forward on the file, or diagonally forward, or sideward on the rank.

2. A single man captures in any of the same five directions; it must continue jumping so long as possible.

3. With choice of captures, the player must take the maximum number of adverse pieces.

4. A single man crowns on reaching the king row.

5. A king moves any distance on an open line in any direction, and captures by jumping to the adjacent vacant square beyond an adverse piece, any distance away.

6. Each captured piece is removed from the board before the captor continues jumping; its removal may therefore open up additional captures previously impossible.

GO

Go is the anglicized name of the Oriental game known in Japan as I-go and in China as Wei-ch'i. It probably originated in China, where historical record carries it back at least a thousand years B.C. Various legends carry it back another thirteen hundred years; one ascribes it to the Emperor Shun, who reigned 2255–2206 B.C. Oscar Korschelt, who wrote one of the first Occidental books on Go, declares it to be the oldest of all games. But the researches of Stewart Culin tend to indicate that Go, Chess, Pachisi, and many other board games, all had a common origin in simpler games of position played with pebbles or cowrie shells.

Go was introduced into Japan in 754 A.D., where it has achieved the position of "the national game." In recent times, courses on I-go have been included in the curriculum of Japanese war colleges.

Go has enlisted a fairly extensive following outside of Japan and China. An American master of Chess, Edward Lasker, says "I really believe that Go is destined to take the place of Chess as the leading intellectual game of the Occident, just as it has reigned supreme in the Orient for some four thousand years."

The rules of Go differ somewhat in China, Korea, and Japan. Unfortunately they have not been codified even in Japan, where, in 1928, a championship tournament was interrupted and suspended for a month by a dispute over rules. A commission appointed to clarify the Japanese rules proposed a code in 1933, but it has not been generally adopted. The description below follows the traditional rules given by Lasker.

During the same millenniums when Chess players were producing a huge literature of technical analysis, Go players compiled little beyond records of games and some analysis of the *Josecki* (corner openings). According to Karl Davis Robinson, who has had much to do with making the literature of Go known in this country, "Until recently, Japanese writers on Go were innocent of the scientific spirit and scientific method."

EQUIPMENT

The Board *(goban)* is a grid of 19 horizontal and 19 vertical lines (see Fig. 1). Pieces are placed upon the points of intersection, not on the squares. There are 361 intersections. The letters and numbers bordering on the diagram do not appear on the board; they are added here to provide a notation for the points. The nine points marked by large dots, d16, k16, etc. are called *handicap points*.

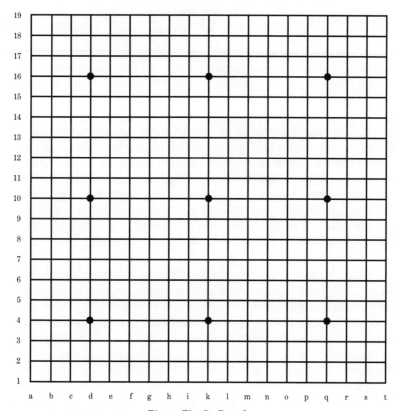

Fig. 1. The Go Board

The Pieces *(go ishi)* are of bone, ivory, slate, or wood, circular and lense-shaped. Each player is provided with about 180 of these *stones* (the standard set has 181 black). The two forces are of different colors, usually black and white. Black plays first.

THE PLAY

Each in turn places one stone upon any intersection. The object of play is to acquire territory, as explained below. Play ends by agreement when both players are satisfied that the ownership of all points on the board has been established.

Connection. Two stones of like color are *connected* when they are adjacent on the same horizontal or vertical line. A group of two or more stones, so arranged that each is connected to at least one other member, *lives* or *dies* as a unit—it cannot be dismembered and killed in part. (*Sei*, live stones.)

Capture. A unit *lives* so long as it is connected to at least one vacant point. (Its "breathing spaces" are *Katsuro*, literally, the four vacant points around a single stone.) A unit *dies* when it can be completely enclosed. If the execution is actually carried out, the player who places a stone on the last vacant point connected to the enemy unit *captures* it entire; he removes all stones of the unit from the board and keeps them in his custody to the end of the game. In many instances the capture does not have to be consummated; the opponent has to concede that his unit is dead if he cannot demonstrate that they can maintain life.

Enclosure. The territory *(chi)* that counts in favor of a player, at the end of the game, comprises *the vacant points which his spaces enclose.* Any point or space entirely surrounded *(kakomu)* by stones of one color belongs *prima facie* to that player. If the opponent wishes to dispute ownership, he must undertake to invade the space and establish a living unit there. The game ends when neither player is willing to attempt invasion of any space that *prima facie* belongs to his opponent.

DETERMINING WINNER

The final score of each player is the total of enclosed points to which he has established undisputed ownership, less the number of stones he has lost by capture. The subtraction is performed graphically by putting the prisoners back on the board, on points enclosed by their own color, and counting the net.

For example, Fig. 2 shows the end of a game during which Black captured 23 White stones and White captured 21 Black stones. Each player first removes the adverse stones that must be conceded to be dead. Black takes k8, l17, t3, t4, bringing his bag of prisoners to 27. White takes n12, n13, o13, s18, with total of 25 prisoners.

Common Points *(dame)*, that is, points connected to units of both colors, belong to neither side. The next step is to fill in common points so that they will not be counted. Stones of either color (from the box, not from prisoners) may be used. In Fig. 2, the common points are f14, h18, m8, o15, t14.

Black puts the White prisoners in the White territory, first filling the smaller spaces—around a15, s18, n13, f8—and the rest in the large territory below n7. White is found to enclose a net of 14 vacant points.

White similarly puts the Black prisoners into Black territory, and Black is found to own 10 points net.

White wins the game, by the difference of 4 points.

EYES

A single point surrounded by four stones of the same color is called an eye *(me)*. An adverse stone placed in an eye has no life unless it effects capture of part of the enclosure.

A unit that contains two (or more) separate eyes is forever safe from capture. The opponent cannot fill both eyes at once, nor successively because the first-played would be removed as a prisoner. The life of any unit depends

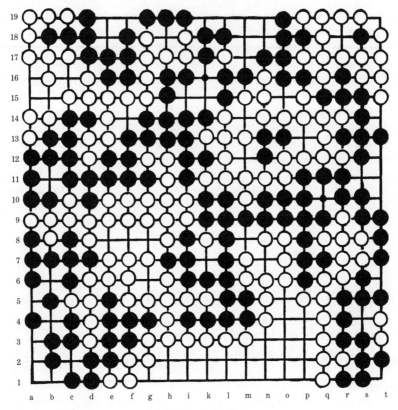

Fig. 2. End of a Game

ultimately upon whether it has both the space and the configuration to make two eyes in defense against attack. Lacking such possibility, a unit must make connection with a safe unit or die.

In Fig. 2, the White group in the upper right corner contains two separate spaces, t19 and r18-s18. The unit is forever safe and needs no further attention; that is why White need not play on r18 to capture s18. Similarly the Black group at the lower right corner is forever safe, having two separate eyes at t1 and the space s4-t4-t3.

False Eyes are those enclosed by stones not all connected in one unit, and susceptible of partial disruption. The White space at e, f, g on the 8th line, Fig. 2, is not a true eye, because it is enclosed by two separate units. Were Black allowed to play upon all three points, he would capture the upper unit. But the invasion could not succeed, for after he played on two of the points, White would fill the third, capturing the invaders, and also connecting the upper unit to the large White unit along the bottom of the board.

632

The fact that an eye is enclosed by separate units does not of itself make the eye false. Two or more units that enclose two or more eyes along their junction are as safe as though they were connected. Examine the White spaces at the upper left edge of Fig. 2. Here are three separate units, enclosing spaces at c16 and a16-a15-b15. It is true that Black might threaten capture of the right-hand unit by filling h18, f14, and b15, for then only c16 would be open. But after the play on b15, White plays a15 and captures the invader. Then all three groups are safe forever. Between the junction of each pair lie two eyes, and Black cannot surround any of the three units.

The Knot *(ko)*. The formation in the lower right corner of Fig. 3 is called a *knot*. White can play on q3 and capture r3. But then Black can play on r3 and capture q3, reproducing the original position. Were no restriction placed upon this situation, the game might result in "perpetual capture." But there is a special rule: When one player captures in a knot, the opponent may not recapture at his next turn. The effect of this rule is to give the

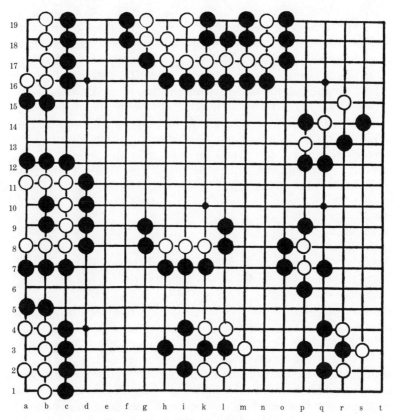

Fig. 3. Various Elementary Positions

first capturer a tempo to close the knot, if he wishes. Thus, White after playing q3 and capturing r3 will have time to play on r3.

The rule applies only to a true knot, and the test of a true knot is that a second capture will reproduce the position before the first. The group at the middle bottom of Fig. 3 is not a true knot. If White plays on i3, capturing two stones, Black may immediately play on k3, capturing one, for the position is then different—White is unable to capture again.

BASIC TACTICS

Fig. 3 illustrates certain fundamental facts about the vitality of small groups.

The Tiger's Mouth is the formation of three stones shown by the White group r4, r2, s3. The formation comprises three separate units, yet it is the best spearhead for many operations both offensive and defensive. If the opponent plays into the mouth, his stone may be captured at once. If he crowds it by *cutting*, as at s4, his stone can immediately be *checked* (threatened with capture).

Cutting is the occupation of a point that otherwise would serve to connect two adverse units. In the upper right of Fig. 3 White has placed a diagonal line of three stones. The attempt to cut or crowd such a formation must look to its own connections. Here Black has cut at p14, and might well complete the cut by playing q13. Instead he plays q15, thinking to press upon the whole line. But White retorts with p15, checking both p14 and q15. He is sure to capture one of them, gaining more life and space.

The Ladder *(sh'cho)*. The two White stones at the middle of the p-line, Fig. 3, are checked. Can White save them? He plays q8. If Black replies with q9, White will play r8. This stone connects with three vacant points, and whether Black can kill the group then depends upon other stones in the vicinity. But after White's q8 Black should play r8. If White tries to escape, he is run to the edge of the board by the *ladder* formation and loses all:

WHITE	BLACK
q8	r8
q9	q10
r9	s9
r10	r11
s10	t10
s11	s12
t11	t12

Outposts. The life of a small unit often depends upon the existence of an outpost to which it can connect if closely pressed. The ladder attack shown above would not succeed if there were a White stone in the path of the ladder, say at s11. The three White stones in the center of the 8th line,

Fig. 3, are doomed. The reader should verify that White cannot save them by playing either i9 or i10. But with an outpost at i11, White could save them by playing i10.

Much of the opening play is concerned with establishing outposts, both for the protection of other stones and to wall off (potentially) sections of territory.

The Impasse *(seki)*. Examine the formation at the middle top of Fig. 3. The five-stone Black unit contains only one eye, at l19. Yet it is immune from capture, for the White wall about it is itself surrounded. Should White play i18 in order to follow with l19, Black answers h19 and takes the whole White force. Yet Black cannot initiate an attempt to capture. If he plays i18 with intention of playing h19, White will answer with l19, capturing six stones and making his unit safe forever.

Such a situation is called an *impasse*. When a large space surrounded by one color is invaded, the defender must do more than save his wall; he must avert the establishment of an impasse that would nullify his claim to the territory.

Killing a Group. The formation at the middle left side, Fig. 3, looks like an impasse. If White plays a9 to capture the two Black invaders, Black takes a10 and captures the whole White unit. If Black starts with a9, White can reply a10 and take the three Black stones. But the situation is not an impasse, because by making this sacrifice Black can eventually capture the White unit. After White captures, Black plays b9, then b10, checking. White can play a9, capturing two, but then has only two adjacent points left. At a sacrifice of one more stone Black kills the whole White group. Between experienced players the diagrammed position would be abandoned and White would concede loss of his unit.

This example illustrates the constant menace of an invasion; capturing the invading force may compel the defender to fill his own "breathing spaces."

CONSTRUCTING EYES

The White group in the lower left corner of Fig. 3 shows the smallest unit that can in itself contain two eyes. Compare it with the White unit at the upper left corner. White to play can make the unit safe by playing a18. Black to play can kill it by seizing a18. Black follows with a19, checking, and White can capture by playing a17. But then there are left only two adjacent vacant points, and by sacrificing one more stone Black captures the White unit.

A unit can be made safe only if it encloses a space of at least three points, and only if the owner can create a *partition* separating it into two independent spaces. With small spaces it becomes imperative to determine which points will make partitions, and whether they must be made at once or can wait until the opponent has commenced invasion. The strongest invasion is of course by occupation of the partition points.

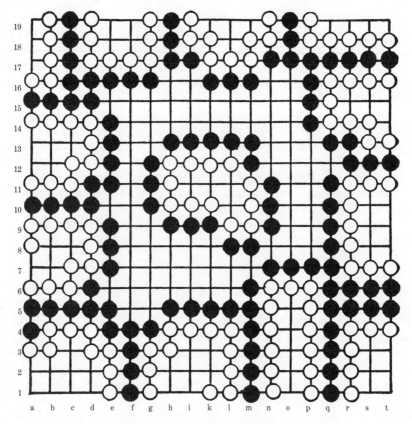

Fig. 4. Defending Against Invasion

Fig. 4 shows a number of White units, enclosing spaces of three points and up. The Go player has to know the merits of these formations, as thoroughly as the Checker player has to know First Position.

Three points (a17, a18, a19) are necessarily in *linear* formation (like beads on a string; the points may form a right angle, but the connection remains purely linear). The only partition point is the middle, as a18. The unit lives or dies according as White or Black seizes this point.

Four points, linear (q19, r19, s19, t19, also r15, s15, t15, t14, also a7, b7, b8, c8). Both interior points, as r19 and s19, serve for partition. The unit is therefore safe, provided that if the opponent takes one partition point the defender immediately takes the other. However, there is an exception to this rule in the "bent four" *(magari shi)* in the corner. In Fig. 4, place White stones on s3 and s2. White will lose the unit if he does not at once make a partition at t1 or t2. For if Black is allowed to play on t2, White's play on the other partition point t1 is useless—this stone is not connected. Black captures it with s1, and the rule of the knot prevents White from recapturing. Black next plays t3 and captures the unit.

Four points, square (e19, f19, e18, f18). No one stone will make a partition; two stones are required, as e19 and f18. The unit is therefore doomed, provided that if the defender plays on any point the opponent takes that diagonally opposite.

Four points, T formation (k19, l19, m19, l18). There is only one partition point, l19. This is equivalent to a space of three points.

More than four points, linear (o1, o2, o3, o4, o5). Every point but the two at the end makes a partition. The unit is safe, and needs defense only if the opponent threatens to occupy the last open partition point.

Five points, augmented square (a13, b13, c13, a12, b12). There is one partition point, b13. But two stones, at a13 and b12, will make a partition. White to play saves his group by playing b13. Black to play wins it by taking b13, and following with a13 or b12. If White takes no action, Black sacrifices four stones to reduce the space to four points in square or T formation.

Six points, augmented square (h1, i1, h2, i2, k2, i3). Imagine k3 to be occupied by a White stone. The only partition point is i2, but two stones on h2 and i1 will make a partition. This is equivalent to the five-point augmented square.

Six points, rectangle (s10, t10, s9, t9, s8, t8). Two stones are required to make a partition. One will have to go on the middle line, s9 or t9. The other can go on any of the three points on the other vertical line. Hence the defender can wait until invasion begins. *Example:* Black plays s9. White must reply t9. If Black continues s8 or s10, White occupies the other, and all is safe.

More than six points. Whatever the arrangement, seven or more points can always be defended against capture of the surrounding wall, even after the invasion has begun, but the defender must beware of an impasse. An example is the seven-point space in form of diagonal squares, h1, i1, h2, i2, k2, i3, k3. White to move can make it safe by playing i2. Black to move takes i2 and threatens to reduce the space to the six-point augmented square, which he can kill by playing back on i2 after his first sacrifice. White can do no better than submit to an impasse by answering i2 with i3. Black plays k2 to block the partition, and White plays h2. Again Black blocks with i1, and there is an impasse. Only h1 and k3 are open. If Black takes either point, White takes the other, captures, and is left with a four-point linear space. White can thus save his unit, but not his territory.

Disconnection. All of the foregoing discussion assumes that the wall about the White space is one unit. If it comprises two or more units, the defender must reckon with the necessity for connections as well as with partitions. A point necessary for connection as well as partition is doubly vulnerable.

In the center of Fig. 4, is a linear four-point space, i11, k11, l11, l10. The rule that White can wait for the attack does not apply here, because the wall comprises two separate units. The point l11, occupied by White, will make both a connection and a partition. Occupied by Black, it kills the White forces. To connect at l10 is useless, because this reduces the space to a linear three, and Black wins by taking the middle point, k11.

OPENINGS

The tabulation of "regular openings" is beyond the scope of this article. One common opening will be discussed to show the principles involved.

Assailed units can form eyes most economically if helped by the edge of the board. The most secure positions, for a few stones, are at the corners. The opening play is therefore almost invariably concerned with staking off small areas at the corners, to form bases from which to extend down the sides or into the center. (The corner openings are called *josecki*.)

The safest first play to take possession of a corner is at the intersection of the third and fourth lines, as d3. The handicap point, d4, does not assure that invasion can be repelled, while the opening on d5 allows invasion at once by d3 (the usual reply to d5).

If White wishes to dispute the corner, after Black has opened d3, his correct move is c5. Among the variations that often arise are the following:

BLACK	WHITE
1. d3	c5
2. b4	c8

Black checks the invasion, but does not press on c5, so White extends up the left side.

2. c4	d5
3. f4	c8

Black checks the invasion and also attacks c5. The defense by d5 also threatens to envelop the right side of Black's area. Black defends by extending, and White extends along the other side.

2. c8	e4

Instead of walling off the corner, Black menaces the invader. White can find safety by direct extension toward the center, by e5 or f5, but there chooses to press the attack on the corner.

3. e3	f4
4. g3	

A characteristic extension.

4.		f3
5.	f2	g2
6.	h2	e2
7.	g1 (1)	c3
8.	d2	c2

White has gained time to invade the corner on the left side. In compensation, Black has a base on the right side. The sacrifice of a few stones that exert momentary threats, to gain time for extension, occurs repeatedly in Go games.

Instead of invading the corner, White may prefer to leave it to Black and give himself a large base for extension into the center; after 6. h2 as above he may play

6.		g4
7.	h3	h4

It is worth noting that after 1. d3, c5, an attempt by Black to pinch off the invader by a closer approach than c8 is inferior. Thus

2.	c7	d5
3.	g3	d7
4.	c8	c3
5.	d2	b3

EXTENSION

To commence play by building a solid wall around a space—as beginners are inclined to do—is to lose by hundreds of points to an experienced opponent. With the same number of stones, the opponent will take possession of the rest of the board.

Since it is the totality of space that counts, no threat by the opponent to acquire a decisive amount of territory can be ignored. At the beginning of the game, threats are exerted mainly by *extension*, the placing of outposts from the corner bases. The lines of extension, even when only two stones are placed, represent *potential* walls; they increase the difficulty of invasion from without and narrow the area open to life for enemies within. The perfection of Go play is to extend at every opportunity, reducing to a minimum the moves made for mere defense, as by making *actual* walls.

In many of the corner battles, the fight is not so much for the space of six to ten points in the corner as for a formation of stones that can quickest expand away from the corner. This explains why many *josecki* terminate abruptly with stones of both colors susceptible to capture, yet neither attacked nor defended; expansion has become more important than the capture of a few prisoners.

Of paramount importance is the initiative *(sente)*, just as in Chess. He has the initiative who is not pressed by necessity to defend, but can look for possible threats against his opponent. In questions of attack and defense on small units, the question of who will emerge with the initiative must be weighed.

HANDICAP PLAY

More than any other board game, Go admits of handicap play without destroying the essence of the contest. There are two methods:

(1) Where there is great disparity between the two players, the weaker takes Black and starts by placing a number of stones on the so-called *handicap points*. With the minimum handicap of two, he occupies d4 and q16. If the handicap is greater, he takes also, in order: q4, d16, k10. For six stones, k10 is left vacant and stones are put on d10, q10. For seven to nine, the added stones go on k4, k16, k10. After the handicap stones are placed, White moves first.

The handicap of four or more stones is about equivalent to queen odds in Chess. In Japan the difference between the highest rank of experts (ninth degree, which class comprises one individual) to the lowest (first degree) is only three stones.

(2) A prefixed number of points may be subtracted from the final score of the stronger player. This method is used when the players are nearly equal in strength.

Illustrative Game

This was played in 1926 between Honinbo, the only living master of the ninth rank, and Karigane, the only living master of the eighth rank. It took six sessions of about five hours each, each contestant being allowed sixteen hours for the whole game. Karigane resigned his lost position with only ten minutes of his time left.

	Black, Karigane				White, Honinbo	
1. r16	r4	7. c15	r10	13. r13	p9
2. p16	d17	8. g17	e16	14. p7	q7
3. d5	d3	9. d13	c16	15. q8	p8
4. c3	c2	10. d15	b16	16. q6	o7
5. c4	e2	11. r12	l17	17. r7 (1)	o6
6. c9	p4	12. r8	q12	18. s10	e5

Black, Karigane   White, Honinbo

19. e6	f5	63. c6 (1)	b9	107. e1 (1)	d1
20. f3	d4	64. b10	f10	108. p13 (1)	s6
21. d6	i4	65. e11	h9	109. a6 (2)	f1 (1)
22. k3	i3	66. g10	b7	110. b15	e15
23. i2	k4	67. a9 (1)	b6	111. e1 (1)	l8
24. k2	l3	68. c5	a4	112. k8	f1 (1)
25. l2	m3	69. k9	a3	113. f14	f13
26. m2	n2	70. a7	g11	114. e14	b18
27. h3	h4	71. h10	i10	115. e1 (1)	e13
28. g4	g5	72. h11	i9	116. d14	f1 (1)
29. n3	o2	73. h12	i12	117. n16	h2 (14)
30. f2	h2	74. l10	h13	118. n17	e12
31. g3	f1	75. g12	i11	119. f11 (2)	d12
32. g1	m1	76. l12	l13	120. c12	h16
33. h1	l1	77. m12	m9	121. h17 (1)	k16
34. e4	b2	78. l9	m7	122. m15	m14
35. g2 (1)	k1	79. l7	g13	123. m16	l15
36. l4	m4	80. f12	k13	124. s7	s5
37. l5	k5	81. d1	c1	125. n9	p6
38. o3	p2	82. a1	a2	126. n6	o10
39. n1	o1 (1)	83. f15	n14	127. n10	o8
40. h5	h6	84. m10	q13	Black resigned. The
41. k6	i5 (1)	85. n13	o13	final moves might
42. i6	h5	86. o14	m13	have been:
43. l6	n1	87. n12	n15	128. e17	d16
44. i1	n4	88. o15	o17	129. a16	a17
45. h7	g7	89. p17	o16	130. a15	d11
46. f6	h8	90. p15	m8	131. c11	q14
47. i7	g6	91. o12	s11	132. q15	q5
48. g8	f8	92. r11	q10	133. p11	p10
49. g9	f7	93. s9	q11	134. o11	f17
50. f9	d8	94. r14	f16	135. f18	o19
51. e8	e7	95. g16	g15	136. o18 (2)	n19
52. d7	e9 (1)	96. h15	g14	137. p19 (1)	l19
53. e10	e3	97. i14	k15	138. d10	t7
54. d9	f4 (1)	98. k18	l18	139. t8	t6
55. e1 (1)	d2	99. e18	d18	140. r6	e19
56. b3	c8	100. i15	i13	141. f19	d19
57. e8 (1)	e4	101. i17	h18	142. r9	r5
58. b5	e9	102. g18	i16	143. k11	k19
59. n5	o4	103. k16	k17	144. o5	p5
60. e8 (1)	c5	104. i18	l16 (1)	145. q7	k14
61. b8	e9 (1)	105. h19	p18	146. i8
62. c7	e8	106. q18	f1 (2)	

No moves remain that would increase the points won by either side.

Black has captured 20 prisoners, including s11. White has won 32, including a1, n3, o3, h15, i15, i14. After the common points (dame) are closed, and the prisoners are put back in the territory won by their own side, Black is found to have 24 points and White 29. White wins by 5 points.

Simplified Go. In clubs, Go is often played on a smaller board, 10 × 10 or 13 × 13, by partnerships of two players each. Partners play alternately, without consultation, using stones of the same color. A time limit of one to five minutes per move is fixed.

Go Bang

Go bang is the anglicized name of the game called, in Japan, Go Maku. There it is played on the I-go board, which is 19 × 19. According to "Berkeley" it was imported to England about 1873, where it was generally played on the 8 × 8 Chess board. It seems patent that Go Maku had a common ancestor with The Mill.

In Go Bang, the two players alternately place counters on a checkered board, and the first to get five of his own color on adjacent squares in any row (lateral, vertical or diagonal) wins the game. If the 19 × 19 board is used, there should be a supply of counters sufficient to cover the board (the Go stones). If the 8 × 8 board is used, each player has twelve counters (Checker pieces), and if neither has won by the time all pieces are placed, the game continues by alternate moves; a piece may be moved to an adjacent vacant square in any direction.

"Berkeley" and others decry the use of the smaller board, declaring that it makes the game too easy. But Mott-Smith *(Mathematical Puzzles)* states that on the larger board the first player can always force a win. It is a fact that in Go Maku the rules bar the establishment of two "open threes" whereby a win is sure. Apparently the only way to make a contest of it is by some such limitation. Limitation of the size of the board and the number of pieces can be carried to the point where it has the same effect, by making two "open threes" dynamically impossible. The effect of extreme limitation is evident in the juvenile "game" Ticktacktoe, which is a draw with correct play by both players. Dudeney has shown that "Ovid's game" (a board 3 × 3, with three counters each, but moving after the pieces are down) is a forced win for the first player, but can be made a contest if an opening play to the center is banned. In The Mill, a *mill* can be forced by the first player, but this is not enough to win (and in many cases loses); the rules require the player to make three-in-a-row repeatedly.

PARLOR
GAMES

♣

♥

Categories (Guggenheim)

Any number may play. Each player is provided with a sheet of paper and a pencil. In a column at the left each writes a list of *categories*, as selected by the players as a whole. The usual practice is to permit each player to name one category. A nomination may be vetoed, however, by majority vote. (In the absence of the right of veto, a player can gain advantage for himself by naming a category with which he alone is familiar.)

To commence a round, the players agree on a key word, usually of five letters with no letter repeated, for example, COMET. Five columns are ruled off on the paper, and one letter of the key word is written at the head of each column.

A time limit for the round is fixed in advance (usually fifteen or twenty minutes). At the signal to commence, each player writes words on his paper, one in each row and column, each word fitting in the category of its row and having the initial letter at the top of the column. For example, a completed paper with four categories and five-letter key might look like this:

	C	O	M	E	T
1. Card games	Casino	Ombre	Michigan	Euchre	Twenty-one
2. Composers	Chopin	Offenbach	Mahler	Elgar	Tschaikowsky
3. Capitals of U.S. states	Columbus	Olympia	Montgomery		Topeka
4. Words containing Q	Croquet	Opaque	Marquee	Equal	Toque

At the expiration of the allotted time, all players must stop writing. The lists are then compared and scored.

Each word scores one point for every other player who *did not* write it in his list. Thus, with seven players, if Ombre was named by only one player, it scores 6 points. If all players wrote the same word for the same category, as Chopin for "Composer" with initial C, none scores for it.

In certain limited categories, there may be no word with the required initial (as there is no U.S. capital with initial E). A player knowing this fact is not bound by rule or sportsmanship to announce it; he may benefit from the fact that others may search for a non-existent word.

In some circles the rule is that, if a player leaves a blank on his paper, for a category in which another has written a valid word, he must deduct one point from his score. The general practice, however, is to count simply zero for a blank.

The player with the highest total score wins the round. The key word should be changed every round, if not the list of categories, and effort should be made to vary the assortment of letters. Key words containing rare letters, as J, Q, X, Z, are usually barred.

It is advisable to agree in advance on some rules as to the admissibility of words. For example:

1. Any question on the validity of a word will be settled by majority vote.

2. There is no score for a word when, if it is challenged, the writer can give no identifying information about it.

3. One point is subtracted for a proper name in a category where a common noun is available (as in "Words containing Q").

4. In categories that call for names of persons, the initial applies to the surname. (*Example:* For "Characters from Dickens," with initial O, the name Oliver Twist is invalid.)

5. One point is subtracted for use of a compound word if a simple word is available. (*Example:* For "Countries," initial N, North Korea is valid but costs a point, while the Netherlands takes full credit.)

6. Only the anglicized spelling of foreign geographic names is permissible. (*Example:* For "European cities," initial W, Wien is not valid.)

The easiest way to avoid arguments is to discuss the limitations of each category as it is proposed. A category should be broad enough to yield a liberal choice of words and at least sixteen initial letters, but not so broad that no player can miss. "Primary colors" would have to be vetoed, as it is too narrow; "Colors" should be construed to include all terms that denote a primary color, a shade or hue, but may well be agreed to exclude proprietary names, fanciful names, and pigments as differentiated from shades. A favorite easy category, "Articles of furniture," often leads to arguments on the admissibility of tools, implements, etc. It should be limited by agreement, say to articles of household furniture of reasonably non-portable character.

The following list of suggested categories was compiled by Edward N. Roberts.

nations	8-letter words
words containing Z	9-letter words
musical instruments	10-letter words
articles of clothing	continental authors
characters from Bible	American authors
place names in Africa	famous streets & buildings
prepositions	American rivers
furniture & furnishings	operas
Presidents	actors & actresses
Governors of states	flowers
occupations	U.S. Cabinet members

Latin words

times & timepieces

battles

mountains

interjections

instruments

chemical elements

Shakespearean characters

publications

islands

names of ships

domestic animals

beverages

vehicles

parts of the body

musical terms

parts of a ship

7-letter words

12-letter words

athletes

birds

mammals

wild animals

bodies of water

games

precious stones

minerals

girls' names

boys' names

rulers

names of sciences

plants

current books

words containing Q

fabulous monsters

characters from Mark Twain

place names in Asia

rivers of the world

card games

opera singers

foods

trees

words containing J

painters

characters from Dumas

weapons

capitals of countries

capitals of U.S. states

scientists

cities in U.S.

American generals

American admirals

characters from Dickens

colors

philosophers

explorers

titles

kinds of buildings

cities in Europe

cities in British Isles

dances

characters from the *Iliad*

monetary units

parts of an automobile

dramatists in English

plane & solid figures

English poets

poets of the world

nicknames

lakes

insects

fabrics

The same selection of categories may be used for several rounds of play, or the list may be changed each round.

Ghosts

Any number may play. Ghosts is a good game to play while riding in an automobile, or wherever equipment and facilities for other games are absent.

One player names a letter; the next in turn adds another letter, and so on in continuous order. The letters are conceived to be set in order as called, from left to right, and the round ends when any player adds a letter that completes a good English word of more than three letters. But the player in turn, instead of calling a letter, may challenge the last player to give a good English word that commences with the series of letters already called. If the challenged player is unable to comply, he loses; if he gives an acceptable word, the challenger loses. In either case the round ends. When a round ends, the next player in turn commences a new one by calling an initial letter.

A player who loses a round, by completing a word, or by losing after a challenge, becomes "one-third of a ghost." His second loss makes him "two-thirds of a ghost," and his third, a "full ghost." Each full ghost is out of the game, but has the duty of trying to make ghosts of the players. No player may talk to a full ghost, upon penalty of becoming a full ghost himself. Full ghosts may talk freely to each other and to the players. Some "house rules" usually have to be agreed upon in advance as to how obstreperous a ghost may become in badgering the players.

The lone survivor, when all others have become ghosts, wins the game.

It is important to note that only the player whose turn it is to call has the right to challenge. Frequently it is necessary to bluff, calling a letter confidently but with no word in mind. The bluffer must not be subjected to exposure by any but his left-hand neighbor. Similarly, players must refrain from saying or even mouthing the words they have in mind, when not challenged, lest they give undue assistance to others.

A dictionary should be kept at hand to settle disputes as to the validity of words. Where feasible, a non-player should be requested to refer to the dictionary.

Fore-and-aft. In this variant of Ghosts, a player may add his letter to either end of the group of letters already named. For example, if it is his turn to add to PRACTICABL, in the regular game he is lost, but in *fore-and-aft* he can add M at the head, aiming toward IMPRACTICABLE.

Word Squares

Any number may play. Each has pencil and paper, and draws a box of 25 squares, 5 × 5. Each in turn calls aloud one letter—any he pleases—until 25 have been called. As the letter is named, each player writes it into his own box—wherever he pleases. The object is to make as many good English words as possible, in the five rows and columns of the box. A word of five letter scores 10; of four letters, 5; of three letters, 2. The player with the highest total wins the game.

Dispute as to validity of a word is settled by reference to a dictionary chosen in advance.

Some play that the first letter called must be placed in the upper left corner of the box.

Skill consists in placing the first several letters so as to allow for the greatest flexibility in the different words that may be formed. It is usually advisable to aim for words with not more than one vowel, because experienced players try to wreck their opponents by calling as few vowels as possible. Often fifteen consonants are called before some player "breaks down" and calls a vowel.

Battleship (Salvo)

This pencil-and-paper game combines luck and skill in about equal proportions.

EQUIPMENT

The paper used must be *quadrille* (also called "cross section," "graph")—divided by horizontal and vertical lines into squares, with four or five squares to the inch. Some game manufacturers print special forms for Salvo.

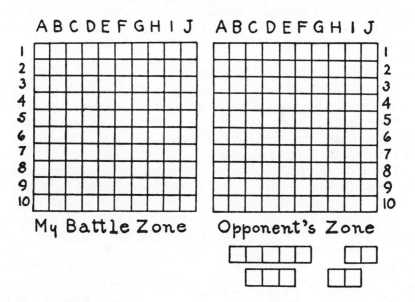

My Battle Zone   Opponent's Zone

PRELIMINARIES

Each player sets up a form on a sheet of quadrille paper, as shown in the diagram. He then distributes a fleet of four vessels in "My Battle Zone." Each ship is a line of blacked-in squares, along any row, column or diagonal. The fleet comprises one battleship (five squares), one cruiser (three squares), and two destroyers (two squares each). Of course the fleet must be distributed out of sight of the opponent. The player has free choice where to put his ships, except that no two may touch at the sides or corners.

649

THE PLAY

First turn is decided by chance. Then the players alternately fire salvos into "Opponent's Battle Zone," trying to sink the enemy fleet. At the outset, each salvo comprises seven shots.

Each player numbers serially the salvos he delivers. To fire a salvo, he writes the serial number into each of seven squares in "Opponent's Battle Zone." He then names these seven squares orally to his opponent, by reference to the column and row coordinates, as "E-8, H-2," etc. The opponent writes the same serial number into the named squares of "My Battle Zone." After the salvo is complete, the opponent must state whether any of his vessels was hit, giving the type of vessel, the number of hits, but *not the square where the hit occurred.* The player achieving a hit on the enemy fleet makes a memorandum of it, by writing the salvo number in the appropriate space below "Opponent's Battle Zone."

The player who first sinks the entire enemy fleet wins the game. A vessel is sunk when every component square is hit. The loss of his battleship reduces the player's subsequent salvos by three shots; loss of the cruiser, two shots; loss of a destroyer, one shot.

STRATEGY

It pays to concentrate on locating and sinking the enemy battleship. The initial salvos should not be too widely dispersed; each should be confined to not more than a quarter of the board. Then when the first hit is made on the adverse battleship, the wastage in trying to hit it again will be minimized. Even if an early salvo has hit a lesser ship, it is advisable to continue the hunt for the battleship.

Having scored one or two hits on the battleship, place subsequent shots where the numbers show the battleship may be. Try to make each shot explore two or more possible lines. Sometimes it is possible to guess the orientation in which the opponent is likely to place his capital ship. The beginner usually chooses a diagonal, feeling that it is harder to find than a row or column.

BATTLESHIP FOR MORE THAN TWO PLAYERS

A good rainy-day pastime, Battleships can be played by as many as five or six players in a slightly varied version. The grid (see page 649) is expanded to 20 by 20 squares, numbered from 1 to 20 on the vertical sides and lettered from A to T on the horizontal sides. To facilitate use of the enlarged size, number both sides of the grid and letter both top and bottom. Only one diagram per player is required.

Because of the increased number of players, some simplification of the game is required. There are still four ships but they are slightly reduced in the number of squares each covers and in the number of shots each can fire. The battleship is four squares long, the cruiser three squares, the destroyer two squares, and a submarine one square. Each salvo is limited to four shots—one per ship—and, as before, the loss of a ship reduces the number of shots available.

The game begins with the first player, decided by chance, calling off his four shots by giving references to the column and row coordinates, as E-8, H-2, etc. Each player then writes the number 1, for first salvo, in each of the four called squares. When the next player "fires his salvo," his four shots are recorded by all in the designated squares as number 2, and so on. The game may require 30 to 40 salvos before a winner is determined, therefore accuracy in recording the correct round number in the proper coordinates is essential.

As in the two-player version, an opponent whose ship has been hit in a salvo must report that hit (or hits), and the type of ship struck, but does not divulge its location.

To keep a record of the hits scored on the opponents' fleet, construct for each player a small diagram of squares similar to that found beneath the "Opponent's Zone" in the diagram on page 649—four squares for the battleship, etc., down to one square for the submarine. When a hit is reported, place the number of the round (2, 3, 4, etc.) in the appropriate player's diagram, under battleship, cruiser, etc.

Once a hit has been announced, the strategy is to concentrate subsequent salvos in surrounding squares. For example, if a hit was recorded in round 15, place your shots in squares surrounding those numbered 15. By luck or a process of elimination, the hit ship will be located and sunk.

The winner is the one who still has a vessel afloat after all those of his opponents have been sunk.

Charades

The game is best with six or more players, and the sides do not have to be evenly matched. Two players are chosen captain, and the remaining players are divided into two teams as evenly as possible. The object of the game is to communicate a word or phrase solely through the use of gestures.

In different parts of the room, or in different rooms, the two teams draft a word or phrase, which is written on a piece of paper for each member of the opposing team. The paper will be given to the opposing team member when it is his turn.

After the teams have reassembled, each player tries to get his teammates to say the word or phrase he has been assigned in the shortest possible time. He may not utter any sound or use any physical props, although he may point to a person, object, place, etc. He may use any actions or gestures that seem appropriate, but may not form letters or words by mouthing them or with his hands.

Teams alternate. A time limit (usually five minutes) is established for each round, and each player's turn is timed. After all the members of the team have played, the total of the times for each team are added and the team that used the least amount of time is the winner. If the teams are unbalanced, say four against three, the number of rounds is limited to the number of players on the smaller team.

To guess the word or phrase a player is trying to convey, teammates should talk and ask questions, and the player may "answer" with appropriate gestures—such as a nod—when part of a phrase is uncovered.

Running Charades is an increasingly popular form of this game. One player drafts a list of five to seven words or phrases, all with a common theme. He stands equidistant between the two teams, who should be in different rooms, and does not take part in the game. To start the game, a member of each team reads the first item on the captain's list, then runs to his teammates and tries to act it out. Whoever guesses the word or phrase runs to the captain for the next item. Play continues until all items on the captain's list have been guessed, and the team that does so first is the winner.

Password

Password may be played by any number of players, but only four should play at a time. There are two partnerships, each partner facing the other. One player and his adjacent opponent agree secretly on a common word. They will become the *pitchers*. One player now gives a clue to his respective partner, who attempts to guess the secret word. The clue may be only one word and may be a proper noun. It may not contain any part of the secret word or rhyme with the secret word. The first clue given must be a synonym or definition of the secret word, but there is no restriction for later clues.

If the first partner does not guess the secret word, the other pitcher gives *his* partner a clue, usually a different one. Play continues until the secret word is guessed. For guessing the word on the first round, the partnership scores 10 points; on the second round, 9 points, and on down to 1 point. If the word is not guessed after five clues are given by each side, there is no score for that round and the secret word is revealed. The team that guesses the word gives the first clue for the next round. Generally partners alternate in giving clues and trying to guess the secret word. Whichever partnership accumulates 21 points wins the game.

No gestures, intonations, or histrionics are allowed. In the popular television game show of the same name there are fewer restrictions on permissible clues or how they are given. The televised Password also differs in that only one partnership plays at a time, and they try to guess a series of seven secret words, one at a time, over the course of one minute.

APPENDIX

APPENDIX

General Procedure of Card Games

AT THE ANNOUNCEMENT of a game of cards, these questions have to be settled: Where shall each player sit? Who shall deal first?

In a family game, or an informal party, these questions can most simply be settled arbitrarily by the head of the household or by the host. In club and formal games an impartial method is necessary, and the method of *drawing cards* has been established in almost all games by long usage.

DRAWING CARDS

The pack of cards is shuffled by any volunteer, and is then spread face down on the table as shown in the illustration. Each player draws one card at random. The draw should not be made from any of the cards at either extreme end of the pack—most games have a rule that the two, three, or four cards at each end must be left untouched. The reason for the rule is that the end cards are the ones most likely to have been exposed inadvertently during shuffling.

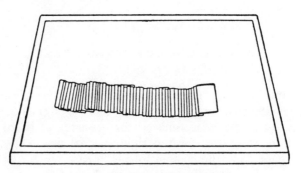

The Pack Spread for Drawing Cards

The drawn cards are turned face up. In club etiquette, no player should show his card until all participants have drawn, but elsewhere this nicety is not important.

The rank of the drawn cards fixes the order of precedence among the players. The cards rank (except in a few games where the rules provide otherwise) just as they do in the game. The highest card gives the drawer the right to choose his seat and to deal first.

If the game is "round"—if there are no partnerships but each plays for himself—the remaining players take places in order to the left of the first dealer. That is, the second-highest card shows who sits at the dealer's left, the third-highest sits at *his* left, and so on. But in many circles this ceremony is omitted; after the dealer takes his seat, the others take places at random.

If the game is played in partnerships, the draw fixes the partnerships unless that has previously been arranged by agreement. In a four-hand partnership game, the two drawing the highest cards play as partners against the other two. Partners sit opposite each other. Thus, if we designate the four sides of the table by compass points, two partners sit North and South, the other two East and West. Some games for six or eight are played in two partnerships of three or four each. In this case, the players of one side sit alternately with their opponents around the table, as A B A B A B.

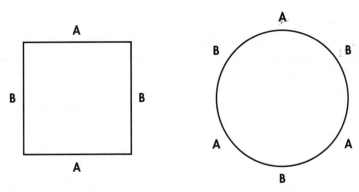

Partnerships in Four-hand and Six-hand Games

If the game provides a ranking of suits as well as of cards in a suit, there can be no ties in drawing. But where there is no rank of suits, players who draw cards of the same rank tie for precedence. If the tie must be broken (as it must if it is for the right to deal first), all tying players must draw again. It is the custom in such a case not to gather the pack and shuffle it again, but to leave it spread, discard the first cards drawn, and draw additional cards.

Drawing cards for places and deal has long been called *cutting*, but this traditional term is best abandoned as it causes confusion with the practice of *cutting the pack*.

Alternative Methods. In many round games it is the custom for all players to take places at random. Only the right to deal first has to be decided. Any volunteer shuffles the pack, then deals cards one at a time face up in rotation to his left, and the first jack that is dealt marks the first dealer. This method is preferred in Poker, Blackjack, and with tables of more than four players generally.

In Europe a third method is used in certain three- and four-hand games. From the pack are first selected a number of cards paired by rank (or suits)—one pair for each player in the game. One card of each pair is laid face up in front of some seat at the table. The remaining cards are shuffled by the volunteer behind his back, then presented face down in a fan. Each other player draws one card at random, the volunteer thus taking the card that is left. Then each player sits at the position with which his card pairs. By advance agreement, one position at the table is fixed as marking the first dealer.

SHUFFLING

After the first dealer is determined, the pack is gathered and shuffled again. It is the duty of the dealer to gather the cards, and by tradition in most games it is his right to *shuffle last*. Most of the time, he is the only one who shuffles. But, as a matter of common law which no special rules for any game can abrogate, every player at the table has the right to shuffle. The exercise of this privilege does not necessarily imply a doubt of the dealer's honesty; if a player suspects that the game is not "on the level," his only safe course is to quit it.

Of several types of shuffle, by far the most efficacious is the *riffle*. This is not only becoming standard for most games but is the only method permitted in most clubs.

How to Riffle Shuffle. Cut the pack into two approximately equal parts, and place them on the table end to end. With the thumbs, raise the touching corners of the two packets, and *riffle* them—that is, release cards one by one (so far as possible) from the bottom so that they spring back toward the table. Interlace the two packets at their corners in so doing. Finally, push the two packets into each other by pushing from the outer sides.

Six or seven reasonably good riffle shuffles suffice to mix the cards well.

CUTTING

After making the final shuffle, the dealer places the pack face down on the table toward his right. It is *cut* by the player at his right. Cutting consists in lifting off a packet from the top and placing it beside the remaining packet. The cut is then closed by placing the former bottom packet on top.

In many games it is traditional for the player cutting the pack to close the cut. But in Bridge the dealer closes the cut, and this practice is gradually being adopted in other games.

The cut should be made toward the middle of the pack, not close to the top or bottom. The rules of many games state that each packet of the cut must comprise at least four cards (sometimes three).

DEALING

After the cut, the dealer picks up the pack and commences dealing. A right-handed player should hold the pack face down in his left hand, the hand being held palm up. Care must be exercised not to turn the palm toward the body—a more restful position—because then the bottom card of the pack may be exposed to view. Nor should the pack be held below the level of the table, in order to screen it from possible exposure. All operations—shuffling, cutting, dealing—must be performed above or on the table, in full view.

Cards to be dealt are slipped off the top of the pack by the right hand. A practiced dealer pushes each card sideward with the left thumb and seizes the projecting edge with right thumb and forefinger or middle finger. There is less danger of exposing a card inadvertently if the corners are seized at the corner farthest from the body, instead of at the near corner.

If more than one card is dealt at a time to a player (as in many games), they should not be detached singly from the pack. The dealer should count off the required numbers of cards from the top of the pack, pushing them one by one with the left thumb and pulling them aside by the fingers of the right hand below, then place the complete packet before the player. But in later drawing from the stock, as in Draw Poker, it is preferable to deal cards singly as a precaution against giving the wrong number.

THE ROTATION

The *rotation* is the direction in which cards are dealt, bids are made, cards are played, and so on. Rotation *to the left* or *clockwise* has become customary for all games throughout the English-speaking world. Formerly, rotation to the right was customary in some games of European origin, but there is no reason for perpetuating this custom. Players who are accustomed to the clockwise rotation should use it in all games.

Eldest hand, the age, the edge, senior, major are various terms all meaning the first player to receive cards in dealing. With leftward rotation, eldest hand is the player who sits at the dealer's left. The first card goes to him in dealing, and the cards continue to be distributed to players in the same direction. In most games, the last card or last packet of the deal therefore goes to the dealer.

The turn to bid or play likewise passes from player to player, leftward.

Eldest hand has the first turn to bid, if there is any bidding, unless the rule of a game stipulates otherwise (Bridge is one of the few exceptions).

MISDEALS

Law or custom provides in every game the number of cards to be dealt to each player, the number of cards to be dealt at a time, and so on. If the dealer departs from the prescribed procedure in any way, any other player may call a *misdeal* and require that there be a new deal. Usually it is an automatic misdeal if any card is exposed in dealing, or if any player finds he has received the wrong number of cards.

Except in a few games where the rules provide otherwise, following a misdeal there is a new deal by the same dealer. The cards are gathered together, shuffled again, and cut. It is a common law of card games that any player who has not looked at his hand may call a misdeal if either the shuffle or the cut was omitted.

No player should look at his hand until the deal is completed. This injunction is written into the rules of many games. The players should keep their elbows and hands off the table while dealing is in progress, so as to avoid striking and facing a card as it is dealt.

IRREGULARITIES

This book contains the rules for rectifying or penalizing all the common irregularities, such as misdeal, lead or play out of turn, revoke. But situations are bound to arise that are not covered by the rules. Even in Bridge, which has a very elaborate code prepared by committees authorized for this purpose, "the book" cannot answer every question.

When an irregularity is committed, and the players can find no specific rule covering it, they should agree upon a procedure in harmony with what rules do exist. Generally speaking, if an offender harms only his own interests, or does not affect the outcome in any way, any necessary correction should be made and play should continue without penalty. If an irregularity fouls the bidding or play, or gives undue information to a partner of the offender, or prevents the natural outcome of the deal from being easily determinable, the offender should be made to suffer, as by losing the hand or game at once, being barred from the bidding, being made to pay antes for all, going *bete*—whatever is the standard penalty in the particular game for offenses of like gravity.

A player so penalized should accept the verdict of the other players without argument, for nothing so destroys the pleasure of games as poor sportsmanship.

SCORING AND SETTLEMENT

As most card games are played, more than one deal is required to complete a *game* in the narrow sense—the fixed minimum of points that one player or one side must amass to be deemed "the winner." A running total of points earned has to be kept. The three common methods of keeping score are: (a) By pencil and paper; (b) by special counting devices; (c) by chips or other tokens in place of money.

When the score is recorded on paper, vertical lines should first be drawn on the paper to make one column for each participant. Each score earned is entered in the appropriate column.

In most games, the score sheet must show each player's current total, so that all may know how near he is to *game*. In Rummy, Oh Hell, Eights, etc., the custom is for the scorekeeper to add mentally each new increment with the previous total and write only the new total. In Bridge and a few other games, there is no totalization until a game is won, since the points credited to a side toward game can be determined by the mental addition of a few items on the score sheet.

As to most partnership games, the rules give the scores to be credited to a partnership or *side*. If the partnerships are *set*, remaining unchanged throughout a session of play, then one column on the score sheet will suffice for each side. But if the partnerships change, as after every rubber in Bridge, and after every deal in Call-Ace Euchre, Skat, etc., individual accounts have to be kept. In this case, every item which by the rules should be credited to a side is entered *in full* in the column for each individual of that side. For example (Auction Cinch), Smith wins the bid at 11, calls the king of trumps, and Jones, who holds the king, becomes his partner; together they win 12 points, or 10 more than the opponents; Smith is credited individually with 10 points and so is Jones. To continue the example, the 2 points taken by the opponents both fall to Robinson; he alone scores 2, his temporary partners Brown and Green earning nothing. In Auction Cinch, Five Hundred, etc., certain items go to individuals, not to a partnership, and in each case the rules note this exception.

If in partnership play all items go to a side, and partnerships do not change often, as in Bridge, it is simpler to keep a column for each *side* rather than for each *individual*. A separate *ledger* (individual score, or "back score") sheet is set up, and the totals earned by each side are credited to each individual thereof on the ledger at the time the partnerships change.

In Bridge, etc., the individual scores are plus or minus, the algebraic sum of all scores being zero. This system facilitates final settlement. The players with final minus scores pay out and those with plus scores collect.

In Skat, Auction Pinochle, etc., although scores may be either plus or minus, their sum is not necessarily zero and extra computation is necessary to determine the settlement. Here the rule is that each player pays or collects according as his final score is above or below the *average of all final scores*. For example, here is the computation on the final scores of a session of Skat:

	FINAL		SETTLEMENT
Smith	42	60	− 3
Jones	91	109	46
Robinson	−18	0	−63
Brown	65	83	20

4)252

average 63

If any score is minus, eliminate the minus signs by adding the amount of the largest minus algebraically to all scores. (This step can be omitted by persons who are not frightened by minus signs.) Total the increased scores, and divide the total by the number of players to determine the average. Determine the amount by which each increased score falls above or below the average. The minuses then pay out and the pluses collect. (When the average has a fractional remainder, it is dropped and the small discrepancy in the net scores is settled in favor of the largest loser.)

Special scoring devices are used for special circumstances. In certain other rapid-scoring games, as Bezique, the use of chips is most convenient. Each player draws chips from a common pool, until he has amassed the number necessary for *game*. Or the process may be reversed: each player is given the *game* number of chips, and returns a suitable number to the pool for ease increment in his score, thus winning when he gets rid of his last chip.

But the commoner use of chips is for scoring where the play is continuous without any division into *games*, as Poker, or where the custom is to make settlement after every deal, as coffeehouse Skat. There are two common methods of using chips. (a) Equal numbers of chips are distributed to all players at the outset, and final settlement is made on the number of chips the player has left when the game ends, above or below his original stack. He pays for any deficiency or collects for any excess. (b) In banking games particularly, each player purchases whatever amount he wishes in chips and uses them as token money. Whenever the player withdraws, the bank redeems his remaining chips in currency.

The Calculation of Chances

A writer on games is frequently asked such questions as: "What are the odds against rolling a 9 or a 7 in two rolls? (Craps.)" "What is the bank's percentage or edge in Chuck-Luck?" "What are the chances of finding one of three cards in the widow? (Pinochle or any of several other games.)"

The following pages were prepared for players who encounter such problems and wish to find the solutions themselves.

Anyone who understands common fractions can follow the explanation given. A warning is necessary, however: Do not attempt to apply any of the formulas or principles given until you have read the entire section and have grasped exactly the meaning of every statement. In other words, do not merely *read* this section: *study* it sentence by sentence.

Arithmetical errors are easy to make in dealing with the large numbers usually involved. Before relying on any conclusion, check the accuracy of your work by performing the computations two or three times. Better still, devise an alternative method of attack and see if it gives the same answer as the first.

ODDS AND CHANCES

When we say that the *odds* are 5 to 1 against rolling a seven with two dice, we mean that for every combination of numbers that total seven there are five others that do not. Another way of saying the same thing is that the chance of rolling seven is one out of six, or ⅙. This way of expressing a chance or probability is the more convenient for computation by addition, multiplication, and so on.

THE MEASURE OF PROBABILITY

It is convenient to let unity (1) represent certainty and zero (0) represent impossibility. Then every probability less than certainty is measured by a common fraction, greater than 0 and less than 1.

THE PREMISE

A die has six faces, numbered from 1 to 6. When the die is rolled, one face and only one must come uppermost. In the absence of knowledge to the contrary, we assume that each face has the same chance as any other to come up. The sum of the separate chances must be 1, since it is certain that some face will come up; consequently, we say that the chance for any one face is ⅙.

This is an *assumption*. We cannot prove it. We may be confident the die was manufactured by a reputable firm, has not been tampered with, and measures true within the limits of tolerance. But this does not prove that there is no factor favoring the six-face, for example, over the four-face. All that we can say is that, knowing of no such factor, we assume it does not exist.

From this assumption or *premise* we deduce a great many facts about dice chances. These are *facts* in the sense that they follow with mathematical certitude from the premise. But it must never be forgotten that the formal mathematical rules are purely deductive. They enable us to infer one probability to another, but at some point the whole chain of inferences rests upon a pure assumption.

The *premise* is rarely stated in making an assertion about chances. In many cases the premise has been established by general agreement, or would be conceded as valid if expressly stated. But in commencing any computation of probability, it is wise to scrutinize the premise and be sure that the calculation is correctly related to it; absurd mistakes are sometimes made through omission of this precaution.

THE PROPER SET

In most problems of chance relating to games, we generate the premise in exactly the same way as for the cast of a single die.

What is the chance that a given event will occur? We make a list of all possible events that may occur, and if we know of no reason why one is more likely than another, we assume that all are equally likely. If the total in the list is n, the probability for each separate even is $1/n$.

Such a list is what we may call a *proper set* if it is both *exhaustive* and *mutually-exclusive*. That is, we must be sure to list all possibilities, and each event must be so defined that its occurrence excludes the occurrence of any other in the list.

PROBLEM. What is the chance that North-South will win the rubber at Bridge, if they have won the first game?

As the problem states nothing about the relative skill of the partnerships, we have to assume that each side has ½ chance to win each game.

A solution sometimes offered goes like this: If North-South win the second game, they win the rubber at once. If they lose the second but win the third, they likewise win the rubber. They lose the rubber only if East-West win both following games. In two cases out of three, North-South win the rubber. Therefore their chance after the first game is ⅔.

This answer is incorrect. It is based on an improper set.

A proper set must list all the ways in which the next two games can be won, thus:

2nd game	3rd game
N-S	N-S
N-S	E-W
E-W	N-S
E-W	E-W

One of these results must come about, and under the premise all are equally probable. In the first three cases, North-South win the rubber. Their chance after the first game is therefore ¾.

The fact that the third game is not played if North-South win the second does not affect the probability.

COMPOUND PROBABILITIES

PROBLEM. What is the chance of rolling either an ace or a deuce with a die?

The chance for the ace is ⅙, likewise for the deuce. Since either roll is satisfactory, the chance of a satisfactory outcome is

$$⅙ + ⅙ = ⅓$$

PROBLEM. I have a table of the relative chances of poker hands. How do I compute the chance that the next hand I am dealt will be no better than two pairs?

From the table (page 39) it can be found that the approximate chance for two pairs is .021; for one pair, .048; for no pair, .424. The desired probability is the sum of these numbers, or .493.

To generalize: The probability that *some one* of several independent events A, B, C . . . will occur is the sum of their separate probabilities.

prob. (A or B or C . . .) = prob. A + prob. B + prob. C . . . (provided that A, B, C . . . are members of a proper set).

CONCURRENT PROBABILITIES

PROBLEM. What is the chance of casting two aces in succession with a die?

The chance for an ace at each roll is ⅙. The chance that both rolls will be aces is

$$⅙ × ⅙ = 1/36$$

To generalize: The probability that *all* of several independent events will occur is the product of their separate probabilities.

prob. (A and B and C . . .) = prob. A × prob. B × prob. C . . . (regardless of whether A, B, C . . . are members of a proper set).

NEGATIVE PROBABILITIES

An event must either occur or not occur; the sum of the chances for the two cases must be 1. If the chance that it will occur is p, then the chance that it will not occur is $1-p$. Many problems are easiest solved by reference to the *negative* probability.

PROBLEM. What is the chance of rolling either an ace or a deuce in three casts of a die?

The chance of getting either number in one roll is 2/6 or ⅓. If we mistakenly apply the rule for compound probabilities, and say that the chance for getting either number in three rolls is ⅓ + ⅓ + ⅓ = 1, we reach the absurd conclusion that we are sure to roll ace or deuce within three trials.

The chance of *not* getting ace or deuce in one trial is ⅔. We can correctly apply the formula for concurrent probabilities and say that the chance of rolling *no* ace or deuce in three trials is

$$⅔ × ⅔ × ⅔ = 8/27$$

The chance of getting at least one satisfactory number is then

$$1 - \frac{8}{27} = \frac{19}{27}$$

THE CONSTITUTION OF INDEPENDENT EVENTS

PROBLEM. A Backgammon player needs a six to hit an adverse blot, which is not protected by any intervening obstructions. What is the chance of getting six (on one die or both together)?

Each die can turn up in 6 ways. Since the dice act independently (or so we assume), the two together can turn up in 6 × 6 combinations. One way to solve the problem is to write out all 36 combinations and count those that provide a six.

Combinations of two dice

1 and 1	2 and 1	3 and 1	4 and 1	5 and 1	6 and 1
1 and 2	2 and 2	3 and 2	4 and 2	5 and 2	6 and 2
1 and 3	2 and 3	3 and 3	4 and 3	5 and 3	6 and 3
1 and 4	2 and 4	3 and 4	4 and 4	5 and 4	6 and 4
1 and 5	2 and 5	3 and 5	4 and 5	5 and 5	6 and 5
1 and 6	2 and 6	3 and 6	4 and 6	5 and 6	6 and 6

It follows from the premise that each one of the 36 combinations is equally likely. They form a *proper set*.

There are 11 rolls with a six on one die. The numbers total six on 5 more rolls: 1–5, 2–4, 3–3, 4–2, 5–1. Finally, the roll 2–2 allows a move of six points, as doublets are taken twice over in Backgammon. The answer to the problem is then

$$(11 + 5 + 1)/36 = 17/36$$

In all the foregoing discussion of compound and concurrent probabilities, it is stipulated that the formulas apply to *independent events*. Error arises if they are applied directly to dependent events. Example: What is the chance of drawing two aces in succession from a pack of 52? The chance that the first card will be an ace is $\frac{4}{52}$. But the chance of getting two aces is not $\frac{4}{52} \times \frac{4}{52}$, because the chances for the second card are affected by the identity of the first.

Nevertheless, dependent events can be dealt with by the same general methods, if due care is taken to tabulate (or conceive) all possible combinations at the point where they are *mutually-exclusive*. There always is such a point. In other words, it is always possible to make a *proper set* of independent groups or sequences of events, even if the events within each group are interdependent.

PROBLEM. What is the chance of being dealt a natural (an ace and face card or ten) at Blackjack?

665

If we deal with each card separately, we have to consider *dependent* events, for the chances on the second card are affected by the identity of the first. But if we make (or conceive) a list of all possible combinations of two cards that may be drawn together from the pack, we have a proper set of independent events. We can then count up those combinations which are naturals.

Without giving the method of computation here, we will state that there are 1300 combinations in the list, of which 64 are naturals. The chance for a natural is then 64/1300 or 16/325.

Backgammon odds can mostly be determined from the table of combinations of two dice. But in many problems, as the Blackjack natural, we have to deal with many more combinations than we can conveniently write out. We have need for methods of computing the *number of combinations* in a conceived proper set. The following sections explain these methods.

PERMUTATIONS

By a permutation is meant a particular arrangement or order of a group of objects.

PROBLEM. In how many ways can an ace, two, three and four be laid in a row to commence a game of Calculation?

For the first card at the left end of the row we have a choice of four cards. Having made our selection, we have a choice of three remaining for the second card, then a choice of two remaining for the third. The total of permutations is evidently

$$4 \times 3 \times 2 \, (\times \, 1) = 24$$

THE FACTORIAL SYMBOL

Similarly the number of orders in which the 13 spades can be arranged in a row is $13 \times 12 \ldots \times 2 \times 1$. The number of arrangements of the complete pack is $52 \times 51 \ldots \times 2 \times 1$. The necessity for writing out such long chains of factors is avoided by using the factorial symbol (!). Thus 52! is read "fifty-two factorial" and means "the product of all integers from 1 up to 52."

Let us use the symbol Pn to mean "the number of permutations of n objects." Then

$$Pn = n!$$

COMBINATIONS

By a combination is meant a group of objects selected from a larger set, without regard to arrangement or order.

PROBLEM. How many fifteens can be counted at Cribbage out of three sevens and two eights?

Since any of the three sevens can be combined with either of the two eights, the answer is $3 \times 2 = 6$.

To generalize: If we must make combinations by selecting one member each from groups containing respectively p, q, r . . . objects, the total number of combinations is the product $p \times q \times r$ . . . .

PROBLEM. How many pairs can be counted at Cribbage in four queens?

For the first card of the pair, we can select one of four queens; for the second, one of the three remaining. However, the answer is not 4×3, as any Cribbage player knows. This computation counts separately the case where we first chose the queen of spades, then the queen of hearts, and the case where we took the queen of hearts, then the queen of spades. That is, it is a count of *permutations*, in which each *combination* is listed twice. The answer is therefore

$$\frac{4 \times 3}{2} = 6$$

To generalize: The number of *permutations* of r objects out of a set of n is

$$P_n^r = n\,(n-1)\,(n-2) \ldots \text{to } r \text{ terms} = \frac{n!}{(n-r)!}$$

The expression at the right is a convenient way of abbreviating what we mean. If the terms of numerator and denominator are actually written out, the denominator cancels all but the first r terms of the numerator.

We saw by the Cribbage problem that in this count of *permutations*, each *combination* is listed as many times as the members of any one combination can be permuted among themselves. This number is $r!$. Therefore the number of combinations of r objects out of a set of n is

$$C_n^r = P_n^r / r! = \frac{n!}{r!\,(n-r)!}$$

PROBLEM. How many different Poker hands can be dealt from a pack of 52 cards? (Hands are to be construed as different according to the identity of the cards, not according to the Poker value of the hands as a whole.)

According to the formula last given, the answer is

$$\frac{52!}{5!\,47!} = \frac{52 \times 51 \times 50 \times 49 \times 48 \times 47!}{5 \times 4 \times 3 \times 2 \times 1 \times 47!} =$$
$$\frac{52 \times 51 \times 50 \times 49 \times 48}{5 \times 4 \times 3 \times 2 \times 1} = 2{,}598{,}960$$

UNDIFFERENTIATED SUBGROUPS

PROBLEM. How many different integers can be represented by laying in a row six cards, of which three are treys, two are deuces, and one an ace?

Hitherto we have dealt with the cards as having separate identities—the deuce of spades is different from the ace of hearts. But in this problem we are concerned with the cards only as numbers; all deuces are alike.

The answer evidently is less than the full number of permutations of six cards, namely 6! = 720. To see how much less, consider any one arrangement, as 3–2–3–A–2–3, representing the integers 323, 123. This arrangement must have been counted in the 720 as many times as there are ways of permuting the three treys in their assigned positions, and the two deuces in their positions. The same is true of every other arrangement that makes a different integer. The number of different integers in the list of permutations must be

$$\frac{720}{3! \ 2! \ (1!)} = 60$$

To generalize: If a set n is made up of p objects of one kind, all identical, q objects of another kind, all identical, and so on, then the different permutations of n are

$$P_n^p + q + \ldots = n = \frac{n!}{p! \ q! \ \ldots}$$

PROBLEM. In how many different orders can the pack come out at Calculation?

Since suits are ignored at this solitaire, the answer is

$$\frac{52!}{(4!)^{13}}$$

PATTERNS

PROBLEM. How many different full houses can be made from the pack of 52? (The cards are to be differentiated by suits as well as rank.)

We have a choice of 13 ranks from which to select the triplet. Having fixed on the rank, we can choose the triplet in 4 ways. There are 13 × 4 = 52 possibilities for the triplet.

Having selected the triplet, we have 12 ranks remaining from which to choose the pair, and 6 ways of selecting the particular cards from the four of that rank. The factor for the pair is 12 × 6 = 72.

For the combination of triplet and pair, we have 52 × 72 = 3,744, the number of different full houses.

To solve this problem, we first set up a *pattern:* triplet and pair, or 3–2. Then we computed the number of different ways each item of the pattern could be satisfied. The final answer was the product of the numbers determined for each item.

The interpolation of a *pattern* is necessary in solving many problems, as in virtually all involving cards and other large "sets." The utmost care must be exercised to relate the *pattern* correctly to the complete *set*.

PROBLEM. What are the relative chances of being dealt a hand of 5–4–2–2 pattern or 5–4–3–1 pattern at Bridge? (Each integer denotes the number of cards in one suit.)

The absolute number of hands of 5–4–2–2 pattern is the product of the number of ways of selecting five cards from one suit, four from another, and so on. But we do not need to compute this absolute number. We are interested only in the ratio between the two types of hands, and in this ratio the factors for the blocks of five and four cards will cancel out. We need compute only the factors for the blocks of 2–2 and 3–1.

By formula, the factors for the 2–2 blocks are

$$\frac{13!}{2!\ 11!} \times \frac{13!}{2!\ 11!}$$

For the 3–1 combination we have

$$\frac{13!}{3!\ 10!} \times 13$$

The ratio between the two products (quickly determinable by cancellation) is 18:11 in favor of the 5–4–2–2 pattern. Is this the answer to the problem? No, indeed! although it has sometimes been proposed.

The premise of the calculation is that any of the 52!/13! 39! possible hands of 13 cards is as likely to be dealt as any other. This count duly treats each card as an individual, regardless of the similarity of its face to certain other cards. The foregoing computation has ignored the suits.

To the computation for each pattern must be attached a factor for the number of different ways in which suit-names can be affixed to the items of the pattern. For, regardless of the rank of the cards, a hand of five spades, four hearts, two diamonds and two clubs is different from a hand of five clubs, four diamonds, two spades and two hearts.

With the 5–4–3–2 pattern, we can choose the block of five cards from any of four suits, and the block of four from any of three suits remaining. After that there is no choice. The factor for suit-names is $4 \times 3 = 12$.

For the 5–4–3–1 pattern, since all the items are different, the factor is $4 \times 3 \times 2 \times 1 = 24$.

The ratio between these factors for the suit-names is 2:1 in favor of the 5–4–3–1 pattern. When this ratio is compounded with the previous figures, we find that the 5–4–3–1 pattern is more likely by 22:18 or 11:9.

PROBLEM. How many different Poker hands of two pairs can be dealt from the pack of 52?

The pattern as to ranks is 2–2–1. For the choice of the rank of the pairs we can select 2 out of 13 ranks in $\frac{13}{2!\ 11!} = 78$ different ways. Having fixed the ranks, we can select each pair out of four cards in 6 ways. For the odd card, we can take any of the 44 cards not of the same rank as either pair. The answer is

$$78 \times 6 \times 6 \times 44 = 123{,}552$$

PROBLEM. What are the odds on rolling each possible total from 3 to 18 with three dice?

Instead of writing out all 6 × 6 × 6 = 216 combinations, let us write out the *patterns* of rolls that sum to 3, 4, and so on. The patterns will be of three types: (a) all three integers different; (b) two integers alike; (c) all three integers alike. Each pattern (a) will represent 6 actual combinations, each (b) will represent 3, and each (c) only one.

We must be sure not to omit any pattern from the list; therefore we follow an orderly plan of writing the highest possible number at each step.

PATTERNS FOR THREE DICE

Total of 3	COMBINATIONS	SUBTOTAL
1–1–1	1	1
Total of 4		
2–1–1	3	3
Total of 5		
3–1–1	3	
2–2–1	3	6
Total of 6		
4–1–1	3	
3–2–1	6	
2–2–2	1	10
Total of 7		
5–1–1	3	
4–2–1	6	
3–3–1	3	
3–2–2	3	15
Total of 8		
6–1–1	3	
5–2–1	6	
4–3–1	6	
4–2–2	3	
3–3–2	3	21
Total of 9		
6–2–1	6	
5–3–1	6	
5–2–2	3	
4–4–1	3	
4–3–2	6	
3–3–3	1	25
Total of 10		
6–3–1	6	
6–2–2	3	
5–4–1	6	
5–3–2	6	
4–4–2	3	
4–3–3	3	27

This is as far as we need go. The last eight totals, 11 to 18, generate the same figures as the first eight, 3 to 10, in reverse order (we leave the verification to the reader). To summarize:

Total of three dice	Combinations
3	1
4	3
5	6
6	10
7	15
8	21
9	25
10	27
11	27
12	25
13	21
14	15
15	10
16	6
17	3
18	1
	216

The chance for any given total to be rolled is the number of combinations over the denominator 216.

"PERCENTAGE"

When a Bank Craps house gives odds of 30 to 1 against the roll of double ace, the actual odds against this event being 35 to 1, it reserves to itself a "percentage." This term is widely-used to denote the "edge" or advantage gained by gamers in laying shorter odds than are theoretically correct. It is a matter of common knowledge that "the percentage" is dependable enough to enable a very large number of gambling establishments to do profitable business without resort to any cheating whatsoever. But many persons, including professional gamblers, are hazy as to how to determine the exact amount of the percentage.

There are in fact two different definitions of percentage, one which proceeds from common sense with the endorsement of mathematicians, and one that is used by gambling houses.

The common-sense definition is: That percentage of a bettor's money which the house expects to win through the discrepancy in odds alone.

Take the case of the double-ace roll. If, 36 times in succession, a bettor wagers one dollar that this roll will be made, and if the abstract probability is exactly fulfilled, he will lose 35 times and win once. The fair odds he should receive are 35 to 1, so that on the one occasion he wins he will exactly regain the $35 he has lost. If he gets odds of only 30 to 1, he wins

$30 while losing $35. The house wins $5 of each $36 that he risks. The percentage to the house is 5/36 or 13.88 . . .

The house, however, defines its percentage as: The amount we can expect to win out of all the money put up. It argues: The bettor put up $36, and we had to cover it (at 30 to 1) with $1,080. Our net profit on the transaction is $5. Therefore our percentage is 5/1116, about 1/10 of 1%.

It must be conceded that there is more reason in this way of figuring percentage than the desire to minimize the apparent edge of the house over the patron. The house has to consider how much capital it has to have to cover the bets and so win anything at all. The *percentage of return on its investment* is actually only 5/1080. The "action"—the amount risked by the bettor—is thrown into the equation no doubt because the house figures that it has to make further capital investment in order to get any action at all.

GLOSSARY

above the line *Bridge.* The place on the scoresheet where premiums are scored.

ace The one-spot in a pack; the one-spot on a die; one dollar.

acey-deucey *Backgammon.* The roll of 2–1 with two dice.

A cheval Placing a bet on a line of a banking layout, so as to bet on both sides at once.

action Betting; opportunity to bet.

Ada from Decatur *Craps.* The roll of 8.

adversary Any opponent; one playing against the highest bidder.

advertise *Poker.* Make a bluff intended to be exposed.

African dominoes Dice.

against *Skat.* WITHOUT.

age 1. ELDEST HAND. 2. *Poker.* The right to bet last after the draw.

alone *Euchre family.* A bid to play without help of partner.

alternate straight SKIP STRAIGHT.

American leads *Whist.* A system of leading to show the number of cards in the suit led.

Ames ace *Dice.* The roll of two aces; also, *Ambsace.*

anchor In pivot or progressive play, one who retains his seat throughout the contest.

angle A situation favorable to a bet.

announce 1. Name the trump suit. 2. Show melds. 3. Predict schneider or schwarz.

announced bet MOUTH BET.

ante 1. A bet made before the deal or before drawing cards. 2. Contribution to a pot which, at the start, belongs equally to all players.

approach bid *Bridge.* One made for information of partner rather than with intention to play the named declaration.

après *Trente et Quarante.* Dealer's announcement that bets are off because of a refait (tie).

ask 1. *Whist.* Signal partner to lead trumps. 2. *Skat family.* Inquiry by eldest hand whether the next hand wishes to compete in the bidding.

assist 1. *Euchre.* Order partner to take up trump. 2. *Bridge.* RAISE (2).

auction The period of the bidding.

authorized opponent *Bridge.* One solely entitled to assess a penalty.

available card *Solitaire.* One which may be transferred elsewhere in the layout.

Avondale schedule The recommended table for scoring Five Hundred.

backer 1. Non-player who finances an active player. 2. Banker.

back door *Bézique.* A sequence in a plain suit.

back game *Backgammon.* The strategy of not advancing runners early, but of using them to catch adverse blots when opponent is well advanced.

backgammon *Backgammon.* The winning of a game when the loser has one or more stones on the bar or in the adverse home table.

back in *Poker.* Come into the betting after checking.

back to back *Stud Poker.* Said of the hole card and first upcard when they are a pair.

bait BÊTE.

balking cards *Cribbage.* Cards selected by non-dealer to be laid away to the crib, which have the least chance of making scores.

banco *Chemin-de-fer.* A bet equal to the entire bank.

bank Gambling house; dealer in a gambling game.

banker 1. Dealer against whom all others bet. 2. The player who keeps, sells and accounts for the chips.

bar *Backgammon.* The division between the inner and outer tables.

barred 1. Estopped from bidding by a legal penalty. 2. Not permitted, as a move in checkers. 3. Not counted, as a roll in craps.

bar-point *Backgammon.* The 7-point, that in the outer table adjacent to the bar.

base value *Skat.* A constant factor in computing the value of each game or declaration.

Basto, or Basta The queen of spades.

bate BÊTE.

Bath Coup *Whist family.* The holdup of the master card to preserve a tenace.

bear off *Backgammon.* Remove stones from the home board in the last stage of a game.

beg *All Fours.* A proposal by eldest hand to dealer that three additional cards be dealt to each hand and that a new card be turned up for trump.

below the line *Bridge.* The place on the scoresheet where the trickscore is entered.

-best (as *third-best*) Ranking in the ordinal position specified, among the cards dealt or remaining unplayed.

best card Highest card of a suit remaining unplayed; master card.

bet Any wager on the outcome of play or of a game, such as that the bettor holds the winning hand.

bet blind Bet without looking at the hand.

bête (pronounced bate) 1. Beaten; having failed to make contract. 2. A forfeit paid by a loser or by a transgressor of a rule of correct procedure.

bet the pot Bet as many chips as there are in the pot at the moment.

bézique *Bézique.* The queen of spades and jack of diamonds.

bid An offer to win a certain number of tricks or points in play; to make a bid.

biddable suit *Bridge.* A player's holding in a suit that meets the systemic requirements for a bid.

bidder 1. Any player who makes a bid. 2. The player who makes the highest bid and assumes the contract.

bidding The auction; the period during which bids are made; competing in the auction.

bid over OVERCALL.

Big Casino The ten of diamonds.

Big Cat BIG TIGER.

Big Dick *Craps.* The roll of 10.

Big Dog *Poker.* A hand consisting of ace-high and nine-low but no pair.

Big 8 *Craps.* A bet that neither 8 nor 7 will be cast in the next two rolls; often, erroneously, a bet that 8 will be cast before 7.

Big 6 *Craps.* A bet that neither 6 nor 7 will be cast in the next two rolls; often, erroneously, a bet that 6 will be cast before 7.

Big Tiger *Poker.* A hand consisting of king-high and eight-low but no pair.

bishop *Chess.* One of the pieces, which moves only on the diagonals. French, fou. German, Laufer.

Blackwood Convention *Contract Bridge.* A system of cue-bidding to reach slams, invented by Easley Blackwood.

blank a suit Discard all cards held in that suit.

blank suit Absence of any cards of that suit from the hand.

blaze *Poker.* A hand composed entirely of face cards.

blind 1. A compulsory bet or ante made before the cards are dealt. 2. WIDOW.

blind lead One made before certain cards are disclosed.

blitz *Gin Rummy.* SHUTOUT.

block A situation in which the player in turn is unable to play, or no player is able to play.

blocking a suit So playing that a partner with the longer of two partnership holdings in a suit cannot keep the lead in that suit.

blot *Backgammon.* A single stone on a point.

Blue Peter *Whist.* A signal asking partner to lead trumps.

bluff *Poker.* A bet on a hand that the player actually does not believe is the best.

bobtail *Poker.* A FOUR-FLUSH or DOUBLE-ENDED STRAIGHT.

bold stand *Loo.* A deal in which the pool contains only the dealer's ante and all must play. Also called a *single.*

bones Dice; dominoes.

boneyard *Dominoes.* The reserve of dominoes from which a player must draw when unable to play from his hand.

booby prize Prize for lowest score.

booby table In progressive play, the table of highest number, to which losers move from table No. 1.

boodle card *Stops family.* Extra cards placed in a layout on which bets are laid.

book *Whist family.* The number of tricks a side must win before it can score by winning subsequent tricks; usually, six tricks.

boost 1. Bet high. 2. RAISE.

borderline bid *Bridge.* A bid on a hand that barely meets the systemic requirements.

bower The jack of a suit. See LEFT BOWER, RIGHT BOWER.

box 1. A device from which cards may be dealt one by one. 2 *Gin Rummy.* One DEAL (2); the score for winning a deal.

boxcars *Craps.* The roll of two sixes.

box numbers *Craps.* Numbered spaces on the layout where bets may be placed on any given number to be cast before a 7.

bracket In any knockout tournament, a group of two, four, eight, etc., contestants scheduled together for a series of elimination matches.

break even *Faro.* Bet on a card equal numbers of times to win and lose.

breaks 1. Luck. 2. Distribution of the adverse cards between the two hands.

breathe *Poker.* CHECK.

brelan *Bézique.* Three of a kind.

brelan carré *Bézique.* Four of a kind.

bridge *Euchre.* Score of four when opponents have not more than 2.

bring in a suit *Whist family.* CLEAR and CASH a suit.

brisque *Bézique.* Any ace or ten.

Bube German. The jack of a suit.

buck *Poker.* A token used as a reminder of the order of precedence in dealing, exercising any privilege or duty, etc.

buck the tiger *Faro.* Play against the bank.

bug *Poker.* The joker, when it may be used only as an ace or as a wild card in filling a flush or straight.

build 1. *Casino.* Combine two or more cards to be taken in later. 2. *Solitaire.* Transfer cards among the tableau cards and foundations.

builder *Backgammon.* A stone in the outer table, especially when brought down from the adverse 12-point.

bull Ace.

bumblepuppy *Whist.* Inferior play, especially in defiance of partnership systems.

bumper *Whist.* A rubber won by two games to none.

bunch 1. Gather cards preparatory to shuffling. 2. *Auction Pitch.* An offer by dealer to play the hand at a bid of two or abandon the deal.

burn a card Expose and bury it, or place it on the bottom of the pack.

bury a card 1. Place it in the middle of the pack or among the discards so that it cannot be readily located. 2. *Pinochle.* Discard it, after taking the widow.

business double *Bridge.* One made for the purpose of exacting increased penalties.

bust 1. A hand devoid of trick-taking possibilities. 2. *Twenty-One.* Draw cards totalling more than 21. 3. *Oh Hell.* Win more or less tricks than the bid.

buy Draw from the widow or stock; cards so received.

by cards *Bridge.* ODD TRICKS.

by me A declaration meaning "Pass."

call 1. Declare; bid or pass. *Bridge.* Any pass, double, redouble or bid. 2. *Poker.* Make a bet exactly equal to the last previous bet. 3. Make legal demand for a card held by another player, as in Callace Euchre, Calabrasella, Authors.

capot *Piquet.* Winning of all the tricks by one player; the score therefor.

capped pawn *Chess.* A marked pawn with which a player engages to deliver checkmate, in giving extreme odds to a weaker opponent.

captain One who has final decisions in a team, as in CHOUETTE play or in certain partnership bidding systems.

capture Remove adverse pieces from the board, as in Chess, Checkers.

cards *Casino.* The score of 3 for winning a majority of the cards.

Carolina *Dice.* The roll of 9. Also *Nina-from Carolina.*

carré Of four parts.

carreau French, the diamond suit.

carte French, card; player's request for an additional card, as in Baccarat.

carte blanche A hand without a face card.

case card The last card of a rank remaining in play.

case-keeper *Faro.* A form for recording the cards as taken from the box; one who so records.

cash Lead and win tricks with established cards.

cash points *Casino.* The scores for big and little casino and aces.

caster One who rolls dice.

castle *Chess.* ROOK; see also CASTLING.

castling *Chess.* A certain compound move of king and rook.

cat See BIG TIGER, LITTLE TIGER.

catch Find valuable cards in the widow or draw from the stock.

cat-hop *Faro.* Two cards of the same rank among the last three.

center 1. *Solitaire.* The foundation piles. 2. *Chess.* The squares d4, d5, e4, e5. 3. *Craps.* Place where bets between the caster and faders are placed.

center bet *Dice.* A bet between the caster and the faders.

challenge *Auction Bridge.* A call proposed to be substituted for "double" when the intent is informatory, but never incorporated in the laws.

check 1. Counter; chip. 2. *Poker.* A nominal bet; usually one which does not require that any chip be put in the pot. 3. *Chess.* Attack the adverse king.

checker Draughtsman; a disk used in many board games.

checkmate *Chess.* Capture of the adverse king, the object of play. Also *mate.*

Chicago pelter KILTER.

chicane Void of trumps.

Chico *Frog.* A game in which hearts are not trumps.

chip A token used in place of money; place chips in the pot.

chip along Stay without raising; make the smallest possible bet.

chiseler One who tries to obtain undue odds in betting.

chouette The participation, by betting interest and right to give advice, of three or more players in a two-hand game.

chow *Mah Jongg.* A meld of a sequence.

cinch *Cinch.* Play a trump higher than the five, to prevent an opponent from winning with a pedro.

cinch hand One that is sure to win.

clear *Hearts.* Having taken in tricks no counting cards.

clear a suit Drive out all adverse cards that can win tricks in the suit.

close 1. *Whiskey Poker.* A call limiting each other player to one more turn, after which there is a showdown. 2. *Sixty-six.* End the period in which cards may be drawn from the stock.

close a board *Backgammon.* Establish a SHUT-OUT.

close cards *Cribbage.* Cards near in rank, as 7 and 9.

clubs The suit denoted by the symbol ♣. French, trèfle, treff. German, Eicheln, Eckern.

club stakes The limitations of betting and rate per point that apply to play in a club, in the absence of any special agreement among the players.

cocked dice Dice which, on being cast, do not each land with one face horizontally level.

cock-eyes *Dice.* The roll of 3.

coeur French, the heart suit.

coffee housing Attempting to mislead opponents as to one's cards by speech and manner.

cold hands *Poker.* Hands dealt face up, as for the determination of the winner of extra chips in dividing the pot.

color Suit; a suit that scores higher than others as trump, as in Solo.

column *Solitaire*. A line of cards extending away from the player.

come bet *Craps*. A bet that the dice will win, treating the next roll as the first of a series.

come in Enter the betting.

come-on *Bridge*. A signal to partner to continue leading a suit; ECHO.

come-out *Craps*. The caster's first roll, which fixes his POINT or loses at once.

comet *Stops*. A wild card, sometimes the nine of diamonds.

comfort station *Backgammon*. The adverse 12-point.

command The best card of a suit; master card; control.

compass game *Duplicate play*. A tournament comprising separate contests among North-South pairs and East-West pairs.

completed trick One to which every hand has played a card.

complete hand 1. *Draw Poker*. The five cards held by a player after the draw. 2. *Mah Jongg, Rummy*. One entirely formed in sets, with no odd cards.

concealed 1. *Mah Jongg*. Still on the player's rack, not GROUNDED. 2. *Canasta*. [Going out] without having previously melded.

conditions *Panguingue*. Certain melds for which the player collects.

condone Waive penalty for an irregularity.

contract The obligation to win a certain number of tricks or points.

conventions Advance agreement between partners on how to exchange information by bids and plays.

copper *Faro*. A token placed on a bet indicating that it is a bet on a card to lose.

counter 1. Chip; a token used in place of money. 2. A card having a point value when taken in a trick.

count out Score the game-winning points before the play is finished.

coup 1. A brilliant play. 2. A winning play or bet. 3. DEAL (2).

court cards FACE CARDS.

cover Play a card higher than the highest previously played to the trick.

crap out *Craps*. Lose by rolling 7 before the point.

craps *Craps*. Roll of 2, 3 or 12 on the first cast, which loses.

crib *Cribbage*. The extra hand formed by the players' discards.

cribbage board A device for scoring.

cross-eyes *Dice*. The roll of 3.

cross-ruff *Whist family*. Alternate trumping of each other's plain-suit leads by the two hands of a partnership.

cross the suit *Euchre*. Name as trump a suit of color opposite from that of the rejected turn-up card.

croupier A banking house employee who collects and pays bets, and sometimes also deals.

crown *Checkers*. Promote from a single man to a king; place a checker on another to show that it has become a king.

cue-bid *Contract bridge*. One that systemically shows control of a suit, especially by possession of the ace or a void.

cumulative scoring *Bridge*. A method of scoring in duplicate play, by determining the net total of the plus and minus scores made on all the boards played by a partnership.

Curse of Scotland The nine of diamonds.

cut 1. Divide the pack into two packets and reverse their order. 2. DRAW (1).

cut in Enter a game by drawing cards for precedence.

cut the pot Take a percentage from the pot.

dame 1. *Cards* and *Chess*. A queen. (French, German, colloquial English) 2. The game of Checkers (French, German, etc.) 3. *Checkers*. A promoted piece, equivalent to a king in English Draughts (Spain, Russia, etc.). 4. *Go*. Common points owned by neither player.

dead card One which cannot be used in play or which has already been played.

dead hand One barred from further participation.

dead man's hand *Poker*. Two pairs, aces and eights.

deadwood 1. *Poker*. The discard pile. 2. *Rummy*. Unmatched cards in a hand.

deal 1. Distribute cards to the players; the turn to deal. 2. The period from one deal to the next, including all incidents of making the trump, bidding, melding, discarding, playing, showing, and scoring.

dealer 1. The player who distributes the cards in preparation for play. 2. Banker.

deal out Omit giving a card or cards to a hand in regular turn during the deal.

deck Pack.

deckhead The card turned for trump.

declaration 1. Call; bid; naming of a trump suit or game; the auction. 2. The trump suit or game as named in a bid.

declarer 1. *Bridge.* The player who plays both his hand and the dummy. 2. BIDDER (2).

declare 1. Call; bid; name the trump. 2. Announce; meld.

defender Contract Bridge. An opponent of declarer.

defensive bid *Bridge.* 1. One made by an opponent of the opening bidder. 2. One made to prevent opponents from winning the contract cheaply.

defensive strength *Bridge.* Cards that are expected to win tricks against an adverse contract.

demand bid *Contract Bridge.* One that systemically requires partner to keep the auction open or to make a responsive bid.

denial bid *Bridge.* One showing lack of support for partner's declaration.

denomination 1. Rank. 2. *Contract Bridge.* The suit or notrump as named in a bid.

deuce Any two-spot.

Devil's Bed Posts The four of clubs.

diamonds The suit denoted by the symbol ◇. French, carreau; German, Schellen, Eckstein, Ruthen.

dis *Pinochle.* The lowest. Also, *dix.*

discard 1. Lay aside excess cards in exchange for others from the stock or the widow; a discarded card or cards. 2. Play a plain-suit card not of the same suit as the lead.

discard pile 1. *Rummy.* Cards previously discarded. 2. *Solitaire.* TALON.

discouraging card *Bridge.* Any played that indicates no desire to have a suit led or continued.

discovered check *Chess.* Check by a queen, rook or bishop disclosed by moving a piece off the line to the adverse king.

distribution Division of cards among the hands, especially as to the number of each suit held by each hand.

dix DIS.

Dog See BIG DOG, LITTLE DOG.

dogging *Mah Jongg.* Saving tiles of various suits, instead of clearing the hand to one suit.

don't come bet *Craps.* A bet that the dice will lose, treating the next roll as the first of a series.

don't pass line *Bank craps.* A space in the layout for bets that the caster does not PASS.

dormitzer, or daubitzer *Jocular.* A low-caliber kibitzer; one entitled to argue with the kibitzers but not with the players.

double 1. *Bridge.* A call which has the effect of increasing the trick values and penalties in case the last preceding bid becomes the contract. 2. *Backgammon.* A call requiring opponent to continue at doubled stakes or resign the game.

double bête *Pinochle.* The penalty suffered by a bidder who has elected to play the hand and has lost.

double corner *Checkers.* A corner of the board which contains a diagonal of two playing squares.

doubled pawn *Chess.* Two pawns of the same color on the same file.

double dummy *Whist family.* A game or situation in which a player knows the location of all the cards.

double-ended straight *Poker.* Four cards in sequence which can be filled to a straight by the draw of a card of next-higher or next-lower rank.

double header A pool not won in the same deal as formed, but left to be won subsequently.

double mill *Mill.* A formation in which the player can close a mill every turn.

double pairs royal *Cribbage.* Four of a kind.

double run *Cribbage.* A hand comprising a run of three cards with one rank duplicated.

doublet *Dominoes.* A bone having the same number on both ends.

doubleton *Whist family*. An original holding of two cards in a suit.

doublets *Backgammon*. The roll of the same number on both dice.

doubling cube A cube with the numbers 2, 4, 8, 16, 32, 64 on its faces, for keeping track of the increase of stakes, as at Backgammon.

doubling up Betting twice as much as was previously bet and lost.

down and out ECHO.

drag down *Craps*. Remove all or part of one's winnings from the pool.

draw 1. Pull cards from a pack spread face down, to determine seats, first deal, etc. 2. Receive cards from the stock to replace discards.

drawn game One which neither player wins, as in Chess, Checkers.

driver's seat *Poker*. Situation of a player who holds what is sure to be the best hand.

drop Withdraw from the current deal.

duck *Bridge*. Fail to cover when able.

duke HAND (1), *slang*.

dummy *Bridge*. Declarer's partner; the hand laid down by him and played by declarer.

duplicate A form of Bridge or Whist play in which all contestants play the same series of deals, which are kept in original form by use of *duplicate boards*.

dutch it CROSS THE SUIT.

Dutch straight SKIP STRAIGHT.

eagles The American name of the fifth suit, green in color, at one time added to the standard pack.

easy aces *Auction Bridge*. Two-two division of aces between the two sides, so that at no-trump there is no score for honors.

echo *Whist family*. A signal comprising the play of a higher card before a lower card of the same suit.

edge 1. AGE; eldest hand. 2. Advantage (from the advantage of being eldest hand in many games).

Eicheln German, the club suit.

eighter from Decatur *Dice*. The roll of 8.

80 kings *Pinochle*. A meld of four kings, one of each suit.

eldest hand The player at the left of the dealer.

encouraging card One played that indicates a desire to have the suit led or continued or indicates strength in it.

end *Dominoes*. The number on one half of a bone.

end game 1. *Chess*. The period of a game after queens are exchanged, or when the immediate goal is to promote a pawn. 2. *Checkers*. The period of a game after one or more kings have been crowned.

endhand *Skat family*. The active player who is third in order of bidding.

endplay Any of several stratagems (especially THROW-IN) that can usually be executed only in the last few tricks of the play.

en passant *Chess*. Capture by a pawn on the fifth rank of an adverse pawn on an adjacent file that has just moved two squares from its initial position.

en plein *Roulette*. A bet on a single number.

en prise *Chess*. Open to capture. Also, *in hock*.

enter *Backgammon*. Move a stone from the bar to the adverse home table.

entry A card with which a hand can eventually win a trick and so gain the lead.

E. P. Abbreviation of EN PASSANT.

establish Make cards the best by forcing out adverse higher cards.

equals Cards in sequence or which have become sequential through the play of the cards of intervening rank.

euchre *Euchre*. Failure of the maker to win the number of tricks contracted for.

exchange *Chess*. 1. Capture of equal pieces by both players. 2. *Win the* —, capture pieces of greater value than are lost, especially to win a rook for a knight or bishop.

exit Get out of the lead; compel another hand to win a trick.

exposed card One played in error, inadvertently dropped, or otherwise shown not in a legitimate manner and therefore (in most games) subject to penalty.

face card Any king, queen, or jack. (The ace is not a face card.)

faced Lying with its face exposed.

fade *Craps*. Bet with the caster that he will not PASS.

fall of the cards The identity and order of cards as played.

false card One selected for play, when there is a choice, to mislead opponents as to the contents of the hand.

false move Illegal move, as in Chess, Checkers.

false openers *Poker.* A hand with which a pot has been opened, but which is not as good as the rules require.

family of games A group associated by a common origin, or by mutual resemblance in important features.

fatten 1. *Poker.* SWEETEN. 2. *Pinochle.* SMEAR.

fat trick One containing valuable cards of more than average total, as in Pinochle.

feed the kitty Set aside a percentage of each pot to defray expenses.

fianchetto *Chess.* The development of a bishop at Kt2.

field *Craps.* A group of numbers, usually 2, 3, 5, 9, 10, 11, 12.

fifteen *Cribbage.* A combination of cards totaling 15 in pip values; the score of 2 for such a combination.

figure Face card.

file *Chess.* A line of squares extending at right angles to the White and Black sides.

fill *Poker.* Draw cards that improve the original holding.

finesse *Whist family.* An attempt to make a card serve as an equal to a higher-ranking card held by an opponent.

first hand 1. The leader to a trick. 2. The first player in turn to CALL.

fish Draw cards from the stock.

fish-hook card Any seven.

five fingers *Spoil Five.* The five of trumps.

flag flying *Bridge.* Assuming a losing contract to prevent the opponents from winning a game.

flash 1. *Poker.* Expose in dealing. 2. *Five-suit Poker.* A hand containing cards of all five suits.

flat bet *Craps.* One between players, other than the caster, that he will or will not PASS.

flowers *Mah Jongg.* Certain tiles which are not formed into sets.

fool's mate *Chess.* The checkmate by 1. P-KB4, P-K3; 2. P-KKt4, Q-R5.

flush 1. *Poker, Cribbage.* A hand with all cards of one suit. 2. *Pinochle.* A meld of the **A, K, Q, J, 10** of trumps.

fold *Stud Poker.* Withdraw from the current deal, as signified by turning one's cards face down.

follow suit Play a card of the same suit as the lead.

force 1. Compel a player to trump if he wishes to win the trick. 2. *Contract Bridge.* By a conventional call, demand that partner bid.

forcee A certain compulsory bid, as in Ombre and derived games.

forcing bid DEMAND BID.

fordern German, lead trumps.

forehand *Skat family.* The active player who is first in order of bidding; eldest hand.

fork *Chess.* Simultaneous attack on two pieces or squares.

40 jacks *Pinochle.* A meld of four jacks, one of each suit.

foul hand *Poker.* One of more or less than the legal number of cards.

foundation *Solitaire.* A card on which a whole suit or sequence must be built up.

fourchette A perfect TENACE against an adverse high card, as **K, J** against the **Q**.

four-flush *Poker.* Four cards of the same suit.

four of a kind Four cards of the same rank, as, four aces.

four signal *Whist.* A method of showing four trumps, by withholding the lowest until the third round.

fourth-best *Whist family.* The fourth-highest card of a suit held by a hand.

frage German, ask, question; the lowest-scoring declaration in some games, as Skat; same as ASK (2).

freak 1. *Bridge.* A hand of extraordinary pattern. 2. *Poker.* A wild card.

free bid *Bridge.* One made voluntarily, not under any systemic compulsion.

free double *Bridge.* The double of an adverse contract which is sufficient for game if made undoubled.

free ride *Poker.* Playing in a pot without having to ante or bet.

freezeout Any variant of a game in which a player must drop out when his original stake is exhausted.

frog *Skat family.* The bid of lowest value. Also, *frage.*

full hand FULL HOUSE.

full house *Poker.* A hand comprising three of a kind and a pair.

fuzzing MILKING.

gag HARD WAY.

gallery Non-playing spectators.

galloping dominoes Dice.

gambit *Chess.* A sacrifice of a pawn or piece for positional advantage.

game 1. A pastime, in the general sense, as Bridge, Poker. 2. The specific number of points that determines the winner of a contest, as 121 points in Cribbage. 3. A contest or division of continuous play complete in itself. 4. The specific number of tricks or points that must be won in play to fulfill contract, as 61 or more in Skat. 5. A declaration, as in Skat. 6. A variant of the basic game named by dealer to be played in that deal, as in Dealer's Choice Poker. 7. A certain card, as the ten of trumps in some variants of All Fours. 8. A system of play.

gammon *Backgammon.* The winning of a game when the loser has not borne off a stone.

gift *All Fours.* The point scored by eldest hand when he begs and dealer decides to play.

gin *Gin Rummy.* A hand completely formed in sets, with no deadwood.

go *Cribbage.* A call signifying that the player cannot play another card without exceeding 31; the score of 1 point to opponent when go is called.

go out 1. Get rid of all cards in the hand, as in Rummy, Michigan. 2. Reach the cumulative total of points necessary for game, as in All Fours, Cribbage; count out.

go over 1. Overcall. 2. Head a trick.

goulash *Bridge.* A practice once fashionable but now outlawed except in Towie (see page 223).

graduated aces *Pinochle.* A scale of bonus payments for holding 100 aces, dependent on the amount of the bid.

grand *Skat family.* A declaration in which only the jacks are trumps. Also, *grando.*

grand coup *Bridge.* A stratagem of play; the trumping of partner's winning plain card in order to shorten a trump holding to advantage.

grand slam *Whist family.* The winning of all 13 tricks by one side.

grounded Melded face up on the table, as in Mah Jongg.

group *Rummy.* Cards forming a valid meld; especially three or four of a kind as distinguished from a sequence.

Grün German, the spade suit.

guarded *Bridge.* Accompanied by as many small cards of the same suit as there are higher cards outstanding, as **Q, x**, x.

gucki GUCKSER.

guckser *Skat.* A declaration in which jacks are trumps and the bidder picks up the skat. Also, *gucki.*

hand 1. The cards dealt to or held by any player; any player. 2. DEAL (2). 3. *Solitaire.* An undealt remainder of the pack after the tableau is laid out.

handplay Playing without use of the widow.

hard way *Craps.* With the same number on both dice, as the number 8 made by rolling 4–4.

head a trick COVER.

hearts The suit denoted by the symbol ♡. French, coeur. German, Rot(h), Hertzen.

heavy bone *Dominoes.* One with a high total of pips.

heeled bets *Faro.* Bets on one card to win and another to lose.

Hertzen German, the heart suit.

high *All Fours family.* The ace of trumps, or the highest trump dealt; the score for holding such card.

high-low ECHO.

Hinterhand ENDHAND.

His Heels *Cribbage.* A jack turned as a starter; the score of 2 to the dealer for this turn-up.

His Nobs *Cribbage.* A jack of the same suit as the starter, in hand or crib; the score of 1 point for such jack.

hit *Backgammon.* Land on a point, where there is an adverse BLOT, and so put it ON THE BAR.

hit me *Blackjack.* Player's request for an additional card.

hock *Faro.* The last card in the box. Also, *hoc, hocly, hockelty.*

hold up *Bridge.* Refuse to win a trick with.

hole card *Stud Poker.* The first card received by a player, which is dealt face down.

home Up to average expectation in total score, as in Cribbage.

honors 1. High cards, especially if they have scoring value. 2. *Bridge.* The five highest trumps, or, if there is no trump, the four aces.

honor tricks *Bridge.* High cards, in hand evaluation.

horse and horse Score of 1–1 in games.

Howell settlement *Hearts.* A method of scoring invented by E. C. Howell.

hustler One who seeks to prey upon the ignorance of his victims.

immortal hand CINCH HAND.

impair *Roulette.* Arithmetically odd.

imperfect pack One from which cards are missing, in which a card is incorrectly duplicated, or which has become so worn that some cards are identifiable from the back.

improve Draw cards that increase the value of the hand.

index The small number and suit symbol printed near the corner of a card, used to read the card when it is held in a fan with others.

individual *Bridge.* A form of tournament in which partnerships change and individual instead of pair scores are kept.

informatory double *Bridge.* A systemic double made primarily to give information to partner.

initial bid OPENING BID.

inside straight *Poker.* Four cards needing a card of interior rank to make a straight, as **9**, **8**, **6**, **5**.

insufficient bid One that is not legally high enough to overcall the last previous bid.

interpose *Chess.* Avert attack from an adverse queen, rook or bishop by placing a piece on the line.

in the box Playing alone against the other participants, in CHOUETTE.

in the hole Minus score, so-called from the practice (as in Euchre) of marking a score as minus by drawing a ring around it.

in the mitt *Pinochle.* Held in the original hand.

irregularity Any departure from a law of correct procedure.

isolated pawn *Chess.* One that cannot be protected by another, there being no friendly pawn on either adjacent file.

jack 1. *All Fours family.* The score for winning the jack of trumps in play. 2. *Hearts.* A pool not won because no hand is clear, and therefore held intact for the next deal.

jackpot *Poker.* A deal in which everyone antes; usually in such a deal a pair of jacks or better is required to open.

J'adoube *Chess.* "I adjust."

jambone *Railroad Euchre.* A bid to play alone and with the entire hand faced on the table.

jamboree *Railroad Euchre.* A hand holding the five highest trumps, which is shown and scored without play.

jasz *Klaberjass.* The jack of trumps.

jetons French, counters, chips.

jeu French, game; hand; system of play.

jeux de régle French, the tabulation of the mathematical probabilities of winning or losing with all types of hands, especially at Écarté.

joker An extra card furnished with the standard pack, and used in some games as the highest trump or as a wild card. See also BUG.

jump bid *Bridge.* A bid of more tricks than are legally necessary to overcall a bid.

kibitzer A non-playing spectator.

kicker *Draw Poker.* An extra card kept with a pair for a two-card draw.

kilter *Poker.* A hand with no card higher than nine, no pair, and no four-flush or four-straight.

king 1. *Chess.* A piece, the protection of which is the object of play. French, roi. German, König. 2. *Checkers.* A piece that has reached the farthest rank from its initial position and has been CROWNED.

king row *Checkers*. Either row adjacent to the Black or White side of the board, where adverse pieces CROWN.

kitty A percentage taken out of the stakes to defray expenses or pay admission fees; a pool to which betes are paid and from which royalties are collected; incorrectly used to mean WIDOW.

knave The jack of a suit.

knight *Chess*. A piece that moves between the diagonal corners of a rectangle three squares by two. French, cavalier. German, Springer.

knock 1. *Rummy family*. Signify termination of play by laying down one's hand. 2. *Poker*. Signify disinclination to cut the pack, or to bet, by rapping on the table.

kong *Mah Jongg*. A meld of four of a kind.

König German. 1. King. 2. An inactive player.

laps The carrying forward of excess points from one game to the next.

last turn *Faro*. The play when only three cards are left in the box.

lay away 1. *Pinochle*. Discard after taking up the widow. 2. *Cribbage*. Give cards to the crib.

lay-down CINCH HAND.

lay off *Rummy*. Add cards to a meld or matched set on the table.

layout 1. A diagram of numbers, cards, etc. on a table top, used for the placement of bets, as at Faro, Michigan. 2. *Solitaire*. The array of cards first dealt out, comprising possibly the tableau, foundations, and stock.

lay suit PLAIN SUIT.

lead Play first to a trick; the card so played.

least *Schafkopf*. The game played if all players pass, the object being to take as few counting cards as possible.

left bower *Euchre*. The other jack of same color as the jack of the trump suit.

L. H. O. *Bridge*. Left-hand opponent.

left pedro *Cinch*. The other five of same color as the five of trumps.

light In debt to the pot.

light bone *Dominoes*. One with a low total of pips.

lilies *Bridge Whist*. The spade suit, when declared for trump at an increased scoring value.

limit *Poker*. The maximum amount by which a player may increase a previous bet.

line 1. PASS LINE. 2. *Gin Rummy*. The score for a BOX (2). 3. Squares in a line, as in Chess, Checkers.

Little Casino The two of spades.

Little Cat LITTLE TIGER.

Little Dick *Dice*. The roll of 4.

Little Dog *Poker*. A hand consisting of seven-high and deuce-low but no pair.

Little Joe *Dice*. The roll of 4.

Little Phoebe *Dice*. The roll of 5.

little slam SMALL SLAM.

Little Tiger *Poker*. A hand consisting of eight-high and three-low but no pair.

live card One still in the hands or stock or otherwise available; one that is not DEAD.

lone player One who elects to play without help of his partner's hand; solo player.

long card One left in a hand after all opponents are exhausted of the suit.

long suit *Whist family*. A holding of more than four cards in a suit; the longest holding in any suit in a hand.

loo *Loo*. Fail to win a trick; the penalty therefor.

look CALL (2).

loose card *Whist*. One that can be discarded as useless.

losing card One that cannot be expected to win a trick.

love Score of zero.

low *All Fours family*. The two of trumps, or the lowest trump dealt; the score for holding or winning such card.

lurch The winning of a game when the opponent has not yet passed the halfway mark.

main *Craps*. PASS LINE.

major The non-dealer in two-hand play.

make The contract; the trump suit; name the trump suit or game.

make a point 1. *Craps*. Roll the point number before 7. 2. *Backgammon*. Occupy a point with two or more stones.

make good *Poker*. Add enough chips to meet the previous bet.

maker   Player who names the trump suit or game.

make up   Gather and shuffle the pack for the next deal.

man   In board games, a piece.

Manille, or Manilla   The lowest card of the trump suit, when it ranks as the second-best trump.

manque   *Roulette*. The numbers 1 to 18 inclusive.

march   *Euchre*. The winning of all five tricks by one player or one side; the score for winning all the tricks.

marker   1. *Faro*. A token placed to show that a bet applies to more than one card. 2. A promissory note.

marking the game   Winning.

marriage   *Bézique family*. A meld of the king and queen of a suit.

martingale   A system of betting on even chances, by doubling the amount bet after each loss.

master card   The highest card of a suit remaining live or unplayed.

matador   Any of an unbroken sequence of trumps from the highest down; any high trump.

matched set   SET (1).

match-point scoring   *Bridge*. A method of scoring in duplicate play.

mechanic   A card sharp.

meet a bet   *Poker*. CALL (2); add enough chips so as to make a total contribution equal to the maximum made by any previous player.

meld   A combination set, or group of cards of value in scoring or in getting rid of one's cards; show or announce such a combination.

menel   *Klaberjass*. The nine of trumps.

middlehand   *Skat family*. The active player who is second in order of bidding.

mid-game   *Chess* and *Checkers*. The period of a game between the opening and the ending.

milking   A method of shuffling, by drawing cards simultaneously from top and bottom of the pack and piling them on the table.

mill   *Mill*. Three pieces of one color on one line of the board.

minor   The dealer in two-hand play.

minor piece   *Chess*. Any bishop or knight.

misdeal   Any departure from the laws of correct procedure in dealing.

misère or misery   NULLO.

miss   1. Widow, as in Loo. 2. *Craps*. Fail to make a POINT.

mistigris   The joker; Poker played with the joker.

Mittelhand   MIDDLEHAND.

mixed pair   In tournament play, a partnership of a man and a woman.

monkey flush   *Poker*. Three cards of a suit, not in sequence.

mort   French, DUMMY.

mouth bet   One made verbally without putting up chips or money.

move   1. A play in turn. 2. *Checkers*. The opposition.

movement   In tournament play, the passage of duplicate boards or of players from table to table; progression; a schedule for the conduct of a duplicate contest.

muggins   *Cribbage*. The right of a player to take points overlooked by his opponent.

multipliers   *Skat*. Factors by which the base value of the trump suit is multiplied to determine the value of a game.

natural   1. Without the use of any wild card. 2. A combination that wins at once; in Blackjack, a face card and an ace; in Baccarat, a count of 8 or 9 in the first two cards; in Craps, a first roll of 7 or 11.

natural points   Those which must be scored on every deal, as big casino, little casino, high, low.

negative double   INFORMATORY DOUBLE.

neutral score   In tournament contract bridge, an arbitrary score assigned by the referee, when regular play is not feasible.

next   *Euchre*. The other suit of the same color as the rejected turn-up card.

Nick   *Craps*. NATURAL (2).

Nina   *Dice*. The roll of 9. Also *Nina-from Carolina*.

no   A declaration meaning "pass," in bidding.

no dice   *Dice*. Voidance of a roll, e.g., because a die is cocked.

noir   French, black.

non-comoquers *Panguingue.* Aces and kings, because they are exempt from a rule applying to lower cards.

notrump A declaration that offers to play the hand without a trump suit.

nullo, or null A declaration in which the object of play is to avoid winning tricks or points.

odd trick *Bridge.* Any won by declarer in excess of six.

offensive strength *Bridge.* Cards that are expected to win tricks at one's own contract.

off numbers BOX NUMBERS.

once around Game fixed at 61, when scored on a Cribbage board.

one-end straight *Poker.* A sequence of four cards either ace-high or ace-low.

one-eyes Face cards on which the face shows only one eye: jacks of spades and hearts, king of diamonds.

100 aces *Pinochle, Bézique.* A meld of four aces.

on the bar *Backgammon.* Awaiting entry, said of a blot that has been hit.

open 1. Make the first declaration or the first bid. 2. *Poker.* Make the first bet, especially in a jackpot. 3. A declaration that offers to play with the entire hand faced on the table. 4. *Stud Poker.* Face-up on the table. 5. Make the first lead of a suit.

open bet *Faro.* A bet on a card to win.

open-ended straight Also called DOUBLE-ENDED STRAIGHT.

openers *Poker.* A holding that entitles a player to open the pot.

opening The first several moves or plays, as in Chess, Checkers.

opening bid The first bid of the auction.

opposition The compulsion to move, in a symmetrical position, as in Chess. In Checkers, called the MOVE.

order up *Euchre.* A declaration by an opponent of dealer, accepting the turn-up card for trump.

original bid OPENING BID.

original hand A hand as dealt, before alteration by discard, draw, play, etc.

ouvert OPEN (3).

overcall Make a bid legally sufficient to supersede the last previous bet.

overs *Casino.* The count of one point for each card over 30 taken in.

overhand shuffle A shuffle executed by holding the pack in one hand and dropping packets from the top into the other hand.

overtrick *Bridge.* Any won by declarer in excess of his contract.

pack 1. Deck; the aggregation of all cards used in a game. See also STANDARD DECK. 2. Discard pile.

packet A portion less than the complete pack, especially in shuffling and cutting.

paint *Hearts.* Discard a heart on a trick won by another player.

pair 1. Two cards of the same rank. 2. Partnership of two players.

pairs royal *Cribbage.* Three of a kind.

pam The jack of clubs.

partie French, GAME (3). Also, *party.*

partscore *Bridge.* A trick score total of less than game.

pass A declaration signifying that the player does not wish to make a bid, or that he withdraws from the current deal. 2. *Hearts family.* The cards exchanged among the original hands after the deal. 3. *Craps.* Win as caster, by rolling a natural or repeating point before 7.

passe *Roulette.* The numbers 19 to 36 inclusive.

passed pawn *Chess.* One not opposed by an adverse pawn on the same or either adjacent file.

pass line *Craps.* A space in the layout for bets that the caster will PASS (3).

pass out a deal Abandon the deal after all players pass.

passt-mir-nicht *Skat.* In a tournee, rejection of the first card turned. [German, "It does not satisfy me."]

pat hand The ORIGINAL HAND when it refuses to discard and draw, as in Draw Poker.

patt German, drawn game, as in Chess.

pattern *Whist family.* A group of four integers, as 4-4-3-2, expressing the way in which a given suit is divided among the four hands or a given hand is divided into suits.

pawn *Chess.* The weakest piece, moving forward on the file. French, pion. German, Bauer.

pedro *Cinch.* The five of trumps, or the other five of the same color.

peg *Cribbage.* A marker used for scoring on a cribbage board; win points, especially during the play.

pelter KILTER.

penalty card *Contract Bridge.* An exposed card that must be played at first legal opportunity.

penalty double BUSINESS DOUBLE.

penny ante *Poker.* A game in which the ante or limit is one cent.

perpetual check *Chess.* Unremitting attack on a king, without checkmate, leading to a draw.

Phoebe *Dice.* The roll of 5.

pianola hand *Bridge.* One that is very easy to play.

picture card FACE CARD.

pigeon *Poker.* A card drawn that greatly improves the hand.

pin *Chess.* Paralysis of a piece because a move off the line would expose its own king to check.

pinochle *Pinochle.* A meld of a queen of spades and jack of diamonds.

pip Any of the large suit symbols ♠, ♡, ◇, ♣ printed on the face of a card (excluding index marks).

pique *Piquet.* The winning of 30 points in hand and play before opponent scores a point; the bonus of 30 points therefor.

pitch *Auction Pitch.* The opening lead, which fixes the trump suit.

pivot A schedule for four players whereby each plays with every other as his partner; the player who remains in the same seat while the others progress.

places open *Pinochle.* Outstanding cards that will improve a hand.

plain suit Any card that is not trumps.

played card One gathered in a trick; one legally construed to be played.

player *Skat.* The highest bidder, who then plays alone against the two others in partnership.

playing to the score Modifying normal strategy of bidding or play when one side is close to game.

playing tricks OFFENSIVE STRENGTH; cards expected to win tricks, but not necessarily high cards.

play off *Cribbage.* Play a card of rank far enough from that of previous cards so that opponents cannot make a run.

play on *Cribbage.* Play a card that may enable opponent to make a run.

play over COVER.

point 1. A unit of scoring. 2. *Piquet.* A scoring combination, the holding of a suit totalling the greatest number of pips; the score therefor. 3. *Backgammon.* Any of the 24 colored lines or triangles on the board. 4. *Craps.* The caster's first roll, other than 7 or 11, which he must roll again before rolling 7 in order to win.

point bet *Craps.* One on the caster to PASS by repeating his point.

point value The count of a card toward GAME (4), as in Skat, Pinochle, All Fours.

polignac The jack of spades.

pone The player at dealer's right; in two-hand play, the non-dealer.

pool POT.

positive double BUSINESS DOUBLE.

post-mortem Discussion of the merits of the bidding and play of a deal.

pot The aggregate of chips or money at stake in a deal, consisting usually of contributions from each active player.

predict *Skat.* ANNOUNCE (3).

preemptive bid *Bridge.* A high opening bid, made to shut out adverse competition.

premiums 1. Royalties. 2. *Bridge.* All scores other than for odd tricks.

progression Movement of players or of boards from table to table in progressive or duplicate play.

progressive A form of tournament play in which players progress according to their scores, the cards being dealt at random at every table.

proil Contraction of PAIRS ROYAL.

promotion The replacement of a piece by one of greater power, as in QUEENING (Chess) and CROWNING (Checkers).

proposal *Écarté.* Request by non-dealer that additional cards be dealt.

protection 1. Cards by which others are GUARDED. 2. To CINCH. 3. *Chess.* Guard of one piece by another. 4. *Contract Bridge.* A bid made in the belief that partner has passed with a strong hand.

psychic bid *Bridge.* One made without the cards to support it, for the purpose of misleading the opponents.

pull down DRAG DOWN.

pung *Mah Jongg.* A meld of three of a kind.

punter One who plays against the bank.

puppyfoot The ace of clubs; any club.

quart *Piquet.* A sequence of four cards in the same suit.

quatorze *Piquet.* Four of a kind (tens or higher), counting 14.

queen 1. *Chess.* The most powerful piece. French, dame. German, Dame. 2. *Checkers.* In many European countries, same as KING.

queening *Chess.* Replacement of a pawn that has reached the eighth rank by a queen.

quick tricks Honor-tricks.

quint *Piquet.* A sequence of five cards in the same suit.

quitted trick One that has been turned face down.

raffle *Chuckluck.* Appearance of the same number on all three dice.

rainbow hand One that can win only by a lucky BUY.

raise 1. *Poker.* Put more chips in the pot than are necessary to meet the previous bet. 2. *Bridge.* Bid an increased number of tricks in a declaration previously bid by partner.

rake-off The percentage of the stakes taken by the house or club, usually by means of a kitty.

ramsch *Skat.* A nullo game which is played if all the players pass.

rangdoodles Variant of ROODLES.

rank 1. The ordinal position of a card in its suit. 2. *Chess.* A line of squares parallel to the White and Black sides.

rearhand ENDHAND.

rebid *Bridge.* A bid made by a player who has previously bid.

redeal A new deal by the same dealer, usually after a MISDEAL.

redouble *Bridge.* A call which has the effect of further increasing the trick values and penalties in case the last preceding bid, doubled, becomes the contract.

reentry A card with which a hand can eventually regain the lead after having lost it.

refait *Trente et Quarante.* A tie in totals of cards dealt to the two rows.

refusal 1. *Écarté.* Rejection by dealer of a PROPOSAL. 2. *All Fours.* Acceptance by dealer of a BEG (hence a refusal to let eldest hand score GIFT).

régle French, a rule of play.

released card *Solitaire.* One made available by the removal of covering cards.

remis French, drawn game, as in Chess.

renege REVOKE.

renounce Play a card not of the suit led.

repique *Piquet.* The winning of 30 points in hand, without play, before the opponent scores a point; the bonus of 60 points therefor.

replay duplicate A form of duplicate bridge between two pairs.

response *Bridge.* A bid made in reply to a bid by partner.

restriction play *Checkers.* Selection by chance of the opening to be played.

revoke Fail to follow suit when able; fail to play a card as required by a law of correct procedure or by a proper penalty.

revolution *Skat.* A variant of null ouvert in which the opponents may pool their cards and redistribute their hands as they see fit.

riffle A manner of shuffling (see page 657).

right bet *Dice games.* One that the caster will PASS.

right bower *Euchre.* The jack of the trump suit.

robbing Exchanging a card in the hand for the card turned up for trump.

rob the pack *Cinch.* Select any desired cards from the stock (the privilege of the dealer).

roll *Dice.* A cast of the dice; the total of the numbers on the uppermost faces.

roodles *Poker.* Any special pot with increased antes or stakes.

rook 1. *Chess.* A piece, moving on the ranks and files. Also, *castle.* French, tour. German,

Turm. 2. A game played with cards equivalent to playing cards.

rope *Panguingue*. A meld of a sequence.

rotation The movement of the turn to deal, bid, or play. In modern practice this is to the left, or clockwise.

rot(h) German, the heart suit.

rouge French, red.

round Any division of the dealing, bidding or play, in which each hand participates once, e.g., the series of deals from one player's turn to his next turn; the series of bids from one player's turn to the next; a trick.

round game One in which there are no partnerships.

round house *Pinochle*. A meld comprising a king and a queen of each suit.

round-the-corner Circular sequence of rank, the highest card being deemed adjacent to the lowest, as, **Q, K, A, 2, 3**; a round-the-corner straight in Poker.

round trip ROUND HOUSE.

row *Solitaire*. A line of cards parallel to the player.

royal flush *Poker*. An ace-high straight flush.

royal marriage *Bézique family*. A meld of the king and queen of trumps.

royals 1. LILIES. 2. The English name of the fifth suit, green in color, at one time added to the standard deck; in America, eagles.

royal sequence *Pinochle*. FLUSH (2).

royalties Payments collected by a player who holds any of certain high hands, in addition to whatever he wins in regular play.

rubber The winning of the first two out of three games by one side.

rubber bridge *Bridge*. A form of play in which rubbers are scored (as opposed to duplicate play).

rubicon Failure of the loser of a game to reach a certain minimum total of points, as 100 in Piquet.

ruff Play a trump on a plain-suit lead.

rule of eleven *Whist family*. The mathematical fact that when a player leads a fourth-best card, the difference between its pip value and 11 is the number of cards higher than that led, outside the leader's hand.

rule of fourth-best *Whist family*. The conventional practice of leading the fourth-best card from a long suit.

rummy *Rummy family*. Get rid of the last card in the hand; lay down a hand completely formed in sets; also, call attention to a play overlooked by an opponent.

run A sequence of three or more cards of the same suit as in Cribbage, Rummy.

runner *Backgammon*. A stone in the adverse home table.

running game *Backgammon*. The strategy of bringing all stones into the home board as quickly as possible; the period of a game after the two forces have completely passed each other.

runt *Poker*. A hand ranking lower than one pair.

run the cards *All Fours*. Deal additional cards, and make a new turn-up when a beg is accepted.

Ruthen German, the heart suit.

sacrifice Relinquishment of a piece to capture, for positional advantage, as in Chess, Checkers.

sacrifice bid *Bridge*. One made without the expectation that the contract will be fulfilled, for the purpose of saving greater loss.

sandbagging Withholding action on a good hand in order to trap an opponent into greater loss.

sans prendre French, without taking the widow.

Schellen German, the diamond suit.

schmeiss *Klaberjass*. A declaration which is a proposal to accept the turn-up card for trump or abandon the deal.

schmier SMEAR.

schneider 1. *Skat family*. Failure of one side to win 31 or more points in a play. 2. *Gin Rummy*. SHUTOUT

scholar's mate *Chess*. The checkmate by 1. P-K4, P-K4; 2. B-B4, B-B4; 3. Q-R5, Kt-KB3; 4. Q × BP.

schwarz *Skat family*. The winning of all the tricks by one player or one side.

score 1. The counting value of specific cards or tricks. 2. The accumulated total of points won by a player or a side. 3. Scoresheet.

second hand   Second in turn to call or play.

second turn   *Skat*. Turn-up of the second skat card for trump.

see   *Poker*. Meet a bet; call.

seeding   In knockout competition, placing the strongest entrants in the brackets in such a way that they cannot meet one another until the later rounds.

see-saw   CROSS-RUFF.

sequence   Two or more cards of adjacent rank, as **8**, **9**, **10**.

serve   Deal, especially in giving addition cards at Draw Poker.

set   1. A group of cards of scoring or melding value, as in Piquet, Rummy. 2. *Bridge family*. Defeat the contract. 3. *Dominoes*. The first bone played.

setback   A deduction from a player's accumulated score; a variant name for certain games, as Cutthroat Euchre.

settlement   Payment of losses and collection of winnings; redemption of chips in money.

seven out   *Craps*. Lose, as caster, by rolling 7 before repeating point.

sextette   *Piquet*. A sequence of six cards in the same suit.

sewed in   *Bridge*. Unable to exit.

shed   DISCARD (2).

shooter   *Craps*. Caster; one who rolls the dice.

short game   Any in which not all the cards of the pack are put into play during a deal.

short pair   *Poker*. In jackpots, any pair lower than jacks.

short suit   *Whist family*. A holding of less than four cards in a suit.

shot   *Checkers*. An exchange of captures precipitated to gain an advantage.

show   1. Meld; expose. 2. *Cribbage*. Count the hand.

showdown   *Poker*. The facing of all active hands to determine the winner of a pot.

shuffle   Mix the cards in the pack preparatory to dealing.

shutout   1. *Gin Rummy*. Winning of a game when the opponent has not scored a point. 2. *Backgammon*. The making of every point in one's home board.

shutout bid   PREEMPTIVE BID.

shy   Short, as said of a pot to which additional antes are due or of a player who owes chips to the pot.

side bets   *Dice*. Bets among players other than the caster.

side card   1. Any of a plain suit. 2. *Poker*. The highest card in the hand outside of a pair or two pairs, referred to in deciding higher hand between two that hold one or two pairs of the same rank.

side money   See SIDE-POT.

side pot   *Table Stakes Poker*. One separate from the main pot, made by continued betting after one player has put all his chips in the main pot.

side strength   High cards in plain suits.

side suit   PLAIN SUIT.

sight   The right to compete for the main pot in the showdown.

signal   *Whist family*. Any convention of play whereby one partner properly informs the other of his holdings or desires.

simple game   1. *Skat family*. The lowest declaration that may be bid; usually same as frage or frog. 2. *Loo*. SINGLE (1).

simple honors   *Auction Bridge*. The holding of three honors by one side; the score therefor.

single   1. A pool containing no chips left over from a previous deal. 2. A game won at the minimum stake.

single bête   *Pinochle*. A forfeit paid by a bidder who concedes loss of the hand, without play.

single corner   *Checkers*. A corner of the board where a playing square abuts two sides.

singleton   *Whist family*. An original holding of one card in a suit.

sink   *Piquet*. Omit announcement of a scoring combination (for possible advantage in play).

sixie from Dixie   *Dice*. The roll of 6.

60 queens   *Pinochle*. A meld of four queens, one of each suit.

skat   *Skat family*. The widow.

skeet   *Poker*. A hand consisting of two, five, nine, and two other cards lower than nine, but no pair.

skip bid   JUMP BID.

689

skip straight *Poker.* A special hand, consisting of a sequence of odd or even cards, as **J, 9, 7, 5, 3**.

skunked WHITEWASHED.

slam The winning of all the tricks by one side.

sleeper A dead or unclaimed bet left on the layout.

sluff, or slough Discard in playing.

small slam *Whist family.* The winning of twelve tricks by one side.

smear Discard a counting card on a trick won by partner. Also, *schmier.*

smoke out *Hearts family.* Force out the queen of spades by repeated leads of the suit.

smothered mate *Chess.* Checkmate by a knight, all squares adjacent to the king being blocked by his own pieces.

smudge *Auction Pitch.* A bid to win all four points.

snake eyes *Dice.* The roll of two aces.

sneak *Whist family.* A plain-suit singleton.

sniff *Dominoes.* The first doublet played, as in Sniff.

snowing MILKING.

soda *Faro.* The uppermost card when the pack is placed in the box.

solo A bid to play without using the widow, or without help of partner.

space *Solitaire.* A vacancy in the tableau created by the removal of all cards of one pile.

spade overs *Casino.* The score of 1 point for each spade won in excess of eight.

spades The suit denoted by the symbol ♠; French, pique. German, Grün, Schüppen, Pik.

spadille, or spadilla The queen of clubs.

splits *Faro.* Two cards of the same rank coming on the same turn.

splitting openers *Poker.* In a jackpot discarding part of the combination that qualified the hand to open (in an effort to better the chances of improvement).

spot card Any of rank **10, 9, 8, 7, 6, 5, 4, 3, 2**.

spread 1. Open; show. 2. A contract that can be fulfilled without playing. 3. *Panguingue.* Any meld.

squeeze 1. Look at one's hand by slightly separating them at one corner to see the indices. 2. *Bridge.* Compel other hands to discard; an endplay dependent upon compelling adverse discards.

stack Pile of chips; quota of chips assigned to each player.

stalemate *Chess.* A position in which the player in turn has no legal move but is not checked, a drawn game.

stand 1. Accept the turned card for trump, as in All Fours. 2. Accept the cards already dealt without drawing, discarding or redealing, as in Écarté, Blackjack. 3. Stay in the game during the current deal, as in Loo.

standard deck The pack of 52 cards (plus a joker, used by agreement).

stand-off A tie; cancellation of a bet by an indecisive result.

stand pat STAND (2).

starter *Cribbage.* The card cut by non-dealer and turned up by dealer, prior to the play.

stay *Poker.* Remain in the pot without raising; meet a bet; call; see.

stenographers Queens (in playing cards).

stich *Pinochle.* Last trick.

stick man CROUPIER.

stiff card LONG CARD.

still pack The one not dealt or to be dealt, when two packs are used alternately.

stock An undealt portion of the pack, which may be used later in the same deal.

stone *Backgammon.* Any of the pieces used in play.

stop 1. *Stops family.* Interruption of play caused by absence of the next card in sequence; the card so missing. 2. *Russian Bank.* A call upon opponent to cease play because of an irregularity in order of play.

stopper A holding by which a hand can eventually win a trick in a suit led by an adversary.

straddle 1. *Poker.* A blind raise of a blind bet. 2. FORK.

straight *Poker.* A hand of five cards in sequence, but not all in the same suit.

straight flush *Poker.* A hand of five cards in sequence in the same suit.

stringer A sequence.

stroke SHOT.

sufficient bid One high enough legally to supersede the last previous bid.

support RAISE (2); cards that are of assistance to partner.

sweep *Casino.* The taking in of all cards on the table; the score of 1 point therefor.

sweepstake *Hearts.* A method of settlement; the pot is won only by a player who is clear.

sweeten *Poker.* Ante again, to a jackpot not opened on the previous deal.

swings Cards in unbroken sequence from the highest of the suit, held by one side or hand.

switch Lead a suit different from that previously led.

system *Bridge.* An agreement between partners on the requirements for various bids and tactical procedure in various situations.

tab CASE-KEEPER.

tableau *Solitaire.* That part of the layout, excluding foundations, on which builds are made. In some games, the entire layout.

tables *Backgammon.* Quarters of the board.

table stakes *Poker.* A method of placing a limit on betting.

tailor SCHNEIDER.

take-all *Hearts.* The winning of all the counting cards by one player.

take in Gather cards from the table, as in Casino.

take-out *Bridge.* The bid of a different declaration from that bid by partner.

take-out double INFORMATORY DOUBLE.

take the lead *Stud Poker.* Make the first bet in a round.

take up *Euchre.* Accept the turn-up card for trump (by dealer).

tally Scoresheet, especially as used in progressive play.

talon *Solitaire.* Waste pile; cards laid aside as unplayable on being turned up from the stock or hand.

tap 1. Signify "pass" by rapping on the table. 2. *Poker.* Bet the whole amount of chips in front of a player.

tempo A gain of time in development, as in Chess, Bridge.

tenace *Whist family.* A holding of two cards in a suit, lacking one or more cards of intervening rank, as **10**, **A**. Perfect tenace lacks one intervening card; imperfect tenace lacks two or more. Major tenace is **A**, **Q**; minor tenace is **K**, **J**.

tenth card Any of pip value 10, as a face-card at Cribbage.

third hand Third in turn to call or play.

three-echo *Whist.* A signal to show three cards of a suit.

three of a kind Three cards of the same rank, as three aces.

threes THREE OF A KIND.

throw-in An endplay dependent on compelling an opponent to win a trick and then lead to his disadvantage.

throw off DISCARD (2); SMEAR.

tierce *Piquet.* A sequence of three cards of the same suit.

tiger See BIG TIGER, LITTLE TIGER.

-timer, as Eight-Timer *Draw Poker.* A hand that will be improved by a draw of any of the specified number of outstanding cards.

tops Highest cards of a suit.

total-point scoring Cumulative scoring.

tournee *Skat.* A declaration which offers to turn up a card from the skat to fix the trump suit.

trail *Casino.* Play a card to the table without building or taking in.

transversale *Roulette.* A bet on three numbers.

trash Useless cards; DISCARD (2).

tray Duplicate board.

trèfle French, the club suit.

trick A round of cards during the play, one card being contributed by each active hand; the packet of such cards when gathered.

trick score *Bridge.* Points made by the declarer for odd tricks; the part of the score sheet where such points are entered.

tricon Three of a kind.

triplets THREE OF A KIND.

trump card Any of the trump suit, or one arbitrarily designated as a trump by the rules of the game.

trump suit   One selected under the rules of the game to have the special privilege that every card in this suit ranks higher than any non-trump card in trick-winning.

turn   1. A player's opportunity, in due rotation, to deal, declare, play, etc. 2. *Faro*. Each draw of two cards from the box.

turn it down   *Euchre*. Reject the turned-up card as a trump.

turn-up   A card turned face-up, after the deal, to fix or propose the trump.

twice around   Game fixed at 121, when scored on a Cribbage board.

twist the tiger's tail   Play Faro.

two-suiter   *Bridge*. A hand containing five or more cards in each of two suits.

unblock   *Bridge*. Avoid or resolve a blocked suit, by cashing or discarding high cards.

undercut   *Gin Rummy*. Show a hand that counts the same or less than opponent's, after he has knocked.

underplay   Play a card lower than the best in the hand, or lower than one previously played to a trick.

under the guns   *Poker*. Said of the first player in turn to bet.

undertrick   *Bridge*. Any by which declarer falls short of making his contract.

unlimited poker   Agreement that there will be no limit on the size of a bet and the number of raises.

unmatched card   *Rummy family*. Any that is not part of a set; deadwood.

-up, as kings-up   *Poker*. A hand of two pairs, of which the higher is named.

upcard   1. *Stud Poker*. One properly dealt face up. 2. *Gin Rummy*. The first card turned up from the stock after the deal; the uppermost card of the discard pile.

valle cards   *Panguingue*. Cards of value; threes, fives, and sevens.

visiting the hamlets   *Skat*. Cashing aces and tens.

void   BLANK SUIT.

vole   SLAM.

Vorhand   FOREHAND.

vulnerable   *Contract Bridge*. Said of a side that has won a game toward rubber.

waste pile   Talon; a pile of discards; cards laid aside as unwanted or as unplayable.

Wenzel   German, the jack of a suit.

whangdoodles   Variant of ROODLES.

whipsawed   1. *Faro*. Losing a bet to win and another to lose on the same turn. 2. *Poker*. Victimized by a form of cheating in which two other players both continuously raise, to increase a third player's contribution to the pot, though only one has a hand he can expect to win.

whiskey hole   A score one point short of game.

whitewashed   Beaten without having scored a point.

wide cards   *Cribbage*. Those too far apart in rank to be likely to form runs.

widow   Extra cards dealt at the same time as the hands, and which usually become the property of the highest bidder. Also called the blind, the skat.

wild card   One that may be specified by the holder to be of any rank and suit.

with, as *with three*   *Skat*. Holding the specified number of top trumps in unbroken sequence from the jack of clubs down.

without   *Bridge*. A call meaning "No-trumps."

without, as *without two*   *Skat*. Lacking the specified number of top trumps, all higher than the best held in the hand.

woo   *Mah Jongg*. End the game by showing a COMPLETE HAND.

wood-pusher   *Chess*. An unimaginative player.

wrong bet   *Craps*. One that the caster will not PASS.

x   A symbol representing any card lower than the lowest specified card of the same suit, as ♡**J x** (♡**J** and any heart lower than the jack).

Yarborough   *Whist family*. A hand containing no card higher than a nine.

younger hand   In two-hand play, the one who does not make the opening lead.

Zugzwang   *Chess*. The compulsion to move; a position in which every possible move weakens the player's defense.